To Jeremy,

On your sixtieth birthday.

Much love,

Bex and Nick

x

THE LAST DAYS OF THE JERUSALEM OF LITHUANIA

THE LAST DAYS OF THE JERUSALEM OF LITHUANIA

Chronicles from the Vilna Ghetto and the Camps, 1939–1944

HERMAN KRUK

EDITED AND INTRODUCED

BY BENJAMIN HARSHAV

TRANSLATED BY BARBARA HARSHAV

YIVO INSTITUTE FOR JEWISH RESEARCH

YALE UNIVERSITY PRESS

NEW HAVEN AND LONDON

Published with assistance from the Nusach Vilne Society

Set in ITC Charter type by The Composing Room of Michigan, Inc.
Printed in the United States of America by R. R. Donnelley & Sons.

Library of Congress Cataloguing-in-Publication Data
Kruk, Herman, 1897–1944.
[Togbukh fun Vilner geto. English]
The last days of the Jerusalem of Lithuania : chronicles from the Vilna ghetto and the
camps, 1939–1944 / Herman Kruk ; edited and introduced by Benjamin Harshav ;
translated by Barbara Harshav.
p. cm.
Includes bibliographical references and index.
ISBN 0-300-04494-1 (alk. paper)
1. Kruk, Herman, 1897–1944. 2. Jews—Persecutions—Lithuania—Vilnius.
3. Holocaust, Jewish (1939–1945)—Lithuania—Vilnius—Personal narratives. 4. World War,
1939– 1945—Jewish resistance—Lithuania—Vilnius. 5. Vilnius (Lithuania)—Ethnic
relations. 6. Klooga (Concentration camp) 7. Concentration camps—Estonia.
I. Harshav, Benjamin, 1928– II. Title.
DS135.L52 V554813 2002
940.53′18′092—dc21
[B] 2002016736

A catalogue record for this book is available from the British Library.

The paper in this book meets the guidelines for permanence and durability of the Committee on
Production Guidelines for Book Longevity of the Council on Library Resources.

10 9 8 7 6 5 4 3 2 1

Unless otherwise noted, all illustrations appear courtesy of the
YIVO Institute for Jewish Research.

Yale University Press would like to acknowledge the invaluable assistance of Donald J. Cohen
(1940–2001), former director of the Yale Child Study Center and chairman of the Committee on
Publications of Yale University Press. Without his unflagging support, the publication of this
book would not have been possible.

[In September 1943, the Vilna Ghetto was liquidated and several thousand remaining Jews, including Herman Kruk, were transported to camps in Estonia, notably to Klooga, near Tallinn. Kruk continued writing his chronicle—in the form of diaries, narratives, and poems—up to the last day. He was killed and burned with most of the surviving Jews just hours before the Red Army liberated the area on September 19, 1944. The following poem, written in Yiddish in precise amphibrachic meter, was found among his writings from this last period and is presented here in a literal translation.]

FOR FUTURE GENERATIONS

Neighbors in Camp Klooga often ask me
Why do you write in such hard times?—
Why and for whom? . . .
. . . For we won't live to see it anyway.

I know I am condemned and awaiting my turn,
Although deep inside me burrows a hope for a miracle.
Drunk on the pen trembling in my hand,
I record everything for future generations:
A day will come when someone will find
The leaves of horror I write and record.
People will tear their hair in anguish,
Eyes will plunge into the sky
Unwilling to believe the horror of our times.
And then these lines will be a consolation
For future generations, which I, a prisoner,
Kept in my sight, things
I recorded, fixed faithfully. . . .
For me it is superfluous,
For future generations I leave it as a trace.
And let it remain though I must die here
And let it show what I could not live to tell.
And I answer my neighbors:
Maybe a miracle will liberate me.
But if I must die, it must not die with me—

The time of horrors I leave for future worlds.

I write because I must write—a consolation in my time of horror.

For future generations I leave it as a trace.

—March 24, 1944

[*The following note was found with Kruk's papers, hidden in the ruins of the Vilna Ghetto.*]

TO THOSE WHO MAY FIND THIS MATERIAL!!

The materials gathered here—the chronicle along with all the documents,

manuscripts, and other texts—were collected, written, and preserved

in the most difficult days of my life, from 1941 to April 1943.

I beg the honest discoverer to respect my wish, preserve the materials,

and carefully ship them to my friends or relatives.

CONTENTS

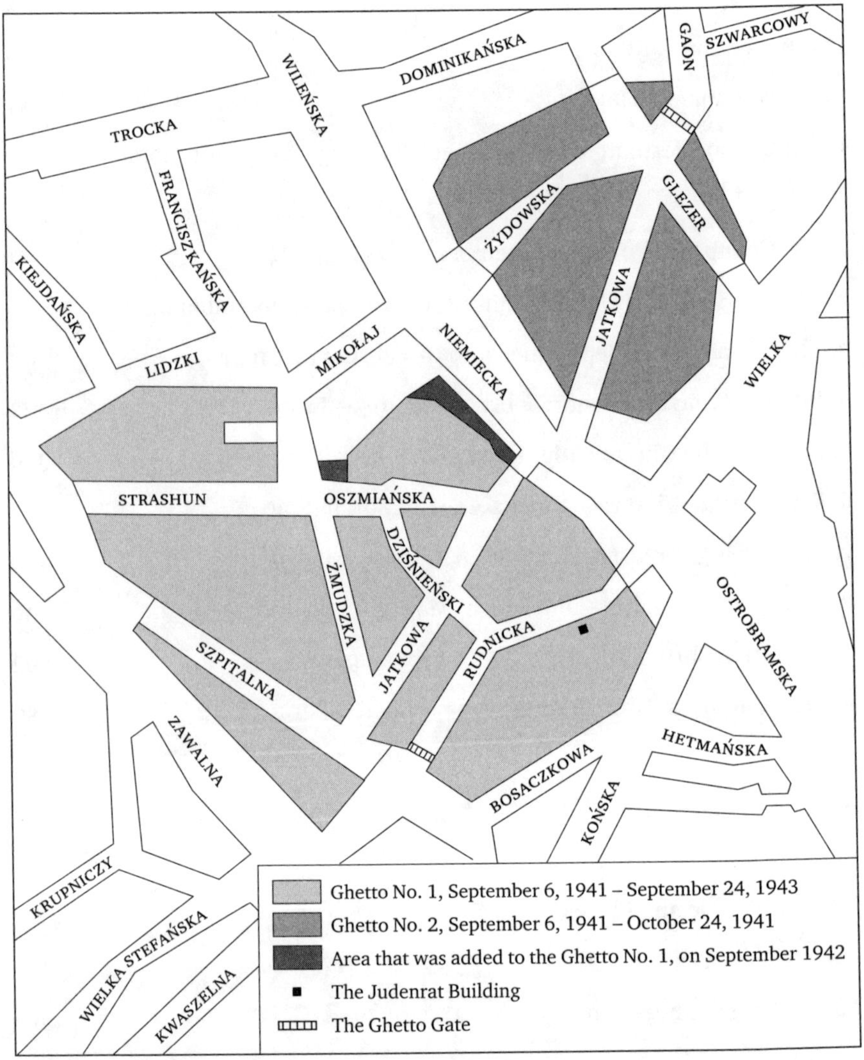

Map 1. Vilna Ghetto. Based on map in Yitzak Arad, Ghetto in Flames *(Jerusalem: Yad Vashem and Anti-Defamation League of B'nai Brith, 1980).*

Map 2. Camps and Ghettos in Lithuania, Latvia, and Estonia.

FOREWORD

Herman Kruk's journal of the Vilna Ghetto and the Estonian labor camp Klooga is a chronicle of daily life as lived under almost unimaginably difficult circumstances. Kruk was aware that he, like many others, might not live till war's end, and he hoped that his diary would survive to illuminate the horrors of the past for future generations. He was correct on both counts: he was tragically murdered at the Estonian camp Lagedi on the eve of liberation, but many pages from his diary were recovered from hiding places after the war. Assembled and published in the original Yiddish by YIVO in 1961, they were among the first full-length diaries of life in the Nazi-created ghettos to be released.

Yet twenty-first-century readers would do well to turn to Kruk's record for inspiration on how to grapple with adversity in any place and time. Blazing forth from every page of his narrative are Kruk's passion to live every moment of life to the fullest, his determination not to relinquish his sense of integrity and justice, his compassion for ordinary people struggling to survive in the face of brutality and daily tragedy, and not least, his success in maintaining his sense of irony and humor.

Many individuals have worked tirelessly to bring this work to publication. At YIVO, Roberta Newman and Dr. Paul Glasser took charge of the final preparation of the manuscript. Ms. Newman also served as the book's photo editor. Michael Cohen, Avinoam Patt, and Aaron Taub provided invaluable assistance. (Additional acknowledgments can be found in the Preface.)

Special thanks go to Yale University Press Editorial Director Jonathan Brent and Managing Editor Jenya Weinreb, who ably shepherded this project through the various stages of production. Charles Grench, former editor-in-chief of Yale University Press, nurtured the project in earlier stages. YIVO Board member Joseph D. Becker provided advice and encouragement on many occasions.

Finally, the publication of *The Last Days of the Jerusalem of Lithuania* would not have been possible without the financial support of the Nusach Vilne Society, which, out of its great devotion to the Jewish community of Vilna, has made this project a focal point of its activities over the past decade.

Carl J. Rheins
Executive Director
YIVO Institute for Jewish Research

PREFACE

Herman Kruk's monumental *Diary of the Vilna Ghetto* is a major classic of Holocaust literature. The YIVO, "Yiddish Scientific Institute," a Yiddish research academy for the humanities and social sciences, founded in Vilna in 1925, shifted its center during the war to New York, where YIVO's founder, Dr. Max Weinreich, succeeded in escaping. When the diary, documenting the demise of Jewish Vilna and the death of the Jewish nation and culture in Europe, was brought to New York in 1947, its publication was obviously an urgent task of the YIVO. Nevertheless, Kruk's book was published only thirteen years later, in 1961, meticulously edited and annotated by Mordkhe Bernstein and introduced by Pinkhes Schwartz, Herman Kruk's brother. The hundreds of names mentioned by Kruk had to be identified and described, the facts and stories checked out against other sources, and the incomplete and damaged manuscript read and supplemented with missing information. Six hundred and seventy-two large pages of the published Yiddish book included almost five hundred long footnotes and dozens of editor's inserts in tiny letters.

The scope of this book, and the extensive knowledge of Vilna personalities and institutions required to understand it, certainly made any translation difficult and contributed to the fact that the book is still unknown in any language outside Yiddish. Yet the main cause seems to be that at the time, the world was little interested in the Holocaust (except for heroism, perhaps), and it was practically impossible to publish translations of such books in English. As the Yiddish poet Yankev Glatstein wrote in 1938, before any ghettos were established by the Nazis: "I do not know if there is a better parallel to ghetto life than writing Yiddish."[1] Now Yiddish culture, in its last flourishing, embraced the Holocaust as its own: "A whole poetry has become monotonic and monothematic," wrote Glatstein.

With that background in mind, Barbara and I gladly accepted the invitation of the YIVO to translate the text and the footnotes into English, and to reedit the book for a new readership forty years after it was first published in Yiddish. It was an emotional experience for me in more than one sense. We tried to maintain precise scholarly standards in the translation and editing; yet in the preface, a few personal words are in order.

I was born in Vilna, "Jerusalem of Lithuania," as we proudly called it. My parents were Jewish secular intellectuals: my mother, Dvoyra Freidkes, was a math-

1. See Benjamin and Barbara Harshav, *American Yiddish Poetry: A Bilingual Anthology* (Berkeley: University of California Press, 1986), pp. 802–4.

ematics teacher and principal of a Yiddish secular school (the Sofye Markovne Gurevitsh Gimnazye), and my father, Dr. Abraham Hrushovski (later, Agassi), taught history in Hebrew schools, the Hebrew Teachers' Seminar, and the Polish-Jewish Gymnasium of Dr. Epstein. In 1940–41, under Soviet rule, they were both Pedagogic Directors of two of the four Vilna Yiddish Gymnasia (a Gymnasium provided the highest level of Jewish education, and in its cultural status was equivalent to an American college).

At dawn of June 22, 1941, Soviet Vilna was bombarded by German airplanes, even before war was declared. After a day and night of bombardments, on the 23rd, my parents, my little sister, and I left our apartment with small rucksacks and hit the road. Only our tenant, old Pati Kremer, the veteran leader of the Bund, remained there. The neighbors were amazed: "You're leaving everything just like that? The Germans are cultured people, they will not touch the city of the Vilna Gaon!" That was how people responded after Kristalnacht, the humiliation of Jews in Vienna and in Poland, and the establishment of crowded ghettos in Łódź and Warsaw. Although those things were unpleasant, no one suspected the "final solution." But my historian father said: "I read Hitler's *Mein Kampf* and I believe him." We went to the railroad station and barely squeezed into the hundred-wagon long train (*eshalon*), the only train that left Vilna before the Germans came, and which was crammed with families of Red Army officers and several thousand Jews. The next day, Vilna was empty of any power, and the Germans moved in. On the old Polish-Soviet border, however, all "Westerners," that is, people without Soviet passports, were forced to leave the train. As Kruk describes it, most of them were trapped, barred from crossing into Soviet Russia; many tried to go back to Vilna, and many of them perished on the way. We, however, my family of four, descended the train on the "wrong" side, and as soon as a German airplane began strafing us with machine guns and the train moved, we jumped back in. Later, we did walk for several days in Byelorussian forests, where I "celebrated" my bar-mitzvah; but eventually we boarded another *eshalon* and two weeks later arrived in the Urals. We were saved.

When I read Kruk's diary, I feel that I could have been on every page of it. I was thirteen when the war broke out. What would I have done when my whole street was taken to Ponar (as it was)? And I knew so many of the names in this book. My best childhood friend, Gabik Heller, worked in Kruk's library (after his father, the historian Dr. Moyshe Heller, died in the Ghetto). Our mutual friend and classmate Itsik Rudashevski wrote a memorable Ghetto diary.[2] Both perished. Boys a few years older went to the partisans (Avreml Zeleznikow, the Lubocki brothers); their leader, Abba Kovner, was a friend of my father's, and we spent the summer before the war near his summer camp of Ha-Shomer ha-Tzair. When Kruk men-

2. Published in Hebrew and English: *The Diary of the Vilna Ghetto* (Tel Aviv: Lohamei ha-Getaot and Ha-Kibbutz ha-Meuhad, 1973).

tions names of people who died in the Estonian camps, I see them before my eyes: my mother's students Zhozik Schreiber (and his father, the director of the Yiddish *Technikum*), the tall, thin Grisha Tsepelevitsh (commander of the Second Battalion of FPO, who perished in Estonia). And so many students, friends, and colleagues of my parents appear here in their last journey: the doctor and cultural activist Pomerants; the teacher and principal of *Real-gimnazye* Mira Bernstein, who organized a Yiddish school in the Ghetto; the modest and splendid scholar Zelig Kalmanowicz (our neighbor in the house owned by the publisher B. Kletzkin); the music teacher Gerstein, who directed a famous choir; and many others. The medieval, narrow streets of the Ghetto were so familiar: I walked there every day on the way to *Real-gimnazye* on Rudnicka Street. And the pastoral, wooded hills of Ponar, which became the slaughterhouse of a hundred thousand Jews, were a frequent place of my family's Saturday outings.

There is a special place in my heart for the YIVO. Its founder, Dr. Max Weinreich, and his family were friends of our family. When I was one year old, I got a printed invitation to their home for the foundation of "Young Vilna" (Weinreich always understood that without a young generation Yiddish culture was doomed; he later used the same title for the budding group of modern Yiddish poets). On the tenth anniversary of the YIVO, in 1935, the historian Simon Dubnow and the artist Marc Chagall came to the conference (from Riga and Paris) and visited the children's summer colony where my father was director. And at the age of 12, I had the honor of serving as a guide at the YIVO exhibition on the 25th anniversary of Y. L. Peretz's death. It was a small, poor wooden house on Wiwulski Street 18, just a few blocks from my home, but it exalted the pure principles of (humanistic) "science." In its poverty, it was a great research institute.

How could I work on Kruk's detailed descriptions without keeping all this before my eyes?

Yet when Barbara and I translated the book with all its footnotes, new problems emerged. Indeed, it was important to keep the first editors' footnotes with minor editorial interference because they collected a great deal of information from Vilna people who survived and were still alive at the time (a large, international correspondence about it was conducted in the early 1950s); this oral history is something we no longer have access to. But at the same time it was imperative to overcome the limitations of that edition.

When the partisans returned from the forests to the ruins of Vilna Ghetto in July 1944, they went to find Kruk's diary in a ghetto cellar where it was buried. Yet the cellar had been broken into by robbers looking for "Jewish gold," and the pages of the diary had been scattered. Eventually, some of the pages (typed and numbered by Kruk himself) were recovered and sent to New York, and some of the pages were taken by Ruzhka Korczak and others to Israel, and stored in Yad Vashem and in Kibbutz Givat Haviva.

The published book was not really Kruk's complete diary; it contained only two-thirds of the numbered pages. The editors of the book interpolated their conjectures as to what Kruk wrote about in the missing pages, but they were often wrong. In an Israeli archive, I found Kruk's own detailed table of contents — 101 pages in his own handwriting — often including ten or twenty topics recorded in one day. Kruk cherished it and saved it separately from his diary, and apparently carried it with him to the camps in Estonia. We deleted the first editor's wrong guesses and inserted all the recovered titles in the text; they read like a skeleton of a horror history.

We also inserted dozens of small pieces into the existing diary, using other copies of the typewritten pages or small fragments, glued together like a half-lost mosaic. This was a laborious job, though it will hardly be noticed by someone reading the integrated text.

Now the nature of the book had been transformed: instead of blindly translating the old Yiddish edition, we were trying to reproduce in English Kruk's original chronicle, insofar as it survived anywhere in the world (including a full translation of the first edition). Indeed, we found hundreds of pages of unpublished Kruk manuscripts, often fragmentary and hardly legible, in the Moreshet Institute in Israel, in the YIVO archives, and in Vilnius! Thus, the English edition is more precise and is 30 percent larger than the old one.

But in addition to corrections in the main part of the diary, there were also problems on a larger scale. The published book presented only two years of Kruk's life in Vilna under the Nazis, June 23, 1941–July 14, 1943. Kruk, however, wrote his chronicles during the five years of his Holocaust: from the collapse of Warsaw in September 1939 to one day before he was killed in Estonia on September 18, 1944. The YIVO was a Vilna institution and was naturally interested in the Vilna Ghetto. But Herman Kruk came from Warsaw, and we cannot properly understand his responses to events in Vilna without reading about the sudden collapse of Poland and the collapse of his own world in the fall of 1939, and his life as a refugee in Vilna in the two subsequent years. We must also include the last stage of Kruk's life and the life of the remnants of Vilna Jewry — the year spent in Klooga and other camps in Estonia, right up to his death. This volume restores the full five-year scope (though, regrettably, not all surviving texts) of Herman Kruk's Holocaust.

Kruk was alert to the problems of genre and discourse in representing the Holocaust (for more about this, see the introduction): to his last day, he collected "objective" documents; recorded witness accounts; wrote diaries; reconstructed diaries in retrospect; wrote narrative chronicles and quasi-fictionalized historical representations; wrote "Ghetto Miniatures" — glimpses of typical, anecdotal situations; and crafted poems — reflecting an individual's experiences in the Estonian camps. He was constantly seeking the discourse most appropriate to the mode of representation befitting the particular situation — and all those genres were mobilized to the telling of the Holocaust. To select only the formal "diary," as the Yiddish edition did, is to misrepresent and impoverish Kruk's record.

And last but not least, when Kruk was taken from Vilna to the Estonian camps, where he survived for another year with 20,000 other Jews, he left his typist and typewriter behind. But he stubbornly continued to write his chronicles, often after 14 or 16 hours of hard labor. This is a direct continuation of his Vilna diaries. He clarifies some issues about the last days of Vilna Ghetto and the partisans, and describes the end of the last remnants of Jewish Vilna. The editors of the Yiddish edition included in their book only texts they found on typewritten and numbered pages, but our task was ten times as hard: the later texts are often scribbled on small pieces of paper, unfinished, and hardly legible. Still, it would be unconscionable if we had knowingly published the old, incomplete, and truncated edition of Kruk's diary while some of the later parts were recovered.

This is the terrible story of Kruk's Estonian chronicles: On September 17, 1944, one day before the liberation by the Red Army, Kruk buried his last diaries in Lagedi camp in the presence of six witnesses. The next day, he and most remaining Jews in Klooga and Lagedi were shot and burned on a pyre. One of the six, Nisan Anolik, hid and survived. He went back to the camp, uncovered the diaries, and brought them to Vilna, to the new "Jewish Museum" founded by A. Sutzkever and Sh. Kaczerginski, where other Kruk manuscripts were located. In 1947 the museum was closed by the Soviet authorities, and the papers were taken away by the NKVD, ostensibly for "recycling" in a paper factory. However, a righteous Lithuanian saved a great many confiscated Jewish books and manuscripts. They turned up half a century later, including hundreds of pages written by Herman Kruk. When Lithuania became independent of the Soviet Union, it became possible to recover Kruk's writings. Sam Norich (then director of YIVO) and the archivist Marek Web acquired copies of the Vilnius Kruk manuscripts and brought them to me. The process of matching the pieces, deciphering them, rewriting them in a typed, standard Yiddish form, and translating them was as labor-intensive as translating the whole book.

From the beginning, I insisted on making every effort to recover all missing parts of Kruk's diary. That was my function as editor and our moral duty toward the *kadosh* Herman Kruk and the memory of the Holocaust. Indeed, we have succeeded in restoring some of the missing parts. The book now covers all five years of Kruk's Holocaust chronicles. Chapters 1, 9, and 10 are entirely new; a window was opened on Jewish life in the Estonian camps, including Kruk's suffering and tantalizing dreams of liberation; and dozens of corrections have been made in the earlier published parts.

Many persons helped in the process. I shall mention just a few: Sam Norich, former director of the YIVO, who initiated the project; the indispensable YIVO archivist Marek Web; Fira Bramson, keeper of the recovered Jewish library in Vilnius; Professor Shalom Luria, the son of Zelig Kalmanowicz, in Kibbutz Merhavia; the archivists of the *Moreshet* Institute in Kibbutz Givat Haviva; Benjamin Anolik, survivor of camp Klooga and director of *Beit Katznelson* in Kibbutz Lohamei ha-Getaot; David Rogow at YIVO, who provided the first draft of deciphered manuscripts; Gitl Schaechter, who put the text on a computer and transposed it into the YIVO orthography; and Andrea Raab Sherman, YIVO production manager, who was sympathetic to the difficulties and helped as much as she could. We are deeply indebted to the first editors of Kruk's diary, who laid the foundations of this work. And *ahron ahron haviv,* the last is most beloved: my wife, Barbara Harshav, invested her indefatigable skill and competence—both as a historian and as a translator—in rendering this vast body of material in idiomatic English, while paying attention to all the subtleties, historical problems, terminologies, and ever again refined elucidations and footnotes.

Benjamin Harshav
J. and H. Blaustein Professor of Hebrew
and Comparative Literature
Yale University

INTRODUCTION
HERMAN KRUK'S HOLOCAUST WRITINGS
BENJAMIN HARSHAV

TWO HOLOCAUSTS

The word *Holocaust,* with its connotations of horror, outrage, and genocide, obstructs our view of the great variety of phenomena, stages, and experiences covered by this term.

In a sense, there were two Holocausts. One was the extermination of several million human beings—Germans, Frenchmen, Poles, Hungarians, Italians, and Russians of Jewish origin. Some of them (like Jean Amery) were Christians, some (like Primo Levi) were indifferent to their Jewishness, some belonged to a synagogue or participated in Jewish life, most were consumers of and contributors to another culture. As individuals, they were persecuted not for what they did or believed but for who their grandparents were. Six million individuals of Jewish origin[1] were slaughtered in the Nazi death machine. From this perspective, many millions of others were killed in World War II, and if you count the numbers of persons killed, there is no difference between them. The questions, however, still remain: What happened to them before they were killed? Why were their children condemned with them to death (unlike the children of every other group except the Gypsies)? What did the Holocaust do to their hearts when they were like hunted animals before they perished, and to the hearts of thousands of other Jews—in Europe and elsewhere—who survived but experienced the horror and fear of their built-in, "genetic" destiny?

But there was also another Holocaust, the Holocaust of the modern Jewish nation and culture, especially as it had lived in Eastern Europe. There was a dense network of Jewish activities, competing ideologies and political parties, youth movements and sports clubs, literature in several languages, publishing and translations of world literature into Yiddish and Hebrew, newspapers and libraries, separate Jewish trade unions and educational systems—a secular, modern, European-type, autonomous Jewish nation—though without power over any territory—that emerged in the nineteenth and twentieth centuries and per-

1. This figure may be somewhat smaller in some accounts, but it may also be larger by 250,000 shot in the occupied Soviet territories that we did not account for before (as Yitzhak Arad argued).

ished in the Holocaust. This was Kruk's world, and he recorded both those Holocausts.

When the German professor (of Jewish origin) Theodor Adorno asked how one could write poetry "after Auschwitz," it was the first kind of Holocaust he was referring to. "Auschwitz" was a death machine and is a symbol of total annihilation. The contemporary cult of the Holocaust deals with it as with a shipwreck we survived, without asking what continent the ship came from, what existed before that shipwreck. Why would the Holocaust be so horrible, why wouldn't it be just part of the general World War II, just 6 out of 50 million killed, if it were not a Holocaust of something, of a nation and a culture that disappeared in it? The Polish poet of Jewish origin Julian Tuwim expressed the problem succinctly: "I am a Pole when the blood is running in my veins, and a Jew when it is running out of my veins." Many people of Jewish origin have a Tuwim Complex. For them, the trauma begins and ends with the word *Auschwitz*.

Those two kinds of Holocaust are related to the two kinds of transformations that Jews underwent in the modern age. The "Modern Jewish Revolution"[2] responded to the criticism of the "medieval" Jewish existence and behavior, expressed both by antisemites and by the internal new Jewish literature. It produced a radical transformation of the Jews, their demographic situation, languages, education, professions, and conceptual world. The harbingers of those changes appeared in the nineteenth century, especially in Western Europe, but the great Jewish masses in Eastern Europe were involved in this process mainly after 1882. The Modern Jewish Revolution consisted of embracing the secular European world, its culture, genres and modes of discourse, and institutional frameworks. And it went in two directions: Intrinsic and Extrinsic. The "Extrinsic" trend brought millions of Jews into the general culture of the respective countries where they were living. The "Intrinsic" trend strove to create an equivalent Jewish culture, modeled on the European system. It was to be primarily in the Jewish languages, Yiddish and Hebrew, but also in the languages of the respective countries. And it was to create a trans-national Jewish cultural nation.

After 1882, all the new Jewish ideologies and parties, literature and art, a network of social and cultural organizations, several networks of Jewish schools in Hebrew, Yiddish, and other languages, all combined to achieve this goal. As it happened, however, the European idea of a nation based on language, culture, and history of an ethnic society did not succeed without territorial power. Only the small branch of the Modern Jewish Revolution that moved to Palestine, reinvented the Hebrew language, and established the state of Israel survived the upheavals of the twentieth century in Europe.

Kruk, however, still lived with the ideals and culture of a politically autono-

2. I described this revolution in the first part of my book *Language in Time of Revolution* (Palo Alto: Stanford University Press, 1999).

mous, secular Jewish nation; in his case, as formulated by his own party, the Yiddishist and Socialist *Bund*. It was from this position, of a Jewish nation in the throes of death, that all the responses to the Holocaust emerged. Each person, naturally, fought for his or her life; but in addition, they participated in finding responses to the state of the nation. It was a whole larger than their own life, embracing them and giving them some raison d'être. It was in the name of this Jewish nation with its proud history that the internal responses arose. Helpless as they were, no matter how little impact they made on the outcome of the war, in their own lives these responses were transforming moves of dignity and achievement. The two major directions of response were: joining the fight against the Germans, in the ghetto or in the partisan forests; or doing everything for "endurance" and "survival," as Kruk did. A few months before the liquidation of Ghetto Vilna, he expressed his opposition to the partisans because their acts might jeopardize the existence of "the last metropolis of the Bund in Poland," as he put it, that is, the Vilna Ghetto, which then numbered about 15,000 inmates.

In the eyes of the last Jews in Nazi-occupied Europe, this was the end of a nation, a millennia-old nation that had lived in Europe for a thousand years, about as long as the other European nation-states and languages. (They rarely considered the American Jewish community in this context, probably because it was not seen as a creative national center.) That is why the Holocaust was called in Yiddish by the Hebrew word *Churban* (something like "total ruin, destruction"), which was the term for the Destruction of the First Temple and the first Jewish state in Palestine and the exile to Babylon, and for the Destruction of the Second Temple, which led to two thousand years of Diaspora around the world.[3] Now it meant the end of the Jewish nation in Europe, as final and as significant as the two destructions in biblical Palestine. It is not by accident that the Zionist establishment in Israel did not want to dignify the death of European Jewry with the term that denoted the end of a Jewish independent nation in the past. "Yad Vashem," the government institution established to commemorate the catastrophe, was called *Yad Vashem la-Gevurah ve-la-Shoah,* "Memorial to Heroism and Holocaust." "Heroism," of course, had the priority, but "Churban" was not mentioned. "Shoah" (like the English "Holocaust") is a natural disaster, an external catastrophe rather than a pivotal historical event in the life of a nation. (With time, of course, "Holocaust" assumed that other meaning as well.)

And there is another sense in which two different Holocausts can be discerned (though not necessarily overlapping the previous division). It was one thing to be taken from your home to a concentration camp or a death camp, and quite another thing to live in the makeshift Jewish polity of a ghetto in your own city. The

3. The term *Churban* was also used for the destructions of Jewish communities in times of persecution in the past (such as the "Churban Ukraine" in 1919, which was the first great wave not of pogroms but of total extermination).

ghetto was drained almost daily, humiliated and terrorized; and yet, in the meantime, a social, cultural, and political Jewish life was carried on. Leon Bernstein, a Jew from East Prussia, said that he would never forgive the Germans for depriving him of his language and culture (German); but for the Yiddish and Hebrew intelligentsia in the Vilna Ghetto no such problem arose. A short time before the end, when the Bundist Grisha Yashunski was removed as director of the education department in the ghetto and the Zionist Leon Bernstein replaced him, Kruk lamented that now the Yiddish schools would be Hebraized! Yiddish or Hebrew —the pre-Holocaust "war of languages"; to live *here,* in the Yiddish Diaspora, or to emigrate to Hebrew Eretz-Israel—this is what really mattered in the long run, not the temporary rule of German cruelty.

The internal life of the ghetto community, in constant counterpoint to the incomprehensible chicanery of the Germans, is what is so outstanding in Kruk's chronicles. It is said that victims remember little of their trauma, yet here we have a richly detailed collective memory, because it is not the memory of an individual suffering unjustly, but that of a dignified nation; not of death, but of life in its shadow. That is why there are so many political parties, institutions, and individuals in this book, all of them remembered and valued, all of them symbols of prewar activity of one kind or another. It is not one death in so many repetitions, but many different and creative lives.

A similar book, Yitzhak Zuckerman's *Surplus of Memory,* written by the leader of the Warsaw Ghetto Uprising, displays the same wealth of social and political detail within a pluralistic Jewish nation in Poland, yet in this case not under the sign of survival, but under that of resistance.[4] An equivalent book, focusing on the growth of the resistance in the Vilna Ghetto and the struggle in the partisan forests, was written by Ruzhka Korczak but has not yet been translated into English. It would be a fitting counterpart to Kruk's very comprehensive book.

MODES OF DISCOURSE

In many ways, Kruk's diary is like Kafka's *Trial*. From the first sentence it is clear that Joseph K. is doomed, an inexplicable denunciation and strange arrest send him on a quest for any avenue that leads to justice, or at least to understanding, which only entangles him more and more in the web of the "system." K. is launched on an inexorable journey toward his own end, yet the end is ever postponed, thus giving us a whole book to explore the absurd rules of the game that is played against him. In the final analysis we don't understand a thing because "the in-

4. Yitzhak Zuckerman, *A Surplus of Memory,* ed. and trans. Barbara Harshav (Los Angeles: University of California Press), 1993. See Barbara Harshav's survey of Jewish parties and youth movements in the introduction.

comprehensible is incomprehensible" (Kafka's parable "On Parables"). When the major aspects of the system are explored, the book is over, and K. is suddenly executed, as a non sequitur to the immediately preceding events and without the trial ever having taken place.

Herman K., too, is suddenly confronted with a total collapse of his world. Yet he lives through stages upon stages of total entanglement in a system that determines his every breath, and Herman tries to confront it with past habits, feverish activity, and attempts at recording and understanding. In a diary, each day is taken in brackets and autonomous explorations of life borrowed for a while are inserted, exposing little human joys and frailties, called "survival," "politics," and "culture." His death is postponed to the very last moment, thus making it possible to describe all faces and stages of hell. And Herman K.'s end too comes out of the blue, apparently unconnected to the immediate context, as if a transcendental fictional hand closed the book when its story had already explored so many unthinkable possibilities.

Herman Kruk was executed by the Germans on September 18, 1944, one day before the first units of the Red Army arrived. He was not in a death camp, but in a German labor camp in Estonia. He was building fortifications for the German defense. Indeed, his Germans told him they were jealous of their Jewish prisoners, for they were surrounded and helpless, the Red Army would liberate the Jews and destroy the Germans. Paris was saved by a German general, but Kruk could not be saved.

We have very few detailed diaries actually written in ghettos and concentration camps. One of the values of Kruk's diary is that it was written during the events themselves, from an internal point of view, without any knowledge of German intentions or plans, without the hindsight of the "final solution," and without the stereotypes and ideologies of the postwar period. In a diary, every delusion is an illusion in its own context, every horrifying event is horrible as it comes; in view of later events, of an immensely greater magnitude, those first impressions would have dwindled, one would be ashamed to even mention them. And this is precisely the value of beginning not from Ghetto Vilna (as the Yiddish edition did), but from the destruction of the narrator's normal life in Warsaw.

In August 1938, in an interview at his home in Riga, the great historian of "the eternal people," the octogenarian Simon Dubnow, said: "The tomorrow of the Jews is tied in with the tomorrow of all of Europe and all of humanity." "The present is indeed very sad, in all the four thousand years of Jewish history there never were such horrifying moments as now." "But," he added, "*Jewish history will go on and continue*."[5] Three years later, Dubnow was brutally killed by a Ger-

5. "'Di yidishe geshikhte geyt foroys un vayter!'—a sho mit prof. Shimen Dubnov," *Idishe bilder* 34, no. 66, Riga, August 26, 1938.

man soldier on his way to the Riga Ghetto. Jewish history did continue, but it was impossible to see it from inside the "New Europe."

Herman Kruk lived in Warsaw, in the capital of the cultural, Westernizing Polish state, and the world center of Jewish life. He was both a consumer of Polish culture and a leader of the modern culture in Yiddish. Nazi-inspired antisemitism raged through Poland in the late 1930s, but Herman was in his own words a "perennial optimist"; he believed in Bundist "*doikeyt*" ("here-ness"), in the necessity and feasibility of building a Jewish autonomous culture in Poland, as Polish citizens. If dark forces were menacing, culture and democratic Socialism would bring equality to everyone, including the Jews.

Therefore, when Poland was attacked on September 1, 1939, and the strong Polish army was overwhelmed in a few days by the first German *Blitzkrieg,* his world collapsed on him. From September 5, 1939, when he left Warsaw and his wife behind, until October 10, when he reached Vilna, he wandered in a daze through defeated Poland, along with everybody else, it seemed. In an article "On the Ruins of Poland" (see Chapter 1), written a few months later, he writes: "Where is the enormously extensive Yiddish press? Yiddish publishing? Not to mention the political movements?! . . . " "The Jewish school system ceased to exist." "Everything is now turned into ruins." By "everything," he means the glorious polyphony of Jewish culture; yet he does not single out the fate of the Jews: "In the Polish world as in the Jewish world—the destruction is horrible." Everything is in ruins, yet the Jewish Holocaust has not yet begun.

And later, when he compiles statistics about the extensive aid to refugees in peaceful Lithuanian Vilnius in 1940 (there were about 20,000 Jewish refugees from Poland added to the 60,000 Vilna Jews, most of whom lived in great poverty), he writes: "A sea of numbers, a terror of anguish and suffering. How terrible it is to tell about it. How anguished and painful are the horror stories."

Yet the first months of the German occupation of Vilna, between June and September 1941—when Jews are snatched in the streets by hired "snatchers," are humiliated, beaten, terrorized, extorted, and when some forty thousand disappear in the still unknown meat grinder of Ponar—are of an entirely different dimension of horror. Perhaps the senses were dulled in those few months, but even later, in the ghetto, there was no such emotionally draining experience as this. And this was only the prelude to the ghetto. And the ghetto was only the waiting room for the dark end.

From the point of view of the final annihilation, all those stages are irrelevant. But if we want to comprehend how it felt when the horrors grew on you, a forward-moving diary is the closest imitation of reality. Especially when it was written "naively," with no knowledge of tomorrow.

Furthermore, Kruk's diary is not just a personal journal, but is in many ways the journal of a community. His entries included three concentric circles: his private life and personal responses to events; the life of his party and extended family, the "Bund" and the Bundists; and the world of the ghetto as a whole. He consciously wanted to record not just his own life, but every angle and event in Jewish existence and annihilation under the Nazi occupation. And he was well placed to do so. He built a large library in the ghetto, which became a center for clandestine activities. Here every day he dictated his notes to a secretary who typed them in three copies. The ghetto knew of his mission and he got help from all sides. He was given the news heard on a clandestine radio and the information of the FPO (*Fareynikte partizaner-organizatsye*—the United Partisan Organization in the ghetto), as well as the inside information from the authorities, the Judenrat. Kruk was not a member of the partisan organization; he admired their wish for heroism, but was also afraid they might provoke the liquidation of all Jews in the ghetto. Yet he had high-placed informants through those Bundists who were in the partisans. Similarly, Kruk's first impulse was to oppose the Judenrat, but eventually he got close to the head of the ghetto, Jacob Gens, and received information directly from him. In addition, he was active in the "Aid Society" in the ghetto and in the Literary-Artistic Association. And he headed the brigade of scholars and writers who went out of the ghetto, to the building of the former YIVO, to sort out the book treasures collected from all over Vilna, which gave him free access to move around the city.

Thus, entries in the diary are daily, as events unfolded, but much of the information is summaries, as reported by various witnesses (for example, about the end of Oszmiana or Święciany), hence not simply forward-moving. In several cases, it is a reconstructed diary, thus, on September 6, 1941, all Jews were taken to the ghetto, but only on the 20th can Kruk go back and write his diary from September 5 on.

Herman Kruk was neither a philosopher nor a literary critic. His culture, the Yiddish culture of the Bund, was populist, suffused with political rhetoric and folklore. There is no profound meditation here about history, culture, or human nature, making it more valuable as a voice from within, expressed in the language of emotions felt by the common victim. In his text, he mixed the reporting of facts with rumors and anecdotes, and added his own emotional outbursts; and he did not spare emotions or criticism in any direction. Yet he was aware of the subjective aspect of his writings and those of various witnesses, and wanted to bolster the objective side of his chronicle.

Thus, the second form of his records was a huge collection of documents of all kinds. Often, his diary reacts to things exhibited in the documentation and is unclear without the documents themselves. But the editors of the Yiddish edition gave up on including the documents, many of which are preserved in the YIVO and other archives. Unfortunately, we had to forgo that too, because it would have taken several more years of work.

The third mode of recording was witness accounts, which Kruk himself recorded in a concise, stenographic manner. We have here the first witness accounts about the slaughter at Ponar, told by escapees at a time when many serious people in the ghetto did not believe it. He has a series of recordings about the liquidations of Jewish communities in small towns all around Vilna. In the Youth Club, he organized students to collect evidence and witness accounts—and in his archives we have several accounts written in a childish hand in Soviet Yiddish spelling. And even in the camps of Estonia, he gathered information about the last days of the Vilna Ghetto and the capture of the Second Battalion of the FPO by the Germans. In Klooga, he collected witness accounts about other camps in Estonia and even about the fate of French and Belgian Jewry.

The fourth mode of discourse was Kruk's narrative chronicles. Kruk realized early on that the diary did not fully reflect the situation. Though precise, it atomized the stories, on the one hand, and in time became repetitive, on the other. Instead of a day-by-day record of a criminal trial in the ghetto, for example, he tells a summary story, rich in background detail. There can be no doubt that his narratives strive toward maximum faithfulness to history, and yet are constructs made from Kruk's position. He himself indicates the constructed nature by talking about a fictional "Vilmen" rather than Vilna. In time, he developed ambitious plans to write large fictional "Books"—many notes and chapters or parts survived (several examples are in this volume). Book 2 was called "Underground Ghetto" and surely inspired A. Sutzkever's long poem "Clandestine Ghetto"; and Book 6 was called "Liberation," describing the camps in Estonia, clearly under the sign of imminent liberation, which never came. Those are vivid pictures of camp life, told not as a narrative but in typical, synoptic scenes. As a Socialist, he was especially attuned to injustice, the exploitation of the weak inmates by the "Strong Ones" in the Jewish camp, and the grotesque yet boisterous Jewish penchant for commerce under any circumstances.

The more time passed and typical events were repeated again and again, the more he was looking for synoptic, quintessential modes of writing that would provide a flash, a glimpse into a basic situation or emotion. That became especially true in Klooga, where he both kept a diary and also described the basic social relations in narrative chapters, yet nothing was happening or changing daily, as in the ghetto. The real world dwindled, and poetry seemed best suited to express his feelings and views of the world. Thus, toward the end he developed two short genres: the "Ghetto Miniatures," written in the Vilna Ghetto and continued as "Klooga Miniatures"; and the poems, written in Klooga in precise, highly rhetorical and symmetrical meters (without rhyme) and often touching on personal feelings or major existential questions, couched in the naive language of the political propagandist he was. Close to a hundred poems survived.

Kruk did not decide between those genres and their rather diverse tones of discourse. He wrote them simultaneously, as complementary kinds of documentation. It seems that he had literary ambitions and wanted to write several volumes of fictionalized ghetto chronicles, based on the diaries—after the Liberation. Fortunately, his literary imagination was limited; his language, though sometimes florid, was rather poor; and precisely for that reason, even the fictionalized writings are authentic documents.

Kruk's chronicles are one of the most detailed documents of daily life, personal and public, written from within the Holocaust without the benefit of hindsight. It was a heroic effort to record the events, experiences, and emotions for posterity, interrupted by the death of its author at age 47. Scholars and readers will be able to compare Kruk's information with other sources and evaluate the details and the author's opinions and judgments. We shall let the diaries speak for themselves.

In the following sections we provide the general context in which the diary was written: What was Jerusalem of Lithuania? What is the importance of a city of 60,000 people, reduced to 16,000 enclosed in a tiny ghetto? What was the historical and cultural situation in which the described events took place? What were the Jewish political parties Kruk refers to? And who was Herman Kruk himself?

JERUSALEM OF LITHUANIA

Vilna, nicknamed "Jerusalem of Lithuania," was one of the cultural symbols of the Jewish Diaspora in Europe, where Jews lived for a millennium. Founded in 1323 by the Lithuanian Grand Duke Gediminas, Vilnius was the capital of the Grand Duchy of Lithuania that stretched through forests and rivers between the Baltic and the Black Sea, and from the Prussian frontier to the outskirts of Moscow. The Duke invited merchants and artisans from Germany and Poland, who constituted the core of the city dwellers. In the fifteenth and sixteenth centuries, the Grand Duchy of Lithuania united with the Kingdom of Poland under one crown, with its capital in Warsaw, and ceded Ukraine to Poland. The Lithuanian aristocracy was culturally Polonized and the city was called Wilno. Its famous university attracted such Polish poets as Adam Mickiewicz in the nineteenth century and Czeslaw Milosz in the twentieth, who came from their Lithuanian estates to study here.

The capital of an immense and diffuse Lithuanian domain separating the Polish aristocratic "Republic" from the emerging Muscovite power, Vilna was a major junction on the highway from Poland and the Baltic to Moscow, later Russia. Napoleon stopped here on his way to Moscow in his Russian campaign of 1812 and on his flight back. Impenetrable forests and swamps supplied wood and furs, trades in which Jews were engaged at different times. Easy access by river to the Baltic sea created a window to the west and linked up with the north-south road, going down to Volhynia and Ukraine.

The medieval Grand Duchy covered a territory at least six times the present-day Lithuanian state, encompassing all of today's Belarus, parts of Russia, Poland, and Latvia, and Lithuania proper. Ironically, these vast boundaries are honored to this day only by the Jews: the whole area with its capital in Vilna is called in Yiddish *Lite* (*Litah*), and its Jews, the *Litvaks,* are marked by a distinct Yiddish dialect and mentality, a penchant for learning, different customs of cooking, and a sense of cultural superiority.

Although few documents are extant, we may assume that the first Jews arrived in Eastern Europe at the beginnings of Christianity there and in the early centuries of the second millennium of the Common Era, coming up either from the Byzantine empire or from the West, via Prague and Germany. In the tenth century, a prominent Jew, Moses from Kiev, is mentioned, and in the fourteenth century, Jewish communities were established in such Lithuanian cities as Brisk, Grodno, and Troki (near Vilna). In Vilna proper, the Christian citizens were warding off a permanent Jewish presence (though the Jews lived in the suburbs), and a regular Jewish Community was legalized only in the second half of the sixteenth century. Individual Jews were lessees of the customs, coined money for the Polish kings, engaged in money-lending and commerce. A Polish king sent a Vilna Jewish merchant to negotiate with the Moscow tsar Ivan the Terrible. And around them, many poor Jews crowded.

In the sixteenth through eighteenth centuries, about two-thirds of world Jewry lived in the Kingdom of Poland and Lithuania, the vastest state in Europe. Vilna—as it was called in Jewish documents from the earliest times—became a Jewish "Principal City" and one of the capitals of the Jewish autonomous governing body. One of the great Talmudic scholars, the "Gaon of Vilna" (the "Genius of Vilna," Elijah ben Solomon, or HaGRO, 1720–1797), dominated the religious establishment of his time and excommunicated the new "irrational" Hasidic movement that was sweeping Jewish areas to the south of Lithuania. Thus, the anti-Hasidic Judaism of the *Misnagdim* (the "opposing ones") was launched, stressing learning, precise interpretation of the literal meaning of the text, and building a network of talmudic academies ("yeshivas") throughout Lithuania. Indeed, in the nineteenth and twentieth centuries, the hundreds of small towns of Lithuania became a breeding ground for Hebrew knowledge, supplying rabbis and teachers to the far corners of the Jewish Diaspora, including Ukraine, Poland, Palestine, and the United States.[6] Here, secular Hebrew literature of the *Haskalah* (Enlightenment) flourished in the second half of the nineteenth century, as did Yiddish literature in the twentieth.

The nickname "Jerusalem of Lithuania" was based on this fortress of Jewish learning and the printing of the whole Babylonian Talmud in Vilna. Yet apparently it was the secular movement, which in Vilna perceived itself as heir to the religious tradition, that invented and promoted this name. In 1859, a Hebrew book

6. For the most recent impact on modern French culture, see Judith Friedlander's book *Vilna on the Seine* (New Haven: Yale University Press, 1991).

by the Maskil (enlightened writer) and scholar Rashi Fin (Samuel Joseph Fuenn) was published, describing the history of Vilna and its Jewish community. The book was called *Kiryah Ne'emanah* (Faithful City), describing Vilna in biblical terms used for Jerusalem. Had the name "Jerusalem of Lithuania" existed, Fin would have used it. It is, rather, the opposite: from the name of the book, the nickname was derived. The Vilna Yiddishist and secular movements, as well as modern Hebrew poetry, adopted the name, proud to continue the tradition of the Vilna Gaon. The Kletzkin publishing house and the YIVO were heirs to the printing of the Talmud. And the widespread thirst for knowledge and education seemed to support that honorific title.

Toward the end of the eighteenth century, Poland was dismantled by its neighbors, Russia, Prussia, and Austria. In 1795, Vilna was incorporated into Russia and became the capital of a Russian Province (*Guberniya*) included in the Jewish Pale of Settlement. The Pale was a huge geographical ghetto confined to the former Polish territories, beyond which the Jewish masses were not allowed to live. The Jews were outside the three legally defined estates in Russia: the gentry, the peasants, and the citizens; they had no voting or other civil rights, and no place in the Russian administration or police. Only a few thousand Jews, who were either merchants of the First Guild or professionals with a university degree, were gradually permitted to live inside Russia or in the capital of St. Petersburg. Since Jewish Lithuania stressed learning, many of its sons were among them: the sculptor Marc Antokolsky, the painter Leon Bakst, the choreographer of the Bolshoi Ballet Asaf Messerer, and the Hebrew poet Yehuda-Leyb Gordon (YaLaG) all lived in the Russian capital. Others went to nearby Prussia (the philosopher Solomon Maimon), Palestine (the standard-bearer of the revival of Hebrew, Eliezer Ben-Yehuda), Paris (Marc Chagall, Chaim Soutine, Emanual Levinas), or America (the founder of the New York Jewish daily *Forward,* Abe Cahan, and the head of RCA, David Sarnoff).

In the Pale of Settlement itself, the Jews constituted about fifteen percent of the population. Yet the demographic structure of their settlements was unusual: they were basically an urban society. In the larger cities, between a third and a half of the total population was Jewish, while in most small towns (the so-called *shtetls*), they constituted two-thirds of the population or more. The Jewish shtetls were surrounded by a sea of Christian villages, where only about one percent of the population was Jewish. The shtetl served as a market place and manufacturing center for the surrounding villages, and as a link between them and the city centers and, beyond them, the markets of Western Europe. It was dominated physically by one or several churches and politically by a Christian administration and police. A shtetl could count between 500 and 5,000 inhabitants and was administratively and professionally different from a village: its inhabitants did not belong to the class of peasants and did not work the land, nor did they possess any land, as the gentry and the Catholic Church did.

This network of hundreds of Jewish communities conducted its separate life in its own three languages: Hebrew of the Bible, the prayer book, the incessant flow of religious books, and official correspondence; Aramaic of the Talmud and Rabbinic knowledge; and Yiddish as the language of home and community life, folklore and modern literature, a language and culture that constituted a bridge between the European world and the traditional religious library.[7] The Jews had their own educational networks, religious institutions, publishing houses, professional organizations, health and philanthropic institutions, and, in modern times, literature, newspapers, libraries, ideologies, political parties, hospitals, and social organizations. Indeed, it was a densely connected social and cultural network, a veritable empire within an empire. Jewish religion had no formal hierarchical organization, and in principle, every rabbi in the smallest community was sovereign. Yet an intense ideological-cultural discourse, conducted in their own private languages, and the authority of the books and of several charismatic scholars, bound them all in one extra-territorial society. In medieval times, the overall framework was religious and defined by law; in modern times, it was secular and voluntaristic. The spreading Hasidic sects, crossing the boundaries of individual communities, and the modern political parties and voluntary organizations cemented this unified network.

In the nineteenth century, European Jewry experienced an unusual population growth: in 1800 there were 2.2 million Jews in the world, and in 1880, 7.5 million. The burden of this growth lay in the confined shtetls of Eastern Europe, especially *Lite,* where poverty was rampant. In 1897, when a major census of the Russian population was conducted, there were 5.3 million Jews in an empire of 120 million. Between 1881 and 1914, about 2.5 million Jews emigrated from the Russian Empire, mostly to America; yet in 1914, on the eve of World War I, there were still 5.5 million Jews in Russia.

In 1897, Vilna had 63,831 Jewish inhabitants; in 1921 their number declined to 46,000, then grew again to 60,000 in 1939. The influx of Jews from the provinces was compensated for by emigration. There were more Jews "from Vilna" around the globe than in Vilna proper; the reason is simple: "from Vilna" meant from Vilna Guberniya, or *Lite* as a whole. Like Jena and Weimar, Cambridge and Oxford, Vilna was a small city, a cultural center serving an immense hinterland. The ties between Vilna and the network of small towns were very close, people traveled back and forth, the city served as a kind of "shopping center" and cultural focus for the whole area, and many small towns fulfilled important roles as well: famous yeshivas were located in small towns, such as Volozhin, Mir, Ponevezh; a major Hasidic sect, *Chabad,* that emerged in eastern Lithuania, had its capital in Lubavitch, a town of 1,667 Jews. Indeed, most Vilna writers and intellectuals were born elsewhere, as for example, the Gaon of Vilna, Max Weinreich, Zelig

7. See my book *The Meaning of Yiddish* (Los Angeles: University of California Press, 1986).

Kalmanowicz, A. Sutzkever, and others. On the other hand, many young people from small towns came to the capital to study in its Rabbinical Seminary or in its Hebrew and Yiddish Teachers' Colleges, then to go back to a small town or emigrate to Palestine or the West.

Hence, when a city of merely 60,000 Jews felt that it was a major center of a worldwide culture, it was because of its cultural institutions and the millions of Eastern European Jews they served and represented. When the intellectuals among only 16,000 remaining Jews in the Vilna Ghetto in 1942 went through the same motions of cultural creativity and competing ideologies, they no longer had that hinterland. Indeed, among the heart-rending parts of Kruk's records are the terse and terrifying chronicles of various liquidated shtetl communities.

In the mid-nineteenth century, when the tsarist censors forbade all Jewish printing except for two cities, Vilna was one of them. The publishing house of the Widow and Brothers Romm executed the extremely complex printing job of the whole Talmud with commentaries, and published Hebrew and Yiddish books for learning and entertainment. In the twentieth century, the publishing house of B. Kletzkin published many of the Yiddish classical and modern writers. Vilna was a center of the Modern Jewish Revolution: Jewish society was transformed from a religious to a national entity, and a new literature in Yiddish, Hebrew, and other languages, as well as a gamut of ideologies and political parties, sprang up almost overnight. In 1897, the year Kruk was born, the illegal Jewish Socialist party, Bund, which would have an enormous influence on the Jewish masses and intellectuals, was founded in Vilna. Half a year later, the Bundists were instrumental in organizing the Russian Social Democratic Workers' Party in Minsk. In the beginning of the twentieth century, Vilna was also the seat of the Zionist and Labor Zionist parties of Russia.

After the Bolshevik Revolution, the Russian borders rolled back. In 1918 both Poland and Lithuania regained independence, and in 1920 the Polish army occupied the city and the surrounding area against Lithuanian objections, and ruled it until September 1939. The majority population of the city was Polish-speaking, and so were the gentry in their estates in the countryside; yet the bulk of the population living in villages was Byelorussian to the north and east and Lithuanian to the west. Under the auspices of the Treaty of Versailles and the League of Nations, national minorities in Poland had autonomous rights to their own cultural activities and education in their own languages. In this framework, a whole rainbow of Jewish political parties and cultural institutions flourished in Vilna and its surroundings. Yiddish, the language spoken by the masses and intellectuals alike, and Hebrew, the language of tradition and of the revived Hebrew society in Palestine, were competing for dominance in the new Jewish national culture; on the other hand, Polish, the language of the state and the universities, exerted its powerful pull. Like Prague, at the crossroads of several cultures, Vilna had an ironic perspective on it all and fostered a modern Jewish culture. It had separate secular schools in Yiddish, other schools in the traditional Ashkenazi Hebrew, yet others in the "Sefardi" Hebrew as revived in Palestine, as well as Jewish schools in the Polish language, observing the Jewish Sabbath; it also had religious schools teaching in Hebrew or in Yiddish, either of a Zionist-and-liberal direction (Mizrahi) or of an ultra-Orthodox kind (Agudes Yisroel), as well as traditional Heders and Talmud Torahs. There were several *Gymnasia* in the different languages (ambitiously academic schools, with a cultural status equivalent to the American college today) and a Yiddish institute of technology, the *Technikum*. Many young Jews went to study in the Polish university, although the antisemitic pressures there were mounting; or in universities in France, Belgium, and elsewhere.

In the interwar period, Jewish Vilna had a dense network of social and cultural institutions and organizations: a Yiddish theater; several daily newspapers; scholarly and popular journals, including the prestigious YIVO-bleter; a literary monthly for children, *Grininke beymelekh* ("Green Trees"); a journal for public health, *Folksgezunt;* Jewish trade unions and professional organizations; sport clubs; public libraries; and so on. Now the Jews could vote both for the Jewish Community Council and for the Polish institutions of city and state. In 1934, several Yiddish writers and artists, including Abraham Sutzkever and Chaim Grade, formed the group of *Yung-Vilne* (Young Vilna), which made a considerable impact on Yiddish literature.

In 1925, the YIVO, Yiddish Scientific Institute, was founded in Vilna by a group of scholars headed by Dr. Max Weinreich and Zelig Kalmanowicz. Members of its governing board included the great Jewish historian Simon Dubnow and Sigmund Freud. The YIVO was a research institute in the Jewish humanities and social sciences, combining the functions of an academy of language and a center of cultural policy. The YIVO competed with the Jewish section of the Soviet Academy of Sciences in Kiev and the Hebrew University in Jerusalem, founded in the same year, yet it was poor in means and could not match a full-fledged university in Jerusalem. In 1939, when World War II broke out, Max Weinreich was at an international linguistics conference in Copenhagen and succeeded in getting to the United States, where he became the moving spirit of the New York branch of YIVO and wrote his monumental *History of the Yiddish Language*. Zelig Kalmanowicz was a spiritual force in the Vilna Ghetto and perished in Estonian camps. The Germans turned the building of the YIVO into a center for collecting and classifying Jewish books to be shipped to Germany for a future *Institute for the Study of Jewry Without Jews*. Herman Kruk, the author of this diary, was the leader of the brigade of Jewish scholars and writers who worked there.

POLITICAL PARTIES

To understand Kruk's diary, a brief description of the range of political parties among the Jews is necessary. With the Modern Jewish Revolution, it became imperative to reunderstand and reformulate the situation of the Jews in the modern world, as well as the human condition in general. After the consolidation of the big nation-states in Europe, the smaller nations also strove to achieve cultural autonomy or national independence. The Jews were an extraterritorial group spread throughout Europe with no majority in any specific territory. Hence they could either merge with the dominant languages and cultures or vie for cultural and political autonomy. At the beginning of the twentieth century it was impossible to foresee the direction and destinies of nationalism and socialism, to weigh the pros and cons of optimism and pessimism. The very existence of the Jews as a culture and as individuals was put in question, hence those ideas about the future deeply touched every person's life and emotions. A variety of diagnoses of the situation and prognoses for the future provided contradictory alternatives which were hotly debated. Hence the justification of a wide range of ideologies, some of which fermented in intellectual circles and crystallized into political parties. When such views and habits of thought and discourse were suddenly caged in a small ghetto, while most of European Jewry was already annihilated, they seemed all nostalgically correct and abysmally irrelevant.

All parties had their antecedents before World War I, and with a few exceptions, constituted nationwide parties throughout Poland or even worldwide organizations. Between the two world wars, Poland was the world center of secular culture in Yiddish. Most parties had their own youth movements and cultural and social institutions affiliated with them. Belonging to a party was like belonging to an extended family that provided most of your cultural needs.

At the extreme left were the Communists. The proximity to the Soviet border, vicious antisemitism in Poland, the appalling poverty of the masses, the hopelessness facing young people in the stagnant economy of the Polish "margin lands" (*Kresy*)—all those, coupled with the closing of the American border and no road to immigration, made the utopia of universal equality an attractive proposition. The Communists were the only general Polish party where Jews were welcome and influential; here they could shed their Jewishness without feeling like traitors to their tribe. Communism also appealed to the idealism and penchant for abstraction widespread among young Jewish intellectuals. Poland, however, became independent in a cruel war with the Bolsheviks, when the Jew Trotsky's Red Army was stopped at the outskirts of Warsaw by "a miracle on the Vistula" in 1920, hence Communism was felt to be Poland's archenemy. Although Poland was legally a democracy, the Communist party was outlawed and its members were put in concentration camps, tortured and humiliated. Several thousand youths crossed the Soviet border illegally, to participate in the "world of tomorrow"; eventually they were all purged by Stalin and many perished, including the brilliant Yiddish writer Moyshe Kulbak. In conditions of conspiracy, the number of actual party members was small, but they were rigorously disciplined and had a wide periphery of sympathizers. The Polish Communist Party got its orders from the Communist International, and in 1938 it was dismantled for alleged "Trotskyism." Yet when the Soviet army took Vilna in September 1939 and again in May 1940, the former Communists were serving the new order, and in the ghetto they were the link to the Soviet partisans and to the only power that could liberate them from the Germans.

A much more popular Socialist party was the Bund, founded in 1897 in Vilna.[8] The Bund was influential in the Jewish trade unions, among the masses and intellectuals alike. It was theoretically Marxist, but anti-Soviet and anti-Communist. It was a pragmatic party, active in all areas of daily life and culture, and believed in a separate Yiddish national culture and in *doikeyt* ("here-ness"), that is, in building a Jewish culture in Poland while simultaneously behaving as full-fledged Polish citizens. It supported Yiddish literature, the Yiddish secular ("worldly") schools, public libraries in the cities and shtetls, and other cultural activities. Not by accident was the first activity of the Bund in the ghetto the establishment of a Social Aid Committee. For the Bund, the Diaspora was a normal way of Jewish existence, if only justice could prevail and Poland could be made more democratic. Yet the non-Jewish Socialists saw the Bundists as hopelessly nationalistic, they were actually expelled from the Russian Social-Democratic Workers' Party in 1903 for nationalist separatism, and even the Russian Menshevik Plekhanov is said to have described them as "Zionists afraid of sea-sickness."

Among the non-Socialist and non-Zionist groups, we may mention the Folkists, populist liberals and Yiddishists, including the admired Vilna social activist Dr. Tsemakh Szabad. Another non-Socialist party was the General Zionists, a middle-class Zionist party with a liberal and a conservative wing, including the head of the Jewish Community, Dr. Jacob Wygodzki. All these parties were secular in outlook and form. Among the religious Jews, there was a national-Zionist party, Mizrahi, and the orthodox and anti-Zionist Agudah (Agudes Yisroel). As in most cities, the religious Jews were a rather small though respected minority; thus, the first Judenrat in Vilna, elected by a group of prominent Jews, had only one representative of the religious in a body of ten. All Zionist parties were affiliated with their counterparts in Eretz-Israel and elsewhere. The Zionists believed in a Jewish home in Palestine, but not many immigrated there.

On the other hand, the radical Zionist movements on both the left and the

8. Its full name was *Algemeyner yidisher arbeter-bund in Lite, Poyln un Rusland* (General Jewish Workers' Union in Lithuania, Poland, and Russia).

right educated the young to activism and immigration to Zion. On the far right were the Revisionists, a party founded by the brilliant Russian, Yiddish, and Hebrew writer Vladimir—Zeev Jabotinsky (who died in New York in 1940), who organized the Jewish Legion in the British army in World War I. He split his movement off from Chaim Weizmann's general Zionist organization, accusing them of talk and inaction. In the late 1930s, Jabotinsky preached a "Catastrophic Aliya," a mass immigration of Jews to Palestine, rightly believing that the ground was burning under their feet. But he could not collect a fleet of ships or alarm Polish Jewry, the British mandatory power would not allow any mass immigration to Palestine, and the Zionist establishment ostracized him. His youth movement, Betar (pronounced "Beytar"), was a disciplined, para-military organization, whose members wore brown shirts and were hostile to both the Diaspora and all socialists. Furthermore, Jabotinsky had contacts with Mussolini's Italy. All that made the socialists (Zionists and anti-Zionists alike) see them as Fascists. The last commander of Betar in Poland was Menachem Begin, a trained Polish officer, who fled to Vilna in 1939, was arrested by the Bolsheviks, then reached Palestine to head the Revisionist underground there, and eventually became prime minister of Israel. When the police in the Vilna Ghetto, and eventually the head of the ghetto (Jacob Gens), were in the hands of former Revisionists, the left had a preconceived image of them.

At the opposite end of the spectrum were several Labor Zionist parties. The most influential was Poalei-Zion (Labor Zionists), a moderately Marxist social democratic party affiliated with Ben-Gurion's Labor party in Eretz-Israel and the largest Kibbutz movement. Poalei-Zion Left was a small party that had tried to enter the Comintern in 1921 but was rejected for its Zionism. Poalei-Zion, which became the larger party, supported Hebrew as the language of the new Zionist society in Israel, yet cherished Yiddish education and literature in the Diaspora; the Left Poalei-Zion, however, was for Yiddish in Eretz-Israel as well. In contrast, Ha-Shomer ha-Tzair (The Young Guard) fostered Hebrew. It was an influential youth organization with no adult political party, because they swore to immigrate to Eretz-Israel as soon as they became adults. They were a scout organization, including uniforms, parades, sport activities, summer camps, and so on; yet they combined it with intense intellectual activities, debating elitist literature, philosophy, and ideology. They also had a strong Kibbutz movement in Eretz-Israel and were perhaps the first intellectual group in the world to combine Marxism with Freud in communes in Palestine after World War I. All Labor Zionist parties had kibbutz movements. Unfortunately, after the British White Paper of 1939, it was almost impossible to immigrate to Palestine, and several thousand *Halutzim,* refugees from Poland, got stuck in Vilna.

The Communists, the various Labor Zionists, and the Revisionists were all radical critics of the situation before the war, and therefore were better prepared to launch a resistance underground in the ghetto.

TWO WORLD WARS

Vilna suffered heavily during World War I. The city was flooded with Jewish refugees, who were expelled by the Russian army from the frontier areas. Large-scale activities were developed to aid the refugees, although the war years were marked by poverty and food shortages. The German army occupied the city from September 1915 to November 1918. The Jewish leadership, headed by Dr. Jacob Wygodzki, maintained a dignified relationship with the Germans. The war was followed by the two Russian Revolutions of February and October 1917. When the Red Army occupied Vilna in January 1919, factions of the leftist parties expressed support for the Communist power, but most Jewish party activities were forbidden. In April, the Polish army took the city back and killed many Jews as "Bolsheviks." The city passed from hand to hand, again to the Bolsheviks, then to the Lithuanians, until Polish army rule was reestablished in October 1920. In March 1922, Vilna and its surrounding area were annexed to Poland and remained Polish until September 1939. The traumatic events of that period molded the attitudes and memories of the Vilna Jewish population and its leadership, and were remembered when they were faced with a new German occupation. But this was an altogether different Germany.

After more than a century of occupation by foreign powers, Poland regained its independence in 1918. It was a much smaller Poland than its medieval predecessor and only about half the Jewish population of the Pale of Settlement was included in it, while the rest remained in the Soviet Union and in the Baltic states. Still, with about 3.5 million Jews toward the end (10 percent of the population, while the Poles made up 70 percent), it was the second-largest Jewish community in the world (after the United States). In cities like Warsaw, Vilna, Łódź, and Lemberg, Jews constituted a third or more of the population. Independent Poland was the major Jewish cultural and political center in the world (Palestine had 80,000 Jews in 1922). Jewish life was bustling with all kinds of activities: political parties, social organizations, schools, literature, newspapers, a news media agency, and so on—if ever there was a secular Jewish nation and national autonomy, it was in Poland between the two world wars. The center of all those activities was naturally in the capital of the state, Warsaw, with its population of more than a million (among them, 353,000 Jews in 1931). The Central Committees of most Jewish parties and organizations had their offices in Warsaw. Vilna, with its 60,000 Jews, was a small town in comparison. Moreover, Jews played a key role in Polish industry, commerce, and literature, and the majority rapidly assimilated to the Polish language and culture.

Jews could vote and were represented in the Polish Sejm and Senat, although Poland was intermittently democratic and dictatorial; and in the late 1930s, Nazi influences rose and the air was increasingly antisemitic. Jewish merchants were pressured, Jewish students at Polish universities had to sit in special ghetto seats and preferred instead to stand at the back of the classrooms; they were often beaten by Polish nationalist students. In 1938, Dr. Max Weinreich went to the Vilna Governor (Wojewoda) and demanded that the pogrom against Jewish students be stopped; on his way home, he was attacked by Polish students and lost an eye.

World War II began with almost the same participants and in the same theater as the previous war, but this time both Germany and the Soviet Union were totalitarian states ruled by extremist ideologies. Barely a year after the appeasement in Munich, in March 1939, the Germans dismantled Czechoslovakia with impunity. At dawn of September 1, 1939, the German army launched a Blitzkrieg on Poland. On September 3, England and France declared war on Germany, and World War II began. It was the first German Blitzkrieg of the war: within a week, the Polish defense crumbled, the legendary Polish cavalry was no match for the German tanks, and Warsaw was surrounded. Pockets of the Polish army fought on for three more weeks, but the government, along with many of the Polish and Jewish political and intellectual leadership, fled abroad. Thousands of residents, especially young men, left Warsaw, marching toward the East. Herman Kruk was among them.

On September 17, 1939, implementing the Molotov-Ribbentrop secret pact, the Soviet army crossed the Polish border in the East, and Poland was again divided between its two neighboring powers. In the first days the Germans humiliated Jews, tortured and killed them, and eventually closed them in walled ghettos in Warsaw and a few other Polish cities. In eastern Poland, now annexed to Byelorussia and Ukraine, the Soviet authorities arrested and exiled or shot Polish officers, "Bourgeois elements" (including many Jewish manufacturers and merchants), and activists of most Jewish parties. The leaders of the Bund, Henryk Erlich and Wiktor Alter, were arrested and eventually executed. Several Vilna intellectuals and political leaders were taken away and disappeared, among them Zalmen Reisen, author of a multivolume lexicon of Yiddish literature and editor of the highbrow Yiddish newspaper *Der Tog,* and the lawyer Joseph Czernichow, who had defended many Communists in Polish trials.

In October 1939, the Soviets turned Vilna over to Lithuania, at the time a semifascist state, which, however, maintained normal relations with the free world. The city was renamed Vilnius and became the capital of the small Lithuanian state. An influx of Lithuanians, including many Jews, filled important positions in the municipal administration and social institutions. Many Jewish refugees from Poland who were stuck in the Soviet zone, especially members of non-Communist parties, Zionist pioneers (Halutzim), writers and intellectuals—the elite of Polish Jewry—tried to cross the new Soviet-Lithuanian border illegally to get to Vilnius. Thousands of refugees filled the city; it was estimated that, in its heyday, Vilna had 80,000 Jews out of a total of 200,000 inhabitants. From independent Lithuania, people who got visas, aided by international organizations, could immigrate to America or Canada via Siberia and Japan, or to Palestine via Odessa. But visas were hard to come by, and only a few thousand were fortunate enough to reach their destinations; some got stuck in Japan and were interned in a ghetto in Shanghai during the war years.

In June 1940, the Soviet army occupied all the Baltic states, and Vilnius became the capital of Soviet Lithuania. All political parties were abolished, all former newspapers were closed, all Jewish schools became Soviet-Yiddish institutions. The immigration of refugees, especially to America, still went on, since the Soviets liked the heavy ransom money that was paid, and Kruk was active in sending comrades out. He himself could not make it, and was caught by the German occupation. In mid-June 1941, just a week before the treacherous and massive German attack on their Soviet allies, a new wave of arrests shook the city of Vilna. Many of those lucky "enemies of the people," who were sent in cattle cars to Siberia, survived the war and the Holocaust.

On June 22, 1941, the German armies crossed the Soviet border and moved east in a Blitzkrieg toward Moscow. World War II was in full rage. Several thousand Jews tried to escape to the east, but most were stopped on the former Soviet border and not allowed into the Soviet Union. They turned back, were betrayed and massacred by peasants and the oncoming German army, and not many returned to Vilna to face the horrors there. Only a few succeeded in crossing the old Soviet border and fleeing deep into Russia. Herman Kruk, himself a refugee from occupied Warsaw, was in a resigned mood, decided not to renew his flight, and instead resolved to keep a diary of the impending events. Actually, it was a continuation of his earlier attempts to chronicle the collapse of Poland and its Jewry.

HERMAN KRUK

Hershl, or Herman, Kruk was born in the Polish city of Płock (read "Plotsk") on May 19, 1897, a crucial year in modern Jewish history.[9] Symbolically, several major political and cultural options were inaugurated in 1897: the first World Zionist Congress was held in Basel; the Bund was founded in Vilna; Simon Dubnow wrote his first "Letter on the Old and New Judaism" formulating the theory of Autonomism; the Yiddish newspaper *Forward* was inaugurated in New York; the Hebrew literary journal *Ha-Shiloah* was published by the spiritual Zionist Ahad Ha-Am. Thus all options of modern Jewish literature and ideologies came of age when Kruk was born. The year 1897 was also the year of the great census in the Russian Empire, which gives us a precise image of Jewish demography and settlement in eastern Europe; it was the year in which a programmatically antisemitic

9. The early biography of Herman Kruk in this chapter is derived from the essay written by his brother, Pinkhes Schwartz, published in the Yiddish edition of Kruk's diary.

ideologue was elected mayor of Vienna and Sigmund Freud joined the Jewish lodge of B'nai B'rith.

Kruk's father, a "scribe" in a vinegar factory, died at the age of 44. Of his six children, three died in infancy. Hershl, the eldest, was 17 years old when his father died and World War I broke out (his sister was 14 and his brother 12). Płock changed hands several times, and when the Russian army ordered the immediate evacuation of all Jews, the Germans marched into town. Herman was a trained photographer and moved around the neighboring towns to record events and support his family. When the German occupation powers made an appeal for workers to pave highways, many young Jews registered, both to become productive workers—as modern Jewish ideologies demanded—and to support their families. For the Jews, the German occupation meant freedom from persecution and oppression: Jewish clubs, unions, and libraries sprang up overnight. The German powers organized factories for preserving fruits and vegetables to be sent to Germany, and Herman Kruk was a supervisor in one of them.

At the same time, he immersed himself in reading and in the activities of the new political trends. At first he was active in Zionist circles and avidly read books he borrowed from Ha-Zamir (Nightingale) library (founded during the revolution of 1905 and managed by a group of Bundists and Zionists). He was fascinated by modern Yiddish literature, and a circle of young people gathered for long evenings at his home, debating Yiddish literature and current events. Political activities focused around Ha-Zamir library and the new Yiddish political-cultural weeklies that arrived from nearby Warsaw. He was especially attracted by the figure of Vladimir Medem, the son of a Russian general, who returned to the Judaism of his ancestors, learned Yiddish, and became a fiery orator and influential ideologue of the Bund; and by Medem's theory of national-cultural autonomy for the Jews. At the same time, Kruk frequented a semi-clandestine Polish leftist circle affiliated with SDKPL (Social Democrats of the Kingdom of Poland and Lithuania), whose leaders included Rosa Luxemburg, and which soon joined the new Communist International. As a Communist, he participated in disarming German soldiers after the German Revolution of November 1918.

When Poland regained its independence, Kruk was drafted into the army, where he continued his clandestine Communist activities but became increasingly critical of Soviet terror and the Communist neglect of the Jewish question. He was attracted to the Yiddish cultural activities of the Bund in Warsaw and became an ardent critic of Communism. Although he had no formal education, he was always immersed in learning and believed in promoting education among the workers. At the National Committee of the Trade Unions in Warsaw he organized a Cultural Department, whose secretary and moving force was Kruk himself. Later, as secretary of the Cultural Department of Tsukunft (the youth organization of the Bund) he organized "traveling libraries." In 1930 Herman Kruk became the director of the Yiddishist Grosser Library at the Kultur-lige (Cultural

League) in Warsaw, and headed its Library Center, which comprised some 400 libraries in towns around Poland. He edited its monthly library journal and published many articles and studies on library matters in Yiddish and Polish journals. In 1936 Kruk became secretary (that is, leader) of the Cultural League.

Herman Kruk's first wife died young, and their child died during birth. He remarried a few years before World War II. The war broke out on September 1, 1939, and on September 5 the Polish government left the city. Kruk left at 4 P.M. with five others, without their wives, assuming that men were in greater danger and would be drafted into the Polish army anyway. In January 1940 he described his wanderings from Warsaw and sent the memoir piecemeal to his brother-in-law in Tel Aviv (the manuscript is in the YIVO archives and is translated in this book).

Kruk managed to cross the frontier to the Soviet occupied zone of Poland, where he met his brother and eventually joined a group of Yiddish writers that reached Vilna on October 10, just before it was turned over to independent Lithuania. He attempted to bring his wife, but she was arrested on the way by the Soviets and exiled to Russian camps. In the summer of 1940, the American Jewish Labor Committee got a number of U.S. visas for writers and political activists who were in danger of being arrested by the Soviets. Kruk's brother, Pinkhes Schwartz, and many others left for the United States via Siberia and Japan. According to his brother's conjecture, the hope of seeing his wife someday prevented Kruk from using an American visa and leaving the Soviet Union. He helped ship others to the United States but didn't make it himself. In Vilna, he researched the history of Jewish libraries there and sent the materials to his brother in New York for a future study.

Finally, Herman Kruk also bought a ticket to Vladivostok in the Russian Far East, but it was too late: the Soviet authorities would not let him go unless he consented to join the Polish army in England and work as a spy for the Russians, which he refused. On June 24, 1941, the German army marched into Vilna.

KRUK IN THE GHETTO

Poland ruled Vilna from March 1921 until September 1939. The Soviets occupied Vilna in September–October 1939 and arrested a number of prominent Jewish intellectuals, politicians, and community leaders and shipped them off to the East. In October 1939 the Soviets transferred Vilna to independent Lithuania in return for military concessions. Vilna was renamed Vilnius and a process of Lithuanization began. The local Vilnaites, Poles and Jews alike, did not know the difficult Lithuanian language, and many functions were assumed by newcomers from Kovno (Kaunas). In June 1940, the Red Army took over all of the Baltic states and the Lithuanian Soviet Socialist Republic was established. The Reds were back in Vilna. A year later, in mid-June 1941, mass arrests were carried out in Vilnius;

thousands of former political "enemies," "bourgeois" persons, refugees, and other "elements" were sent to Siberia. Many of them were freed from Soviet camps during the war, as former Polish citizens; many died in exile. But many didn't know how lucky they were, and survived the Holocaust in Russia; as former Polish citizens, they could return to Poland after the war, and from there, most left for Israel, the United States, and other countries.

Vilnius was still paralyzed from the great purge when the Germans attacked their Communist allies and marched on Moscow. Vilnius was taken on June 24, 1941. The horrors of the first months under the Nazis are described in Kruk's diary, and we shall not preempt it here. On September 6, 1941, the surviving Jews were herded into the tiny ghetto, encompassing seven narrow streets in a former slum and medieval "ghetto" area (there had never been an official ghetto in medieval Vilna). Of an estimated 76,000–80,000 Jews before the war, about 40,000 were crammed into two ghettos. Forty thousand Jews were summarily executed in Ponar—it was the first mass execution of Jews the Germans undertook when they crossed into the territory of the Soviet Union. Soon, the smaller "Second Ghetto" was liquidated and most of its inhabitants were sent to Ponar.

When the underground in Warsaw Ghetto learned about Ponar, they concluded that this was the beginning of the extermination of all Jews in Europe, an ideological policy rather than a unique case.[10] The same conclusion was drawn by Abba Kovner, the leader of the Ha-Shomer ha-Tzair youth movement in the Vilna Ghetto, who on New Year's Eve 1942 called for an end to delusions and for armed resistance.

The sense of a vibrant Jewish city between the two world wars, which lived in the memories of most Vilnaites, as unique in its richness and vitality, was based on a multitude of cultural and political options, arguing and competing with each other. There was in Vilna a highly intelligent, alert, and erudite youth, oriented toward culture and ideas. Some of them left to study in Western Europe; others perished in the Soviet Union, in the partisans, and in the Holocaust. There was a "war of languages": between Yiddish and Hebrew, between traditional Ashkenazi Hebrew and the Zionist "Sephardi" Hebrew, and between all of them and the language of culture, Polish; and there was an uninterrupted argument between all the political trends. But all those were dialogues conducted on one stage; they hated each other, enriched each other, and yet needed each other.

Now a United Partisan Organization, FPO, was formed in the ghetto, with members of all youth movements sharing each cell of five. After all, they spoke one common language. Their story was tragic; the envisioned revolt in the ghetto did not sweep the masses and did not materialize. Nevertheless, several hundred

10. Antek (Yitzhak Zuckerman), who was born in Vilna, heard about Ponar in November 1941 and concluded: "This was the beginning of the end. A total death sentence for the Jews." See his book *A Surplus of Memory*, pp. 154–155.

of them reached the forests and fought in the Soviet partisan movement, and many of them survived. Kruk had contacts with the partisans, part of the Bund organization joined them, but he himself was reserved about them. Eventually, when the liquidation of the ghetto came, he accepted the next German lie and persuaded people to leave for the "work camps" in Estonia.

In the less than two years before the ghetto, Kruk was occupied in various social functions and refugee activities. Only in the ghetto did he become a visible figure in Vilna's cultural and social life. We must remember that Vilna was stripped of most of its Jewish leadership. Some were arrested by the Soviets in 1939 and in 1941; some emigrated during the window of independent Lithuania and even in the last Soviet year, especially to the United States and Palestine. And some were killed by the Germans in the first months of their occupation, among them the old leader of the community, Dr. Jacob Wygodzki. Thus, some central positions in the ghetto were occupied either by outsiders or by young people. The head of the ghetto, Jacob Gens, was a Lithuanian army captain; the director of the Youth Club, Leon Bernstein, was from Prussia; Kruk was from Warsaw; Abba Kovner was twenty-three years old and had to make crucial decisions concerning the life of the revolt and the lives of its soldiers, while all senior party leaders had left. Kruk was a Bundist and felt like a fish in water in the political and social life of the ghetto.

Kruk was a librarian and the builder of the library in the Vilna Ghetto. When the hundred thousandth book was borrowed, he made a special celebration. When abandoned secular and holy books were found in the liquidated "Second Ghetto," he organized an expedition to save them. For the sake of the Rosenberg Institute, he collected Jewish books from the Polish university and from around the city, for which he got German permission to move freely in the city. Kruk, Sutzkever, and others tried to save rare books and manuscripts from the YIVO collections, smuggle them into the ghetto, and hide them in cellars. The wise old man Zelig Kalmanowicz told them: "*Kinderlekh,* don't even try, the Germans will do it better than you ever could." For the YIVO workers, it seemed terrible that they had to pack the books in crates for shipment to Germany. But paradoxically, Kalmanowicz was right: those books were saved, found after the war, and shipped to YIVO in New York by Lucy Dawidowicz and others.

We may conclude this section with two vignettes (both quoted in Pinkhas Schwartz's "Biography of Herman Kruk" in the Yiddish edition of this book).

Dina Abramowicz tells about the "*Aktion* of the yellow permits" in October 1941, when those without such permits were sent to Ponar. "When the column of Judenrat employees began to move, we suddenly saw, to our amazement and fear, a strange couple: Herman Kruk walked in his short coat and beret, with firm strides and lifted head, and on his arm the ancient Pati Kremer, who, with her grey hair and wrinkled face, looked like his grandmother." Pati Kremer, 75 years old, widow of the founder of the Bund Arkady Kremer, was a veteran leader of the

Bund and its moral authority in the ghetto. By a miracle, they passed German muster as husband and wife. Pati was saved for another year or two.

The Vilna University librarian Anna Šimaite, who often helped her Jewish colleagues, writes: "Like a little mouse, gathering grains one by one for its nest, Herman Kruk himself brought and encouraged others to collect books in the ghetto. . . . It was amazing to see the consistency and patience with which he dug into the materials. When he came to the [university] library, he was always restrained, calm, and polite. Some university employees said: 'When this little Jew with the yellow patches on his chest and his back comes to us—we want to stand up and bow our head to him.'"

Kruk was not the only one who wrote diaries in those days. Even before the war, writing autobiographies and diaries was cultivated by most intellectual circles. The experiences of World War I and the precarious situation of the Jews linked the present to its historical roots. The circle and the journal *Yunger historiker* (Young Historian) in the late 1930s heightened this awareness; Emanuel Ringelblum, the chronicler of the Warsaw Ghetto, was one of the young historians. Herman Kruk was a parallel figure in the Vilna Ghetto, and he was well positioned to collect information and documentation, and well known enough for many to bring him materials.

ESTONIA

The partisan movement in the ghetto was in a difficult dilemma: a real base for their anti-Nazi activities could be found in the Soviet partisan movement in the deep forests around Vilna. But they had decided to stay with their people and lead the masses in an uprising before the liquidation of the ghetto. The leadership of the FPO were young representatives of the major youth movements in the ghetto (except for the religious, who were negligible and didn't have such ideas). The Commander of FPO was the veteran Communist Itzik Wittenberg, an "elder statesman" in his mid-thirties, while the others were in their twenties. The Communists were a strong and disciplined group, experienced in underground work. It was also natural to have a Communist at the helm because he could establish contacts with the only resistance movement outside the ghetto, the Communist party in the city and the Soviet partisans who got orders and weapons from Moscow.

For more than a year there was a lull in the Vilna Ghetto (January 1942–March 1943), the mass persecutions seemed to be over, the remaining Jews were so productive that they would be saved to contribute to the German war effort. Law and order and social and cultural activities dominated ghetto life. No one knew about the Nazi decision on the "final solution." But in March, the persecutions and deportations began again; the Jewish communities in the small towns were liquidated one by one, their remnants crowded into the Vilna Ghetto.

In April–May 1943, an uprising in the Warsaw Ghetto reverberated in the world media. It was crushed by the Germans but became a heroic page in the book of Jewish resistance. Suddenly, in July 1943, the Vilna Gestapo demanded the extradition of the FPO leader Itzik Wittenberg *alive,* or else they would destroy the whole ghetto. The head of the ghetto, Jacob Gens, incited the masses with the slogan: 1 or 20,000. Underworld characters and Jewish police, masses of ghetto Jews besieged partisan headquarters with screams: "We want to live!" The Germans were staying out of it. For the partisans, it made no sense to start the uprising then and there because that would mean fighting the Jews rather than the Germans. In a terrible bind, the partisan leadership decided to let Wittenberg go alone to the Gestapo. He apparently got hold of a cyanide capsule and committed suicide the same day.

This was the beginning of the end. "Wittenberg Day" changed the direction of the FPO, and they began sending people to the forests. The Germans learned about the existence of a partisan organization in the Vilna Ghetto and wanted to avoid the Warsaw experience. The new ruse was to send people to labor camps in Estonia.[11]

After the liquidation of the small Jewish community in Estonia in 1941, Jews from Theresienstadt and Germany were brought there in September 1942—90 percent of them were liquidated. Then, about 20,000 Jews from Vilna (and Kovno) were brought to work for the German war industry. They were taken from Vilna in four waves: on August 6, 1943; August 24; September 1–3; and September 23–26, at the final liquidation of the Vilna Ghetto. The first wave provoked a revolt of the Jews who were to be sent; they were fired on and many died or were wounded. To calm the atmosphere, the Germans sent several Jewish brigadiers to Estonia to see the situation for themselves, and organized personal letters from those in the Estonian labor camps. The purpose was to convince the Vilna Jews that, for a change, Estonia meant not extermination but work. Kruk, who did not opt for the partisans, walked from house to house to convince the hiding Jews to go voluntarily. Hundreds of Jews were hiding in underground *melinas* (hiding bunkers, equipped with all necessary provisions). But the Estonian police and the Germans found the melinas, broke in, and took them out by the hundreds.

The background for the expulsions to Estonia was both the decision to liquidate the Vilna Ghetto and Himmler's order of June 21, 1943, ordering all able-bodied Jews transferred from the ghettos of "Ostland" to the concentration camps, and all "unnecessary" ones liquidated. Estonia was close to the Leningrad front, and Hitler's ambition to take that city was thwarted. On August 11, 1943, Hitler ordered the construction of an "Eastern Wall," a defense line stretching

11. Most of the information on the camps in Estonia in this section is based on M. Dworzecki's book *Vayse nekht un shvartse teg* (*White Nights and Black Days: The Jewish Camps in Estonia* [Tel Aviv, 1970]). There were also a Hebrew and a shorter French version.

from near Leningrad to the south. The Jews were to help in building that wall in the north.

The inmates were constantly shifted from one camp to another, both to fill various needed works and to confuse the prisoners. Kruk himself was apparently sent to Estonia in September (23?), 1943. He wrote a diary from September 1943 in the main camp, Klooga, and continued in camp Lagedi, where he was taken on August 22, 1944, until his death on September 18, 1944.

In the summer of 1944, the Red Army pushed into Estonia, first cutting it off in a cauldron. The final offensive began on September 15. On September 16, the German army was allowed to retreat from Estonia. On September 18, Obersturmfuehrer Otto Brenneisen, Commandant of all Estonian camps, arrived in Lagedi, promised to transfer the Jews to a warmer camp, gave them food, and loaded them on trucks. That was the usual German lie. They were taken to a place 40 kilometers from Lagedi, where a big pyre of wooden logs was prepared. The Germans tied 10–12 Jews with ropes and ordered them to lie on top of the logs, where they were shot. The others were kept at a distance. The process lasted from 11 A.M. until dark. In the end, the Germans set fire to the pyre. On the 19th, a mass slaughter finished the largest Estonian camp in Klooga. Soon, the Soviet army marched in and found the pyres with the burned bodies. Only a very few survived.

The day before, on the 17th, Kruk wrote his last sentences and buried his diaries in the presence of six friends; only one of them, Nisan Anolik, survived, went back to Lagedi, retrieved the diaries, and brought them to Vilna. From there, some of Kruk's manuscripts were taken to Israel and preserved in the Moreshet Institute, and others were confiscated by the Soviets and kept for half a century. Some of them miraculously survived.

THIS BOOK

This book contains, first of all, an English translation of the whole edition of Kruk's diary published in Yiddish under the title *Diary of the Vilna Ghetto* (New York: YIVO, 1961). The editor of that edition, Mordkhe V. Bernstein, and Kruk's brother Pinkhes Schwartz, who wrote a sketch of Kruk's biography, did an invaluable job of reproducing Kruk's text and identifying and annotating dozens of names, allusions, and events. In the early 1950s, they conducted a worldwide correspondence with witnesses of Kruk's life; they also compared Kruk's entries with other published accounts of the events. That evidence by survivors and Kruk's contemporaries is irreplaceable; therefore, as far as possible, we have kept the original annotations and inserts. We did not continue their comparative work—that would lead us too far afield, and it is the task of the historian to compare and clarify what actually happened. But we updated the annotations, whenever necessary.

That first edition was based on the manuscript dictated by Kruk to his secretary in the ghetto library. It was typed on long, single-spaced, densely packed pages. Out of 757 pages, only 510 survived: 380 pages were sent to the YIVO (probably by A. Sutzkever) in 1948, and an additional 130 pages were brought in 1959 from Yad Vashem in Jerusalem. For some reason, the editors did not look for any materials in the institutions of Ha-Shomer Ha-Tzair, brought from Vilna by Ruzhka Korczak and Abba Kovner.

The editor of the Yiddish edition read other sources on the history of the Vilna Ghetto and inserted into the text his conjectures about the events described in the missing 250 pages. But in the Moreshet archives in Israel we found a manuscript of 101 pages in Kruk's handwriting, listing the precise table of contents, often recording ten and twenty topics per day. Kruk kept it as a separate document, apparently to be able to reconstruct his diary in case the diary itself was lost. In April 1943, after the liquidation of the small towns and the "Purim scare" in the ghetto at the end of March, Kruk hid his diary and wrote a plea to anyone who might find it (reproduced in this book). The table of contents, however, was concluded on May 10, and was apparently taken to Klooga because it survived in Israel along with other Klooga papers.

But the first editors did not touch any manuscripts in longhand, or did not get hold of them. We inserted the missing titles (which are printed in italics in this book), thus providing a continuous story of Kruk's diary. Naturally, whenever the conjectures of the first editor went astray, we changed them.

In spite of the title *Diary of the Vilna Ghetto,* the printed book included also the important period under Nazi occupation *before* the ghetto, when the spirit of Vilna Jews was really broken and their first Judenrat brutally murdered.

Yet the great puzzle is: Why does the manuscript break off in mid-sentence on July 14, 1943? There can be no doubt that Kruk continued writing his diary in the good conditions he had in the ghetto, for he did it even in the harshest conditions of Klooga, after 14 hours of physical labor (and Kruk was taken to Estonia apparently on September 23). It seems to me that there is only one explanation: the text we have was abruptly cut off before the two tragic days of Itzik Wittenberg's delivery to the Gestapo.

We can reconstruct the situation as follows. When the Soviets came back to Vilna in July 1944, they immediately instituted their party and secret police. To them, the Wittenberg affair was the betrayal of the partisan leader in Vilna, the delivery of the commander by his own troops to the Gestapo (which it was, but the tragic circumstances of the abnormal Jewish situation must be taken into account). They perceived that treachery as especially egregious, since Wittenberg was a Communist and the others were not. An investigation was conducted to discover who betrayed Wittenberg. Kruk's manuscript was in the new Jewish Museum; a little note shows that he himself was posthumously investigated: was he for the partisans or not? The Yiddish poet A. Sutzkever, who was in charge of the Jewish Museum, was close to the Lithuanian Soviet powers. The Lithuanian President Justas Paleckis was his patron: in Lithuanian jails in the 1930s, Paleckis had learned Yiddish from fellow Communists, and in 1940 he translated some of Sutzkever's poems into Lithuanian. He was instrumental in bringing Sutzkever out of the partisan forest to Moscow in the middle of the war.[12] And now he awarded the poet and partisan Sutzkever with the prestigious Soviet medal of the Red Star.

Sutzkever told me that he hid 17 pages of Kruk's diary, dealing with the Wittenberg affair, in his locked drawer in the museum, because it was a "sensitive issue." We don't know whether those pages were destroyed or confiscated by the NKVD. In any case, apparently to avoid suspicion, not just the Wittenberg pages but the whole last part of the manuscript was deleted. Thus, we have nothing for July 15–September 27, 1943, unless it surfaces somewhere else.

As explained above, we added some of the available material covering the periods before and after the ghetto, and we divided the book into ten chapters to make the long chronicle more manageable for the reader. Manuscripts that predated the ghetto had been typed, but the handwritten manuscripts, either drafts from the late ghetto period or texts written in the camps, were especially difficult to decipher. In some cases, the photocopy obtained in Vilnius transferred both the front and back writing on thin paper, and we had to disentangle the positive side from the negative. Often the pages were scattered and renumbered arbitrarily when they arrived in the Vilnius Jewish Museum. Some of the poetry was retyped in the museum by someone using the Soviet spelling, who often made mistakes in reading the original.

The major problem of Kruk's book is that he wrote it as a two-level record: he collected a large number of documents and referred to them in his daily entries. The documents included official German orders, ghetto regulations and official ghetto statistics, excerpts from newspapers in several languages, private letters, poems, ghetto publications, recordings of witness accounts by others, and whatnot. The purpose was to give his subjective voice an objective foundation. Often it is hard to understand the diary entries for lack of the documents they refer to. The hundreds of documents, however, were apparently placed at the end of the diary. To the extent they were found after the Holocaust, they were scattered around the world, especially in Israel and the YIVO. The editor of the Yiddish edition often marks the number of the YIVO file where the document can be found, and more often, when Kruk writes "document attached," the Yiddish book says, "document not attached."

Regrettably, we followed the first editor's practice. Finding the documents now would take much longer and at least double the size of the book. Furthermore, today, more than half a century later, it makes sense not to separate the

12. See my introduction in A. Sutzkever, *Selected Poetry and Prose,* trans. Barbara and Benjamin Harshav (Los Angeles: University of California Press, 1993).

documents collected by Kruk from other documents, but to publish a large critical edition of Vilna Ghetto documents. The rich Sutzkever-Kaczerginski collection at the YIVO and the collections in Israel provide a good start.

As mentioned above, Kruk had literary ambitions. He clearly planned a thinly disguised fictional account of the Holocaust, where instead of the daily diary entries, prototypical situations and individual characters would be vividly described. There are various notes, detailed lists of points to be developed, and beginnings of many chapters. The names are often authentic or thinly disguised; yet there are specific signals that it is fiction, such as that "Vilmen" is a code word for "Vilna."

Book 2, "Underground Ghetto," apparently influenced Sutzkever's conception of his long poem "Clandestine Ghetto." It is interesting that the descriptions of Klooga were titled "Book 6: Liberation"; in July–September 1944, when this was written, Vilna was liberated (Kruk wrote poems about it), the Germans were losing the war, Klooga was not a death camp, and the Soviet Army was just around the corner. It is in the perspective of the imminent liberation that the internal social tensions in the camp are portrayed. Socialist ideology and criticism of the "Strong Ones" merge here with the jealousy of the underdog toward those who wine and dine in the camp. Jewish trade is seen in a grotesque light, as a negative and unreal feature, although Kruk understands at the same time that it served Jewish survival. Unfortunately, there was no time to present all that material here, but we did include several relatively finished sections in Chapters 9 and 10.

It is interesting to note that Kruk, a prominent activist in Yiddish culture in Warsaw, made spelling mistakes in Yiddish and did not observe the new spelling rules established by the YIVO. He makes typical dialectal mistakes, confusing "I" and "U" (thus confusing *in* and *un*) or hypercorrecting them in the literary-Lithuanian dialect. He also constantly misspells the Hebrew words in Yiddish (systematically spelling, for example, *shokhn* ("neighbor") with a *het*).

Kruk observes the world with a chronicler's eyes but through the lens of his party rhetoric. Various expressions have to be read in light of this discourse. A typical case is his use of *khaver* ("comrade" or "colleague") for any Bundist (party comrade), "friend" for non-party colleagues, and "Mr." almost as an offensive title, or an indication of an official or bourgeois figure. Naive as he was, Kruk used various devices of conspiracy that anybody who reads Yiddish could easily decipher. On sensitive matters, he wrote about himself in third person, calling himself "K." or "H."; and names are often given in reverse: Rebayrsh for Schreiber, Shtivelepets for Tsepelevitsh, and so on.

A major problem is the transcription of names of persons and places. We use the YIVO transcription of Yiddish (which is basically similar to the non-phonetic transcription of Russian), yet allowing for several exceptions in cases of familiar American spelling (for example, *Chaim* rather than *Khayim*). But for names of persons or streets which are clearly non-Jewish, the respective spellings were used: Polish, German, Lithuanian.

This practice needs explanation. Vilna was a Yiddish cultural center, and it would be offensive to Polonize or Germanize it. Yet many Jews did precisely that. Thus, it is customary in the United States to spell Jewish names in the German way—*Goldstein, Eisenstein*—yet in a transcription they are spelled, as in Yiddish, *Goldshteyn, Ayzenshteyn*.

The Poles ruled in Vilna for only 18 years: 1921–1939. Many of the persons discussed here lived in that period and had to adjust their official names to the language of the state; therefore they often appear in books in the Polish form. In 1940 came the Lithuanian spelling, and before 1920 it was Russian. But the names themselves were much older in Yiddish. For example, the Polish spelling *Jaszunski* was, before the revolution, *Yashunskii* in Russian, and after 1940, *Jasunskas* in Lithuanian. We left the Yiddish pronunciation: *Yashunski*. Or how shall we spell the name *Zajdsznur* (Polish), *Seidschnur* (German), or *Zaydshnur* (Russian and Yiddish)?

Since the Jews lived in that area for five or six hundred years, their names need no adaptation to passing powers and fashions. This is also true for names of streets and towns, many of which had different Yiddish names or Yiddish variants. The Jewish *Zezmer* is Polish *Zhazmiry* and Lithuanian *Zazmeriai*. The Jewish *Baranovitsh* was Polish *Baranowicze* for 21 years, and since 1939 it has been the Byelorussian *Baranovitshi;* so why spell the Polish way? The reader would not find it on a modern map of Belarus. *Glezer* (Glazier) Street in Vilna—a Jewish street—was translated into Polish—*Szklana*—and had a different name in Lithuanian; why not keep the old Jewish name?

A contrary example is the striking collection of photographs in the Washington, D.C., Holocaust Memorial from a Jewish town they call *Ajsziszki,* but this artificial Polish name was imposed on the town for only 17 years; since 1939 it has had a Lithuanian name, *Eisiskiai,* whereas it was a predominantly Jewish town for centuries, and its memory should be preserved as *Eyshishok*.

EPILOGUE: THE END OF JERUSALEM IN EUROPE

We called this book *The Last Days of the Jerusalem of Lithuania*. "Lithuania" is not the small Baltic country that carries that name today, but the vast area between Poland and Moscow that was the multilingual Grand Duchy of Lithuania in medieval Europe, whose official language was Byelorussian, later Polish, and whose towns and markets resounded with Yiddish, and whose spaces were eulogized by Czeslaw Milosz and preserved in Jewish popular myth.

The Jewish religion and national consciousness are symbolized not by a person but by a place. The longing for Jerusalem throughout two thousand years of Diaspora provided the pivotal axis for the self-perception of the Jews as a nation in Exile, waiting for Redemption. The last two terms are often used as an ideological pun: *GoLA–GeuLA,* as if the two concepts of Exile and Redemption were inseparable twins. Indeed, from the very beginning of Jewish mythology, the moral image of man hinges on a two-place axis: one you were exiled to and one you are yearning for. Adam and Eve are banned from the Garden of Eden, which remains forever their measure of ideal values; the first father of the nation, Abraham, is exiled "from your country and from your homeland and from your father's house" in Aram of the Two Rivers (Mesopotamia)—and sent to the Promised Land; the Exodus from Egypt and the return to the Promised Land, celebrated every Passover, is the great parable of Jewish existence. The modern return to the Holy Land is used as a response to the Holocaust.

By calling their city "Jerusalem of Lithuania," Vilna Jews stressed this bipolar existence. On the one hand, it means "wherever we are, we are longing for Jerusalem"; on the other hand, it implies "whatever we have here is a substitute for Jerusalem"—if not in power, at least in spirit. There were other communities that called themselves "Jerusalem": Frankfurt am Main; Charleston, South Carolina. But Vilna was embraced as such by the whole modern Jewish culture.

By calling this book *The Last Days of the Jerusalem of Lithuania,* we indicate that it is not just about the sufferings of one person, the refugee Herman Kruk who was stranded in Vilna; or about the monstrous, stupid, and sadistic liquidation of a town of 60,000 Jews; but about the end of the Second Jerusalem. For more than a millennium, dating from the beginning of the Christian era, Jews lived and created in Europe, longer than they had been sovereign in their original independent state in Palestine.

Jews have always remembered the first Jerusalem as the utopian home of their dignity as a nation. The recent *Churban,* as the survivors called it, the Destruction of European Jewry, is of the same magnitude as the two Destructions of the Temple and the state in the ancient Land of Israel. Now that a worldly third Jerusalem has been built in its original place, we must not forget the Second Jerusalem in Jewish history.

THE LAST DAYS OF THE JERUSALEM OF LITHUANIA

CHAPTER 1
THE COLLAPSE OF POLAND
SEPTEMBER 1939 – JUNE 1941

THE FLIGHT OF A WAR REFUGEE

[*After devouring Austria and Czechoslovakia, the German army marched into Poland on September 1, 1939. Two days later, Poland's allies, England and France, declared war on Germany, and World War II began. The German* Blitzkrieg *was so swift that Poland, in spite of heroic resistance, collapsed in a matter of weeks. The Polish government, along with several politicians and intellectuals, fled via Romania to England. On September 17, the Red Army crossed Poland's eastern border and occupied the eastern part of Poland, as agreed between the* USSR *and Nazi Germany. The German-Soviet border was established on the Bug River. On October 10, however, the Soviets ceded Vilna to independent Lithuania in return for military concessions. The city, renamed Vilnius, was the capital of independent Lithuania until June 1940, when the Soviets annexed all Baltic countries.*

Herman Kruk left Warsaw on September 5, 1939, when men, especially Jewish men, were advised to leave. After a long and difficult trip, he reached Vilna on October 10, 1939. This story of his flight was written retrospectively in Vilna in January 1940, possibly based on diary notes.]

Author's comments:

1. On September 5 [1939], when it became clear that I was leaving Warsaw, the question arose of whether to go alone or with my wife. I decided to leave my wife behind in Warsaw, because I assumed I'd be conscripted into the Polish army within two or three days and didn't want her to be all alone in a strange place.

2. A group of six of us left Warsaw: myself, my friend Ber-Yitskhok Rosen, a journalist;[1] Marek Kozik, a vinegar manufacturer;[2] and his three brothers-in-law (Frankenstein, Fleshel, and Reiseman). Frankenstein is a wealthy man, a build-

1. Ber-Yitskhok Rosen, born in 1900 in Warsaw, was an active Bundist and writer; the secretary of the Warsaw Yiddish Journalists' Union in the 1930s; and a member of the staff of the Yiddish dailies, *Express* and the Bundist *Folkstsaytung*. He reached Vilna and, in 1941, made it to Japan, was interned by the Japanese in the Shanghai Ghetto during the remainder of World War II, and eventually got to Australia, where he died in 1954. For his biography, see *Generations* 2:466–468.

2. Marek Kozik went with Kruk to Vilna and was in the ghetto there; in April 1943 he was arrested by the Gestapo and disappeared.

ing contractor and the owner of several houses; Fleshel owns a haberdashery store on Theater Square; and Reiseman is an employee of a film enterprise.

3. Thanks to Frankenstein's efforts, we obtained a wagon [and horses] for absolutely nothing. A friend of his, owner of a big coal yard on Towarowa Street in Warsaw as well as a brick factory in Otwock, gave us a broad, deep coal wagon and two horses.

4. The group elected the author of these comments its "commander" and undertook a strict discipline.

SEPTEMBER 6

From noon on, people are snatched ceaselessly for work [building trenches around Warsaw]. We avoid being taken and reach the meeting point, where we are supposed to leave from. On the way we are regularly hindered by airplane attacks. Three times we had to hide inside gates [of buildings] and in air raid shelters. Our departure was set for 1 in the afternoon. Because of the obstacles, we didn't gather together until 3, and we set out at 4. The owner of the wagon went with us. He is going to his brick factory, which is on our way.

The wagon is black and dirty with coal dust. We spread some hay on it and feel happy because, if not for the dirty coal wagon, we would have had to go on foot. From Sienna Street, we turn into Żelazna Street, via Jerozolimskie Boulevard to Poniatowski Bridge. Everywhere traffic is heavy and nervous. Most of the people are trudging along with bundles. The closer we get to the bridge, the more refugees we see. At the corner of Nowy Świat and Aleje, we see a great many wagons and cars—all filled with bundles, all going toward the bridge. Right at the bridge are anti-aircraft cannons. On the Praga side,[3] near the bridge, the road was blocked with pillars to stop an eventual tank invasion. . . .

The street around Skaryszewski Park is full of fleeing people: cars, carts, military cars, bicyclists, masses of provincial police, and masses of pedestrians. The street is almost completely blocked.

We turn right, on the road to Otwock. Once more, an air raid. We get out of the wagon and hide inside one of the nearby gates. The air battle lasts a half hour. As soon as it is calm, we go on.

The highway presents an extraordinary picture. Traveling is almost impossible. The road is completely blocked. You drive barely a few feet and you have to stand still for 15 or 20 minutes. Small cars squeeze through somehow. Military convoys hurry by; municipal and intercity cars rush. From time to time, big units of firemen from Warsaw and the provinces break through:

"Where are they going? They're fleeing from Warsaw. . . ."

3. Praga is a suburb of Warsaw on the eastern side of the Vistula River.

The road is full of wagons, masses of bicyclists, hundreds and thousands of pedestrians. Dust tears your throat. Our horses, used to walking harnessed to a little cart filled with bricks, refuse to drag the heavy, wide coal wagon. The trip to the brickworks, three kilometers beyond Otwock, would normally take two hours, but this time it lasts from 4 in the afternoon until 2 in the morning. Tired and worn out, nervous and depressed, we come at 2 in the morning to Teklinek, the village where the brickworks is.

The brickworks is in a forest. Near the brickworks, in the thick part of the forest, we are suddenly surrounded by soldiers pointing their rifles at us. It turned out that we had come into the middle of an artillery position; all around us is a big camp of motorized heavy artillery.

After we explain that we were going with the owner of the local brickworks, and after a meticulous check of our documents, they announce to us: okay, we'll let you in, but you must be quiet—don't go out of your room, and don't light any matches; or else—a bullet in your head!

The workers in the brickworks greet their boss excitedly. Two of them have already been arrested—and threatened with shooting. Their wives greet us, weeping. My traveling companions regret that we got waylaid here.

We spend the night in the office of the brickworks: one on the sofa, some on the ground, some simply propped up in chairs.

Every rustle makes us nervous. Only at dawn do we notice that there is a telephone in the room and that we can get in touch with Warsaw. Marek Kozik is the first to call. His wife cries and begs him to come back home. The group is very nervous. Except for me, they all are in favor of going back to Warsaw. I get in touch with my home. My wife is frightened by my sudden telephone call. But she answers with determination that we should run wherever our eyes carry us. Once again, my friend Kozik gets in touch with his home. This time he gets an answer: go on running!

SEPTEMBER 7

We get new horses for the wagon and an addition—a light carriage with a third horse. We set out in the direction of Otwock-Garwolin. Now, traveling through the forest, we see where we had wandered during the dark night: the forest all around is full of gasoline barrels, and deeper in the forest stand big cannons; the army is maneuvering here nervously.

The highway we are traveling on is even more crowded with refugees than yesterday. Everyone is running, rushing as if he were pursued. Everyone gives the impression that he knows he is too late. We learn that at dawn today on the radio all men were ordered to leave Warsaw. Now the nervousness of our wives when we spoke with them by telephone earlier today becomes clear.

People who left Warsaw today tell horrible stories. The fields around the capital are flooded with people: thousands of pedestrians—Jews and Christians, men and women, old and young, a sea of limousines, military cars.

At about 9 in the morning we had the first air raid, and it lasted all day without letup. That day was extremely hard. Dozens of times we ran from the carts to hide from the bombers. Horrible scenes took place in the forest. People look for family members who got lost in the dark of night. Women and children shudder. Men, tired from running, throw off their shoes and run barefoot. Horses are frightened by the bombing and run away with the wagons, leaving the passengers in the forest. Everyone trembles with fear. As soon as we hear explosions, people cling to each other. People can't lie still and simply run off aimlessly. People chase after one another. In some cases people lose their senses and run away from the crowd, thinking this will save them. People run after them and bring them back. Everybody's eyes blaze. The ground shakes. The forests rise up. The rattling of machine guns is jolting, and the fear keeps rising. The road from Otwock to Garwolin was then a horrible hell.

In the forest, people relate stories to each other: An old couple were staying in an Otwock boarding house. In Warsaw they had a safe. On Wednesday, September 5, the owner went to Warsaw to open the safe. He was one of the last to be allowed in. Excited and nervous from the sudden changes, the owner of the safe packed up the money: there should have been 350,000 zloty, tens of thousands of dollars, and a large amount of valuables. By then it was hard to get a train to Otwock. The Jew, with his property, hastily jumped into a cart, promising a big payment. In Świder, as he jumped off the wagon, the package fell apart and the highway was strewn with tens of thousands of zloty, dollars, jewels, etc. Everyone who was there began to grab. Meanwhile, a suspicion arose that the money came from a robbery. The police, passing by, intervened, collected the money, and arrested the owner.

People tell about horrible cases of death:

Four men were killed during the air raid—the fifth was thrown up a tree where he broke his spine.

A bomb hit a horse, and as it ran in horrible torment, it trampled two pedestrians.

A woman went mad and was taken, tied up, to Garwolin.

Many cars ran out of gas. People left them and continued on foot. The number of "dead cars" on the highway steadily increases.

The wildest rumors circulated on the highway. A Chevrolet passed by and a captain shouted out the window:

"Let everyone know that, in Germany, a revolution erupted against Hitler!"

But the airplanes don't stop tormenting.

Suddenly, not knowing how it happened, we were horribly sprayed with bombs and strafed with machine guns. Later, that was repeated many times. It was a tactic of the German pilots! They stayed so high that you didn't even hear them flying, and suddenly, they would dive down and spray the highway with bullets, bullets, and bullets.

The refugees had a word for it: "mowing"—they're mowing as with a scythe.

We quickly turn into the woods, and our wagon breaks down. We don't have any time to think. We abandon the wagon, load the belongings onto the small carriage. We hitch two horses in front and tie the third one up in back. And follow on foot. . . .

About 6 in the evening, we arrive in Garwolin, barely alive.

In and around the town are thousands of people, wagons, and cars. Everybody rests or prepares for the road. We take pains to get water for washing ourselves. In the middle of washing, we have to escape from an air raid.

When we are somewhat rested, the question arises: What now? The wagon was left on the highway; to travel with the carriage is impossible, even though we have three horses.

Finally, my friend Kozik saves the day: a big wide wagon harnessed with one horse that is going with refugees from Płock to Lublin. One horse is harnessed to the wagon; it is exhausted and can't pull the load. There are seven people in the wagon, a lot of bundles, feather beds, etc. We make an arrangement: we give them our horses and little carriage. The little carriage is to remain their property, but we are only lending them the horses. For that price, we arrange to travel to Lublin together. We harness our three horses to the wagon, and we let the fourth horse walk behind, tied with a piece of rope to the wagon. The carter sold the little carriage on the spot.

We get settled in the wagon and burrow into the bundles, sacks, and feather beds. Meanwhile, the owner of the wagon learns that I was born in Płock, and he informs me that my sister and her two children left Płock and fled toward Gąbin. Where her husband is, I can't find out. Is she alive? Isn't she? Who can tell? . . . [4]

Late in the evening, we leave Garwolin for Lublin. The main street that leads from the town to the Lublin highway is cluttered with wagons and masses of military cars. The officers nervously issue orders. The road is crammed with a lot of heavy artillery. It seems that this is the same unit we saw this morning in Teklinek.

Are they fleeing with us?

So what will happen to Warsaw?

Every few minutes, the road is blocked and everyone stands still. People are again upset as if they were pursued. The enemy seems to be breathing down your neck.

All 13 people are curled up and sleeping. Only at dawn do we realize that our

4. Kruk's sister was Golde Torner (b. 1900). See Kruk's diary for May 18, 1942. After September 1942, he received no information from his sister; she perished in the Warsaw Ghetto.

fourth horse has disappeared. The rope came untied and the horse walked off. We make jokes about our luck, and thus we reach the town of Ryki.

SEPTEMBER 8

For the first time since we left Warsaw, I meet an acquaintance, my party comrade Kleczewski, an old Bundist. He tells us that no one is allowed into Lublin. He advises us to turn toward Brisk.[5] But we nevertheless decide to go toward Lublin.

Freezing from the damp autumn chill, we go on.

Again hundreds and thousands. People travel in wagons and cars, but you mostly see people on foot. People trudge along tired and worn out. They beg to be taken on at least for a short stretch. Some run behind the wagon, some hold onto one of the boards of the wagon and let themselves be dragged along by the horses. The road forks: ahead, the road to Lublin; right, the road to Kock. Military guards do not allow traveling ahead. So we are forced to go toward Kock. Pedestrians circumvent the road through fields and break through in the direction of Lublin. Patrols of Polish pilots examine our documents.

On the road, in the woods all around, one is struck by a great many cars, and around them pilots and thick barbed-wire fences. In the distance, we see half-covered hangars. We decide to stop in a nearby village. But an air raid soon comes. We hear anti-aircraft cannons. We interrupt our rest and decide to leave the area. We quickly depart. The closer we get to Kock, the more frequent the air raids become.

We feel as if we are in a trap—it makes no sense to get out of the wagon, for there is no cover, just open fields all around. The woods are far from the road. Some of us cling to a stone, some to a ditch. The attacks are now so frequent that there is no time to climb into the wagon and jump out again. The women and children decide anyway not to get out. Whatever happens will happen!

Exhausted, we drag ourselves into Kock. Like all previous towns, Kock is full of escapees. The whole town is in the street. Young people tell us that people have been running there day and night—for three days already.

It is Friday evening. We negotiate with a woman and we get a room in her house and full board. At night we go to a workers' club to hear the radio. A few people busy themselves with the radio. We hear a few fragmentary sentences in Polish, but unfortunately we don't understand a single word.

5. This old town in Jewish Lithuania, on the Bug River, was part of the Soviet Zone in the 1939 partition of Poland.

SEPTEMBER 9

On Saturday morning, we decide to try to telephone Lublin. We get a connection to the apartment of my party comrade Dr. Hershenhorn. But it turns out that Comrade Hershenhorn is in the army. Mrs. Hershenhorn can't tell me very much. We agree that I will get in touch with her again in about an hour and by then she will invite Comrade Bella Shapiro, the leader of the Lublin Bund. Meanwhile, I go back home and eat breakfast.

As from under the ground, I suddenly hear a few familiar explosions. The whole house is lifted. The attacks are repeated several times. There is an extraordinary turmoil in the town. Within a few seconds, the townspeople pack their things and run toward the fields. Horses and livestock tear out of the stables and also run into the fields. The shouts rise up to the sky. Jews leave their Sabbath prayers and run with their *tallises* [prayer shawls]. Women wring their hands and scream. Children run in their nightshirts and cry.

The bombings upset us so much that people lose their senses. One of our group jumps into bed and thus considers himself "covered." Another has an attack of hysteria and laughs so loud that one could go mad from that laughter. From the street come screams that the town is burning. The whole town is indeed wrapped in a thick smoke. The town is burning in three places. Frankenstein and a few bold fellows from among the refugees and local people run to put out the fire. The town is swept clean as with a broom.

As soon as it calms down, I hurry to the post office. Unfortunately, I don't get a connection anymore. The telephone operator tells me secretly that the telephone connection with Lublin and the surrounding towns is broken—that Lublin is now bombed horribly, etc.

The post office official and I suddenly have to hide somewhere near the post office because multitudes of airplanes are again flying over us. People say that the planes are thus "strolling" to Lublin and back.

In my mind's eye is a picture: a man, who is both the city doctor and the city president, stands in the middle of the street and bandages a wounded woman, with a wounded breast. The doctor can't manage, and a peasant helps him out. We look from our hiding place at that stubborn doctor and admire his boldness. Two men and a woman come from a side street. All three carry rucksacks. They go toward the doctor, and I hear how they shout at him:

"Lunatic, leave everything and come with us!"

The woman literally begs him:

"Jacek, leave it and come with us."

The doctor raises his head from the wounded woman, and with a stoic calm, he answers:

"Go on, I'll be the last one out. . . ."

The post office official lying near me tells that those were the municipal notary, his wife, and their secretary. It was the notary who called the doctor crazy.

Across from us, we see the prayer house of the Kotsker Rebbe.[6] Most of the Hasids have left the prayer house. But the Rebbe hasn't left, and a few of the faithful are standing with him at the Eastern Wall and praying. . . .

Now the town is completely evacuated. The smoke from the fires all around covers the whole town. Only a few people are seen from afar, latecomers who are still dragging themselves into the field with their few belongings.

In a little while Frankenstein comes back filthy and bleeding. It turns out that, while putting out the fire, he was hit. We bandage him, pack our things together quickly, and leave Kock, going toward Radzyn.

Airplanes constantly accompany us on the road. Somewhere anti-aircraft cannons thunder, and we feel trapped, just like yesterday. It is impossible to go on, and we can't stay on the highway. We drag ourselves to a wood and stay there until dusk. The woods are full of people. Entire groups are hiding here. Wagons and cars "rest"—among them a large number of automobiles with police from the provinces of Poznań and Pomerania. From here we see whole groups of cars with air force personnel constantly maneuvering back and forth, a few anti-aircraft cannons are moved from place to place, as if they wanted to block all the holes. At sundown we move onto the road.

Farther on, as we move toward Radzyn, we see the horrible results of today's bombing. Fires are seen in several places. Gigantic craters have been torn on the highway and around it. Trees are torn up by the roots. Telephone lines hang uselessly from the poles—torn by the bombs. All the roads around Lublin have been destroyed. We see this, and people passing by tell us the same thing.

A few kilometers outside Radzyn, we learn that Radzyn is burning. People advise us not to stop in Radzyn—better to turn to the right, to Wisznice. That is another trip of fifty kilometers.

Two kilometers beyond Radzyn, there is a crossroad: ahead is Radzyn, to the right is Wisznice. The road here is so destroyed that it is impossible to get through. The fields around are plowed up from scores of bombs. At the crossroad, a peasant's hut is burned down. The smell indicates that the fire was just put out. Next to it sits a peasant, eyes frozen on the dung heap that is all he has left from the hut. I ask him for advice on how to go. He answers:

"I don't hear, Pan. Today I have become deaf! . . . Bombs . . . I don't hear. . . . Don't hear nothing! . . ."

Peasants passing by stop us from going to Radzyn. A street bridge was torn up, and we can't get through anyway. So we turn right, toward Wisznice.

6. Kock was the capital of an influential Hasidic sect and dynasty, headed by the Kotsker Rebbe (the rebbe of Kock).

The horses are tired and barely trudge along. The road here, too, is so torn up that very often we have to circumvent the highway and travel in the fields—from the highway to the fields and from the fields back to the highway. Thus we drag along for a few hours.

Not far from the burned hut, we meet a woman holding an icon. Her movements are very strange. She looks crazy. The woman—we find out—has gone crazy today; she is the wife of the deafened peasant. From that fire, she saved one icon and went into the world with it.

Soon it is completely dark. Our road now goes through forests. In the distance we again hear an incessant cannon fire. In the nearby forest, we see large groups of people. Some of them go out onto the highway and ask us for advice on how to go. The faces are terrified. Women weep. We stop our wagon and go into the forest. Scores of families from Radzyn are there: with bundles, bedclothes, everything they could grab—they lie on the ground and cry to one another. Even men cry.

Everyone asks us what to do. Two freight wagons from Warsaw stand apart from the group. Around them are about 50 men from Praga. All of them are tall, healthy men, dressed in jackets and boots. They all look like butchers, horse traders, etc., but they are all despondent and feel like lost children. Two of them lie wounded on the ground—victims of the air raid here on the highway. People have torn up their shirts and bandaged their wounds. They have been lying here a few hours and are afraid to pick up their heads:

"We can't anymore," they plead. "We have decided: whatever happens, we're going back to Praga."

We console them and encourage them not to go back but to come with us. They obey like children, quiet and obedient, and harness their freight wagons.

When we move from the place, a whole caravan goes with us. They are also going to Wisznice.

Our horses barely drag along. We, too, are hungry and look for something to eat. The dark sky is red with the fires all around. The shooting somewhere doesn't stop. At the first hut, we stop and get off the highway—maybe we'll get bread, or some milk.

Everything around looks dead. There is not even a dog on a chain. We knock on a window. After a long time we hear that something is moving there. A middle-aged peasant comes out. His answer is half frightened, half depressed.

We find out:

Today, he buried his wife, a cow, and . . . the dog—all three were killed by a bomb, here, not far from the hut.

"I don't have any bread. Milk? I can give you some—that is the last milk of the cow. . . . That is the last work of my wife. . . ."

Naturally, we don't take the milk. We take a few bottles of well water, buy some fruit, and go on in order to use the dark of night.

SEPTEMBER 10

At dawn, we trudge up to a village. None of the peasants want to let us in. They are all sympathetic but they are afraid:

"Right after you, the airplanes will come. . . ."

"You'll bring airplanes!"

An old peasant woman took pity and let us in. We drive to her yard with the wagon, buy peasant bread and butter, and rest there until 2 in the afternoon. It is quiet, and we decide to go on to Wisznice.

Not until dusk do we drag ourselves into the town of Wisznice. There, in the marketplace, we are surrounded by the townspeople. Everyone wants to know where we come from, what's going on. The town doesn't know anything and various rumors are circulating.

We divide up the work: one goes to look for a radio, I and another person go to the police station to ask for advice about what direction to go, and second, to glance at the map and maybe even to come up with a plan.

In the police station we come upon a strange scene—they are interrogating a spy. A frightened peasant stands there, stammering. When they arrested him, he was wearing a military overcoat, and they assume he is spying. I don't want to stay there long. From all the information we have collected, we conclude that a big battle is being prepared around the River Bug—near Dęblin and Lublin. Therefore we decide to cross the Bug and go to Chełm through Włodawa. At 9 in the evening, we leave Wisznice, and at dawn we come to a village not far from Włodawa.

SEPTEMBER 11

No one advises us to stay here. Nearby is a big railroad junction. Around the railroad tracks are sawmills, and not far from there is the big bridge over the Bug.

We set out for Włodawa. Hearts pounding, we drive over the enormous bridge. Everyone urges us to hurry. Police patrols, passersby—everyone hurries us on. But they don't let us into Włodawa. We are advised to go on, to Chełm.

We turn off, park the wagon, and three of us set off for Włodawa through side roads. The remaining people in our group stay with the wagon until we come back.

Włodawa is full of refugees. We encounter scores of acquaintances from Warsaw. More important: there are already refugees from Lublin.

One of those from Warsaw is an old Bund activist, author of the book *Over the Years: Memoirs of a Jewish Worker*. There also I see the Warsaw Bundist councilman Nosn Szafran; the activist from Tsukunft (the Youth Bund), Berke Shnaydmil, and others. From Lublin, we see Lerer, the chairman of the local central committee of the trade unions; Engelsberg, the secretary of the Lublin Kultur-lige;[7] and a great many Bundists and Tsukunftists from Warsaw and Lublin.

The Lubliners are especially nervous. Events happened so unexpectedly that they simply can't deal with them. The whole thing is like a dream; they feel that they were plucked out of reality. I learn that Bella Shapiro's apartment was burned down and everything she owned was completely destroyed. I get regards from my brother Shmulik [Pinkhes Schwartz], who left on September 6 with a group of evacuated Jewish and Polish journalists. Lubliners tell me that Comrade B. Shefner[8] is very excited, and my brother twisted his leg jumping. In any case, I can't find out from anyone what happened to them. The Lubliners know only that because of the great bombardment, no one had seen them again.

"What happened to them, are they saved?" No one can give me an answer. . . .

Finally, from a comrade whom I don't remember, I learn that they said they were going to Lwów.

The Lubliners advise us to continue our flight. The comrades from Warsaw are a little restrained and advise waiting it out at the Bug. Some young comrades want to go back to Warsaw and stand on the barricades.

My group agrees with the comrades from Warsaw that we mustn't go too far and must stay at the Bug. We decide to wait somewhere in a village between Włodawa and Chełm.

Our wagon goes in the direction of Chełm.

Tired and exhausted, we all are wrapped up in the wagon and have a difficult sleep. Not until dawn do we realize we are soaked with rain. We are hardly 13 kilometers from Włodawa, and the horses are literally falling off their feet. Around us is a forest. We decide to stop at the nearest village.

SEPTEMBER 12

It is still dawn. We go into the woods toward the village of Luty.

In the village, we have encountered several wagons full of people who, like us, have come here to hide. Every one of the newcomers has taken pains to "get hold of" a better hut, a few trees where you should be able to hide, or something like that. On one of the village huts we noticed a Jewish name. We go in—they really are Jews!

We spent three days in that village, with that Jewish family.[9] We arrived there a day before Rosh Hashanah and left after the holiday was over.

7. The "Cultural League," headed by Herman Kruk in Warsaw, was a central organization for promoting Yiddish culture, schools, and libraries.

8. A Yiddish writer and prominent Bundist, who managed to get to America.

9. They arrived in Luty on September 12, at dawn, and left on the night of September 13–14. There must be some mistake either in Kruk's dates or in his counting.

Soon after we came to the village we decided that some of us should go back to Włodawa to find out what was going on.

"A trifle, what could have happened since last night!"

The news we bring from there is bad: you can't get back over the Bug. The town is regularly bombed. The sawmills are burning. Nevertheless, we decide to wait some more.

SEPTEMBER 13

We spent the night in an attic with hay. Frankenstein, Kozik, and I start out in a White Russian [Byelorussian] peasant's wagon—once more on our way to Włodawa to get news. It is foggy outside. We are all satisfied about that: may it remain like that—at least we will be able to rest from the airplanes. The peasant is gregarious and answers questions fluently. He tells us: almost all the men of the village were in prison at one time or another. The Poles always suspected them of Communism.[10] "My brother has just returned from prison in Siedlce," he says; "they have released all those who were arrested."

The peasant is furious at all Poles.

Unfortunately, the weather improves, and in Włodawa itself we encounter a new series of bombardments. We run from one gate to another, from one courtyard to another, and finally out of the town.

We run with challahs we have bought and eat as we run. The horrible bombing forces me to cling to a fence. Frankenstein and Kozik stand across from me in a gateway and observe me. They recount later that when the whole town caught fire and everything around trembled with the bombing, I didn't let go of the challah, but tore off pieces of it and ate them with great appetite. . . .

We watch the heavy army movement on the highway. Everyone here is nervous. From everything we see here, we conclude that great events are about to take place close by.

In the bustle all around, we suddenly hear familiar voices next to us. We turn around. Behind us stand the leaders of the Left Poalei-Zion: Yitskhok Lev, Buchsbaum, and other activists. They look terrible. Lev can barely trudge along; it is hard to recognize him. Buchsbaum tries to make a joke.

You can't stay there for long—you aren't allowed to stop. Lev also advises not to stay there. There is a smell of gunpowder in the air! We take leave of each other warmly and go back to Luty.

More friends:

The editorial staff of *Robotnik*[11]—Klibanski and Jan Dąbrowski and his girl-

10. The Byelorussians were a prominent minority in northeastern Poland. Culturally close to Soviet Byelorussia, they would allow for Communist influences.

11. A Polish Socialist newspaper.

friend, the Bundist Liszczyńska—trudge along in a farm wagon. Rejoicing, we agree to meet in Chełm.

A half-kilometer beyond the town we see this event:

A few tanks ride in the middle of the highway. Suddenly one of them makes an abrupt left turn and falls into a ditch. Some soldiers soon jump in, and from under the tank they pull out two soldiers—killed or wounded, it is not clear to us.

As night falls, we hear a heavy bombardment. The darker it becomes, the more distinctly the fires in the area are seen. Once again, villages are burning, Włodawa is burning!

We leave Luty and go on the highway that leads to Chełm. Our road goes through heavy sand. In the distance, the highway looks horrible. Once again, as between Otwock and Garwolin, everyone runs. The highway is full. Among the refugees—hordes of military cars, pontoon bridges, anti-aircraft cannons—everything is running toward Chełm. Suddenly everything stops as if it were over. We are frightened:

Are we really the last ones? . . .

I stand next to the carter and command:

"Faster, don't spare the horses!"

We drive like that for six hours. Before dawn, we come to Chełm.

SEPTEMBER 14

Chełm looks like a besieged city. The streets are filled with soldiers. Chełm has suffered greatly from yesterday's bombardment. Two bombers were shot down in the center of the city. Some houses are still burning.

Going among soldiers and refugees, we are blocked by a crowd:

The fence of a garden is smashed; in the garden, a broken German airplane. In a corner are two shining boots. A few meters down lies a scorched piece of body. You can see a hand reaching out to an ear. Some singed hair is still on the head. There is no clothing; all that remains is a leather belt, buckled around the burned body. The other part of the body is gone. The air is full of the smell of burned flesh. . . . The hut that stood is still smoldering there.

Shortly after, another surprise: our good old friend from Warsaw, the silk merchant Dovid Sadowski of Marszałkowska Street. We want to take him with us, but he doesn't want to go. He is stubborn: he is going to enlist in the army as a volunteer. He parts from us and goes to enlist.

We find a courtyard in which to park our wagon. In the same courtyard, we are given a big apartment belonging to people who escaped from Chełm only yesterday.

That means Chełm is also running?

The police did leave last night.

As soon as we have rested, we go to a neighbor to hear the radio. In the ardor of listening to the news, someone calls me: Marek Kozik shouts to me to come down at once. I run out and see:

In the gate stands a Polish non-commissioned officer—Kozik's older brother Albert—with six soldiers. The bayonets are fixed on their rifles. Albert accidentally met his brother and our whole group. I arrive when Albert, always a calm and mild person, shouts at his brother in a typical military slang:

"No tricks. At four o'clock you have to report to me with the whole group."

Marek is a bit confused by that encounter. Albert would gladly take us, hence he talks with us as if we have to obey his orders. Thus he will legitimize us for his soldiers.

The issue is explained precisely by Dovid Sadowski, whom we had met this morning. They didn't want to take him into the army, claiming that they didn't need any volunteers. In the courtyard of the army headquarters, he encountered Kozik's brother, the non-commissioned officer. Thus the plan emerged to take us officially to Kowel. On Sadowski's instructions, Albert Kozik had searched for us.

So we have to part from our Płock group, the owners of the wagon, with whom we have been groping our way ever since Garwolin. We left them the horses and all the supplies, and parted with them very warmly. To our great regret we had to leave a good and fresh lunch on the table. The plates were on the table and steaming. But we couldn't delay. No use, we left everything and reported at the determined time at the railroad station.

We are taken out to the tracks with great pomp—with a military guard. But it is very hard for us to get into a railroad car. Everything there is full. Anyone who is strong enough pushes his way in. No one buys a ticket. Not even the cashier is working. Finally, the non-commissioned officer succeeds in grabbing a cattle car, and we occupy it. A captain also squeezes in with us. He shivers with cold. He is sick and feverish. He asks for something warm. The soldiers get hold of some warm water, and one of us gives him his overcoat. We lay him down in a corner, on a dung heap. He falls asleep.

We wait in the car from 4 in the afternoon until about 9 in the evening. Finally the train moves toward Kowel. It drags along a few kilometers, stands still, goes back, goes forward again.

The railroad line is simply jammed with people walking close to the tracks. The train goes so slowly that people jump in while it's going. A soldier suddenly jumps into our car. As soon as he is in the train, he starts cursing horribly. He abuses Poles, the Polish army, and the officers. He tells us that he had been thrown from one front to another; the officers were everywhere the last into battle and the first to run away. The soldiers were hungry, he says, and disorganization prevailed!

Our non-commissioned officer can't stand it that a soldier in uniform would say such things. He asks the soldier why he does this, but the soldier talks back to him. In the darkness, he doesn't see that he is talking to an officer.

A quarrel arises between them. At a certain moment, the non-commissioned officer lights an electric lamp and illuminates himself. The soldier sees the uniform and becomes very confused. Not thinking much, the soldier jumps out of the moving train.

The incident made quite an impression.

SEPTEMBER 15

Our train stands still. At dawn we found out that we are standing on a side track in Maciejowice. We have traveled 36 kilometers.

Day dawns. To stay in the car is dangerous. People say that the railroad yard was bombed yesterday. A bomb hit a moving train. Two cars were blown up. The front part of the train went on, and the back part, along with the destroyed cars, stood still and was strafed again. Such things happened a lot, they say.

The first ones who are in favor of leaving the train are the group of soldiers with our non-commissioned officer. They are nervous. They consider that the danger is great and we should get away as fast as possible.

We go on foot. All side roads are full of people, wagons, and cars. The same scenes as before. Everyone is hurrying. Every few minutes a new airplane squadron comes. All around, a heavy bombing is heard. Meanwhile, the airplanes passing by drop some bombs. Behind us there is a shudder. Smoke rises to the sky, and shouts are heard.

Two hundred meters behind us are some engineers. A bomb exploded. Their wagon spun into the width of the highway, was damaged, and turned upside down. Four people are torn to pieces. The carter is seriously wounded. The fifth engineer was thrown to the side—he is not hurt. He was only hit in the ribs. The horse, however, was cut in two. The front part of the horse—both front legs—fidget, as if they would like to go on.

In minutes the road is cleared. Horses and wagon are flung off to a side. The human limbs are gathered up. A soldier brings a shovel. A mass grave is dug. The fifth engineer is despondent and looks on at the burial of his friends. He practically doesn't react at all. When everything is taken care of, the surviving engineer sits in a wagon and goes on with everybody else.

The tension increases every minute. Our soldiers are falling off their feet, more from tension than from weariness. It is simply impossible to control the people. We go into the fields because we dread going on the road. It is warm. We are all sweating heavily, but there is not a drop of water to be had. It is as if we were hurled into some desert. I suggest to our group to lie down on the ground and cool our cheeks on the grass growing under our feet. . . . Only at sundown do we again come to the railroad track and jump on a passing train. The train is open: plain platform cars. A Christian boy of 10 or 12 sits next to me. He is very sad. Those sitting around him give the youngster sugar and bread. He takes the gifts and weeps. He collects them for his mother, who is stuck in another car. His grief is great because, just a few hours ago, he was traveling here in a train that was exploded by a bomb. His father and grandmother were killed on the spot. He and his mother ran away. The mother jumped into one car, he into the other. They plod along, not knowing where and to what.

About midnight we come to Kowel. The trip of about 90 kilometers from Chełm to Kowel lasted 28 hours.

It is pitch dark at the railroad station. So as not to get lost, we decide to leave in single file, each holding on to the coat of the one in front of him. Thus we drag ourselves out of the cars, and we can barely press through the railroad station. People are lying there on the ground, on the stairs, on the tables of the buffet. We climb over legs, walk over bundles, and finally come out into the street.

Here the darkness is almost palpable. It is very late, but the streets are still full of people hurrying, groping in the dark. We search for bread and a night's lodging. Unfortunately it is impossible to get anything. After an hour and a half, we give in. We find some corridor—here we will sleep. The lower part of the corridor is already filled with refugees. People are also sleeping on the stairs. We walk around among the sleeping people, and on the first story we lie down on the floor. But just as we get settled, a door opens and a woman standing in the door invites some of us in. I go in and tell her that we want to use the corridor to spend the night. So as not to upset the woman, I show her Rosen's and my journalists' passes. The woman bursts into tears. She asks us all in and puts her whole apartment at our disposal. It turns out that only the day before, her husband, a local pharmacist, ran away from Kowel. She can't fall asleep, thinking about the fate of her husband. . . .

She makes a bed for us and is probably thinking about her husband. . . .

SEPTEMBER 16

Early in the morning, we send a few of us out to find out what is going on. Our soldiers go to register at the local headquarters. I and two others stay home. The door opens and the writer Alter Kacyzne[12] drops in on us, and behind him is

12. Alter Kacyzne (1885–1941), a well-known Yiddish writer and photographer, was born in Vilna and lived in Warsaw between the wars. In 1939 he went to Soviet-occupied Lwów, and in 1941, when the Germans advanced, he tried to escape again and was caught by Ukrainian collaborators and beaten to death.

Dovid Naymark[13] of the editorial staff of the *Folkstsaytung*.[14] Naymark cries like a baby; he is sick. He can't walk anymore and asks me what he should do. Kacyzne decides not to move. He is with his wife and two children; he can't go on. He goes out to look for an apartment and promises to come back.

A while later I get another guest—Mandelman, of the staff of TSISHO.[15] He is completely broken. He is hungry. When he sees tea, bread, and butter, tears come into his eyes. He weeps and can't control himself. We hide our faces so that he won't see our tears. The anguished scene is interrupted only when another guest stands in the door—our friend Staszek Broder, a partner in a big boardinghouse in Otwock. He heard about our arrival and came to inquire. He stands before us in a military uniform—he is a sergeant.

Joyous at meeting everyone, Staszek Broder tells his story:

He is coming now from German captivity. He fell into German hands near Prasznice, was there four hours and escaped. He went with a horse and wagon for three days and three nights. He traveled with a priest and two soldiers, who escaped with him. Here they parted from one another. But he keeps the Christian with the wagon. It is a wagon with two horses, which he got at a farm. He puts the wagon and himself at our disposal. He reports to us that he hasn't a cent, he is hungry and horribly dirty.

Again there is tea and bread. First he washes. Albert Kozik, the non-commissioned officer, reports to us that he is putting some of his soldiers at the disposal of the city headquarters. We remain with only him and two of his Christian fellow soldiers.

Thus we again have a wagon with two horses. Our camp is thus: there are 6 of us who have traveled from Warsaw, our friend the silk merchant Dovid Sadowski, the officer Albert and his 2 colleagues, and Sergeant Broder. With the driver, this is a group of 12 people.

The soldiers who go on with us claim, Everything is pretty much lost. The military authorities send us from place to place to look for our regiments. The higher authorities have run away anyway. The ability to fight is broken.

Where is the road? Where is the way out of their situation?

At sundown, we leave Kowel for Sarny.

13. Dovid Leyb Naymark (1891–1960), a Bundist journalist, was active in Warsaw. He fled to Vilna and from there to Canada in 1941. He died in New York.

14. *Folkstsaytung* ("People's Newspaper") was an influential Yiddish Warsaw daily, the organ of the Bund.

15. Mandelman was born in 1895 and died in 1963. TSISHO is the Central Yiddish School Organization, a network of Yiddish secular schools in Poland, founded in Warsaw in 1921.

SEPTEMBER 17

At dawn we arrive in the Volhynian village of Holoby, where we stay until 2 in the afternoon. From there we shall push on through Mielnica to Sarny. At 7 in the evening, we arrive in Mielnica.

In the outskirts of the town, a young man meets us and asks if we want to eat. He takes us to a house that looks like a place where one can get a homemade meal. The house is full. Refugees are eating there, Jews and Christians, policemen, soldiers. Everyone is grateful and touched by the hospitality. They don't take any money from anyone. The host and hostess in the house are busy, they cook soup, they serve. People come and go.

Later we found that in that town, the Jews do miracles. For a whole week they have been cooking, baking bread, taking care of lodging—they do that for everyone with no distinction of Jew or Christian.

People were especially interested in our group because they learned that Rosen is a journalist from Warsaw. A young man takes me to a radio and tells me on the way that rumors have been circulating that the Bolsheviks are coming to help Poland. On the radio I immediately come upon Molotov's speech, and I hear loud and clear: the Bolsheviks are going to liberate Western Ukraine and White Russia from the Polish yoke.[16]

I tremble all over. The impact is shattering. I go back to my people and tell them what I heard. The tension reaches the highest level in all of them. We decide not to move from the place and to wait. Our soldiers stay with us.

Both young people who have become especially interested in us take care of finding us lodgings. They put our horse and wagon away in a suitable place, and we sit at the radio waiting for further news. People come in and go out. Everyone talks about Molotov's speech. At about 10 in the evening, we are still all sitting in the City-Hostel.

Someone knocks on the door. We invite him in. In the door is an unpleasant face in the uniform of a prison warden, and behind him are a civilian and then another warden. The first one excuses himself: he heard, he says, that we know something about current political affairs and he asks us to inform him.

Who are the three people?

The first is a warden from the Święty Krzyż prison, near Kielce; the second is a district attorney; the third is the assistant of the first.

We tell them about the radio broadcast.

16. According to the Hitler-Stalin Pact, the USSR occupied the eastern half of Poland and annexed it to the Ukraine and Byelorussia. Indeed, most of the peasants in the areas were of those nationalities.

SEPTEMBER 18

Early in the morning, our non-commissioned officer learned that a colonel called a meeting of officers. He goes and comes back looking mysterious. He tells the result of the officers' meeting only to me, as commander of the group. The order given at the meeting was: the Bolsheviks are taking the entire region; more precise details are not yet known and therefore, for the time being, the orders are as follows:

Not to mount any resistance and even to let oneself be disarmed—but all soldiers had to leave for Łuck to join the entire Polish garrison of the Volhynia province.

Once again a turmoil. We don't understand what is going on there. All of us go out to the highway where, about 12 kilometers from the town, the road splits: right, to Kowel; left, to Łuck.

The movement here is two-sided—people are running toward Łuck, and people are hurrying to Kowel. We can't find out why some go to Kowel and the others to Łuck. We stand at the crossroads, stop people, and ask, but no one can give us an answer. One man runs to Łuck, he himself hardly knows why; another rushes to Kowel because—where else should he rush?

A tragic chaos!

We decide to go to Kowel. We travel for an hour and a half when a new wave arrives: "Where are you running?" they yell at us. "You want to go to the Germans?"

We stop again. Talk with people again—now everyone advises running to Łuck. . . .

We turn around and take the road to Łuck.

The highway becomes fuller from one minute to the next. Everyone is drawn to Łuck. A military truck rushes by, and strange equipment is thrown out of it. The glass of the equipment sprays, and the highway becomes flooded with splinters of glass and tin. For kilometers we drive over papers and papers. It turns out that those papers were identity cards that were scattered on the highway by someone who wanted to get rid of them. On a side, on the right, stands a long line of cars. The soldiers are distributing underwear, uniforms, and shoes to everyone without exception.

A colonel and his officers stand on the side there and watch the soldiers rule. Soldiers, police, farmers, Jews—everyone gets what they want and there is an abundance for everyone. . . .

We look around. Kozik stands fraternally with yesterday's chief of the Świętokrzysk prison—he is there, too, and he persuades my friend to take:

"Should it fall into the hands of foreigners? Better your own people should enjoy it. . . ."

Two of our group are convinced, and in a few minutes they come back to us on the road with a veritable warehouse: warm underwear, sheets, socks, etc.

It is clear that the war is finally lost. We are confused and cannot make any sense of the quickly unfolding events. My friend Kozik has tears in his eyes. He circles around me and sighs into my ear:

"Lost, all is lost. . . ."

About three in the afternoon comes a new wave; everyone is going back to Łuck.

Passersby, seeing us running toward Łuck, laugh at us:

"Where are you going, why are you going to Łuck?

"Go home, it's all over—*Demobilization!*"

They can't say anything more precisely about what is going on. The highway is full as usual with police, soldiers, farmers, escaping Jews, etc. Hordes of cyclists are rushing by as if they want to get home as fast as possible.

We stop again, we stop people to talk with them, and we learn:

The Bolsheviks entered Łuck; they disarmed and released all Polish soldiers and sent them home.

Tens of thousands of people are now running from Łuck; hardly hundreds are now going toward Łuck.

Nevertheless, we decide to go to Łuck and, once there, to figure out the situation.

About 10 kilometers outside Łuck, we learn that the peasants all around are attacking the Polish soldiers and disarming them.[17] Suddenly we hear violent rifle shots. Everyone runs into the woods and stretches out on the ground. The first ones who run there are the soldiers who were passing by.

I am also very frightened:

"We've already had such a difficult trip. We've already overcome such horrible bombings and suddenly, here, to die from a saboteur's rifle bullet?"

Fortunately, things calmed down around us. On the highway a mixed group gathered: soldiers and civilians are standing together there and everyone is consulting about what to do next.

An officer explains:

"The peasants are attacking us—we absolutely must get into Łuck because here the peasants can slaughter us. I will give rifles to everyone who can shoot; we must absolutely get into the city!"

Many civilians get rifles, others only cartridges. Armed against any attack, we get into a long convoy of soldiers and civilians. Some of us direct our rifles to the left side of the highway, others to the right side.

It is late in the evening when we see the first column of Soviet tanks in front of us. They are drawn up in the field on both sides of the highway. Nobody prevents

17. That is, Ukrainian peasants. Volhynia is currently part of Ukraine.

us from entering the occupied territory. Only after 20 minutes of traveling between the Soviet tanks are we stopped by a group of officers. They demand that we give up our weapons and calmly order us to drive to the city.

In the city, there are almost no Soviet soldiers to be seen. Marek Kozik and I go to look for a night's lodging for the group. Somewhere in a side street, someone shouts at us:

"*Kladis!*"[18]

Opposite us stands a civilian with a rifle aimed at us.

We drop to the ground. Only when he learns what we are looking for does he let us go on.

It is already 2 in the morning. We are on one of the main streets of Łuck. A passing car promptly stops. A soldier jumps out and points a revolver at my heart:

"Documents!"

I show him my documents; he asks my pardon and goes on.

We have no choice: we spend the night in a movie house on a stone floor.

SEPTEMBER 19–OCTOBER 6

In Łuck, we came on a new wave of people.

"All Warsaw is in Łuck," claims one of our group.

Among others, we meet the Zionist activist Dr. Kleinbaum;[19] a contributor to *Nasz Przegląd,*[20] Attorney Nowogródzki; one of the directors of the organization of cooperatives in Poland, Shmoysh.[21] We also meet Bella Shapiro and her husband, editor of the *Lubliner Togblat,* who have fled from Lublin.[22] I have written about them, describing the bombings in Kock. The Lublin Bundist councilman Dr. Hershenhorn is here, a captain in the military. There are a great many workers and worker activists from Warsaw: Comrade Hershl Ramet, the veteran president of the Leather Workers' Union in Warsaw, the youth activist Bornstein, etc. Once again, we meet Berke Shnaydmil, whom we met before in Włodawa.

Everyone tells of horrible events. They share their first impression of the Bolsheviks. But all of them are penniless, they are hungry, and they are naked and barefoot. Shnaydmil calls me aside and shows me: he doesn't have a shirt. On his

18. "Drop to the ground!"—a command in Russian.

19. Dr. Moyshe Kleinbaum was then a well-known Zionist leader and editor of the Yiddish daily *Haynt*. In 1940 he immigrated to Israel, changed his name to Sneh, became the chief of staff of the underground Hagana, and was later a Communist member of the Israeli Knesset.

20. A Zionist newspaper in Polish, which had appeared in Warsaw since 1923.

21. Shmoysh was also active in Jewish journalism and in the management of the Medem Sanitarium, an institution of the Jewish children's welfare organization (CENTOS).

22. Bella Shapiro's husband was Avrom Bornstein (1910–1942), a Bundist; he was active in the Bund in the Warsaw Ghetto and was murdered along with his wife and child.

naked body he simply wears a woolen sweater. I give him one of my shirts and a pair of warm underwear. We, too, especially Rosen and I, are penniless, and we have also been hungry for long days. There is no bread there to be gotten. You can't even dream of other food. Rosen is afraid for my health; he sees that my strength has declined, and he left to ask for food for me.

In fact, a carpenter whom Rosen confided in was strongly taken with our situation, and for a few days he takes care of us like one of his own. He is really extraordinary. But the carpenter doesn't stop there. He brings us into his home. He gets bread for us, fruit, he brings butter, eggs. It does indeed turn out that there is everything. But speculators are hiding it.

Dr. Kleinbaum accidentally learned of our plight. He came to us and said that until today he had been penniless. He got something to eat because he was taken in by rich Zionist activists. Only today did he get a little money and he wants to share it with us. We take some and are moved by his extraordinary concern.

A few days later, on my own responsibility, I call a meeting of a few local and refugee Bundists. I propose to do something to get urgent aid at least for a group of close comrades. The meeting decided: the Łuck members collect a little underwear, clothing, bread. We ourselves start getting some financial support for the neediest. Comrade Shmoysh is the first to contribute a big sum. He and Dr. Hershenhorn promise to make an agreement with TOZ[23] about the establishment of a kitchen.

Within a few days, a kitchen is organized at TOZ. We were able to distribute some clothing, bread, and financial support. When I left Łuck on October 6, the TOZ kitchen was distributing 250 lunches a day.

I want to mention three of the various events in Łuck:

1. The day after the entry of the Bolsheviks, groups of the new militia disarmed Polish soldiers. A Jewish fellow stopped a high Polish officer and challenged him to give him his weapon. The officer gave his revolver, which he carried on his belt. Finally, the young militiaman began removing the medals from the officer. The officer complained that he couldn't take them from him. The fellow threatened him with the rifle. The officer then took another revolver out of a holster and shot the militiaman on the spot. The officer was arrested.

2. A group of Polish prisoners of war and other arrested persons are being led through the street. Suddenly a female shriek is heard in the street. A woman and child who are accidentally standing on the sidewalk fall into the arms of a soldier,

23. OZE—Obshtshestvo Zdravookhraneniya Evreev (Russian for Society for Protecting the Health of the Jews)—was founded in Russia in 1912 and worked worldwide in promoting health and health awareness among Jews (especially among the poor), fighting epidemics, restoring the physical strength of children, and publishing journals on medicine and public health. In independent Poland, it was renamed TOZ (Towarzystwo Ochrony Zdrowia), but the Vilna intellectuals were steeped in the Russian language and often switched to the old name of OZE. Kruk vacillates between the two names.

who came out of the line. Both wept profusely. She is a refugee. She had simply gone for a walk in the streets of Łuck, and there she met her husband. The scene made such a strong impression that the whole street literally wept along with them.

3. The Bolsheviks call a meeting of working intelligentsia. A great many refugees come, including one speaker who asks the Bolsheviks in the Presidium why they don't take Warsaw. Several of those present applaud. A few members of the Presidium also welcome the wish of the Polish citizen. After that speech, one of the Presidium members stands up and announces that none of those sitting here in the Presidium support the wish of the last speaker to liberate Poland.

All those present look around and understand that the Bolsheviks, who went hand in hand with the Germans, aren't "allowed" to agree with such demands from a Polish citizen. . . .

Meanwhile, Comrades Mandelman and Naymark come to Łuck; we had already met with them in Kowel. Both are now sick in bed. Comrade Nayman is all swollen, and we take pains to put him in the hospital.

Among the newcomers we see the former senators Professor Schorr and Trockenheim, and the deputy Mincberg. Among them was also one of the richest Polish Jews, the former president of the Warsaw Jewish Community Council, Elye Mazur.

I use all possibilities to find out where my brother Shmulik is. I already know that he is not in Lwów. A Polish journalist said that he had to be in Krzemieniec. I do everything I can to learn the truth. It turns out that he isn't there either. I decide to go through Bialystok to Vilna. Suddenly I get a note from comrade Sh. Gilinski—going through Łuck to Brisk, he had given it to someone for me—that my brother, along with Shefner and the whole group of Jewish journalists, is going from Galicia to Vilna.

On October 5, my brother comes to me from Równe to Łuck. It turns out that the whole group of writers and journalists are now in Równe. Learning that Naymark, Rosen, and I are in Łuck, they invite us to join the group and go with them. They delegate to us my brother and the journalist Flinker from *Togblat*. On the morning of October 6, we all leave Łuck for Równe, and on October 8, we leave with the whole group for Vilna.

The trip lasted barely two days. We arrived in Vilna on October 10.

ON THE RUINS OF THE GREAT CALAMITY[24]

Between Łuków and Włodawa, not far from the Polish fortress of Dęblin, was the little town of Z. The town was surrounded by a network of highways and side

24. This story was typed single-spaced by an inexperienced hand, with Kruk's typical dialectal errors in Yiddish and with several of Kruk's own handwritten emendations. The events are based on Kruk's experiences at the outbreak of the war in 1939.

roads, which all led from the town to the fortress and from the fortress to the whole world.

On a side street not far from Butcher Street lived The Oak, a tall, broad-shouldered Jew with a big wide beard and a red suntanned face that smelled of sun and woods. The Oak was the nickname of the town cobbler, Reb Nokhem. And Reb Nokhem, with his pipe always in his mouth, really looked like an oak uprooted from the nearby woods and admitted into the town to become the town cobbler. . . .

Nokhem "The Oak" worked quietly, lived quietly, and quietly and without turmoil had raised two daughters and three sons. All week he pulled threads, pounded wooden studs, and on market days Reb Nokhem went to the market with both daughters to sell his wares.

In his quiet life, The Oak had put one penny with another, collected, and . . . thought about the daughters' dowries and, in any event, about hard times. Two sons went off to the Polish army, and the third, along with his father, pounded wooden studs into shoes and sang songs, and they told each other everything that people chatted about in the town.

The wife and the younger daughter were busy keeping house. In the stall was a white goat that gave licorice-sweet milk; poultry pecked around in a flower bed; a hen clucked and laid eggs as regularly as a clock; Pudel, their faithful guard dog, warmed himself in the sun, and from time to time leaped up howling, with no purpose in the world. Reb Nokhem would use the goat's milk for the harsh cough he had lately suffered from. The older daughter used the eggs for her languor.

The quiet and cozy life of the family of The Oak seemed like a blessing from the Good Lord. Everything there was as it should be, everyone was healthy, and they couldn't complain about their livelihood.

That's how it was until the World War of September 1939.

When a turmoil arose in the town about the war between Poland and Germany, The Oak groaned, which should be interpreted as "my two sons," and . . . as if nothing had happened, went on spitting the little studs and pounding them in to the beat of a cobbler's hammer. His wife wrung her hands, wept over her woe, and started singing dirges in advance for her poor sons. . . .

When the first German airplanes appeared over the town and the houses began trembling and jiggling, the windowpanes flying, and the women shrieking, only then did The Oak shake and really understand that the war had indeed begun, that he didn't live far from the fortress, and that the danger could be great. When he saw with his own eyes the hosts of refugees fleeing Warsaw, The Oak once again shook:

"This means," he said to nobody in particular, "this means that people are already running." Reb Nokhem remembered World War I from 1914. He also remembered the refugees from those years. That they are running is bitter, but nevertheless, he thinks, one mustn't do it, they shouldn't run.

"One mustn't make oneself miserable. Running means to bury yourself with your own hands. . . ."

This was his war philosophy—a result of his war experiences from 1914 to 1918.

When the town was honored with the first bombardments, when the townspeople, under the influence of the plague of refugees, began hiding in the fields and the surrounding woods, Reb Nokhem laughed quietly and sedately:

"A soldier shoots and the Master of the Universe sends the bullet. If it has to hit me, there's no point in running, why ruin yourself?"

The golden Polish autumn threw sunbeams as in midsummer; by day it was hot, which facilitated the war operations of the German tanks. At night it was cool and autumnal—a relief for the refugees, who could run quietly, not fearing the bombs and the attacks of the German pilots. By day the town was recklessly strafed by the German bombardiers; at night it was swarming with people running and fleeing.

A large part of the town's inhabitants had taken to the road quite a while ago, bolting behind them all doors and windows, covering them with boards and not sparing any nails. Some abandoned everything, saving only themselves and their families. Reb Nokhem and his son stood all night in front of the house and watched how people ruined themselves, how the strangers, the Warsaw people, and others ran into the hollow hell, into the abyss.

[*Two lines are missing.*]

"We shall not run!"

All night the town seethed like a cauldron; it swarmed like a beehive. The army runs as if driven by an approaching enemy. Fire departments of cities and towns are on the run. Police run, priests run. People ride in buses, in trucks, in cars of private companies, in wagons and carts; people trudge, out of breath, on bicycles, dragging behind them a cow, in front a basket. People travel with dogs, cats, and, at the least, bundles. The highways are clogged with vehicles and the side roads with hordes of pedestrians breaking through on foot. A drink of water is a cure, a piece of bread a rare thing. A high Polish officer chews on a raw carrot and is happy; a soldier asks for a cigarette and is ready to give up everything for it. Barely five days of war and everything is like a ship without a rudder. People become animals and people become angels. Some are prepared to strip themselves naked and help one another with everything possible; some bury everything for themselves and neither see nor hear, blind to everything around!

But he, Reb Nokhem, won't move.

Whatever happens, he won't uproot himself from the sap of his soil. Here he has lived and here he is ready to die. Isn't he in God's hands?! . . .

He won't be broken or crushed! . . .

And another day came and a night. Another night with all its horrors. The town was burning on all sides. The townspeople, the few who were left, pack up their belongings and run. Through the town rush the last refugees, the last army units. It is clear as day: any minute the Germans will enter.

Reb Nokhem, The Oak, stands in the doorway like a dog in front of his doghouse; he isn't going and he won't go! . . .

The quarrel has been going on for a day and a half already. The Oak won't budge—he's not going!

The son went with the stream of humanity and fled. The daughters stay with their mama. They are waiting for their father, and Reb Nokhem, their father, like a rooted oak, stands in the doorway, looks at everything that's going on, and persists, stubbornly:

"Go where you want, I'm staying."

"I'm not moving. . . . "

"I'd rather die, go where you want!"

At sunrise, the town again gets the first portion of bombs and grenades. The front is approaching. The hours are numbered; every minute could bring death. The town has already been burning for two days and nights. Reb Nokhem, The Oak, doesn't budge. One of his daughters lies unconscious and the other one is already half mad; it doesn't matter. Reb Nokhem doesn't heed the crying and pleading. He won't be influenced by anyone now. No one will convince him: "Run where you want to, I'm not moving."

An incessant fire has begun spraying from the sky. The smoke all around makes you choke to death. The whole town is pelted with corpses. The town burns, and its flames encroach more and more. Not a brick is left standing. Not a person will remain alive, and everyone who runs by screams to The Oak:

"Why do you stand there, Jew? Why are you protecting your threshold? Run away where your eyes carry you. . . . "

Like the oak in the forest, Reb Nokhem doesn't budge from his hut. He barely breathes. Blackened with smoke, he stands at a bucket of water and douses himself from time to time to refresh himself, and to take heart. His wife, half out of her mind, got away with her daughters. Everyone has left him, and he persists stubbornly—he's not budging!

A home waits with everything in the world, waits for the flames that will engulf it any minute in their whirl and annihilate it.

And Reb Nokhem waits too. He knows that everything is doomed—he knows it, he knows that the fire won't spare his home either—he knows that. Yet, he knows something else: he knows that he won't be uprooted from here. . . .

He will die but he won't run away from here! . . .

"Better die at home than perish in an alien place. . . . "

Twice did Reb Nokhem faint and both times he recovered by himself. A piece of wood fell on his head and doused him with blood, and a strong explosion threw him on the ground so that he didn't know what was going on with him. But both times he didn't give in—he will fight to the end. A man can't live without roots. He won't let himself be uprooted! . . .

Two hours later The Oak was torn out by the roots. His hut was ruined by shrapnel, and everything was so enveloped by fire that it was impossible for him to save even a shirt. In the afternoon, a wind blew the fire and carried it over every corner of the town. In the evening, a strong shower with a delayed thunderstorm put out the fires in the burned town.

At dawn, when the German army marched into the town, the first advance units, between the posts and the burned ruins, came upon Reb Nokhem sitting on a stool with a bandaged head, wearing nothing but his shirt and trousers. The always red, suntanned face had become black as a gypsy's, and the red flowing beard and the rest of his appearance frightened everyone around. Pudel, his faithful dog, who for years had guarded the house, had, in his terror of fire, broken away from the rope and lay at his master's feet.

"Like the destruction of Jerusalem," murmured the first Germans. They offered the lonely Jude some cigarettes, water, coffee, rum. They photographed him with his dog on the background of the ruins, and they went on their way.

For a whole day The Oak crept around among the ruins like a crow among tombstones, seeking and searching.

The next morning, two Germans almost went out of their minds at the horrible howling of a dog that went on continuously for hours, overflowing in dreadful lamentations of a great calamity.

Ready to kill, with their fingers on the triggers of their guns, they went in the direction of the howling and suddenly stopped as if frozen.

On the chimney of a burned hut, on a rope thrown over sooty bricks, hung a tall Jew with a huge disheveled beard, and facing him stood Pudel, Reb Nokhem's dear and last servant, howling at his calamity. . . .

The chimney was the last vestige of the worldly possessions of Reb Nokhem, The Oak.

Here he lived and here he died. . . .[25]

The Germans took a photograph and, looking one another in the eye, they silently returned to finish their breakfast. . . .

—Vilna, July 14, 1941[26]

25. In Yiddish "Do hot er gelebt un do iz er geshtorbn"—an image of the Bundist ideology of *doikeyt* ("here-ness"): the Jews belong "here" in the Diaspora and will live and die "here."

26. This date is amazing: the piece was written after the Germans occupied Vilna, amid the panic of Lithuanian Snatchers catching Jews in the streets, ostensibly for forced labor (see Kruk's diary entries of July 13–14) and apparently without German participation.

REFUGEES[27]

[*The following section was written in independent Lithuania, in the capital Vilnius (Vilna), where about twenty thousand refugees from Poland arrived, fleeing both the Germans and the Soviets, and adding to the sixty thousand Vilna Jews.*]

1. Early Days

The hundreds and thousands who arrived in Vilna were huddled together, terrified, hungry, and exhausted. Stooped—with a habit of bending over at the sound of every exploding bomb. Terrified of all that happens around them with such lightning speed, such terror and tragedy.

A week ago a landlord, the director of a bank, an industrialist; today hungry, naked, and hunched up. Ten days ago a merchant, a factory supervisor, a cobbler, a baker; today naked and barefoot, crushed.

Tortured and worn out, they look fearfully at tomorrow. Fear brings people together, strangers become intimate, people cling to one another. The Jewish engineer befriends a Polish factory worker; a Jewish tailor is with a group of Polish students. Everything was so simple then, so human, so equal. All were brothers and all were close, facing the thousand lurking dangers. If someone is bleeding, you tear off your shirt and bandage his wounds. If someone falls down, you carry him along, so as not to abandon him in the wasteland.

The earth trembled at its foundations. Towns and villages were burning. One wave came on the heels of the next. Yesterday's factory managers, begging along with their workers, for a peasant's piece of bread—hunger! Yesterday's landlords begging along with their tenants for a roof over their heads—even a peasant's stable, even with the cattle, just a roof over your head!

Such was the reality in those days, and this is how they came to Vilna: hunched up, terrified.

A woman lost her husband, a man searches for his child, children ask about their parents—everything is mixed up, confused, and lost. Here is a woman running wearing only her shirt, covered with a coat—fleeing her burning home. A man on a bicycle: in front of him a child, in back of him a little dog—all his remaining property. . . .

Lubliners ask Plotskers, Plotskers seek among refugees from Warsaw, people from Łódź crawl up to those from Kalisz—a confusion, a tangle of such dreadful loneliness, of such scared madness—the war tremors of Hitler's invasion!

Such were the horrifying days of September–October 1939.

The sea overflowed and flooded Vilna.

A place to lie down is a dream. A piece of bread is rare. A shirt—who thinks

27. This report is extant in two versions: a manuscript subtitled "On OZE Activity in Vilna" and an article in two installments published in the journal *Folksgezunt* (Public Health) (nos. 2–3 and 4, 1940). The two versions are markedly different. Here, we have compiled parts of both to include all the information recorded by Kruk.

now of shirts? . . . Soap is a luxury. Warm food a fantasy. Every room that looks normal makes you tremble: a room!? Do people still have rooms? . . . Are people still sleeping in beds? . . . Are they sleeping?! Every refugee trembled when he saw that normal life is still going on somewhere and not everything is destroyed and crushed.

2. Vilna, October–November 1939

Thus they trudged over the streets of Vilna, refugees from all over Poland. Workers from Warsaw, yeshiva students from Lublin, merchants from Katowice, engineers, doctors—plodding through the medieval alleys of Vilna, seeking refuge. Searching for an open door, some water to wash with, a board to lie down on.

Over it all, the siren of alarm. Everyone responded in his own way and everyone wanted to help somehow, but . . .

The first days were one big confusion of need and anguish. Who will take care of the tens of thousands of refugees? Who will feed them? Who will console them?

Vilna was busy with its own troubles, its own anguish and suffering. Vilna had just shaken off the nightmare of war, the German bombardments, the dark nights and mortal days. Cut off from the world, Vilna was hungry and no one in those days had a mind for refugees.

No one? No, that would be too much. Let it be said for posterity—the first was the Joint.[28] Then OZE [in Polish, TOZ] jumped in. The refugee campaign began—everything was thrown into the aid of the oncoming stream of people.

When others just made noises and meanwhile wanted to exploit the need for their party's purposes, when others talked much and did little, the representative of TOZ came and declared, pure and simple:

"We have a nursing school with all its facilities—let the uprooted Yiddish writers come and occupy this building, let them feel at home here, let the bright rooms of our nursing school substitute at least a little for their abandoned homes, their studies, their familiar atmosphere."

When the representative of TOZ, Mr. Hirsh Matz, presented this plan to the committee of the uprooted Warsaw writers' family, they all accepted this initiative with the emotion it deserved—gratitude.

The Joint, on the one hand, and TOZ, on the other—and overnight at Sadowa 9, there was a shelter for the most prominent Yiddish writers and journalists who reached Vilna. And if, along with writers and journalists from Warsaw, they also feed and care for Vilna victims of the turmoil as well—writers and journalists, too—this is understandable and natural. This is the second achievement of TOZ.

28. The American Jewish Joint Distribution Committee (JDC), commonly called the Joint, founded in 1914, was the major worldwide Jewish aid organization, especially during the two world wars.

After Sadowa 9 came the dormitory for the intelligentsia and social activists at Kviatova 7, the dormitory for the intelligentsia at Wielka Pohulanka 17, the home for mothers and children, the large-scale sanitary and hygienic supervision, the medical service, the bath, the central laundry—and so on and so forth.

3. The Transition

But until then, everyone responded in his own way. Everyone wanted to contribute, to help:

On a side street, in a remote courtyard, at the top of a crooked staircase, was an attic. The landlord's son, a young student, persuaded his father: "Let the attic be for refugees. It is empty anyway. For the intelligentsia!"

The daughter added: "Papa, just look at them: professors, doctors, engineers, writers."

And the response was: "Let them live there, by all means!"

. . . The window in the attic is crooked and distorted—bent with old age. Professor X cannot straighten his back here—can he push up the ceiling? So he sits bent over. . . .

Where can one sit down? A box in a corner, a bench with three legs—you sit wherever you can. Sitting is important. . . .

Six refugees live in this attic: a doctor from Warsaw, two engineers from Częstochowa, an engineer from Katowice, a professor from Cracow, and a teacher. An old desk serves as a dining table, the windowsills are covered with everything from pieces of soap, toothbrushes, a crust of bread, to a belt and razors. The doctors forgot the rules of hygiene. On the table is a big bowl of potatoes in their jackets. Even when you aren't starving, this is an excellent dish! . . . The professor from Cracow peels the potatoes and wipes his fingers on his pants. . . .

The Warsaw doctor is humorous and hums a song: "Tomorrow will be worse. . . ."

Suddenly one of the six comes with the good news that TOZ is opening a dormitory for intelligentsia. A pessimist from Częstochowa interrupts him: "Again beds, again as in the [Jewish Community] Council offices? . . ." The newcomer calms him down: "Everything is arranged! In two days we move to TOZ—everything is arranged."

The appetite for potatoes increases. The people are happy and the sulky teacher mumbles: "A bath, better they should give us a bath." The newcomer consoles him: "Six rooms, board, a radio, a bathroom, a toilet—all that in the dormitory."

The appetite grows with the eating. The potatoes creep out of the bowl and the people eat heartily:

Full board? . . .

To sleep in beds? . . .

A piece of soap and a towel? . . .

A bathroom?
A toilet?

4. Refugee Aid

Yes, but what will happen to the other refugees? What about the six or seven thousand under the auspices of the refugee committee of the Jewish Community Council?

True, a considerable percentage doesn't need any refugee aid. In human terms, their situation is the same as that of any other refugee: uprooted, lonely, out of contact with their friends and family; but as for material means, they brought enough with them. . . . But aside from them, there is an endless number—thousands of hungry, isolated, uprooted, hollow, with not a penny to their name. What about them?

Vilna sounded the alarm. Everything calls for mobilization. The Refugee Committee builds refugee homes, soup kitchens, and so on. The Jewish Community Council opens its doors. Entire yeshivas arrive and settle in synagogues. School buildings are occupied, etc. Zionists take care of halutzim, labor activists build workers' homes—Vilna is flooded, Vilna is steeped in an inundation of refugees.

We visited the dormitories supported by the refugee committee. At Pohulanka 14, six rooms and . . . 94 people. Almost all sleep on the floor. All mixed together—women, men, children: dirty, cold, one toilet for all of them, and you should have seen that toilet. Sleeping? They sleep on the ground!

In the synagogues, the zone of the yeshivas—dirty, cold, they sleep on the floor, on benches. The Pinsk yeshiva settled in a prayer house of the laborers (Niemiecka 6). A long dark corridor with stairs, as if going up to the sky, and no one even thought about a lamp. Ninety-seven yeshiva students are lying there, sleeping on desks and benches, freezing cold. The room is full of feathers, straw —a poorhouse that should at least be disinfected.

On Strashun Street, women live. On Subocz, 450 persons, on Zawalna 112, on Zygmuntowska 18. And almost everywhere are dirt and darkness.

Where is the Refugee Committee of the Community Council? Where is the activity of the offices?

At Pohulanka 14, especially made beds stand for weeks, but everyone sleeps on the floor. The beds cannot be used—no straw mattresses, because there is no straw. . . .

In other places, even worse:

Someone acquired a board from a ping-pong table and turned it into . . . a bed. Six people sleep on it. A sick woman along with her sixty-three-year-old husband who sleeps in his pants because he's cold. Next to him, four more, like a family.

Thousands lie on the ground and have nothing to put over their heads. People with fever lie with nothing to cover them. No shirt, no clothing. A piece of soap is a problem, a towel a rare sight. The autumn brings colds. They lie in fever, cough, have runny noses. Their feet are bleeding from running. Their heads are buzzing with what they went through: alarm, alarm!

And Vilna OZE took on the mission: to bring medical aid! To supervise hygienic conditions among the refugees. A doctor. Medicine. A bandage.

5. People Huddle Together

A TOZ hygienist writes in one of her reports: "There are several dozen centers here, refugee homes or soup kitchens. The refugee homes have a regional character, others have a social-ideological essence." Indeed, in part, this is so: some homes are filled with Czechoslovak refugees or with students from several yeshivas who naturally stay together: from Białystok, Grodno, Lublin, Ostrów-Mazowiecki, Międzyrzec, Pinsk, and other places. All those are yeshiva students who fled both from the Germans and from the Bolsheviks.

The dormitories that are directly affiliated with TOZ are homes with full board. The writers at Sadowa 9 have renewed Tłomacka 13 here.[29] The ideological debates haven't stopped, but they eat dinner and entertain themselves at the same table: the Zionist Y. M. Nayman with the Bundist B. Shefner, the Folkist [populist party] Noah Pryłucki with the Socialist Kh. Sh. Kazdan, the Orthodox D. Flinker with the secular Lazar Kahan, the religious Zionist B. Jeuschsohn with the fanatical Bundist P. Schwartz.

Everything is equalized here: the editor of [the daily] *Togblat* with the editors of [the Zionist daily] *Haynt,* along with the colleagues from the [Bundist] *Folkstsaytung*—the whole Yiddish press of Warsaw, contributors to the greatest Yiddish newspapers in the world—everything here is together. Whoever lives on his own gets his food at home. Similar arrangements prevail at Kwiatowa 7 and Pohulanka 17.

As the writers' home has a corporative character, so do some refugee homes have a regional and often social-ideological character. Aside from the homes for yeshiva students, there are homes for workers, halutzim, etc. In American parlance, these would be called branches: a Lublin branch, a Czechoslovak branch, a Bundist branch, etc.

It's good that everyone huddles together. To be together with someone from your home town or someone close to you socially [i.e., politically] is better than being jumbled up in a herd of faceless uprooted refugees, with no common character traits, no common ideology.

6. Among Refugees from Czechoslovakia

I went to the Czechs. In a Christian neighborhood. Somewhere in a school building, in the heart of the university quarter—at Universytecka Street 9—104 Czechoslovak refugees are stacked away. Some of them have fled two or three times. A few are running for the fourth time.

29. The famous Warsaw Yiddish writers' club, the center of Yiddish literature in Poland.

"The first time," one of them says, "we fled from the Sudetenland and from the occupied parts of Hungary to [Czech] Prague, then from Prague to [Polish] Cracow, from Cracow to [Soviet] Lwów, and then from Lwów to [Lithuanian] Vilna."

Here, among the Czech refugees, there's a homey atmosphere. They do not let gloom get the better of them: "Why think about it?" Indeed it's good that they don't let gloom take over. If they had thought about it all the time, it would have been worse. Nevertheless: "Who can control the pillows soaked with tears . . . " He smiles at the word "pillows."

One hundred and four refugees benefit from this home. Some eat only dinners, some are on full board. Forty-seven sleep here. But there are only . . . 23 places to sleep, including a few beds and hardly 21 blankets.

"Food?" They take me to a room that once was a classroom and is now a dining hall. In a large room, school benches are arranged together. While sitting at the table, the refugees have to fit into children's benches. The plate cannot stay still—the school tables slope! So they hold the plates in their hands and . . . eat.

About 90 percent of the Czechs are intelligentsia: 12 engineers, 9 attorneys, 4 doctors, 3 journalists—altogether 85 men and 19 women, including 4 under the age of 16.

The rooms are dirty. The Czechs explain, "There is nothing to sweep the floor with, nothing to wash the floor with, no spittoons, no hangers for clothes." In small rooms, each shared by several families, clotheslines hang over the broken beds or straw mattresses. "We wash clothes in kitchen pots," explains Dr. L. The woman sitting on a small bed reads a book. She closes it and I observe: Thomas Mann. . . .

I ask someone: "Did you get any clothes?" The answer is ironic: "Yes, we got a promise: for a hundred and four people, thirteen pieces of underwear." "And the underwear?" I ask. "Yes, that's what I mean, the underwear? That's what we've got a promise for. . . . But they rarely come to us, the only one that visits here is the TOZ."

7. The Aid of OZE

In November OZE served 26 centers with about 3,000 refugees. In January, there were already 87 centers with 8,660 refugees. In March, 94 centers with 8,524 refugees. Forty doctors were mobilized to serve the refugee army. A staff of nurses and orderlies.

Refugees, naked and barefoot, keep on wandering [across the borders]. At −30°C, −35°C, even −40°C, they continue their pilgrimage to Jerusalem of Lithuania.[30] Scores have frozen limbs. Tragic cases arrive. Arms are amputated, legs

30. "Jerusalem of Lithuania" was the honorific nickname of Vilna, recognizing its importance as a cultural center. Vilna was annexed to independent Lithuania, and Polish Jews had to sneak over the Soviet-Lithuanian border to get out of the Soviet domain.

are cut off—OZE must be everywhere. Out of the hospital and into an infirmary. The infirmary is a home of horror and tears.

"Nurse, I want a pillow."

"Nurse, we have no sheets."

"Nurse, please, a straw mattress."

A garbage can, a spittoon, a towel, a toothbrush, tooth powder—OZE does whatever possible, invests a great deal of effort.

In January, 1,007 kilos of soap were distributed. In January 18,803 people went to the bath, and in March 17,000.

At the initiative of OZE, along with the Refugee Committee, a big campaign for collecting clothes was undertaken. Four thousand garments were collected, as were linen, shoes, and underwear for men, women, and children. Altogether, the clothing was valued at 17,000 Lit.[31] Sixty doctors and their families, bereft of everything, have been neglected and abandoned—refugees among refugees. OZE conducts a special activity among them: five thousand Lit a month are distributed as financial support. Language courses, refresher courses in various fields of medicine, etc., are organized for them.

With the aid of OZE, a dietetic kitchen is established for sick refugees. The regular clinic of TOZ was turned into an open clinic. Hundreds of visitors a day, thousands a month. In the first quarter of 1940, 12,260 patients were treated in the clinic. In the dental office, 5,862. Thousands with eye ailments, hundreds with nervous disorders or skin diseases, women and children needing surgical treatment, and so on.

The quartz lamps radiated 819 persons. In the three months, 2,387 laboratory tests were done, their own drugstore produced and distributed 13,054 medications. Hundreds of first-aid kits were distributed in the dormitories and soup kitchens.

The home for infants issued thousands of daily rations, the sanitarium for consumptives provided 4,244 person-days of hospitalization, the children's sanitarium, 1,847.

A sea of numbers, a terror of anguish and suffering.

How terrible it is to tell about it. How anguished and painful are the horror stories.

8. Infirmary

Those winter days will remain in memory forever. At −40°C and under −40°C, hundreds and hundreds wandered from country to country, from border to border, seeking a home, seeking a place to hide.

"In a field in no-man's-land on the border between one country and another, a group of frozen people was discovered."

31. The official currency of independent Lithuania (1918–1940).

"In the Vilna [Jewish hospital] Mishmeret-Holim [Watch of the sick], two young people had their legs amputated. The cause: they were frozen while crossing the border at under −40°C."

Such news is printed in the daily press. OZE began to organize aid for the unfortunate. An infirmary was established, a transit point from hospital to recovery. Dozens passed through it, and many of them remained without arms or legs.

On New Year's Eve [1940], he walked over the border, and now? . . . Now, one of them sighs: "Now we don't walk anymore, we drag ourselves." He grabs the two sticks, stands up as in a race, and . . . drags his two paralyzed legs. "At first we didn't even feel it," says the unfortunate man, as if he wanted to justify himself; "there was no pain. Only later did it come. . . . The legs grow numb, heavy, and you drag them like poles."

"And then?"

"Then came OZE, Mishmeret-Holim, and—as you see—I'm an invalid for life: three toes on one foot, two on the other. . . ."

A young man walks by on crutches, another one limps, wearing on his only foot a black felt boot and a rubber shoe as an embellishment.

One of them talks to me: "How can I go back home?" Another one speaks as if to himself: "With these two hands, I supported my father and mother, married off a sister, fed a grandmother. With these two hands?!" He raises his voice and breaks off as if scared of his own voice. His face turns scarlet. He looks at his bandaged hands, gazes at his friends, burrows deeper under the blanket, and . . . I pretend not to see it. He cries. But he quickly restrains himself. Pretends to be calmed, and I hear his young, energetic voice calling out: "Who needs me now? Who do I need to stay alive for?"

I see his young, energetic face, but his eyes, like two extinguished candles, tell of a merciless resignation: "Who needs my life now?!"

This is the nightmare scream of the inhabitants of the OZE infirmary. The broken, ruined human skeletons are cared for attentively. Everything possible is done to ease their misfortune. But is there a power that could return their lost limbs?

Here in the infirmary are patients who rarely smile, who are rarely warmed by the spring sun—patients ashamed and hiding from life. On all fours, as if he had escaped from slaughter, head thrown back, half-sitting and half-leaning on a chair, a man pushes on, moves the chair and slides forward. A hollow half pant leg is seen on the chair. He wipes the sweat with his hand and we see that the hand is also missing fingers. . . .

The young dark fellow is a carpenter's assistant from the Zawiercie district. He worked with his father in construction, and now? When the war broke out, he was in the Polish army. With the twentieth regiment of the Cracow infantry, he went to Silesia. On that front, he was hit by a series of bullets. He shows me his hand—what remains is a crippled piece of flesh with two crooked fingers.

"When I was released from the Łuck hospital," he recounts, "the Bolsheviks were already there. At minus thirty-five [Celsius], I walked toward Vilna. My goal," he smiles, embarrassed—"then my goal was Vilna, to go to Eretz Israel."

"And today?"

"Now," he explains, as if I couldn't see for myself; "now, my right hand is not a hand and my leg, maybe I'll be able to walk with a prosthesis and maybe not—am I fit for Eretz Israel?" The question mark remains hanging in the air, as if he wanted to save something. . . .

The twenty-two-year-old Jewish war invalid, the carpenter's apprentice from Zawiercie district, bows his head as if seeking consolation on the floor.

9. Children

In the sea of bitterness there is one consolation: children.

In the flight, people left everything behind: their property, their workshops, all the achievements of dozens of years of work. "Just to save your life!" And the youngest refugees came with their parents and . . . silent fear in their childlike eyes. A strange gloom gazed out of their black, beautiful little eyes. . . .

The Vilna OZE created a home for those refugee children. Gradually, the gloom disappeared. The children of the "Children's Republic" of OZE turned tears into song. . . .

The press tells of it: Dozens of refugee dormitories exist in Vilna, and every dormitory, every assembly center has its own "music." True, you hear just minor keys, sounds of grief and anguish, but the individual notes play out a great symphony, the war symphony. Strain your ear and in this symphony you will hear the whistle of shrapnel, the crack of exploding bombs, the cry of women and children. . . .

One place, one little corner exists in Vilna where a different music prevails, a joyful, even dancing music. There you hear not sighs but songs. This is the food and rest center for the youngest war victims, for the smallest refugees, the Moysheles, Shloymeles, Rivkeles, Soreles, who ran with their fathers and mothers, some without fathers and mothers—ran over highways, walked over swamps, swam over rivers, crossed over borders—to escape the destruction.

Here, in their joyous Republic, you meet children who experienced much more than adults. You see children who experienced the expulsion from Pultusk, children who don't know to this day where their father is or children whose mother is left behind somewhere, cut off, unable to get here. . . .

But in the children's home, everything is done to make the little souls forget the evil. The refugee children sing, play, cavort, and laugh. The summer peeps through the windows. The children hear talk of providing them with a forest and fresh air; something is being prepared for them. And when you see the Pinyeles and Soreles sit at little tables, on low benches, you unwittingly remember the words of [the popular song] "Afn Pripetshik [At the Fireplace]": "Children, when you grow up, you will understand what lies in all that, how many tears, how much weeping. . . ."

That is the description of the OZE Children's Republic in Vilna. In the winter months, OZE organized a winter camp for children of refugees and of the Vilna poor. The camp existed for two months, and more than 90 children passed through it. Here, too, in the abundance of snow and winter sports, a white Children's Republic was created.

The figures of the OZE activity among children tell their own story: in the first quarter of 1940, the OZE clinic treated 468 children. In the tuberculosis dispensary, 1,040 children were treated. The children's sanitarium served 1,847 children's visits. The home for mothers and infants provided 5,540 feedings per day, and so on.

On the waves of grief and pain, in a sea of anguish and loneliness, the Vilna OZE was a little flame that warmed—an instrument of aid that brought salvation to the suffering and tortured people.

10. May God Take Pity!

"The Vilna refugees went through fire and brimstone," a refugee said to me. "And yet they still cannot stand on their own feet, no small thing to go through the childhood diseases of a refugee! . . . And when we do stand on our own feet, only then will the real refugee hardships come." There's a lot of truth in that: every refugee somehow managed to settle, found a roof over his head, obtained some clothing and lunch in a soup kitchen, overcame registration number one, survived registration number two, and . . . the childhood diseases of a refugee are not yet over—he still cannot stand on his own feet. . . .

The winter was unusually harsh—as if to spite the half-naked refugees. Despite the frost, the streets were teeming with refugees. Something drove them, something made them run: but what?

Very simple: how can you sit still? The telegraph section in the post office is always overfull. Everyone is jealous of everyone else. What for? He himself doesn't know, but in the meantime, he's jealous:

"Aha, he's cabling to America!"

"See, that one got a cable from Palestine!"

Everyone would like to do what the other one does. Everyone imagines that he was fooled, that someone else knows better. . . . People live here on the hope each has built for himself:

"An uncle in America . . . "

"A brother in Argentina . . . "

"A certificate . . . "[32]

"An affidavit . . . "[33]

32. The official document needed for immigration to Palestine.

33. The document needed for immigration to the United States.

And everyone is running around the city. Everyone has a secret and keeps it to himself, in the meantime pricking up his ears at this one and that one, at anyone who shows a smile on his face. . . .

"Aha, he's smiling!"

May God take pity! How can you live without hope?

And they live with this Menakhem-Mendl[34] wish that the great prize will come out of the blue, the certificate, the affidavit.

May God take pity! . . .

II. "Skalbiklaying"

How do the refugees fill their day? Jews give advice to Chamberlain[35] and reproach him:

"Why won't he shoot? . . ."[36]

"How long can they be silent? . . ."

But meantime you remember that you are nothing but a sinful refugee and . . . you gather up the two dirty shirts, you run with them to the [Refugee] Committee or to TOZ. There it is—got a coupon to wash a few pieces of laundry.

Attorney X. cannot stand the wrong that the world has done to him: for six months he has no longer been an attorney. He trudges through the streets of Vilna, stands in lines for the honor of having his eight pieces of laundry accepted in the TOZ laundry.

Young people standing in the line have fun:

"Berl, where are your pajamas?"

A lady who has fallen on hard times and must also depend on OZE cannot stand it: "You found something to joke about. . . ."

Everyone has his own interests. Engineer Z. . . . is a chemist and got intrigued by the *Skalbikla* ("laundry" in Lithuanian). "This is no small thing: a laundry that services fifty thousand pieces of laundry a month!" The director of the laundry is pleasant and explains: "The laundry works in three shifts. We have fifty-eight workers and employees, Jews and Christians. The best specialists in town work here. We serve all Jewish refugees, on average seven thousand customers a month, mostly refugees in dormitories, soup kitchens, and kibbutzim.[37] Today it is one of the largest Jewish enterprises in Vilnius."

I make a tour with the engineer around the unique TOZ refugee laundry: I

34. Sholem Aleichem's proverbial character who plays the stock market and has fantastic dreams, only to fall on the ground, facing reality.

35. British Prime Minister Neville Chamberlain, who signed the Munich Pact appeasing Nazi Germany and who promised "peace in our time," which was shattered by Hitler in short order.

36. That is, when will England fight Germany?

37. Members of Zionist Pioneer youth movements, mostly refugees in their late teens or early twenties, lived together in communes called *Kibbutz Hakhshara* ("training kibbutz" or, in the plural, "kibbutzim"), waiting for an opportunity to go to Palestine.

count twenty-two persons at the washbasins. The laundresses sway with hard efforts—refugee laundry. They explain:

"If you'd only seen the laundry! Filthy isn't the word to describe it. If you'd only seen the laundry—how can you wash such things?"

A laundress pulls a piece of laundry out of her washbasin; it's hard to tell whether it's a shirt or . . .

The director explains:

"Actually, we planned to establish a mending center in the laundry. But it turns out that you have to mend ninety percent of the clothes. Who can do it? It would have devoured a huge budget. Where do we get money for it? We use up half a ton of soap a month here. Twelve pressers work twenty-four hours a day. To be able to serve everybody on time, we had to set up a mechanism to dry the laundry fast. We achieved the maximum—to dry a whole shipment of laundry takes three hours.

"There are also special machines to wring the laundry: they save us seventy-five percent of our work. The OZE-TOZ thinks of mechanizing the whole laundry, buying machines, and changing the site—this will further rationalize and accelerate our work."

We look at the laundry: clean, washed without bleach, and . . . the jokes in the line do not stop.

The young woman taking in the laundry explains that such torn laundry is hard to wash. Two younger refugees help her:

"Good idea, give me a note to the Refugee Committee, maybe they'll issue a new shirt?"

Another one takes it up:

"Comrade, write a 'Request' and enclose your shirt with it. When you wait a month, then . . ."

"Then you'll get your refusal," the first one supports him. . . .

The refugee crowd, as we see, is joyous and jokes at the expense of refugee suffering.

12. Sanitary Medical Supervision

The doctors and hygienists supervising the refugees are happy with the results of their work. They remind me of the sad situation I wrote about earlier. "Today it is considerably better," they tell me with a smile. "Today we serve about nine thousand refugees. Most of them are housed in dormitories, many use the various soup kitchens. Altogether we now serve ninety-one centers."

The hygienic situation has improved considerably. There are many more beds, linen, furniture; the larders are better equipped. In some dormitories, reading rooms of the Yiddish and non-Yiddish press have been set up. I learn from the reports: 19 sanitary doctors and 3 social hygienists carry out the work in those 91 centers. Just in February the doctors and hygienists visited their institutions 448 times.

Nevertheless, they complain, in many dormitories two persons sleep in one bed. Nevertheless, the hygienists report, in many dormitories it is cold. One of them reports: in all the centers of Ha-Shomer ha-Tzair, there are sixty to eighty sick persons per day. The sick must be fed properly. . . .

"But," one doctor tells me, "between February and today we have accomplished a lot."

"For example," adds a sanitary worker, "in February alone, we had 16,436 visitors to the disinfection bath. Seven hundred kilos of soap for personal use were distributed in the same month!"

In the weaker sanitary centers, the sanitary brigades worked 17 times. In February the doctors visited 812 patients in bed and treated 356 patients in dormitories. Through the medical supervision of TOZ, hospital aid was given to 145 people with a total of 2,659 hospital person-days.

They explain:

According to the report for the month of February, the TOZ clinic treated 5,648 refugees. They distributed 4,534 prescriptions. The refugee dormitories received 103 portable apothecaries.

The reports are filled with figures, their authors are beaming with happiness over the results, but . . .

But how long can you throw figures around? . . .

Nevertheless, the refugees are still scattered and upset. Something drives them, something makes them run, something . . .

"How can you sit still?"

"An uncle in America . . . "

"A brother in Argentina . . . "

"A certificate . . . "

"A visa . . . "

What a pity! . . .

ON THE RUINS OF POLAND[38]

The recently extinguished fires are still smoking. Corpses are regularly dragged out from under the ruins. Bombed-out houses collapse, covering passersby.

Who knows how many years, perhaps decades, it will take to heal the wounds of the destruction of Jewish Poland.

For two decades Poland has built,[39] and the annihilation took only three weeks.

38. This section was written in Vilnius, the new capital of the (still) independent Lithuania, into which the city was incorporated. The article was published in *Kultur un dertsiung* (Culture and Education), New York (May 1940), pp. 7–9.

39. After more than a century of foreign occupation, Poland regained its independence in November 1918 and lost it again in September 1939.

All of Poland has been destroyed, the Jewish community of Poland is in ruins, and a great cultural treasure of Polish Jewry lies in ruins. It is precisely about that destroyed cultural treasure of the Jews in Poland that I want to write.

1. Numbers

For better or worse, about 1,000 Jewish Community Councils were active among the Jewish population in Poland. Now, not a single one of them exists in their old form—in a few places, there are simply *Älteste Raten der Juden* [Councils of Jewish Elders].

Nine central school organizations existed in Poland, including 1,500 educational institutions with close to 200,000 children. The Central Yiddish School Organization (TSISHO) alone numbered about 170 institutions. There were also [the Hebrew secular] Tarbut schools, Orthodox schools, vocational schools, institutions of ORT,[40] CENTOS, etc. CENTOS alone is a union of nine central Jewish societies for children's protection and care of orphans,[41] with about 350 institutions in more than 200 cities and towns in Poland.

Extracurricular education: there were a network of evening courses, public libraries, hundreds of cultural and educational institutions.

The Jewish Scientific Institute (YIVO), the crown of modern Yiddish cultural society, had hundreds of collectors'[42] groups in Poland and 1,755 subscribers to its scholarly publications in 210 cities and towns. The actual number of subscribers is much larger because these figures don't include such cultural centers as Warsaw, Łódź, Cracow, and Białystok, which have undertaken to enlist larger numbers of subscribers. Warsaw alone distributed 100 copies of the third volume of *Historishe shriftn* [Studies in History]. In fact, we must count more than 2,000 subscribers to YIVO publications.

Kultur-lige [the Cultural League] had 160 branches, and hundreds of public libraries were affiliated with its Library Center. Several public universities operated under its direction, as did many choruses, orchestras, and drama clubs. There was an extensive tourist activity, summer and winter camps, etc.

Where is the enormously extensive Yiddish press? Yiddish publishing? Not to mention the political movements?! . . .

Everything is now turned into ruins. Everything lies in dust, and only in a few places can you retrieve some embers, remaining bits and pieces, as a souvenir of the destruction.

40. The Russian initials for the Society for Spreading Work among Jews. It had a network of professional and vocational schools and, to this day, is active around the world.

41. CENTOS is an acronym meaning "Federation of Associations for the Care of Orphans in Poland."

42. Collectors of archival material and folklore.

2. Greetings

Thousands run across the borders and look for a roof over their heads, a bit of straw on which to stay overnight, a temporary lodging, some broth to warm their insides. They come bringing the most horrible and anguished greetings:

The Jewish school system has ceased to exist. A few schools are active here and there, but mostly they are no more than food distribution centers. There are almost no classes anymore. Of the whole system of Yiddish secular schools, barely six are still active: in Warsaw three, in Łódź two, in Lublin one. In Lublin, classes are proceeding. . . .

The famous children's sanitarium in Miedzeszyn, named for Vladimir Medem, has experienced the war with all its horrors.[43] Grim battles took place around it. The sanitarium has been turned into a hospital. The sum total: the splendid kindergarten has been filled up with graves—it is a cemetery. The walls are sprayed with blood. All the inventory was rescued by the devotion of friends and comrades.

Once again, there is a sanitarium there, and once again, there are more than 100 children there. . . .

3. Something about Writers, Books, and Artists

In the Polish world as in the Jewish world, the destruction is horrible.

One piece of information is more awful than the next:

The famous Yiddish writer Shimen Horonczyk, escaping from Warsaw under a hail of bullets, couldn't bear the pain: not far from Warsaw, in the small town of Kałuszyn, he committed suicide.

In Łuków, the Nazis shot the old Yiddish journalist Lipe Kestin and his son. In Otwock (near Warsaw), the unique Jewish-Polish writer Urke Nachalnik was shot; he was a former criminal who had become a writer.

For several months Indelman, the chairman of the Yiddish Journalists' Union in Warsaw, was held in a German concentration camp.

The Nazis have removed the book collection of the famous library of Judaic studies in Warsaw.

The only representative Jewish theater, the Nowości, is completely burned. Ida Kamińska and her family, barely alive, fled to the Soviet zone. Many other Jewish actors did the same.

The writers Y. Perle and Leon Finkelstein are in Lwów; others changed their skin and are prominent in Białystok.[44]

As you now know from the press, a group of forty writers has reached Vilna unharmed. These include Noah Pryłucki, B. Shefner, Dr. Kleinbaum, Vladimir Ko-

43. The Medem sanitarium, named after the leader of the Bund, was situated near Warsaw. It was affiliated with the Central Yiddish School Organization (TSISHO) in Poland.

44. That is, they turned into Communist sympathizers. Białystok was incorporated in Soviet Byelorussia.

sovski, B. Jeuschsohn, Kh. Sh. Kazdan, Bernard Singer, Sh. Mendelson, Y. M. Nayman, Lazar Kahan, M. Moses, Dr. Y. Kruk, Victor Shulman, P. Schwartz, and others. Now more and more people arrive—the forty has already become sixty.

As is also known from the daily press, in the territories occupied by the Soviet army, the leaders of the Bund—Henryk Erlich, Wiktor Alter, Anna Rosental, and several dozen others—have been arrested.[45] In Vilna, those arrested and deported by the Soviets include the leader of YIVO, Zalmen Reisen, and his son; Attorney Czernichow and his son; and all Bundist members of the Municipal Council.[46] In Galicia, the Soviet authorities arrested the Jewish-Polish journalists and editors of the Polish-Yiddish daily newspaper, *Nasz Przegląd:* Wagman, Schwalbe, and Wołkowicz. They were deported to Tbilisi, where they work in a . . . sawmill.

This and similar news items come from all corners of the country—each item more tragic than the last.

In cities and towns, there is total destruction. In Bełchatów, near Łódź, two days after the Germans invaded, on Yom Kippur, a bonfire was set up in the marketplace and books—holy books, and everything that wasn't German—were burned. They ordered all Jews to put on prayer shawls and dance around the auto-da-fé. The same thing was repeated in dozens of towns.

And in the Soviet occupation zone?

A reliable comrade tells us:

In Lwów a commission came to the building of the Cultural League. There they found the local banner of the Bund and the cultural office of the professional unions. The commissar tore up the banner and left those who accompanied him to finish the job. They tore the pictures of worker activists down from the walls and trampled on them.

That's the news from there.

4. Individual Rays of Light

The catastrophe isn't over, nevertheless, here and there, cheerful and encouraging rays of light appear:

The Jews of Poland work with devotion to save whatever is possible. The Jewish proletariat does heroic work. But it is still too soon to write about that. Young people have thrown themselves into battle with all devotion, and miracles grow on the ruins.

In Vilna, there is now a publisher, TSISHO. Its task—not to lag behind—is to publish a book for young children and one for older children every two weeks.

45. The Bund, as a Socialist party, was considered the enemy of Communism. Its leaders, Henryk Erlich and Wiktor Alter, were shot on Stalin's orders during the German-Soviet war.

46. The Soviets ruled Vilna in September–October 1939, during which period they arrested many intellectuals and political activists and evacuated the radio factory, Elektrit, to Minsk. They then turned Vilna over to independent Lithuania, but they occupied all of Lithuania in June 1940.

Textbooks, etc., are put out. As these lines were written, the anatomy textbook of Dr. [Yisroel] Biber [in Yiddish] was reprinted. Now a new series of textbooks is being prepared for printing, adapted to suit the new Lithuanian curriculum.

A one-time publication, *Shul un vegn* [School and ways], has already appeared, displaying again the names of the experienced pedagogues: Sh. Mendelson, Kh. Sh. Kazdan, G. Pludermacher, Sh. Gilinski, and others.

Lithuania turned the Jewish primary schools in the Vilna district into state schools, including the Yiddish secular schools. Only the Vilna Yiddish Real Gymnasium[47] and its primary school were not taken over by the state. The nationalization of the schools caused a series of difficulties—this story would constitute a chapter in itself and not an easy one, but this isn't a topic to be discussed today.[48]

The Vilna TSBK[49]—the school organization of Vilna—is also active. The TSBK is about to open a new series of children's homes, which Vilna badly needs now. All institutions remain under the old direction so far.

In Kovno and in the Kovno part of Lithuania there are eighteen [Yiddish] schools. They are unified and are directed by a pedagogical commission. A contact between Kovno and Vilna has now been established to unify the activity in the whole country. A comprehensive plan for extracurricular activity, children's clubs, and houses is to be worked out. Particular attention is being paid to work among the children of refugees.

As for the material existence of the Yiddish secular institutions, the material care for the schools remains in force. Many teachers, aside from those of the Real Gymnasium and its primary school, will be refused government positions. Nor will the government support positions in the children's homes, and certainly not in the children's clubs. The enormous impoverishment of the local population, the high level of unemployment, and the number of war casualties are reflected in reduced tuition. The material difficulties do not shrink but increase.

Nevertheless, the general mood of the faculty is good. They all believe that the school will again develop and show new achievements. And they all believe in the attachment of the Jewish masses to the Yiddish language. According to Lithuanian law, parents play a large role in the management of schools. Hence the great hope that with the opening of new schools and new classes in the next school year, the number of schools will increase considerably.

An unpleasant chapter in Poland has been written by the so-called *szabasówkas* (official schools for Jewish children with Polish instruction).[50] When the Bolsheviks entered Vilna, these schools immediately switched from Polish to Yid-

47. The Yiddish high school for science.

48. For fear of censorship.

49. In Yiddish, Tsentraler Bildungs-komitet, or the Central Educational Committee, which oversaw Yiddish secular schools in Vilna.

50. Literally, "Sabbath schools," that is, schools conducted in Polish for Jewish children, who rest on the Sabbath.

dish. As soon as the Lithuanians came in, these schools joined the central organization of Yavne [religious schools]. Some of the teaching is done in Yiddish, some in Polish. The tendency is to switch to Lithuanian as quickly as possible. The nests of Polonization have changed into nests of Lithuanization![51]

The former Jewish-Polish small shop—the Jewish-Polish gymnasium—has now changed into a gymnasium with Yiddish as the language of instruction, and it now bears the name of Y. L. Peretz. Let us hope that the shopkeeper tradition will soon be forgotten and that the gymnasium will be unified with Yiddish secular schools and their administration.

Now in the area of the former Kovno and Vilna, there are forty educational institutions with Yiddish as the language of instruction, including four gymnasia. Altogether, there are about four or five thousand students.

Unfortunately, the Lithuanian government cannot decide to form a special department for the Yiddish school system. Such a project was proposed by the Yiddish school circles, but nothing has come of it. Let it be recalled for posterity that back in 1920, when Vilna still belonged to Lithuania, there was such an office. The director of the Yiddish secular schools was then the meritorious pedagogue G. Pludermacher.

Efforts have been made by the circles of friends of Yiddish to establish a chair for the Yiddish language and literature in the humanities faculty of the only university in Lithuania. Candidates have already been mentioned.

In the area of Yiddish publishing, there has been tangible movement: in the first weeks, as the local population caught its breath from the German bombings, several Yiddish books appeared: the Tomor publishing house put out the second book by Y. Y. Trunk about Sholem Aleichem's Tevye the dairyman, *Fate and Trust;* a collection devoted to the founder of the Bund, Arkady Kremer, appeared; a book of poetry by the poet A. Sutzkever (of the Young Vilna group) came out, and as mentioned above, the anatomy book of Dr. Biber was reprinted. YIVO is preparing to print the second edition of *The Way to Our Youth,* by Dr. Max Weinreich. In the YIVO publishing house, the ninth volume (book 6) of the *History of the Jews,* by Professor S. Dubnow, is in print. Volume 15 of YIVO-bleter (nos. 1–3) and *Yidish far ale* (no. 15) are about to appear.

The Vilna daily press also resumed its activity: thus far, the *Vilner Togblat* and the *Vilner Ovnt-kuryer* have appeared.

In short, out of this great destruction comes just a small consolation that little fires flicker, keeping the flame alive.

This flame, we believe, will flare up again with the brightest light!

51. An allusion to the assimilationist tendencies of the Jewish Orthodox.

CHAPTER 2

THE DESTRUCTION OF JEWISH VILNA

JUNE 22, 1941 – SEPTEMBER 6, 1941

[*The first four pages of the diary are missing; the headings listed in Kruk's table of contents provide an idea of their topics. The Germans attacked the Soviet Union at dawn on June 22, 1941. Vilna was bombed all day and all night. Some tried to leave Vilna on June 23 with the retreating Red Army, which Kruk mentions in the entry of July 7. It appears that Kruk himself considered fleeing the city but gave up the idea.*]

JUNE 23, 1941

War Between Germany and the Soviet Union
Six in the Evening: People Are Fleeing
I Give Up[1] and Rely on God's Will
No Authority in the City[2]
I Resign Myself [to Destiny]

Young people are taking off their leather jackets and trying to appear European.[3] People look one another in the eye as if each one wanted to ask the other: What shall we do? Where shall we go?

In front of the gates of many houses, groups of people stand watching aimlessly. People are running, here one person, there another. What shall we do with ourselves?

No more strength to take the walking stick in hand and set out again on the road. I'm staying with my brother-in-law.[4] The heavy shoes are off, the rucksack is unpacked—I'm staying! . . .

1. I.e., Kruk gives up on fleeing and stays in Vilna.

2. On the evening of the twenty-third, the Red Army had left the city.

3. During Soviet rule, many young people wore leather jackets, commissar style, indicating that they were Bolshevized. At this point, anticipating the invasion of the Germans, everyone removed all signs that might occasion a suspicion that they had been affiliated with the Reds.

4. Hersh Horowicz, the brother of Herman Kruk's wife, Paula, came from Warsaw to Vilna as a refugee. In the ghetto, he became director of the Aguda kitchen. He later was deported to Estonia (Kaczerginski 1947:211).

I START WRITING

Wavering, trembling like a fish in water, running to Pati[5] and from her back to others, I make a firm decision: I leave myself to the mercy of God; I'm staying. And right away, I make another decision: if I'm staying anyway and if I'm going to be a victim of Fascism, I shall take pen in hand and write a chronicle of a city. Clearly, Vilna may also be captured. The Germans will turn the city Fascist. Jews will go into the ghetto—I shall record it all. My chronicle must see, must hear, and must become the mirror and the conscience of the great catastrophe and of the hard times.

I have decided to write a chronicle of the events of Vilna.

NIGHT OF JUNE 23 – 24 [1941]

All night long, bombs thumped and airplanes roared over our heads. The windowpanes were blown out, and I and the others sleeping here, exhausted and nervous from the day before, lay in bed as if it didn't concern us. Not until 6 in the morning did we grab our clothes and go down to the corridor. There the neighbors, pale and scared, are gathered. An elderly Jew huddles up to his wife and cries in fear. A Christian doctor clasps her two daughters. The windowpanes fly, and the roar drowns all our voices out.

JUNE 24 [1941]

THE DRAMATIC DAY

This night had more airplanes than the previous night. This time we didn't get undressed, and every few minutes we went to the corridor, which had to serve as a bomb shelter. Every shriek of the bombs that tore over our heads confused and scattered our thoughts. Not until six in the morning was everything quiet.

The day is full of dramatic events. I can't convince myself that I'm staying here and have to wait for the Germans, yet I feel that fleeing is a futile effort, an effort you can't complete.

The Germans push forward with a dreadful force and thrust with an enormous speed. The Bolsheviks are running in disorder. Individuals are still fleeing.

5. Pati Kremer (1867–1943), of the pioneer generation of the Bund, was the widow of the Bund's founder, Arkady Kremer. She kept the secret treasury of the Bund's money. Despite her age, she remained active and was the moral authority of the underground organization of the Bund in the Vilna Ghetto. During the final liquidation of the ghetto on September 23, 1943, she was sent to the "left"—to death. For biographical data, see the collection *Arkady* (1942) and *Generations* 1:130–137.

Columns with Red Army groups, on foot and in trucks, are still marching, individual military groups are still rushing through. But the city is already cleared of every power.

I GATHER INFORMATION

Comrade Dr. [Shloyme] Hershenhorn,[6] Bundist councilman from Lublin, demobilized captain of the Polish army and refugee, who wanted to go with me to America—he escaped.

Janek Dąbrowski,[7] the Polish writer, author of several works of fiction and collaborator on the former *Robotnik, Tydzień Robotnika, Wolna Myśl,* and other periodicals—he also escaped. His former wife, Erna,[8] cries because he asked her to come with him but she didn't want to go on the road anymore. He left without her.

50 RUBLES[9]

Dr. Antoni Pański,[10] a member of the Polish Socialist Party and my comrade in fate, who like me and for the same reasons wasn't allowed to go to America,[11] found me and stuck 50 rubles into my hand. He had received some money. And just as I had shared with him [in the Soviet period], he now wants to share with me and pushes the money into my hand.

6. Born in 1888 in Lublin. Hershenhorn joined the Bund at an early age and remained active in it until the end of his life. In September 1939, he fled to Vilna. In the first days of the German-Soviet war, in June 1941, he succeeded in escaping to Russia. In 1943, when the Polish Corps was created in the Soviet Union, Hershenhorn was appointed chief of medicine in a military unit. He returned to Poland with the Soviet army and became active in the Bund as the vice-chairman of the Central Committee. In 1948, during the liquidation of the Socialist movement in Poland, he immigrated to Israel. Later he moved to Australia, where he was also socially active. He died in Melbourne on January 2, 1953. For his biography, see *Generations* 2:99–103.

7. An activist in the Polish Socialist Party (PPS) who wrote for the Polish-language publications of the Bund. As a refugee in Vilna, he was close to Bundist circles.

8. Erna (or Esther) Liszczyńska was born in Warsaw, where she was active in the Bundist academic circle, Ringen. In Vilna, she was active in the general Refugee Committee, and during Lithuanian rule she ran a home for working refugee intelligentsia. She saved her life by hiding on the Aryan side and eventually moved to Buenos Aires.

9. In Kruk's table of contents, a similar title is dated August 6.

10. See the entries of July 2, 1941, and January 15, 1942, for more about Kruk's relations with Pański.

11. They were blocked by the Soviet NKVD.

LATER AT NIGHT

WORDS FROM THE HEART

There are no words for my suffering. This day has turned me into an old man. No, not an old man. I want to be young, strong, and persevering. To make it through—I want to and will make it through!

Everything is really lost. This is how I think when I hold the ticket I paid for at Intourist[12] for the Kovno-Vladivostok train. No more going to America.[13] The Bolsheviks saw to that. All they've got for me is a piece of advice: either to go to the Polish Legion in Canada and from there inform for them . . . or they procrastinated for six months until . . . until I am among those submitted to the trials of the German Huns.

Unless some miracle happens, everything really is lost. What is happening around us says clearly that, first of all, we are hostages of Germany. It's the beginning of a new era, perhaps the hardest in my life.

I put myself in the hands of fate and wear the yellow patch,[14] as Christ wore the crown of thorns. This is how I shall go with the [. . .]

[*Pages 7–9 of the diary, from June 25 to June 28, 1941, are missing. On June 24 and 25, the Germans took as hostages 60 Jews and 30 Poles. They were jailed in Łukiszki Prison, where they stayed until July 22, 1941. Of the 60 Jewish hostages, only 6 were freed; the rest did not return (Dworzecki 1948:29–30). On June 27 and 28, a wild snatching of Jews for forced labor began. Often, those who were snatched did not come back. The following titles from Kruk's table of contents indicate the topics of the missing diary entries.*]

June 25, 1941

Germans in Vilna—The Jail Is Plundered

I Go toward Them

I Am Tired

12. The official Soviet international tourist agency.

13. Here Kruk refers to the large operation of sending Jewish refugees from Soviet-ruled Vilna to America. In late 1940 and early 1941, the American Jewish Joint Distribution Committee (JDC), the Jewish Workers' Committee, and several other international Jewish organizations procured American visas for a few thousand Jewish social activists and for students in several Lithuanian yeshivas and their leaders. Many traveled with Intourist by train through Siberia to Vladivostok and from there to Japan on Japanese transit visas. Many reached the United States on time, but many others were exiled to Shanghai, where they spent the war under Japanese occupation. Herman Kruk was able to get an American visa, but because of family matters, he could not leave Vilna right away. By the time he was ready to leave, the Bolsheviks refused him the necessary permission to go, unless he would agree to serve them as a spy.

14. Kruk uses this image only symbolically, to indicate that he is accepting the historic Jewish fate; the order for Jews to wear insignia (patches or armbands) was given later.

June 26 [1941]
Lines
I Collect an Archive
The City Is Dead

June 27, 1941
People Are Snatched for Work
Back to Vilna
Face to the Wall

June 28 [1941]
Dead Bodies Are Found in the Streets

[. . .] learned that, in recent days, people who had been shot were found on Legionowa Street, under the railroad bridge, on Piwna, in the park near the cathedral, and other places.

This is what I heard. But people tell much more.

I ESCAPE FROM THE LINE

You have to stand in line for three or four hours to get a kilo of bread. Just a few days after the war broke out, the city goes all topsy-turvy—you have to fight tooth and nail for bread.

To keep my brother-in-law from having to wait on me, I went to the line at 5:30 in the morning. And I was perhaps the 500th person. In the distance, I see a similar line on Chopin Street. There, as here, people are fighting each other. They slander each other to the Lithuanian policeman. He drives them away and is the only judge.

Suddenly everything disappeared. In a few days, all those who hid under the guise of [international] solidarity[15] have suddenly turned into animals ready to devour one another.

The policeman has fun and abuses people. I feel as if the blood is draining out of me. I escape from the line and remain without bread.

JUNE 29 [1941]

JEWS POSING AS CHRISTIANS

Jews who don't look semitic take advantage of the situation and set out for non-Jewish streets so as not to have to wait in a long line.

15. A reference to the principles of "international solidarity" and friendship between nations, promoted by the Soviet regime. As soon as the Soviets left, all ethnic tensions were unleashed, especially antisemitism.

POLES OFTEN OBJECT

It often happens that Poles object to letting Aryans cut into the line. Such a person is often insulted or, in some cases, even beaten.

JEWISH LINES AND CHRISTIAN LINES

Today, the Lithuanian police introduced something new wherever there are lines at the stores: one line is Aryan and one is semitic, a line of Jews on one side and a Christian line on the opposite side.

An attempt to impose the Nuremberg Laws using . . . Lithuanians.[16]

■ ■ ■ ■ ■ ■

JULY 1 [1941]

WHY IN ŁUKISZKI PRISON?

I have now learned that many of those who were snatched for labor were sent to Łukiszki jail. According to rumor, that was to be the gathering place from which they were to be sent to work. Many women gather in front of the prison.

TWO DEATHS ON THE BRIDGE

Before dawn today, a group of Jewish workers who were being driven across the so-called Strategic Bridge on Śnipiszki[17] came upon two corpses who had been shot. People assumed that it was for violating the curfew.

■ ■ ■ ■ ■ ■

JULY 2 [1941]

DR. PAŃSKI COMES TO VISIT ME

My friend Dr. Antoni Pański, who had directed with me the flow of emigration of those Polish and Jewish labor movement activists who wanted to leave the Soviet Union, found me today, and we had a long discussion.

All our plans for emigration have produced nothing but a soap bubble. Everyone who had been sent off by us has left, and we . . . we stayed behind. Now [. . .]

[*The rest of the page is torn off. The beginning of the entry for July 3, 1941, was probably on this page.*]

16. Kruk does not seem to think of the Lithuanians as a superior race.

17. In Yiddish this bridge is called *Grine brik* (the Green Bridge). *Śnipiszki* is a suburb of Vilna on the other side of the Wilija River.

July 3 [1941]
Prof. Noah Prylucki[18] Does Not Go Out in the Street
They Snatch Whole Streets

[. . .] In the past two days, the snatching assumed a mass character. It is dangerous to leave your home.

PEOPLE ARE DRIVEN OUT OF THEIR APARTMENTS

Most recent events: they come at night, drive the whole family out of the apartment, take the men away, and the rest remain with their belongings in the open courtyard. The apartment is sealed. And there isn't anybody to protest to.

JULY 4 [1941]

HOW A JEWISH REPRESENTATIVE BODY CAME INTO BEING IN VILNA

On July 4, 1941, an automobile arrived on Żydowska Street, in front of the Synagogue Yard,[19] and two Germans emerged with rifles on their shoulders. They went into the Synagogue Yard and asked for the chief rabbi of Vilna. The municipal sexton, Khayim-Meyer Gordon, a big, tall Jew with a white beard, was brought to them.

Asked if he was the Vilna rabbi, Gordon answered no. He explained that the first rabbi, [Isaac] Rubinstein, was in America, and the second rabbi, Haim Ozer Grodzenski, died.

The Germans couldn't understand how Vilna could be without a chief rabbi, and they ordered him: From now on, you're the rabbi. And they also announced:

"We order you to set up a Jewish representative body today and present it to us tomorrow."

Gordon the sexton went to the former secretary of the Jewish Community Council, Mr. Yisroel Werblinski. Werblinski called a meeting of a few persons, where it was decided to call a bigger meeting in the evening. Meanwhile, three persons—Rabbi [Shmuel] Fried,[20] Dr. Gershn Gershuni,[21] and Gordon—went

18. Prylucki, a distinguished Yiddish linguist and literary critic from Warsaw, came to Vilna in 1939 as a refugee. There he organized a historical committee to study the Nazi destruction in Poland. When Vilna became Lithuanian, and later, when Lithuania was Sovietized, he assumed the position of professor of Yiddish Literature at Vilna State University. For details of his work on the Rosenberg Task Force and his arrest, see Kaczerginski 1947:303–304; Sutzkever 1946a:108.

19. In Yiddish, *Shulhoyf,* several connected yards with dozens of synagogues and prayer houses, located in the center of the old Jewish Quarter.

20. An activist in the religious Zionist party Mizrahi, military chaplain of the Vilna district under the Poles, and deputy of Rabbi Isaac Rubinstein. For health reasons, Rabbi Fried refused to join the Judenrat but promised to participate in preparing the list of candidates for the Judenrat. Soon after, he was incarcerated in Łukiszki Prison by the Nazis. From there, he was taken with others to Ponar. Because he was too weak to walk, people carried him to his death in Ponar.

21. Born in Grodno on June 8, 1860, to a distinguished family. In Vilna, he played a large role

to the district commissar, Mr. Kalendra, asking him to put them in touch with the representatives of the German military administration concerning the creation of a Judenrat. Kalendra answered that the German administration did not want any direct contact with Jews, and that everything had to be arranged through him. He also informed them that a Judenrat of ten persons had to be composed within 24 hours.

That same night, a meeting is held; 57 persons participate, including representatives of the Zionists, leftists, intelligentsia, artisans, former merchants, literati, teachers, and others.

[Dr. Jacob] Wygodzki[22] was deliberately not invited because he had been the chairman of the Vilna Anti-Hitler Committee and they were afraid to expose him.

Dr. Gershuni took over the chairmanship of the meeting. In his opening speech, he said: "We thought that Jerusalem of Lithuania would avoid the persecutions because, here in Vilna, are the graves of the Ger-Tsedek and the Vilna Gaon.[23] But that didn't happen. We must create a Judenrat. And although we are aware of the danger we face, we have an obligation to do it. If I were younger, I would join it myself. Therefore, I determine that those selected must accept it." And he presented himself to serve at the disposal of the Judenrat.

With those words, the speaker burst into tears, as did most of the participants. During the election, however, not a great many were eager to be chosen. After a break, it was decided that anyone who was selected must sacrifice himself and become a martyr.

Thus, the following were selected:

1. Rabbi Yosef Shub[24] (religious Jews)

---

in Jewish social life in general, especially in medical circles; he was a Zionist activist, chairman of several institutions, and honorary chairman of the Vilna Jewish Medical Association. During the first days of the Vilna Ghetto, he was taken to Łukiszki Prison and was one of the few to come out alive. After a month in the ghetto, his wife died. After her funeral, he committed suicide in the ghetto hospital. For his biography; see Yeshurin 1935 and *Lexicon* 2:421–422.

22. Wygodzki was born in 1855 in Bobruysk. He spent the last 57 years of his life in Vilna, where he assumed a leading role in Jewish life. He was the Jewish representative who established good relations with the German administration during World War I. In World War II, in the first months of Nazi rule, he was tortured in Łukiszki Prison and died in 1941. For his biography, see Yeshurin 1935 and Dworzecki 1948:46ff.

23. The Ger-Tsedek and the Vilna Gaon were the two "guardian angels" of Jewish Vilna. The Ger-Tsedek, or Righteous Convert, was Count V. Potocki, an influential Polish magnate who converted to Judaism, assumed the name Abraham son of Abraham, and was tried and burned at the stake in 1749. His ashes were buried in the old Jewish cemetery. The Vilna Gaon (Elijah ben Solomon, or HaGRO, 1720–1797) was one of the major talmudic scholars of modern times. He organized opposition to the emerging Hasidic movement, launched the Misnagdim movement, and stressed religious learning, as realized in a network of famous yeshivas, founded by his pupils.

24. A well-known Vilna Rabbi. In September 1941, the Gestapo took him, along with some

2. Eliezer Kruk[25] (artisans)
3. Avrom Zaydshnur[26] (merchants)
4. Attorney Pinkhes Kon[27] (writers and working intelligentsia)
5. Shoel Trocki[28] (industrialists)
6. Engineer Anatol Fried[29] (working intelligentsia)
7. Dr. [Rosa] Szabad-Gawrońska[30] (doctors)
8. Dr. [Elye] Sedlis[31]

---

others, from the Judenrat building for not presenting the requested "contribution" on time. He was taken to Łukiszki Prison and from there to Ponar. For his biography, see *These Will I Remember* 1:247–257.

25. One of the distinguished Jewish activists in Vilna, especially among the artisans. He was vice-chairman of the Vilna Artisans' Association, a member of the Jewish Community Council, and alderman on the City Council. He was captured in September 1941 and did not return. For his biography, see Abramowicz 1958:152–162.

26. A prominent member of the Jewish Community Council. During the liquidation of the ghetto, the Gestapo discovered him and his daughter in a hiding place. He was arrested and tortured and died in prison in 1943.

27. Born in Łódź, he came to Vilna as a student. After studying law at Vilna University, he became an attorney. He grew attached to Vilna and devoted himself to studying the history of the city. He belonged to the Vilna Journalists' Union, was active in YIVO, and was a member of its historical section; his writings were published in YIVO publications. At the liquidation of the first Judenrat in early September 1941, he was captured by the Gestapo and killed.

28. Co-owner of the Kurland oil factory in Vilna. He was a senior member of the Vilna Jewish Community Council and alderman on the Vilna City Council. Taken from the Judenrat building by the Gestapo in early September 1941, he was killed in Ponar.

29. An assimilated Jew, he was director of the Communal Savings Bank in Vilna. On the eve of the liquidation of the ghetto, in 1943, he was taken to Estonia. He was killed in Kaiserwald, near Riga.

30. Born in Vilna in 1882; her father's brother was the famous Dr. Tsemakh Szabad. One of the most popular pediatricians in Vilna, she was a school physician for many years and was active in the Organization for the Protection of Children. She was one of the founders of TOZ/OZE and wrote for the Yiddish medical journal *Folksgezunt,* edited by her uncle. On the doctors' committee for the state of health in the Vilna Ghetto, she devoted herself primarily to children. She directed the children's kitchen at Strashun Street 12 and was the founder of the orphanage in the Vilna Ghetto. During the liquidation of the ghetto in September 1943, she had the option of being saved by Christian friends on the Aryan side; however, she would not leave the ghetto children. She went with them to Majdanek, where she was killed. For her biography, see Goldshmidt 1935:409–410.

31. A well-known Jewish doctor in Vilna before the war. He was born in 1886 in Širvintos, in the Vilna district, to a distinguished rabbinical family (he was a grandson of both Rabbi Shmuel Mohilever and Rabbi Hillel Salanter). Sedlis directed the ghetto hospital. He survived the ghetto and the camps and died in New York in September 1958. For his biography, see Goldshmidt 1935:417–418.

9. Yisroel Werblinski[32]
10. Yosef Szabad

In spite of this, a great many refused the office, including Dr. Sedlis and Yosef Shalit.[33] Shalit argued that he must not accept an official position because he wrote anti-Hitler articles before the war. Engineer Anatol Fried spoke, and finally, many withdrew. Thus they succeeded in patching up a committee in the following way:

Chairman—Engineer Shoel Trocki.
Vice-Chairman—Engineer Anatol Fried.
Secretary—Avrom Zaydshnur.

The next day, Saturday, July 5, at noon, the Judenrat was received at Magdalena 2, in the office of Kalendra, the Lithuanian in charge of Jewish affairs, by his secretary Cubirgas.[34]

PEOPLE FLEE FROM THEIR HOMES

Staying overnight at home isn't safe anymore. Massive surprise assaults occur every night. They come in and order all the inhabitants to leave the house in ten minutes. The apartments are sealed and the men are taken away. The rest of the family are left in the courtyard.

People have started running away from their homes and staying with Christians. Some of those who work in the Judenrat office all day stay there at night for fear of coming home.

LANGBORD'S ACHIEVEMENT

[Arn] Langbord,[35] the former director of the Jewish Bank, received a document from the Fourth Police Precinct[36] stating that the Judenrat office may accommodate 30–50 people overnight, and this group can serve as a reserve in case workers are urgently needed at night. . . .

This achievement is a salvation for the group of Judenrat activists.

32. An activist with the General Zionists. Until the outbreak of World War II, he was the administrator of the Jewish Community Council of Vilna. He was killed in early September 1941 in Ponar.

33. The name *Shalit* is not on the list of Judenrat members. Kaczerginski (1947:215) mentions a *Moshe* Shalit as a member of the first Judenrat in Vilna, but he is not mentioned by Dworzecki, nor by Korczak. The argument Kruk cites—that Shalit was unwilling to belong to the Judenrat because he wrote anti-Nazi articles—does indeed fit the Moshe Shalit that Kaczerginski describes.

34. Later, this name is mentioned as *Cubirgas.* Obviously, Kruk had only heard the name; he had not seen it written.

35. Also spelled *Langbort.*

36. This police precinct included the main Jewish area.

A STREET SCREAMS

During the recent robberies at night, they come to take everything that can be taken and also take the men, beating them murderously. Those who are affected react by screaming. The screams are soon taken over by the neighbors and are carried from neighbor to neighbor and from courtyard to courtyard.

It often seems that a whole street screams.

Such cases have happened twice in the past 24 hours. Once, when people were taken from Wielka Stefańska Street at about 4 in the morning. A second time was at 7 in the morning, when they surprised the inhabitants of Chopin 4. The streets actually screamed along, and the more the shouts were heard, the more they irritated the Snatchers[37] and drove them wild.

JULY 5 [1941]

PEOPLE ARE TAKEN AWAY IN GROUPS

The women who gathered in front of the prison say that large groups of men are being taken out of there. The groups are taken in the direction of Legionowa Street.[38]

Women who gather in front of the prison are often dragged into the jail.

A STREET SCREAMS AGAIN

The picture must be drawn:

On Kwaszelna Street,[39] Lithuanian Snatchers are leading a group of Jews. One of them is an old man, the rabbi of Kwaszelna 21. His face and snow-white beard are bloodied. Just the sight of him, without a hat and with red blood marring his majestic appearance, would make the stones scream.

The Lithuanians are so wild and nervous—they drive you mad. The screams of several dozen women and children that accompany them for half a street drive them nuts. They shove the prisoners fast, as if they want to escape from the wailing. The crowd grows, and the shouting rises to the skies. The rabbi falls down and gets up. Several young people in the group pick up the old man and try to carry him, but the hooligans won't let them. He has to walk by himself. Either he walks or he won't make it. Whether he made it or not is really not clear. But one thing is clear—he certainly will not come back.

All day long, the whole neighborhood talked about the agonizing incident.

37. In Yiddish, *Khapunes*.

38. The street that led toward Ponar.

39. Kruk lived half a block away from the location of these events, at Kwaszelna 21/23.

JULY 6 [1941]

ARM BANDS WITH A STAR OF DAVID

Today an order is posted that, from July 8 on, every Jew over the age of twelve must wear an armband.[40] The bands must be ten centimeters wide and worn on the right arm.

Not complying with the order is punishable by death.

In short, either wear it or . . . die.

WHO CATCHES AND WHO SNATCHES?

A wild chase has ensued. Germans demand Jewish workers. Groups are formed and sent to the designated work sites. But on their way they meet Snatchers from the Lithuanian Ipatinga,[41] who turn the group around and take them wherever they want.

During the past few days, many such cases have been recorded. There have even been cases where Snatchers took away whole groups from the courtyard of the Judenrat at Strashun 6.

The Germans curse and threaten; they don't want to know anything—they demand that their orders be carried out precisely. The Lithuanians don't want to know anything either, they attack and . . . snatch. Thus, it's hard to figure out the game—who catches and who snatches? . . .

THE STREET SCREAMS AND . . . LIBERATES

A painful picture was seen in the street yesterday afternoon when several Jews were snatched from Kwaszelna Street; they were taken toward Łukiszki, and several dozen women who "escorted" them lamented, accompanied by the whole street.

40. Various sources display contradictory information, revealing the panic vis-à-vis the constantly changing German orders. Kruk writes about armbands; Dworzecki (1948:27) states that they first had to wear patches and later armbands. Kaczerginski (1947:29) says that the order referred to patches. Yitskhok Rudashevski says in his journal that the order is for patches in front and back. The same is mentioned by Korczak (1946:10). From some of the entries in Kruk's journal, it seems that the order was first for patches and later was changed to armbands. Dworzecki and Kaczerginski say that the order was issued by the military commander of Vilna, Lieutenant Colonel Zehnpfennig; but according to Korczak, the order came from von Neumann.

41. The full name of this paramilitary quasi-Fascist organization was *Ipatingas Buris* (Lithuanian for "the elite group"). In Vilna, they were located at Wileńska Street 12, and their assistant leader was Second Lieutenant Norvaisas. The Snatchers were recruited from the Ipatinga, and members of this organization carried out the executions of Jews in Ponar, as well as in Kovno, Šiauliai, and other Lithuanian towns.

Several elderly Jews were beaten horribly by the Snatchers because they could not keep up with the fast pace.

At this dreadful sight, the street raised such a commotion that the Snatchers got scared and, in confusion, freed the old Jews. . . .

THE EXILED HAVE TO BE SETTLED WITH UNEXILED JEWS

Rumors tell of an order that all the homeless families who were recently evicted from their apartments must settle in Jewish apartments that have not been touched. But Jews may stay with Christians.

THE JUDENRAT ISSUES COUPONS FOR A PLACE TO SETTLE

In this regard, the Judenrat issues coupons for apartments where the homeless can move in. Moving in without such a coupon is forbidden.

JULY 7, 1941

THE END OF A SAD GAME

We have often noted the tragic events that took place on June 22 and 23 during the evacuation and escape of many civilians, mainly Jews.

For example, we wrote[42] that on Monday the 23rd, among the thousands of escapees was the Vilna teacher, Dr. Moyshe Heller,[43] and his family; the teacher Y. Trupiański,[44] and many, many friends and acquaintances.

Heller and his family didn't actually get on the train because it was so crowded.[45] The train, full of old people, children, and baggage, was not only

42. This entry is missing.

43. Born in Zbaraż, Galicia, Heller studied in Vienna, where he received his doctorate in history. After World War I, he came to Vilna, where he was a teacher in the Yiddish Teachers' Seminar, and when the Seminar was closed by the government, he taught Jewish history in the Vilna Yiddish Real Gymnasium (the high school for science). He became an active member of YIVO and a member of the board of the Vilna Friends of YIVO. In the ghetto, he wrote a study, commissioned by the Rosenberg Task Force, of the old Jewish ghetto in Vilna from 1633 to 1861, with an appendix of facts and figures about the new ghetto under the Nazis. That study is published by Korczak (1946:303–309). For the later fate and death of Dr. Heller, see the entry of November 8, 1942.

44. Born May 15, 1909, in Vilna. Trupiański (also spelled *Trumpyanski*) was a graduate of the Yiddish Teachers' Seminar in Vilna. Before World War II, he was a teacher in the Bundist Medem Sanitarium for children, near Warsaw. He came to Vilna with the refugees. In the ghetto, he was a director of the soup kitchens. He was deported to Estonia and, from there, was taken to Germany. On November 17, 1944, he died in the German slave labor camp of Schömberg-Dautmergen. For his biography, see *Teachers' Memorial Book* (1954:180–184).

45. This train, of several dozen cars and thousands of people, carried families of Red Army of-

blocked from inside but was also plastered with people hanging on outside. Instead of leaving at one in the afternoon, it didn't move until eight in the evening. The trip was dreadful. Because of frequent alarms [for air raids], they often had to leave the cars and get back in them—a hell!

At noon on Wednesday, the train was standing in a field. It turned out that it was five or six kilometers beyond Radoszkowicze, the Polish-Soviet border [until September 1939]. Suddenly an order came that everyone, with bag and baggage, had to get off the train for a border check. Only a few, the so-called Easterners, remained on the train.[46] When the train was evacuated, the NKVD [People's Commissariat of Internal Affairs, i.e., the security police] watched the cars and the train moved on. In the field, 3,000 unfortunates remained, led astray and deceived.[47] Many of them were Communist activists, teachers, writers, and journalists, including the [Soviet] inspector of the Jewish schools, Mrs. Maler, and her husband, director of the Peretz Gymnasium, both of them longtime Communist activists.[48]

In the great chaos and despair, NKVD agents appeared among the people and advised them to consult the Radoszkowicze authorities. Radoszkowicze was already evacuating, there were no more trains, and there wasn't anybody to talk to. Some of the desperate people went forward; the rest went back. There, on that road, was my friend Trupiański, the Ewzerow family,[49] and others.

On Wednesday, the 25th, early in the morning, the teacher Trupiański came upon some Germans. A heavy aerial bombardment took place, and there was a great air battle. Trupiański and his family got away on side roads and went through Iwje, Mołodeczno, and other towns. After 17 days of wandering, they came back to Vilna on the night of July 6.

---

ficers as well as refugees. It was apparently the only train that left Vilna before the Germans entered the city.

46. Easterners were those who lived in the Soviet Union before September 1939 and had Soviet passports. Those who lived on the Polish side of the old border and were former Polish citizens were called Westerners. The Soviet regime distrusted them and barred them from crossing the old border to the Soviet Union; they were thus returned to their fate under the Nazi occupation.

47. A few people did nevertheless jump back on the train (from the back side) and succeed in getting to Russia; among them were Benjamin Hrushovski (Harshav)—the editor of this book—and his family.

48. Mr. and Mrs. Maler, originally from Lithuania, came to Vilna in 1940, when it became Vilnius, the capital of Lithuania. He became the director of a Vilna Yiddish Gymnasium, and she was a school superintendent. In early July 1941, both of them were shot in Ponar.

49. Mordecai and Libe Ewzerow were a well-known Bundist family in Vilna. Aside from his official position as director of the Jewish Cooperative Bank, Ewzerow devoted himself to bibliographical work, especially to the history of the Bund. He was "snatched" in the early days of the occupation and was killed at Ponar. For his biography, see *Generations* 2:129–131.

On the first half of their trip, the Christians were friendly and humane to the Jews, but when our wanderers approached Mołodeczno, going toward Vilna, through an area where the peasants already understood that the Bolsheviks had lost and the Germans were winning, attitudes toward the wandering Jews changed completely. The peasants stayed away from the Jews, didn't let them into their homes, mocked them, etc.

Such stories are now told by hundreds of furious, bitter, disappointed and . . . deceived people. It really is the end of a sad game.[50]

JULY 8 [1941]

JEWS MAY NOT APPEAR ON EVERY STREET

An order was posted that Jews are not allowed to appear on many streets, for example, Wielka, Niemiecka, Trocka, Zawalna, Mickiewicz, etc. Jews who live on those streets must go to the closest corner and walk from there through side streets.

At the same time, it was posted that as of today, Jews must wear a Jew sign—a patch on the right arm (unlike all other patches, which you wear on your left arm). The patch is a white band with a star of David and a *J* (for *Jude*) sewn on it.

JULY 9 [1941]

LITHUANIANS SNATCH AND GERMANS RELEASE

The snatching of organized groups who are intended to work for the Germans has become a daily event. No intervention helps. The Germans respond that they don't know anything about the matter, and the Lithuanians respond that they have orders. . . .

Often a simple German passerby frees Jews from the Lithuanians. Jews often appeal to Germans passing by; they explain what is happening and the Germans, either nicely or by force, often even slapping the Ipatinga people, release the Jews.

Where to look for the guilty? Who does what and out of spite to whom?

Meanwhile, the Jews fall victim.

50. I.e., a sad game that the Soviets played with the previously "liberated" people.

JULY 10 [1941]

SNATCHERS

The whole city is depressed about the men who have disappeared. Groups of Snatchers wander around the streets and courtyards, snatch men wherever they can, and drag them off. The excuse is that they are taken "for work," but seldom does anybody come back. Most of the snatched groups are taken to Łukiszki [Prison]. More and more often, groups sent by the Judenrat for work are snatched on the way and taken to Łukiszki. Sometimes, Germans themselves come for workers and take them to their work sites.

Who are the Snatchers? Nobody knows what their purpose is, and it's hard to figure it out.

SNATCHED AT NIGHT

Tonight, the Snatchers came to the courtyard of Kijowska Street 4[51] and entered several apartments, searching and digging around. From some, they took money, gold, etc.; from others, they took healthy young men. Eight men were snatched like this—tenants in my courtyard.

Snatching at night has become a frequent event.

GOOD INTENTIONS, BAD RESULTS: A TALE OF 150

All the while, the Judenrat has sought a solution to the unbearable situation of the Snatchings in the streets and houses. When the Judenrat received information that the matter is related to the Ipatinga at Wileńska St. 12, the former secretary of the Jewish Community Council, Mr. Werblinski, went there. Werblinski proposed that the Snatching be stopped and that the Judenrat provide workers in an orderly way. The Ipatinga liked the idea and agreed. The Judenrat made a mistake: How can you send people when there is no guarantee where the people disappear?

In connection with this "agreement," there soon came a request for 150 men. The Judenrat wanted to get out of the situation and voted 24 to 1 not to send them. But to comply with the "agreement," an announcement was made. Fifty-three persons signed up. When the time came to go, only 21 remained.

The "agreement," indeed, could not survive. The group of 21 went off and did not return. Now the wives, mothers, and brothers attack the Judenrat for delivering Jews to the Ipatinga with their own hands.

The intention was good but the result was bad. So the "agreement" is void and the Ipatinga are snatching again in the wildest way.

51. This is where Kruk lived before the creation of the ghetto.

THE YOUNG GENTILE HAS GONE WILD; HE DISPERSES THE JEWS AND THE GERMANS PHOTOGRAPH IT

At Kijowska St. 4, in front of the bakery, stands a line of about 200 Jews. A Lithuanian hooligan, a civilian holding a gun, has gone wild, and there is nothing we can do about it. He doesn't talk, he only beats. Christians go in without waiting in line, and whatever Jews he does let in, he beats, kicks, and insults unmercifully.

A Christian who observed the scene made a terrible scandal, scolding the Lithuanian guard for his behavior. The arrogant hooligan lowered his voice and calmed down. But as soon as the Christian left, his wildness grew tenfold. He stood in front of the shop and didn't let a single Jew in. When the Jews also started rebelling, he beat them terribly, whacking on their heads and anywhere he could with his rifle butt. The result was that the line dispersed and the arrogant young man stood triumphantly and smiled at his achievement.

It is worth noting that on the other side of the street, a group of Germans looked on smiling and joking, and one of them photographed the scene "as a souvenir." . . .

JULY 11 [1941]

LIKE A CAT WITH A MOUSE

It's impossible to stick your nose out. As soon as you appear in the street, you are engulfed by the many Snatchers lying in wait there. You see almost no Jewish men in the streets. The Snatchers come into the courtyards and drag people right out of their apartments. They search and rummage around in the beds, under the beds, in the closets, in the attics. Often they beat you bloody. Sometimes men flee and are hunted as a cat hunts a mouse.

In general, it looks like a wild chase. Whoever can, saves himself; whoever can't is caught.

JULY 12 [1941]

GUARDING MY OWN BONES

Like all those who want to save themselves, we decided to get a *melina*.[52] In the house, I found a mezzanine, blocked it up with old baskets, machinery, and an old broken cupboard, and arranged it all so that before anything happens, we go up there, the ladder is taken away and hidden, and we, my brother-in-law and I,

52. In thieves' jargon, a melina is a place where thieves would hide stolen goods. The word was used in many ghettos to indicate a hiding place.

the landlady's son, and somebody else we dragged along, stay there until the danger is past. Once, the Lithuanians rummaged about in our apartment and didn't find anything. The women claimed that the men had already been snatched for work. But the issue becomes ever more serious. For the past two days, we have taken turns standing guard. For almost sixteen hours each day, we stand watching the gate of the house. Whenever something seems amiss, we hide in the melina and the guarding is taken over by our wives, the landlady, Mrs. Bek (who, incidentally, is from the Stupel family, relatives of Wirgili-Kahan),[53] and her daughter.

Guarding: every man stands guard for two hours. It is a systematic protection of our lives. It is a system introduced into hundreds of Jewish houses where there are men. Often the gate is guarded by women or young children who are used as messengers to sniff out the situation in the street, before the enemy appears in the courtyard.

Can we hold out like this for long? . . .

JULY 13 [1941]

STRASHUN STREET 6 — A SPRINGBOARD

Until recently, the courtyard of Strashun 6[54] was the only place in Vilna where a Jew felt safer than at home. Jewish labor forces would be taken from there and returned to there. Lately, not only has that ceased to be the case, but on the contrary, Strashun 6 has become one of the most dangerous points. Actually, it is the address where Jews can most easily be caught.

Recently, a fashion was introduced: Gestapo or Snatchers drive around in trucks and snatch. They drive into a courtyard, drag off a group of men, and the hunt goes on.

At six last night, Snatchers drove up in front of the gate of Strashun 6 and snatched all the officials and guards. They announced that they must have 20 men for the Wehrmacht. Mr. Langbord opposed it, claiming that he can't give anybody because he is authorized to keep a reserve of 50 men. After an intervention of the Fourth Police Precinct, they still demand, if not 20, at least 15, then they agree to 10 and are even ready to take only 5.

Mr. Langbord gives in and 5 are delivered, including both sons of Rabbi Shub, Sholem and Shmuel Shub. Both were sent immediately to Łukiszki. After Mr. Langbord intervened with the Lithuanian Committee, they were all released at 10 the next morning.

53. The Stupels and the Kahans were well-known Bundist families in Vilna.

54. The site of most of the offices of the first Judenrat and other ghetto institutions.

DOVID UMRU[55] IS SNATCHED

Like thousands of young people who remained in Vilna, the editor of the *Vilner Emes* hid from the Snatchers. Recently, he left his apartment and went to his friend Shloyme Bartenstein[56] (at Ostrobramska St. 2, apt. 4). In the street, in front of the house, he was stopped by the Snatchers, who dragged him into a taxi and took off in an unknown direction.

THE SAMBATYON[57] DOESN'T REST

Not a single night goes by when you don't hear of a hunt for men and of whole families thrown out of their homes into the street. Night after night, men are dragged off and their families are left in the street with their meager bundles.

This time, we learn of new victims at Pohulanka St. 11. All the men are assembled, the families are thrown out of their apartments, and as usual, the men are dragged off. Among the men in that courtyard was one Goldshteyn, a refugee from Warsaw, a journalist with the Warsaw Jewish Telegraph Agency (YITA). His wife and several children remained in the street.

JULY 14 [1941]

SNATCHED RIGHT IN THE MIDDLE OF THE DAY

The game of snatching men becomes more menacing from one minute to the next. Initially, they snatched groups. They would entice them to go to work and, on the way, would turn to Łukiszki. They would come at night, when everyone was asleep, and snatch men. Now, the same job is done right in the middle of the day, without any cover. They come, they let you take only the most necessary things, and then they carry you off.

Yesterday, Sunday, at about 10 in the morning, a truck came to Nowogródzka St. 28. All the men were ordered to assemble in the courtyard. They were not allowed to take anything with them. All they could take was money, a handkerchief, and some soap.

Thus, several dozen men were dragged off from Nowogródzka 28.

55. A young Jewish poet from Kovno. When Lithuania became Soviet, he came to Vilna. As a Communist, he edited the Soviet Yiddish daily newspaper *Vilner Emes* (Vilna truth), which was published instead of all the former Yiddish newspapers, which were shut down. He fled east during the German advance, but as a Westerner, he was not allowed to cross the old Soviet border and returned to Vilna.

56. Bartenstein, also from Kovno, was the assistant director of the Yiddish State Theater in Vilna under the Lithuanian-Soviet regime. In 1941, he was killed in Ponar.

57. The legendary Sabbath River, beyond which the ten lost tribes of Israel were exiled. According to legend, the river's roaring torrent calmed down only on the Sabbath, when the Jews were not allowed to cross.

THE TEACHER YITSKHOK MANN IS DRAGGED OFF

A child who saw what happened at Nowogródzka 28 came to the flat of the teacher Mann[58] and warned him they were snatching men. Comrade Mann went out into the street to disappear. But there he was accidentally stopped by a passing taxi. Asked by one of the Germans what his profession was, he replied that he was a teacher. The Germans ordered him to get in. In the same way and with the same taxi, the teacher Mowszowicz was also dragged off. He had previously been caught in the courtyard of Nowogródzka 28, but had escaped and set off for Piłsudski Street. There he was stopped by the same taxi as Comrade Mann. Thus, both of them disappeared in a strange way.

JULY 16 [1941]

WILL THAT STOP THE SNATCHING?

According to the official tasks set for the Jewish Committee [Judenrat], it must become the only source of Jewish labor. For that purpose, the Judenrat appointed district representatives of the inhabitants to set up an order according to a list, and thus it will be possible to regulate the supply of labor and stop the Snatching.

Will this really stop the wild Snatching?

JULY 17 [1941]

JEWS SNATCHED FROM THE ZARZECZE QUARTER

On the night of July 16–17, all over the Zarzecze Quarter, Jews were assaulted.[59] Popławy, Safjaniki, Bakszt, and other streets were surrounded. As a result of that piece of work, about four hundred Jewish men of all ages were taken off, including Borekh Fishman, son of the Artisan Union activist [Yoyel] Fishman.[60]

The Snatchers are making progress. They have progressed from snatching individuals to carrying off entire courtyards. Now one more step forward and they'll be taking over entire districts.

58. Yitskhok Mann, born in 1906, was the older brother of the writer Mendel Mann. He was a graduate of the Yiddish Teachers' Seminar in Vilna. He was also a Bundist and worked as a teacher in several Jewish grammar schools and in the Medem Sanitarium near Warsaw. From 1939 on, he worked in the Pedagogical Museum of YIVO in Vilna. For his biography, see *Teachers' Memorial Book* (1954:335–336).

59. Zarzecze was a suburb of Vilna on the way to the new Jewish cemetery. Dworzecki (1948:497) states that the Jews of Zarzecze were taken out on July 14.

60. Yoyel Fishman was a shoemaker, an activist in the Vilna Socialist Artisans' Union, and a Bundist. He was a member of the Vilna Jewish Community Council and was later killed in Estonia.

JULY 19 [1941]

FEAR AND A NARROW ESCAPE

About ten in the morning, everyone in our courtyard was startled. We barricaded ourselves as usual in our melina and waited for the result.

Not until things calmed down and we could creep out of the melina did they tell me that one of the Snatchers stopped a Jew on the street. The Jew had run into our courtyard. The Lithuanian—a civilian, by the way—ran after him and shot at him. The Jew went to a Christian neighbor. The "hunter" with his revolver searched, rummaged around, cursed, and finally left frustrated and empty handed.

The bird got away. . . .

The courtyard breathed a sigh of relief. A narrow escape and a brush with fear only.

JULY 20 [1941]

WHAT IS HAPPENING IN PONAR?

On the tenth of this month, a rumor came to the Judenrat that people were shot in Ponar.[61] The Judenrat didn't want to hear anything and considered it an unfounded rumor.

[*The continuation of this page of the journal is damaged. We present the part that can be read.*]

Five days later, reports came to the Judenrat from var[ious] people who secretly repeated the rumor [about what is happening] in Ponar. One of them was a maid of N. In [. . .] on Skopówke. She said that her boss was [. . .] taken prisoner in Łukiszki. She used to bring him [a package] every day. When she waited to be allowed in with her [package, she saw] a group of Jews taken off, including [her boss]. She ran after the group until they were [brought] to Ponar. Scared and crying, she demanded [that they] go with her to the field commander because she [. . .] all the Jews were shot.

The Judenrat didn't believe it this time either, [but] the next morning, there came to the Judenrat [. . .]

[*Page 23 of the journal is missing. This page presumably contained the information about Ponar that was given to the Judenrat.*]

July 22 [1941]
A Policeman Guarding the Judenrat

61. Ponar, a village about ten kilometers from Vilna, became the valley of death for about a hundred thousand Jews from Vilna and its surroundings. For further details, see the entry of September 4, 1941.

July 23 [1941]
Jews Want to Accompany Them. . . .

JULY 24 [1941]

A JUDENRAT OF 24 PERSONS

Today an order was issued that the Judenrat must be expanded from 10 to 24 persons.

The enlarged Judenrat included Engineer [Shoel] Trocki, Yosef Szabad, [Shmuel] Pietuchowski,[62] Attorney P. Kon, Attorney G[risha] Yashunski,[63] Yoyel Fishman, [Shoel] Ofman,[64] L. Kruk, [Attorney Shabse] Milkanowicki,[65] [Attorney Nokhem] Soyfer, [Dr. Jacob] Wygodzki, Mrs. Dr. Szabad-Gawrońska, Rabbi Katz, Rabinowicz, [Avrom] Zalkind,[66] Mrs. [Dr. Lyuba] Kholem,[67] Engineer Fried, A. Zaydshnur, Yosef Szkolnicki, [Attorney Boris] Parnes,[68] Berl[69] Werblinski, Attorney [Leon] Katzenelson, and Dr. Liber.

62. Former deputy mayor of Šiauliai, Lithuania. He came to Vilna when the city was annexed to Lithuania. He was taken in early September 1941 and killed in Ponar.

63. Son of the well-known ORT activist Joseph Yashunski (in Polish, Jaszunski). A Bundist, he came to Vilna from Warsaw in 1939 with the refugees. After the war, he lived in Poland and was active in government.

64. Ofman, a shoemaker, was born in 1880 in Kielce, where he belonged to the first groups of Poalei Zion (Labor Zionists). Because of his activity among the shoemakers, he was arrested by the tsarist police. He was exiled in 1908 to Kovno and a year later to Vilna, where he settled and owned a shoe factory. He was active in the Jewish Merchants' Union and in the 1930s was a member of the Jewish Community Council. During the ghetto period, he worked in a big shoe factory outside the ghetto. At the time of the liquidation of the ghetto in 1943, he was deported to Estonia, where he perished.

65. Milkanowicki, a Doctor of Jurisprudence, served many terms as vice-chairman of the Jewish Community Council in Vilna. He originally belonged to Poalei Zion and was later considered an independent Zionist. He wrote several works in German about the British Mandate of Palestine. In the ghetto, he represented the Independent Zionists in the Zionist Coordinating Committee, the so-called Zionist Umbrella. Deported to Estonia and later to Camp Dautmergen, he died on April 1945, two days after the Liberation. (According to Dworzecki, he died in Alach; according to Kaczerginski, in Bergen-Belsen.)

66. Director of the Jewish Merchants' Union in Vilna. He was killed in Ponar in 1941.

67. Neé Soloveichik, wife of Dr. Emmanuel Kholem. She was the only woman in the Vilna (or any other) Judenrat. She perished in Camp Klooga, Estonia.

68. A Zionist activist who owned sawmills. For a time he was chairman of the Vilna Jewish Community Council. In 1941 he was killed at Ponar.

69. The Yiddish edition listed him as Yisroel Werblinski; here reconstructed from the manuscript.

JULY 25 [1941]

SNATCHERS SNATCH AND GERMANS RELEASE

Incidents are happening that deserve to be recorded. Jews snatched by Lithuanians often stop Germans and ask them to release them. Some Germans take Jews under their protection, often scolding the Snatchers and dragging Jewish victims out of their wild hands.

Snatchers often come into houses, and if the Jews manage to tell the first German in sight about it, he comes and . . . releases. There have even been incidents of the Germans honoring the Snatchers with . . . blows.

JULY 27 [1941]

A CONFLICT OVER HOUSING JEWS WITHOUT INVOLVING THE MUNICIPAL HOUSING DEPARTMENT

Because the Judenrat has issued coupons for the homeless to be housed among other Jews, a representative of the Judenrat was summoned to the Fourth Police Precinct and asked to submit to them a list of where the Judenrat had quartered the homeless. The Housing Department had also interfered in the matter.

I learn now that the palms are already "greased." The matter cost five 30-ruble notes.

The Judenrat is once again saved from a scandal.

Would it be only a scandal?

JULY 30 [1941]

COMRADE NOKHEM WAPNER IS CAUGHT

Wapner[70] has been a Bundist activist for many years, active in schools, a former member of the Vilna Jewish Community Council, etc. Lately, Wapner, along with many social activists in Vilna, has devoted himself to serving the Vilna Judenrat. In recent days, he even negotiated with the Judenrat for the participation of representatives of the B[und], including himself.[71]

70. Wapner was born in 1881. In his youth he was a joiner, and later he became a bookkeeper. He joined the Bund at a very early age and was arrested during tsarist times. In independent Poland, he became a member of the Central Educational Committee (TSBK) in Vilna, which supervised Yiddish schools. When the Red Army took over Vilna in 1939, he was arrested by the Soviets as a Bundist and spent nine months in prison. He was one of the Bund delegates involved in the formation of the Judenrat.

71. According to Yosef Musnik (1945), the delegation to negotiate the representation of the

This morning, as every day, Wapner went toward the Judenrat, but he hasn't come back. People say that he was captured by the Snatchers on Zawalna Street and taken to Łukiszki. At three in the afternoon of the same day, he was taken out of the prison with a big group and led toward Ponar. . . .

■ ■ ■ ■ ■ ■

July 31 [1941]

THE ŁÓDŹ EDITOR KH[AIM]-Y[ANKL]
BRZOSTOWSKI IS DRAGGED OFF

The dragging off by the Draggers [Yiddish: *Shlepers*] doesn't stop. What is there to say about it?

[*This page of the journal is damaged. We present those parts of lines that are complete and legible.*]

[. . .] Before dawn, Lithuanians came to the apartment of the Łódź refugee Khayim [-Yankl] Brzostowski[72] (former editor of the Łódź *Folksblat,* [. . .] at Wielka Stefańska. 27), pretending to be looking for a Communist. They didn't find [the] Communist, but meanwhile, they did take Brzostowski, Dr. Lejbowicz [. . .] Altogether, they dragged [. . .] victims out of that house, took them [to] Łukiszki and, as I now know, soon transported them from there [to Po]nar.

■ ■ ■ ■ ■ ■

AUGUST 1, 1941

AGAIN A JUDENRAT OF TEN

[. . .] the Lithuanian liaison Cubirgas brought an order [from the district] commissar that the Vilna Judenrat must consist not of [24 but of 10 per]sons.

How Was It Composed?

To the general demand that he absolutely must be in a Judenrat of ten, Mr. Trocki set as a condition that the committee include a group of men whom, he [says, he] can depend on. He demands: Fried, Pietuchowski, [. . .] Engineer Szabad from the Dutch oil factory, [Eliezer] Kruk, and Dr. Sedlis. [Everyone] agreed to his proposal. All that remained was to choose three more [per]sons. [Eliezer] Kruk then demanded that, without elections, a representative of the Jewish labor move-

---

Bund in the Judenrat comprised Grisha Yashunski, Yoyel Fishman, Berl Widman, and Nokhem Wapner.

72. Born in 1893 in Łódź. He was active in Poalei Zion. In his last years, he was co-editor of the Łódź Yiddish newspaper *Folksblat*. He came to Białystok in 1939 with the refugees and reached Vilna in 1940. For his biography, see Fuks 1958. The *Lexicon* states that he was sent to Ponar in November 1941, Kruk's diary indicates that that happened several months earlier.

ment be added, and he nominated Grisha Yashunski. The proposal was accepted unanimously. [Two] more persons were elected—Mrs. Soyfer and Zalkind. Five more candidates were elected; these were Fishman, Zaydshnur, Milkanowicki, Srolowicz,[73] and Wygodzki.

[Pages 26–32 of the journal, from the beginning of August to about August 6, are missing.]

August 3 [1941]

Patches, Don't Walk on the Sidewalk, Walk in Single File, Don't Use Transportation, Don't Greet Each Other

[Page 33 (which is badly damaged) and the following pages tell of the "contribution" of 5 million rubles imposed on the Vilna Jewish community, which had to be collected by the Judenrat.]

August 6

5 *Million Contribution*

Panski Sticks 50 *Rubles in My Hand*

In the Yiddish edition, a similar item appears earlier; see the entry for June 24, above.

Vilna Again Gets a Bund

How Did It Happen?

The First Consultations

The Foundation [of the Bund in the Ghetto]

We Get Representatives in the Judenrat

[On those days of missing entries, Hingst, the first civilian district commissar for the city of Vilna and organizer of numerous slaughters of Jews, issued Order Number 1, commanding Jews to wear a yellow star of David, and imposed many other evil decrees on the Jews. This and the "contribution" were the first steps of the Nazi civilian administration concerning the Vilna Jews.]

August 7 [1941]

They Squeeze Out Contribution Money

[The Nazi deputy for Jewish affairs, Franz Murer, met representatives of the Judenrat.]

[. . .] Zaydshnur tried to anticipate: "So we'll be punished."

[The German responded:] "Not punished, shot!"

He finished speaking and waved his hand imperiously, as with children after they have been whipped:

"Get out!"

Thus came the order of the Contribution.

73. A well-known activist among Zionist students.

One more detail:

This was to be the procedure: at 9 in the morning of the 7th,[74] the first 2 million rubles had to be dep[osited]. Soon after, at ten, the [representative of] the Judenrat was to come to him. According to Murer[75] and the interpretation of his words, those [who] came at 10 in the morning would have to take the dead bodies of [those who were] shot if . . . the money wasn't presented by 9 in the morning.

When the delegates came to the Judenrat and told what was demanded, terror prevailed: you may walk in the city only until 6 in the evening. Many streets are closed to Jews altogether. How could you get such a sum by tomorrow morning?

Old Dr. Wygodzki raised the spirits and shouted that this was not a time to despair; they had to start collecting.

The news about the 5 million spread like wildfire through the city. Spontaneous collecting groups formed. Men took off [their watches], women took off rings—by 6 in the evening, [a handsome sum] was collected. Throughout the night, 667,000 [rubles] and a half kilo of gold were collected, including a great many jewels and . . . about [200 g]old watches.

[. . .] In the morning, this was all packed up in a good leather valise, and the three representatives from the previous day went off with it to the same alley where M[urer had] met them the day before. Murer was already waiting there. When asked [if the money] was there, the delegation answered, intending to drag it out until [after] 10 in the morning, that they didn't know precisely because [it still had to be c]ounted. Murer took them to a cellar room. Everything was laid out on a table and, after he counted it, he asked [where is] the rest. To the reply that the Judenrat was continuing the collec[tion, he] announced that the decision must be carried out and [. . .]

A Lithuanian policeman came in and announced that all three [were to be] shot. And, because there were Jewish workers in the courtyard, they [had the] right to indicate which of the Jewish workers [would receive th]eir clothes. . . .

[When the po]liceman left, Murer came back and [asked the representatives] what their professions were. Zaydshnur answered that he was a merchant. [Kruk answered that he was] an artisan; Pietuchowski, the deputy mayor of Šiauliai. Then he [said] to Zaydshnur the merchant:

"[Go b]ack to the city and tell the Judenrat that, instead of 10 in the morning, they should be there at [. . .] 11, but with all the money."

[The two] remained. Zaydshnur met the Judenrat on the way. The delegates decided not to return but to enter at once.

74. The Yiddish edition of the book says "twenty-seventh," but this is obviously an error.

75. The deputy for Jewish affairs, who worked under District Commissar Hingst. Murer was a Nazi officer, a barber by profession, who had been trained in the Hitler Youth. His presence caused dread among the ghetto inhabitants. The Jews called him The *Mem* (the Hebrew letter *M*, for Murer and for *Malekhamoves*—Angel of Death).

Of the 24 members of the Judenrat, 2 were missing (Fishman and Katz). Murer wants to know who is the oldest one there. Dr. Wygodzki assumes that he meant oldest according to age, and points to himself. Given that opportunity, he requests that the time to collect the money be extended by 10 days and tries to explain the difficulties, the poverty, etc.

Murer then roars:

"Stupid old man! It has to be brought immediately!"

Dr. Lyuba Kholem, an elegant lady who speaks excellent German, attempts to explain the situation of Vilna. Murer interrupts her and shouts:

"Shut up, damned woman!"

He takes Dr. Liber, Dr. Sedlis, and Shoel Ofman out of the room and announces that those three share the same fate as the previous ones who didn't produce the sum at nine in the morning.

Right after that, Murer left for parts unknown with the valise of money. The Judenrat decided to go to District Commissar Hingst; perhaps they could save the prisoners. The delegation included Shoel Trocki, Yosef Szabad, and Lyuba Kholem.

In the corridor, Murer stopped them. There he was much milder. He advised them to collect what they could and deposit it in the bank every day. The impression was that the sentence against the prisoners was lifted. That same day, at 1 in the afternoon, the prisoners came back.

The collection was continued. Altogether, a total of 1,490,000 rubles, 16 1/2 kilos of gold, and 189 watches were collected. No one received any receipt. The impression was that everything was calculated at the official rate, i.e., 3 rubles a gram.[76] But no one could know the true account.

[*Pages 36–102 of the diary are missing, but this is probably an error in the numbering of the pages. According to the table of contents, only twelve entries are missing; it seems that Kruk read "96" instead of "36"—the seven missing pages would reflect the average proportion of entries per page in the rest of the journal. During that time, Order Number 2 of District Commissar Hingst, dated August 12, 1941, was issued in German and Lithuanian, regulating public commerce in Vilna and designating six sites for marketplaces. On August 13, Hingst issued an addendum for the registration of all motor vehicles. On August 14, 1941, at eight in the morning, all owners of vehicles had to present them at Łukiszki Square. The topics of the missing parts follow, as listed in Kruk's table of contents.*]

August 10 [1941]
How I Extract Information

August 12 [1941]
Bentsien Kit [?] Is Taken in the Middle of the Street

76. On the black market the rate of gold was immeasurably higher.

August 14 [1941]
Tribute

August 16 [1941]
They Beat Atrociously in Porubanek
How They Beat G[?] . . .

August 17 [1941]
My Neighbor Returns from Jail

August 18 [1941]
What Is Ponar

August 19 [1941]
Jews in the Role of Snatchers

August 23 [1941]
Now Women Are Also Being Snatched

August 24 [1941]
How Did Vilna Pay the Tribute?
In the Street

GIVE BACK THE MEN!

Yesterday, about 400 women gathered in the courtyard of the Judenrat and demanded that the Judenrat bring back their husbands, who had been working for three weeks, and send others in their place. The women selected a delegation of two to negotiate with the Judenrat. The policeman on guard there wanted to arrest the women. It was possible to calm the Lithuanian, but the women attacked and screamed. Then the director of the Labor Division, Mr. Emes, attempted to explain; he told them that, unfortunately, the men couldn't be exchanged because nobody knew where they were. After a whole day of wrangling, the women dispersed, once more . . . without their husbands.

AUGUST 26, 1941

PEOPLE ENVY THOSE WHO WERE EXILED

The Bolshevik roundup on the eve of the outbreak of the German-Soviet war, when they loaded whole families onto cars to ship them to Russia, had such a depressing effect at the time that even the former Reds were ashamed of it.[77]

77. On June 14, 1941, just a week before the Nazi attack on the Soviet Union, the NKVD carried out a big purge in Vilna and in all of Lithuania. Thousands of so-called dubious elements were arrested and shipped to the far north. These included many well-known Jewish social activists,

Now, after all the painful experiences, those "lucky ones" who were exiled are envied.

Thus, one misfortune is traded for another.

August 26, 1940 [should be 1941]
An Original Chapter: An Article about Vilna and Its Social Activities
The Vilna Ghetto
People Sell Everything Fast

TWO TRAGIC HISTORIES

A comrade sits in front of me, my friend Nekhame.[78] She can't stop crying.

What happened?

Her father lives at Piłsudski St. 28. All his life he had a store. The mother and sister worked in the store, the father and brother-in-law had other occupations. The Bolsheviks took the little shop, and the father and brother-in-law got jobs in an artisans' cooperative. That's how they "made their bread." Now my friend Nekhame is also at work. At home, there is the father, sixty-nine years old, deaf in one ear and disabled in one leg.

Last night, they assaulted their courtyard and came to their apartment. They threw the certificate that the father is sick on the floor, refused to read it. They beat the old man and when, greatly agitated, he told them he was sick, they threatened to shoot him. They pointed a gun at him, and the old man, not losing control, shouted: Please shoot. . . .

When they wanted to take him away by force, the older daughter, a mother of two children, wrapped herself around her father's leg and shouted: Shoot us; I won't let you take him in such a condition! . . . They beat her terribly, right in front of her children. The little sparrows cried terribly and, with childish fists, threw themselves on the executioners. The latter didn't pay attention; they ordered her to get dressed and come with them. She did. There was a dreadful wailing in the house. Finally, they released her and took the father. They beat the mother because, meanwhile, they had tried searching the cabinets and the mother dared to follow them. . . .

Meanwhile, the group was summoned to another apartment, apparently with better opportunities. They left our apartment and . . .

. . . And today, after the event, her sister walks with a black eye, the old man keeps crying, and the mother looks for a place for her husband to be admitted to forced labor.

---

merchants, and industrialists; Lithuanians who had been officials in the previous Lithuanian government, etc. The families of those who had been arrested and shipped off earlier to prisons and camps were also sent off.

78. Probably Nekhame Trupiańska, the wife of Yankev Trupiański.

One of the thousand tragedies in today's Vilna homes. . . . From the same house, they dragged off an old man, a widower, who lived with his 82-year-old mother and his 11-year-old daughter. He was the only one who served and fed them. Now the two remain orphans. Who will take care of the old woman, and who will look after the 11-year-old girl?

Last night, the Germans took five Jews from the courtyard of the Jewish Committee (Strashun 6). Today the Jews came back beaten and crushed, two of them fatally, the rest severely.

I GO TO WORK! . . .

Everybody congratulates me sincerely today, and I'm the only one who feels bad about it.

Worse than bad!

Thousands of people have worked, thousands have been dragged off, thousands went off voluntarily. Only I, the whole time, for 10 weeks, have been hiding, however threatened with the severest consequences. I shall not willingly crawl into the jaws of the wolf. That's what I've decided.

Today, my friend Hersh[79] came and "invited" me to do it. He works and is a commander of a labor brigade. It's good there, and he'll be able to keep an eye on me. He advises me [to go].

Two days ago, his wife[80] came to me about it. All my friends and relatives advise me to go to work and stop hiding. I have decided, and tomorrow I go to serve the Germans with forced labor.[81]

I even have a pass in my pocket. But I admit: I am breathing freely now. Tomorrow morning, I'll be able to look at the street freely.

Am I doing the right thing? . . .

Tomorrow, I'll become a slave for Hitler! . . .

We intervened to accept my roommates, my brother-in-law Hersh [Horowicz] and my friend Kelson, to work with me.

79. Hersh Gutgestalt, a Bundist activist in Warsaw, who came to Vilna with the refugees. In Vilna, he was active on the historical committee, led in 1939–1940 by the linguist and literary critic Professor Noah Prylucki. He was arrested by the Soviets when they occupied Lithuania. For his biography, see *Lexicon* 2:173–174; *Generations* 2:330–334. He died in Camp Klooga, Estonia, in September 1944.

80. The wife of Hersh Gutgestalt, Miriam Rotkop-Gutgestalt, was in Vilna with her husband and their son Gavriel. She was killed in the final liquidation of the Vilna Ghetto in September 1943. For her biography, see *Lexicon* 2:175; see also the biography of her husband in *Generations* 2:330–334 and *Teachers' Memorial Book* 1954:87.

81. This dilemma is not just personal but also concerns the principle of serving the enemy's war effort.

WEDNESDAY, AUGUST 27, 1941

I've finally finished my first day of work. Carried bricks in a wheelbarrow, swept a courtyard, worked in a warehouse. And the most important thing—for the first time, I walked freely in the street . . . with a pass!

Recently there has been a new fashion in Vilna:

A few days ago, Germans came to the courtyard of the Jewish Committee with a truck and demanded five Jews. They left with the quintet, and as I have told before, these Jews were beaten horribly.

What have they done with them?

The Jews were taken to a forest near Ponar and beaten atrociously.

The next day, there was another incident. Two Germans selected two Jews, took them away, and brought them back half dead a few hours later. In the courtyard of the Jewish Committee, the Germans bragged that they did that since, because of the "shitty Jews," they can't end the war . . . they do it for the sake of . . . Persia,[82] and they will do even worse to the Jews. . . .

A new fashion, it seems, a Persian style! . . .

An interesting incident: at the railroad station, many Jews work at forced labor. Today, a great many prisoners of war[83] were brought there. A Jew took up a collection of food among the workers, and a Christian, whose task it is to watch the Jews work, turned the collected food over to the Bolsheviks. You could hear about it all day among the working Jews.

I learned that Noah Pryłucki is no longer in Łukiszki. It is assumed that he was sent somewhere to work. . . .

The news on the radio that the Gestapo in Lwów murdered Prof. Bartel, the former Polish premier, made a strong impression.

Another interesting story: an acquaintance of mine, a locksmith, is often visited by a Christian friend, another locksmith. Recently, the Christian took my acquaintance into a corner and asked him for a wrench. He told my acquaintance that, the first chance he got, he would unscrew the railroad tracks. "You think we'll keep quiet?" he said.

In Vilna today, it passes from mouth to mouth, I talked to someone who had seen it, so the following information is reliable. In the city, last night and today, cigarettes were distributed among friends and relations. . . . In the cigarettes were proclamations against the German occupation.

Today I got a personal, written message from all my relations in Warsaw. They send greetings and promise aid.[84]

82. I.e., to avenge what the Jews did in Persia in the biblical story of Esther.

83. I.e., Red Army soldiers who fell into German hands.

84. By "relations," Kruk means the Bundist underground movement in Warsaw. It is clear from further entries that there was a connection between Warsaw and Vilna concerning aid.

THURSDAY, AUGUST 28 [1941]

Warsaw. Shouldn't I be ashamed to say it? It's hard for me to mention it, but how many times have I wept for my home town since I left it in my exile? Today, once again, my eyes filled with tears when I listened to a detailed and extensive message from Warsaw.

Some twenty years of social activity in Warsaw. I know every stone there. Everything in me was feverish when they told me about it. What is happening there?

Before [June], we've been sealed off by a German-Soviet border. This is the first message [with both cities] under German rule. In short, what do they tell?

In Warsaw, 500 people die every day. There is so much poverty and hunger that there is often nothing with which to bury the dead. The solution: the dead bodies are thrown in the street. Simply and without ceremony. At the same time, there are a lot of Jews who have become millionaires under the Germans.

A brand-new plutocracy!

These "New Men" there live as before the war. Nothing is lacking in the ghetto; you can have whatever you want as long as you have money. They say that the Jewish Community Council even determines the . . . exchange rate of the dollar. The Jewish Community Council there has so much power. The Warsaw Courthouse on Leszno is the central point where they meet with the outside world. Jews go in on Leszno. From Ogrodowa enter the non-Jews. The courtyard is the meeting place. Only individual Jews get permission to leave the ghetto. Most of them are military suppliers, members of the Community Council, etc.

In Warsaw, a Yiddish newspaper of the Bund is published illegally, also a paper of Tsukunft and a Tsukunft paper in Polish.[85] Three Polish daily newspapers also appear illegally. One of them is the organ of the PPS, *Wolność Równość Niepodległość*.[86] In the whole country, there are 46 illegal newspapers. The PPS and the Bund cooperate closely.

I record the news from there only because in the future, if I live to see it, I will be able to check how news reached us. It is characteristic of the situation and of the sad state we find ourselves in.

Isolated from the world and cut off from the milieu that was dear to us.

85. Tsukunft was the youth organization of the Bund in Poland. For the publications of Tsukunft in the Warsaw Ghetto, see Zeldin 1947.

86. The paper was known as *WRN*, which stands for *Wolność, Równość, Niepodległość* (Freedom, equality, independence).

FRIDAY, AUGUST 29 [1941]

This is the third day I've worked. Have already swept the courtyard, pushed a wheelbarrow, and now I drag iron, locks, screws, and so forth. Am I content? In fact, yes. I am content because I am, unfortunately, an active participant in whatever the masses of Jews live through. I feel their pains, see them as pariahs forced to assist Hitler in his defeat, which must come sooner or later.

The gigantic enterprise where I work was formerly a base of metal production and, earlier, a big Jewish metal factory. Recently, Bolshevization took place,[87] now Hitlerization. I observe:

The Lithuanians run the enterprise under the leadership of a German. None of them knows anything about this profession, and none of them understands anything about it. For that, there is a Jew with a patch, who works with the same rights as I. He had been taken to work in the peat bog. The Germans found out about him and dragged him out of there. Now he's the only expert. Everybody comes to him, and he explains and interprets for all of them.

I observe. All the clerks there got bonus food rations today, white flour, gray soap, matches, rice, and so on—all things worth more than gold in our current condition. But none of us gets them, obviously; even the Jew, the expert, the specialist, one of their most important workers, doesn't get it. It's probably more than swinishness.

But go talk to "them" about being a swine. . . .

VELFKE

Unfortunately, just today did I learn that the famous Velfke was arrested long ago.

Who is Velfke? The owner of a literary café at Żydowska St. 4, in Vilna. Velfke, the restaurateur, became involved with Yiddish literature not only through the Vilna writers but because of many, many Jewish writers and artists throughout the world. To visit Vilna and not go to Velfke's meant not to know Vilna.[88]

So Velfke is also a victim!

A JEW DOESN'T NEED ANY DOCUMENTS

An acquaintance, released by the Bolsheviks when they fled, once brought me a message from my friends Fishgr. and Bl.[89] He was stood against the wall with them in Lida by the Bolsheviks. Now, while working for the Germans, he acciden-

87. All private enterprises were confiscated and nationalized under the Soviets.

88. Volf Usyan, nicknamed Velfke, was a popular figure in Jewish society. His restaurant was a meeting place for Yiddish writers, bohemians, and underworld figures. Thus, when the novelist Joseph Roth visited Vilna, he was taken to Velfke's.

89. Persons arrested by the Soviets in late 1939 and early 1940 for crossing the border of the Soviet-occupied part of Poland on their way to Vilna, which then belonged to independent

tally lost a document. The Germans attested to his identity, but, for ten days now, he has been running around from one office to another asking them to issue him a document stating that he really is he. One sends him to another, and no one will do it. Everyone finds another excuse. At last, today, a police official gave him an answer, short and sweet:

"We don't do such things. A Jew doesn't need any documents."

Short and sweet!

SABOTAGE

The following is circulating as a fact: the highways around Vilna are often covered with glass. German car tires burst on the glass. This is presented as proof that sabotage takes place.

An announcement in today's local Polish newspaper: because Jews are not permitted to marry non-Jews, the civilian registry office announces that it will issue documents to Jews only if the marriage is between Jews.

A brand-new decree! . . .

SATURDAY, AUGUST 30 [1941]

More about my work. This time about the non-Jews who work with me. As soon as I started working, an elderly Christian came to me:

"Don't rush, it's bad for your health. Let them pay you, then you'll work. . . ."

Later, he told me, little by little:

His two sons went off with the Reds. They are in a training school for lieutenants.

"If they're killed," he once told me, "what can we do; at least they'll know why."

Another time, he consoled me:

"Don't be ashamed of the yellow patch. The ones who made you put it on should be ashamed."

And he hinted that you may not talk about it aloud. . . .

Another man, a Polonized Lithuanian, sees me working in decent trousers and asks me if I don't have any working pants. I explained to him that this is all I have, and unfortunately I have to work in these pants. The next day, he almost forced me to borrow a pair of overalls from him. . . .

An interesting fact: last night, as I mentioned, all the employees received food. The two Polish employees on the crew did not get those rations. . . .

Lithuania. They were jailed in Lida prison. One of them was Salo Fishgrund, a Bundist activist from Cracow. Another Bundist activist from Cracow, Leon Feiner, was arrested along with Fishgrund. The identity of Bl. is not clear. He might have been the Warsaw Bundist Khayim-Ber Blondman, a typesetter at the *Folkstsaytung*.

DR. JACOB WYGODZKI IS ARRESTED

Dr. Jacob Wygodzki is arrested. That news made an understandable [. . .]
[*Pages 107 and 108 of the journal, from the end of August, are missing. The most revered Jewish leader of Vilna, Dr. Wygodzki, was arrested on August 24 or 28.*]

Question Ghetto
Licentiousness and Banditry
Banditry

August 31 [1941]
A Joy among the Jews

[*The new page (109) begins with the end of the entry about the registration of Jewish property that was to be carried out by the Judenrat.*]
[. . .] The registration of Jewish property was revoked.

REGARDS FROM 87 VILNA JEWS

Yesterday, a railroad worker from near Minsk came to a Jewish home and brought a list of 87 Vilna Jews. They asked him to convey that they were alive and working near Minsk.

Those who were concerned came running in amazement to look at the list. You're joking!—the men were re-discovered. . . .

MONDAY, SEPTEMBER 1, 1940 [SHOULD BE 1941]

TWO YEARS AND TEN WEEKS

Today it is two years since the outbreak of the war[90] and 10 weeks since the outbreak of the German-Soviet war.

Two years ago, I still had my normal social activity, my job, my home, and my wife next to me, my brother, his child, and all my near and dear ones.

Two years ago, on the first of [September, at] exactly 10 in the morning, was the first air battle over Warsaw. I and [my family] watched it from the balcony of my apartment, and we thought that what had begun would [. . .] but, at the same time, salvation would come. That [was the main reason why we] had been prepared to suffer.

[Two years ago, I didn't] yet think how soon I would be a refugee and didn't understand [the situation]. Now I understand, I understand.

[. . .] This is the balance of my family: my wife left [Warsaw] on her way to me; at the German-Soviet [border . . .] 1940 she was stripped naked and searched and accompanied to [. . . At the] Russian-Lithuanian border on March

90. The day the Germans attacked Poland and World War II began.

17, 1940, she was [arrested[91] and remained in] Oszmiana prison for more than a year. Only then was she sentenced to [. . .] Since spring 1941, in Siberia, in the Marinski district [. . .] Maybe she's already free and maybe not, who [knows].

[My brother Pinkhes and his wife] and child managed to break through and [are] in America.[92]

[My brother-in-law, after] the Germans entered, fled from Płock to Warsaw. [My sister and the] children were driven out by the Germans and [wandered around] in the Radom district for many weeks. Now my brother-in-law stays in [Warsaw, and my sis]ter and the two children are in Tomaszów [Mazowiecki].

My fellow party members, my colleagues, and my friends are scattered to the four corners of the globe, some in Palestine, some in Japan, and some in my old home. Here in Vilna, we remain [. . .] isolated and abandoned by everyone.

THE BLOODY PROVOCATION ON *GLEZER STREET*

The second anniversary of the outbreak of the war was celebrated here in Vilna in a un[ique way].

Early in the morning, it became clear that the city militia were not letting Jew[ish wom]en into the street. Why? Nobody knew. People thought it might have something to do with possible demonstrations that were supposed to take place today. So why don't they let the Jews out, especially the women? . . .

On the way to work, they checked the men, took passes away from some of them and let them go, and arrested a few. Another rumor spread that they weren't letting the women out because they were going to take the men [out] of Vilna today, straight from work. They didn't let the women out so they wouldn't make a scandal. . . .

A third supposition: an important person is coming to Vilna and they don't want any Jews in the streets. . . .

Meanwhile, news came from the street: on Glezer Street, a German was shot yesterday, supposedly by a Jew. . . .

The Lithuanians and Poles have allegedly settled accounts between them. Several dead: three Poles, one Lithuanian, and one German.

The city seethed all day, but no one could say anything for sure.

Now, at 4 in the afternoon, I have found out: on Glezer Street, a shot was fired, wounding a German in the arm. Yesterday, Sunday, August 31, there was unrest because of that. Windows were broken, houses robbed, furniture thrown out of windows—a real fancy wedding.

Now, people [coming] from that district say that, since this morning, they have been expelling residents of Glezer, Gaon, Szawelska, and Strashun Streets,

91. By the Soviets.

92. Pinkhes Schwartz, born in 1902, reached the United States and lived in New York until his death in 1963.

and a handful from Niemiecka Street.[93] When the [men] went off to work, the [women] and children were expelled [from those streets].

I cannot walk over and check it out. It is dangerous to go into the street. So I register what people tell and the way they tell it. This is characteristic of the kind of life in Vilna. So far, [we know] very little. Tomorrow, we may be able to have a final account of this day.

[From the sa]me source: last week, the Germans taunted the Jews, as I described before; now, they feel they had gone too far, and in recent days they have treated the Jewish workers so well that they feel as if they were in Paradise. [They] get good food, are given cigarettes, cigars, chocolate, etc.

Isn't this the calm before the storm?

Look what has become of Jewish happiness in Vilna. . . .

Cut Off Half a Beard

[The boss] of the Jewish workers on the railroad is wild [. . .] Today, for no reason at all, he ordered [. . .] They beat him up thoroughly and cut off part of his beard [. . .] a religious man.

Because of Regret

THE YESHIVA STUDENT

In Jewish Vilna, there was a very popular so-called yeshiva student who read palms.[94] Some talk about him with complete seriousness. Some, even non-Jews, take his opinions very seriously.

Now they say that for a long time, the yeshiva student has been saying that between Rosh Hashanah and Yom Kippur, great changes will take place. People interpret that to mean we'll be rid of the *D*'s ["*Daleds*"], as they are called here.[95]

May it come true!

Because of the events in the street, Pati [Kremer] sent her sister to find out what had happened to me.

The old woman[96] watches me like the apple of her eye. . . .

TUESDAY, SEPTEMBER 2, 1941

ABOUT THE PROVOCATION ON GLEZER STREET

No matter how much horror my entries contain, what has been going on since Sunday night is a game for which I can find no expression.

93. Jewish streets in the poor downtown area of the so-called medieval ghetto (there never was a formal ghetto in Vilna).

94. He lived at Kwaszelna Street 15.

95. *D*'s—for *Daytshn*, i.e., Germans. *Daled* is the Hebrew letter *D*.

96. Pati Kremer, the moral authority of the Bund in Vilna.

What happened?

On the corner of Niemiecka and Glezer Streets,[97] a shot was heard. They say a German was wounded. Soon there was a commotion, and someone point[ed] to a Jew from a house on that corner of Glezer and Wielka Streets, [as] the one who must have shot the German. . . .

People soon appeared there; the Jew was beaten horribly, everything was thrown out of his house, and a pogrom against Jewish property spread over Glezer and Jatkowa Streets.

This did not finish the game. At night, they started driving the tenants out of their apartments. This goes on today, too. To yesterday's list of streets where people are expelled, I can add Zawalna 32, 38, 40.[98]

So far, it is hard to determine the extent of the destruction. It is estimated [that] about 5,000 Jews were driven out, including old people and children.

[. . .] people tell. The picture was so horrifying [. . .] and wept too. Poles and Germans wept, [. . .]

[. . .] a picture:

[. . .] old people and sick people. They lead a blind woman, they drag bundles and [. . .] pursue and push on. Women weep and look like crazy [. . .] 80 percent of those driven out are women. The men were [taken earlier] at work. In the meantime, the people at home [were driven out] . . . Yesterday, there were [cases of] men coming home and [finding the gate] locked and the families gone. There were [cases when] the people from an entire area were gathered in a big courtyard and [later] driven on. Szawelska St. 1, for example, was used as such a courtyard.

Thus far, people have somehow settled into a normal (if you can call it that), sad, but more or less stable life. There has been less snatching. For the men, work has become something normal. They have sold their belongings and have somehow lived and toiled on in the gloomy situation. The streets have taken on a normal appearance. There was movement in them, and between 4 and 6 in the afternoon (when people come home from forced labor), traffic in the streets was heavy. Lines of people march on both sides of the street, winding behind one another—all with yellow patches. It was gloomy, horrible, anguished, but as with everything, you got used to that, too. Now there is another upheaval.

No one knows whom fate is waiting for, and the whole city is packing. People are ready to take to the road at any order. Bundles lie in the rooms—everything is ready!

As I said, on Monday morning, no women were allowed in the street. The men's passes were checked, and some men were arrested.

97. This is certainly a mistake. It must be the corner of Wielka and Glezer Streets.

98. This was probably a list of the courtyards from which Jews were expelled. The list was not found.

HINGST'S ORDER

This morning, Vilna Commissar Hingst distributed an order around the city that the murderers of the two Germans killed by Jews on Sunday were shot. To prevent similar cases, Jews are allowed to be in the street from 10 in the morning until 3 in the afternoon, except for men and women with passes, indicating they must go to work later.[99]

So all the Jews are punished. Two Jews have already been shot, and thousands of Jews have been driven out, not knowing why or where. Moreover, today's order restricts the possibilities of movement by Jews.

Despite today's order, after 10 in the morning, the women were not allowed into the street. Not until 2 in the afternoon were the women allowed to move around. The sadism lies in the fact that women can go to market only between 10 and 12. By forbidding the women to be in the street, they were deprived of the possibility of buying anything in the market.

Christians say that at 3 o'clock this morning they saw groups of people being led away, most of them in nightgowns or other night clothes.

Most of the groups were taken toward Łukiszki.

THE PROVOCATION ALSO INCLUDES POLES

The second anniversary of the start of the war was a day of mourning not only for Jews but also for Poles:

I learned that in the electrical plant, all the workers were gathered and a Lithuanian listed the names of all the Communists and ordered them to go into an adjoining room where the po[lice] were waiting for them.

[. . .] This is how the Lithuanians got rid [of the Polish workers in] the electrical plant. There were similar cases in [other enterprises].

[. . .] Thus 2,000–3,000 Poles were arrested.

[. . .] This second anniversary was thus prepared [. . .] not just for Jews but for Poles as well.

Registration of Jewish Property

[. . .] carried out a survey of Jewish property. Recently, the order has been withdrawn.

Today the press again reports that Hingst has ordered a forced registration of Jewish property. The registration must be completed by the eighth of this month. The police commissioner of each precinct is responsible for this task.

Thus, the registration is taken away from the Jewish Committee and placed in more reliable hands. . . .

99. That order, in three languages—German, Lithuanian, and Polish—was published in Mowszowicz 1947; also in Kaczerginski 1947 (only the German text) and Dworzecki 1948.

TEN CARTS. THE JUDENRAT IS SNATCHED

(Schweinenberg's First Appearance on the Scene)[100]

The Judenrat Is Taken Away

On September 1, the Judenrat was ordered by the Lithuanian Ipatinga (Wileńska St. 12) to deliver 10 carts the next morning. There were no Jewish wagons at all, since they had been taken away from the Jews. The order for the ten carts was received by Attorney P. Kon, the member of the Judenrat. He attempted to carry out the order. But he didn't succeed. He was helpless. On the morning of the 2nd, the Judenrat hired five Christian carts and sent them to the Ipatinga. The wagons arrived on the scene late: instead of 9, they didn't arrive until 10. The Ipatinga didn't accept the carts and sent them back.

At about 11 in the morning, a German and three civilians came to the building of the Judenrat at Strashun 6. The German raged around the office and asked who took the order for 10 carts. P. Kon answered that it was he. The German, a certain Schweinenberg,[101] roared wildly:

"So, you didn't carry out the order?" And, looking P. Kon straight in the eye, he went on: "You are far too lazy and have lost your senses. I will make you fewer so you will suffer less. . . ."

He came to the table and inquired about the protocols, and ordered everyone to stand in a row and show their passes. All the present employees of the Judenrat stood in a row in the room, along with a few clerks and some people who were there by chance. After checking the documents thoroughly, he took 16 persons and ordered them to stand on the other side. The other 6 stayed where they were.

WHO ARE THE 16?

The 16 who were selected are: Engineer S. Trocki, Yosef Szabad, Attorney Nokhem Soyfer, P. Kon, Avrom Zalkind, Boris Parnes, Yosef Szkolnicki, Pietuchowski,[102] the director of the Mefitsei-Haskalah [Disseminators of Enlightenment] Library [Fayvl] Krasny,[103] Tabarowicz, Rabbi Katz, and others. The visitors took all 16. The remaining 6 were: Engineer A. Fried, A. Zaydshnur, Attorney G. Yashunski, Y. Fishman, Srolowicz, and the staff member Emes.

100. This subtitle in Kruk's table of contents is obviously a later addition.

101. A Gestapo officer. From his office at Wileńska Street 12, he directed the atrocious acts of the Lithuanian Fascists, the Ipatinga. He was the most brutal organizer and executor of bloody provocations in the ghetto.

102. This is not clear. From previous entries in the journal, as well as from other publications (e.g., Dworzecki 1948:497), it seems that Pietuchowski and Eliezer Kruk had been killed in August.

103. An artist and photographer. He was not a member of the Judenrat.

THE FIRST SMACK

When they showed the passes, Y. Fishman stayed somewhat farther away than the swine Schweinenberg demanded. For that, he gave him a blazing smack.

SZAWELSKA AND STRASHUN STREETS "PURGED"

Yesterday, the Jewish quarter around Szawelska and Strashun Streets was purged. All the inhabitants of the streets were taken, with their little bundles, toward Łukiszki.

Those who saw it describe dreadful scenes. The wailing reached the sky. The young were leading the old. They were dragging sick people and children. There were dozens of well-known and distinguished Vilna Jews in the groups. Those who saw it wept with them.

Szawelska and Strashun Streets contained about 1,000 inhabitants.

ELIEZER KRUK IS DRAGGED OFF

I learn that yesterday the Vilna community activist Eliezer Kruk (a member of the Judenrat, a former vice-president of the Vilna Jewish Community Council, and Chairman of the Vilna Artisans' Union) and his family were thrown out of their apartment, at Niemiecka 23, and from there were taken off, with the other inhabitants of that house, in an unknown direction.

LANGBORD IS ALSO GONE

The indefatigable Langbord, the energetic, ingenious, and devoted member of the Judenrat, was arrested at 12:30 yesterday at Strashun 15 and has not yet returned. Apparently, Mr. Langbord has also gone the way of those who were dragged off. One of the central nerves and boldest members of the Judenrat has been taken away.

A LOCK ON THE DOOR OF THE JUDENRAT

Now, late at night, I learn that, after the events described above at the Judenrat building, someone from the authorities put a lock on the door and sealed the offices.

So we remain completely abandoned.

I AM CONFINED TO MY HOUSE

I am again confined to my house. At 3 in the afternoon, I come from work and, since then, I have to sit at home until 8 the next morning, when I will once again go to my so-called workplace.

I have great difficulty and often take real risks to get information. My family often scolds me for it.

PEOPLE ARE AFRAID OF DISMISSALS

Good or bad workplaces. But now, when there are rumors that the number of Jewish workers in several units will be reduced, the fear of Łukiszki hovers over everybody.

The perspectives here grow "better" from day to day.

SEPTEMBER 3 [1941]

THE FIRST SUMMARY OF THE DESTRUCTION

The destruction in the city is just beginning to be felt. Moans and groans reach me from all sides. People mourn for neighbors, relatives, close friends, and acquaintances. Mostly, for those who were dragged off on the night of Sunday/Monday. The streets are even deader than they have ever been. No one dares to set foot in those streets where they dragged off the Jews. Everyone is terrified for himself. The apartments there are empty and sealed.

Everyone seeks his own. My neighbor's son is beside himself today. From Lidzki [Street], they took off his girlfriend, a beautiful girl, along with her mother. With them in the apartment lived a Lithuanian militiaman, who always assured the family that nothing would happen to them. Now, he himself has thrown out not only his own landlady but all the neighbors in the courtyard. . . .

A Hasidic Jew tells me that among those who were dragged off is the popular Vilna preacher [Arye] Zuchowicz.[104]

I also learned that they dragged off my landlord's mother-in-law and a sister-in-law with two children.

There is hardly a home today that hasn't been directly affected, orphaned, and darkened. Every few minutes I obtain new information, often through the neighbors coming from work, often through special messengers, through letters from friends and acquaintances, and through information given to my janitor by those on their way from work.[105]

Lately I feel like a dumb animal. At 8 in the morning to work, at 3 in the afternoon at home. Back to work in the morning and back home in the afternoon. You can't go out because walking in the streets is allowed only until 3 in the afternoon [. . .] on the pretext that I'm going to work, they don't even let me [. . .]

You don't see your friends, you don't know whether they're alive or whether they've been dragged off, you live like a dumb animal.

104. Known as the *Baranovitsher Magid,* the Preacher of Baranovitsh.

105. The Christian janitor of Kruk's house had apparently agreed to accept information and notes for him.

Jewish hearts rejoiced today: the Vilna radio ordered yesterday that not only are the [bomb] shelters not to be destroyed, on the contrary, they are to be cleaned and prepared for any eventualities. . . .

What [will console] us today?

Once more, Jewish hearts rejoice: the radio broadcasts that the Russian counteroffensive is moving toward Smolensk. They also say that yesterday the Russians bombed Memel and Königsberg. That and the news about the preparation of the bomb shelters warmed Jewish hearts twice today.

We console ourselves with bubbles in the air.

Soviet Prisoners of War

Today, on the way to work, I came upon two trucks loaded with Russian prisoners of war. The trucks stopped on [the corner of] Kijowska and Słowacki Streets. People on the street pelted the prisoners with bread, cigarettes, etc. The Germans allowed it and even helped. Their hunger for bread and cigarettes has become so great it just breaks your heart.

When the truck moved, the people in the street, incidentally only Christians, blessed them warmly.

My friends envy me: good working conditions. My fellow workers, Lithuanians or Germans (and certainly Poles) treat me very well, often even amiably. Today, the local superintendent found coveralls and a smock for me so I won't ruin my own clothes. The pity makes me nervous. But, in all, in the eight days I've worked here, several thousand kilos of iron have passed through my hands, sometimes I have been hurt and paid for it with my blood.

For whom? Why?

THURSDAY, SEPTEMBER 4, 1941

HOLD ON!

[*In the Yiddish edition, this section and the following one are placed at the end of September 4, but Kruk's table of contents corrects the order.*]

Today at work, a piece of paper was put in my hand. I read it; it was written in Polish by a Christian who works with me. Passing through with a heavy load, he thrust this at me.

I read: the Germans are taking such a beating that everything happening today around us looks like their last gasp. Hold on. We must hold out. . . .

I'm holding on, comrade; I'm holding on, friend—hold out! . . .

My friend Comrade Erna, whom I visited for a moment to find out how she was, greeted me with kisses and cried like a baby:

"I'm scared, I'm frantically scared; if you can't help me, at least stay in touch with me. Drop by. I can't move about and you can do it better. . . ."

I looked at the awful situation of the helpless person, my comrade, my close co-worker, and with a heavy heart, I assured her: I will be with her, I'll stay in touch with her.

Comrade Pati [Kremer] asks me to drop in on her. But it is risky. How can I do it? Nevertheless, tomorrow, I'll go.[106]

Panic. Terror. Dreadful helplessness!

Where do you get the strength to hold out? Where do you get the nerves to bear it?

Masses of Poles are fired from work. A lot of them are arrested and sent to Łukiszki. All the Polish employees of City Hall are released from their jobs.

Today a notice was issued that Jews must hand over all their property immediately to the police precinct: money, gold, silver, and valuables.

The Jews do bring a lot. Others hand in the completed questionnaires. They hold on to their property as a piece of their life, and they stay with it for the time being. . . .

I CONSOLE MYSELF

[My comrades] Grisha [Yashunski] and [Yoyel] Fish[man] were accidentally saved from being dragged off with the Jewish Committee.

At least a small consolation in the great misfortune.

Another consolation: my wife, who is now in the Soviet Union, released from exile, is probably enjoying the right of all interned Polish citizens. If she did not volunteer for the Polish army, she is at least granted an apartment and food.[107]

On English and Soviet radio [it was announced] that the arrested and interned Polish citizens were in camps maintained by the Polish Red Cross.

So, it's good that she'll have a little piece and quiet now. Good that at least she will finally be freed and saved.

THE FIRST MESSAGES FROM PONAR

With trembling hands, I write the words. All I have heard, all I have written here is hardly a fraction of what [. . .]

[*Page 117 of the journal is missing.*]

106. At the time, Pati Kremer lived at Węglowa 12, about half a mile from Kruk's home at Kijowska Street 4.

107. The news had reached the Vilna Ghetto that Polish citizens in Soviet camps were released, but no one knew their situation. The release was the result of the so-called Sikorski Amnesty, an agreement between the Polish government-in-exile in London and the government of the Soviet Union, stipulating that all Polish citizens be released from Soviet prisons and camps and that those who had been sent into exile in "free" villages be allowed to leave those places. (The agreement was named for General Sikorski, prime minister of the Polish government-in-exile.)

OUT OF THE GRAVE!

It sounds like an echo from the other world. Indeed, that is what it is. What I describe here is truly a scream from the grave. But the people we shall hear about really do come out of the grave after the execution and have reached the Jewish hospital in Vilna.

The persons I'm talking about are related to our entry of September 4—the first information from Ponar.

Through friends and efforts, I gained access to a few of the six who came from Ponar.

The 11-year-old child is Yudis Trojak of Szawelska Street 11, apartment 26. She has undergone an operation, and I find her frightened and weak on a hospital bed.

WHAT DOES YUDIS TROJAK TELL?

Of the whole family—mother, father, three boys, and two girls—the only ones left are our narrator Judith and her father, who works in a peat bog in Rzesza. And one brother who escaped with the Bolsheviks in time.

How did it happen?

On Sunday, September 1, there was a commotion; what the commotion was, she doesn't know; she knows only that people were talking about events on Glezer Street. The next day, she learned that not far from their house, a lot of people were taken. Everybody gathered in a neighbor's apartment and everyone brought news of the events. At about 8 in the morning, Lithuanians suddenly appeared and ordered everybody to get dressed and go down to the courtyard. There they were lined up in rows.

> The janitor took everyone's keys to their apartments and then they took us from there to jail. We stayed in jail from Monday to Tuesday.
>
> On Tuesday morning, they led us all out into the jail yard, and all were sure that we would be released. But an order came to leave all our belongings and get into the waiting trucks. Traveling in the covered trucks, a woman saw that we were riding through a forest. Later we heard shooting. A wailing arose. We didn't understand what was happening with the men because they were led away on foot.
>
> When we got out of the trucks, we were taken to a forest, among sand hills, and there we waited.

Earlier, the child tells, the men were taken. Only Lithuanians took care of that. All day long, they heard shots. There were a lot of quarrels; people cried. "Not until 5 in the afternoon did they take the 10 of us. From there, we walked about five minutes. They blindfolded us and stood us in front of a pit." When I asked her how she could see the pit with blindfolded eyes, she laughed cunningly: "I adjusted the cloth like this so I could see. . . . There in the pit lay a lot of dead bodies, whole mountains of them!"

[*Here a few sentences are probably missing.*]

She was dragged out of the grave by a woman. Five or six women gathered there, all of them wounded, all of them emerging from the mass grave. On the road, they came on a Lithuanian who asked them where they were going. They replied that they were hurrying to the city, and, scared that he would turn them in, they set off for the forest, in the opposite direction. There they came to a Lithuanian's house. Some stayed there until the next day and some went on. "I and the woman who dragged me out of the grave, and a few others, stayed there overnight. The next day, a peasant woman took us to the city." From there, she came to the hospital where she was operated on.

Now her arm is crippled and she doesn't know if she'll be able to move it.

The doctors say that her arm will heal in a few months. The bullet went into her left arm under the armpit.

WHAT DOES THE SECOND GIRL TELL?

The second one is Pesye Schloss, 16 years old, who lived at Strashun 9.

She tells: on September 2, at about 4 in the afternoon, the Lithuanians came to their home, ordered them to come along, and didn't allow them to take anything with them. All they permitted was a package of food. They were taken to Łukiszki. They stayed there until four in the morning. Then they were ordered to dress, ostensibly to be taken to work. They were led out to the prison yard on foot. From there, the men marched ahead, the women behind. The children were taken away and loaded onto trucks. They got to the place only at about 10 in the morning.

> Few people knew that we were in Ponar, and few imagined what they were going to do with us there. But we saw it with our own eyes, as the shootings were taking place no more than 200 steps from us. The men were numbed with blows to the head and only later were they shot. There were whole mountains of people lying. They all surrendered, obeying orders. All the work was done by the Lithuanians. They were supervised by one German.
>
> Groups of 10 people were led to the place of the executions. Early in the morning, there was a lamentable weeping. Later, people "calmed down," got used to it, and made less commotion.

The narrator came to the execution in the very last group of 10. It was already sunset. She walked to the grave with 5 relatives. They were ordered to blindfold their eyes and hold hands. Like that, in a row of 10. Then they were shot. She got a bullet in the arm, a bullet that came to her as a "legacy" from her mother. The bullet went through the mother, who held her arm behind her, as if she wanted to protect her. But the soldier noticed she was alive; he took off her shoes and put a bullet in her foot. She thinks she lay in the grave for no longer than 15 or 20 minutes. When she woke up, she pulled herself out of her mother's arm, and then she heard talking. She saw a woman with a child. Four persons gathered. One wasn't wounded at all and went to the city right away. "The three of us," she says, "went off toward a village." There they spent the night. One Lithuanian gave them milk, another washed their wounds. The next morning, the Lithuanian woman took all three of them to the city and thus they came to the hospital.

This is the sum total: on Thursday, July 26, the Snatchers took her brother. They dragged her father away somewhat later. The continuation was what happened to her and her mother. She is left with a brother, and there is a sister she doesn't know anything about.

[*Some lines are missing, which probably contain more testimony from those who had been saved from Ponar.*]

[. . .] so far were recorded and certainly with regard to what I must record today. I don't know if I will ever live to see these lines, but if anyone anywhere comes upon them, I want him to know this is my last wish: let the words someday reach the living world and let people know about it from eyewitness accounts.

Can the world not scream?

Can history never take revenge?

If the heavens can open up,[108] when should that happen if not today?

The dreadful thing is hard to describe. The hand trembles, and the ink is bloody. Is it possible that all those taken out of here have been murdered, shot in Ponar?

Six wounded people, including a 12-year-old child, lie in the Jewish hospital. They all tell: they shot us with machine guns. In the ditch lay thousands of dead bodies. Before being shot, they took off their clothes, their shoes. The peasants who brought the people to the hospital tell the same thing. The fields reek with the stench of the dead bodies. . . . A few crawl out of there, and a few drag themselves to villages. Six of these few are now in the Jewish hospital. As I write these lines, a 12-year-old child is lying on the operating table, and they are taking a bullet out of her arm. The child mentions names of those she saw shot. . . .

A woman dragged herself to a peasant and asked him to take her to the Jews. After what she saw and after all her loved ones were shot in front of her eyes, she considered her life worthless. But she wanted the Jews to know, and that's the only thing that led her to the peasant.

Let the Jews know!! . . .

It is hard to find out how many were shot. We have to wait for that. Now I understand the behavior of our German[109] toward us, his workers. For the past two days, he has warned our leaders that we shouldn't walk around in the streets and

108. To accept our supplication. According to Jewish folklore, the heavens open once a year, at the end of the holiday of Sukkoth.

109. I.e., the supervisor of the place where Kruk worked.

that we should sleep at work. The Jewish workers have been sleeping in our center (HKP)[110] for two nights. Apparently he knew about the horror and didn't want us to fall victim too. . . .

How can you write about all this? How can you collect your thoughts?

If heaven is heaven, it should start pouring down lava; let all that is still alive be washed away once and for all. Let a greater world destruction than this one come—let a new world rise on the ruins!

"Arise ye wretched of the earth . . ."[111]

It's quiet in my house now, as if a dead body were laid out here. In fact, a lot of dead bodies lie here; none of them weeps, nobody talks, nobody comments.

It is pitch black in the middle of the day. . . .

What is there to talk about?

Whom to complain about?

Whom to argue with?

Horror upon horror, dread upon dread!

SEPTEMBER 5 [1941]

THE BURIAL DEPARTMENT IS OPENED

As we know, on [September] 2, after the 16 men of the Judenrat were taken, all the rooms of the Judenrat building, at Strashun 6, were sealed, including the Burial Department.

For a few days now, corpses have been lying around and cannot be buried.

Nevertheless, after many efforts on our part, the Lithuanian Burakas,[112] commissioner for Jewish affairs at City Hall, came to Strashun 6 today and opened the office of the Burial Department, thus allowing the department to carry on with its work.

[*Several lines are missing.*]

He declared that there is in fact no [Jewish] Committee [Judenrat] now, that the entire issue is not yet clarified, and that he will make a special announcement about the situation.

110. HKP is the abbreviation for *Heereskraftpark,* one of the most important units the Jews worked in. The German management of HKP took the workers of their unit and their families out of the ghetto and lodged them in Subocz in the former "cheap houses" housing project. That unit lasted until 1944, almost until the Red Army captured Vilna, and the Jews considered it an excellent workplace.

111. The first line of the "Internationale."

112. The following item appeared in the Lithuanian newspaper *Naujoji Lietuva* (The New Lithuania), no. 19, August 24, 1941: "F. Burakas was appointed Commissioner for Jewish Affairs in Vilna. His office is in the municipal administration building, Dominikańska St. 2, Room 51" (YIVO Archive, Kaczerginski-Sutzkever Collection).

On Wednesday, September 3, another delegation called on Burakas, and he again replied that the situation was not yet clarified. On that occasion, they explained to him that the cemetery had not been in operation for several days. There were corpses that could not be buried because the Burial Department was in Straszun 6 and the building was sealed. He answered that the Burial Department would be reopened on Thursday.

On Thursday morning, the department was in fact opened.

On the same day, a delegation called on the mayor. The reception was especially polite, even friendly. He hinted that the Lithuanians were not responsible for what was happening; it was purely a German matter. He also declared that he was making great efforts to release Dr. Wygodzki, unfortunately without result; that he was continuing his efforts and that he had experienced great unpleasantness in the matter. . . . He is helpless.

When asked what would happen to the Judenrat, he replied:

"There will be a Judenrat."

When asked about a ghetto:

"There must be a ghetto. . . . "

This is the chronicle of the events.

The Liquidation of the Judenrat and the Following Events: According to September 2

MORE INFORMATION ABOUT THE EVENTS IN PONAR

On Wednesday, the 3rd, four slightly wounded women came to the Jewish hospital. They didn't come with peasants, as was said, but on foot. They told [the following story]:

They were taken from Lidzki [Street] to prison and from there to Ponar. On the spot [in Ponar], a group of Lithuanians, commanded by Germans, started shooting them with rifles. They were shot from behind as they walked. Some of them were told to sit on the edge of a ravine and were shot from behind. All the women and children were killed. When asked how many people might have been there, one of them replied several thousand, others a few hundred.

In the hospital, there is a woman who says that her four children were shot right in front of her eyes. . . .

Today, a fifth person came to the hospital. This person also confirms everything chronicled here.

ONE CONTRADICTION SUPERSEDES ANOTHER

Characteristic of this week is that, on Tuesday, the news appeared in the press that a registration of Jewish property would be carried out between the first and the eighth of the month. Two days later, on Thursday, an announcement was posted that Jewish property must be turned over immediately. All local and foreign currency, money, gold, silver, jewels, precious stones, merchandise and [. . .] roundups.

One order contradicts the other!

A registration form that the Judenrat was to distribute to the population indicates that people are allowed to keep up to 100 rubles. Now, people are ordered to turn over every last cent. Not until the second day did the precincts announce that people can have up to 300 rubles. . . .

Because everyone has until today to turn in the registration forms, the time for walking in the streets has been extended to 5 P.M.

They say on good authority that house searches will be made starting today.

GHETTO

The whole city is shaken. Everyone has forgotten the recent bloodbath, and people are already trembling about a new decree—ghetto![113]

They say that sometime soon there will be an order for a ghetto. Incidentally, I know from reliable sources that today meetings were held about a Jewish ghetto.

Somebody comes with information that all residents of the Fourth Precinct must leave their apartments tonight.

Somebody else says that at about 6 this evening searches were taking place on Ogrodowa [Street].

I also learn that a neighbor from a nearby street sent a note to someone in my courtyard, saying that there they were ordered to pack up and go to the ghetto.

Even before 6 P.M., people started running from the Fourth Precinct to friends and relatives in other precincts. A woman from Kwaszelna Street came to our courtyard.

At about eight in the evening, I learn that there is an order in the street that all owners of horses and carts must appear with their full team at the lumberyard at 5 o'clock tomorrow morning.

People rack their brains. Why horses and wagons from all Vilna? Who has to be transported?

Nobody will sleep tonight.

At 8:30, the *Upravdom*[114]—by the way, a fine and dignified Pole—shows up and says that all the Jews who live in the Fourth Precinct are being taken to the ghetto. The Jewish quarter of the city center has been designated for the Jewish ghetto. First of all are included the streets from which the Jews have been dragged out, that is, Glezer, Strashun, Szawelska, etc. If this is true (unfortunately I can-

113. At the time, there were already Jewish ghettos in the major cities of Poland, such as Warsaw and Łódź.

114. A Soviet term for the manager of a building nationalized by the Soviets—actually, a concierge. The Upravdom—who was usually a non-Jew—was in charge of registration books and generally supervised the residents.

not go into the street because it is too late), it means that we are finally going into the ghetto and that the ghetto will be in the city center.

I must wait until tomorrow morning for an answer to that horrible question.

A night like a year!

THE HEAD IS SPINNING

The people who are dearest to me in Vilna are in the Fourth Precinct. On Kwaszelna Street live my friend Marek[115] with his family and my friend Eydl.[116] Daniel[117] and Erna also live there. What's happening now with the old lady, my friend Pati [Kremer], and with Grisha [Yashunski] and Leyke?[118]

Where will they be dragged off to? Where will I meet them? Will I ever meet them?

Better stop thinking. But how?

It is 11:30 at night. Everyone is awake. My house borders the district of the Fourth Precinct. I listen to the nocturnal silence. Maybe I'll hear something. Neighbors go from door to door and don't know what to do with themselves.

Maybe pack? Pack what?

In the street, I hear shots.

My friends, where are you? What's happening to you now? Will I ever see you again?

The hours drag on like years! . . .

SATURDAY, SEPTEMBER 6, 1941

THE HISTORIC DAY—WE GO TO THE GHETTO

(6:30 A.M.–7:00 A.M.–12:00 noon[119])

It is now 5 in the morning. Through the night, we all waited. Waited and waited. So far, nothing has happened.

115. Marek Kozik, Kruk's friend from Warsaw.

116. Eydl Feinsilber (née Segalowicz), wife of Bundist activist Avrom Feinsilber, who was arrested and sent off by the Bolsheviks (and who eventually moved to New York). She was a teacher in the TSISHO (Yiddish secular) schools. During the liquidation of the ghetto, she and her son Henekh were sent to Ponar or Majdanek. For her biography, see *Teachers' Memorial Book* 1954:282–283.

117. Daniel Augenfeld, a Bundist activist from Warsaw. He survived the war and moved to Montreal.

118. Leyke Glezer, later the wife of Grisha Yashunski. She was an activist in the Vilna Tsukunft organization and in the Bund. She survived the war and lived afterward in Warsaw and Paris.

119. This heading may be partially incorrect. According to the entry, the last section was recorded not at noon but at two in the afternoon.

At 7:30 in the morning, it is as if nothing has happened; we must go to work. No one can say what happened here during the night. Only after 6 in the morning may a Christian woman go out and bring the first news.

One of the most anguished nights I have ever experienced is past. What kinds of nights are still to come? . . .

Outside, I hear carts hurrying by—to whom and for what are they moving?

Almost all the tenants of my house are awake. Now that it is light, I see: every once in a while, a face appears at one window or another, looking out into the courtyard with terrified eyes.

The dog barks, everyone comes to the window. . . .

The janitor sweeps the courtyard, and terrified glances are cast again at the windows. . . .

Every rustle makes you tremble!

Yesterday, September 5, it was two years since I left my wife, my home, my loved ones, and the child, my brother's son Henyo.

Recent events upset even my equanimity. Unfortunately, yesterday I forgot the sad anniversary. My departure from Warsaw has not yet been described. I have already recorded the parting from my brother. Today is not the time to write about those events. Today's agenda presents a brand-new event—a ghetto, or maybe the final road to infinity.

I want to hope that everything will turn out well. It is hard to think that this is the end.

My neighbors are happy: another night in their bed . . . their own home . . . among their loved ones. . . .

Money and valuables must be turned over. Furniture is taken. Yesterday they collected linens, took whatever they liked. Now taking is not the issue; just to live to take the most necessary things with us and, at best, to be thrown out like a dog in the middle of the night—alone, without money, without things—into the ghetto.

Maybe it's good that I'm alone now. My loved ones don't have to share my grief and anguish. Maybe when I meet them again, they'll be all ears when I tell them about it.

Maybe . . .

Half Past Six in the Morning. Ghetto.

You might think that, in spite of everything, going to the ghetto would be considered a terrible act of isolation, a curse of fear and terror. But no. Vilna accepted the announcement of the ghetto, cool, calm, and collected.

Going to the ghetto did not take place by order, as in many cities. Here it was done much more simply. They came before dawn today and gave half an hour to pack and take whatever you can. Sadism has reached such a stage that just yesterday (as I mentioned), all wagons with their horses and drivers were ordered to appear at the lumberyard at 5 this morning. The purpose: people should not be able to transport their belongings. . . . Furthermore, today, on the eve of the eviction from home, flocks of wagons drove in and, right in front of the inhabitants, who were already gathered in the courtyard, the last pieces of furniture were dragged out of their abandoned homes. . . .

Seven in the Morning

As soon as I hear that we are to be driven into a ghetto, I go out to see my friends. The police stop me. I make an effort, invent some pretexts, and finally get to Kwaszelna St. 23.[120] They don't let me go in the house. But everyone is already in the courtyard with their bundles. There I meet Comrade Erna. She kisses me tearfully but is sober and cheerful. We agree to meet in the ghetto. A soldier on guard tells me that the ghetto will be in the Jewish center. I am informed that Kwaszelna Street is assigned to Rudnicka , and so is Chopin. Christians come to their neighbors, but this time they are frightened; they want to help somehow and are ready to carry things away and hide them. On Makowa Street, I see in the distance how all the people from Develtov's Courtyard[121] are already in the street with their bundles—they will probably move off soon.

Men are dressed in two or three coats, women wear winter coats, etc. In the street, you see a few Germans bringing the men back from work to help the women move to the ghetto. A few Germans even come with trucks and take a lot of things.

Everyone is impressed by this humanitarianism. . . .

At about eight in the morning, it is 100 percent clear that we are going to the ghetto.

9 in the Morning

Groups of Jews are being carried off. Everyone is padded; they wear several coats, they drag packs, they take things on baby carriages. People make improvised litters carried by two and cart things on them. People push wheelbarrows. The picture is awful.

Christians come to help—friends, comrades, fellow workers. Others come to buy for almost nothing; others come like jackals—already waiting for Jewish belongings. Good old friends appear, a former nurse of a Jewish child, a former

120. Kwaszelna 21/23, or Kletzkin's Yard (at the corner of Kijowska Street, half a block from Kruk's home), was a large courtyard with several four- to five-story buildings, including the B. Kletzkin publishing and printing house, which published the best of Yiddish literature. Residents there included Zelig Kalmanowicz, Arkady Kremer (who died in 1936), Pati Kremer, the teachers Dr. Abraham Hrushovski and Dvoyra Freidkes-Hrushovski, and other Vilna intellectuals.

121. Several connected yards between Kwaszelna and Makowa Streets, bordering the yard mentioned above.

maid. Some of them also come to help, and some take a legacy from the living. . . .

The groups drag themselves with their heavy coats, sweating.

Dogs, as if they knew something, are barking and howling. Thus they take leave of their former masters. . . .

People get information from the street: the ghetto is enlarged, Zawalna is also part of the ghetto, as are the side of the Jewish hospital, a part of Niemiecka, and probably also Trocka Street. Our Upravdom says that our house has two more days because we don't have to move to the ghetto until the eighth of the month. A little later he will know precisely where the residents of our house will be transferred. . . .

Chopin Street was taken away.[122] They go to Rudnicka.

2 in the Afternoon

We're all in a state of anticipation. Trade is feverish here, people sell everything for pennies. Crowds of buyers come. . . .

News from the street:

On Bosaczkowa,[123] people were given five minutes to pack. They drag bundles wrapped in sheets; some just drag the bundles over the stones. Soldiers drive them like cattle.

People say that going into the ghetto is like entering a darkness. Thousands stand in line and are driven into a cage. People are driven, people fall down with their sacks, and the screams reach the sky. The mournful trek of being driven out of your home into the ghetto lasts for hours.

Meanwhile, the landlady has sold her chairs. Today, we eat lunch here (perhaps for the last time), while sitting on the packed bundles. . . .

The landlord orders:

"Eat up everything, don't leave a thing. Eat and drink and don't leave anything. . . ."

122. Chopin Street is the continuation of Kijowska Street, two buildings away from Kruk's home at Kijowska 4.

123. A marketplace near Zawalna Street.

CHAPTER 3

THE VILNA GHETTO

SEPTEMBER 7, 1941 – FEBRUARY 17, 1942

SEPTEMBER 20, 1941

[*For reasons that will become obvious, the events of September 5–18 were reconstructed only on September 20. Because Kruk provides the dates of the events he describes, the diary entries for this period seem to be out of order.*]

VILNA GHETTO I

It has been 14 days since I've held a pen. The past two weeks have been not weeks for me, but years. Since that last day when I wrote that we expect a lot of news—mainly that people are talking about a ghetto—ever since then, we have gone through a dreadful hell. Everything we had lived through and gone through here is child's play compared to what these last 14 days have brought. Now, after an interruption of two weeks, everything that can be said here will be poor and pale compared to what happened.

For the entire two weeks, I haven't held a pen in my hand because it was truly physically impossible. Tired and exhausted from everything around. The pen fell out of my hand, and my brain wasn't strong or calm enough to think up an idea. Let us hope that from now on, I will do everything possible to record my notes.

Before I went into the ghetto, I buried all the entries I had made until then, and all my manuscripts. I have only a part of them with me, and I hope that in time I will pull them all together to form a whole.

I shall reconstruct everything that happened:

On the Events between September 8 **and** 20

On Friday, the 5th, the whole city said that any day now we would be driven into a ghetto. That night, an announcement was posted that all carts and horses must be brought before dawn on Saturday to the lumber market. The news spread through the city that the Jewish population would be taken out "somewhere" that same night. "Somewhere" meant to the places where they had recently taken the residents of the Jewish quarter—Glezer St., Strashun, etc.[1]

1. On August 31–September 1, the Jews of those streets were taken to Ponar.

The night was restless and anguished. In tens of thousands of homes, no one undressed. Some sat, packed and waiting. At about five in the morning, the scraping of the carts on the cobblestones was heard. At six in the morning, no one was allowed out of the houses. By 7 in the morning, it was clear—ghetto!

The entire Jewish quarter was closed off. In some of the streets, people were packing; some were already led away. Where was the ghetto? Where were the people taken? Nobody knew anything.

I have already written about it, but I have to do it afresh.

I succeeded in sneaking out of my house and went to my friends on Kwaszelna Street. Lithuanian militia stopped me a few times, but I did get to my loved ones: in the courtyard were bundles of things. Everyone was dressed in winter clothes. People were wearing galoshes, two or three winter coats, each person wore more than the last. In short, you wanted just to take as much as you could. The inhabitants packed in about an hour, they would soon leave their homes, taking only what they were strong enough to carry.

Where are they going?

The soldiers say to Rudnicka. The inhabitants are calm. People are crying somewhere, but generally those are just some of the women who find it hard to leave their warm, cozy homes. On the whole, the news about the ghetto is accepted as something long expected. Often as a relief that people will finally be with their own and not exposed to all sorts of provocations.

I bid farewell to them all, sure that we will soon meet, and that anyway, the ghetto is in the center of Jewish Vilna.

All the inhabitants of Develtov's Courtyard on Makowa Street are already in the street, sitting on their bundles. More people in winter clothing and more of the same. Now and then, a sob is heard. In general, people accept the decree calmly.
[*Pages 124 and 125 are partially destroyed, consisting of half lines.*]

My courtyard is waiting, all is [. . .]
The nervousness is because here [. . .]
will go. Suddenly there is a [. . .]
several ghettos. And if there are already several, who knows [. . .]
loved ones.

All the inhabitants are already packed so when even [. . .
A few mi]nutes will suffice. . . .

In many homes people constructed litters [. . .]
to carry as many things as possible. Some pack children's carriages [and others stuff it] all in mattress covers.

From the street comes news:

The carts are used to take away the Christian [population that has previously] lived in the area where the ghetto is to be.

Jews are not allowed to use any vehicles to [transport their] things.

In the ghetto, you are granted 2 [square] meters a person! . . .

About 2 in the Afternoon

In the streets, groups are led from all sides toward [the ghetto]. Everywhere the same picture: loaded with clothes, people drag bundles, people strain beyond their strength. They help each other. The "Gentile world" looks at it all and doesn't understand. Germans look and are amazed.

3 in the Afternoon

Two Lithuanian soldiers come into the courtyard and order people to get ready. Meanwhile, many Christians come and take away a lot of things from their Jewish friends to keep until "better times." Some of the Christians take things out to sell, and in a few [minutes] they are turned into money. Thus the Jews get "travel expenses" on their way. Christians perform genuine wonders, often great wonders.

We eat our last lunch. The landlady managed to sell the chairs—six chairs for 40 rubles a chair. The sale is really a pittance. Therefore, we sit not on chairs but on [the bundles] with which we will soon leave for a new ghetto exile. The [mood] at lunch is peculiar—everyone is silent, as before a funeral.

Meanwhile, the inhabitants drag out [. . .]
each one spreads out his little bit of poverty on the road [. . .]

Devoted a life, worked, toiled, [and remained with a little] bundle in hand [. . .]

All that is left is a little bundle on your back [. . .]

"With the traveling stick in hand"—and a young man takes up the song:

"Without a home, without a land . . . "[2]

Morris Rosenfeld's poetry sounds like a voice from the other world.

I am loaded from head to foot. A backpack [. . .]
tied with straps, to be able to [. . .
of our] courtyard get the final order [. . .]
We have to go through Makowa Street, through [. . .]

"It means we are going" [. . .]

"It means" [. . .]

THE MARCH INTO THE GHETTO

When the people moved, a [. . .]
was heard [. . .
The street is] thick with Aryan onlookers. Some pass by and [do not] want to [. . .]
the gloomy picture. Superficially it makes a [. . .]

2. From the popular song "Goles-marsh" (March of exile), by the American Yiddish poet Morris Rosenfeld (1862–1923): "With the wanderer's staff in hand, / With no home and with no land, / No friend or savior on the way, / No tomorrow, no today, / Chased, not suffered in our plight, / Ne'er a day where spent a night, / Always pain will knock, knock, knock, / Always walk, walk, walk, / Always stride, stride, stride, / While your strength can still abide" (translated by Barbara Harshav and Benjamin Harshav).

Everyone has taken more than they have the strength [. . .]
human mass. Everyone is soaked with sweat. People just can't drag [. . .]
Some find a way of moving it: 10 steps forward, leave [a bundle there], go back again for the rest, another 10 steps [forward, and again go back]. Thus they drag themselves in installments. . . .

Two neighbors drag along with an overloaded wheelbarrow. They [drag and it] turns over, and everything falls in the mud. . . .

Others, unable to carry, scrape their bundles on the bare pavement. Just so as not to leave them on the street.

The Lithuanian army is spread out in the street; soldiers push, people drag along, everyone is electrified, irritated, exhausted and . . . weeping.

German soldiers hunt with Leica cameras and photograph it all.

MY KNEES BUCKLE

I feel that my legs won't carry me anymore; a Lithuanian soldier [consoles?] [. . .]
Downhill, from Makowa through Nowogródzka in [. . .]
Dark, the cameras working away, standing [. . .]
I with my last strength on the right [. . .]
the face. But I don't raise it and fall down [. . .]
German stands ready with his camera. I am soaked [. . .]
among the four valises, the big rucksack, and packed full [. . .]
comrades help me. Sima, the daughter, a strong, healthy girl [. . .]
and hurries with it in front. My brother-in-law cannot go on walking [. . .]
I [pick up] one of his bundles and drag myself on [. . .]
the leica is ready and waiting for an opportunity
In the narrow little Lidzki Alley, I feel that the m[ood] grows [. . .]
too many police. They are driven here with more [. . .]
The rain grows stronger, darkness falls [. . .]
Lidzki is lined with a narrow lane of po[lice . . .]
A narrow neck of a sack through which you [are] fa[lling]

LIDZKI ALLEY

On Lidzki, the neck becomes narrower and [. . .
Everyone] feels—he has fallen into a jam [. . .]
great nerve. The street is really filled, everything [. . .
people are] lost and look for each other. Everyone is entangled [. . .]
finally to get to the end of the horrible way.

GHETTO

Finally we dragged ourselves to the place. The gate of the ghetto [. . .]
In your heart. Ghetto! . . . But meanwhile, people tear [. . .]
People from all corners of the city. Everyone is pushing [. . .]

loses the other. It is dark and [people shout out the] names of the ones they've lost. It is already [. . .]
My way from Kijowska Street to Strashun [. . .]
dead and exhausted, I [landed . . .]

[. . .] in the courtyard of Strashun St. 13. The courtyard is crammed with people and bundles. I estimated about 1,000 people, old, young, women and children, infants, etc. I sat down in a corner of the courtyard not far from the water faucet. Everyone comes here to fetch water, to rinse their weeping eyes, to quench their thirst, or just to wash their hands. Thus, exhausted, amid the hurly-burly of hundreds, I fell asleep.

At about eleven at night, I woke up. A heavy rain was falling, and I had slept like a corpse. Wet from the rain, wet and sweaty from my "stroll" [to] the ghetto, I was very cold. My brother-in-law had started looking for a place where we could hide, and we went into a damp cellar. That was already full, too. Everything was taken. . . . Nevertheless, we somehow made do, and I slept soundly until dawn in my sweaty linen in a wet cellar.

SUNDAY, SEPTEMBER 7 [1941]

THE FIRST NIGHT IN THE GHETTO

Such nights must be remembered. Soaked in my own sweat, at about half past eleven at night, I fell back to sleep. The wet cellar didn't bother me. The hard bundles I was half sitting, half lying on didn't disturb my sound, drunken sleep. A child cried in its mother's lap, a woman wept to herself, men were busy with their bundles—none of this had any influence on me; I woke up only temporarily and fell back into a heavy, weary sleep, as after a hard day of work.

Dawn. Everything is stuck to my body. My shirt has dried, but now, dry and stiff, it sticks to my body. A strange dawn cold grips my body.

"Don't give in!" shout all my limbs. "Don't allow bad thoughts!" the survival instinct dictates. . . .

I leave the wet cellar to find out where I am in the world. The world? . . . The world is steeped in a damp autumn morning. As I emerge from the cellar, my friend Rivke Epstein[3] catches sight of me. She envies me for at least having a cellar. She herself was sitting with hundreds of others in the courtyard, without even a place to hide from the rain. From the world!

I am not in this world. I am in a cage that was once the entrance from Zawalna

3. One of the popular Bundist activists of Vilna, particularly in the movement of professionals. Epstein, born in 1884, joined the Bund at an early age and remained a member until she was killed during the liquidation of the Vilna Ghetto. She was a sister of Lazar Epstein of New York, the famous labor activist. For her biography, see Hirsz Abramowicz in *Generations* 2:103–107.

to Strashun Street. But the entrance there is blocked by a wall of boards. On the other side, at the entrance from Szawelska to Strashun, is another wall. Strashun St. is nailed shut on both sides. On the Szawelska side, there is an opening a meter wide, where people are still allowed in as into a cage. Jews from the city are still dragging themselves, and fragmentary and half-drunk regards come to us from the street:

On the street, you see bundles with belongings thrown away.

You come upon groups going in the opposite direction from the ghetto. . . .

Lidzki Alley looks like the aftermath of a disaster. . . .

It is still very early, but Strashun St., nailed shut, looks like an anthill. The courtyards are crammed; people creep out of holes like mice. The streets are flooded full of people, and people are pushed in from the city regularly and incessantly. . . .

A GHETTO ADMINISTRATION IS CREATED

In the presence of Engineer Fried, Attorney Milkanowicki, Attorney G. Yashunski and Y. Fishman, a meeting of the former staff [of the Judenrat] from before the ghetto period was called. About twenty staff members attended the meeting, including Notes, Solomon Gens,[4] [Khayim] Tropido,[5] Słucki, Trocki, R. Kahane, M. Giligitsh, and M. Emes.

Engineer Fried called on those assembled to continue on the staff. He added that, for the time being, nobody should hope for big wages. Almost everyone decided to stay on and help set up the ghetto administration.

[*A few pages of the original are missing here.*]

[. . .] The homes in the entire area were sealed off because, as we know, the residents were driven out a few days ago. . . .

What a nice piece of work. First one part was vacated, and now they throw us in as a second part.

Why the exchange? . . .

G. [Grisha Yashunski], a member of the former Judenrat, announces that he is attempting to open the wall between Strashun and Szawelska Streets to create a free passage between Rudnicka, Zawalna, Szpitalna, and Strashun Streets.

Meanwhile . . .

Meanwhile, I learn that everyone who was behind me last night, from Zawalna through Lidzki to the gate of the ghetto, was driven into the gates of Lidzki

4. Brother of Jacob Gens, the future head of the ghetto. Later Solomon Gens was in the ghetto police.

5. Administrator of the Kovno newspaper *Yidishe Shtime*. In Kovno, Tropido was active in the General Zionist movement, in the Et Livnot (Time to Build) faction. In the Vilna Ghetto, he was the representative of Et Livnot in the Zionist umbrella organization. Later he directed the Food Supply Department of the Vilna Ghetto.

and late at night was driven out of there in an unknown direction. People console themselves: maybe to Łukiszki. . . .[6]

Meanwhile, I realize that yesterday, before I went into the ghetto gate, my bag and rucksack were taken from me by my landlady's daughter, and I haven't found my landlords and I don't have my things either. So, I remain with a small valise without linen, without clothing, without belongings—once again, like two years ago, naked as Adam. . . .

Meanwhile, I meet hundreds and hundreds. People hug and kiss one another—just to see one another alive. . . .

THE FIRST "GOOD MORNING"

Meanwhile, it has already started.

In the courtyard of Strashun 1, someone hanged himself—a young man, Hirshman, who had completed three university degrees.

A woman doctor asked me to locate her husband: last night, he had a heart attack and was taken to the hospital, while she was driven into the ghetto. . . . The wife of Dr. Zeldowicz, of Wileńska 28.

Meanwhile . . .

At night, in two different places in the courtyards of Strashun Street, women had miscarriages. A major manufacturer and merchant, Goldman, died of a heart attack. . . .

Early in the morning, the Lithuanians burst into the ghetto and took 15 men away for work. . . .

Does this mean we won't have any quiet here either? . . .

Various rumors are circulating [about] those snatched from Lidzki and other [streets]. Entire families [were] separated by the event. People say that some of them are still lying on Lidzki [. . .] crammed on Szawelska Street in that part of the ghetto; others, they say, [were taken] to prison. . . .

[*The rest of the page is damaged.*]

[Solo]dukha,[7] a wood merchant, a big tall man, remained here [with his] parents-in-law, a sister, and a four-year-old daughter. His wife, a young [. . .] didn't arrive. He is desperate, the rest of the family were [. . .]

Meanwhile . . .

Meanwhile, those who dragged themselves into the ghetto try to help each other.

Among those lying in a courtyard, someone sets up a Primus stove, and people cook something hot for the children. . . .

At Strashun Street 13, there is a big built-in kettle, and people cook hot soup. . . .

6. Rather than directly to Ponar.

7. Kaczerginski (1947:282) mentions Solodukha, a wood merchant, who was captured in a melina during the liquidation of the ghetto.

"A little hot soup . . ."

People drag wood from a cellar; a Jew, a "former" resident there, prepared a supply of heating material.

A melina is discovered. People carry toiletries out of a cellar: little packets of Vaseline, soap, powder, perfume. Apparently, a toiletries dealer hid part of his shop there. . . .

By now it is noon. People are still coming continuously from the city into the ghetto. Thus people come from Niemiecka Street, even though it's only a hop, skip, and a jump away. They come from more distant places. They bring sick people; they lead old people. People are already getting sick in the ghetto, and doctors offer help on the spot. Others are taken to the hospital. Doctors and nurses distribute hot water in the street. . . .

Soon Grisha [Yashunski] informs me that Murer has established a new Judenrat of five persons, including himself, Engineer Fried, Fishman, Milkanowicki, and Engineer Gukhman.

He says that the wall blocking Strashun Street from Szawelska Street will soon be opened and both parts will be united. When he and I cross the threshold of that wall, we witness a dreadful scene:

There, on the other side, just like here, men look for their wives and wives for their husbands, children ask for their parents and parents look for their children. But it becomes clear that many people have not reached the ghetto. From Lidzki Street and other areas, people were driven to Łukiszki. As the wall is now opened and people are finding each other, the joy is so great that they are crying and laughing at the same time. It means that those who aren't there are, unfortunately, those who were dragged away from Lidzki.

The calculation is that about 6,000 people were dragged off. . . .

Are they just in prison? And from there? . . .

The heart stops with grief.

But everything around here turns like a magic wheel, a kaleidoscope where you can't catch everything all at once. Here you must not grieve too long. If you ponder for too long, you are late. In the meantime, a representative of the Judenrat suggests that I take care of the Mefitsei-Haskalah [Disseminators of Enlightenment][8] Library and obtain permission to occupy one of the library rooms.

THE DISSEMINATORS OF ENLIGHTENMENT LIBRARY

In the good days, that library was a piece of Vilna. It was founded in July 1911 as a division of the Society for the Dissemination of the Enlightenment [among Jews], endured the [oppression of the] tsarist regime, then the war of 1914–1918, and now was examined first by the Lithuanians and finally by the Germans.

8. An organization founded in the nineteenth century in St. Petersburg for spreading education among the Jews of the Pale of Settlement.

At the outbreak of the war in 1939, the library numbered 45,000 books.

[*Page 129 of the journal is missing. What follows are more entries that Kruk made about the first days of the ghetto.*]

September 8 [1941]

A New Proposal

A Preliminary Summary

On the first day of the ghetto, there were five funerals.

A madman stood at the end of Strashun Street, at the corner of Zawalna Street, and started throwing stones over the ghetto fence. A commotion arose, people feared a provocation, and the madman was led away with great pomp to the hospital.

A DOG

He strayed into the ghetto with his owners. Went everywhere with them and didn't leave them for a minute.

A poor dog, could have had a good life in the city, and came with his family to ghetto exile. . . .

PEOPLE KISS EACH OTHER

I meet people. Great joy. Even half-strangers fall on each other and kiss:

Just to be alive! . . .

KHAYKL LUNSKI

It sounds symbolic:

A few days before going into the ghetto, the old, popular librarian Khaykl Lunski[9] returned from prison.

How does this modest, quiet, marginal man belong in prison? The Germans dragged the veteran librarian of the Strashun Library into prison, demanding that he give them the incunabula preserved in the library. He showed where they were hidden and was released.

Thus six incunabula were lost.

Khaykl Lunski, the bibliophile, chronicler of the old [medieval] Jewish ghetto in Vilna, was freed a few days before the entrance into the new ghetto. Apparently, the chronicler of the Vilna Ghetto was to be present at the crossing of the threshold into the brand-new ghetto.

It sounds grotesque!

Meanwhile, a day has passed. The courtyards are full; we are not yet allowed to occupy the apartments because official representatives will come soon and re-

9. Scholar and head librarian of the Strashun Library; he was a well-known figure in Vilna.

move the seals. The ghetto Jews are rotting here for the third night, and nobody is concerned about that.

What will happen next?

RUMORS

Meanwhile people tell of conversations.

[*The end of the page is torn off.*]

[. . .] Does that mean that everything is not yet lost? . . .

People say that all the Jews who worked in the peat bog of Kiena (not far from Vilna) were driven out.[10] The wives who remained in the ghetto were desperate.

TRIVIALITIES

Friend K[11] lives at Strashun Street 6, in the building of the Community Council. The morgue is also there. In the courtyard, they build coffins for Jewish corpses. The Burial Department is in the same courtyard.

Christians from the street come into the ghetto wearing yellow patches, and bringing bread and clothing. Christians cry more than Jews. . . .

Today there was a fire at Lidzki 7. Yesterday, a small fire on Szawelska Street.

Jews are happy: the ghetto is burning. . . .

All the apartments are still sealed. People are not allowed to pry them open. People lie around in the street for the third day. Some don't give a damn about the rules and pry the apartments open. Everything and everybody are fair game. People take over apartments filled with other people's belongings and settle down in them. Some of the closed apartments are opened, some by the police.

OLD PEOPLE

Eighty old people have lain for three days and three nights now in a store on Strashun. Nobody takes care of them. They don't even get the little bit of water distributed in the street. They lie on a stone floor and die of hunger.

CHRISTIANS

Today, at Ostra Brama,[12] there was a prayer in honor of the martyrdom of the Jews. People say that Jews are now bringing in full bundles, which they got in the city as gifts from Christians in the street.

10. Kiena is a small town about 30 kilometers from Vilna. There was a camp there, and several hundred Vilna Jews and 70 Jews from Kiena itself worked in the peat bogs. That camp was liquidated on July 8, 1943, when the Jewish peat bog workers were surrounded by a group of German and Lithuanian soldiers and shot on the spot. For testimony from that camp, see Kaczerginski 1947:151–153.

11. Kruk means himself. He often writes about himself in the third person.

12. The "Pointed Gate"—a gate in the old city wall; also the name of a church attached to it. Over the gate was an icon of the famous Ostrobramska Madonna. When people went through

In the street, at a Maistas,[13] masses of Christians bought packages of meat and distributed them to the Jewish workers marching to the ghetto.

The sympathy of the Christian population, more precisely of the Polish population, is extraordinary.

HELPING THE JEWS

Friends say that German employers of Jews take their Jews into their former homes and help them save whatever they can. Often, a truck filled with Jews' belongings drives into the ghetto.

VARIANT NUMBER 2

This was told by a man who witnessed it:

An elegant gentleman, a Christian, was walking from Antokol alongside a group of Jews. The whole time, the Jews were driven and mocked. Somewhere at a corner, the gentleman made contact with the abusive guards, evidently gave them money, and . . . they started treating the Jews well. Now they are allowed to drag themselves along the sidewalk, walk slowly, not rushing, rest a while, etc. The Christian walks along, watches, and wanders with the group up to the gate of the ghetto. . . .

SEPTEMBER 12, 1941

WHAT DOES GHETTO MEAN?

Friend Kalman[owicz][14] relates: one Jewish woman explains to another: "*Ghetto* comes from the word *get,* divorce, to cut yourself off. We've cut ourselves off from our homes and so now we live in a ghetto. . . ."

INSTEAD OF A CORRECTION

The dates of my last few entries may not be precise. I made the last entries from memory because, as I said, for about three weeks I haven't been able to write. Now I'm only filling in the blanks.

---

the gate, they had to take off their hat, kneel, and cross themselves. Pious Jews used to go far out of their way to avoid the gate.

13. A Lithuanian name for a meat cooperative of the Soviet government.

14. Zelig Hirsh Kalmanowicz (1891–1944), born in Latvia, settled in Vilna in 1929. This famous Jewish scholar was one of the founders of YIVO and editor of its scholarly journal YIVO-bleter. A great deal has been written about Kalmanowicz's activities in the ghetto. Several of his own writings were published in YIVO-bleter in New York, including his "Diary of the Vilna Ghetto" (YIVO-bleter 35:18–92). He perished in Camp Klooga, Estonia.

M. SHALIT

I learn that the writer [Moshe] Shalit[15] has been dragged off.

A RUSSIAN WOMAN IN THE GHETTO

I met a Russian woman in the ghetto. Her husband is a Jew, and she has come here with her husband. . . .

HOLES

People make holes in the walls so they can go from Strashun to the courtyards of Lidzki. The front of Lidzki Street doesn't belong to the ghetto, but the courtyards do. Therefore, people are allowed to make openings so they can use the courtyards from behind. Such openings are made at Lidzki 5 and 7, from Strashun 8 to Lidzki 9, etc.

PHYSICIANS AT WORK

The physicians are active. The street is full of doctors, nurses, etc. They run to help, and they do a lot.

THE TWO GHETTOS: THEIR TOPOGRAPHY AND POPULATION

Now that the borders of the two Vilna Ghettos have been defined, we can talk about them more precisely.

Ghetto 1 consists of these streets: Rudnicka, Dziśnieński, Jatkowa, Szpitalna, Szawelska, and Strashun. Ghetto 2 includes Żydowska, Antokolska, and [. . .] [*Page 133 of the journal is missing. Aside from the streets mentioned here, Ghetto 2 also included Gaon Street, Glezer Street, and the side streets and passages around the Synagogue Yard. It is estimated that about 10,000 Jews lived in Ghetto 2, which existed for only a few weeks. Ghetto 2 was designated for unskilled workers. In reality, it became a transit point for those condemned to death by the Germans. From Ghetto 2, the way led straight to Łukiszki and Ponar.*[16]]

15. Longtime chairman of the Yiddish Writers' Union in Vilna. He was especially creative in the area of regional Jewish history of Vilna and environs. Kaczerginski (1947:215) claims that he was taken to Ponar on July 29, 1941. For a biography and essay on Shalit, see Abramowicz 1958: 186–192.

16. For details about Ghetto 2, see Dworzecki 1948:116–121, 134–137.

Kr[uk] Becomes Director of the Library:
A Post Office Is Initiated, the First Bread Cards Are Distributed
The Ghost of Ponar
Again Ponar
Friend Kr[uk] Tells:

BLOWS INSTEAD OF BREAD

In the past few days, a few members of the Judenrat of Ghetto 2 were beaten up by Germans and Lithuanians who made demands of the Jewish Committee. The committee members refused to carry them out, demanding a written order. The "order" consisted of blows. One member has been in bed for several days.

SCHWEINENBERG

In a space where 4,000 people used to live there are now 29,000. It is no wonder that thousands of residents fill the streets. The low-ranking German officer Schweinenberg, the real boss of both ghettos, can't stand it. That scene annoys him, and he orders the streets cleared. Today, he drove into the ghetto at top speed, running over a woman and a child.

Schweinenberg cooled his sadistic, hot blood:

"He will crush them like worms" . . .

This is the anointed ruler of our ghettos.

SEPTEMBER 15 [1941]

It is still very hard to understand it. Hard to say precisely what they intend by this. Suddenly, the German authorities decided to ease the crowding of the ghetto and took 3,550 persons out, ostensibly transferring them to Ghetto 2. But only 600 persons arrived there. What happened to 2,950 people? . . .

From Strashun St. alone, 1,100 people were taken away. And how many did the other ghetto streets and alleys contribute?

Where are the rest? . . .

What's happening to them now? . . .

HUNGER

People say that there have already been cases of illness resulting from hunger.

Christians come to the ghetto. People say that Christian friends and acquaintances often come. Today a priest came to me, looking for his Jewish friends.

■ ■ ■ ■ ■ ■ ■

SEPTEMBER 16 [1941]

Today the Lithuanians watching the entrance to the ghetto confiscated the food that the workers wanted to bring in as they returned home. The confiscated food was piled in the street [before the gate], and the street was full of food. Aryans from outside grabbed it and were happy. Late at night, the guards changed their minds and ordered the remaining food thrown into the Jewish side of the gates. Here the Jews started grabbing it. Mostly, the Jewish police were in on it.

JEWISH POLICE

Militia. After serving as deputy chief of the militia for three days, Friend H. [Kruk?] went to the chairman of the Judenrat and asked to be released. Why?

The argument about the formation of a militia or a police force ended in favor of a police force. [Jacob] Gens, the police chief,[17] a former captain in the Lithuanian army, and his comrade, [Yosef] Muszkat,[18] a degenerate character, are both trying to set up a police force in the ghetto.

"Beatings. We have to have beatings, otherwise they won't listen to us."

This was the "ideology" of the two chiefs. All arguments of Comrade Kr[uk] about the role of such a militia, if it adopts other methods, didn't do any good. Meanwhile, the two men are enrolling many Betar[19] members in the militia; they enjoy life on the backs of the ghetto residents.

The chairman asked to postpone the resignation. But Kr[uk] does not want to and resigns.

He didn't want to be connected with the administration, especially Betar and

17. In the literature on the Vilna Ghetto, a great deal has been written about the activities of Jacob Gens. Gens, a Lithuanian Jew married to a Lithuanian Christian, was an officer in the Lithuanian army and had been active in the Zionist Revisionist paramilitary organization Brit ha-Hayal in Lithuania. Kruk's diary contains many entries about Gens's role in the ghetto. Before the final liquidation of the ghetto, Gens was shot by the Gestapo. Allegedly, Salek Dessler, another boss of the ghetto police and an open collaborator with the Gestapo, had a hand in that. (For more on Dessler, see the entries of December 26, 1941, and July 11, 1942.)

18. An attorney and Revisionist activist from Warsaw who came to Vilna with the refugees in 1939. He was appointed to a high-ranking position in the ghetto police and became chief of the first police station in the ghetto. He organized the children's brigade, Yeladim, and employed children to spy on the FPO (the United Partisan Organization). He was in one of the last groups sent to Estonia and probably died there.

19. Betar was a radical rightist Zionist paramilitary youth movement affiliated with Jabotinsky's Revisionist Party and hated by the Left as Fascists. The leader of the Polish Betar, Menachem Begin, was arrested near Vilna in 1939 and exiled by the Soviets. Eventually he reached Palestine, became the leader of the Irgun underground, and then Israel's first rightist prime minister.

its chief, Muszkat. In the militia, a unique ethic about the residents developed. You beat them, you steal from them, and you do any possible evil.

A HOUSE — A STREET. A STREET — A CITY

Today the sealed apartments were finally opened. Today we know that, based on the number of people who live in the apartments, we get ninety [square] centimeters per person (? . . .)

They say that every apartment is a street and every street, a city.

This is absolutely true.

A German came from Ghetto 2 with 100 Jews and demanded a place for them in Ghetto 1. Such incidents often happen. Everybody wants to arrange things well for his own Jews. As I said, this happens frequently.

SEPTEMBER 17 [1941]

RUMORS

Very serious rumors are circulating that those who have been sent away are in Jagiełłonów, an estate beyond Ponar.

KASPER-SEREBROVICH'S VISIT TO THE GHETTO

[. . .] a guest came from Kovno. The visitor, one Kasper-Serebrovich,[20] was in the apartment of Police Chief Gens, at Szpitalna 11. A witness told about it: a young, handsome, lively fellow came into the room and, during the visit, insolently tore open the coffers full of things found on Lidzki Street. He took out chocolate, leather gloves, leather, cloth, etc.

When my informant, who was supposed to take the valises with the things to the Judenrat, asked Mr. Gens why he allowed this, Gens answered [with] a wave of his hand—just let him take the things and shut up. . . .

My informant guessed that [he] should take. . . .

[*A few lines are missing here.*]

20. Kruk is mistaken about the name; it is not Kasper-Serebrovich but Kaspi-Serebrovich (in Russian, *Serebrovich* is equivalent to *Silverman* or *Kaspi* in Hebrew). This man left a blot on the history of the ghettos in Kovno and Vilna. Before the war, he was a Hebrew teacher in Rokiškis, where he was active in the Zionist movement, but he often shifted from one party to another. He was a master of intrigue. Eventually, directors of the school where he taught sent him out of town. Later, he was involved in forging documents and went to prison. Because of his relations with the Lithuanian Fascist Tautinikas, he was released. When the Soviets occupied Lithuania, he was re-arrested and released only when the Germans took Kovno. He was an official employee of the Gestapo. For details of his dark role in the ghettos of Kovno and Vilna, see Gar 1948 and Garfunkel 1959. His masters did not reward his devoted service, and he was eventually liquidated.

SEPTEMBER 18 [1941]

THE JEWISH POLICE HAVE A LIVELIHOOD

Jewish police and their business. The "heroism" of the Jewish police and their business has often been mentioned. If you stand at the gate, you take money for letting people bring in a package. If you walk into the city, you bring bundles that Jews left with Christian friends, etc. And you take bribes for this, too. In short, the Jewish police do business. The homes of the Jewish police are full of everything: bread, butter, fat galore.

Really, police work is the best livelihood!

Apropos police, to show what ignoramuses the Jewish police are, I quote an exact copy of a police order:[21]

Police Order
Hereby it is ordered that all residents of the ghetto must wear on chest and back a yellow star of David, at such time as they be in the city.
Leiter
I. Kom. Jud. Pol.

REGISTRATION OF THE 50-YEAR-OLDS

Today in the city, a lot of Poles were arrested. Men up to the age of 50 were registered in the city.

LIDZKI ALLEY

I have visited all the abandoned houses on Lidzki. I found dreadful scenes there, showing how the inhabitants left their homes. Documents of silent pain and gloom.

The description of the pogrom in Bialik's "City of Slaughter"[22] is nothing compared to Lidzki Alley. Korolenko's scream in "House Number 13"[23] is a joke compared to what you see on Lidzki.

The original inhabitants were dragged away on that night after the provocation of Glezer Street.

Where are they?

By now it is almost a hundred percent certain that they are victims of Ponar.

When we entered the ghetto, on the night of [September] 6–7, Lidzki Alley again experienced Dantesque scenes. Suddenly people were forbidden to enter

21. The original Yiddish text is written in a pretentious pseudo-German grammar and spelling characteristic of people trying to sound more educated than they are . . .

22. A long poem by the Hebrew poet Hayyim Nahman Bialik (1873–1934), written in Hebrew and translated by Bialik into Yiddish, describing the horrors of the pogrom in Kishinev in 1903.

23. V. G. Korolenko (1853–1921) was a Russian writer; his story "House Number 13" is a denunciation of the Kishinev pogrom.

the ghetto. They were crammed in masses into the courtyards of Lidzki and, at night, they were all dragged off to Łukiszki. From there, it is awful to put this on paper, . . . from there to Ponar! . . .

The blood ebbs out of your veins. . . .

What do I see of the remains on Lidzki Alley?

In one home, everything is scattered about, a cabinet stands open!—they had no time to close it. The bed is half unmade—they were dragged off, apparently, in the middle of the night. In the sewing machine, a piece of linen lies in the middle of a stitch. The clock is stopped—there isn't anyone to wind it.

A life was torn apart. . . .

Another tableau: everything is scattered. A poor little home. Pillows uncovered. The smell of a carcass. A little chicken is tied to a bed with a string. The chicken lies dead. Apparently it died of hunger in the abandoned home. On the side, on a shelf, are two candle holders, a mirror, and a few books. On top, a book by Hector [Malot], *Without a Home,* which won a prize from the French Academy.[24]

Without a home . . .

Where are the owners of the home? Where are the readers of the book if not [. . .] somewhere, at best, without a home?

THE LIBRARY

The library, which is already functioning under the supervision of Comrade Kr[uk], has become a real cultural center. The books are put in order. All the literati, or those who had any connection with culture, literature, etc., meet there.

Many come to the library to be put to work. It's not so much for the employment as in order not to sit at home, which is not a home. Moreover, and this is also a consideration—for a pass.

Writers come, beg, and cry: Moyshe Zilburg,[25] Editor [Khayim] Levin,[26] [Naftole] Weinig.[27] There are also the wives of [Dovid] Umru, [Shloyme] Beylis,[28] and others.

Among the remaining writers is Dr. [Avrom] Gliksman.[29] Intelligentsia come

24. Co-editor of the Warsaw Yiddish daily *Express*. Originally from Mołodeczno in the Vilna province, he came to Vilna with the refugees in 1939. He was unable to adjust and was killed in Ponar.

25. Hector Malot (1830–1907), a French writer, was the author of the novel *Sans famille*.

26. Editor of the Vilna Yiddish daily *Tsayt*. He was killed in Ponar.

27. Pseudonym of the folklorist and critic Norbert Roze, a teacher in several Vilna schools. According to Kaczerginski (1947:191), he died in Camp Narva, Estonia, in 1944. For his biography, see *Teachers' Memorial Book* 1954:147–148.

28. A graduate of the Mefitsei-Haskalah Yiddish school. Until World War II, he wrote for the Yiddish press in Vilna. His wife went to the ghetto by herself; he escaped to the Soviet Union.

29. Gliksman, who had a Ph.D., wrote for the Warsaw Yiddish press. He came to Vilna with the refugees in 1939 and perished in 1943 in Treblinka. Several manuscripts he wrote in the Vilna

from the whole city, among them teachers, attorneys, engineers, scientists, and artists.

The former co-director of YIVO, friend [Kalmanowicz], showed up for work, as did the wife of Zalmen Reisen,[30] who was arrested and taken off by the Soviets. Here are the scholar and former director of one of the Vilna gymnasia, Dr. [Moyshe] Heller; the veteran [Bundist] activist Comrade Rivke Epstein; the wife of a Bundist activist, Eydl Feinsilber; and [the daughter] of the Bundist Wapner, who was dragged off by the Snatchers.[31] Here the librarians in the ghetto huddle together.

[. . .] is again here a librarian; Mrs. Sackheim, director [of the children's lib]rary is also here, working in her profession, with the help of her assistant, Dina Abramowicz.[32] Kalman[owicz] is busy with Pinkhes Kon's legacy, the library that [. . .] arranged separately; he helps save the children's library of the Real [Gymnasium], climbs over abandoned stairs, seeking books, objects, old valuables. Poor [Khaykl] Lunski is confused, nevertheless, he isn't abandoned—he is here among books and readers. . . .

[At the out]break of the war in 1939, the library numbered about 45,000 books. Nine thousand books [are missing] from the library, including 1,500 books that were carried away by the ghetto Jews.

DOLLARS

On Szpitalna Street, a radio was found. Because of that, the entire ghetto lives in fear.

Characteristic. Even in the ghetto, we don't lag behind. Not even at the sight of everything that happens here. A dollar in Ghetto 1 is 15 rubles more than in Ghetto 2. There are more customers here, fewer takers there. . . .

THEY BEAT

Once again, they beat people in the barracks. Workers from the railroad and the barracks were stabbed with bayonets.

Those who beat are Storm Troopers. Many people are wounded and bandaged.

Ghetto are in the YIVO Archive (Kaczerginski-Sutzkever Collection). For his biography, see *Lexicon* 2.

30. Zalmen Reisen was a prolific Yiddish literary critic, author, and editor. He wrote a multivolume *Lexicon of Yiddish Literature* and was editor of the Vilna Yiddish daily newspaper *Der Tog*. He was arrested by the Soviets in 1939 and liquidated. For the fate of his wife, Miriam Reisen, see Kaczerginski 1947:213–214.

31. Paye Wapner, who was later a teacher in the ghetto and who was subsequently interned in several camps in Latvia and Germany. She survived the war and moved to Buenos Aires.

32. Later a partisan, Dina Abramowicz survived the Holocaust and for many years was the famed YIVO librarian in New York. She died in 2000 at age 90.

SEPTEMBER 25 [1941]

[*Here ends Kruk's reconstruction of September 20.*]

FERMENTATION

People say for sure that Lithuanian intelligentsia, intellectuals, clergy, and professors are working to prove to the masses that what the Lithuanians are doing to the Jews will remain a blot on the history of the little nation.

Will this effort have any results?

FIVE DEAD JEWS

A woman who came to Vilna says that on the way from Rzesza,[33] not far from the road, she came [upon] five dead Jews tied to five trees.

MORE DEAD JEWS

Christians say that dead Jews are found in many areas. . . .

THE JEWS OF WIELUCIANY ARE SHOT

Terrible things are heard from Wieluciany.[34] In Niemenczyn, three kilometers from Troki, a great many Jews were shot.

JEWISH CRIMINAL POLICE

But Jews don't lag behind. [A criminal] police [is added] to the [normal ghetto police.] . . . It [the ghetto] becomes a kingdom with all the accoutrements, even criminals. . . .

33. One of the peat bog camps, 15 kilometers from Vilna. A few hundred Jews from Vilna and other cities worked there. A song about Rzesza, "Peshe from Reshe," was sung in the Vilna Ghetto (words by L. Rosental, music by M. Weksler, published in Kaczerginski 1948:168). A revue with the same name was also performed in the Vilna Ghetto. At the time of the liquidation of the camps in Bezdany and Biała Waka (see note 37), those in Rzesza were brought to the Vilna Ghetto. Hirshke Glik, author of the Partisan Anthem, wrote his songs in the Rzesza camp, which existed until August 1943. In the YIVO Archive (Kaczerginski-Sutzkever Collection, no. 249), there is a report on that camp, listing such information as the number of workers, etc.

34. Wieluciany is twelve kilometers from Vilna. Before the war, there was a facility for juvenile delinquents there. On Rosh Hashanah 1941, Jews from the small towns around Vilna—Jaszuny, Andrilishok [?], Miedniki, Kiena, Szumsk, Nowa Wilejka, Krzykowka, Rukojnie, etc.—were brought there and shot (for eyewitness accounts, see Kaczerginski 1947:69).

SEPTEMBER 27 [1941]

LICENTIOUSNESS

They tell not only comic stories about the police, but tragic ones as well. Yesterday, the police exiled someone from Ghetto 1 to Ghetto 2 because he dared . . . to turn on a light at an hour when it is forbidden.

VISITS FROM THE GESTAPO

In one of the local courtyards, there was suddenly a commotion. Gestapo in the middle of the night. What happened? Apparently, they were looking for a Jewish girl. . . .

Another time, Gestapo agents came to see how people slept. . . . They went through the rooms, shone lights in the eyes of the sleeping people, and determined that people weren't living hygienically here! . . .

A DRUNK IN THE GHETTO . . .

Today a drunk was seen in the ghetto. The drunk isn't a goy,[35] in fact, but a Jew who lives in Ghetto 1.

DISTURBING RUMORS—WIELUCIANY

For a few days now, disturbing information has circulated that the inhabitants have been taken from New Wilejka, Gudogaje, and Kiena and driven to Wieluciany, an estate where there used to be a reformatory.

Fifteen Jews from Kiena escaped on the way; they say that the Jews are being shot in groups. The wife of the Kiena [Polish] landowner ran away. Jews arrive from there every day: today another one came who had been shot. He says that the local landowner's wife bandaged him. And she told that on the first day, 160 people were ordered to dig a pit. On the second day, they were ordered to sit around the pit and were shot. But many ran away. Many were shot while running.

This is the case of Wieluciany.

SPECIFICS

Lately, the press has reported that the sanitary inspectors visited the Vilna Ghetto and examined the sanitary conditions of the apartments there. The proper orders were issued concerning the case.

35. Allusion to a folk song and proverb, *Shiker vi a goy* (Drunk as a Gentile): "He is drunk, / Drink he must, / Because he is a goy,"—a Jewish stereotype.

GHETTO FURNITURE

You look around—people are making furniture: they make tables from boxes, build bunks, shelves grow out of the walls like mushrooms after a rain—a new style, ghetto style.

BARBERS CUT THE GHETTO'S HAIR

Barbers cut hair. A barber stands in the courtyard of Szpitalna 4 and people come for a shave and a haircut. The razor lies on a stone, the dish with a brush sits on a brick.

Ghetto Janitors

Jewish janitors.[36] On Rosh Hashanah, the Jewish janitor stands and sweeps the street of the Jewish ghetto. The janitor on the other side of the street has a degree from the Sorbonne. . . .

SO FAR, I HAVE SAVED MYSELF

Often, people don't want to let themselves be slaughtered like sheep. At night, a group from Ghetto 1 was taken to Ghetto 2. [On the way] they were turned around, toward Łukiszki. On Niemiecka and Trocka Streets, seeing that they were being taken in quite a different direction from Ghetto 2, the people made quite a fuss. Those who were taking them got scared and withdrew. The group was turned back and taken to Ghetto 2. . . .

After the cases in which Jews were snatched from provincial towns and from the areas of the peat bogs,[37] the men started running away from the peat bogs.

SEPTEMBER 29 [1941][38]

FROM GHETTO 2

The Jewish Committee of Ghetto 2 includes Lejbowicz, Levin, Sznajderowicz, Dr. Ran.[39]

Just as in Ghetto 1, an address office, a post office, and several other institutions were set up. The two address offices conduct a lively correspondence with each other. You get information about residents, etc. In both ghettos, there are post offices, and an intensive correspondence takes place.

36. Before the war, most janitors in Jewish houses were non-Jews.

37. Along with the peat bog camps of Kiena and Rzesza, there was also one at Bezdany (25 kilometers from Vilna), and at Biała Waka (14 kilometers from Vilna).

38. In the table of contents, this entry is dated September 30, probably in error.

39. According to an eyewitness account in Kaczerginski 1947:62–64, the Judenrat of Ghetto 2 included Yitskhok Lejbowicz (a pawnbroker), Feldman (a refugee from Poland), Levin (owner of a distillery), Sznajderowicz (owner of a restaurant), and Nokhem Khayet. Several other individuals were added later.

KASPER-SEREBROVICH

Always and everywhere the same thing. Jews who have "merits" and are properly compensated for their "merits" hang around. Kasper-Serebrovich, a man with a disgusting past—a Kovno Revisionist, by the way—is one of them. Here, in this sad situation, he has emerged as a patron of Kovno Jewry. He shouts, he orders, and everybody . . . trembles.

Of course, he walks around without a patch, walks on the sidewalk like a person. Rides on the train. Often comes from Kovno to Vilna and tries to extend his rule here, too. He shouts, curses, and doesn't hide the fact that he can. . . . That he is . . . etc.

In short, he really is, he really can . . . and . . . people really do tremble.

A SIGN OF THE TIME

These lines should remain as a sign of the time in which I write them, as a memory of this difficult and terrifying time:

These lines so far, the pages from [. . .] to [. . .] and the pages [. . .] to [. . .],[40] were written in the most awful chaos and in the most dreadful circumstances. The physical and mental situation, the housing conditions, and the entire milieu all must be my witness to the murderous [conditions] contained in these lines.

There is no time to check it all. Perhaps some of my notes repeat themselves; they must all be put in order. Let us hope that such a time will come. . . .

TUESDAY, SEPTEMBER 30 [1941]

KOL NIDRE[41]

This Yom Kippur Eve in the ghetto is unique. In the apartments, people are cooking in big pots, as if nothing is the matter. People are washing and scouring (as if everything around them were normal).

On the gate of the ghetto, the Germans have hung a sign: *Seuchengefahr,* danger of epidemic. People run from here as from leprosy. The Jews are happy. Germans won't come into the ghetto. And, since they won't come in, we'll have peace and quiet.

Workers coming from the city say that the Germans released them for Yom Kippur. . . .

People go to Kol Nidre service. Kol Nidre must be over by 6:30 in the evening. The Judenrat ordered this. People recite Kol Nidre in the dark here. The prayer

40. Apparently because of an oversight, Kruk did not enter the page numbers.

41. *Kol Nidre* (Aramaic "All Vows") is the prayer with which the evening service of Yom Kippur, the Day of Atonement, begins. Yom Kippur, the holiest day of the Jewish religious calendar, occurs on the tenth day of the Hebrew month of Tishri.

houses are full to bursting, people stand on the steps, in front of the entrance. The courtyard, the street—everything is bursting, everything is desolate.

Jews come to me in the library and ask me to lend them prayer books.

During Kol Nidre, there were cases of spasms; people fainted. In short, it was Yom Kippur, with all the trimmings.

People tell a fact. The Germans in one place ordered their Jews to come to work shaved. . . .

FACTS OF BULLYING

The beatings in the barracks continue. Yesterday, in the barracks on Kalwaryjska, people were again beaten terribly. The women were ordered to dig a pit and were forced [to cover] one of them up to the head, and only then were they ordered to dig her up.

People run away from the work. But the Germans don't calm down. In another place, where 53 girls were to report to work yesterday, only 3 came. The Germans are irritated and threaten.

YOM KIPPUR, WEDNESDAY, OCTOBER 1 [1941]

Yom Kippur began early in the morning with the militia's ordering everyone to appear at their work places as on a normal day. At about 9 in the morning, the Gestapo came into the ghetto and started snatching people for work. They didn't touch those with permits or certificates of employees of the Judenrat institutions.

When the Gestapo came into the ghetto, there was a great commotion. People started looking for hiding places. Jews in prayer shawls ran through the streets looking scared. The prayer houses emptied out. Everyone looked for a hole to hide in.

At about three in the afternoon, the Gestapo boss Sch[weinenberg] demands 1,000 Jews. Either they will be given to him by [. . . , or] he'll take them himself. The Judenrat decides that it's better to give them to him, [. . . to sel]ect among those without a work permit. In the [ghetto, there is an in]describable commotion. The police hunt and chase; the residents [hide wherever] they can. Everybody knows that when the chairman of the Judenrat was asked if [they would] be transferred to Ghetto 2, the answer was no. It is not clear [where they will] be taken. The residents of the ghetto already smell prison and later, as before, Ponar. . . .

It is now 7:30 in the evening; there is a commotion in the street. They're saying that 1,500 people were taken out of Ghetto 2 today. Where? Toward Łukiszki. . . .

PEOPLE TRADE

In the ghetto, people gradually start to come alive. At about 4 P.M., battalions of workers come from the city. Everyone brings either wood or a sack of potatoes or two loaves of bread. No wonder [. . .] Meanwhile, we must note, in [complaining], may it not get worse. Life consists also of the fact that, in the street, a small, tiny trade is felt: a woman would part with half a kilo of tomatoes; she stands with it in the street and . . . trades. . . . In a shop, you see a few kilos [. . .]

A young man sells cigarette paper.

THE EVENTS OF THE DAY

Yom Kippur today was really Yom Kippur. The commotion of this day indicated a mood of resignation. People believe that hell will never end.

Resignation grows worse from one minute to the next.

We will be dragged to the slaughter in installments!! . . .

Eight in the Evening

Nine P.M. Now it is clear: by 7:30, only 46 (!) men appeared at the gate. At 8 P.M., the German Schweinenberg, the 23-year-old lord of our life and death, came to the ghetto. He ordered all the Jews of the ghetto driven out to the gate and the designated number—1,000—selected. Right away, a group of Germans and Lithuanian militia came into the ghetto. A wild bacchanal began. The Jewish militia ordered, and the Lithuanian militia chased. In the dark night, the depressed and exhausted inhabitants of the ghetto started dragging themselves with their possessions to the gate, where they had to "show a permit." Anyone who could, hid and avoided the registration at the gate. The most horrible scenes occurred. People dragged themselves with sacks, with all their possessions and property. Some chose not to take anything with them because . . . you can go to death without things. In the [dark] of the night, I hide on the balcony of Strashun 6 and watch:

[. . .] arm-in-arm to the gate, tied and bound [. . .] begs to go faster because . . . it's a waste of time! . . .

Meanwhile, the houses of Rudnicka 19, 23, and 17 were completely cleaned out. For Schweinenberg those are the courtyards closest to the gate. In the courtyard of Rudnicka 19, the Lithuanians gave [. . .] minutes to get out.

Old P[ati Kremer] was dragged out of her apartment and taken to Rudnicka. Here, a militia man pushed her into a doorway and saved her.

Saved?—Yes, all who went out the gate are who knows where. . . .

From the gate, the crowd of 1,200 heads was driven not into Ghetto 2 but through Trocka Street and, from there, toward Łukiszki Prison.

In the same way, people were dragged off in installments from Ghetto 2: at 1:30 P.M., 800 people; at 6:30 P.M., 900 people. Altogether 2,900 people.

Not until 3 in the morning did the St. Bartholomew's Night start to settle down.

Thus Yom Kippur passed in the year 1941 in Vilna Ghetto 1 and its subsection, Ghetto 2.

■ ■ ■ ■ ■ ■

THURSDAY [OCTOBER 2, 1941]

NOCTURNAL CAROUSING

[To those] we have already noted, I will add:

[. . .]

[Pages 134–232 of the diary, from October 2 to December 22, are missing. Those were difficult and dramatic days. During that time, Ghetto 2 was liquidated and the Germans and their Lithuanian assistants carried out bloody massacres of Vilna Jews. The dates and figures of the slaughters, Aktions,[42] *and liquidations for that time are listed in Herman Kruk's "Statistics and Mourning Statistics," which he added to his entry of May 7, 1942.*

The account of the murderer Yankl Avidon probably appears in the missing pages. In the entry of March 25, 1942, Kruk refers to an entry of October 23, which is missing (see also the entries for March 17, June 4, and June 5, 1942).

During this time, something evidently happened at the ghetto gate, where things used to be taken from the Jews who had to pass through. On October 10, 1941, Avrom Zaydshnur issued an order to the gate guards that they would bear responsibility for the objects taken (Kaczerginski-Sutzkever Collection, no. 172).

The calendar of events in the Vilna Ghetto (Dworzecki 1948:498) mentions that on November 15, all the Jewish inhabitants of Woronów, and a few hundred Jews who escaped from Vilna to Woronów, were shot.

Kruk's table of contents for this period follows (the handwriting is often difficult to decipher).]

Podbrodzie
Ghettos of District Towns and Regions

October 3
People Are Fastidious
People Expect . . .

October 4
They Tear Families Apart

2,000 [Taken from Ghetto 2]

October 5
A Consolation
The Vilna "Yeshiva Student"
Again 6,000

42. The term *Aktion* (Yiddish *aktsye*) is specific to ghetto life in the Holocaust. It indicates an "action" taken by the German police and their helpers, in which Jews are rounded up and deported to death camps.

Rumors

Tearooms

October 6

People Go Voluntarily. . . .

News from Riga

October 7

The Thing Doesn't Move at All

Our Accounts . . .

My Name Becomes Popular

News

A Consolation . . .

A Letter to Uncle Abram

October 8

Still the 5,000

New Aristocrats

The Heroine from Jaszuny

From Ghetto 1 to Ghetto 2

Forbidden to Bring in Food

Militia

A Chapter of Anigst

A Third Ghetto?

October 9

People Share

From Outside the Ghetto

October 10

Today the Ghetto Is Hermetically Sealed

Prices High and Rising

Kailis

People Flee the Ghetto

Chaos

October 11

Kamker [?]

A Meter and a Half per Person

Arrests among Christians

October 12

Again Kamker [?]

Prison! . . .

Reductions in the "Pension"

News from Kovno
Demoralization

October 13
People Become Animals
They Beat Again
Pariahs
How Many Are in Ghetto 1 Today?
Two Funerals

October 14
New Evil Decrees
2,300 Heads
We Are Being Separated
Taken Down from the Gallows
News from Ponar
Division of the Ghetto into Blocks

October 17
Permits for Employees of the Judenrat
400 Instead of 1,440
The Lot of Thousands
People Are Running
44th Anniversary [of the Bund]

October 20
The Day of Destiny
A Chapter of Bridegrooms
Germans—Lithuanians

October 21
Again They Are Taking [People] Out!
The Hero Schwartz
Ghetto 2 Liquidated
Office of Vital Statistics
People Look for Matches
A Little Psychology
They Cut Beards and People Stand at Attention
Permits
How They [Make Business?] for Jews

October 22
Germans Save Jews and Jews Steal from . . . Jews
Vilna Seen through the Window of the Ghetto
The Chronically Ill, Crippled, and Insane

October 31

Murer and Schweinenberg (Two Character Sketches)

The Plans of the District Commissar Foiled by the Gestapo

Crumbs . . .

Where Is Safer? . . .

Even If You Shoot Us We Won't Move!

Faces

Death

News from the Other World

Between Yes and No

Everything Makes You Nervous

An Echo from the Thirteenth Century

November 1

From 70,000, Only 17,000–18,000

Shot on the Spot

A Permanent Assembly of "Whites"

A Madhouse

People Take Their Destiny in Their Own Hands

They Think about Us

A Proposal to Impose Yet Another . . . Contribution

November 2

The Conscience of Vilna? . . .

An Opportunity to Hang

The Culmination of the Situation

Steps about Contribution

A Contribution to Our Lifestyle—Matchmaking!

November 3

Aktion to Move from Ghetto 1 *to Ghetto* 2

You Are in the Apartment of Comrade Wirgili-Kahan

The Veker [The Awakener]

Reminiscences

Melinas

November 4

At My Bed

News from Ghetto 1

November 5

I Cry . . .

A Stroll through Ghetto 2

Escape with White Permits!

"Details" That Have to Be Recorded

November 6

Back in Ghetto I

The First Estimates

My Investigations

Suicides

November 7

Trifles

A Great Achievement

News from Warsaw

November 9

One Does Want to Return Home . . .

Rumors

Demoralization

Enough!

Observations

November 11

Unrest, Anxiety, Calm . . .

Look for the Thief!

November 12

Yellow Permits

Blocks

November 13

Again Second Ghetto

Opposition!

The Number of Permits

Blocks

Gershon Pludermacher

November 15

Trifles

November 16

A Block and . . . Łukiszki

A Good Initiative

Destinies

It Sounds Like a Joke

November 18

Schweinenberg the Haman of Vilna Ghetto

Stabilization

The Aid Society and the Bund

November 19

The Last Position of Ghetto 2!

It Gets Stabilized

A Robbery

An Interesting "Average"

A New Monster—Additional Permits

Porubanek

A Suspicion

November 20

Schweinenberg Back from a Vacation

About the Melina on Niemiecka 22

November 21

A Picture of Both Ghettos

The Tragedy of Comrade Mrs. Mikhtom

Oberhardt

November 23

We Push the Cart

Typhus

Family Permits

Police Act over the Head of the Judenrat

The End of Mrs. Zusman

November 24

Kailis

Marek

A Robber's Assault

Reductions

Ghetto Terminology

November 25

People Build a New . . . Life

News from the Ghetto

About the Illness of Fr[iend] Marek

Under a Question Mark . . .

November 27

Assistants . . .

Glazman

Marek Is Well

Schweinenberg Has Fun

November 28

The Humanist Shriftzetser and the Poet Sutzkever

A Trial Expedition to the Second Ghetto

November 30

Back from the Expedition—the First Results

Saved 14

A Treasure

Parades

Why Have Vilna Jews Been Eliminated?! . . .

News from Słonim

Culture in the Ghetto

Collecting Cultural Treasures

We Buy Our Lives

Saved Cultural Values

An Incident

December 1

An Incident with Gens

December 2

The Expedition Works

The Chronicle of Niemenczyn

December 3

They Purge among the Underworld

Murer and Torah Scrolls

Flogging . . .

Cashier in the Aid Society

The Poet Sutzkever's Mother

December 4

About the 67 Underworld Characters

Aktion Late at Night—Kailis Blocks

Permits

Poet Sutzkever in Mourning

Kozik

How Did Fried Become an Obmann?

The Ghetto Trade Is Flourishing

December 5

The Events in the "Gestapo" Block

They Try to Feed

All Because of Money and Impotence

December 18

It Comes to an End, It Comes to an End

We Become a "Kingdom"

Zaydshnur

A Page

Ghetto Uniqueness

Silent Boils

Arrests

Radio

The Aid Society

December 19

A Palace Revolution

Rumors about a "Purge"

Commissar General of Lithuania Dr. von Rentlen

December 20

The Aktion of December 20 and 21

December 21

The Aktion Continues

Białystok, Dropping in at a Bad Time

Old People

An Echo

The people in the ghetto, those who remained, stagger around—the community is once again diminished. . . .

Is it really true that all those who are taken out of here are taken to the slaughter?

Is it that horrible?

DECEMBER 22 [1941]

THE AKTION CONTINUES . . . IN KAILIS[43]

We haven't yet caught our breath. Everyone feels as if his heart were sliced open. This time it cost a lot of young lives. No one can calm down.

43. *Kailis* is Lithuanian for "hide" or "fur." Before the war, there was a fur factory in Vilna with the name Kailis, where Jewish laborers worked. Fur production was especially important to the Germans, because they needed furs and gloves for the soldiers on the Russian front. The Germans took the Jewish fur laborers and their families out of the ghetto and housed them in two blocks outside the ghetto, in the former radio factory on Szeptycki Street, Elektrit, which was evacuated by the Soviets to Minsk. Conditions in the Kailis block, which had up to 1,500 inhabitants, were better than in the ghetto. After the liquidation of the Vilna Ghetto, Kailis still re-

This morning, we again looked with frightened eyes to the gate:

Are they coming, aren't they coming?

Now, at about one in the afternoon, it seems that, for the time being, they aren't coming.

But meanwhile, work is going on in the Kailis block outside the city.[44]

Will they still come here? Almost no one knows.

HEROIC ACT — MOYSHE HAUZ

Yesterday, two melinas at Szpitalna Street 13 cost the lives of two men. One of them, the young bookbinder Moyshe Hauz, resisted and refused to go. The hero Hauz got a bullet in the head and fell dead on the spot.

His funeral was secretly held this morning.

In daytime, people say that the committee of the Bund met and decided to call the population to the funeral of the two murdered men.[45] A poster was drafted, which is to be posted before dawn:

> COME TO THE FUNERAL OF
> 1. MOYSHE HAUZ
> 2. GOLDSHTEYN
> The population of the Vilna Ghetto is summoned to stand en masse at the funeral of the murdered men, which is to start from the Jewish hospital today, exactly at . . . in the morning.
> Honor their memory

Later, when it turned out that the hero Hauz was no longer in the ghetto, instead of that obituary a leaflet with the following contents was posted:

> SUNDAY, ON SZPITALNA STREET 13
> HAUZ AND GOLDSHTEYN
> WERE MURDERED

Thus Vilna ended her latest tragedy with another 400 murdered lives.

THE BEST WISH

At noon today, news spread that there is unrest in the city, and that Polish men were raided and sent away. Later, when sirens were heard, a rumor went through the city that there is an air-raid alarm in Vilna. An old Jew shouted out gaily: "If only they'd shoot us all! . . . "

---

mained as a work camp until the beginning of July 1944. A week before the Red Army entered Vilna, the Kailis residents were liquidated.

44. Kailis was in the city. Kruk means "outside the ghetto."

45. Kruk was, of course, at that meeting. He covers up his presence by reporting the information as hearsay.

OUR DREAM

Reliable information comes from the city: the supreme commander of the German army, von Brauchitsch, has resigned and has been replaced by Hitler!

Hitler appealed to the army to persevere.

Goebbels appealed to the German population to use the holidays (December 27 to January 2) to contribute warm clothing for the soldiers on the Eastern Front. . . .

Meanwhile, English radio [BBC] broadcasts that during the Russian offensive, 1,600 cities and towns were taken back from the Germans, that the Germans flee 20 kilometers a day, that they are now 400 kilometers from Rostov, etc.

We swallow every word and ask ourselves: Will we hold out? Will we endure our fate to the end? . . .

PALACE REVOLUTION

Back to our "palace revolution."[46]

The Judenrat lived disgustingly and died even more disgustingly. It is de facto dead. Power is almost completely and solely in the hands of the police—that is, the trio of Gens, Oberhardt,[47] and Glazman.[48] The latter is surely the diplomat and leader.

After the police took over the post office, they also monopolized the issuance of so-called protective permits. Their relatives were provided first of all. Now the police Revisionists[49] have invented a system: permits are issued only to young men and only to those women who can still give birth (??).

An exchange of words during the meeting when Gens imposed a director of the hospital is typical.

Fried asks: "Will you also order me soon?"

46. This probably refers to something on the missing pages.

47. A Viennese Jew. In the ghetto, Oberhardt was feared and considered a shady character. Kaczerginski 1948:45 contains a song about Oberhardt by Gita Sudeńska. The note to the song says: "Because of his 'merits,' [Oberhardt,] along with the leader of the Jews Gens, Dessler, and a girl (Lili Reszańska), had permission to walk around without a patch. Was formerly a commander of a big Jewish labor group working in gasoline. After the Gestapo shot Gens, Oberhardt became the leader, but only for a short time. He later hid in the Jewish labor camp 'Kailis,' where he was caught by the liquidator of the Vilna Ghetto Kittel, who took Oberhardt and his wife to Ponar."

48. Born in Alytus, Lithuania. Yosef Glazman was the commander of Betar in Lithuania and editor of the Revisionist journal *Ha-Medina*. When Lithuania became Soviet, he moved to Vilna. Later entries in the diary tell about his position in the ghetto after he was deposed as deputy chief of the ghetto police. He was a member of the staff of the clandestine FPO (United Partisan Organization) in the ghetto and was killed in the forest on October 8, 1943, while leading a group of partisans.

49. The Revisionists were the right-wing Zionist followers of Jabotinsky. Gens, a Revisionist himself, staffed the police with his comrades. Before the war, they were considered Fascists by the Jewish socialists or socialist Zionists.

Gens answers: "I'll do the same with you as with the others."

Fried: "Even with a stick?"

Gens answers: "Yes, even with a stick."

Fried: "Your hand's too short. . . . "

Fried is really scared. He tries to defend himself but Gens knows his weakness—he will surely subdue him. . . .

POLICE ORDERS

While we're on the subject of the Jewish police, we shall quote two typical [police] orders:

ORDER NUMBER 22

From the Police Chief of Vilna Ghetto, December 6, 1941

1. Be it known that any persons found in the ghetto without the star of David (yellow insignia) or whose insignia is not securely fastened at all corners will immediately be fined 5 rubles.
2. Gathering in groups on the streets of the ghetto is strictly forbidden. For not following point 2, there will be a fine of 3 rubles.
3. Going out of the gate of the ghetto without a yellow permit or a special permission from the chief of police is strictly forbidden.
4. Those attempting to go through the gate of the ghetto will be fined 10 rubles.

December 12, 1941

Chief of Police

Those are the guardians of the star of David (sometimes a yellow insignia, sometimes a yellow permit . . .)!

Here is the watching to ensure that the corners are securely fastened!

Here is the watch to prevent, God forbid, going out of the gate without a permit, etc.

Another order:

ORDER NUMBER 26

From the Vilna Ghetto Police Chief of December 18, 1941

I order all inhabitants of the ghetto to inhabit the domiciles assigned to them by the Housing Department.

Those found in apartments not designated for them will be punished severely—and may even be expelled from the ghetto.

Chief of Police

Here you have style: inhabitants dwelling in apartments, punishment by deportation from the ghetto, and the elaboration of a precise price scale of punishments. . . .

Thus, the police budget constantly has a surplus. . . .

DECEMBER 25 [1941]

A HALF YEAR SINCE THE GERMAN-SOVIET WAR

The 23rd[50] of this month marked a half year since the first explosions were heard in this area—war between the Soviet Union and Germany. Today, making a bit of an account of the sad past, we know that Jewish Vilna is torn to pieces. Instead of 65,000 Jews, we now number 13,000, and the 13,000 find themselves in a ghetto in conditions probably unlike those of any other ghetto in Poland.

Two letters have accidentally reached me from Ghetto 2, written before people were snatched out from among us and thrown into Ghetto 2, and then came a wild chase for two or three days to rescue people from there. Two such importuning letters are before me:

A certain Sergey Smorgonski writes to Comrade [Avrom] Chwojnik:[51]

To the director of housing in the Housing Department of the ghetto:

We are in the second ghetto, about ten house managers and two employees of *Butus Skirius,*[52] Misses Ginsburg and Krantz. Our situation is dreadful; we have no possessions, no money. This is the second day we haven't eaten. Everyone has betrayed us. They took care of their own families, but one of our own[53] has been forgotten. Oberhardt took care of Zlatin only and completely forgot about us. When he took us to the second precinct, he promised he would come get us out the next morning but as of noon, he has not kept his word, as usual. Save us, you are a decent man. Alarm Gukhman, Friedman, and do everything you can. Our possessions are safe in our apartments (?). My belongings are in Rudnicka 10, apartment 4, with Burabishkin. We are waiting for an immediate answer.

If you want to, you can save us.

My address is c/o Adentia, etc.

This is how helpless people were. And this is how naive they were, thinking that Oberhardt would keep his word and that everyone else had betrayed them.

Today, the letters are already "old" documents. Since then, we have survived much harder times. Nevertheless, I consider it important to present both documents as they came to me.

[*The second letter is missing.*]

50. It should be the 22nd.

51. Chwojnik was born in Różana about 1907. Just before the outbreak of World War II he was a Bundist activist in Vilna, and he became a prominent leader of the Bund in the ghetto. In addition to his several general functions, he was the representative of the Bund on the staff of the FPO (United Partisan Organization). Later entries in the diary contain some details about his activity in the ghetto. The Germans hanged him publicly on September 24, 1943, during the liquidation of the ghetto. For his biography, see *Generations* 2:508–513.

52. In Lithuanian, the Housing Department in the city administration.

53. This probably means a member of the Bund.

Hardly half a year, and it was only a few days ago that we suddenly received equal rights. I present here an order from the city secretary, Dr. Preissler, about the *Strafrechtspflege* (Criminal Code) against Poles and Jews for the annexed *Ostgebiete* (Eastern Districts). In addition to this order, I will only add—we have lived to see ourselves made equal to the Poles. Progress, nevertheless! . . .
[*The order is missing.*]

While we're talking about Ghetto 2, we must mention that with the last purge, Ghetto 2 has finally been closed and none of us can go there.

All expeditions to look for museum valuables, to continue transferring books from the Strashun Library, etc.—all that is henceforth forbidden.

The Strashun Library was sealed by the authorities several days ago.[54]

MRS. ŠIMAITE

Mrs. [Anna] Šimaite,[55] who visited me recently, tells that Burakas says that all Jewish things remaining in Ghetto 2 belong to the Germans, and no one dares touch anything there. . . .

Apropos Mrs. Anna Šimaite, she is an elderly Lithuanian woman and a veteran social activist. She often comes to visit her Jewish friends in the ghetto. This time she visited the library (she herself is a librarian in the Vilna University Library) and the museum valuables. Two days later, she wrote a letter to her Jewish friend asking her, among other things, to give regards to the gentleman who showed her around.[56] She thanks him and admires his great strength and courage to have the will in such a terrible and difficult time to collect such things everyone turns away from. . . .

GHETTO KITCHENS

A corner of ghetto life: there are five kitchens here.[57] The kitchens distribute 3,500 lunches a day, 1,000 of them free. The best of the five is the kitchen at Strashun 12.

54. The Straszun Library, founded in 1892, was a major library of Judaica, including rare books as well as modern secular books based on the collection of the nineteenth-century *maskil* ("enlightened writer") and Jewish scholar Matthias Strashun (1819–1885). It served as a central public library for young and old in Vilna. Many of its books were gathered at YIVO under the German occupation and were transported to Germany; after the war, they were salvaged and brought to YIVO in New York.

55. An unusual woman—a genuine Righteous Gentile. She was a member of the SR (Socialist-Revolutionary Party) in tsarist Russia. During the war she maintained contacts with those in the ghetto, including Herman Kruk. She saved Jewish cultural treasures as well as Jewish lives, and hid Jewish children. Later she was arrested and sent to a concentration camp in France, from which she was liberated after the war. Thereafter she lived in Paris.

56. I.e., Kruk.

57. According to Dworzecki (1948:177–178), the ghetto contained at that time the following kitchens: (1) the Zionist soup kitchen at Strashun Street 2, where the Halutz Youth would gather

A BATH IN THE GHETTO

Another part of ghetto life—a bath in the ghetto. Since the 23rd of this month, a bath has been operating in the ghetto, which has many showers.

Now we won't be led to the bath[58] from Ghetto 1 to Ghetto 2—Ghetto 1 fortunately has its own bath!

GHETTO CONFISCATIONS

We have often written about the enormous expenses incurred by this ghetto.[59] Yesterday, for example, a holiday eve for the Christians, the ghetto distributed holiday gifts of about 100,000 rubles. Is it any wonder they have to take from the dead and the living?

From the dead, the Lithuanians take; from the living, the Judenrat of the Vilna Ghetto takes.

There was a time when the Judenrat was a partner in found possessions. The owners would get . . . 20 percent of their possessions, the Judenrat "legally" would take 50 percent, and 30 percent would be stolen.

Now, when they need money, the Jewish police go to various inhabitants who are denounced and . . . foreign currency is confiscated. If 50,000 rubles are found on someone, he gets "hush money" of 5,000 rubles. Some get nothing. Today, such a thing happened to my friend B., the leader of the local Orthodoxy.[60] They came to search a neighbor's house and meanwhile found 162 dollars on B.'s wife.

B., left without any money, has to go ask for a free lunch for himself and his children. How will the Judenrat deal with the case? We will try to intervene.

---

and where Zionist consultations would take place; (2) the children's kitchen at Strashun Street 12, organized by the children's clinic of the Health Department and directed by Shifre (Stefanya Lvovna) Szabad (widow of Dr. Tsemakh Szabad), to which groups of schoolchildren would come with their teachers during recess; (3) a kosher soup kitchen at Szawelska 5, known as the religious kitchen, in which no meat was ever cooked because meat in the ghetto was mainly nonkosher horse meat (religious Jews would meet there); (4) the Bundist soup kitchen at Rudnicka 17, which served as a meeting place for Bundist activists and circles close to the Bund (cultural events would often take place in this kitchen, organized by the Association of Writers and Artists and the Teachers' Union); and (5) the largest kitchen, the Judenrat kitchen at Rudnicka 6, designated for the ghetto police and later for all Judenrat employees, and where large festive events of the Association of Writers and Artists and Brit Ivrit (the Hebrew Language League) would take place.

58. A pun: the Yiddish idiom "to lead someone to the bath" means to trick, cajole, and catch him.

59. This was probably in the missing pages.

60. This probably refers to Rabbi Aaron Hacohen Berek, a representative of the religious Jews in several ghetto institutions. He died in the ghetto hospital. For his biography, see *These Will I Remember* 3:73–77.

FOR GETTING A FEW BOARDS

Not only for such things do people come to me. I also have "bigger distinctions." A friend sleeps regularly on the ground, and I got him boards for a bed. His joy is so great, and his gratitude even greater, that I truly can't describe it.

A GOOD APPROACH

A Jew comes, a quasi-intellectual: he has a manuscript; he doesn't have anywhere to hide it. If he lives and survives, he wants to have it whole; if he doesn't live, he wants it to remain in safe hands. Where do you go? He begs me.

Received and promised—will any of us survive? . . .

MY CO-WORKERS

People come to me and say: I'm going crazy. Nowhere to hide. Give me work. I'm not asking for any money. Let me assist in your fine, painstaking work.

Thus, 20 volunteers are already working for me. New ones come and old ones often go away. Writers, journalists, doctors, and professionals work here.

People bring books. Where to dispose of them? Let them stay with you. With you, at any rate, they won't be burned. Maybe some of them will survive? . . .

POLICE-MILITARY DICTATORSHIP

An excellent witticism heard today from a speaker at a meeting:

"Here in our ghetto, a police-military dictatorship[61] now rules."

So we are equal to other nations: our own economy, our own . . . police and . . . a police-military dictatorship.

If only it weren't so sad!—Unfortunately, it's the truth. . . .

DECEMBER 26 [1941]

"RULERS" IN THE GHETTO

Not long ago, we told of the "palace revolt" in the ghetto. Later we passed on the witticism that a "police-military dictatorship" rules in the ghetto. Today people tell how much fur those "rulers" have grown.

To get acquainted with a Revisionist in the ghetto is an enormous achievement. If the acquaintance is direct—i.e., with one of those close to the powers—this is truly a heroic act. So you take advantage of the most remote acquaintance of an acquaintance through an acquaintance to get "connections" with somebody like that. To get to the new candidate, the present leader of the local Revisionists, Mr. Glazman, for example, is invaluable. The most remote acquaintances reach

61. This was the usual description of quasi-Fascist regimes in the small countries of Europe—Poland, Lithuania, etc.—in the late 1930s.

him through his father-in-law, the local ritual slaughterer, Reb Nisn [Yofe],[62] who is to speak to his daughter so that she will agree to talk with her "officially registered" husband.[63] It's real acrobatics. Nevertheless, it is done. People rack their brains about who knows Glazman's father-in-law, who knows the ritual slaughterer's daughter, who studied with his daughter in school, and so on and so forth. In short, people will soon pay a lot of money for such an acquaintance.

This is how the police-military rule looks in our ghetto.

WOOD IN THE GHETTO

It is barely minus 8 or 10 degrees Celsius. Nevertheless, all of us at work here are freezing. The offices are truly paralyzed. People look at every piece of wood with "pity"—not a small thing in the ghetto, a piece of wood! . . .

No wonder then that the poorer ghetto residents rip wood right off the wall. People rip boards up from the floor, they burn doors with the frames, they cut up stairs from abandoned houses.

From the outside, Strashun Street looks like a ruin with makeup on. All the shops are torn open, doors and gates are torn off, floors are torn up. You walk in the street and in front of you are gaping holes. Through the holes you can see what's going on in the courtyard because even the windows at the back are torn out and you can see through the back side of the house, as if through a cloth riddled with holes.

This is how all the courtyards of the ghetto now look.

AN IMPORTANT PERSONAGE IN THE GHETTO

You have to see this. You have to face it head on. Twenty minutes before the event, Jewish police beat passersby; they curse and drive them through the gates. Jews are silent, take the blows, and run.

"Is this an Aktion? A new purge?" Meanwhile, people start hiding. There is a panic, and meanwhile . . . meanwhile, a procession is seen: two policemen drive

62. A religious activist in Vilna and former secretary of the Vilna chief rabbi, Haim Ozer Grodzenski. Yofe was the representative of Agudat Israel (the religious Orthodox party) in many ghetto institutions. He worked on the Rosenberg Task Force. During the liquidation of the ghetto, he was discovered in a melina and killed at Ponar.

63. Some people who did not have permits had been registered as "wives," "husbands," "parents," or "children" of those who did have permits. This practice was intended to save the lives of those without permits. Reb Nisn Yofe's daughter, Ester, was Glazman's "wife," for the purposes of the German documents. Born in 1916, she was a Revisionist activist before the outbreak of the war. Though one of the first members of the FPO, she later belonged to another partisan group in the ghetto. She escaped to Kovno with Aryan papers. According to Kaczerginski (1947:218), she was recognized in Kovno and killed; according to Korczak (1946:317), she was denounced as a traitor and agent provocateur and condemned to death by the FPO, but she escaped to Germany with Aryan papers and her fate is unknown.

the rest of the people from the already cleared street. In the middle of the street, like the leader of a parade, walks police commissar [Salek] Dessler.[64] Behind him is a German lieutenant, Meler,[65] the vice-chief of the Vilna Gestapo, led on one side by Gens, the head of the ghetto militia, and on the other side [by] his adjutant, the unruly fellow Smulikowski.

This procession leads the guest around the ghetto, and the visitor, taking leave of the officials, thinks it necessary to state that he really doesn't understand the "dumb Jews" of the ghetto. He "sees" that everything here is "*in Ordnung*." Jews live in peace, and he is sure that nothing will happen to anyone; so why do so many Jews escape from the ghetto? . . .

The officials listen obediently to the reproach of the great man, Lieutenant Meler, and in minutes, the "golden words" circulate with delight through the ghetto.

Is this a sign of slavery, weakness, or just helplessness?

BATH

The bath in the ghetto is finally finished. But in the ghetto, people joke that the clothes that go to be disinfected don't come out of there alive.

That's how it is: several garments have emerged burned.

DECEMBER 27 [1941]

BREAD CARDS

The ghetto probably will not get bread cards. The City Council sends food into the ghetto for the 13,000 inhabitants there, and the ghetto is to distribute it as it likes.

The ghetto administration intends to print about 14,000 [cards] (including the "whites"[66]), so the food is also distributed to the "whites." Thus, the situation of the remaining "whites" is legalized.

64. Son of a rich Jewish merchant of Vilna. Dessler was a university student and belonged to the Revisionist Student Corporation, Hasmonean. He was an open collaborator with the Gestapo and one of the most hated of the ghetto police. In the ghetto, a song was written about him: "The Jew from the Ghetto" (Kaczerginski 1948:31). After the liquidation of the ghetto, he hid out in a bunker that he had built in the city, outside the ghetto. The partisans were searching for him to kill him. The Germans were also searching for him, since they considered his escape a betrayal. They found him and killed him.

65. Here the text has the spelling *Meer*—probably a mistake, later corrected to Meler.

66. Holders of white permits. In the Vilna Ghetto, there were permits of various colors. Those who had white permits were in fact condemned to be liquidated. They were constantly in danger of being taken out of the ghetto. (For more precise details about the permits, see note 83 below.)

APROPOS "WHITES"

Meanwhile, however, with the introduction of registration books, people say that "whites" won't be able to live in the ghetto anymore because . . . they won't be allowed to register.

INTRODUCTION OF PASSPORTIZATION

There is talk of introducing passports. They say that the ghetto will also have a passportization, and obviously not all those who have permits will get passports. This is also seen as a chapter of Ponar.[67]

FUR COATS

Around the 22nd of this month, the German press published an appeal by Dr. Goebbels for a collection of fur coats and warm underwear for those fighting on the front. The collection is scheduled from December 27 to January 4. In the Polish press, too, the appeal was published under the headline "A Voluntary Collection."

We attach the appeal in German.

[*The appeal is missing.*]

Today at noon, a group of Germans came into the ghetto, and soon after, Jewish policemen went from house to house announcing the following:

All fur coats, fur collars, muffs, etc., must BE PRESENTED TO THE JUDENRAT IN HALF AN HOUR. THE ALTERNATIVE IS THE DEATH PENALTY.

The inhabitants soon started bringing, and at about 8 in the evening, the building was full of hides and other furs. A group of Germans watched the Jews bring muffs, and the Jewish [police] took the furs from them and put them in a special room.

In the street, you now see many people with collars of stiff canvas instead of the cut-off fur collar. . . .

Has everyone really given up his furs? Unbelievable. A great many fur coats are hidden in melinas.

OLD YASHUNSKI IS SIXTY YEARS OLD

We accidentally learned from Councilman Y[ashunski] that his father [Joseph is sixty years old today. On his [Grisha's] initiative, a few of us have written him a card.

THE HOLIDAY ATMOSPHERE OF THE GERMANS

The atmosphere in which the Germans celebrate this year's Christmas is characterized by the half-page greeting in the holiday issue of the [. . .]

[*The name of the journal is missing.*]

67. In other words, the rumored introduction of passports was seen by Vilna's Jews as yet another way to identify and single out the ghetto's residents for extermination.

Alle unsere Kunden und Freunde grüssen wir zum Weihnachtsfest und Jahresbeginn 1942. Wir wünschen, dass das kommende Jahr für uns alle erfolgreich verlaufen und uns einen *dauerhaften Frieden* bringen möge.

Der Staatsverlag in Kauen mit seinen Zweigstellen in Wilna und im gesamten Gebiet.

Kauen, im December 1941.

[We wish all our customers and friends a Merry Christmas and a Happy New Year, 1942. We hope that the coming year will be successful for all of us and will bring us a *long-lasting peace.*

The State Publishing House in Kovno and its branches in Vilna and the entire [Eastern] District.

Kovno, December 1941]

DECEMBER 28 [1941]

The "Voluntary" Collection of Fur Coats in the Ghetto

The appeal to give up fur coats was carried out with fear yesterday. The order that anyone who did not bring their fur coats would be shot resounded loud in the ghetto, and people brought their fur coats en masse. This morning, the first truckfuls of furs departed.

It looks like Purim.[68] Ladies usually known to wear fur coats are walking around the ghetto today in light autumn coats. . . . Men's collars are skinned of their fur, and the wadding is visible.

At the gate, they searched, and those who wanted to take out fur coats were stopped.

Some people cut up their fur coats and lined their shoes and boots.

This is how Jewish property was shared and how the voluntary collection campaign looked in the ghetto.

Meanwhile, in the city, the campaign is "only voluntary." No one knows how it will end.

This evening, the Jewish police still thought it necessary to go from house to house searching for fur coats. In many apartments, they did indeed find expensive and valuable fur coats.

Another fine chapter in the history of the Revisionist police of the Vilna Ghetto.

MY NEW APARTMENT

I forgot to tell this: I am finally living in the block of Judenrat employees.[69] Many neighbors envy me, not for a good apartment but for a more comfortable apartment. . . .

68. A holiday and merry costume festival.

69. At Strashun Street 6.

GOOD WISHES

A great frost today, but Jews are happy: may we freeze, and "them," may they get frozen in. . . .

DECEMBER 29 [1941]

FUR COATS

Once more, fur coats. The population of the Vilna Ghetto lives on what is sold. Foreign currency is sold; not everyone has it. Some who do have it are scared to show it. So they sell clothing. Now in winter the best sales occur: warm underwear, fur coats, etc. But the recent "voluntary" collection of fur coats put an end to it. Those who gave up their fur coats lost anyway—there's nothing to sell. Those who didn't give them up can't enjoy them. They can't wear them and they can't sell them. In short, the trade is finished.

But that trade is not finished for everyone. Today, a few men—the chairman of the Judenrat, Mr. Fried; Judenrat member Mr. Yashunski; and chief of the Jewish police, Mr. Gens—received personal invitations from the district commissioner to appear before him at three in the afternoon.

Those invited were nervous:

"Is there special news again?"

When people talk about special news in the ghetto, in ghetto language this means really special. Ponar has not been dropped from the agenda.

Late at night, I find out:

This time, the representative of the district commissioner, actually his deputy for Jewish affairs, the famous Murer, received them calmly. He greeted "Chief" Gens a bit better and carried on a light, amusing conversation with the others. The subject: fur coats.

He regretted that the Gestapo got there first and had already taken the fur coats, but he wants some too and asked them to get him fur coats. . . .

Those waiting for the result of the visit have calmed down—the mountain has produced a mouse. The specter of a new Ponar is postponed.

Who knows for how long?

DECEMBER 30 [1941]

IF IT ONLY STOPS WITH FUR COATS . . .

Suddenly and unexpectedly, at 8 this morning, 60 Germans and 200 Lithuanians marched into the ghetto.

When the commotion in the ghetto calmed down, it was clear that they would search again. But this time, they would search for fur coats.

People come out of the ever-ready melinas and throw into them the . . . fur coats. Those who have not yet given them up decide to hide them again. Some throw the hidden fur coats into the corridors, onto the steps, into garbage cans, etc.

The inspection by the Lithuanian soldiers was generally quiet. Here and there they took a piece of leather; here and there a piece of soap crept in. All in all, quiet.

They really found little, and what was found was unimportant and worthless. The campaign had a happy ending: as they left the ghetto, the Germans searched their Lithuanian "colleagues," took fur coats from some of them, and other little items from others. Some of the robbers were arrested on the spot, some publicly slapped. All this took place in front of the Jews, and the Jews were secretly happy that these evil executioners of Ponar [the Lithuanians] were publicly disgraced here.

A revenge on the bedbugs: the house is burned down. . . .

A REPORT ABOUT THE GHETTO

Last night, H[erman] K[ruk] was suddenly called to the "chief," Mr. Glaz[man], where he was received very nicely. Ultimately, a request: write the history of the Jews in the ghetto. When Kruk asked why he should do this when there are others who are Vilna natives and writers, the answer was: because he had the material. When he asked for whom this was to be written, the answer was "Jewish interests."

After explaining to Glazman that "Jewish interests" were like a bird in the sky, that he had to know precisely for whom it was to be written, he refused to do it.[70] Mr. G[lazman] replied that he would consider it until the next day. The same day, G[lazman] explained to a friend that he needed it for the delegate of the Polish government.[71] But the entire issue came to nothing because, in the meantime, he[72] got sick.

NEWS FROM THE FRONT

Meanwhile, great events are happening around us.

Today's report of the battles from the Führer's headquarters said, among other things:

[*The report is missing.*]

70. Kruk refused because he saw Glazman as a Zionist nationalist and a Revisionist Fascist, and he was afraid that his material would fall into German hands. He didn't know that Glazman had sympathies in the opposite direction and would become one of the clandestine leaders of the Vilna partisans.

71. Probably the Vilna delegate of the Polish government-in-exile in London.

72. Apparently, "he" means Kruk.

Moreover, there is an interview of the Foreign Minister of the Reich, von Ribbentrop, with Artisek, a representative of the Spanish Press Agency EFE. There the minister says:

[*The interview is missing.*]

This is how the front looks and how they are beginning to talk about it in German circles.

DECEMBER 31 [1941]

ZAYDSHNUR

The leaflets distributed in the streets of the Vilna Ghetto really do have an effect. Pressured by this unusual special "public opinion," Zaydshnur, a famous hero for us, has finally been thrown out.[73]

A NEW LEAFLET

For the new year, a new leaflet appeared,[74] which has made a tremendous impression in the ghetto. . . .

We shall quote this leaflet soon.

FUR COATS

Again fur coats. Last night, they also searched for fur coats in the city among the non-Jewish population. Even Burak[as] expressed his amazement at how a voluntary collection had become a compulsory one.

Too bad for his fur coat. . . .

That same Burak[as], in a conversation in his own home today, found it necessary to say that the Germans admired the Jewish workers for their productivity. He expressed his opinion that the situation of the Jews will improve in 1942. . . .

THE BATH IN THE GHETTO

The new bath in the ghetto now processes 300 patrons a day.

MORE ABOUT FUR COATS

The district commissioner is sorry that the SS got all the fur coats and that the poor Jewish police must accommodate everyone in . . .

We quote Order Number 28, issued on December 31, 1941:

73. It is not clear what sort of leaflets were distributed or who distributed them. Nor do we know who the "hero Zaydshnur" is. There were several people named Zaydshnur in Vilna. Apparently this Zaydshnur was discussed in the missing pages.

74. Probably Abba Kovner's call for resistance, claiming that all Jews of Europe are marked for annihilation and that armed struggle is the only response.

Ghetto inhabitants who own fur coats, fur jackets, or other furs outside the ghetto must report to a police station, by January 2, 1942, at 9 P.M., the precise address of the goods left outside the ghetto.

Those who do not follow the order will be severely punished.

Chief of Police

More about furs: the Jewish police cannot bear the idea that Jews hid their furs somewhere, thus the order. The Germans, by contrast, arrest everyone in the street who goes to work with a skinned collar. They consider this a demonstration of robbed fur collars.

JANUARY 1 [1942]

NEW YEAR

The Judenrat of Jerusalem of Lithuania: if all the Vilna Gaons could rise from the dead; if the Vilna minds, scattered over the world, could look and spit in your faces; if I could at least be sure my efforts would become public—how relieved I would be, and how calmly I would prepare for the uncertain tomorrow! . . .

But I am full of confidence, full of hope for the great new times that the new year, 1942, will bring.

It's better not to write about the past year. For that you have to use blood [not ink], and with us in Vilna, Jewish blood, the still warm blood of women and children who were ripped away from us with their children, their mothers, often with fathers and relatives. It's better not to write about them.

But let me note for memory how our ghetto accompanied the old year out last night, December 31, and greeted the new year.

The meeting of the Judenrat decided to do away with the free lunch they had been distributing to the "whites" through the Aid Society. The explanation: the Aid Society should not do any favors for the "whites" with our money. . . .

Il Duce of the ghetto,[75] the Revisionist police chief Gens, held a New Year's Eve party, attended by 25 persons, in his apartment. At 12 o'clock at night, Il Duce took the floor and said that despite the hard year this was and despite his hard work, he recalls how he stood at the gate and saw Jews taken away; some we may never see again, others we may perhaps meet sometime—nevertheless, he thinks he has done important work. . . .

What this important work consists of, we have written about quite often. Who knows how many more times we will have to write about it. . . . But in fact, Gens spoke, the women cried, and what the chief said was received with great "understanding"—

75. Kruk, the Socialist, resents the "Fascist" Revisionists. In fact, the Revisionist Party did have contacts with Italian Fascists in the 1930s.

. . . He has done important work.

The Judenrat was represented there by the "Obmann" [chief] Mr. Fried, and the masses, by policemen of various ranks. . . .

At 2 o'clock in the morning, Hering[76] and his gentlemen graced the party. He was welcomed by his friend Gens and colleagues, and the party ended at dawn.

A small but interesting background detail:

Gens's wife is a [Christian] Lithuanian, a nice person, seems honest. She came into the ghetto with flowers (she lives outside the ghetto). In the course of the "sad amusement," she was perhaps a bit intoxicated, and admitted to some women that she knew that people have great resentment for her husband, that he is suspected of ugly things. But she "guaranteed" that he is a decent man and is doing important work. And not in vain did she wander like a beaten dog outside the ghetto walls whenever she knew that an Aktion was going on in the ghetto. . . .

The women drew out the chat and commented on it like women. . . .

Our New Year's Eve took place at my bed. Around me, Hersh [Gutgestalt], Shmulke [Kapliński],[77] Pati [Kremer], Grisha [Yashunski], Leyke [Glezer-Yashunski], and my brother-in-law. In sad silence we assembled, and in sad silence we wished each other to hold out, survive, and be able to tell about all this!

Meanwhile, we consoled ourselves with the latest information:

Kerch[78] has fallen. Kaluga[79] has fallen. An Italian regiment surrendered[80] and promises to fight against the Germans. On the front 2,000[81] are found frozen. . . .

This means that not only atmospheric conditions strike the Germans. Kerch, where it is now warm, proves that the Bolsheviks have the upper hand militarily. So the Russians are coming back and hitting back at the enemy. Moreover, the German-Italian army is faltering in the east as well as in Africa; now the English are marching hundreds of kilometers deep into Tripoli. The Italian empire is no longer an empire. This is the reward for Italy's participation in the war. . . .

We wish each other to hold out, to survive, and to be able to tell [about it].

76. August Hering, adjutant of the Gestapo executioner Schweinenberg. Hering was one of the organizers of the slaughters and provocations in the ghetto.

77. Born in Zdzięcioł in 1914. His father, Khayim Kapliński, was a pioneer Bundist (who was exiled to the Soviet Union and later lived in Israel). His brother, Nyomke, a Bundist activist in Zdzięcioł, was arrested by the NKVD and sent to a camp, where he perished. In the Vilna Ghetto, Shmulke was a member of the committee of the Bund and was its representative in the FPO, occupied especially with the preparation of weapons. He eventually went to the forest, where he led a partisan unit. His wife, Khyene Borowska, was a Communist activist in the ghetto. They survived the war and lived in Vilna.

78. Kerch, in the Crimea, was recovered by the Russians.

79. Near Moscow.

80. To the Russians.

81. I.e., Germans.

NEWS FROM WARSAW

Lately, through various channels, horrifying letters come from Warsaw, filled with dread about our fate in Vilna. . . .

They want to know if we're alive, what we're doing, and . . . if we don't plan to come [to Warsaw].[82] It seems that only lately have they heard in Warsaw about the events in Vilna.

PERMITS

From everything we have written here, it is clear: once there was a problem of "white permits"; later a matter of life or death—"yellow permits." Recently, there was a struggle for "pink permits," also called "family" and "protection permits." Now there is a struggle to get "pink permits," "affiliated permits," "blue permits."[83]

The struggle continues on, and we shall probably talk about it again.

23 DEGREES BELOW ZERO

Today the temperature was 23 degrees below zero (Celsius). Heating material is extraordinarily hard to get in the ghetto. We know the living conditions in the ghetto more or less. Nevertheless, everybody comes to work today in a happy mood—23 below. If it only lasted for at least two weeks. . . .[84]

APROPOS NEW YEAR'S EVE

Concerning the stormy New Year's Eve at the "chief's." His adjutant, young Smulikowski, has become a father. He went to the Judenrat explaining that he wanted to honor the birth with a New Year's Eve party, and asked for a . . . loan. They refused him the loan, but a New Year's Eve party did take place. The guests: all the commissars and several "civilians." Most important, along the noble company, there were several "girls" who are famous in the ghetto for being close to the Germans. One of them [is] a former employee of a pharmacy, Miss Lili Reszanska.[85]

This is a local detail I considered it necessary to note. . . .

82. The slaughter at Ponar was a terrible shock, even in the Warsaw Ghetto, which had seemed stable at the time. For those who faced reality, Ponar was the first sign that the Nazis intended the total annihilation of the Jews. See Yitzhak Zuckerman, *A Surplus of Memory,* ed. and trans. Barbara Harshav (Los Angeles: University of California Press, 1993), p. 150ff.

83. In October 1941, all permits were abolished, and yellow permits were introduced, which were valid for a family with two children under the age of 16. Such permits were issued only to 3,000 families (about 12,000 people). During the second Aktion, blue permits were introduced. A yellow permit was no longer enough to stay alive—a family member also had to have a blue note. In December 1941, several artisans who did not have yellow permits were issued pink permits (see Dworzecki 1948:101, 126).

84. They were hoping the Germans would freeze on the front.

85. Collaborator with the ghetto police. She was "famous" in the ghetto and was one of the few who walked around without the Jewish patch.

My guess that not all of those taken out of Vilna were shot gets more support. Recently, messages were received from several people who were taken out of Vilna, for example, from the son of the Vilna conductor [Avrom] Slep.[86] The son, who was picked up by the Snatchers about half a year ago and taken away, passed through the streets of Vilna a few days ago telling everyone he met that he was healthy and working.

Lately, as we said, there have been a few such cases.

JANUARY 2, 1942

LITHUANIA, LITHUANIANS

Not only on the front are things happening, but in the rear as well.

Rumors are circulating that Lithuania will be proclaimed an independent state and will have to pay for that with 200,000 soldiers. . . .

Great changes have been noticed among the Lithuanians in their relations toward Jews:

The last searches for fur coats went differently from all previous ones.

The Lithuanians have eased up considerably in their guard duty at the ghetto gate.

They say that [Antanas] Smetona,[87] in exile in America, has created an emigré government and has declared war on Germany.

They say that the Vilna Ghetto is to be opened and only a district for Jews will remain here. A similar quarter, they say, presumably already exists in Kovno.

After the series of shootings of various Jewish agents, people say that it will soon be the turn of the famous hero Serebrovich. People say he has been shot to death recently.

After the New Year's Eve party at the "chief's," last night a New Year's party was organized by the police of the third [ghetto] district, at Strashun 13. Among the speakers, a Lithuanian policeman of the fourth precinct complained that the Lithuanians are worse off than the Jews. The Lithuanians are in the grip of dark, foreign forces. They are compelled to act in what will remain a dark chapter in the history of the Lithuanian nation. When Lithuania is liberated, the Jews will go free and pure, as martyrs; but the Lithuanians will always remain in history with a bitter testimonial. . . .

86. Music teacher, conductor of choruses in Jewish schools, and director of Yiddish and Hebrew choruses of adults. He continued his work in the ghetto and was killed in Camp Kivioli in Estonia. For his biography, see *Teachers' Memorial Book* 1954:278–279.

87. Former Lithuanian president. He came to power on December 17, 1926, as the result of a revolt of the Tautinikas, an organization of Lithuanian nationalists, and retained power until June 15, 1940, when Lithuania was Sovietized and Smetona fled to the United States.

The speech, a truly sincere one, could not, however, have been heard during the entire six months of the German occupation. Now suddenly other winds blow, and now such utterances are ripe.

We repeat—something does happen today; there is no doubt of it.

THEY SEARCH AGAIN

Today, suddenly and unexpectedly, Jewish police began roaming from house to house and requisitioning sacks.

If there was a sack of potatoes, they threw out the potatoes and took the sack. A few weeks ago, they took a valise from someone. The things were thrown out and packed in a sack. Now the things lie on the ground once again because the Jewish police have also taken the sack.

Who is to use the sacks, the Judenrat or the Germans? We shall try to find out.

THEY ARE FREEZING ON THE FRONTS

Today the railroad workers said that in recent days, masses of soldiers have been brought to Vilna with frozen hands and feet.

They tell this with a sadistic smile on their lips. . . .

And the latest radio communiqués brought from the city give us great relief.

The Russians are 50 kilometers from the Latvian border.

As a Jew counts the days of the Omer [after Passover], so we count the kilometers and every sort of movement of the Germans and . . . the Russians.

LACONIC

Another news flash about the nature of the Jewish police in the Vilna Ghetto: a policeman "Elder," a Jew from Kalisz, Henryk Zag[ajski],[88] told me this. During an Aktion, he reported to his boss that a new melina had been found with a certain number of people. Not thinking much, the boss muttered militarily:

"Too few . . . "

The fact is 100 percent true. The reporter is alive, and there are witnesses who are also alive [. . .]

PATI'S 76TH BIRTHDAY

Today, January 2, we may end on a happy note.

Today, the old Pati [Kremer] is 76 years old. We gathered together at my bed and celebrated her birthday. Only a few and, as she put it, only the closest were told about it.

88. Zagajski, who was not from Kalisz but from Kielce, worked in the ghetto administration. He came to Vilna with the refugees in 1939 and was subsequently in the partisan organization. After the war he lived in New York.

We made potato pancakes with tea and saccharine. In honor of her birthday, Pati brought a little can of preserved *kishke*.

Thus we spent a few good hours among friends.

THE GENERAL DESTRUCTION IN LITHUANIA

Six weeks ago, we promised to note the great general destruction of the Jewish population in all of Lithuania, which has been carried out systematically.

On Saturday, October 26, about six days before going to Rudnicka 6 during the general purge in Vilna—on that same Saturday, under various pretexts, the Jews were led out of Kovno Ghetto, Niemenczyn, Olkieniki, Rudziszki, Troki, and Landwarowo; thousands of Jews were shot in a beastly way. In Kovno alone, about 1,000 Jews were shot, as we wrote at that time.

There is another fact which we note only now, after a delay of several months. Now we know it accurately and precisely. When the Jews entered the Vilna Ghetto, masses of Jews were taken out of Lidzki Street to prison and from there to Ponar. Similarly, thousands of Jews were liquidated, ostensibly taken from their homes to the ghetto, but actually driven to an unknown place.

Sober minds only now estimate that that sad number reaches 7,000 liquidated Jews!

JANUARY 3 [1942]

COMRADE NOYEKH IS DEAD

We received the news that Comrade Noyekh,[89] one of the last of the legendary pleiad of old Bundists, has died in America. He was the Bundist chancellor, the eternal chairman of the last Central Committee. At the B[und] conferences I had the honor to attend, Comrade Noyekh was the only man we all revered.

Honor to his memory.

EMPTY RUMORS

After the alarming news that the trucks to Warsaw and Białystok were detained,[90] after the alarm that Dr. [Ayzik] Goldburt[91] was caught, that Engineer

89. Pseudonym of Yekusiel Portnoy, also known as Józef. He was one of the pioneers and leaders of the Bund and served as chairman of the Central Committee of the Bund in Poland. He lived in Warsaw before the war and came to Vilna in 1939 with the refugees. At the end of 1940, he arrived in America; he died in New York on September 27, 1941. For his biography, by Kh. Sh. Kazdan, see *Generations* 1:68–122.

90. A reference to an organized attempt by a group of Vilna Jews to move to those other ghettos, which were presumably safer.

91. A physician who went to Białystok with his wife and who was sent from there to Treblinka in August 1943. For his biography, see Goldshmidt 1935:433–435.

Chwat is in Łukiszki—we know now for sure that the former is in Białystok and the latter in Warsaw. All the rest have reached their destination in peace.

APPEAL FOR AUXILIARY LABOR TO GERMANY

As if nothing had happened, as if, for example, the Germans had never carried away 2 million Poles for forced labor in Germany, as if so far nothing had happened with those citizens who were used for penal servitude, I suddenly read an announcement in the press:

[*The announcement is missing.*]

Truly a disgrace: if you want to come, we will treat you with great care. If they at least were able to take care of themselves. . . .

But, since nobody comes and nobody adjusts to it, the same comes in another way:

[*The text of the announcement is missing.*]

So it is clear that if they won't go willingly, they will be taken by force. Just as with the voluntary registration of fur coats, just as they collected skis and ski shoes, just as they collected electrical appliances, etc.

Soon, if they succeed, we'll be naked.

FROM VILNA TO GRODNO

Recently, 150 Jewish workers, who had been working until now in the fifth regiment, were sent to Grodno (?).

MORE RUMORS

The rumor that the gates of the ghetto will be opened on the fifth circulates stubbornly in Vilna. Today it was noted that people can come in and go out of the ghetto freely:

"Where is the guard?"

BREAKING IN AT THE GATE OF THE JEWISH HOSPITAL

Interesting: the main entrance of the Jewish hospital is from Zawalna. When the ghetto was created, the iron door was nailed up with boards. On the night of the 2nd–3rd, those on duty in the hospital heard wood boards breaking. No one dared go out. Not until morning did it become clear that half the boards had been torn off. People interpreted this in various ways. Either the breaking of the gate was a demonstration by the Poles or . . . a simple attempt by bandits to break in. . . .

In today's mood, the first notion can make sense.

WITHOUT ELECTRICITY

For a week now, some streets, or one side of several ghetto streets, have no electricity. This is the punishment of the electric plant for using too much electricity.

FROZEN GERMANS

They say that twenty-six train cars of frozen German military personnel were brought to Vilna yesterday.

IN AND AROUND KOVNO, THERE ARE NO MORE JEWS

Had a conversation today with a Lithuanian railroad worker who lives and works in Kovno. He says that Jews from Czechoslovakia and Belgium have presumably recently been brought to Kovno. He says that it has become easier in the Kovno Ghetto. That a lot of Jews live outside the ghetto. He also tells of the already described auction of Jewish objects, which presumably took place publicly in the cities and towns of the Kovno district. The main thing he reports is that in the area of Kovno, in all the little towns in the region, there are absolutely no Jews. . . .

And he's not the only one who tells about that! . . .

JANUARY 4 [1942]

SAVING JEWISH BOOKS

We have already mentioned people who come and ask me to help them save the treasures of books scattered and neglected in their abandoned houses. Lately, people have been coming with the same complaint about books from Ghetto 2.

Today, Betsalel Jakubson, brother of Vladimir Jakubson, a member of the Labor Group organization[92] and former deputy to the Russian *Duma*[93] from Grodno Province, came to me. He says he is the brigadier of a group of municipal workers who have been sent to collect belongings from houses in Ghetto 2. There, he has seen thousands of Yiddish books, religious books, and Torahs. He says the Strashun Library is completely abandoned. Until Friday the door was sealed, but then it was torn open. A Polish Christian directs their work and is willing to help save books. Jakubson wants me to advise him. Naturally I did. Bring them—do what you can to save the books.

A shoemaker tells me we have two guests today—two district commissars. One is General von Pensel, commissar of Orel District; the other, General von Hils, commissar of Smolensk District.

Both came from those Russian districts as if escaping from a fire. Both shaggy, unshaved, and looking awful.

The shoemaker says that the district commissars have run away from their districts.

Orel and Smolensk . . .[94]

92. I.e., *Trudoviki,* a Russian democratic party.

93. The parliament of tsarist Russia.

94. Russian cities west of Moscow. This scene is evidence of the Russian counteroffensive, which pushed the German army back from the outskirts of Moscow in the winter of 1941–1942.

HOW THE SITUATION LOOKS IN FACT

Two days ago, the Jewish workers for the SS were suddenly told that they were released from work for today. Tomorrow, at the regular time, they are to appear for work as usual.

The Germans were edgy and absent-minded.

What had happened?

Eight days ago, their unit went to the front. Today they were informed that the unit had been totally destroyed.

As a sign of mourning, they have stopped work in the SS unit.

WHAT SITUATION IS CREATED?

Yesterday a German acquaintance, a railroad worker, came to a private home. He says that most of the German railroad workers have been sent out of Vilna—that altogether forty German railroad workers are left and that the Lithuanians will substitute for the Germans. German semi-invalids, who will eventually be convalescents, will provide assistance. . . .

HOW THE WAREHOUSES OF THE VILNA JUDENRAT ARE EMPTIED

Searching in the clothing warehouse, the wife of a member of the Judenrat, Mrs. Gukhman, found a valise with "good things"—a fur coat, bed linens, etc. She asked for it, and the valise wound up with Mrs. Gukhman. Now the incident is exposed, and Mr. Gukhman, a decent and honest man, does not feel terribly comfortable about his expensive wife. . . .

Enough about Mrs. Gukhman. Then comes Mrs. Fried. She complains; why shouldn't she complain, isn't she the wife of "Mr. Fraud"?[95]

Why should she fall behind Mrs. Gukhman? . . .

JANUARY 5 [1942]

FRIED, THE OBMANN OF THE VILNA GHETTO

Here is a Jew who spent his whole life in Vilna, and no one in Jewish Vilna knew anything about him. His trademark was white gaiters and a pair of light-colored gloves. His "importance": he was director of the Vilna Communal Fund. In the city, wicked people called him *cocotte* [whore] or . . . gangster. We have already talked about that.

Now, unfortunately, someone suggested to the Germans to appoint him to the Judenrat. And that is indeed what happened—from a simple member of the first

95. In the Yiddish, "Herr *Obmann*," a pun: ***Ob****mann* in German means "Elder" or "chief," but in Russian, *Ob**man*** means "fraud."

Vilna Judenrat, Fried became its vice-chairman and then the Obmann of the Judenrat in the ghetto.

Did anyone want him as chairman? No one. The day after the Jews entered the ghetto, a new Judenrat of five was appointed. When the five nominees met to deliberate, it somehow happened that Fried presided over the meeting. That was a year ago, and Fried still presides over the meetings; thus, he is the chairman, in our language, the Obman [Fraud]. . . .

Is he big enough for the job? No. Can he pull it off? Yes.

Who couldn't lead here? The police beat. The Judenrat does all that is ordered. The population is treated like dogs.

Who couldn't do such work?

That's how the ghetto is, and that's how Fried is.

POST OFFICE IN THE GHETTO

The ghetto has gotten a post office. How is this post office different from all post offices in the ghettos we know about? Everywhere else, you can write letters in Polish and German. Here in Vilna, only in German.

If someone intervened, perhaps they could do something about it? No one says anything because it doesn't interest anyone, and Jews torture themselves to write German letters.

While we're on the subject of correspondence, we have to mention again the contribution of the Vilna Judenrat for the good of the population. The Vilna Judenrat receives masses of letters asking about friends and relatives. Thousands of the relatives are already in the next world, and about thousands nothing is known. The relatives are dying for a word—doesn't everybody know what happened in Vilna?

Did the post office department become interested in the enormous coll[ection] of names without addressees?

The letters are lying about, and they will soon be thrown away. . . .

COOPERATION

There are three cooperatives in the ghetto: a police cooperative, a cooperative in the Jewish hospital, and the recently established cooperative of Judenrat employees, whose purpose is to share the food of the "white permit" holders.

The Judenrat decided to give up to 50,000 rubles' credit to each cooperative. However, it set a condition for the last cooperative. It gives 50,000 rubles on condition that the cooperative sell its merchandise only to members.

Naturally, the cooperative thus loses its idealism, and the members withdraw completely from the credit.

Better to rely on your own strength than to set off on the path of Judenrat social work.

AID SOCIETY AND A REPRESENTATION OF PROFESSIONALS

As a cooperation of Judenrat employees, the cooperative assumes the task of a professional representative of employees. Hence, a delegation went to the abovementioned Fried and asked for a raise for the employees. Fried answered: Impossible. Anyway, he thinks all day about the employees, but unfortunately he has no means.

The departments now elect their representatives to the professional committee, and the committee will probably teach Mr. Fried to deduct from other expenses and transfer them to a minimum salary for the Judenrat employees.

Today I'm writing constantly about the Judenrat: the lunches, as we said, were stopped because of the arrogance of the chairman of the Judenrat. The society therefore was forced to send all their lunch-takers back to the Judenrat. Hundreds stand there and fight in the corridors for a . . . lunch.

Registration books have been introduced. "White permits" will not be registered. The "white permits" thus remain doomed to destruction. What Schweinenberg, Murer, Hering, et al., have not succeeded in doing so far will finally be accomplished by the Vilna Judenrat.

The Aid Society called a conference of all units concerning all these questions. Representatives of eight large units attended the conference: Kailis, HKP, supply camp, field command, war hospital, etc.[96] Altogether they represent about 1,000 workers of the ghetto.

The speakers emphasized that they felt fortunate because, for the first time since they have been in the ghetto, they were able to attend an assembly where they didn't talk about undermining one another but talked about mutual aid.

The conference will soon speak sharply with Fried about all the enumerated issues.

CAKES AND MURER

The few free days in the ghetto have had an effect. A heavy trade has begun in the ghetto. People are trading in the street. At the gates, they sell meat, bread, cigars, cigarette paper, matches, saccharine, onions, etc.

Today the ghetto is flooded with cakes. Five rubles a cake. Suddenly the joy is destroyed. A guest has come into the ghetto—Murer. Murer has indeed come and stood at the gate to check those returning to the ghetto. If anyone had "too much" food, Murer ordered it taken away. If anyone came alone from the street when he should have come with the group, his permit was taken away and . . . meanwhile, he was allowed to return to the ghetto. Today, 27 permits were taken away. What end awaits the 27, no one yet knows.

96. These are units that worked for various German military groups. After the liquidation of the ghetto, the war hospital unit became a work camp where as many as seventy Jews worked.

CHRISTIANS

Incidentally, concerning today's commotion at the gate. Christians went over various areas of the city, warning the Jews what was happening at the gate. Naturally, more than one person was thus saved, and food was rescued from Murer's robbery.

LITHUANIANS THEN AND LITHUANIANS NOW

In Ruzele, a suburb of Vilna, not far from Subocz, 30 Jews were arrested in the homes of various peasants. After an investigation, they were gathered and taken away . . . to the ghetto. This time, they didn't touch a hair of the Jews' heads. This was done by Lithuanians. . . .

Times change. Lithuanians in Vilna not long ago and Lithuanians in the same Vilna today.

NEWS FROM THE OTHER WORLD

Today we got information that a lot of Jews were taken out of Głębokie and Lida.

When this happened and where they were taken are hard to find out right now.

WITHOUT ELECTRICITY

Three-fourths of the ghetto, including most of the institutions of the Judenrat, are still without electricity.

Either you can't work because of the cold, or because there's no electricity, or because of . . . Aktions.

JANUARY 6 [1942]

BLACKOUT

Just as a religious Jew carefully observes the time to light candles, so the German press carefully observes the time of the blackout. For example, here is one of the hundreds of press calendars you find in every newspaper:

[*The press calendar is missing.*]

The Polish press, more Nazi than the Nazi press, makes it even more precise:

[*The extract is missing.*]

So, the non-German press is more Catholic than the Pope himself. . . .

NEW WINDS, NEW SONGS

Jews tell. At the railroad, they saw a gigantic train today with skis. Jews console themselves: it's too late. . . .

Carloads full of sleds pass by, and Jews don't give in—too late. . . .

Today, 50 carloads of frozen soldiers passed through Vilna, and Jews console themselves—it's all too little, may the cold not relent. . . .

Two long trains of Lithuanians were sent to the front: it will be as much help as medicine for a corpse. . . .

Jews mustn't think badly of them, it's not their fault. They were forced to do it. Lithuanians have nothing against Jews.

TILL TIME COMES TO CONSOLE, YOU'LL GIVE UP YOUR SOUL

Meanwhile news comes that Jews are being taken out of several cities in Byelorussia. They are being taken out of Biała Waka[97] and Rzesza. Some people report that only the sick are taken away because there is supposedly typhus there; but others say they are purging, purging, purging. . . .

PEOPLE TAKE FROM THE DEAD AND FROM THE LIVING

Those close to the rulers of the Vilna Ghetto make believe they don't know anything. People go through houses here, and where they find a whole bed, a decent piece of furniture, a chair, a table, etc., they record it, and the next day, the blue-banded Jewish policemen come and take everything away with the explanation that this is what the Germans ordered.

What the Bolsheviks in their day and then the Germans and later the Germans and Lithuanians together didn't manage to do is now done in the ghetto by the Jewish policemen.

A holy mission!

PEOPLE "AMUSE" THEMSELVES

The big shots in the Jewish police "amuse" themselves together with their German colleagues from the Gestapo and others.

The ghetto provides . . . the chief's apartments, girls, brandy, and recently an orchestra is also organized for the purpose. . . .

TILL THE FIRST BITE OF BREAD

At first, the Housing Department of the Judenrat took 7 rubles a month from a ghetto resident for rent; later it was 12, and now we have to pay 30 rubles.

The average salary of a worker is 300 rubles. With a family of three people, it comes to this:

97. A village fourteen kilometers from Vilna, where there was a camp even before the Vilna Ghetto was established. In the summer of 1941, when the great snatchings were going on in Vilna, hundreds of Jews working in that peat-digging camp were saved from the Aktions in the city. In the spring of 1943, the Biała Waka Jews were taken to the Vilna Ghetto. Later a few hundred were again selected and sent back to Biała Waka. The camp ended in a bloody liquidation. Additional details of the events in the camp are given later in the diary. In the YIVO Archive (Kaczerginski-Sutzkever Collection, no. 250), there is a report of the camp from August 18, 1942, including the number of employed, etc.

Apartment	90 rubles
Three bread cards	9 rubles
Water and "block"[98]	9 rubles
Electricity	? rubles

Before the bread, about 130 rubles. A kilo of bread now costs about 40 rubles. . . .

JANUARY 7 [1942]

HAUZ, MOYSHE

We have already written about the martyr's death of Moyshe Hauz, who, refusing to be taken to Ponar, fell heroically in the last purge.

Hauz has remained the hero of the ghetto, the first to dare to resist, adhering to the position that circulates here:

Better to die on the spot like a human being than like a dog in Ponar. . . .

Everyone repeated it, but no one dared do it. Moyshe Hauz was the first who dared.

Who is that Hauz?

Hauz was born in Zamość on February 12, 1902. His father, Leyb, was a barber-surgeon; his mother, Yokheved, a midwife. Moyshe completed a Polish grammar school, studied electronics and worked in Zamość until 1937. After his marriage, he settled in Warsaw, and in September 1939 he fled Warsaw, arriving in Vilna in January 1940. From here, he wanted to immigrate to Palestine. The German invasion threw him, along with the whole population of Vilna, into the ghetto, where he remained with his wife without any means to live and without a yellow permit. At every purge, he was forced to hide in a melina with all the unfortunate "whites."

He wandered like that with his wife in cellars and attics, and meanwhile he sold everything he could, was often a porter, sold newspapers and cigars.

At the last purge, on December 22, 1941, he was caught in one of the melinas at Szpitalna Street 13 and refused to go with the Lithuanian hangmen. A bullet in his head, and Hauz died in the arms of his wife. Now she lives in the ghetto.

She says her husband was an active member of the Right Poalei Zion.[99]

I attach his picture.

[*The picture is missing.*]

98. Probably a tax for cleaning the block.

99. An essay by Shlomo Schwarzberg (1957:731–732) tells about the Hauz family of Zamość, a well-known family of medics. Avrom Żeleznikow, former chairman of the Youth Club in the ghetto and later a partisan (now living in Australia), claims in his memoirs (1949) that Moyshe Hauz was a Bundist. According to Kruk's entry, this is incorrect. Żeleznikow, only a youth at the time, probably got the impression that Hauz was a Bundist because the Bund issued a leaflet about his death.

A LETTER FROM KHAYKL LUNSKI

A letter received by a certain Herman[100] concerning the "white permits," from a popular Vilna resident, Khaykl L[unski], says, among other things:

Dear Herman!

My fate persecutes me dreadfully. All my friends have forgotten me and look at me with scorn and contempt. All sorts of boys and girls have obtained yellow permits, and I, who have given my life for Vilna, have not obtained a yellow permit and cannot register and protect my only daughter, a highly educated person, my one and only friend in life. She remains without protection, without bread, and without work. The two of us cannot live on 120 grams of bread a day. There is nothing to sell, and to live on the charity of friends [is] very hard. So we are often starving. But even worse than starving is the menace of Ponar. Everyone is deaf to all my requests for a protection permit for my daughter. Nobody wants to talk to me; I cannot even get to them.

I have no more strength to bear the torments and grief. I walk around like a madman from the fear and terror of Ponar, and often—thinking of the thousands of innocent, pure souls murdered in Ponar for the Sanctification of the Name, of the devastation of all our holy objects, of the destruction of our cultural institutions, and so forth—I don't want to live. Rather than be killed by a murderous hand in the pits of Ponar, it is better to be killed by myself and at least have a Jewish grave.

We are bitter and desperate, and we appeal to you, dear Herman, take pity! Be the agent of the Lord of the Universe and save us from destruction!

We appeal to your great soul, your noble heart, your conscience, your great possibilities!

Take pity, take pity!!!

Kh[aykl] L[unski]

December 31, 1941

SOCIAL ACTIVITY IN THE GHETTO

Two quick facts that are typical of the social "activity" of the local apparatus of the Judenrat and the Vilna population's relation to it:

I accidentally entered Fried's office. There stands a citizen of the ghetto, talking excitedly:

"You want to bathe in my blood?! . . ."

I left the office, not wanting to listen to the conversation. Obviously, they again took some savings from a Jew to cover the broad expenses of the ass-kissers of the Judenrat "for the good of Vilna Jewry." . . .

Then I went into another office, to the director of the Sanitary-Hygienic De-

100. Kruk means himself.

partment, Commissar Goldman. Two women stand at his desk; both request to be released from punishment. One begs him:

"I don't have anything to pay with. My only food is the soup I take from the kitchen. Where should I get it?"

The "commissar," the rich Warsaw Jew, [former] director of [the] Europa insurance company, does not take the bitter words to heart and answers:

"Why is your place dirty? If you're dirty, you've got to pay!"

Her arguments don't help, and the woman gets angry:

"The Germans at least give us death, but you take our lives from us. . . ."

From there, I went to police headquarters. Behind me, someone is talking to himself:

"Snatchers, their bellies should burn. . . ."

Three different cases, but each of them, in its own way, shows how the tormented and beaten Vilna people relate to the rulers of the ghetto.

THE GHETTO SNATCHERS

Snatchers. Here they are indeed called *Khapunes*. In the ghetto police, there is a special group of 10 Snatchers, whose job is to snatch people wherever needed, to denounce melinas whenever necessary, to guard, to search and rummage around where it is ordered and where it is not.

Snatchers—that's what they're called.

GHETTO STRONGMEN

But there is another part of our police—strongmen, *shlegers*. There are cases when they want to or have to squeeze out something, and there are two special "heroes" for that. One of the beaters is Seidel, a Vilna butcher, who has already risen to the rank of sergeant; and the second is just a hooligan whose name I shall try to find out and register.

So, as we see, a kingdom with kingdoms, a police as in other nations. . . .

ABOUT THE ARRESTED DR. JACOB WYGODZKI AND ABOUT HIS WIFE

The chairman of the former pre-ghetto Judenrat [Dr. Wygodzki] was arrested despite his advanced age. All efforts to free him have not produced the slightest result. His wife, an old woman, has remained alone and helpless. When she was dragged into the ghetto, the group of doctors took pity on her and kept her in the Jewish hospital. Now she has come for aid. The Judenrat has just now provided her with a "pink permit." . . .

PROCLAMATIONS IN THE GHETTO

We present one of the typical proclamations that swarm and teem in the ghetto.

We present the language and orthography just as they are in the original:[101]

101. Kruk's indignation is directed at the proclamation's semi-literate Yiddish, mixed with distorted German.

PROCLAMATION NO. 30
From the Police Chief of the Vilna Ghetto
January 5, 1942

For spreading incorrect information and panic among the population, I have punished two inhabitants of the ghetto with imprisonment on January 3, 1942.

I call your attention to the fact that I shall severely punish anyone who commits the same offense.

Chief of Police

CONCERNING THE "VOLUNTARY" COLLECTION OF FURS

We already know about the "voluntary" collection of furs that occurred recently throughout the German Reich and all occupied countries. We know about it especially in the ghetto and in Vilna generally.

Now the results, as reported today in the press, become comprehensible to us: [*The extract is missing.*]

GHETTO 2

In today's newspaper is a note that says that the so-called Ghetto 2 is designated as a residential area for Aryans. I attach the article. Interesting, however, to know which Aryans will settle there.
[*The article is missing.*]

SUMMARY RESULTS OF OUR EXPEDITIONS

As a result of our efforts with the expeditions to Ghetto 2, until January 1, the objects and museum valuables were saved by us according to the attached lists:

1. List of objects and museum valuables.
2. List of chronicles collected in the prayer houses.[102]

[*Both lists are in the YIVO Archive (Kaczerginski-Sutzkever Collection, nos. 476/7, 476/8)*]

Inventory of [Religious] Objects and Museum Valuables Now at Strashun Street 6
126 scrolls
9 scrolls
170 Prophets and *megillot*
26 shofars
13 Hanukkah lamps and menorahs
12 silver, brass, and copper candleholders

102. Both lists are in the YIVO Archive (Kaczerginski-Sutzkever Collection, nos. 476/7, 476/8).

15 chandeliers and wall lamps
11 tin plates from columns
21 parts of ornaments for the Holy Ark
2 pairs of doors for the Holy Ark
1 Simhat Torah torch
7 engraved tablets
5 cardboard Torah crowns
5 *mezuzot*
6 seals of prayer houses
1 lock of an iron safe
11 spice boxes
10 silver, metal, and wood pointers
17 Torah scroll plates
4 silver and metal chalices
1 tobacco case
2 *ethrog* cases
5 walls of a Holy Ark
3 clocks
61 pieces of metal parts (silver, etc.)
10 lavers and pitchers for hand-washing for Cohens
12 charity boxes
12 Trees of Life (white metal [and?] silver)
39 parts of Trees of Life
16 parts of Trees of Life, wooden and ivory
34 metal letters from the curtains of the Holy Ark
4 Torah crowns (2 silver, 1 tin, 1 broken)
Tombstone [?] from the Gaon's Prayer House
4 pulpits
4 carved little doors to [named synagogue seats]
21 curtains of the Holy Ark and *kapoyres*—complete
24 *paroykhes* (curtains of the Holy Ark)
37 kapoyres
110 Torah covers
11 tallises
24 tallis bags
7 pair of *tefillin*
17 tefillin bags
14 tablecloths
21 small tablecloths
1 silk shawl
4 banners of *Ha-Shomer ha-Dati*
3 trimmed cords

3 ornamental strips
2 yarmulkes
17 pictures
1 picture of M. Strashun
2 prayerbooks (a cover-all *mahzor,* volume 1, made of parchment)
The same, volume 4
3 engravings in frames
2 oil paintings
1 scissors to cut wicks
2,464 books from Strashun Library
20 manuscripts
Parchment of banners from Jogiches Prayer House (*Shivah Kruyim*)
1 box with a scroll of the counting of the *omer*
The *bima* of Elyashberg's Prayer House
Vilna, January 2, 1942
(—) H. Kruk

List of Chronicles Collected in Prayer Houses, Now Collected in the Library of the Judenrat
Donations of the Painters' Prayer House, 1887 (Malarska)
Talmud Society in the Elyashberg Prayer House (1904)
Hospitality Fund of the Jewish Community of Żoludek (1870)
Yortsayt Book of Dvoyre Ester's Prayer House
Torah Students in the New Painters' Prayer House
(New Malarska Prayer House) 1902
Welfare Society in the Painters' Prayer House, 1902
New Mishna Society . . . Prayer House of Rabbi Elyashberg, 1907
Record Book of Yortsayts of the Mishna Society of Elyashberg, 1914
Women's Section (Donation Fund) of the Chimney Sweepers' Prayer House, 1893
Record Book of the City Talmud Torah of Yortsayts (1905)

STREET COMMERCE

Trade in the ghetto is lively lately. Jews bring in things, and often non-Jews sneak in as well.

Here is an example:

At Strashun 3, there is a hole that leads easily out of the ghetto. Almost every day, a Christian comes through, bringing butter, eggs, chickens, etc.

Today I saw him alone holding a sled with a basket of ducks. He negotiated a good price for it, and Jews buy and . . . pay.

Apropos trade. Because of Murer's last visit, it has again become harder to bring food into the ghetto. The food is often confiscated at the gate.

Today, for example, they took two pounds of fat from a Jew there—clearly a trader, clearly a speculator, earning thousands of rubles a day. Those do indeed buy ducks to eat, and they can afford it. Others don't buy, and live from the little soup they get in the cheap kitchen of the Judenrat.

On the one hand, speculation, robbery, and thievery; on the other, misery, hunger, and terrible poverty.

JANUARY 8 [1942]

Street Commerce

Street commerce in the ghetto becomes ever more active. Some Jews brought wagon loads of wood into the ghetto and sold them there openly.

Today a woman selling cakes advertised her wares in rhymes:

"Gather round, soon it won't be found!"

In a [courtyard] gateway stands a young man holding chunks of chocolate on a plate—five rubles apiece.

This trade is likely to be stopped soon. Today a big sign was posted at the ghetto gate, announcing that bringing food and wood into the ghetto is forbidden.

That is the consequence of Murer's last visit in the ghetto.

Apropos the 27 permits [see the entry of January 5, above], for the time being Murer has them all. It might be possible to get them back.

PASSES

Whoever has a finger in the pot, or has the pull to bring in something in partnership for the ministering angels of the ghetto, has received a pass in a few hours allowing him to go into the city alone.

Today, when Mr. H.[103] once again appealed, arguing that with his connections he might be able to save the Strashun Library, which has remained abandoned in the territory of the second ghetto, Fried granted his request—he would attempt to get a pass to go out once or twice.

The marauder gets an unlimited pass. To save the Strashun Library, they agree to give a pass for one or two days. . . .

And go talk to a Jew Vilna calls a *cocotte* and who has the innate mentality of a banker.

What interest can such a person have for a "miserable Jewish Strashun Library."

FOREIGN CURRENCY

Once again, people relate that another large fortune in foreign currency was found. Those who had the good fortune to find it had a big drink on it.

The drinks cost 2,000 rubles.

103. Kruk means himself.

JANUARY 9 [1942]

SOME INFORMATION ABOUT GENS

Before the war, he was a teacher of the Lithuanian language in Kovno, a bookkeeper for the Kovno prison, and, at the same time, one of the leaders of the Brit ha-Hayal [Revisionists]. At the inception of the ghetto, he was director of the Jewish hospital, and later he became commander of the Jewish police.

PROSCRIPTION LISTS

In certain circles, they say that the Jewish Communists from the ghetto are making a proscription list of all those who will have to be sentenced to death by the future wo[rker's] regime.[104]

TWO GHETTO POLICEMEN ARRESTED

Yesterday, two Jewish policemen were arrested by Murer himself outside the ghetto and taken to Łukiszki.

Murer

Today Murer came back to the ghetto and once again arrested several people who were walking alone to the ghetto.

JANUARY 10 [1942]

Today we report several tragic events that happened to Jews in the Lithuanian towns.

The stories are the destruction of Lithuania in miniature.

[*In the original diary, two lines were crossed out here, with the following note: "See appendix 'Destruction of Lithuania.'" The appendix is missing.*]

TYPHUS . . . AND THE PATTERN OF READING IN THE GHETTO

Because of the so-called typhus epidemic, the ghetto administration has thought it necessary to close its only library, the Mefitsei-Haskalah Library. Hundreds of borrowers come, old people and children, and ask with concern:

"When will you open?"

The head of the Epidemics Department, Dr. Goldman, promises to make an effort. The rest procrastinate and take their time.

Meanwhile, the library does its internal work, and thus we learn a lesson on the nature of reading in the first three months of the Vilna Ghetto:

104. The Communists themselves put out such rumors so that people would be afraid of later acts of revenge. The ghetto leadership did indeed seem to be in awe of the Communists.

Readers in the Library

September 1941	1,485
October	1,739
November	2,260
December	2,560

Books Read in the Library, by Language

October	Number	Percent
Polish	6,277	80.41
Yiddish	1,306	16.72
Hebrew	61	0.78
Lithuanian	67	0.86
Russian	87	1.12
French	5	0.07
English	3	0.04
Other	—	—
Total	7,806	100.00

November	Number	Percent
Polish	7,156	77.62
Yiddish	1,743	18.88
Hebrew	45	0.5
Lithuanian	138	1.5
Russian	92	0.8
French	14	0.15
English	14	0.15
Other	32	0.40
Total	9,234	100.00

December	Number	Percent
Polish	6,338	74.5
Yiddish	1,884	22.2
Hebrew	38	0.4
Lithuanian	125	1.4
Russian	50	0.6
French	18	0.2
English	36	0.4
Other	23	0.3
Total	8,512	100.00

On December 19, the library was closed.

JANUARY 12 [1942]

NO LONGER RUMORS

Not only do we hear rumors, but it's now certain—we're entering a new age.

In all likelihood, the Germans are cracking. Finland, they say, is laying down its weapons. Battles are fought on the fields of Smolensk, the same Smolensk where the Germans lost hundreds of thousands last fall.

Latvia and Lithuania are bombed [by the Russians]. Daugavpils, Tallinn, and Kovno have been bombed. Vilna already had an alarm. Everyone waits impatiently. The first bombing will be the first symphony, which will sound like the most brilliant concert.

EVERYTHING AS BEFORE

Again they say in the city that young Poles are being snatched off the streets. They lay siege to some streets and take off young men just as they did to us right before the ghetto. . . .

Few Christian men are seen in the streets. Just as before, as with us, everything as before, right before the ghetto. . . .

JANUARY 13 [1942]

A SAD DOCUMENT

The tragic words of the helpless Mordkhe Wileńczyk speak to me like an echo of the not-too-distant past. Although the letter is from the end of October 1941, I present it in full and untouched as a document of the suffering of those tragically condemned men. As I write these lines, the people of Ghetto 2 are no longer alive, and no one knows where their bones have come to rest. But one thing is certain. The letter was written from Ghetto 2 after people had been dragged off from Ghetto 1, and there, in Ghetto 2, they were dying of hunger, hiding in melinas, and hunting a mouthful of bread like birds of prey.

I attach the document as a sad remnant of that time. . . .

[*Wileńczyk's letter is missing.*]

THE NUMBER OF INHABITANTS NOW IN OUR GHETTO

Another appendix: we have already written that the ghetto got [no] bread cards for January. The Judenrat receives a quantity of food, which must be distributed independently—of course, only among residents who have the right to register. The Judenrat, therefore, printed special Jewish bread cards, and I attach one as an example.

[*The bread card is missing.*[105]]

The remaining "whites," of course, are once again omitted.

Altogether, 13,600 bread cards have been distributed, including to all holders of permits, even protective permits (1,600). Altogether, it is estimated that 15,000 residents now live in the area of our ghetto. Thus, about 1,400 holders of white permits are still among us.

The professional representatives received an answer to their request to raise the fees of the employees. The answer was a raise of 100 rubles a month, irrespective of the category the employee belongs to.[106] However, this makes an average raise of 80 rubles per person.

Practically, it amounts to this:

1st category earns 687 [rubles] or 69 marks	(a raise of 25%)
2nd category earns 562 [rubles] or 57 marks	"
3rd category earns 435 [rubles] or 44 marks	"
4th category earns 375 [rubles] or 38 marks	"
5th category earns 338 [rubles] or 34 marks	(a raise of 40%)
6th category earns 280 [rubles] or 28 marks	(a raise of 35%)

JANUARY 15 [1942]

DR. ANTONI PAŃSKI

Today I received some sad news that my friend and comrade Dr. Antoni Pański died in Łukiszki, abandoned and alone.

Antoni Pański was one of the few quiet activists in the PPS. In 1916, he was arrested in Kovno by the German authorities and spent several months in the Kovno Seventh Fort.[107] Like me and many other refugees from Poland, he was supposed to leave for America. But the Russian NKVD set their sights on him and didn't grant him an exit visa. When the Germans entered Vilna, he stayed here, and as a convert from childhood, he did not wear the yellow patch and stayed outside the ghetto with his Christian friends.

105. Reproductions of bread cards from the Vilna Ghetto are in the YIVO-bleter 30:141; Korczak 1946:261. There were also forged bread cards; see Kowalski 1954:57.

106. This sentence seems to contradict the following chart. According to the chart, the raise was between 73 and 137 rubles, which is closer to Kruk's calculation, in the next sentence, of an average of 80 rubles.

107. "The nine Fortresses built by the Russian czars to protect the city of Kovno were used by the Nazis for the torture and massacre of 100,000 persons, 70,000 of them Jews" (Nora Levin, *The Holocaust* [New York: Schocken Books, 1973], p. 249).

All of a sudden, he was arrested, stayed in prison for several months, and in the past few weeks, was thrown out of a general cell into a Jewish one. There he died, lonely and forsaken.

Honor to his memory.

WHO SEEKS PROTECTION FROM WHOM

The wheel turns. There is commotion in the city. Christians are afraid of being arrested and sent to Germany to work.

Today I know of several cases of Poles asking Jewish friends to take them into the ghetto for the night.

The wheel turns.

IN THE WHIRLPOOL OF PERMITS . . .

Those who had pink "protection permits" had to get blue permits. Now it turns out that the blue permits will remain deposited with the Judenrat. Those who have protection permits will receive only a stamp on their permit indicating that their blue permit is in the possession of the Judenrat. What the Judenrat means by this device is not yet known.

JANUARY 16 [1942]

CAN IT BE?

Lately, it has been relatively calm in the ghetto. There is a battle for Smolensk, and everywhere you hear about a retreat of the German armies. The street is alive with new hope that it can be.

And can it be?

The most awful of awful we have already. . . . Could it be behind us?

Can it be, can it be that the ghetto's days are numbered? Let us therefore round out our entries to a whole. Let us start trying to penetrate corners of our ghetto life that we have had no time or possibility for up to now.

Let us carry our notes to obtain a plausible reflection of daily life in the Vilna Ghetto.

This is what preoccupies me now. We will gather material here and, as far as possible, will record it precisely.

ABOUT THE DEPARTMENT OF SOCIAL WELFARE IN THE JUDENRAT

We have mentioned the activity of this department in its first days. Now we will present some figures of its activity for December 1941:

1. The office distributed lunches (gratis)

	Total	Sum
A. Directly through the department	18,430	2,416.80 [Marks]
B. Through the Aid Society	4,720	627.40 [Marks]
C. Through Mr. Dessler's mediation	3,500	460.00 [Marks]
D. Children's daycare in the hospital	300	38.00 [Marks]
Total	26,950	3,542.20 [Marks]

2. Hospital treatment was given to 59 persons, 508 hospital days.
3. Ambulatory treatment and prescriptions: 43 persons.
4. Released completely or partially from rent: 57 exemptions, 161 persons altogether.
5. Acknowledged financial support for 47 exemptions, total of 306.26 Marks.

This is what the pitiful social provisions of the Vilna Judenrat looked like in December 1941.

JANUARY 17 [1942]

JOCHELSON, DANIEL

Just yesterday we mentioned the relative calm, but today we have to record another dramatic event:

Groups of Jews work in Porubanek unpacking and sorting various weapons and ammunition. A few days ago, two Jewish workers were accidentally killed by an explosion. The incident made an obvious impression in the ghetto.[108]

Something even sadder happened yesterday. A group of twenty-some people went out, as every day, to the area around Porubanek to buy food for the workers and their families. Just then, the area was surrounded by a group of Lithuanians. The Jews ran away. The Lithuanians shot at them. Two escaped, but the third—Daniel Jochelson—was hit by two bullets and fell dead on the spot. Another man, Blumental, was wounded. The rest were taken to Łukiszki.

Daniel Jochelson's body was brought to the ghetto on a peasant's sled and the funeral is tomorrow, Sunday.

The man who died so tragically had been an active member of the Youth Bund, Tsukunft, in Vilna for many years.

FIRST CONCERT IN THE GHETTO

Today I received a formal invitation from a founding group of Jewish artists in the ghetto announcing that the first evening of the local artistic circle will be held on

108. Because it implies that they were preparing a bomb.

Sunday, January 18, in the auditorium of the Real Gymnasium at Rudnicka 6. A dramatic and vocal musical program will be presented.

I felt offended, personally offended, about this whole thing, let alone the festive evening. In every ghetto you can amuse yourself; cultivating art is certainly a good deed. But here, in the doleful situation of the Vilna Ghetto, in the shadow of Ponar, where, of the 76,000 Vilna Jews, only 15,000 remain—here, at this moment, this is a disgrace.

An offense to all our feelings.

But as we know, the real initiators of the evening are the Jewish police. Furthermore, important guests, Germans, will come to the concert. Lyuba Lewicka, the brilliant Jewish singer, is even trying to have some German songs "on hand."

In case, God forbid, a German will ask for them! . . .

You don't make a theater in a graveyard.

The organized Jewish labor mov[ement][109] had decided to respond to the invitation with a boycott. Not one of them will go to the "crows' concert." But the streets of the ghetto are to be strewn with leaflets:

> about today's concert:
> YOU DON'T MAKE THEATER
> IN A GRAVEYARD

In this atmosphere, the ghetto will bury its victim—Daniel Jochelson. The police and the artists, along with the Germans, will amuse themselves, and the Vilna Ghetto will mourn. . . .

BIAŁYSTOK

We wrote that Dr. Goldburt left for Białystok. Later, that he was arrested on the way and is now in Łukiszki; later still, that the news about the arrest was not certain and that he is in Białystok.

Recently we obtained some information: with the participation of that doctor, 40,000–50,000 rubles have been collected to rescue us from the Vilna Ghetto.

With tears in our eyes we rejoiced at the fine comradely initiative.

CALENDAR OF THE SOVIET-GERMAN BATTLES FOR THE WAR YEAR 1941

I attach here a newspaper extract of a calendar of the Soviet battles for the war year 1941.

[*The newspaper extract is missing.*]

What the German soldiers look like on the Eastern Front is indicated by the aid suggested in the German and pro-German press.

I attach the extract of that suggestion.

[*The extract is missing.*]

109. I.e., the Bund.

“REDS” AND THE AID SOCIETY

We already mentioned the advice given us lately by the Zionist social activists.[110] Lately, they have talked to us on their own behalf and on behalf of the . . . “R[eds].”[111] The latter denied this at first. Recently, they came themselves and demanded the same things as their comrades . . . the “R’s.” However, the “R’s” have negotiated with us for . . . cooperation.

Finally we reached an agreement: 3 of ours remain in the administration, the “R’s” send 2 (so they, too, get 3), the Zionists send 3, and that leaves in addition 1 Trop[112] and 1 Berek.[113] Moreover, at our suggestion, the “R’s” promised to create a faction within the administration consisting of our representatives and their representatives. That means a minimum of 6 out of 11, eventually 7 out of 11, including Trop.

Let us hope that the crisis of the Aid Society has thus passed and that the society is in proletarian hands for a while.[114]

JANUARY 18 [1942]

ANTISEMITISM IN POLAND, IDEOLOGICAL SLACKNESS OF THE REDS

I have received information about Polish social activity in . . . London, Warsaw, and . . . Vilna.

In London, the Endeks[115] left the government.[116] One of the causes: their unwillingness to grant equal rights to national minorities.

Warsaw does as London and Vilna do. The Vilna comrades cannot understand why Jewish workers are seeking a connection with them:

“How can you help us?” asked the leader of the Vilna PPS, with a thin smile.

“What will that contact really give us?”

Antisemitism is blowing again from the Endeks to the PPS.

The “R’s” have not learned much either. They make overtures, we are told;

110. This advice was probably mentioned in the missing pages. Apparently, it was a move to create a larger political base for the Aid Society, initiated by the Bund.

111. I.e., the Communists.

112. *Trop.* is Kruk’s abbreviation for Fayvl Trupiański, well known Socialist-Revolutionary (SR) activist in Vilna, and brother of Yankev Trupiański.

113. Rabbi Aaron Berek, chairman of Agudat Israel (the religious Orthodox party).

114. The Aid Society was founded initially by Bundists, who administered it. Later, it became a source of interparty haggling for influence. At this point the Socialist parties (Bund, Communists, Socialist-Revolutionaries) have a majority.

115. *Endek* is the nickname of the ND, or Narodowa Demokracja (National democracy), an antisemitic right-wing Polish party.

116. I.e., the Polish government-in-exile.

they talk with comrades from the "B[und]" and negotiate simultaneously about the very same issue with the Zionists of Mr. Milkanow[icki's] trend.

It smacks of prewar ideological slackness. Didn't even the Reds learn anything during the second bloody world war?[117] . . .

PERMITS

After long months, the tragic chapter of the permits now comes to an end. According to the attached order, the holders of all sorts of permits must register with the Jewish police. That office will completely legalize the registrees.

In the attached order, we underline the artificial Yiddish and call attention to the Yiddish-German style.[118]

[*The order is missing.*]

JANUARY 19 [1942]

ABOUT THE FIRST CONCERT IN THE GHETTO

The concert we have already written about is over. In general, it was a success. The singers Lewicka, Rechtig, and [Shabse] Blacher[119] took part in the concert.

Seventy percent of those gathered in the auditorium were Jewish policemen, their wives, and their children; the rest were all brands of Zionists, Judenrat members, and others.

A poster hung at the entrance:

"There must be no hungry person in the ghetto." At the entrance, about 4,000 rubles were collected.

The notices posted in the streets (see the entry of two days ago) made a colossal impression. The police sent a special brigade into the streets to tear them down. Nevertheless, throughout the day, leaflets were distributed in all the public places of the ghetto: the kitchens, the clinics, the post office, the Judenrat building, etc.

ACTS OF SABOTAGE

While the first concert was performed in the ghetto, the whole city was illuminated by a big fire. The fur factory, Kailis, burned.

117. As a prewar Bundist Socialist, Kruk dislikes the idea of a common front with the Zionist and "bourgeois" parties, with whom the Communists are prepared to join in a tactical coalition. Underneath all this was a move to create a "popular front" coalition as a basis for the partisan organization in the ghetto, which Communists, Labor Zionists, General Zionists, and the Bund participated in.

118. This offense to the literary Yiddish language indicates that the police did not include Yiddish intellectuals, or that it was dominated by Germanized Jews from Lithuania.

119. Born in Vilna in 1907. He was a member of the Vilna Troupe Theater and died in Camp Klooga, Estonia. More details about him below.

As far as I know, 25 percent of the finished products were burned there. . . .

As I discovered, this is the third fire in Vilna in recent days.

A few days ago, the former Polish Technical School on the Holendernia also burned down, today the workshops of the German HKP.

JANUARY 20 [1942]

ASSOCIATION OF WRITERS AND ARTISTS

This Sunday in the ghetto, an association of Jewish writers, authors, and artists was created. So far, 20 writers, 22 stage artists, 16 musicians and singers, and 6 painters have joined the association, and there is also a list of 15 families of writers and artists who were taken away.

The purpose of the association: to provide mutual aid and an inducement to artistic creation in the context of the ghetto; to put together a chronicle of Jewish writers, artists, and intellectuals who were taken off; to collect works abandoned by those who were taken off; and to prepare material for a literary and artistic almanac from the ghetto.

The following were elected to the leadership of the association: Kalman[owicz], Herman [Kruk], [Yankev] Gerstein,[120] [Shabse] Blach[er], [Abraham] Sutz[kever], [Hersh] Gut[gestalt] and [Yankev] Sher.[121]

ELECTRICITY

The extinguished electricity in several streets makes it clear that the ghetto will receive electricity only occasionally. The inhabitants of the ghetto will be allowed to use electricity from 6:30 until 9 in the morning and . . . from 9 at night.

Clearly, it will be impossible to cook on electricity, and the evenings will be unbearable, with people forced to sit in the dark until 9. A small candle in the ghetto costs 15 rubles.[122]

FORCED LABOR BEFORE THE GHETTO

We attach two tables of figures on the magnitude of forced labor before the establishment of the ghetto: the tables include the months of July [1941], from the 11th

120. A pioneer of the Yiddish secular schools and director of school choirs. In 1908, he participated in the first illegal Yiddish teachers' conference in Vilna, under Russian tsarist rule. He died in the ghetto. More information about him is provided in later entries. For his biography, see *Teachers' Memorial Book* 1954:109–111; *Lexicon* 2:325–326.

121. A prominent painter, who was later sent to Camp Vaivara in Estonia. He died in 1944. For his biography, see *Teachers' Memorial Book* 1954:430–431.

122. Order Number 33, dealing with limitations on electricity, was issued by the leader of the ghetto on January 19, 1942, and is in the YIVO Archive (Kaczerginszki-Sutzkever Collection, no. 18).

to the 31st, and August, from the 1st to the end of the month. In addition, it must be emphasized that the number of workers supplied by the Judenrat is no more than a third of those recruited by the Lithuanians and Germans snatching Jews off the streets (see appendix).

[*The appendix is missing.*]

JANUARY 21 [1942]

THE AID SOCIETY

What happened today with the Aid Society must be noted here:

When absolute darkness reigned in the ghetto, and no one was interested in anything, a group of people[123] came and created the [Aid] Society, as we noted above. New winds came from the outside world, and suddenly the Zionists became interested in the activity and the "Reds" began to understand that they had to be properly represented in the [Aid] Society.

The Zionists and the Reds formed an alliance to pressure the org[anizers] and began to disturb and destroy. In the Kailis block, they insisted on uniting all the forces of the ghetto, otherwise they wouldn't pay. Owing to pressure by the Zionist member of the Judenrat,[124] payments were stopped—that is, the 10 percent for the Judenrat employees. Suddenly the Communists together with the Zionists demanded management on a parallel basis. When the org[anizers] agreed to that, too, the most interesting thing happened: the Communists voted to change the chairman, and both partners elected the Zionist member of the Judenrat as chairman. The former chairman quit, and along with him, all the other founding members of the organization refused to work in the presidium of the [Aid] Society.

Thus, the only organ[izers] of the [Aid] Society were pushed out by the Reds and their partners, Zionists of all varieties.

KAILIS

Massive arrests were carried out today among the Kailis workers. Various numbers of people arrested are cited. More precise information when we get it.

Today's Vilna newspaper reports more fires, including a fire in the surgical instruments factory at Dominikańska 7. Of course, the frequent fires are inter-

123. I.e., the Bundists.

124. I.e., Shabse Milkanowicki. Minutes of the Aid Society, published by Mark Dworzecki (1948: 377–379), show that the political composition of the Aid Society was as follows: "Zionist umbrella": S. Milkanowicki, Avrom Pińczuk, Deul, Mark Dworzecki; Communists: Mire Bernstein, Rokhl Brojdo, Leyb Opeskin, Yankl Kaplan; Bund: Abrasha Chwojnik, Herman Kruk, Hersh Gutgestalt, Grisha Yashunski; unaffiliated: Fayvl Trupiański; religious Jews: Rabbi Aaron Berek, who later fell ill and was replaced by Wygdorczyk.

preted as caused by . . . overheating apartments. Meanwhile, there is a terrible wood crisis in Vilna. . . .

ONCE AGAIN GHETTO 2

Ghetto 2 was liquidated long ago. The gates have been opened to Gentile residents. Yet a big cache of fabrics, finished suits, footwear, and woolens has recently been discovered there. A few days ago, a large storehouse of hard and soft leather was also discovered.

The people [of Ghetto 2] and the owners of the storehouse were liquidated long ago, but gradually and in stages, the veils of a past life are lifted.

JANUARY 22 [1942]

"CHITS"

We have already mentioned the "notes" distributed in the ghetto.[125] In a conversation with the chief of police and his deputy, the chief, as if bursting out, asked his interlocutor,[126] whom he sees as one of the instigators of the "notes":

"Tell me, please, do you know who posted the notes?"

The answer was:

"Why ask me? Don't you understand—if I know, I won't tell you; if I don't know—why ask?"

The answer was:

"Listen, so far, I've closed my eyes to all your 'politics.' Now that's over. An end to 'politics.'"

Half serious, half smiling, the interlocutor enlightened the "chief":

"With politics, if you drive it out the door, it comes in through the window. Politics is bread. Bigger 'bosses' than you have fought against politics and lost badly. Do you think this is something for you to take on, and here in the ghetto to boot? . . ."

The chief accepted this with a smile, and the interlocutor took it as a warning: an end to politics. The next day, a rumor circulated that the chief had ordered a list of Bundists and Communists in the ghetto.

Yesterday, two days after the conversation, the chief came to the Judenrat and reported, short and sharp:

Because the cooperative of Judenrat employees is involved in politics, it is to be closed, and all Judenrat members who want to join the police cooperative must enroll in it as members.

125. This probably refers to the leaflets about Moyshe Hauz and Goldshteyn, who were shot, and to the pamphlets against the theater, both issued by the Bund in the ghetto.

126. Probably Kruk himself.

The cooperative must be liquidated by February 1.

As the chief speaks, the Judenrat is silent, and the Judenrat has been practically silenced. . . .

The 500 members of the cooperative must join the police cooperative, which has 200 members altogether. And the 500 can eventually have three representatives in the general cooperative administration, along with four members from the police administration. . . .[127]

In response, the administration of the cooperative has decided that it is prepared to renew negotiations for the merger of the two cooperatives and that, in case that does not occur, it considers the decision of the police arbitrary, and more such nice words.

The continuation will be played out soon.

KAILIS

Today I found out that 36 Jewish workers and 2 Polish workers were arrested yesterday and taken to Łukiszki. All those arrested were employed in the workshop that burned down.

Early this morning, there were more arrests. People assume that no danger threatens and that this is only an investigation.

A SERIES OF SNATCHINGS

For a few days now, snatchings for work have started again in the ghetto. Germans and the Jewish police arrest Jews in the ghetto, and all those who have blue permits and are unemployed are taken for work. They also go through houses and take people out for work, as before.

WHO IS THE CHIEF? . . .

When asked why the Obmann of the ghetto bows under the boot of his subordinate, the "chief [of police]," the Obmann answers that the other man, the chief, is the real head of the ghetto. That the other man is really the one who gets things done with the authorities, the Gestapo, etc.

And he also tells us:

An order came to make buckets. When it was argued that the ghetto cannot make such things because there is no material, etc., the reply was:

"You could have made the whole war?[128] So make buckets!"

When Gens went to the authorities, the issue of the buckets was closed. . . .

Such cases are not unique. . . .

127. The political issue here is that the Bund and other trade-union veterans dominated the union of Judenrat employees, while the Revisionists dominated the police.

128. This is the German accusation that the Jews unleashed World War II.

CONCERT NUMBER 2

It turns out that the police liked it. Today, people are walking around selling tickets to the second concert, to take place next Sunday.

That's how it is: the police got tired of beating and applied themselves to concerts. . . .

■ ■ ■ ■ ■ ■ ■

JANUARY 25 [1942]

THE CHIEF THREATENS WITH . . . PONAR

And this very evening, the chief came to the Judenrat with the order to liquidate the only democratically elected cooperative [of employees] because "there's politics there." The chief ordered in a dictatorial tone: let the Judenrat know that if "leaflets" appear in the city again, he will send Kr[uk], Chwoj[nik], and their comrades[129] to . . . Ponar!

Of all the bourgeois representatives in the Judenrat, the only one who censured this coarse and vulgar statement was Engineer Gukhman. Although everyone understood that the chief wouldn't go that far, they nevertheless decided to take steps against him and his statement. Before you know it, it turns out that the chief instigated his commanders to use every opportunity to show these two "conspirators" who the Jewish police are.

Today, an accident happened in Kr[uk's] office. When the office was closed, they forgot to turn off an electric lamp, and the light shone in the street. Commander Oberhardt ordered the administrator of the office arrested immediately for the crime of leaving a light on. Two sergeants and two policemen, that is, four persons, came to Mr. Kr[uk's] apartment and "unfortunately" did not find him. Kr[uk's] friends went to Commander Oberhardt, who screamed that he had to arrest Kr[uk]. But Grisha [Yashunski] intervened with the chief, arguing that precisely because Kr[uk] had been threatened two days earlier with Ponar, he should be released immediately; otherwise, this would be interpreted as the beginning of the harassment of Mr. Kr[uk]. This argument convinced the chief, and he immediately ordered his assistant Oberhardt to withdraw the arrest order.

Meanwhile, the police had come back to Kr[uk]'s home and, not finding him home this time either, were waiting. It was only the order to release him that led the two guests back to the station.

Until late at night, Kr[uk's] friends stayed with him: the old Pati [Kremer], Hersh [Gutgestalt], Grisha [Yashunski] and his wife, Notes, and others.

Clearly the chief has shown his claws. He doesn't take you to Ponar, but he teaches . . . respect!

129. I.e., the Bundists.

Until late at night, they interpreted the behavior of the police in various ways. They pointed out that whenever such incidents of burning lights occurred, fines were issued, but in Mr. Kr[uk]'s case they wanted arrest and nothing else.

The trend is too obvious. . . .

Why the war with the few people around us?

We were the first in a dark ghetto who roused the consciousness of the Jewish masses. We were the first to oppose to the antisocial Judenrat a society with a social understanding. The employees' cooperatives, the professional representation, and most important, the Aid Society. All these institutions forged a social force, and the Judenrat had to consider it. The chief and the Obmann, who are afraid of this social power, try to challenge it. The game is far from over! . . .

FINES, FINES, AND FINES

The Jewish police force in the ghetto is a big consumer. Aside from the hundreds and thousands of confiscations of gold and money taken from ghetto residents, the police budget is full of income from . . . fines. Fines rain down on the inhabitants more fiercely than blows from the Germans. People are fined for everything. Recently it was decided that, aside from their permits, all inhabitants of the ghetto had to register with the police. This registration was done by houses. Anyone late for his appointment pays five rubles. You can light an electric lamp only at certain times. Anyone who doesn't obey this and is caught with a lamp on or heating an electric teapot pays a fine. They take away the burner and they . . . impose a fine. . . .

A fine for not attaching the star of David precisely at every corner. . . .

A fine for walking after 7 in the evening (three rubles).

A fine for bringing too big a bundle of supplies. . . . They fine by taking the supplies. . . . Fines, fines, and fines.

No small thing, the Jewish police in the Vilna Ghetto!

JANUARY 26 [1942]

ABOUT MY ARREST

The first attempt by the paper commander to get at me—the order to arrest me and its withdrawal—made a big section of the ghetto interested in me.

From dozens of circles, they ask me and my comrades for the reason. Even from police circles. Everyone considers it an arbitrary act, and everyone condemns it.

REPERCUSSIONS ABOUT SENDING ME TO PONAR

That incident that was noted here has caused a lot of excitement. Those who know about it pass it on by word of mouth, and everyone shakes his head in disgust against the "saying."

The committee of the Aid Society, which also discussed that matter with its proletarian majority, has censured that behavior. The two representatives of the Judenrat will duly call the paper boss to order, mocking him and his threat.

For his feeble reaction, Ja[szunski] has been called to order at a meeting of his comrades.[130]

CONCERTS

The first concert, organized by the police, brought a profit of 3,896 rubles. The sum was put at the disposal of the reconstituted Aid Society.

The second concert, on Sunday, the 25th of this month, was held in the presence of German and Lithuanian guests. These included the drunken head of the German Labor Exchange, Burakas, and the leader of the Ipatingas (Lithuanian Snatchers, including one of the most dreadful heroes of all the Aktions), and Hering, who came in civilian clothes this time. After the first part, the three drunkards of the Labor Exchange left. The rest remained until the end. During the concert, Brojdo, the Jewish representative of the Labor Exchange, appealed for explanations in German as well. Of course this was done immediately.

Thus, at the second concert, the chief murderer of all the Aktions, Hering, and one of the greatest sadists of the Aktions, a member of the Lithuanian Ipatinga, were duly entertained.

Thus the police have taken up art! . . .

SOCIAL AID

To the figures we noted concerning social aid in the Judenrat, we want to add that in January, 65,000–75,000 rubles were put at the disposal of the department.

HOW MANY "WHITE PERMITS" ARE STILL IN THE GHETTO?

To the figures of ghetto inhabitants, we add: it is estimated that 3,000 "white permits" are still in the ghetto.

Thus, the number of inhabitants is:

Breadcards	14,200
Whites	3,000
Total	17,200

KOVNO

People say there are 17,000 Jews left in Kovno.

It turns out that there is a post office for Jews in Kovno. Recently, on about the 24th of this month, the first shipment of letters reached the Vilna Ghetto

130. I.e., a meeting of the committee of the Bund.

post office. Until now, letters from Kovno have arrived through private channels.[131]

FIRES

Because of the frequent fires, the press is full of announcements and warnings about preventing fires. They even threaten capital punishment.

Those arrested in Kailis for the fires have not yet been released. Today, Glik, the director of Kailis, was apparently arrested. We once wrote in detail about him.

LINES

The press writes that because of contagious diseases, lines will be formed so that people will stand a meter apart from one another.

The order is reminiscent of the last days before the Russian Revolution. There was such an order there too, and it didn't help then, either. . . .

Is it really an order against contagious diseases, or is it caused by fear of other diseases?? . . .

TROKI

The Yiddish poet Sutz[kever], who was in Troki with his German [labor] unit, reports that there isn't a single Jew there.

Two thousand Jews in Troki have been annihilated. Many of them were driven into the Troki lakes.

JEWISH BETRAYAL

Typical of the relation of the population to the local Judenrat is the popular pun. Instead of "Yidn-rat" [Jewish Committee], people say "Yidn-farat" [Jewish betrayal, or betrayal of the Jews]. . . .

IN THE VILLAGES

Typical of what is happening in the villages is the following slogan printed by the press:

[*The slogan is missing.*]

We can conclude that things in the villages aren't cheerful either.

131. We have precise details about the Kovno Ghetto post office, which was organized illegally, with the knowledge of the Kovno Judenrat and the cooperation of the Lithuanian railroad workers. The organizer of that secret post office, Ephraim Silberman (1948), wrote about it; see also Gar 1948:377ff. This information was also confirmed by Attorney L. Garfunkel (1959:121), one of the leaders of the Kovno Judenrat. The dates in all these sources match.

ABOUT THE BUND IN THE GHETTO

Received from a reliable source. The conversation was overheard from behind a door. The German authorities inquired if there were any Bundists in the ghetto. The police replied in the negative.

NEWS FROM ŁUKISZKI

From what we hear, it becomes clear: those arrested in Łukiszki Prison are so badly off that for three kilos of bread, they give up their boots and sit barefoot in winter. . . .

JANUARY 27 [1942]

ORDERS

Yesterday, the chief of the Jewish police called a meeting of brigadiers of the units and issued orders:

1. Five kilos of potatoes, three kilos of bread, a bottle of milk, and, . . . secretly, some fat can be brought through the gate of the ghetto.
2. It is forbidden to drink brandy in the ghetto. The chief says he has to do this for the Jews' own good. . . .
3. No one is permitted to play cards!
4. The regulations about electricity must be followed.

Nevertheless, I am informed that several thousand rubles in fines for the illegal use of electricity flow into the police coffers every month.

FROM THE BATTLEFIELD

On the battlefield, it looks worse than bad [for the Germans]. Mozhaysk has fallen, Vyaz'ma is taken [by the Russians]. They're already talking about Latvia. Pskov and Velikiye Luki are supposed to have been captured. A series of articles appeared in today's press: people are warned not to listen to the Jewish-Bolshevik lying propaganda, and then comes an extraordinary order about the radio:

1. People are not allowed to listen to foreign broadcasts.
2. Spreading foreign communiqués will be punished by death.
3. The order goes into effect on January 13 [?].

Signed: Commissar of the Eastern Lands

Because of the order, all radios were confiscated in the city today. And so were . . . sewing machines.

A brand-new "collection"—phonographs, gramophones, and records. This is necessary to cheer up the German soldiers in the farthest outposts.

In any case, that's how the collectors explain it. . . .

ARREST OF TROPIDO

The director of the Food Supply Department of the Judenrat was stopped and arrested yesterday in the city while making purchases for the ghetto. Despite many efforts, he has been held for twenty-four hours and has not yet been released. In Judenrat circles, there is much uneasiness about this.

RABBI HAIM OZER GRODZENSKI

To this day, in the Women's Shul, there is a treasure of books and holy books[132] from Rabbi Haim Ozer Grodzenski. His library was famous for unusual editions. The books are being carried away. The janitor of the synagogue courtyard has already hid a lot of holy books himself. Now Dr. Daniel Feinstein[133] has set himself to it. In conjunction with me, he has created a group of volunteers who went into Ghetto 2 and took a few dozen rare holy books out of the Women's Shul. Dr. Feinstein wants to repeat his daring expedition.

The holy books were given to the Disseminators of Enlightenment Library.

RED TERROR IN LITHUANIA

An exhibition of this name has recently opened in the Kovno museum. The press writes of it: the exhibition was organized by the office for the study of Bolshevism and Judaism. The exhibition presents an overview of Jewish-Bolshevik terror in Lithuania from 1918 to 1941.

For example, 40,000 were exiled by the Bolsheviks! . . . This and similar facts are supposed to show the Jewish-Bolshevik terror in Lithuania. . . . That this was done almost entirely by Jews is proved by the undeniable photographs. . . .

JANUARY 28 [1942]

Jews from the Peat Bogs Return to the Ghetto

Today, some ominous information has spread that the Judenrat received an order to assure that all Jews who have been working in the peat bogs *are to be well received* and accepted back in the ghetto.

Why does Murer demand that they be well received? This is Murer's secret. But why are seven or eight hundred Jews being sent back to the ghetto? Very few can answer that. But one thing is clear—hundreds of Jews are coming back to the ghetto, often with their wives and children.

132. "Holy books" means religious canonical texts or study books.

133. A Ph.D. and author of several works in Polish on Yiddish ethnography. In the ghetto he was an active lecturer. He was killed two days before the liberation of Vilna, in July 1944, in the HKP labor camp.

JANUARY 29 [1942]

JEWISH POLICE AGAIN

The Jewish police are more German than the Germans. The Germans once ordered furs taken. They took what they could, and it calmed down. But the Jewish police never rest. Just yesterday, they "uncovered" a radio and 15 furs. Oberhardt, the commissar and leader of the expedition, was proud of his achievement. . . .

WOOD AND LIGHT

In the ghetto, it is now cold and dark. Cold because there is no wood, and it doesn't look like there will be any. The city doesn't have any wood, either.

There are thousands of cubic meters of wood around Vilna. But nothing to transport it in. The Germans use all the wagons to send human material to the east.

There is no light either. The ghetto is in darkness from 4:30 until 9 in the evening and from 7 to 9:30 in the morning.

It is dark and cold in the ghetto. . . .

JANUARY 30 [1942]

A train with Jews passed by here today. The Jews said that they are being taken to work from Sosnowiec[134] and the surrounding area. The train left in the direction of the Eastern Front.

RIGA, LATER KOVNO

Rumors have spread in the ghetto that all the Jews of Riga have been taken out. Yesterday, a similar piece of information was spread about Kovno. Both pieces of information, it turns out, are false. But the rumor, which comes from Lithuanian circles, is typical. . . .

Meanwhile, Jews are looking for melinas in the city.

FROM THE SERIES OF VILNA TRAGEDIES

It happened like this: a few months ago, her husband was snatched and there is no trace left of him. The woman went to work and settled in the workshop of the Gestapo, sewing linen. A few days ago, a high officer sent some linen to be mended. Among that linen, the woman came on one of her husband's shirts. At first she thought she was dreaming, but later, when she was sure it was her husband's shirt, with his initials, etc., she fainted. The Germans calmed her and assured her that her husband is . . . alive.

134. In Polish Silesia.

ASSOCIATION OF WRITERS AND ARTISTS

The founding committee of the Association of Writers and Artists has finally been created. The board includes H. Kr[uk], Kalman[owicz], [Yankev] Sher, [Abraham] Sutzkever, [Avrom] Slep, [Hersh] Gutgestalt, and [Shabse] Blacher.

The first general meeting is to take place on February 7. The chairman is H. Kr[uk]; the board includes Kalman[owicz] and Blacher. Kruk opens the meeting. Hersh [Gutgestalt] and Kalman[owicz] lecture.

JANUARY 31 [1942]

KAILIS

Kailis is celebrating a major holiday today. The 36 Jews and 2 Christians captured because of the fire in the Fur Department have been released. Everything confiscated during the search has been returned to them. The only one left in prison is Glik, and his wife was summoned today—these days, that's a bad sign. . . .

HORSE MEAT

An expression is making the rounds of the ghetto: "Prrr," as you say to a horse [to stop him]. The "Prrr" is related to the horse meat that has recently been sold here. Thousands refuse it but . . . thousands buy it and assume a satisfied face—meat! . . .

THE NUMBER OF GERMAN UNITS

How many German units does the ghetto serve now?

Altogether 188 units and little tiny "subunits."

RABBI HAIM-OZER'S COLLECTION OF HOLY BOOKS

We have already written about Rabbi Haim Ozer's collection of holy books. His treasure of holy books remained in the second ghetto in the Women's Shul of the Great Synagogue. Jews take the holy books as heating material and toilet paper. The only one who protects the books is the janitor of the Synagogue Yard. He rescued many of them and hid them in a secluded room in his house. The rest were saved piecemeal by the comrade whose name we have already mentioned.[135]

135. I.e., Dr. Daniel Feinstein. In the YIVO Archive (Kaczerginski-Sutzkever Collection, no. 345), there is a report for January 1942 signed by Herman Kruk about all the offices at Straszun Street 6. A special entry is made about the collection of holy books and manuscripts brought by Feinstein from Rabbi Haim Ozer Grodzenski's library and archive.

HOW A GERMAN SAVES A WOMAN

He is young, a German of 23 or 24. Every day, he leads his group of "SS" (20 people)[136] to make various purchases. Marching with his Jews on the main street of Vilna (Mickiewicz),[137] he noticed a Lithuanian soldier taking a Jewish woman in the opposite direction, to Łukiszki Prison. Seeing Jews, the woman pleaded, "Save me." The 23-year-old German asked his Jews what she wanted. Meanwhile, the Lithuanian shoved the woman. When the Jews translated for him, he ran to the Lithuanian who was taking the woman, stopped him and chatted with him, meanwhile ordering the woman to join the group of Jews. The "chat" ended with the woman's marching off with the group and the downcast Lithuanian's going off to Lukiszki . . . alone.

The woman now works regularly in the "SS" and lives in the ghetto.

THE TRAGEDY OF THE ARTIST SHER

Just before the war, he ran away from Switzerland to his homeland, to Jerusalem of Lithuania. Now he goes to work like all the Jews of the ghetto. He works in the "SS," painting pictures of the old ghetto.[138] Of the new—God forbid. . . .

The Germans have taken dozens of his paintings. So fast they don't even have time to help him obtain paint. He's a good artist; they snatch his artistic productions out of his hands. Paint—the damned Jew artist should bring it up from wherever he can, either heaven or hell. They hardly are interested in that. And Sher complains: they took his finest paintings, and he can't do a thing about it.

HOW I COMMUNICATE WITH A COMRADE FROM KAILIS

He came to me to help them create a local library, asked for a lecture, and when he emphasized a lecture with a special attitude, I asked him what he meant by "attitude." He pointed to a picture of Comrade Wirgili[139] hanging on the wall:

"You understand, that one was close to my heart. If I could get help from his comrades . . ."

I understood him and am interested in his case.

RADIO

Yesterday, the English radio reported several German defeats on the Eastern Front. Three German divisions were demolished, 2,000 cannons were captured, along with 6,000 vehicles, 102 train cars, 2 locomotives, and a lot of ammunition.

136. I.e., Jews who worked for the SS.

137. Formerly Mickiewicz Street, the main street of the Polish part of Vilna.

138. I.e., of the old Jewish quarter, a poverty-stricken area going back to the Middle Ages, encompassing roughly the streets where the new ghetto was established.

139. Borekh Wirgili-Kahan, a famous Bundist leader in Vilna, who died on January 31, 1936.

Velikiye Luki is surrounded [by the Russians], and they go from Bryansk toward Smolensk. On the same day, we read in the papers a long speech by the Führer honoring the ninth anniversary of the National Socialist takeover. Among other nonsense, repeated dozens of times in the past, it says:
[*The text is missing.*]

Knowing the reality and reading the Führer's speech, the simple reader does not understand what is really going on, and who is really the bigger liar, the English radio broadcaster or the Führer of Great Germany. . . .

FEBRUARY 2, 1942

WHY DO JEWS TREMBLE?

It is now February 2, and the Jews are worried: after all, things don't go as easily as people thought. It is now February, and in the spring, the Germans will be back on their feet like a bear. . . .

PERMITS END. WHAT HAPPENS NEXT? . . .

Meanwhile, history doesn't stand still. Pessimistic Jews point out that permits are valid only until March 31 and that March 31 is approaching.

"What will happen next?"

Meanwhile, Murer, the deputy for Jewish affairs in the Vilna commissariat, has come into the ghetto and proclaimed: he wants to organize a factory to make good furniture to send to Germany as soon as possible. The Judenrat is now busy with the proposal and is indeed about to establish such a furniture factory.

"Does this mean they won't liquidate us yet?"

Meanwhile, the Jews are thrown back and forth as in a fever! . . .

IN THE GHETTO, THERE IS EVERYTHING . . .

Again, the ghetto has everything. Everything as in normal life. But everything is retarded by a thousand years. A kilo of meat is sold out of a woman's hand in a doorway. A merchant carries matches in his pocket. A woman is looking for candles and shouts: "Who's selling a candle?"

And with all that, the ghetto has a good feeding trough, a so-called restaurant at the home of the janitor at Strashun 2. Supper, 180 to 240 rubles. They drink brandy, eat goose, everything just as before the war, as if nothing had happened.

Recently, the police discovered a bordello. A bordello with three women. In short, the ghetto has everything! . . .

FRIED AND HIS ROLE IN THE GHETTO

Everything connected with that time of Aktions and the transfer of Jews from one ghetto to another is now referred to in the Vilna Ghetto as an inconceivable nightmare. Unfortunately, only now have I found out things about the Obmann of our ghetto that makes your blood run cold.

When hundreds and thousands were torn away from us and transferred from Ghetto 1 to Ghetto 2, they would often send letters to our ghetto telling how they could be rescued. This didn't always help, but even from all the stories we told here, something could be accomplished in a great many cases. Having no other addresses, they sent those letters to the Judenrat and only today did I find this out:

During Yom Kippur, the ghetto was ruthlessly purged, and many of the unfortunates were temporarily thrown into Ghetto 2. In the Judenrat offices, there were about 1,000 letters. The room was full of relatives waiting for a word from their unfortunate relatives. A few young ladies sorted the letters alphabetically so they could be distributed. Suddenly Fried appeared and, banging a stick, shouted to employee Zaydshnur in Russian:

"This is a *bezobraziye* [outrage]. Contact with Ghetto 2 is not allowed. Who let letters be brought? Burn all the letters at once! . . ."

Women began disruptions, wives started begging and crying, even Zaydshnur tried to calm him. It didn't help. A Jewish policeman, Mowszowicz, took the letters and threw them into the fire. But one of the women, Comrade Troup., snatched up a considerable bundle of letters and took them to a private apartment, where they were distributed.

The precise details of the case were confirmed by Police Sergeant Mr. Fleshel.

This is the Obmann, the leader and anointed ruler of the Vilna Ghetto. . . .

JEWISH POLICE METHODS

The Jewish police is a world unto itself. It includes, as we have written, a group of Snatchers, a brigade of beaters, a criminal division, civilian agents, female police and women agents. In short, everything necessary.

The wife of Engineer . . . says that, while searching, they stripped everybody naked, and women searched other women's private parts. . . .

In short, police with all the mannerisms.

A treasure of up to 100,000 rubles was confiscated from that engineer.

FEBRUARY 3 [1942]

From a Letter from Kovno I Learn

In a letter from Kovno, I find out that there were four "purges" in Kovno. Now there are 17,000 Jews there. A few days ago, the authorities ordered that some of the streets of the ghetto were to be abandoned. A group of German Jews who were supposed to be brought in were to settle there. So far, they haven't come, and people say that the vacant streets are to be restored to the ghetto.

The staff of the Kovno Judenrat earn 100 rubles a month, which is worth a bit more than a pack of cigarettes. In the apartments, they're freezing, there is no wood.

All the towns in the Kovno area are completely purged of Jews. There are Jews left only in Šiauliai.[140] There, too, out of 15,000 Jews, 4,000 remained. . . .

RIGA

In Riga, writes the same well-informed person, instead of 30,000 Jews, 4,000 are left. Ten thousand Jews were brought to Riga from Germany, so altogether there are 14,000 there. . . .

BOMBINGS

Yesterday, they talked about bombings of Vilna [by the Russians]. Today, loud explosions were heard. People talk about a new bombing.

Whether this is true is hard to say. . . .

AFTER THE TYPHUS EPIDEMIC

After the Mefitsei-Haskalah Library had been closed for six weeks because of the "typhus epidemic," an order came today allowing the library to function again, but with a limited circulation.

FEBRUARY 5 [1942]

JEWS MUST NOT HAVE ANY CHILDREN

> And the king of Egypt spake to the Hebrew midwives, of which the name of one was Shiphrah and the name of the other Puah:
>
> And he said: When ye do the office of a midwife to the Hebrew women, and see them upon the stools: if it be a son, then ye shall kill him; but if it be a daughter, then she shall live.[141]

Pharaoh, Hitler's forefather, was more restrained than the ruler of the Great Reich.

Today the Gestapo sent for two members of the Judenrat and announced to them:

"As of today, no children may be born among Jews." The officer was half ashamed to announce this and added that he got orders from Berlin.

So the order is from Berlin.

The impression made by the news in the ghetto yesterday is indescribable.

140. The third-largest ghetto of Lithuania.

141. Exodus 1:15–16.

Everyone quoted the Book of Exodus where Pharaoh, the king of the slave-state of Egypt, forbade Jews to give birth to sons.

The Pharoah of the twentieth century is more horrible and dreadful—absolutely no births among Jews! . . .

Right after the news of the decree came out, the question of several pregnant women was raised:

Mrs. Hela Tarakinska is about to give birth any minute. And it was arranged with the Jewish hospital. She will go there and her birth will be recorded as having occurred two weeks earlier. . . .

Thus, the first fruit after the new law will be saved.

THE GANGRENE OF THE VILNA JUDENRAT

An important and entirely decent member of the Judenrat staff, Mr. G., divulged:[142] Trojecki is a rich Jew in the ghetto who deals in gold, and he is one of those who receives the gold from the Judenrat. He's a hero of the Obmann's business. A man came to friend G. and wanted to sell a large quantity of wood for 500 rubles a [cubic] meter. G. goes to the Obmann and the deal is almost concluded, but as soon as Trojecki finds out about it, he goes to friend G., tells him not to interfere in his business and to get out of the deal. G. did this gladly and didn't want to get in Trojecki's way. Two days later, it turned out that the Obmann bought the same wood but for 650 instead of 500 rubles. Of course, the 150 rubles were divided between the gold dealer Trojecki and the Obmann, Mr. Fried. Thus the ghetto pays 150 rubles more for wood, and those who don't have the wherewithal to pay are freezing dreadfully.

HOW THE JEWISH POLICE PLEASE MURER

Yesterday Murer visited the ghetto and stood at the gate to observe what Jewish workers bring in from the city. Naturally, everything everybody had was confiscated. One kilo of bread and three kilos of potatoes per Jew were left. Because Murer was convinced that Jews are bringing "too much" food into the ghetto, proof that the Jewish gate guards aren't following his orders, he scolded the police and announced that if this didn't change, he would have all the police on gate duty arrested.

Because of yesterday's events, the police command in the ghetto decided the following:

Commander Aster is to leave gate duty and take a high position in the second precinct. Lev, popularly known as Levas,[143] remains commander of the gate. Thus, Levas is promoted from sergeant to commander.

142. Kruk may have meant Hersh Gutgestalt, who did indeed work in the Workshop Department of the ghetto.

143. The Lithuanian form of *Lev*.

The hero Levas is famous in the ghetto as a horrible adventurer, denouncer, and [. . .]

[*Part of the following pages was destroyed. We present here only the legible beginnings of the lines.*]

Levas assumed his role: no one has brought [anything into]
the ghetto. People are searched. They [. . . The]
women were examined around their breasts, between [. . .]¡
To help the hero Levas came the pers[. . .]
Chief Smulikowski who has terribly [. . .]
those who dared to bring in food [. . .]

On the other side of the street opposite the gate of the ghe[tto . . .]
observed that and didn't understand why [Jews . . .]
like this with their own Jewish fellow citizens from [. . .]
Incidentally a very young man, the Christians had before their eyes [. . .]

"Hey, Komsomolets,[144] come here to [. . .]
this is how you should hit. . . ."

[*The following sections are missing.*]

News from Minsk

Liquidation of the Ghetto

February 6 [1942]

10,000 Rubles for Writers

Poland Is Not Yet Lost . . . [145]

Christians

The Policemen Against Their Comrade Levas

Khaimson-Bastomski[146]

ESTABLISHMENT OF THE ASSOCIATION OF JEWISH WRITERS AND ARTISTS

Today, in the soup kitchen, the charter meeting of the Association of Writers and Artists was held.

The walls were decorated with drawings of the ghetto, and the meeting was opened with a poem by Bialik, read by the excellent actor Bergolski. Mr. Kr[uk] opened the meeting (speech attached). Mr. G[utgetstalt] spoke about the goals of the association, and Mr. Kalman[owicz] spoke on the topic: "The Artist in the Ghetto." About eighty writers, authors, and artists, actors, singers, musicians,

144. "Young Communist" (here ironically meaning "youth, apprentice").

145. The first line of the Polish independence anthem.

146. I.e., Malke Chaimson-Bastomski, a well-known Vilna teacher, writer, and editor of children's books, and wife of Shloyme Bastomski, a publisher and editor of a children's journal.

and graphic artists participated in the evening. The following were elected to the board: Kalman[owicz], Kr[uk], Gut[gestalt], Sutzkever, Sher, and others.[147] [*Kruk's speech is missing.*]

A CHILD NAMED MELINA

The teacher [Khayim] Stolicki[148] has had a hard life lately. He and his wife were lined up several times to be taken to Ponar. The wife was then pregnant. Finally they got out of Ghetto 2 and came to Ghetto 1. Here they lived in melinas and experienced all seven circles of hell.

Recently his wife had a baby, and the parents named the little girl Melina because she was conceived in the dark melinas of the Vilna Ghetto. . . .

SAVED HIS HEAD

Yesterday someone was supposed to bring a radio for family purposes[149] and install it secretly. When the comrade with the radio approached the gate and saw Murer with his soldiers, he ran away and saved his head. . . .

A CARICATURE OF A LIFE

Even here in the ghetto, a caricature of a life emerges. Trade in the street increases and becomes more widespread. The gates of Szawelska and Strashun Streets are full of buyers and sellers.

You hear: "Who wants butter?" or "Who's buying butter?" You don't see the merchandise. You hear only:

"Who's buying butter?"

"Who's got bread?"

This is how they establish contact and trade. . . .

FEBRUARY 9 [1942]

ARTISTS AND WRITERS TAKEN AWAY

As a contribution to the documentation of the tragic events with the Snatchers in Ponar, I attach the list of names of actors taken out of Vilna, and families of writ-

147. Aside from those listed, the following were also elected: Yankev Gerstein, Shabse Blacher, Yeshaye Szadowski, and Yosef Glazman.

148. Originally from Lida. He studied mathematics at Vilna University and was then a teacher in the Yiddish Real Gymnasium in Vilna. He perished in a camp in Estonia. His wife, who was a nurse, and his child, the Melina of the entry, perished in Majdanek. For his biography, see *Teachers' Memorial Book* 1954:271.

149. I.e., for the Bund.

ers who remained orphaned here after their husbands and fathers were taken away.[150]

[*The list is missing.*]

HERING STROLLS IN THE GHETTO

It is now 11 at night. With a special police permit, I can walk in the streets late in the evening. The Jewish police on guard are now frightened, and at the inspection they tell me, in trembling voices:

"Hering is in the ghetto."

"He's personally inspecting permits. . . ."

Whether I want to or not, I also tremble. Hering in the ghetto. This is the night of February 8–9.

"LIQUIDATION"

Rumors about the liquidation of the ghetto are circulating again. People are dying of terror:

"Is the liquidation really on the 15th?" . . .

THEY SEEK AND FIND ME

Recently I have received a collection of [religious] objects, including a Torah cover with embroidery in Russian and Hebrew (text is attached):

[*The text is missing.*]

Apropos objects and collections: we have recently received new and extremely valuable archival material, including material about Dr. Theodor Herzl's visit to Vilna in 1903, a file with correspondence of the World Zionist Organization and its Central Committee in Lithuania, a large quantity of letters from Rabbi Haim Ozer Grodzenski to famous Jewish personalities, etc.

While we're on the subject of the various collections, we must mention:

As we said, people still hurriedly carry things away from the abandoned Strashun Library. Dr. Daniel Feinstein played the most important role in this.

A German from the Rosenberg Task Force[151] is now sniffing around the li-

150. The YIVO Archive contains a list of 28 actors taken to Ponar (Kaczerginski-Sutzkever Collection, no. 424). This may be the list that is missing here.

151. The Rosenberg Special Unit in the Nazi party. The director of the "task force" was Alfred Rosenberg, the "expert" in Jewish affairs. The function of the Rosenberg Task Force included "studying" the Jewish problem. For that purpose, books and documents about Jewish life and problems were stolen from the libraries and archives of the occupied countries. In Vilna, the "special unit" occupied the YIVO building, at Wiwulski Street 18. Later chapters of the diary contain a great deal of information about this task force. For details about the nature and work of this institution, see Weinreich 1946:82, 112, 114. On the activity of the task force in Vilna, see Pupko-Krinski 1947:214–222; Sutzkever 1946a:108–113.

brary. He demands to be put in touch with [Khaykl] Lunski and [Herman] Kruk from the ghetto.

Jews looked for Kr[uk] in the ghetto, and no one wanted to point him out. Finally they found out where Kr[uk] was, and Kr[uk] expects that tomorrow or the next day, Mr. K[ruk] will be summoned. What this is about isn't certain. Meanwhile, people are now clearing out the most valuable materials. . . .

FEBRUARY 10 [1942]

A CARICATURE OF A SOCIAL LIFE

We have often written that in the ghetto, a caricature of a life is taking shape. Everyone is busy with his own concerns and doesn't have any free time. Better not to be alone.

The establishment of the Aid Society, the establishment of the cooperative, the professional representation, the establishment of an Association of Writers and Artists—all that now creates something of a social life in the ghetto.

The Judenrat also obtained the right to establish a court in the ghetto, with its own judges, prosecutors, and attorneys. Recently, trials have been held, and once more everything here gives the impression of a life. They investigate, people are arrested, in the preliminary arrest people are forced to sign statements, etc., etc.

On Saturday the 7th,[152] the founding meeting of the Association of Writers and Artists took place. On Sunday the 8th, there was a founding meeting of jurists. Eighty jurists participated in the meeting. The goal: mutual aid. The attorney from Kovno, B. [A?] Dimitrovski, was elected dean, and he is also secretary of the police command.

On Tuesday the 10th, another founding meeting was held of a union of professional musicians. The goal is the same as that of the jurists. Fifty musicians participated.

HINGST IS COMING TO THE GHETTO

Yesterday the ghetto lived in fear. Hingst is coming. Why? They're talking about the liquidation of the ghetto!

It turned out that they really came, but Hingst was not among them. Murer visited the building where the furniture factory is being built. . . .

152. According to Sutzkever (1946a:103) and Dworzecki (1948:238), the meeting took place on February 17. From Kruk's entry and the later dates in the same paragraph, it is clear that the meeting was on February 7.

FEBRUARY 11 [1942]

ROSENBERG TASK FORCE COMES TO KRUK . . .

Today the ghetto is once again terrified that Hingst is coming. Yesterday Mr. Kr[uk] was informed that Rosenberg's adjutant was looking for him.

The Jewish police have started driving people off the streets. There was a fright. The streets were empty. Three Germans appeared at the gate of the ghetto and ordered to be taken to Strashun 6. Accompanied by the Judenrat and a horde of police, the three Germans came to Strashun 6. The director, refined and elegant, asked for Kr[uk], questioned him about his work, and inquired about old books. Among other things, he asked about the director of the Strashun Library and the director of YIVO. Khaykl Lunski and Kalmanowicz were introduced to them, and after a long conversation, Messrs. Lunski and Kruk were asked to come to his office. When this happens, they'll inform us again.

With that, they left. The fear is past, and the ghetto population breathed a sigh of relief.

So once more, not Hingst. Just the adjutant of Alfred von Rosenberg![153]

ASSOCIATION OF WRITERS [AND ARTISTS]

On Monday the ninth, the charter meeting of the board of the Association of Writers [and Artists] was held. Kalman[owicz] was elected chairman, Kr[uk] vice-chairman, and Blacher secretary.

With the establishment of various commissions, the committee began its work.

DR. LAZAR EPSTEIN

A name, you would think, with a fine past. For what can be finer than a Jew who came from near Łódź and made a name for himself in Lithuania not only as a physician but also as a central figure in the Lithuanian Socialist movement?

What can be better? But the Lithuanianized Dr. Epsteinas turned out to be one of the ugliest characters in the region. His little history is a chain of the most dreadful careerism. Now, in the ghetto, he has become typical of those ugly characters with which the Vilna Ghetto has written a black page in history.

Who is Dr. Epstein?

He was born in Zdunska Wola near Łódź. After the war of 1914–1918, he came to Kovno and settled there. As a good neurologist, he was respected by the locals. He was also a veteran member of the Lithuanian Socialist Party, which was legal and respectable at that time. E[pstein] became a close friend of the leading veteran activists, Engineer Stefan Kairis, Attorney Mrs. Purenas, Bazis [?], etc. In time, he became close to the Central Committee, speaking at meetings and party conventions. During the elections for the third Lithuanian democratic parliament, he was

153. The "von" was added by Kruk.

in fourth place on the Social Democratic list. The Social Democrats were then aiming at getting the votes of the radically inclined Jewish sector. Epstein was a deputy and a member of the Social Democratic faction in the parliament until it was dispersed after the Smetona-Valdemaris[154] takeover in December 1926.

Epsteinas went back to medicine but stayed in touch with the Social Democrats. He even went abroad as a representative of the Lithuanian Social Democrats at the international [Socialist] congress. Nevertheless, this did not prevent him from carrying on a policy of good relations with the powers that be. He got a good position and became director of the Center for School Medicine in the Kovno city government. L. Epstein is one of those who distanced themselves from Plečkaitis (who, in 1928, organized an uprising against the Fascist order) after Plečkaitis 's escape to Vilna.[155]

He had nothing to do with Jewish social life. But he showed some sympathy for the Right Poalei Zion. In the conflict between Lithuania and Poland, he always maintained that Vilna must be Lithuanian, although the Lithuanian leaders of the Social Democrats were in favor of a plebiscite in the Vilna region.[156]

This is his tendency—always to travel with the extreme Lithuanian nationalism, even on purely Socialist issues.

When there is talk in Lithuania about forbidding Jewish slaughter, L. Epstein comes out and defends it.

When the Red Army comes to Kovno, it doesn't hurt Dr. Epstein to declare himself loyal to the Stalinists. His former friends, the bolder ones, soon wind up in prison. Naturally, this helps him. Epstein is soon inspector general of sanitation in the health commissariat of the LSSR [Lithuanian Soviet Socialist Republic]. After a visit to Moscow, he understands that he has to give speeches about Soviet patriotism.

The invasion of the German army didn't hit Epstein hard, as he soon started adapting to the new conditions and, with the help of his good Lithuanian friends, tried to "achieve something." Unfortunately, this time it didn't help much. But for all that, he became one of the "big shots" in the Vilna Ghetto, and here again behaved as an unrestrained boss. He is the leader of the sanitary-epidemiological unit [of the Health Department]. He starts threatening to turn over employees to the Germans. He refuses to accept employees without permits, although in all other departments they have not done that for a long time. He threatens to throw [out] nurses.

This is the kind of characters the Vilna Ghetto possesses, and who are its spokesmen! . . .

154. Valdemaris was the leader of a right-wing Lithuanian nationalist party.

155. I.e., out of Lithuania, since Vilna was then in Poland.

156. Vilna, though the historical capital of Lithuania, was populated mainly by a Polish-speaking urban population and by Jews; thus a plebiscite would have left the city and part of its surroundings in Poland.

In terror of the 15th, the ghetto again experienced some fear today. The commotion happened because Rudnicka Street was suddenly closed. It turned out to be a visit from the Germans.

500 JEWS IN KOVNO

As soon as this was over, a rumor circulated that in Kovno, 500 Jewish workers were suddenly assembled from a German unit at the airport and sent off to work.

A WORLD WITH LITTLE WORLDS (CONCERNING THE GHETTO COURT)

For some time, a court has been functioning in our ghetto, carrying on its work by authorization of the Judenrat. Of course, wherever there is a police with a criminal department, a local Jewish prison,[157] a secret police, etc., there must also be a court. And of course, wherever there is a court, there must be a prosecutor, a judge, lawyers, secretaries—the full show.

Chief judge of the court is the Vilna attorney Srolowicz, the judges are Abrasha Chwojnik, Y. Notes, and Deul.[158]

On Tuesday, February 9, a public trial was held, which had the genuine stamp of gangsterism. Khayim Rayman, Holts, and Glezer were on trial. All three hired lawyers—[Moyshe] Ornstein, [Nosn] Gawęnda, and Teitelbaum.

What is the trial about?

GANGSTERS OF THE GHETTO

Rayman has a wife and children; his mother was taken away. A child, too. He himself has no permit. Another Aktion is expected in the near future. Rayman decided to save himself by committing an act of violence to obtain money to buy a permit. He tempted the money changer and gold dealer Herman Feigenbaum to his home with a story that he wanted to buy foreign currency from him. As soon as Feigenbaum crossed Rayman's threshold, he was attacked by Rayman and Holts. The two forced him to give them all the money he had on him. Feigenbaum gave them 18,000 rubles, 1,600 RM [Reichsmarks], 5 pounds sterling, and a watch. Rayman brought out two bottles of liquor and Feigenbaum had to have a drink with them.

The trial lasted until late at night, and not until morning was the following verdict handed down:

Rayman was found guilty and sentenced to six months in prison and a 200-

157. The ghetto prison was on Lidzki Street, where the Rosenberg and Shriftgiser printing press had been. The prison was nicknamed Lidzki.

158. The YIVO Archive (Kaczerginski-Sutzkever Collection, no. 331) contains the protocol of February 8, 1942, concerning the creation of a Juristic Collegium in the ghetto, consisting of thirty-eight men. The document is signed by A. Dimitrovski.

Mark fine. Holts and Glezer, three months in prison. The pretrial detention is included, and they have the right to appeal to the Judenrat.

(The text was taken from the court files, number 53.)

This is how the trial of the three looked. The hall was packed: police, lawyers, witnesses, and onlookers. The accused were taken off to prison, and this morning the ghetto once again trembled for them:

Hering with Two Lithuanians

Hering and two Lithuanians went to the prison, and through a back door (from Strashun 3 to Zawalna), they took the three accused, along with a fourth Jew, Lev.

How did the Germans find out about the three? Who told Hering that they were in prison? There is a lot of talk about that in the ghetto today. The events made a strong impression and roused much bitterness in legal circles.

Naive people! They think the judges weren't properly recognized, and unfortunately, they weren't independent. . . .

THE ROSENBERG TASK FORCE IS SATISFIED

After yesterday's visit of the German celebrities to the Disseminators of Enlightenment Library, two young men, who had showed the Germans around, came to Mr. Fried today and recounted the satisfaction the Germans expressed about their visit to the library yesterday.

Mr. Fried is also satisfied! . . .

FEBRUARY 13 [1942]

MORE ABOUT THE CONDEMNED

Today came a sad sequel to the story of the three condemned men who were taken. The Lithuanians are searching for the families of the three men. The whole thing has a distinct character. In the corners, people say that someone denounced the judgment to the Gestapo and they reacted as they thought fit.

So now they are searching for the wives and children.

OBERHARDT

The famous commissar of the Jewish police, actually a member of the high command and a figure we have often talked about in the columns of our chronicle, has suddenly vanished from the arena.

For a few days now, rumors have been circulating that Oberhardt is resigning. In the ghetto, this was interpreted in various ways. He was often suspected of all sorts of machinations, etc. Oberhardt was also suspected in the sad conclusion of the recent trial. Now the issue is somewhat clearer. . . .

On the evening of Friday the ninth, the entire ghetto police force was assembled in the auditorium of the Jewish Real Gymnasium (Rudnicka 6) under the direction of Major [Isidore] Frucht.[159] There they received the leaders of the unit, Messrs. Glazman and Oberhardt. Oberhardt said farewell to his fellow policemen, thanking them for carrying out his orders so well. Glazman said that at 12 o'clock that day, Oberhardt had handed the chief his resignation. The chief accepted it, and now he is saying goodbye to him and thanking him for his service in the police force.

Typically, the chief did not appear in the auditorium, and the resignation was quickly accepted. This led to the most varied interpretations.

Was the Oberhardt case connected with the three condemned men? Perhaps the course of history in the ghetto will eventually shed more precise light on it.

PERMITS

A few weeks ago, it suddenly became clear that the Jewish police had received the right to distribute so-called protection permits. The ghetto population was satisfied with this—a new opportunity for permits. The Judenrat shrugged: How come? Behind the back of the Judenrat, the police obtain a monopoly on permits? . . .

Later, a new chapter of protection permits began. To acquire a protection permit, it was most convenient to appear as a Revisionist, Zionist, etc. Later, businesses began paying for a permit, giving a broker's fee, etc. It has gone so far that some well-informed people think that the issue of protection permits was really [started by] a stock company of individuals in the police and . . . the Germans who hang out with the police. There too, people mention Commander Oberhardt mockingly.

WHO IS OBERHARDT?

He is a German refugee (so they say), an engineer (no one is sure). He works for the Germans at the gasoline station and is simultaneously co-chief of the Jewish police in the ghetto. During all the Aktions, he was most active: he uncovered melinas, took charge of releasing prisoners, and most important, he's a good fellow, doesn't refuse anybody anything and . . . doesn't arrange anything for anybody. Recently, he has indulged in big "enterprises"—releasing prisoners for money. Took 40,000 [rubles], took more, and they stay in jail. Only a few of the discovered furs got as far as the station, they say. Everyone has something to say about him. Nothing is certain in all this. I note it only as a reflection of what the ghetto allows.

159. A former major in the Polish army. He took part in the first meeting to create the partisan movement, and in 1943 he joined the partisans in the forest.

A BORDELLO

Recently, another bordello has been discovered in the ghetto.

It looks as if people don't sleep. . . .

SPANISH LEGIONS

Workers coming from the city told this today, as a fact: in the city, there is a unit of the Spanish Legions for the Struggle Against Communism. Recently they received orders to march to the front. People say that the unit resisted the order. Some of those who resisted have been arrested.

A 15 PERCENT RAISE

Under pressure from the professional representation, the Judenrat decided to raise its employees' salaries by 15 percent.

A BUND CONFERENCE

Reliable sources[160] report that the first city conference of the Bund took place yesterday. Thirteen delegates with voting rights and four with advisory rights participated in the conf[erence].

In the opening address, the chairman of the organization announced that this is the organization that continues the work of the General Jewish Labor League (Bund). He spoke of the reasons for dispersing the Bund in Poland and argued that now is the time to sing "We are coming!" [*mir kumen on!*][161]

He mentions the comrades who were taken out of Vilna[162] and hopes they will soon return and take over the leadership. He calls us to stand in honor of the dead: Noyekh, [Vladimir] Kosowski,[163] Leyzer Levin,[164] and Engineer Mark Idelson.[165] Another person then takes over the chair. The agenda is: (1) political lec-

160. I.e., Kruk himself.

161. From a hymn of the Bund Medem Sanitarium for children.

162. I.e., Bundists who were arrested by the NKVD and sent off in September 1939, when the Red Army took Vilna. Those included Anna Rosental, Leybl Weinstein, Yosef Aronowicz, Yankl Żeleznikow, Attorney Teitel, and Avrom Feinsilber.

163. A pioneer of the Jewish workers' movement and a founder of the Bund. He came to Vilna with the refugees from Warsaw in 1939, immigrated to America with the help of the Jewish Labor Committee in New York, and arrived in New York in April 1941. He died on October 18, 1941. For his biography, see *Generations* 1:11–67.

164. A Bund activist who worked on the Warsaw *Folkstsaytung*. He came to Vilna in September 1939. On September 16, when the Red Army crossed the border to take the eastern parts of Poland, he crossed the border to Lithuania with a group of Bundists. He died in the Kovno Jewish hospital in the summer of 1940.

165. A senior Bundist in Vilna and a teacher in the Yiddish Technical Institute. He was known as a great bibliophile and devoted much energy to the YIVO in Vilna. His biographies (in *Teachers' Memorial Book* and in *Lexicon,* vol. 1) state that he died in the ghetto in 1942, but according to Kruk he died at the end of 1941.

ture; (2) report; (3) miscellaneous; (4) elections of the leadership. The conference lasted from 9 in the morning until 8 at night. All problems were discussed on a high level. I attach the resolutions adopted, along with part of the reports. [*The resolutions are missing.*]

FROM THE REPORT: INTERESTING DETAILS ABOUT THE ESTABLISHMENT OF THE JUDENRAT BEFORE THE GHETTO

In July [1941], the authorities ordered the formation of a Judenrat. At a meeting attended by religious Jews, Dr. Wygodzki, Kruk, Pinkhes Kon, and others, a Judenrat of 9 persons was selected. A later order required the Judenrat to have 24 members. A council of the Bund decided to send 4 persons. One of them, Comrade Wapner, was snatched that day; the second was not confirmed. So only 2 entered. This, more or less, is the part of the [report] about how our 2 representatives entered the first Judenrat before the ghetto. We have already written about the second Judenrat, consisting of the current 5.

FEBRUARY 16 [1942]

A batch of small but typical orders:

1. Potato peels may not be thrown away. Gather them up and dry them, eventually give them to others.
2. Bones are not to be thrown away but given to the janitor.
3. Ashes are not to be thrown away but also given to the janitor.

If these are the orders, it's clear what the near future is liable to bring.

PLASTIC SURGEON BREZMAN

We learn only today that the plastic surgeon Brezman was killed in the early days of the German-Soviet war during the attack on Vilna.

RIGA

Another bit of news from Riga. A Christian from Riga who visited Vilna says that in Riga, all the Jewish women and children were shot; only the healthy men were left alive. Altogether 3,000 men are left.

WEISKOPF

Today there is a famous person in Vilna, a name that circulates.

Weiskopf is the king of the ghetto. He saves Jews from prison, gives the most charity, helps people with everything he can, and the ghetto says that Weiskopf alone does more than anybody else in the ghetto. He is more than the Judenrat. . . .

Who is Weiskopf?

Before the war, he was a mid-level artisan who had a secondhand clothes shop. An energetic Jew with a lot of initiative. With the Germans, he suddenly emerged as leader of the so-called Tailor Establishment (*Schneiderstube*), simply—a tailor shop. But the workshop has reached such a level that by now 150 Jewish laborers work there. Germans order from them, clothes are bought there; in short, it is an enormous undertaking from which this Weiskopf is becoming a multimillionaire.

When Weiskopf gives charity for a social purpose, the smallest sum is 5,000 rubles. He gives generously, talks about it aloud so everyone will see and know.

Weiskopf gives to everyone. For me, he says, there is no difference, criminal or politician—all are equal and I help everyone.

Weiskopf hates "party people." He is for all Jews, he claims.

Suddenly, the ghetto discovers that Weiskopf's wife is arrested for selling a fur coat. How that happened, for what reason—never mind. What is important is that even in prison, Weiskopf is an aristocrat. Weiskopf's wife is put into a special room. Germans provide her with plenty of delicacies. Still, it costs 50,000 rubles, and she is released. When Weiskopf's wife is released, her husband buys out a whole performance from the police and distributes the tickets among all his employees to let them know that his wife is free! After the performance, Weiskopf throws a gigantic ball: the Obmann, the leaders of the police force, and all the actors who took part in the concert gather at the police chief's house. Brandy and vodka flow like water; people eat roast chicken and dishes you don't see in the ghetto.

Weiskopf makes a speech, tells all he is doing, what he will do, and people discover that he is bringing carloads of food, wood, and other things for the poor. Soon he will open a big factory for patching and mending underwear for the Germans. "He will give work and, because of him, people will live. He will give, give, give. . . . " Everyone is silent and knows that Weiskopf, the primitive man, the current emperor of the ghetto, will keep his word.

Weiskopf is an interesting chapter of the ghetto.

BERL SHTEPER

My comrade Berl Shteper,[166] along with all my friends and comrades, immigrated with his family of five to America. He didn't succeed and apparently remained stuck in Japan.

Now I learned that in November 1941, a letter from him came to Vilna saying that he got stuck in Shanghai and his situation is difficult.[167]

Berl Shteper was a popular name in Warsaw. He was an active Bundist, former

166. Berl Ambaras. He survived the war and lived thereafter in New York. The nickname *Shteper* means a sewing machine operator.

167. After the bombing of Pearl Harbor, Jews who could not proceed from Japan to America at that time were sent to a ghetto in Shanghai.

leader of the Warsaw sewing machine operators, a Warsaw *Dozor*[168] for many years, and a popular speaker at mass assemblies.

DOGS IN THE GHETTO

We have often written about the dogs that didn't want to stay in their old homes and came to the ghetto with their masters. Now, after six months, you don't see a single dog. All of them gave up their obstinacy and, sooner or later, left the ghetto.

The Vilna Ghetto remains dogless. . . .

A MESSAGE FROM FLOWER

Another letter from Flower.[169] Again he asks me about all the friends, again he asks about the trip to Warsaw, and again he begs me to keep in regular contact with him.

KOVNO

We have received many interesting and authentic pieces of information about the life of the Jews in Kovno since the German invasion. We already know some of the attached information. But we won't censor it now and will attach it here.

KOVNO AND THE ROUTE OF ITS JEWS (FROM JUNE 22 [1941] TO FEBRUARY 1942)

The First Days.

The German army entered Kovno on the evening of June 24 [1941], but the annihilation of the Jews had already started on June 23 at 12 noon. Groups of Lithuanian Fascists were soon maiming and robbing Jews. As the Soviet soldiers were retreating on the main streets and as the German army was marching in from the other side, the pogrom against the Jews was simply reinforced and lasted two weeks in a row.

First they broke into Jewish homes, mainly in the crowded Jewish [quarter] Slobodka, in the Old City, killing Jewish men and maiming women and children. Later they started arresting masses of men and women. Those arrested were taken to the Ninth Fort. About 5,500 Jews were assembled there, and thanks to the intervention of non-Jews, 73 of them were released. The rest were machine-gunned by Lithuanian Fascists in the presence of German military representatives.[170] Apart from that, in Slobodka, there was a mass execution of more than 600 Slobodka Jewish youth in the Eleventh Fort. A few thousand Slobodka Jews,

168. A voluntary guard of the Bund.

169. In the typescript, *Kwiatek,* which is Polish for "flower." Kruk means Abrasha Blum (*Blum* means "flower"), the leader of the underground Bund in the Warsaw Ghetto. From the entry, it appears that the previous information from Warsaw also came from him.

170. According to all published reports about the destruction of Kovno, the greatest killings took place at the Seventh Fort, not the Ninth Fort.

including masses of women with small children and infants, were concentrated in one place, where they were tortured for 10 days. Altogether, in Kovno and the surrounding area, in the first three weeks after the 22nd, 9,000–10,000 Jews were killed.

Jews Come and Jews . . . Disappear.

Jews have disappeared from the streets. The Snatching of Jewish males, ostensibly to send them to work, has started. The newly formed Jewish Community Council consists of several persons who have just come out of Bolshevik prisons. These include Attorney Y. Garfunkel; Attorney Yankev Goldberg; former general-secretary of the Association of Rabbis, Dovid Icykowicz;[171] and others. They have already organized the voluntary registration of Jews for unpaid labor. And you might have thought that things had calmed down.

Before Kovno's going into the ghetto (on September 15), a stream of Jewish refugees flowed in from the Lithuanian provinces. In the small towns with little Jewish communities, the real hell had started, and anyone who could and would rushed to salvation in the bigger Jewish community, Kovno. In the opposite direction, a stream of Jewish individuals and families went from Kovno, escaping from there to towns and forests, to friends and relatives. Non-Jews started profiteering.

The Kovno Ghetto

On about July 15 [1941], Jews in Kovno were ordered to leave their apartments in the front houses [of courtyards] and be shoved into the deeper back parts. Simultaneously, wearing "patches" was introduced. In a few weeks, a ghetto was set up for Kovno Jews in Slobodka. The transfer to the ghetto was scheduled for August 15 to September 15 [1941]. Transfer into the ghetto was divided by districts. The first ones into the ghetto were the Jewish residents of the New Town and hillside districts, and the last ones were from the Old City districts and the suburbs. During that time, Jews could select apartments, exchange apartments with non-Jewish residents of the ghetto district, transport everything they wanted, and more or less settle down in the "new place."

The ghetto consisted of: (1) the big ghetto district (right of Jurbarkio Street), and (2) the small ghetto district (left of Jurbarkio Street). The two ghetto districts were united by a viaduct bridge over Jurbarkio Street. The living area in the ghetto was enough for about four square meters per capita. But aside from Kovno residents, the Kovno Ghetto also included almost the entire Jewish population of Jonava and many Jews from the area around Kovno and the surrounding small towns. Altogether, there were more than 30,000 Jews in the ghetto. (Kovno itself previously numbered 33,000–34,000 Jews.)

171. In the typescript, the name is misspelled Micykowicz.

At first, life in the ghetto went on more or less calmly. Jews who had previously worked "voluntarily" for the Germans and Lithuanians still went to work in groups. The inspection at the gate was very strict: they were prevented from bringing in food, and upon their return to the ghetto, the work brigades were inspected carefully to ensure that the same number of Jews returned to the ghetto as had left in the morning. The inspection was carried out by Lithuanians and the Gestapo.

In the ghetto itself, a ghetto administration was set up. An old, well-known physician, Dr. [Elkhonen] Elkes, was nominated as president, and as deputy, Attorney Leyb Garfunkel. The first is a General Zionist, the second, Right Poalei Zion. The former director of the insurance company Lietuvas Laidas, [Mikhl] Kopelman (a non-party man), was appointed chief of police. But the strongest influence over the ghetto administration was exercised by the Revisionists and their representative in the Judenrat, Hirsh Levin. The latter is a young man of 30, a former owner of two big buildings. During the Soviet regime, he was kept in prison for a long time. Hirsh Levin, Attorney Yankev Goldberg, and the general-secretary of the Lithuanian Association of Rabbis, Dovid Icykowicz, shared the actual government of the ghetto.

As soon as the Jews of Kovno were closed in the ghetto, the attitude of the non-Jewish population toward them changed. On Sundays, the non-Jewish ghetto guard could not ward off the masses of non-Jewish women, men, and youngsters who clung to the ghetto fences, tossed in packages of food, goods, letters, etc. We must add that because of local conditions—i.e., that the ghetto in Slobodka was on a broad area covered with small wooden huts—the ghetto was fenced only with barbed wire and people could easily throw things inside. The Gestapo and the fanatic Lithuanian Fascists weren't happy that the Christian population "stuck with" the Jews as they did. Blows from rifle butts didn't help; they used bullets, which killed a few non-Jews and Jews. Only thus did they succeed for a certain time in separating Jews from non-Jews. Once during such Aktions, a gang of Fascists burst into the ghetto, beating left and right, and severely wounding the president of the Judenrat, Dr. Elkes, among others.

Kaspi-Serebrovich

The ghetto has suffered great aggravation because of a certain Jew, Yosef Kaspi-Serebrovich, who had been in prison during Soviet rule; he soon appeared so "useful" to the Germans that he and his family (a wife and two daughters) were allowed to live outside the ghetto and to be generally in a privileged position. He regularly came into the ghetto to make a fuss in the Judenrat, and to extort money and valuables, ostensibly to bribe the high dignitaries of the Gestapo, etc. True, along with that he also did favors for others, but woe to those with whom he previously had private accounts.

The First Provocation

The first provocation that shocked the Slobodka Ghetto was thus:

Five hundred intelligentsia were ordered to be delivered for work in the Central Government Archive. In the course of a few days this number was increased, but from the first day, they disappeared. Only later did it become clear that the whole group had been shot near the archive, in the old fort. The group included young doctors, lawyers, bank employees, teachers, journalists, and other professionals. Those murdered included the former editor of the Poalei Zion newspaper *Dos Wort* and leader of the Right Poalei Zion in Lithuania, Efroim Greenberg; the former assistant editor of the General Zionist paper *Yidishe Shtime,* the talented young journalist Uri Glazman; the well-known young Jewish lawyers Yofe, Kisiniszski [??], Niewiażski, and others. People assumed that the ghetto would at least be calm. The Judenrat took pains to find out the fate of those who disappeared. But they [the Germans] openly mocked the Jewish intercession.

With Blood and Fire

New terrorizing and decrees began to rain down. People were ordered to turn over all their money (leaving no more than 100 rubles or 10 Marks per capita), gold, silver, and precious stones. Then they came with trucks and took all the better furniture. Soon people were ordered to hand over all good clothes and fur coats.

The non-Jewish lords of the ghetto thought the Jews had too much room there. One fine morning they ordered the inhabitants of the "small ghetto" to leave their ghetto homes immediately, taking only what they could carry. The so-called small ghetto was completely liquidated, and the viaduct over Jurbarkio Street was torn down.

That was the start of the game of decreasing the number of ghetto residents by taking people away. The Judenrat received an order from District Commissar Kramer's deputy, Jordan, to surrender 2,000 heads. The Judenrat tried to oppose it, but. . . . A group of armed Lithuanians led by Gestapo agents carried out the demand with a large overhead.

Such exports were repeated on a smaller scale.

People Run Anywhere

In that atmosphere, it was impossible for many people to breathe, and many who had non-Jewish good friends slipped out of the ghetto in the dark of night with Christian documents. For a long time, those who remained didn't want to believe that their relatives had been taken away to be destroyed, but they soon became convinced that the process of annihilation had indeed taken place. For example, Jews coming back from work noticed young Christians selling in the marketplace the clothes of those who had just been taken away. The number of those taken away reached about 7,000 persons, including old men, old women, and children.

Chapter of "Professional Permits"

In mid-October [1941], they tried to introduce a system of special "professional permits" for Kovno Jews. But the Judenrat was informed that the number of permits was limited to 4,500 and that, in all, including families, about 13,000 persons could be protected by permits. This meant that more than half the remaining ghetto population would be destroyed. The Judenrat was assigned to distribute the permits by itself. That is, with their own hands, one group of Jews was to authorize [a verdict on] another part. The Judenrat refused categorically. Then the Gestapo also renounced the permit system. On October 28, the entire ghetto population was driven into one place and simply divided at random, one part for life, the other part for annihilation. On that day, 10,000 persons were taken away for destruction. Officially, 13,000 Jews remained in the ghetto, but in fact, about 17,000 Jews remained in the Slobodka ghetto.

An additional action took place that shook the nerves and minds of the ghetto population.

Sick People Are Burned Alive

On the pretext of a typhus epidemic, they came into the ghetto, surrounded the department of contagious diseases in the Jewish hospital (established in the new brick building of the Slobodka Yeshiva), and burned it along with the few dozen patients inside. The next day they came and took the inhabitants of the old age home and the children's home for destruction. Both the Judenrat and the inhabitants of the ghetto had to look on and swallow it.

The Non-Jewish Population Wakes Up

These actions also agitated the non-Jewish population, which saw that the country was being dragged into the mire and openly began showing sympathy for the persecuted Jews. The Gestapo was forced to counter such manifestations with threats and warnings.

Still, it seemed that ghetto life was becoming stabilized because for a long time people went to work and no new provocations took place.

New Hordes of Jews, Executions, and a Resistance

The only disturbing thing was that masses of Jews were driven into Kovno from the Czech area, from Łódź, Upper Silesia, Belgium, and Germany. The Slobodka Judenrat calculated that they would settle those Jews in the ghetto, but it turned out that the Jews were brought to Kovno for destruction. Non-Jews later told that when a group of such Jews was brought to be executed, the Jews put up a vigorous resistance against the small number of executioners and ran away in the turmoil. From then on, the destruction in Kovno has been stopped.

Six Streets

On January 22, the residents of six streets in the ghetto were suddenly ordered to leave their ghetto homes in four hours and move somewhere else. Ostensibly the place was being prepared for a large group of German or other Western Jews who were brought to Kovno. The order was carried out with violent haste and . . . blows. But, within a few days, the six streets were given back to the old ghetto residents. The German Jews didn't come. Information about what was actually done with those Jews unfortunately doesn't exist.

The Working Ghetto

What is typical of the Kovno Ghetto is that almost the entire able-bodied population of the ghetto, about 7,000–8,000 persons, works only at the airport. All other places of work were gradually purged of Jews, and only a few places remained with a few dozen Jews who were irreplaceable specialists working in their profession.

FEBRUARY 17 [1942]

ŁÓDŹ

A woman who just came from Warsaw says that in Warsaw, they're very worried about the fate of the Łódź Ghetto. For three weeks now, Warsaw has not had the slightest contact with Łódź. They assume that the Łódź Ghetto is being liquidated.

You don't need to waste words explaining to a Vilna resident what it means to liquidate a ghetto.

Apropos Warsaw. A letter came from Warsaw.

Someone who recently left the Vilna Ghetto in panic and fear writes:

"If you can survive in Vilna, don't move from there." Another person adds: "My parents and I are starving. Don't come, because there's nothing to eat. . . ."

CHAPTER 4
BETWEEN YIVO AND PONAR
FEBRUARY 19, 1942 – JULY 9, 1942

FEBRUARY 19 [1942]

GRAVEDIGGERS OR SAVIORS

Two days ago, Alfred von Rosenberg's representatives sent for me, Kalman[owicz], and Khaykl [Lunski]. After we met with them, it became clear: they are transferring the Strashun Library to the university building. I am to direct the work. Kalman[owicz] is to be my deputy; Lunski is to serve as an expert. Twelve workers are harnessed to transfer the books. We have been given a large suite in the university building where, during the time of the Bolsheviks, the Marxist-Leninist seminar was held (Universytecka Street 3). Khaykl is beside himself; he is nervous and distracted.

[*The end of the page is damaged. We present the parts of the lines that can be read, with additions by the editor of the Yiddish edition.*]

But he lends a hand to take out the [treasures of the Strashun Library, where he worked and which he guarded] for forty-five years! . . .

Kalman[owicz] and I don't know if we are gravediggers or saviors. If we succeed in keep[ing the treasure] in Vilna, it could be our [great ser]vice to some extent, but if they take the library away, we [will have] had a hand in it. But I am trying to insure myself for [all cases].[1]

1. So far, we have already, as noted above, taken some 3,000 books out [of the Strashun Libr]ary;
2. The janitor of the Synagogue Yard is hiding a few thousand [. . .] holy books in his house;
3. Today we got the decision from Dr. Müller[2] th[at we will re]ceive duplicates;
4. We also take out books little by little we [. . .] thus, in case we go away

1. Probably an insinuation that he is trying to hide certain important material from the Rosenberg Task Force. The following list clarifies what Kruk's "insurance" consists of.

2. A member of the Rosenberg Task Force. Aside from him, the staff consisted of the Nazi "Jewish specialists": Dr. Pohl, famous as the "Hebrew" (Kruk mentions him often); Dr. Wulf, Dr. Gotthart, Willi Schaefer, Sporket, and a Polish "supervisor," Wirblis.

[are deported]. But if [we succeed in preserving the library], we will remain victorious because the library remains in the building of the university library, in safe hands!

This is how I secured myself from both sides. . . .

Our new "taskmasters," as we said above, are intellectuals, and it seems they are people we can get along with. But it is harder to get along with my colleagues, the workers from the ghetto, who come here to carry the books. When I talk with the Germans, they stand around and prick up their ears; they treat the books like wood—no relation, not even the slightest traces of understanding.

A worker finds an old illustrated Haggadah[3] and wants to throw it in the fire; Kalman[owicz] barely saves it from his hands; Kalmanowicz says that the worker wants to burn the Haggadah because there are pictures of Pharaoh's bodyguard whipping Jews.

"He doesn't want the Germans to see that Jews were also whipped in the past. . . . He doesn't want that and so he grabs it to burn it."

One of our supervisors comes to me enraged and frantic. He can't understand the dullness of the . . . Lithuanians. Today, he stopped two trucks full of books. It turned out, he says, that somewhere on Vilna Street (Vilna 2), there is a "Hasidic synagogue," and they were taking the books from there. Worse—they were taking them to a paper factory to shred them! . . .

The German was flushed with excitement but calmed down when he arranged it. "The books will come to me and I will have them." . . .

I discover that they will assemble here all the Jewish material—from YIVO, the Strashun Library, and all the others. Here we are to segregate the books, make a selection, and draw up precise lists. The workers are happy—it will be work for months. . . .

Apropos YIVO. Only now do I find out that the Germans shipped part of YIVO a few months ago. Ostensibly the better and more important holy books.[4] In fact, however, parts of the cases were emptied, and in place of the discarded material, they filled them with loads of bacon to be smuggled into Germany. The discarded material was lost, and what was stained with bacon grease was surely spoiled.

Thus, some of the YIVO materials were put in order. The other part, they say, is to come to me.

As we said, we were given a whole suite for our work—an enormous hall with a few rooms. The library of the Marxist-Leninist seminar is in the hall. The hall is to be cleaned out for the Jewish holy books, and I decide to transfer the Marxist

3. The compendium of benedictions, prayers, midrashic comments, and psalms recited at the seder (ritual meal) on Passover.

4. Kruk uses the term *sforim* (rather than *bikher*, "books"). *Sforim* is usually reserved for religious books, but here he clearly means to include not just holy books but also secular books, and the term highlights their "holiness" for Kruk.

literature to a side room. The secretary of the university library, who knew me from before the Soviet-German war, embraces me, questions me, and among other things, asks me to protect the Marxist-Leninist library.

"I beg you, do it . . . with your whole heart," she asks me, as if she wanted to stir a spark of sympathy for Marxist literature in me. . . .

I promise her, and therefore she promises me to cooperate, that some of my Jewish books will gradually escape from here and meanwhile find shelter in a safer place.

This is our transfer!

I am beginning to like the place at Universytecka Street 3 as a "meeting place." My new office can serve, serve . . . serve me.

Everyone is happy about my idea.

But meanwhile, I am preparing a new team to make lists and catalogue the works we are putting together.

Another group of intellectuals will be saved with a few rubles a day, some with permits . . . and even work. Salvation from idleness. . . .

THE GIRLFRIEND OF HINGST'S GIRLFRIEND

A guest today, a Christian friend. He tells me something he's sure of. Today a girlfriend of Hingst's girlfriend told him that the tale of the Jews in Vilna isn't yet over. . . .

The blood curdles in our veins.

VILNA IN FEBRUARY 1942

The Germans entered in June [1941], now it's February, seven long months now. But Vilna still doesn't seem to have awoken. A kind of lethargic sleep hangs on the city, on her narrow, crooked side streets, her church towers, and on the dead walls that divide the city from the ghetto, from Ghetto 1 and from the barely remaining traces of Ghetto 2.[5]

The stores are locked up with a holiday calm. The dulled courtyards of the Jewish district are frightening in their emptiness. Niemiecka [Street], the main artery of the Vilna business district, is a quiet, calm alley, which doesn't remember life. The Poles I meet on the street look at me, frightened. All around, a dead emptiness and, over the city, from one end to the other, a terrible melancholy circulates—a city has died.

Vilna in February 1942.

GHETTO AIRSTRIP FOR VILNA CHILDREN

The Vilna Ghetto doesn't relinquish winter sport.

The Vilna children from the ghetto don't want to know about anything. It is

5. To get from the ghetto to the university, Kruk has to cross the once-bustling Jewish commercial streets.

winter, and the children themselves selected a hilly courtyard (Szpitalna 11) and turned it into a sledding airstrip. Dozens of children with and without sleds come here, as if everything were normal. With great noise and bustle, they amuse themselves with winter sports.

Another such strip on Szawelska 8. The mountains [of snow] covered the local garbage crate, and from the garbage crate in the courtyard, the children made a big, long path to sled on. Masses of children come here and amuse themselves merrily and lively with sleds.

The children don't want to know about anything.

A LETTER FROM BERL SHTEPER

Berl Shteper, one of the most popular activists and an original type of a simple laborer, a guardian of a synagogue, a good speaker, a leader of the Sewing Machine Operators' Association, etc., went, along with hundreds of Jewish labor activists, through Japan to America. Only today do I receive a letter from him. The letter comes from Shanghai, sent on October 6, 1941.

What does he write? He left Kobe for Shanghai. He has been in Japan for seven months. He asks about all our friends. He doubts that he will be able to leave for America and sends regards to everyone.

The letter from Berl seems like a letter from the other world. . . .

FEBRUARY 22 [1942]

VISITING THE ROSENBERG TASK FORCE

My new incarnation of work in the university building assumes new forms. Yesterday, I was informed that, at 2:30 on the dot, I had to appear at the secretariat of the Rosenberg Task Force, at Zygmuntowska 18. The Obmann, Milk[anowicki], and Kalman[owicz] had to appear there with me. We were received politely, even amiably. A new bigwig asked questions and requested information. First he requested our confirmation of his addresses of Vilna prayer houses, libraries, museums, archives, etc. Then he asked us to help them with that, and if we did it well, he promised a trip to the "neutral countries." Our smiles amazed him a bit. He said he didn't offer it to us but . . . if one of us would like it. There was then an informative conversation. For example, why is there a war between Yiddish and Hebrew, why is Hebrew connected with Zion? What attitude did the Bolsheviks have toward Hebrew? From the opinions and interpretations, we infer that these people are interested in the questions and that they already have some information about all these subjects. Finally, they asked for cooperation in collecting books, holy books, artwork, and museum valuables. Our conversation ended on a friendly note.

WORKERS FOR RIGA

There has recently been a secret fear among the ghetto residents on this question. People say that thousands of Jewish workers will soon be sent to work in . . . Riga. Now they're talking about 300. In any case, there is a fear on this score.

NEWS FROM WARSAW

Rare as it is, it is strange and unique to us:

1. In the Warsaw Ghetto, there is a church (on the corner of Karmelicka and Leszno), where the converts gather on every Christian holiday.[6] A regular attendant there is the . . . chief of the Jewish police. The church is full of people praying. . . .
2. An illegal German newspaper, *Der Soldat,* has penetrated the ghetto. It is an illegal military publication for German soldiers. Just such a paper comes into the ghetto. . . .
3. In Warsaw, three illegal Endek newspapers appear. All of them are antisemitic. But they fight with each other over how to get rid of the Jews. . . .
4. All shops are busy. All of them full of customers. You can even get oranges there. Nevertheless, hundreds of people are starving to death. Corpses lie in the streets.

THE "PARK" IN THE GHETTO

[*The end of the page is partially torn off. We present here the remaining portion of the lines, with bracketed additions by the editor of the Yiddish edition.*]

[We're] just like everybody else. Our ghetto also has its park in a courtyard [. . . No.] 6, there are two little gardens on about 20 square [meters.] Dozens of mothers with [their children] gather here every day. People stroll around the low walls of the garden and . . . [it feels like] a park.

Once again Messages from Those Who Were Exiled

[. . .] buried tens of thousands, for them it sounds [like an absurd . . .] nevertheless this is how it is. We have often [presented in]dividual letters from those who were taken. Recently, [the issue has] once more revived: a Jew in the uniform of a German [. . .] traveling through the Vilna railroad station left several [messages from Jews] from Vilna who now work in Vitebsk. [They are really] newly found. They long ago [. . .] their families. All those from whom [the letters] came today were taken on July 13, 1940.[7]

6. I.e., Jews who converted to Christianity. According to the Nazi Nuremberg Laws, a person with one Jewish grandparent was considered a Jew, even if he or she had been a Christian for two generations.

7. I.e., they were deported by the Bolsheviks.

OUR GHETTO KING IS CAPABLE OF ANYTHING

Concerning Weiskopf's banquet in honor of his wife's release, that same host donated 25,000 rubles to the Aid Society.

An important king—*Znaj pana!* [Polish: "Don't I have class!"]

February 24 [1942]

THE GHETTO IS FRIGHTENED AGAIN

March approaches. The holders of the thousands of permits in the ghetto tremble when they remember that their permits will soon no longer be valid. They live in fear.

The issue of workers for Riga is not yet over. It is not yet known how many will have to leave the ghetto or where they will be sent.

I Organize Units for the Rosenberg Task Force

[*The end of the page is torn off. From individual words, it can be seen that the missing section concerns the sending of workers to Riga and the Rosenberg Task Force. The new page seems to begin in the middle of an entry showing how artisans advertised in the ghetto.*]

Repairs

[. . .]

THE TAILOR ACCEPTS
REPAIRS
SZAWELSKA STREET 4, APT. 46

JUST NOT TO BE IN THE GHETTO

You go through the Vilna streets and often meet a peasant man or woman. But often the peasant is a Jew who ran away from his home town and wanders through villages, or settles someplace where no one knows him. He lets his mustache grow, sinks into high boots, with a peasant fur cloak, and acts . . . a peasant. Women imitate the game, playing peasant women. Some couldn't prevail upon themselves to do it but have decided to give their children to peasants, with whom they will be safe.

Dozens, maybe hundreds, of children live like that with peasants, and the peasants protect them, often as a good deed, more often for a good payment, seldom for friendship. . . .

FEBRUARY 25 [1942]

Sometime in the past, about four weeks ago, we said that the leader of the Food Supply Department in the Judenrat, Mr. [Khayim] Tropido, was arrested. We said that he was arrested in a strange way and that, in time, we would tell more about the case.

Now the case can be told: everything that comes into the ghetto is done through bribes. This time, like every time, Mr. Tropido went to Maisto Prekiba[8] with a bundle of gifts (material for a child's coat and other things). The thing was denounced, and Tropido was arrested. It happened on a Saturday, January 26 of this year. The giver and the taker were both arrested. Tropido was transferred to the Gestapo and from there to Łukiszki Prison. Most important—they demanded that he tell who was giving the gifts. Tropido took the whole thing on himself, unwilling to denounce the Judenrat. First, because that would make a big social scandal; second, because the ghetto would then remain without food. He was hardly interrogated until February 13. In contrast, he was beaten severely at every opportunity. On February 19, Tropido was released.

IN ŁUKISZKI PRISON . . . A GHETTO

The fellow who was just released tells that there is a ghetto in the prison. Jews are separated. The Jews' food is also different. Jews receive half the portion of non-Jews. If a Jew falls ill, no doctor comes to him. Therefore, there are many cases of people dying without receiving any help.

PRISONERS OF WAR IN PRISON

To what we have already told about Jewish Bolshevik prisoners of war, we will now add:

A large number of Bolshevik prisoners of war were held in Nowa Wilejka. The situation there was such that as many as fifty a day died. One day they announced that a ghetto was being created for Jews. The Jews were taken out of the camp and brought to Łukiszki Prison. In the prison, there were also prisoners of war from Vilna. They were there for no reason, dying of hunger and cold.

A GHETTO OF PRISONERS

On Subocz [Street], two houses were occupied by the wives and children of former Russian officials; their husbands couldn't take them along.[9] Recently, large and small groups have been taken out of there every day.

Where are those groups taken? No one can answer that.

In short: Vilna has yet another ghetto, the ghetto of the Bolshevik women and children.

8. Lithuanian for "Center for Food Supplies."

9. Russian officials and army officers fled Vilna on the second day of the war.

[*The following entry is badly damaged. Parts of lines are missing. We present the parts of the lines that are legible.*]

TWO CHILDREN'S SONGS

While we're on the subject, it is interesting to add two children's songs. One was written by a nine-year-old boy in Subocz. The second is a response to it by a Jewish [boy]. The first was written in Russian to the melody of a Bol[shevik song], the second in Yiddish. The first, the product of a nine-year-old Russian prisoner, is pessimistic; the second, the Jewish [song, was] written by a Jewish child in the ghetto, and sprouts with hope and [faith]. The Russian boy thought it necessary to send his song [to] the Jewish children in the ghetto. The Jewish boy, reading [the Russ]ian song, answered his Russian friend in Yiddish.

I consider both documents interesting exhibit[s. . . .] I attach them as they are written.

[*The songs are missing.*]

We have written once about the great destruction among the books of the Disseminators of Enlightenment [Library in] the ghetto. A part was taken by the Lithuanians from Smet[ona's time.] Later, the Reds purged the library, and even la[ter] the Lithuanians along with the Germans; finally books were car[ried off by] the Jewish inhabitants themselves. The last and final [destruction was] made by the librarians, who took from the treasure of books [those works that] might be suspicious.

To illustrate this, we attach two [pages] torn out of the ruined catalogue. Let this remain as a mem[orial for] generations.

[*The catalogue pages are missing.*]

UKMERGĖ

We write a separate report about the destruction of Ukmergė, as [told] by an Ukmergė Jew who saw and heard it all.

[*The report is missing.*]

FEBRUARY 28 [1942]

WINDS OF UNREST BLOW THROUGH THE GHETTO

Again, a wind blows through the ghetto: execution of Jews in Lida, Baranovitsh,[10] etc. The fire seems to envelop Byelorussia. Rumor has it that there are Jews in Vilna who ran away from those places.

10. Kruk wrote an extensive report, based on the statements of eyewitnesses, about the destruction of Baranovitsh. The report can be found in the YIVO Archive (Kaczerginski-Sutzkever Collection).

I learn that the Vilna Lithuanian Snatchers have been sent to Byelorussia.

I learn that the executioner Hering said that Jews will have to pay a lot to get into the Vilna Ghetto. . . .

Mrs. Matz of Vilkaviškis (see the report on Vilkaviškis), who has just arrived in Vilna, says that the Lithuanians are hopeful that the business with the Jews is not yet finished. They think of finishing with them during the approaching spring. Unease blows through the ghetto! . . .

[*The report of Mrs. Matz is in Chapter 9.*]

OSTENSIBLY FOR SPECULATING

In the city today, a group of about 400 Christians were driven by in a transport: for speculating and charging high prices.

People say that the group was taken from Łukiszki Prison to the train; they are probably being taken to work in Germany.

While we're on the subject of being taken to Germany, it became clear that the group of Soviet women we recently wrote about are being taken out of Subocz for Germany, presumably for work.

People claim that this was how the arrested people from Łukiszki Prison, who have already been [sentenced,] were transported.

MUSZKAT WITH AN HONOR GUARD AT THE HEAD

Workers at the Jewish hospital tell that a member of the Jewish police in the ghetto, the famous Muszkat, is in the hospital. But that "commander" can't bear to be alone and is regularly attended by a police honor guard.

That isn't funny, but it is typical of the local Jewish police.

MY NEW INCARNATION

After much deliberation with my Rosenberg bosses, it is clear that YIVO, the Anski Museum, the Children's Library, all the libraries of the Jewish gymnasia, the warehouse of Kletzkin publishers, and others will all be in my hands.

Meanwhile, my new boss has gone to Berlin. He will return in a few days, and then everything will be decided.

Meanwhile, the Strashun Library is in the university building. The holy books from the Gaon's Prayer House, from the Old Prayer House, from the Glaziers' Prayer House, and others have been sent there.[11]

11. The Gaon's Prayer House was in the Synagogue Yard, opposite the Strashun Library; the Old Prayer House was on the second floor near the Great Synagogue. The Old Prayer House, home to rare old holy books, was probably built in 1440. The Glaziers' Prayer House was at Żydowska Street 9, in one of the so-called passage courtyards there (Shik 1939:207, 215, 230).

A JEW IS SHOT IN BURBISZKI

A Jewish worker was shot today in Burbiszki[12] by the German supervisor there. The fellow went off to buy something; when he was called to stop, he ran away. He was wounded by the bullets, and after he was brought into the ghetto, he died.

RECOGNIZED HIS STOLEN HORSE

Today a group of workers from my unit brought a cart of wood into the ghetto. As soon as the cart came through the gate of the ghetto, a Jew standing on the sidewalk started running after the cart of wood. It turned out that the Jew recognized his own horse, which the Lithuanians had stolen from him. Now it is the property of the local German administration. The Jew looked at the horse brokenheartedly, examined his hooves, and looked at him like an old friend. The incident made a strange impression on those around.

A LITERARY EVENING DEVOTED TO HAMAN . . .

Last Saturday night, the second literary evening took place, organized by the Association of Writers and Artists. The evening was accompanied by great applause. There were many guests in attendance. Many of them came to warm themselves in the circles of Jewish literati and artists.[13]

The next evening takes place on March 7, 1942, and will be devoted to Haman. . . .[14]

PEOPLE SEARCH FOR . . . WORK

Another wave of interested people comes to me. The fact that I [will] put together a unit with three or four detachments has pushed a new wave to me, most of them workers and working intelligentsia. People give as credentials that they know languages, know Hebrew, etc.

INSTEAD OF IRON SEMAPHORES — WOODEN ONES

Meanwhile, I learn that the iron semaphores are taken from the Vilna railroad station and replaced by wooden ones.

Do they have such a critical shortage of iron in Germany?

12. A village outside Vilna.

13. The evening was held in the kitchen of Szawelska 17. Invitations to the evening for A. Sutzkever and for Malke Chaimson-Bastomski are in the YIVO Archive (Kaczerginski-Sutzkever Collection, nos. 440, 443).

14. The date indicates a Purim celebration, but *Haman* (the villain of the Purim story) was a code name for Hitler (partially because the names are linked by alliteration).

BRIGADIERS

That sort has become a plague and a robbery in Vilna Ghetto life. Who are the brigadiers? They are those who ran first to the units, ingratiated themselves with the German or Lithuanian leaders, did business with them, and established such customs as that the leaders get regular salaries from the . . . Jews. They bought them gifts and didn't take the payments.

The brigadiers are the partners and project-proposers. The brigadiers take thousands of rubles for allowing you to work and several thousand for helping you get a permit.

There are brigadiers who became very rich. They don't work and are occupied primarily with trade and manipulations.

The fellow workers are their slaves, work for them, and are dependent on them for a job, a permit, and . . . their body and soul.

MARCH 1 [1942]

SPRING

Spring is approaching. Although winter is still in full swing, it is clear that the worst is past. Soon real spring will come and, with spring, . . . But the ghetto man must not think of that. On the 31st, his right to a permit ends. The permit is a thing to which his whole life clings. If the permits are extended, you live; if not, life is over!

Meanwhile, rumors circulate that they will be extended. People even say that instead of a permit, they will be given an identification card, just like the Lithuanians. But Jews will have an ID with an addition.

PURIM IN THE VILNA GHETTO

Purim was celebrated in the ghetto this year.

The most patriotic Revisionist police arranged a Purim party attended by the commanders, the chief of police and his Christian wife, and others.

A group of Hasidim made a big Purim celebration. They drank brandy, sang, and were happy as if everything were normal.

The following paradox is interesting: there is no Book of Esther in the ghetto, so they had to come to the Socialist H[erman] K[ruk] to ask him to lend them scrolls out of his collection.

Such cases happen often. . . .

MARCH 3 [1942]

ARRESTS

Today I learn that there have been arrests in the city among Polish actors, converted Jews.

A great many arrests, they say, took place among Polish clergymen and monks.

I BECOME A GERMAN "BOSS"

Today I received a written appointment as supervisor of the work of ordering the Jewish books. The work has been done so far in the university library building and in . . . the ghetto. A warehouse of Jewish books is being set up in the ghetto.[15]

This is the fruit of my first labor.

MARCH 4 [1942]

A LIVING MESSAGE FROM PONAR[16]

Everything I tell here will surely sound like an invention. I have carried death on my shoulders; with his claws he clasped my neck, choked my throat. But listen:

In the beginning of December 1941, I was brought to Łukiszki Prison. My crime was that I was a Jew. By the time I reached Łukiszki, I had gone through an episode with the Gestapo where I was murderously and bloodily beaten. Only in Łukiszki did I begin a life constantly in question. Some were there because they had gone into the street without a pass. Others were apprehended in Christian homes; still others while buying bread for their families, and so on.

The prisoners receive 500 grams of bread a day. Those who are "agile" and get on well with the guards, who charge them a high price, endure the hunger that others unfortunately can't bear. Because I gave the guards some of my clothes, which were hidden in the city, my bread ration was a bit larger and I was allowed to keep up a written communication with my relatives.

Therefore, I was hopeful that something would be done and I would soon be out of there. It went on like that for a week. On December 5, we learned that an Aktion had taken place in the ghetto against the Jewish workers in the

15. I.e., a hidden warehouse, which the Rosenberg Task Force didn't know about.

16. The following quotation is a testimony; it also appears in Korczak 1946:64–65. There, the witness is identified as someone named Kagan.

Gestapo,[17] and as a result, 800 men were arrested. I learned that the Gestapo workers and their families were already in prison. Later, we found out that the actual collaborators of the Gestapo and some of their families were released. But all the "reduced" Gestapo workers remained here along with the parents of all Gestapo workers and those who were imprecisely or incorrectly recorded as "family members."[18]

The next morning, December 6, all of us were taken out of the cells and united with the Gestapo Jews remaining in prison. About eighty Poles were also added. All were loaded into trucks. I had the "honor" of being in the first car. Schweinenberg rode in front of us, and in back I saw five or six big trucks. Only then did we realize we were going on our last journey. I felt that I was already half dead. The trip lasted no longer than about 10 minutes, until we were taken to a fenced-in area called Ponar.

All hope vanished. We already saw the prepared graves, and we were aware that there were hundreds and thousands there who had ended as we were to end. . . . We wanted it to happen as fast as possible; there was no time for reflection. Moreover, it was impossible. All the Jews were lined up, and Schweinenberg stood in front of them. Men, women, and children were separated, and we were ordered to take off our outer clothing. Anyone who had good underwear had to give that up, too. The temperature was 25 below zero, Celsius. We were quickly driven to the graves. Those who hadn't undressed were beaten murderously with rifle butts.

In front of the grave stood six Lithuanian soldiers with rifles. The victims were stood in rows of six, and as soon as a row was arranged, a Lithuanian gave an order, there was a salvo, and six people fell into the grave. Another row of six was driven up, again shots, another falling of victims into the open grave, and so on.

I can't remember whether the victims cried or shouted; maybe some of the women or children did. I wound up in the fifth group of six. We remained facing our executioners. I didn't see who was standing on my left or my right. I was calm because I didn't really exist anymore. . . . Only my body was standing there, waiting indifferently for the bullet. I know I fell to the ground and there was a heavy mass on me. I lay in a swoon in my underwear in the snow and frost. I heard a lot more shots, and everything became denser and tighter around me. Now I understood that I was lying in a grave and that what I heard were the shots of more executions. What I felt was the mass of the murdered constantly falling into the big mass grave.

17. Here and later, mentions of "Jewish workers in the Gestapo" or "Jewish Gestapo people" refer to the Jews who were employed in the work unit that carried out various jobs for the Gestapo.

18. Some people without permits were identified on official documents as family members of permit holders. Members of a fictive "family" usually belonged to the same social or political group.

How long I lay there like that I don't know. Human blood flowed over my body. It must have lasted about four or five hours because it began to get dark. I looked around and didn't see anybody; I tried to get up, to get away from the pyramid of bodies, and a bit farther on, I saw the Lithuanian murderers still standing and dividing up the remaining clothes. But they stood with their backs to our grave and were absorbed in what they were doing. I crawled out of the grave. I was naked and covered with red blood spots, but I wiped myself off with snow and crawled along the ground. Later I stood up and ran as I never had before until I came to the wire fence of the death place. I quickly crawled through the [barbed wire], badly wounding my hands, feet, and shoulders, and dripping blood from my wounds, I came to a village. Of the few huts there, I went to the smallest, the poorest. It was [the home of] a Pole who worked in the area for a rich Lithuanian landowner. I explained my situation to him. He immediately gave me warm water to wash off my bloodstains. I drank and ate, and only then did I feel that my bones were frozen. The peasant gave me his own bed. I lay there until six in the morning almost in a lethargic sleep. When I was out of bed, the peasant gave me clothes and brought me back to the ghetto. For the two months since then, I have been in the hospital.

MARCH 7 [1942]

CHILD CRIMINALS

Today, in the Child Education Department, a unique meeting took place, attended by the public prosecutor of the Jewish ghetto court, Attorney [Adolf] Povirsker;[19] commissioner of criminal police, [Henryk] Zagajski; representative of the Jewish police unit, Mr. Muszkat; chairman of the Jewish ghetto court, Attorney Srolowicz; and the staff of the Child Education Department, Miriam Gut[gestalt], [Rokhl] Brojdo,[20] and [Moyshe] Olicki.[21]

Why was that meeting held?

It dealt with the fact that a gang of child criminals has been discovered in the ghetto; 13 of them are in the ghetto jail. About 40 children are estimated to be in the gang.

19. Died of dysentery in Stutthof.

20. Born in Troki. In the Vilna Ghetto she worked as a teacher in the Jewish schools. She belonged to the Communists and the FPO. In September 1943, during the liquidation of the Vilna Ghetto, she was sent to Majdanek. For her biography, see *Teachers' Memorial Book* 1954:69.

21. Chairman of the Hebrew Teachers' Association in Vilna. In the ghetto, he and his wife, Esther, were teachers in the school of the labor camp Kailis. He was killed in an Aktion at that labor camp in March 1944.

After considering several proposals, the council decided to create a workshop for the displaced children.

VILNA IS INEXHAUSTIBLE

At last, as we have said, the books from the city were delivered to the ghetto warehouse. The deliverers were Jews, the leaders of the so-called Rosenberg Task Force, [whose overseers] had turned the whole job over to Jews. The leader is H[erman] K[ruk].

Today H. Kr[uk] went with Kalman[owicz] to reconnoiter in the former Ghetto 2. The result: several thousand holy books are still to be taken out, meaning weeks of work. Once again, we ascertain that Vilna has been a city of learning, an inexhaustible sea.

HAMAN EVENING

This is Purim week. It is the Saturday night after Purim.

Now, at midnight, I have just finished the fourth literary gathering. This time the evening was named Haman Evening. H. Kr[uk] conducted the evening. The most distinguished people of the ghetto participated.

The next evening will be devoted to the Jerusalem of Lithuania.

[There was] a Purim evening of the Hasidim.

MARCH 8 [1942]

PONAR

It gnaws like a worm. Rumors come from all sides: spring will bring new sad events for Vilna Jews. However, if the Germans have to withdraw from the area, who knows what they will do with the Jews.

Lithuanian friends advise escape. Escape because you can expect great misfortunes. A reliable person comes, a man who has good connections among highly placed persons. He says they are already digging graves in Ponar. A man with extensive acquaintances sent someone to Ponar to investigate. Meanwhile . . . the splendid spring comes and a pain gnaws in the depths of the soul and no one dares talk about it.

Where to flee? Where can you flee? . . .

Thus the Vilna Jewish masses are waiting in a line. The noose is thrown around their neck and they wait for the hangman to come and pull it. . . .

CELEBRATIONS AND MEMORIALS

Nevertheless, life is stronger than anything. In the Vilna Ghetto, life begins to pulse again. Under the overcoat of Ponar a life creeps out that strives for a better morning. The boycotted concerts prevail. The halls are full. The literary evenings burst their seams, and the local hall cannot hold the large number that comes there.

Today was a little Yom Kippur for me. I couldn't control myself, my tears flowed like a spring:

The Child Education Department in the Judenrat arranged two memorial commemorations in the two schools. The first service, in the school at Szawelska 1, was held from 10 to 11; in the second school, at Strashun 12, from 11 to 12.

The commemorations are dedicated to the dead teachers Shloyme Bastomski, [his wife, Malke] Chaimson-Bastomski, Gershon Pludermacher,[22] and Engineer Mark Idelson.

The participants in both commemorations included the Judenrat, representatives of various institutions, writers, artists, teachers, parents, and others. Several hundred residents of the ghetto attended the commemorations.

Here, for the first time since I have been in the ghetto, I felt the children's performance as an echo of that Warsaw life of tremendous mass assemblies. I felt the breath of the Medem Sanitarium, the schools on Krochmalna, those on Karmelicka, and others.[23] Here, for the first time in the ghetto, I was overcome by the Ponar tones of Grieg's "Valse Triste," Chopin's "Funeral March" and . . . a hall full of people crying. It's hard to explain what it means to cry today in Vilna Ghetto. . . .

The music reopened the wounds left by tens of thousands taken away, murdered and slaughtered fathers, mothers, sisters, brothers, and loved ones. The hall wept, and the tears flowed like peas. No one was ashamed of the tears. One woman speaker even said: "The schools unite us. The tears elevate and purify. And although we cannot visit the graves of our loved ones, we are joined with them in spirit and are hopeful that, although we are physically weak, we stand tall spiritually and will hold out through it all."

The children sang, recited, and read, and among other things, they read two poems created by a child of eleven who died recently. I attach the poems.
[*The poems are missing.*]

At one in the afternoon today, a new celebration took place: the opening of a children's home at the Health Department. The air there is different. The atmosphere is like that of a Jewish community council. The children keep expressing their gratitude for the children's home. It's cold, a wind is truly blowing.

In the coming days, we shall record several biographies of the children from the home and their hymn. It's good work, nice work, but—it smacks of cursed philanthropy.

Incidentally, it is interesting to note: the home is set up in the building of the

22. The Bastomskis and Pludermacher were among the pioneers and builders of the Yiddish school system. Their biographies are in *Teachers' Memorial Book* 1954.

23. Kruk refers to the Yiddish secular schools of TSISHO at Krochmalna 36 and Karmelicka 29 in Warsaw.

former Elyashberg Prayer House, Szpitalna Street 1. The celebration took place in the auditorium of the prayer house. The former pulpit before the Holy Ark is the lectern. The Holy Ark has not been touched, and it makes a strange impression: what the Bolsheviks didn't do with the prayer house, the ghetto Jews have managed to do.

KAILIS — THEY SEARCH FOR . . . CHRISTIANS

On Friday evening, the 6th of this month, a search of documents took place in the Kailis block. It seems they were looking for . . . Christians.

Lately, many Christians have been hiding, not wanting to be sent away for forced labor. . . .

SPRING IN THE GHETTO

An interesting contribution to the recent mood in the ghetto is the writing of poetry. The attached document, "Spring Evening, 1942," is very typical of that. [*The poem can be found in the YIVO Archive (Kaczerginski-Sutzkever Collection, no. 627).*]

MARCH 9 [1942]

DOES SPRING BRING — SPRING?

The same question is on everyone's lips. Everywhere the same. Everyone draws conclusions and analogies to the question: Will the spring really bring spring?[24] . . .

The events on the major fronts have not always had the proper impact on us. We know little about what is happening. Information here is dreadfully thin, but nevertheless it is almost clear—spring is bringing something new. New winds are blowing, new birds are bringing new songs.[25] . . .

Everyone is getting ready for that and making preparations. The masses live with hope and are certain that soon, in the very near future, salvation will come. The Aryan world keeps on reassuring us that the time is at hand. Others advise running away again because spring is bringing new troubles for the ghetto.

Just yesterday an appeal was circulated in the city, calling on the population to hold out because . . . liberation is at hand. Christians come into the ghetto to hide out with their friends because that is now the safest melina for them. . . . The Jewish police, who understand that spring for all doesn't bode hope for the ghetto police, are preparing melinas in the city. . . . Jewish and non-Jewish social activists are preparing melinas for the time of transition. . . .

24. Spring is a metaphor for liberation.

25. A line from a popular Socialist song.

Meanwhile, people tell, with 100 percent reliability, that at 2 o'clock yesterday morning, Wilejka[26] was bombed and that there was an air raid alarm in Vilna. They tell of 12 dead.

Meanwhile, the German powers are not falling behind.

The leader of the Rosenberg Task Force consoles me that I will have . . . work—the selection of Jewish books will last until August. He has time. Others suspect that this is his way of hiding out so as not to be sent off to the front.

Although the German organization is limping badly, nevertheless. . . . Nevertheless, they begin a "voluntary" collection in the Balkan countries. Not fur coats this time, but metal, brass, etc.[27]

How this voluntary collection will end is hard to predict.

One thing is clear—spring is ushering in a lot. May it come to pass.

MURER IN CIVILIAN CLOTHES

On Sunday he stood like that at the gate, stopping all those going in or out. If they were people simply going out of the ghetto, he stopped them and ordered them put in the Jewish jail and shouted at them: "Even on Sunday they want to stink up my streets." . . .

He caught several people like that.

BAGELS, DOUGHNUTS

As if nothing had happened. In the ghetto, you get fresh and tasty bagels and people snatch them out of your hand. A bagel costs five rubles.

Bagels like the prewar ones, fresh, well-baked, and crispy. You also get doughnuts here. Ten rubles apiece.

The ghetto does not succumb. On the one hand, people are dying for a mouthful of food; on the other, people are living in luxury.

MARCH 11 [1942]

Visiting Kailis

Yesterday I went on invitation to Kailis. Kailis is tucked out toward the Jewish Scientific Institute [YIVO] and opposite the famous Vilna radio factory. From the ghetto, I go there through Nowogródzka Street. On the way, the wood market is

26. A town not far from Vilna.

27. In the YIVO Archive (Kaczerginski-Sutzkever Collection, no. 15) is the order from the police chief of the ghetto (no. 24, March 10, 1942) demanding that all kinds of metal—lead, copper, brass, etc.—be turned in.

empty. Zawalna is empty. The building at Zawalna 60 is boarded up; the big, noisy house is desolate and empty.[28]

Nowogródzka Street reminds me of the march into the ghetto. A soldier shoved me with a bayonet, I fell under the weight of my packs, and the German on the side . . . photographed me in my "humiliation."

Painful memories . . .

Here, at Makowa [5], I lived; I held meetings at Nowogródzka 10, and now, in snow and blizzard, I stride in the middle of the street with the yellow patch of the ghetto to the isolated buildings called the Kailis blocks.

The two Kailis blocks look like two islands, torn out and isolated from the surrounding world. About 500 Jews live in each block. Going out of the block is a risk, a danger to your life.

Kailis looks like some provincial place. The best—[. . .] to travel into the big world. Here the saying goes: "That's what they say in the ghetto."

"They say in the ghetto . . . "

What can you do but stand "at attention" . . .

Kailis is indeed a provincial place compared to the ghetto.

MARCH 12 [1942]

SPRING BRINGS ITS MESSAGES . . .

The ghetto breathed a sigh of relief today with "spring." Outside, the snow is like winter but "spring" brings its messages.

Today, between 10 in the morning and 12 noon, Vilna was in a state of alarm. Machine guns and rifles, etc., were heard.

The ghetto revived. The ghetto drew in fresh air. . . .

All evening, the Jewish police demanded the strict observance of the blackout—that was the strict order of the Lithuanian authorities.

JEWS FROM GERMANY

A rumor has suddenly spread through the ghetto that 2,000 German Jews were brought to Subocz Street.[29]

28. This was the house of Anna Rosental, leader of the Vilna Bund (who was later shot by the NKVD). Before the war, the activists of the Vilna Bund used to meet in that house. In the first months of the war, her house was a meeting place for Bundist activists who came to Vilna as refugees from Poland.

29. "Subocz Street" refers to the popular Cheap Houses, built in 1899 by the IKA (the Jewish Colonization Organization). These were two big six-story buildings of 100 apartments each. Later the houses became the property of the Jewish Community Council. Until World War II, poor Jews lived there along with students and others. In 1939–1940, the houses held a concen-

Why were they brought in?

Why were they taken to Subocz?

Meanwhile, nobody knows anything. Everyone asks, and question marks remain hanging in the air.

THE YELLOW PATCH OF A GERMAN JEW

Today I got a gift from Mr. Gens—a yellow patch from a Western European Jew. Along with it, he says: a few weeks ago, a large group of Jews from Belgium and Holland were brought to Kovno. There they were to be shot. They resisted and many managed to hide. The patch comes from one who was shot. . . .

YIVO IS OPEN

It is hard to convey [my feelings on] my first visit to YIVO. Aside from my relations to this institution, let alone the days and weeks I spent under the roof of the Jewish Scientific Institute [YIVO], yesterday I saw a picture that truly crushed me.

I have already written about where part of YIVO went. The remaining parts are lying in a cellar. The condition of things is thus: it is really impossible to go into the cellar. The cellar is stuffed from top to bottom. I step on the excellent card catalogue of the Bibliographical Center. The cards are lying on the floor in a heap half a meter high. Along with them, all mixed up, lies the card catalogue of the YIVO library, the cards of the press. Underneath are pictures, works of art, Yankl Adler's[30] "two soldiers," etc. The books from the library shelves, which are in the same cellar, are strewn and confused, piled more than a meter high. Between the cabinets are letters, documents, photographs, pictures, etc., etc.

The hall where the Peretz exhibition was recently held is empty, the exhibits thrown into a side attic.[31] Peretz's manuscripts are lying there, mixed up with sand. There are Peretz's objects, pictures. Everything is broken, torn, soiled.

My first order is to save the Peretz exhibition, bring everything from the exhibition into room number 10. The second order is to lock the cellar temporarily.

---

tration of "training kibbutzim" (*hakhshara*), consisting mostly of refugee members of Halutz youth movements from other parts of Poland.

30. Yankl (Jacob) Adler (1895–1949), a Jewish painter, was born in Łódź and studied at art school in Germany during World War I. After the war he returned to Poland, where he painted works with Jewish themes and co-edited and illustrated a literature and art magazine, *Yung Yidish*. During the interwar period Adler relocated to *Düsseldorf*. In 1937 the Nazis removed his paintings from German museums and included several of his works in the "Degenerate Art" exhibition they organized in Munich. Adler fled to France and served with Polish army units during World War II. After the war he moved to England, where he became a prominent abstract painter.

31. A major exhibition was held at YIVO in 1940, on the 25th anniversary of Y. L. Peretz's death in 1915, and it lasted until 1941, which was assumed to be the ninetieth anniversary of his birth (he was probably born in 1851).

The entire YIVO building is at the disposal of my unit, actually at my disposal. In this building, as in the university, the ghetto, and other [places], we shall collect holy books and books from the city.

How all this will end, as we have said more than once, is the question of who will get whom first. . . .

The warehouse of books and holy books in the ghetto is already filled to the brim. I am looking for more warehouses. The first warehouse in the ghetto is in a store at Rudnicka 5.

ANOTHER NEW INITIATIVE

On the tenth of this month, through our initiative,[32] a founding meeting took place for the creation of a school commission designed to provide care, warmth, and material support to the Yiddish schools.

The meeting was attended by twenty school and cultural activists, teachers, etc.

The meeting was opened by Comrade [Berl] Widman,[33] the lecture on the mission was given by Dr. [Jan] Antokolski,[34] and the meeting was chaired by Dr. [Leyb] Pomeranc.[35]

The lecturer said: The schools should not be isolated from social life in the ghetto. The committee should provide material support for the schools, supply them with instruments, and preserve the character of each school. The legal status of the Jewish teacher should be improved. The number of schools should be increased. The good mood of the children should be maintained.

After a discussion by Comrades [Leyb] Turbowicz,[36] Dr. [Yitskhok] Rucz-

32. Probably the initiative of the Bundists. The leaders of the meeting were certainly Bundists. The meeting was also attended by those who were involved in the Yiddish secular school system.

33. Born in 1896 in Biržai, Lithuania. A painter by profession, he had joined the Bund in his youth. He was a deputy of the Bund in the Vilna Jewish Community Council and was particularly active in the Central Education Committee (TSBK) and the Central Parents' Committee (CEK). In 1939–1940 he was active in the Refugee Committee. In the ghetto he was a member of the committee of the Bund. He was killed in a camp in Estonia.

34. Also known by the name Antokolec. He was among the young Bundist activists in Vilna. After attending Vilna University, he practiced medicine. He was also the Vilna correspondent for the Warsaw *Folkstsaytung*. After the liquidation of the Vilna Ghetto he was sent to Estonia, where he organized the escape of Jewish inmates in the Estonian camp Ereda. He was killed in the forests of Estonia in August 1944 (Kaczerginski 1947:179).

35. Born in 1894 in Święciany. He completed a gymnasium education in Vilna and then studied in Switzerland. He was active in building the Yiddish school movement in Vilna and the Vilna district. In September 1944 he was killed by the Nazis in Klooga, Estonia. For a detailed biography, see *Teachers' Memorial Book* 1954:306–307.

36. One of the most popular pedagogues in Jewish Vilna. He was principal of the Yiddish Real Gymnasium. In the ghetto, he directed the school system. He was killed in a camp in Estonia. For his biography, see *Teachers' Memorial Book* 1954:172–174.

nik,[37] M[iryem] Gutgestalt, [Yitskhok] Senicki,[38] and [Borekh] Lubocki,[39] the following was decided:

1. The council declares itself a plenum of the School Committee.
2. A temporary presidium of the School Committee should be elected.
3. Nine persons were elected to the presidium.

WHAT DO THE SCHOOLS LOOK LIKE IN THE GHETTO?

From a report submitted to the aforementioned council by the School Department, it becomes clear:

At the beginning of September 1941, a group of teachers met to establish a Department of Child Care. A registration of teachers and children was carried out at that time. Three thousand children were listed in the registration. The first school was located at Rudnicka 13. Later the school moved to Strashun 12. The second school settled at Szawelska 1. The Judenrat confirmed 40 positions for teachers. Because of the various events, the number of children regularly "decreased." On October 12, 1,073 children remained, only 900 of whom attended school.

As of today, March 10, 1942, there are two school locales. The daily attendance amounts to more than 700 children. There are 10 classes. Twenty teachers are employed in the two institutions. There is a lack of furniture, supplies, heating wood, etc. Some of the children eat lunch in the children's kitchen. All the children receive imitation coffee at the long recess. Ninety-two children receive free bread and coffee at breakfast. The children attend school from 9 in the morning until 2 in the afternoon.

At first, they did not study at all but were limited to systematic discussions. Later, studies were introduced in Yiddish, arithmetic, nature, hygiene, crafts, and singing, drawing, and finally music.

The number of teachers who worked at the time of the distribution of permits was 43. Instead of the promised 30, only 10 permits altogether were distributed. That was the hardest event in the life of the Vilna teachers. The distribution of the 10 permits was done almost at random. *(Pludermacher and his wife; Turbowicz, the former principal of the Yiddish Real Gymnasium; Chaimson-Bastomski; and others remained outside.)* [Italics are Kruk's.]

Only later was the question resolved in the form of protection permits. But meanwhile, dozens of teachers were gone. . . .

37. A popular ophthalmologist in Vilna. He was killed in Estonia in 1944.

38. A well-known educator in Vilna who was director of the Dinezon School. He was killed in a camp in Estonia. For his biography, see *Teachers' Memorial Book* 1954:284–285.

39. An educator who was active in the Jewish Democratic Party in Vilna. He was sent to Kivioli. From there, he was transported to Stutthof and later to a camp in Schömberg, Württemberg, where he was killed on November 22, 1944. His two sons were partisans in Rudnicki Forest and were killed in action.

Aside from the two institutions, children's groups in the Kailis blocks have now been opened. There are now 123 children in these groups. Six teachers are employed there.

Under the direction of the Health Department, as we mentioned, a division for abandoned children has been opened.

Now there is activity toward creating vocational classes. Groups of child apprentices have been created in the technical workshops of the Judenrat.

The Judenrat has rejected the appeal to introduce gymnasium classes.

Because of the large number of criminals among children, an institution for delinquent children is now projected.

OUR POLICE STRAIGHTEN OUT . . .

For a long time now, the Jewish police in the ghetto have behaved like human beings. At first they snatched up the group of actors, promised them permits, and made them organize the famous police concerts. Later a series of lectures was introduced for the police to stir them up for . . . Palestine.[40]

Recently, the process of humanization has gone even further. The police leadership is trying to persuade the police to reduce their brutality toward the ghetto inhabitants. . . . We hear that police "beg" groups of people to break up. They're not shouting as often as before and are behaving less arrogantly.

Nevertheless, the spoiled young man Levas, commissar of the gate guard, "broke down" again yesterday and beat Berl Widman's daughter[41] just because she brought three kilos of potatoes from work. The man on the street wanted to lynch the licentious fellow. In spite of that, he threw her in jail, into a little room used to store wood. At 11 at night, he took her to prison and didn't release her until 5 in the morning.

A lot of water will flow before the dissolute Revisionist police of the Vilna Ghetto will really turn into human beings.

Not in vain do the leaders understand that in case of a change, they'll have to look for melinas. . . .

ABOUT THE OBMANN, MR. FRIED

We have often written about that great hero of our ghetto. Now a few character traits to show how the ghetto thinks of him.

When the Obmann's name is mentioned, the ghetto inhabitants call him *Yobman,* and Russified Jews call him *Obmán*.[42]

Recently the Judenrat employees invented an amusement for themselves: one

40. The police consisted mainly of Revisionists, right-wing Zionists, whom Kruk, as a Bundist, detested.

41. Widman's daughter, Esther, died a week before the liberation of the ghetto.

42. The first half of the word *Yobman* is from Russian; the expression translates as "Fuckman." *Obmán* means "deceit" or "fraud" in Russian.

of them wrote a four-line poem about the "boss." The staff had several copies typed up and gladly distributed it among their colleagues.

This is the poignant and typical poem [in Polish]:

Getem niby rządzi Fryd,
Zblazowany pseudo-Żyd.
Ale w tym tkwi cały sens,
Że go w d . . . ma P. Gens.

[The ghetto's boss is Mr. Fried,
He's a blasé pseudo-Yid.
Yet therein lies the real sense:
He's up the ass of Mr. Gens.]

MARCH 14 [1942]

MORE TERRORISTS SHOT

In our little Lithuania, the number of "terrorists" is very big. Regularly and incessantly, the local press becomes alarmed about Communists who carry out "acts of terror," murder, arson, who use printing presses, distribute leaflets, have at their disposal gold bullion, radios, arsenals, etc.

This is the song of the 1880s, of the time of the terror of 1905, 1918, and 1919, and now, too.

Recently, the local press reported that 37 terrorists were shot in Kovno. About two or three weeks ago, they reported 62 terrorists shot, and some time ago, a group of 5.

We in the ghetto thought that it was calm in Lithuania. Meanwhile, we discover that the "terrorists" of the 1880s have been raised from the dead.

We attach one of the latest news reports on the execution of 37 "terrorists." [*The report is missing.*]

THE DREAD OF LIDA. THE TRAGIC EVENTS OF THE RUSSIAN ORTHODOX PRIEST

For about three weeks now, people have been telling of terrible events around Lida.

We know that a group of Lithuanian Ipatinga left Vilna for Byelorussia. The purpose of such a trip is clear. Now we learn more:

In Lida, on Kościuszko Street, there lived a Russian Orthodox priest. He was a man with a good reputation and recently did a lot for Jews. He hid them and gave them all possible support. All of a sudden, the priest was attacked in a robbery. While defending himself against one of the attackers, he was knocked on the head with an iron bar and fell down, wounded.

One of the escaping men dropped a jacket with a yellow patch. Obviously the bandits were Jews. In the rage that arose against the Jews, the German authorities ordered the Judenrat to deliver the Jewish criminals within ten hours. Otherwise, they themselves would take 1,000 Jews. . . .

The Judenrat felt forced and . . . gave the authorities Jews from the underworld, with the premise that some of them might have been the murderers. Wanting to save themselves, the six [Jews from the underworld] denounced the Lida Judenrat for making [false] passports for Jews who had escaped from Vilna. The Judenrat reportedly took dollars for it, etc. Seven persons were immediately arrested.

About two weeks afterward, in early March, an order was suddenly issued that on Sunday, at a specified time, all Jews from the city must appear in the marketplace. A temporary gate was put up in the square, and they all had to pass through it. The police entered the apartments of those who did not appear in the square at the specified time, and shot them on the spot. Thus a great many Jews were killed.

Byelorussian police, Gestapo agents, and two . . . of the six arrested Jews (the father and son Olkienicki, carters) stood on either side of the gate. Their task was to indicate all those who came from Vilna. Seventy-five or eighty people were selected. All those arrested were taken to prison and, ten days later, were all shot, along with the Judenrat. Three of the condemned Vilna Jews (Genski, Szykczulski, and Perlman) saved themselves. At the execution square, they threw themselves down among the dead and later disappeared. . . .

For a while, it was calm there, and rumors again reached Vilna: all the Jews were expelled from Lida. . . .

Few among us react anymore to such news. Either we are dulled or petrified—more than 80 dead, no big deal. . . .

Disturbing news has recently arrived from Byelorussia.

2,000 GERMAN JEWS

We have already noted that 2,000 German Jews are in the Municipal Houses on Subocz. Now I know that the group of Jews is from Austria, most from Vienna.

So far, we have not been able to make contact with them.

THEY DIG! . . .

In Ponar and Jaszuny, they are constantly digging pits. . . .

200 POLES AND A FEW JEWS

I just received word that this week, in Ponar, 200 Poles and a few Jews were shot, including the Jew Glik (the famous director of Kailis) and others. Thus, our Glik of Kailis is also done in.[43]

43. In Yiddish, *Glik* means "happiness," "good fortune."

FROM THE PROVINCE

For the time being, Vilna has stopped being hell. Conversely, there is unrest in the surrounding area. I know precisely that many people have recently come to Vilna from the surrounding area.

Many protection permits have been distributed recently; yet there are still thousands in the ghetto without permits. It should be emphasized that the ghetto now numbers about 18,000 inhabitants.

JEWISH SUITCASES

From the Gestapo in Vilna, where a lot of Jews work, we hear that the Gestapo took a lot of suitcases and valises from the train. The suitcases and valises are covered with labels from world-famous spas. The suitcases come from Jews. And the Jews? . . .

The Vilna Jewish workers in the Gestapo were assigned to unpack the suitcases. Aside from the rich and elegant things found in them, they also came upon knitting that was begun and not finished, books laid down in mid-read, socks incompletely darned, etc. The impression left by the unpacking is hard. It seems as if the owners of the baggage were unexpectedly taken away from their last bit of property. . . .

And perhaps the owners of the baggage were the Austrian Jews in the Cheap Houses? . . .

MURER'S REQUEST

At Murer's request, the head of the ghetto police has recently commissioned a history of the Jews in Vilna with special attention paid to the medieval ghetto and a survey of the current ghetto. The work must be accompanied by a map of the old ghetto, two maps of the contemporary ghettos, and a drawing of the territory of the ghetto on the map of Vilna today.

The committee selected for that purpose will do the work fast. We shall attach a copy of it.

A HORRIBLE STORY

Our story today is both typical of the stories and legends often told in the ghetto, and unique.

A Kovno Jew, Judelewicz, an employee of the Judenrat, says he received a letter from Kovno announcing that one of his friends has had a baby. But the baby was born with the mark of a star of David on its body.

How much truth there is in this is not important. What is typical is the case and the idea.

Perhaps there really is a spot there that looks like a star of David?

Stakhanovites Receive Food Bonuses in the Ghetto —Each Stakhanovite Receives a Kilo of . . . Sausage

It is typical of our life here. Extraordinarily, the ghetto received 200 kilos of sausage. The police took a third of it. The Judenrat distributed the rest in portions of one or two to three kilos for each department on condition that the heads of the departments distribute it only among the best workers as prizes. . . .

So much for Stakhanovism.[44]

"WE WERE SLAVES OF PHAROAH IN EGYPT" . . . MATZO FOR THE GHETTO

Nevertheless, the world is not lawless. Even this year, Jews won't be left without matzo in the Vilna Ghetto. A committee of Orthodox [Jews] has already thought about that. On the March food card, ghetto inhabitants receive a "portion of matzo," a quarter kilo for 10 rubles. Some inhabitants might get half a kilo more. In short, as we said, the world is not lawless. There will be matzo, and Jews will be able to say "We were slaves of Pharoah in Egypt . . . "

FURNITURE IN THE GHETTO

As we said, Murer ordered a furniture workshop set up. Most important was, first of all, an order for furniture for himself. He comes to the ghetto every morning to see if his order is progressing.

Recently, he sent in sausages—a gift for his furniture-slaves.

FANTASIES

Today a rumor circulated that the area around Vilna was bombed. There are even those who saw stars.[45]

It sounds like a fantasy, *A Thousand and One Nights* . . .

MARCH 15 [1942]

Yesterday's literary evening, the fifth in the series, was very good. The crowding was a bit disturbing. The evening was conducted by H.[46] The evening was titled "Jerusalem of Lithuania." The next evening is devoted to Lithuania. Pati [Kremer] and the librarian Khaykl Lunski, two of those remaining from the former Vilna, were elected to the committee this time.

44. Kruk mocks the Bolshevik methods of the Judenrat.

45. I.e., Soviet planes.

46. It is not clear whether Kruk means himself or Hersh Gutgestalt. Dworzecki (1948:239) says that the following lectures were given that evening: Dr. Milkanowicki, "Vilna, the Cradle of the Haskalah and Hibat-Zion"; H. Gutgestalt, "Vilna, the Cradle of the Jewish Labor Movement"; and Reuven Cohen, "Vilna, the City of the Vilna Gaon."

PONAR

We recently noted that 200 people were supposed to have been shot in Ponar. Now I find out more precisely that in fact, 54 Jews and 14 Christians (men and women) were shot.

In this regard, I learn that Łukiszki Prison ordered the ghetto police to take back packages for arrested people, left for them by their relatives. Why? It turns out that packages for seventy people were returned. Why? The arrested people aren't there. . . .

THE POET CHAIM GRADE IS ALIVE

Information from Vitebsk has recently arrived in Vilna, including the news that many Vilna people are there. They assure us that the Vilna poet Chaim Grade[47] is there.

UMRU IS ALSO ALIVE

As far as I know, the editor Dovid Umru is living and working in the Jaszuny district.[48]

PERETZ'S GLASSES A CHILD'S TOY

We have already talked about the situation at YIVO, the objects in the Peretz exhibition, Peretz's things, etc. Today, the janitor's child was found playing with glasses. Comrade [Uma] Olkienicka[49] recognized Y. L. Peretz's glasses. . . .

Thus, treasures are now found in the filth in Vilna.

Something similar happened involving a letter from the Vilna Gaon found in the gutter in Ghetto 2.

MARCH 17 [1942]

TWO CHILDREN'S HOLIDAYS

On Sunday the fifteenth, the Department of Child Care in the ghetto arranged two children's celebrations, which were the first children's performances in the ghetto.

I haven't felt like this for a long time. Hundreds of children. They sing, and

47. A major Yiddish poet and novelist and a member of the Young Vilna literary group in the 1930s. He fled to the Soviet Union and eventually settled in New York. He could not have been in Vitebsk while it was under German occupation.

48. A false rumor. Umru was shot by the Germans in 1941.

49. An artist. She was married to YIVO activist Moyshe Lerer. Before World War II, she was director of the theater-museum at YIVO named for Esther Rachel Kamińska. In the ghetto, she worked on the Rosenberg Task Force. She was killed during the liquidation of the Vilna Ghetto in September 1943. For her biography, see *Teachers' Memorial Book* 1954:443–444.

when children sing, everyone weeps. The stage is full of children. Over the width of the stage stretches a pipe of an iron stove, the only heating in the auditorium. The children press forward in a stream.

A mother sits and weeps. I know her. She is weeping because her child is outside with her Christian nurse.[50] Another, because her sister and brother have gone to Ponar. Thus they weep here. . . .

And who doesn't have something to weep about? . . .

On the stage there is skating. The children act out their fantasies. No skating in the ghetto, so they do theater-skating. . . . The children skate, scrape their feet to the beat of the music, and . . . They create an illusion for themselves. . . .

THE MURDERER OF THE LIDA PRIEST IS CAUGHT

The Vilna Ghetto experienced a strong emotion yesterday: the Vilna police caught the murderer of the Russian Orthodox priest of Lida. The horror of Lida was told on March 14. Now I learn:

On October 23, we told of Murer and his excitement about finding the guilty man who stabbed a Jewish policeman. The murderer then went to Lida. We reported that in our entry of October 31 of last year. Now it turns out that the same Yankl Avidon took part in that murder. He had recently escaped, and now they have caught him. Now the horrible 35-year-old murderer is in the ghetto prison.[51]

CHILD CARE IN THE GHETTO

We should add to the report on the activity of the [Department of]Child Care.

On September 6, we entered the ghetto, and by September 12, the Judenrat had received a memorandum about the establishment of a Department of Child Care. The Judenrat then set two conditions: no party involvement and no studies. At first, the schools worked in two groups daily. Nine hundred children attended school—32 percent of the children in the ghetto. After the events of Yom Kippur, daily attendance fell to 450. Only in November was there an attempt to introduce systematic studies. The "stability" that ensued helped in that.

Now, 800 children attend school daily. In Kailis, 120 children. Altogether, this comes to 80 percent of the children in the ghetto. Interesting that altogether 12 teachers have yellow permits!!!

Children are now occupied in the institutions for 30 hours a week. They study Yiddish for 6 hours, along with the history of culture, the history of inventions and discoveries, hygiene education classes (with 48 children regularly going to the bath), natural science and geography, arithmetic and geometry, painting, gymnastics, singing, and music.

50. I.e., on the Aryan side—passing as a non-Jewish child.

51. The entries of October 23 and 31, 1941, are missing. Regarding the case of the stabbing of a Jewish policeman and of Yankl Avidon, see the entries for June 4–5, 1942.

Now a plan of compulsory study is being worked out. There is a plan to establish a class for musically gifted children. Children receive free notebooks, clothes, etc.

Textbooks are lacking, but Jewish workers make all sorts of efforts to bring books from old Jewish apartments outside the ghetto, although this involves great danger.

The department helped build dormitories No. 1 and No. 2.

We shall once again be occupied with additional information about these children's institutions so that, over time, we can draw a picture of how the Jewish grammar school in the ghetto existed and worked.

MARCH 18 [1942]

A MESSAGE FROM KOVNO

Two Jews came from Kovno today. They say that there are two ghettos, called the Big and Small Ghettos. Between the two ghettos lives a Christian population. Communications between the two ghettos is made possible by an overhead bridge above the residences of the Christian population. Seventeen Gestapo men live in the ghetto. Altogether there are only 17, but they make enough trouble for hundreds.

Among other things, the two say that the Bundists who were once arrested [by the Soviets] for forging false documents to emigrate to Japan were released soon after the Germans entered. He could name two of them, Nekhame Dzwonek[52] and a director of the Warsaw Nutrition Association, Comrade [Betsalel] Bibering.[53] Bibering was taken by the Lithuanians; Dzwonek lives in the Kovno Ghetto.

MARCH 20 [1942]

LITHUANIA ACQUIRES INDEPENDENCE

The independence is so unclear that no one understands anything about it. The German authorities remain as they were. Somewhere there will be Lithuanian regional elders. What else?

52. This is an error and surely refers to Shakhne Dzwonek, a Bundist born in Włocławek (brother of Zalmen Lichtenstein of New York). He was a refugee in Vilna and later in Kovno and was arrested while attempting to leave Lithuania with the so-called Japanese Visas. Shakhne Dzwonek did indeed spend time in Kovno prison.

53. Born in 1906 in Stanisławów, Bibering later lived in Lwów. He was a member of the Lwów Committee of the Bund. In 1936 he moved to Warsaw and was appointed secretary of the Nutrition Association. He came to Vilna as a refugee in 1939. When Lithuania became Soviet, he moved to Ukmergė, then to Kovno, where he was arrested, along with Shakhne Dzwonek.

Privately, the Lithuanians are ashamed. For weeks they worked in Berlin, wrote declarations, and really crept on all fours. Now they obtain autonomy, for which Lithuania must have a mobilization.

The disappointment is horrible.

ROSENBERG TASK FORCE

From a conversation with the director of the Rosenberg Task Force, it is clear: apparently we won't get to the cataloguing of the books.

Does this mean we will be taken away? For the time being, it doesn't mean that. For a while there is suspicion.

Meanwhile, I brought in new people for the work, including the poet Sutzkever (he already has a position), the artist Olkienicka, and others.

A VISIT TO WEISKOPF

Finally I had the "good fortune" to meet the king of the Vilna Ghetto, Mr. Weiskopf, in person. Dozens of people from the ghetto pass through his home, he talks to everyone and tries to help them. I was thinking of Sholem Asch,[54] why he isn't with us and doesn't see the ascent of the real ghetto. This is how the ghetto is and this is how her archetypes are. Weiskopf sits in a deep armchair, at his right his secretary, at his left Kalman[owicz] and me. He is self-confident, talks at ease, and radiating from his simple face are a lot of energy and goodwill, but even more pride and love of flattery.

"I'm talking!" he interrupts a woman weeping in front of him.

"Who's talking to you?"—he doesn't let anyone speak.

"That's why my name is Weiskopf!"

"Go, it's already taken care of."

He does a lot and, most important, he wants everyone to know he does:

"I do, I will do, and no one will tire me. . . . "

He tells of big plans, contracts with Göring for five years, and often utterly imaginary things. Fantasies, fantasies, and more fantasies.

MARCH 21 [1942]

TRADE FLOURISHES IN THE GHETTO

Once again, we return to trade in the Vilna Ghetto.

In the beginning, people wandered around trading a . . . half kilo of butter, a quarter kilo of meat, a candle, a cigarette, some candy, etc. The seller could carry the whole "shop" in his hand. . . .

54. Asch (1880–1952) was a Yiddish writer whose novels, stories, and plays often depicted shtetl life.

Now, people carry on free and open [commerce] in cigarettes, tobacco, matches, etc. You can see a basket of onions, a sack of potatoes, here stands someone with a big bundle of wood—next to him is a quarter meter of wood for sale. In a doorway, people sell small parcels of wood of three or five kilos. . . .

Little shops are opened in the ghetto. In the shops are a few kilos of flour, potatoes, candy. The whole shop is on a little table. A few partners moved into a ruined store and spread out their merchandise: cigarettes, cigarette paper, candles, a few pieces of soap, cakes, bagels. Next to a quarter of a kilo of meat is a lemon, next to the lemon, a kilo of sugar, etc.

Peasants who come in to take out garbage bring merchandise into the ghetto, and there is a trade in the ghetto the likes of which have never been seen. By now, they're dealing in live poultry, fish, etc.

Outside the ghetto, they say that the Jews in the ghetto live better than the residents of the city. There's some truth to that. In this respect, the ghetto is much livelier and more active than are the inhabitants outside the ghetto.

SSSR — A JOKE

The Jews in the ghetto made up a joke:

What is the ghetto? It is SSSR.[55] The four main streets of the ghetto:

Szawelska, Szpitalna, Strashun, Rudnicka.

MARCH 22 [1942]

THE FIRST CHILDREN'S RECITAL IN THE GHETTO

We have written about the children's celebration held in the ghetto a week ago Sunday. The finale of that children's celebration was today's children's recital, organized by the Department of Child Care in the Judenrat of the Vilna Ghetto. Both existing children's institutions (no. 1 and no. 2) participated. The recital was held in the big auditorium of the former Vilna Real Gymnasium. The program is attached.

[*The program is missing.*]

Like all such assemblies in our ghetto, the recital was held in the shadow of the horrible ghetto events. The program was carried out perfectly. The context of the work, the entire milieu, made a grotesque impression. The children were happy, as lively as in the good old days, and all those looking at them couldn't control themselves.

"Oh, don't say the world is lawless!"—they recite Y. L. Peretz.

At eight in the evening, to close that children's celebration, there was tea for the teachers and the cultural activists in the soup kitchen at Rudnicka 17.

55. The Russian acronym for the USSR.

The evening passed in a warm atmosphere. Those who didn't have passes to return from the evening later than allowed were given the password "child." With that password, they received the right to walk in the street at the late hour.

SIXTH LITERARY RECITAL

Last night, the sixth literary meeting, devoted to Lithuania, took place. The vice-chief of the Jewish ghetto police, friend Glazman, spoke about Lithuania. This time the graphic artists adorned the evening with two beautiful montages.[56]

HOW A POLICE PERFORMANCE ENDED IN THE GHETTO

The individual police precincts often organize police amusements for themselves, with brandy, food, etc.

This time, the Second Police Precinct tried to introduce something new—an evening of amusement for the police, for representatives of the units and the Judenrat. A concert with tea was organized, and at the end, jazz was played on the instruments and the guests began to . . . dance.

This time, the members of the Judenrat and Mr. Glazman demonstratively left the frolicking company.

The demonstration didn't have much effect, and the crowd went on having a good time.

This is how it looks when people make a "party" in a graveyard.

THE GHETTO IS TO BE TRANSFERRED TO NOWOGRÓDZKA

Suddenly, without knowing how or by whom, a rumor spread like wildfire in the ghetto that the Vilna Ghetto is to be transferred from the center of the city to Nowogródzka.[57] In minutes, the whole city was talking about the strange news.

Whether the rumor has a foundation is hard to say.

SOUP KITCHENS IN THE GHETTO

We have the reports of the soup kitchens in the Vilna Ghetto. To understand their nature, we record some facts here:

In December [1941], four kitchens (Rudnicka 6 and 17, Strashun 2, and Szawelska 6) distributed 72,202 lunches for the entire month; 47,139 of them were paid for, and 25,063, or close to 35 percent, were free.

In January 1942, the same kitchens distributed 75,843 [?] lunches; 37,416 were paid for and 40,609 (54.5 percent) were free.

In February, 73,701 [?] lunches; 26,538 were paid for, 47,133, or 64.7 percent, were free.

Thus we can see how poverty increases in the ghetto from month to month.

56. According to Dworzecki (1948:239), Dr. Tsemakh Feldstein also spoke on that evening (see the entry for May 6, 1942).

57. A poor suburb of Vilna.

The number of free lunches [grows] from 35 percent to 54.5 percent and then to 64.7 percent.

If we add the children's kitchen (Strashun 12) and the police kitchen to the number of February lunches, in all six kitchens the total number of lunches distributed in the ghetto was 103,357.

■ ■ ■ ■ ■ ■

MARCH 23 [1942]

BY THE CALENDAR, SPRING; BY THE SOUL, AUTUMN

Only yesterday it was the middle of winter here. The temperature was close to minus 25 degrees Celsius. Today, on the third day of spring, it all ended, as with a magic wand. Water runs off the roofs, the snow sweats and melts. The sun is pleasant and warms, and the mood in the ghetto takes on an autumnal appearance—because of the spring.

All hope lay in a big and hard winter. The war would come to an end during the winter. Instead of 1812, it will be 1942. . . .

Spring is at the door, and for the time being, hopes have not been justified. People warm themselves in the nice spring sun, and in their soul, there is an autumnal cold.

Instead of hope, spring of 1942 in the Vilna Ghetto brings a loss of courage. Regardless of the harsh winter conditions of the ghetto, everyone would be willing to return to the great [gray?] winter days, horrible as they are and hard as they may oppress—if only hope would be greater and the horizon broader.

Meanwhile, March 23 has to do with the ending of the permits. Today we know that the permits were extended for another month. Not until April will there be a new hunt, a second series of permits. . . . Your hair stands on end when you even think about it—for everyone and especially for those who are among the "most fortunate" (as the yellow permits are called). The blood runs cold in the veins of the "registered" in the "family permits," "protective permits," etc.

In the ghetto, people calm each other: everything will be okay, but after the sad experiences no force can calm us.

The sun warms, by the calendar it is already spring; but by the soul, it is deep autumn. . . .

DR. [YISROEL] BIBER IS ALIVE

The splendid spring sun today brought good news. We have learned that one more of the 76,000 Vilna Jews was found. This is Dr. [Yisroel] Biber,[58] the brilliant writer, teacher, and scientist.

58. A biologist, teacher, and prominent school activist. He wrote textbooks and other books on biology in Yiddish. For some time, he worked in the Medem Sanitarium. The information

Perhaps another one is saved, and this time one of the best.
As on this first day of spring, may the rest not be worse.

ONLY FROM 6 TO 9 IN THE MORNING
AND FROM 3 TO 6 IN THE AFTERNOON

To go out of the ghetto, you must have a special "pass permit." As of today, that is no longer valid either. You can leave the ghetto only from 6 to 9 A.M., and from 3 to 6 P.M. Those who have to walk around in the afternoon receive a special pass supplement from the Jewish police command.

As you see: a brand-new "permit"!

MARCH 23, 11:30 AT NIGHT

AN AIR RAID ON VILNA

After our current pessimistic tones, a spark of hope. Is this really hope? Maybe harder and bitterer times are coming for us? . . .

At about 9:30 this evening, we suddenly jumped up. The windowpanes began to shake, glass started breaking, and the corridors, staircases, and courtyards were soon full.

Bombs! At first it started pouring as from a porous sack. The city shook and shattered. Rockets appeared in the sky, then came another bombardment and another rocket. This lasted an hour. The ghetto residents took it calmly, and a woman doctor quietly exclaimed:

"Blessed be the hands!" . . .

But some wrung their hands. Others started groaning and some even took a practical approach. For example, that tomorrow you shouldn't go into the street. After such an event, the Fascists would be outraged and might start looking for holes in the whole thing. Others assume that the Lithuanians will be as soft as butter tomorrow.

They tell an anecdote: the Lithuanian soldier on gate duty in the ghetto left his post and ran to the nearest police station. They say that many Jewish police—thinking that this wasn't a joke—pulled the police band off their sleeves. . . .

The street is full of glass, as in the "good old days."

Nine months ago, I heard the first bomb—war between Germany and the Soviet Union. Today, nine months later, once again we endure—the Soviets have woken us from a lethargic sleep and reminded us that they are alive and fighting, a tangible proof. . . .

---

about Dr. Biber that Kruk reports here turned out to be incorrect. He was taken by the Snatchers even before the ghetto was established and was killed in Ponar. For his biography, see *Teachers' Memorial Book* 1954:41–47.

The ghetto revived. It is 11:30 at night, and no one here is asleep. Everyone lies in his clothes, ready for anything.

"Ready for anything"—in the ghetto this means reminding yourself of a "memento mori."

And perhaps, perhaps, on the third day of "spring," the new, real spring has also come for us!

Perhaps? . . .

MARCH 24 [1942]

Today, unlike yesterday, isn't like spring anymore. The sun isn't shining, the snow doesn't move, and it seems as if we are between winter and spring. It is no longer winter, but it is not yet spring.

Except that the mood among the ghetto residents is more springlike today than yesterday and the day before.

Last night's events have put the whole city on its feet. For the past nine months there hadn't been as much movement in the city, outside the ghetto, as there is today. As if to spite the world, masses went out into the street to see with their own eyes what they didn't believe with their own ears last night.

They say that last night, as soon as one Jewish policeman on guard was convinced that the explosions were from a Bolshevik attack, he shouted into the middle of the street the blessing:

"Blessed be He who has kept us alive and sustained us to reach this present time. . . ."

Jews who met each other in the street today generally had smiling faces. Various news began to come from the street. It turns out that Kovno, Mołodeczno, Wilejka, and other places were also bombed last night.

In Vilna, everybody waits curiously for the newspapers. But in the papers there isn't a word about it. People started coming back from the street and it all became clear.

At the railroad, a bomb fell on the third platform. A few train cars were damaged. There were 10 dead.

At Zawalna 51 and 53, not far from the Halles marketplace, opposite the railroad tracks, a bomb fell and killed two Lithuanians.

Traffic on Niemiecka Street next to Jatkowa stopped—a bomb fell on Niemiecka 17 and another one on the only Lithuanian church on Dominikańska Street, which is attached to the ghetto walls. A Lithuanian priest was killed there, and Bishop Rainis was badly wounded. The result of the bomb on Niemiecka is not yet known.

The Ignatov Barracks suffered a great deal. They say that this morning, four trucks carrying dead Lithuanian soldiers were taken out of there.

Poles were cheerful: the Lithuanians suffered 90 percent; the rest of the population, only 10 percent. In truth, it does seem that the bombs were specially hunting Lithuanians. The Lithuanians are depressed. They maintain that this was a toast to their independence. . . .

In the outskirts of Vilna, the Bolsheviks dropped leaflets, calling on the population to hold out. At Porubanek, they found masses of leaflets calling upon the German soldiers not to believe Hitler and to throw down their weapons.

Fort mit Hitler!
Nieder mit dem Krieg!
Gibt Euch gefangen. Die Parole ist:
"Leb wohl Moskau. Nieder mit Hitler!"
Russisch: "Proschaj Moskwa. Daloj Gitlera."[59]

The leaflet is nicely printed with illustrations and a series title:

"Was geht in Deutschland vor?" [What's going on in Germany?]

The publication is number 77, of February 1942.

Workers returning from the city heard rumors that the ghetto was spared because the Jews threw rockets and showed where to aim the bombs. Therefore, a lot of bombs scored a direct hit.

The ghetto lives in fear of provoking the authorities. The Jewish police ordered people to stay out of the street after seven in the evening. Windows must be rigorously blacked out.[60] At a meeting of house administrators, following an order from the city, all houses were ordered to build shelters and keep sand in the attic.

Now I learn that one bomb fell in the courtyard of City Hall. The fire department building was badly damaged. There are victims. Opposite Trocka and Niemiecka, the Hotel Europejski was badly damaged—there were deaths there, too.

The first "concert" looks like a success. In the city, people are amazed at how nicely this piece of work was done.

The ghetto is right in the middle of events,[61] but yet it is completely outside and undamaged. The only damage here is to the windowpanes. Most of the windowpanes in the two children's schools on Szawelska and Strashun are out. The

59. The German reads: "Away with Hitler! / Down with the war! / Give yourself up. The password is: / 'Long live Moscow! Down with Hitler!'" However, the Russian in the last line is faulty: it reads "Goodbye Moscow" instead of "Long live Moscow"—one wouldn't have gotten through the front lines with such a password. Hitler is called "Gitler" in accordance with Russian usage. (There is no "h" in the Russian alphabet.)

60. The YIVO Archive (Kaczerginski-Sutzkever Collection, no. 16) contains Order Number 26, of March 24, 1942, issued by the ghetto chief, which says that as of that date the curfew hour is 19:00 and includes several instructions for how to behave in an air raid and how to execute the blackout of the ghetto.

61. The ghetto was located in the ancient center of the city.

Judenrat has already tried to obtain glass—unfortunately this won't happen so fast. But there is a promise of plywood. Meanwhile, they issued an advance: nails for the plywood.

AID SOCIETY FOR LAST MONTH

A report of the Aid Society for last month shows that more than 100,000 rubles were distributed during that time. Aside from food, the sum was distributed to about a thousand persons. Now there are another 1,000 requests for assistance. The more than 100,000 rubles were collected: 36,000 thousand from the Judenrat employees, a similar sum from the German labor units, the rest from "charity" from police circles and the organized police concerts.

ARCHIVE AT THE JUDENRAT

Following H. Kruk's initiative, an archive of ghetto activity was established in the Judenrat. The archive is at Strashun 6, directed by H. Kruk.

The archive will also contain valuable old documents, manuscripts, et al.

MARCH 25 [1942]

NOT A WORD ABOUT THE BOMBARDMENT

Yesterday the press didn't report a word about the bombardment. Everyone believed that this would be technically impossible today. Everyone was sure: if not that day, it would surely be in the next day's papers, if not the whole truth, then an approximate one. Today, the press printed a big item about blackouts, about preparing "shelters" and sand in attics. Again, not a word about the events.

Today's Vilna radio did take courage and announced that the city was attacked by three squadrons and . . . they were all shot down. In fact, it must be noted here that no anti-aircraft fire was heard in Vilna. So the squadrons were shot down without anti-aircraft artillery.

And why is there no word about the damage? . . .

Today information comes again about dreadful losses caused by the bombardment. For example, on Kwaszelna Street two people were killed by shrapnel. Something similar happened on Bosaczkowa, where two Lithuanian policemen were killed. Some of the houses mentioned yesterday were completely ruined.

The city, especially the outskirts, was strewn with leaflets. Aside from yesterday's leaflet, we saw another one today from the same organization, titled "Weist du wofür du kämpfst?" [Do you know what you're fighting for?]

The leaflet calls on the soldiers to strengthen the Red Army and throw down their weapons because: "Diejenigen von Euch, die in den Reihen der Okkupanten bleiben, werden vernichtet werden" [Those of you who remain in the ranks of the occupiers will be destroyed], etc.

Lithuanians flee the city en masse for the villages. Their motive is: "Who knows what will happen to us here in the city?"

Jews are frightened again—people are afraid of provoking the authorities. The Jewish police are on guard, and the ghetto inhabitants avoid everything that can bring down a provocation.

MRS. KHASYE TURBOWICZ DIED

The former director of the only Yiddish secular academic gymnasium in Vilna has completely broken down in the ghetto. He is old, bent double, he turns his head toward you as if he doesn't hear what you're saying.

We have told how long he was hiding without a permit and how none of the Judenrat wanted to have anything to do with him. Now, when the ghetto has calmed down a bit and the teacher Turbowicz has obtained some work in the children's institutions and started reviving, he has suddenly been struck with a misfortune:

This morning his wife, Khasye, died in the Jewish hospital, and the funeral was at 3 this afternoon.

Her death depressed the ghetto teachers.

MARCH 27 [1942]

"CONCERTS"

This time it is not a bomb-concert but a real concert in the ghetto. We have already said that, aside from the police symphony concerts, a new cheap kind of review concert has taken place. The Second Police Precinct has recently started producing such concerts.

Such a custom was established here. Police beat, police rob, and police . . . entertain.

The review concert was supposed to be performed just once—to entertain the families of the police. Today we know that that concert was repeated a second time, and persistent efforts have been made to produce a regular review.

The program: besides a series of good and well-performed numbers, there is an ugly imitation of Krukowski[62] with cheap cabaret jokes and ugly dances by a disgusting maid. The pieces about current events, some quite excellent, revolve around the higher police staff, flattering them, making them out to be like other people . . . [who] put on shows for themselves.

In short, the bleeding Vilna Ghetto . . . plays theater.

62. Leopold Krukowski, a popular Warsaw review actor (of Jewish origin), known under his nickname, Lopek. He performed in the Warsaw vaudeville theater Quid Pro Quo.

SECOND ALARM

On the night of the 25th–26th, another loud alarm occurred. People got out of bed, went down to the cellars, and spent one and a half hours there. It didn't amount to a bombardment. Nevertheless, people slept in their clothes, often even stood guard.

I was the only one who slept through the night without interruption and learned of the alarm only the next morning.

More news about the bombardment: I also learn that eleven houses were destroyed in the suburb of Lipówka, near the radio station. So they were aiming at the radio stations, too.

A JOKE ABOUT THE BOMBARDMENT

We have told the joke of why the ghetto is called SSSR. Today, after the bombardment by the Reds, people say:

"Why didn't the Bolsheviks bomb the ghetto?"

"Because they don't bomb their own territory."

"Why is the ghetto their own territory?"

"What do you mean why? That's the SSSR—Szawelska, Strashun, Szpitalna, and Rudnicka. . . ."

CATHOLIC AND ORTHODOX PRIESTS

Yesterday they began again on the clergy. All day, groups of [Catholic] nuns, priests, and Russian Orthodox priests were led through the city. The monasteries, they say, are sealed. Even Ostra Brama is closed. The Poles say that the last priests were taken away.

MURER AS A GUEST IN THE GHETTO. JEWS ARE BEATEN AND WHIPPED

Yesterday Murer paid another visit to the ghetto. Again he visited the workshops, and again he noted that the Jewish police are not following his orders and are letting Jews bring in food. He ordered food taken and the Jews beaten. The commander of the gate guard, the infamous troublemaker Levas, proved to Murer what he could do. Murer praised him for being the only one who understood the issue. He went so far as to whip a Jew on his naked body in that police precinct. Levas went so far overboard that he became nauseated and left half fainting.

The result: food was taken from hundreds of Jews. . . .

ELECTRICITY AGAIN AN ISSUE

For many, electricity in the ghetto became the only means of heating and cooking. The electric works ordered them to save electricity or the meters would be closed altogether. Those who didn't follow the order soon had their electricity cut off. They wanted to complain about it but . . .

But it turns out that the electric works had to collect [for the] electricity used by the inhabitants of the former Ghetto 2. Because, unfortunately, none of those who used electricity are there, the electric company started demanding it from the Judenrat in Ghetto 1. The Judenrat put up an argument. But the electric company wasn't stopped by anything and denounced the Judenrat of Ghetto 1, demanding that they pay for about 300 inhabitants of the other ghetto.

The irony is that every one of those who used the electricity has long been in the other world, and the Judenrat of Ghetto 1 is ordered by the city administration to pay their debt . . . though that was an entirely different Judenrat.

ABOUT KOVNO

From the mail just arrived from Kovno, I learn that a kilo of bread there costs 75 rubles (here it is barely 35).

I learn that 500 Jews were taken out, as we wrote on February 6, 1942.[63] The Germans demanded that the Judenrat there give them 500 Jews from the underworld. The Judenrat answered with dignity that there weren't any such people in the ghetto. On the above-mentioned day, all Jews were ordered to appear on the locally famous square. Six thousand Jews were gathered there, and 500 Jews were selected and transported. People say they were sent to Riga. Moreover, they [the authorities] accept correspondence only for Riga.

What is happening to them in Riga? For now, we must be silent about that.

A TRIAL OF THE LOUSE . . .

This is purification week in the ghetto. In connection with that, a lecture by Dr. Epstein titled "A Trial of the Louse" was announced.

WHEN LITHUANIA IS ENLARGED

The Lithuanian "autonomous government" receives a larger territory. The Brasław and Oszmiana districts have been appended to it.[64] But although everything is fine, a terrible tragedy has befallen the Jewish population there. Jews flee their homes en masse. Delegations come to Vilna for advice. They come on foot and in cars. Today about 50 or 60 Jews from those areas came to the ghetto.

As Lithuania is enlarged, Jews run. . . .

63. No mention of this incident has been found in the entry for February 6, but it is mentioned in the entry for February 11.

64. The addition of those areas to the Vilna district was designed to please the Lithuanians—their "Republic" was enlarged. The districts belonged to Poland during the interwar period and to Byelorussia under the Soviets (and to this day). In those areas there were many Jewish small towns. In the Brasław district were Druja, Miory, Nowy Pohost, and Widze. In the Oszmiana district were Smorgonie, Dziewieniszki, Holszany, and Krewo.

THE SECRET OF MY UNIT

What can be more innocent than the cultural activity of my unit? But it turns out that it is concerned not only with holy books and museum items but also with living, profane things. Not everything there is spiritual. . . .

They kept a large group of Russian actors in Vilna; they fed them, paid their hotel, had a good time with them, and . . . caroused. One of them, who was drunk in the kitchen, intimated to the forced laborers:

"You think we don't know what they want from us?" . . .

Another time, two wooden valises, like Russian military valises, were ordered from a cabinetmaker. The valises were taken to the hotel where the Russian actors were staying. Since then, two of them are missing, have been harnessed [?] to the boxes and sent away somewhere. . . .

This is the secret of my unit. . . .

We are occupied not only with holy things but also with profane things![65]

AGAIN THE TRAGEDY OF LIDA

We will add to what we have written: the sad events in Lida took place on Sunday, March 14.[66] Sixty persons who did not appear in the square were killed. Of those [in the square] who were pointed out as being from Vilna, another 80 persons fell, including 6 members of the Judenrat, among them both Cederowicz brothers; Lichtman, who was considered a bright figure in Vilna; Cukiernik, commander of the Jewish police; Kotok; and Keisler. Kotok, Lichtman, and Keisler are in a separate grave in the cemetery. Those who were shot there include attorney Cederowicz, a brother of the Warsaw Cederowicz, who was once chairman of the Warsaw ZTK.[67] All of them were shot in the prison courtyard and later were turned over to be buried in the Jewish cemetery, as were those shot in their homes.

The execution of the 60 "Vilna" Jews took place in the prison courtyard: on Saturday night, the men were shot; on Sunday night, the women. Three escaped. They were shot with dumdum bullets so that some were literally ripped up, and hence 9 couldn't be identified.

A Christian who lives near the prison tears his hair out: the wild sounds of the two night executions are still ringing in his ears.

Two of the seven thieves the Judenrat had turned over were also shot, and five of them were released.

65. The editor of the Yiddish edition assumed that Kruk hints here at the orgies. By "we," Kruk almost certainly means the Germans in the unit, not the Jewish forced laborers, i.e., the scholars.

66. See the entry for March 14, 1942. In the YIVO Archive (Kaczerginski-Sutzkever Collection), there is an eyewitness account by Zkharye Jutan, partly reprinted in Kaczerginski 1947: 242–249.

67. Initials of the Żydowskie Towarzystwo Krajoznawcze, the Jewish Geographical Society.

The reporter, a man from Lida who just came, says he won't go back to Lida again. Until now, he had lived outside the ghetto as a Christian. Now he prefers to remain in the Vilna Ghetto because in Lida, there is a special Aktion of ostensible Christians.[68] One squeals on the other. He also says that the severely wounded Orthodox priest often tried to make them stop shooting Jews. . . .

TWO AND A HALF THOUSAND JEWS ARE SHOT IN BARANOVITSH

It sounds like a wild invention. For the inhabitants of the Vilna Ghetto, it is a simple and "understandable" matter.

Twenty-five hundred Baranovitsh Jews were shot.

This was at the beginning of March, as the chauffeur who was there, our friend Nikra,[69] says, more precisely, two and half weeks ago. All of a sudden, everybody was ordered [to come] to the marketplace. They checked the passes. Specialists were placed on one side and the others on the other side. There was a commotion, and one group began running over to the other. The Germans were terribly excited at the "chutzpah" and issued another order:

Three left, one right, and thus on one side there remained one group of Jews, and on the other—two and a half thousand. The execution took place on the spot. Right in front of everyone.

MARCH 28 [1942]

MORE ABOUT THE BOMBARDMENT

A few days have passed since Wednesday's bombardment, and there is not a word in the local press. New items come every day.

Today, for example: "What is the Meaning of the Signals of an Air Assault?" As if nothing has happened, as if they don't mean anything.

In the chronicle, there is an item about the funeral [of] the Lithuanian priest Kibaras, another victim of the recent bombardment. Again, a dryly worded piece, as if nothing had happened.

This evening, the seventh literary and artistic meeting took place. The subject was the Jewish renaissance. After a lecture by Comrade Kalman[owicz], an alarm suddenly went off. Everyone in the audience went home.

Apropos the Wednesday bombing, Niemiecka Street, from Trocka to Wielka, looks like a ruin. The houses on the corner of Żydowska and Niemiecka 8, 11, 13, and further down are completely destroyed. The courtyards are literally a large

68. Jews who lived outside the ghetto with Aryan papers.

69. He probably means Arkin. Often, for the sake of conspiracy, Kruk reversed people's names. In his work on Baranovitsh (Kaczerginski-Sutzkever Collection, no. 617), almost all the names are written like that: *Kavon* for *Novak, Ikswomarba* for *Abramowski,* etc.

mountain of debris. More than one Jew of those remaining can thank God for saving his life. If they had been living there, hundreds would have fallen victim.[70]

For everything, you must have luck. . . .

GHETTO JOKES

The pessimist: "If it lasts so long, we will all have to go begging."

The optimist: "From whom?"

This is the perspective of the future in the ghetto.

I BRING ARMCHAIRS

After all my struggles for the slogan that you don't make theater in a graveyard, I received thanks today from the very one—he should live and be well—the "chief." He thanked me for using my possibilities and bringing 100 armchairs from the destroyed former YIVO into the ghetto auditorium.

MARCH 30 [1942]

THE DISGRACE OF THE VILNA GHETTO

On Wednesday, the 24th of this month, Jews were whipped in the ghetto. We told about it on the 27th. Today, some more precise information. How wretched is the Jewish police . . . wretched, how rotten to the core is our ghetto kingdom; nevertheless none of us could have imagined how dreadfully low life is all around. Two facts:

Fact 1. The Vilna Haman—Murer—came into the ghetto. In a conversation with Obmann Fried, Fried appealed to Murer for exceptional permission to walk on the sidewalk without a patch. Murer refused, half joking, half serious.

People say that a few days ago, Fried made a similar proposal to the Lithuanian representative for Jewish affairs, Mr. Burakas.

For Fried, everything is fine; his only care is to be allowed to walk on the sidewalk and be free . . . from the ghetto patch.

Fact 2. People say that the chairman's proposal infuriated Murer so much that he took out all his anger at the gate.

At the gate, he arrested a Jew for bringing in more food than is allowed. Murer ordered the Jewish police to whip him. Levas, the commander of the gate guard, intervened for his police and carried out the task himself. The whipping took place in a shop in front of the ghetto gate (the "glazier's shop").

Two Spanish anti-Bolshevik legionnaires and a German officer happened to be present. After the whipping, Levas fainted and had a nervous breakdown.

It so happened that on the same day, the commander of the police station in

70. Before the ghetto existed, these were Jewish streets, but they were not included in the ghetto.

the ghetto, the haughty major (he was apparently a major in the Polish army), Mr. Frucht, ordered . . . a Jew whipped.

What for?

A certain tailor, Gordon, works in Weiskopf's "tailor shop." This Gordon had a run-in with Weiskopf because of Weiskopf's arrogance. Weiskopf, the so-called king of the ghetto, denounced him to Frucht. Frucht is supported by Weiskopf, and naturally, Major Frucht did what had to be done: he summoned the rebellious tailor to the station and, for "10,000 sins," ordered him to be given 25 lashes. The policeman Gordon was to carry out the order, but he refused. It was done by another policeman, Wasserman. When a third policeman, Lubocki, scolded Wasserman for doing that, especially when Gordon had refused to carry out the order, a fourth policeman, the Revisionist activist [Ayzik] Averbukh, took the case to Major Frucht. Frucht had both of them arrested, policeman Gordon and the "agitator" Lubocki.

The police command is apparently investigating the case. Frucht may be rebuked. Meanwhile, the tailor from the "tailor shop" received 25 lashes, and the policemen Gordon and Lubocki were called in for "breach of discipline."

It is interesting to mention that the sick sadistic commander Muszkat, who recently returned to the police force, was also present at the whipping.

No one from the Vilna Ghetto will be able to wash off that disgrace. Neither Obmann Fried's regret nor the reproof of the Legionnaire[71] scoundrel, Major Frucht, will help.

Fact 2:

THEY TAKE BOOKS

From a letter that just came from Kovno, I learn that the German authorities took all the books out of the ghetto there.

Now the Jewish police in Vilna plan on their own to carry out a selection of kosher and non-kosher literature. The chief of police has appealed to H. K[ruk] to organize that censorship. H. K. categorically refused.

POETRY IN THE GHETTO

Because of my important function in the literary association [the Association of Writers and Artists], people come to me with various literary creations. Among them are often splendid lines, talented paragraphs. Most, as usual, are [nothing more than] "graphomania." I present an excerpt of a better poem today:

PONAR

A straight highway, lined with stone,
Wide fields with trees, like a riddle.

71. An allusion to Piłsudski's Polish "Legions," hinting at Frucht's service in the Polish army.

The Wilija winds, with grass overgrown,
A tavern with a big chimney—in the middle.
What is it?—Ponar!

In the winter, a mountain covered with snow,
You slide, see no danger, near or far.
Always full of happy shouts, aglow,
It echoes all around with glee—Ponar!

Ponar!—Lovely place, where youth and joy did reign,
Your good name is gone and will not return again.
Now, murderous and cold for eternity will you sound,
With trembling will they walk through your forest ground. . . .

The excerpt from that poem was written by Rikle Glezer, dated February 17, 1943.[72]

In another place, the same poet writes a poem she calls "Ghetto":

My mama does washing and poverty rules the house
I forget all that when I dream of freedom. . . .
Though I look at a pole, I think . . . it's a tree.[73]

RETURN FROM PONAR (A TALE THAT FREEZES THE BLOOD IN YOUR VEINS)

All of this is reported precisely by the Vilna teacher Tsak.[74]

Grieving, she tells:

Late Saturday night we went to the ghetto and, barely alive, were dragged to the courtyard of Strashun Street 14. The yard was packed with people. It was

72. The date should be 1942, not 1943. Rikle Glezer was born in Vilna, the daughter of a jeweler. She studied in the Yiddish Sh. Frug School of the Central Educational Committee (TSBK), and then in a Polish school. She started writing poems at the age of 12, was active in school circles, and belonged to SKIF (the Socialist Children's Association—a Bundist children's organization). In the ghetto, she wrote a great deal. The Snatchers took her father at the very beginning of the German occupation. Her mother and a little sister lived until the liquidation of the ghetto in September 1943, and all three were taken out together. But Rikle jumped out of the car when it was 15 kilometers from Vilna, and she reached Rudnicki Forest, where she joined a partisan unit. She returned to Vilna with the partisans and army units that liberated the city from the Germans. After the war she lived in Israel with her husband, also a former partisan. Her poems were published in several collections (Kaczerginski 1948) and were also translated into Polish and Spanish.

73. The published poem is called "It Is Gray and Dark in the Ghetto" (Kaczerginski 1948: 10–11).

74. Once again, Kruk turns the letters around. He means the famous Vilna teacher Teme Katz, who worked in the school for retarded children. During the liquidation of the ghetto, she was taken to Estonia. For her biography, see *Teachers' Memorial Book* 1954:370–371.

raining, and everyone looked for some cover for himself, his children, his family. My husband, our son, our two daughters, and I went into a cellar, huddled together, and dozed off. When I heard noise up above, we went out and saw everyone packing their things, ready to go on the road.

The Lithuanians are chasing us!

We, too, took our bundles and went on the road. Now we saw that they were driving us back to the city. We came out of Niemiecka Street, and only then did we understand that they were taking us toward Łukiszki. Through the whole street, groups of Jews surrounded by soldiers were plodding along. In the streets were traces of a horrible destruction. Torn bundles and strewn-about suitcases blocked the streets. In the middle of the street were bedding, linens, shoes, remainders of belongings thrown away or stolen by others, all scattered around. We couldn't understand the solitary figures hiding in the gates, sitting on their bundles or without anything, peering at us with frightened eyes, not knowing whether to envy us or themselves. Nevertheless, they began to understand something. At any rate, they decided to hide and stay away.

The light was still dim, and yet we already met groups of Jews being driven toward us, apparently into the ghetto.

In Łukiszki they separated us. My husband and son were on the men's side, I and my two daughters (Feyge, 17, and Mine, 10) remained with the women. The courtyard was already overflowing with thousands of Jews brought from Lidzki, Makowa, and other streets.[75]

"What can we expect?" We were sure that sooner or later, they would send us back to the ghetto. No one dared think otherwise. . . .

For two nights, we lived outside. On the third day, barely alive, we were closed in a cell. Only there did we find out that the groups taken out of there were led to Ponar. But we never dared to think that so many people were being taken to be shot.

We sat there until Thursday, at 2 o'clock in the morning.

The prison yard was suddenly flooded with searchlights. We were driven and loaded onto freight trucks. On every truck were a few Lithuanians armed with rifles and 50–60 Jews. Thus we were shaking, driven hastily to Ponar.

At 6 o'clock on Friday morning, we came to a hilly forest area, and we lay among the sand dunes, tired and scared, as on an outing. . . .

Even then, none of us could imagine the gravity of our situation. Not far from us burst salvos of rifle shots. Germans gave orders and Lithuanians carried them out. The Lithuanians began to arrange us in groups of 10. They led the groups between the hills where the shots were coming from. And then they came back to take new groups. . . .

75. Lidzki was cleaned of its Jews before the ghetto was established there; Makowa was outside the ghetto.

All at once, as if an electrical current were running through us, the situation became crystal clear to all of us. The women began pleading with the Lithuanians, trying to bribe them with wristwatches, clothing. Others fell on the ground and kissed the Lithuanian soldiers' boots. Some began tearing their hair, ripping their clothes. Nothing helped. The Lithuanians took everything but cursed and mocked and beat them to the place of the slaughter. At 12 noon, when everyone was convinced that our fate was sealed and no one would get out alive, there was a turning point. When people's turn came, they stood up, quiet and resigned, no protests, no pleas. Thus family after family walked their last steps.

Mrs. Ts.'s young, haggard face burst into weeping:

My oldest daughter hugged me by the waist. The younger one, weeping, was lying, leaning on my knees.

People who didn't want to wait went voluntarily to join a group of 10. But I decided to wait—I had time. Maybe a miracle. . . . Maybe. But I didn't know what "maybe" I was waiting for.

The place around us cleared a bit. Some women, in despair, rolled face down in the sand. Others sat quietly as if nothing had happened. Sitting petrified between my daughters, I schemed once again to be among the last.

At about 5:30 in the afternoon, our turn came. I set out with my daughters. On the way, between the hills, we met other groups, which, like us, were waiting for their fate. They stood us in a front line, and I felt my older daughter's hand slip out of mine. . . .

When I came to, I felt packed in, with people walking over me; I was wet and covered with some acid. . . .

I grasped that I was lying in a mass grave among corpses, that I was soaked with human blood—and that I was alive and wounded. Although it was late, a young man was running around sprinkling lime, digging and searching in the pit. I lay still, holding my breath, listening to every rustle and quiver. Sighs were still heard in the grave, quiet moans, and at times, a death rattle.

I felt a pain in my calf and understood I was wounded and had fallen into the mass grave among corpses. . . . I didn't see my two children anymore, and I didn't even look for them. Late at night, I felt someone dragging himself around among the corpses. It turned out that a woman, looking for a way out of the mass grave, had investigated the whole area and had found no one there. We both dragged ourselves to some barbed-wire fence and from there to the gate. No one was there either. The gate was tied with a piece of wire, which could easily be opened. Through the field to the road and through the road to the nearby forest. There we made bandages from our shirts to bind our wounds and decided not to move until dawn. At daybreak, we somehow cleaned off the blood and lime and cautiously went toward the nearby village of Nowosolsk, six kilometers from the forest. There, in a peasant's house, we washed, cleaned up, ate, etc., and under the direction of a local peasant, went on to Sorok-Tatary. We stayed in that village from Saturday until Monday, and on Monday morning we left for Biała Waka, where the two of us spent a week. From there I later came back to Vilna alone and back to the ghetto.

Mrs. Ts. wept for her two daughters, even though she was a stepmother. When asked who else she met there, she mentioned the names of the two sisters, the teachers [Ester and Rokhl] Notik,[76] the teacher Etl Eisenstadt of Kovno,[77] the teacher [Noyekh] Łozowski[78] and his wife (both taught in the Vilna Real Gymnasium), and others.

(Vilna Ghetto, told on October 15, 1941)

WHAT BECAME OF TEACHER TS.?

For months, the tortured teacher Ts. searched and rummaged through the ghetto and could not get a permit. But she didn't want to go back to Ponar, and she fought with all her might. She dragged herself around in melinas, did any dirty work, and now, in March 1942, she lives on a protective permit and works in the ghetto laundry as a laundress. People say that two weeks ago, she fainted twice in one day, unable to bear her hard work.

This is the tragic finale of teacher Ts.

This story came to me after a delay of a few months, although I have known about it for a long time. Why this happened is hard now to write.

We may still be able to write about that more precisely.

MARCH 31 [1942]

PERMITS

Today the validity of the permits was to end. Meanwhile

[*Pages 348–353 of the diary are missing, from April 1 to about the middle of April. During that time, no special events in the ghetto are recorded in any other publication. The* YIVO *Archive (Kaczerginski-Sutzkever Collection, no. 20) contains Announcement 42 of the ghetto police, stating that as of April 15, the curfew time is extended to 8:45 in the evening.*

Kruk's table of contents lists many entries for this period.]

76. Born in Vilna. Both were killed in Ponar. For their biography, see *Teachers' Memorial Book* 1954:262–264.

77. A well-known Yiddish teacher from Kovno, who came to Vilna in 1939, when the city was transferred to Lithuania. She was principal of a Vilna Yiddish high school.

78. One of the builders of the extensive Yiddish school system in Vilna.

About 19,000 in the Ghetto

April 5, 1942
Pesach in the Ghetto
The 27th Anniversary of Y. L. Peretz's Death
Slogan "Seder"
Lit. Artist Meeting

April 7 [1942]
Recitals
Weiskopf
Doctors on Pesach

April 9 [1942]
History of the Ghetto
A Trial of the Louse
Forged Bread Cards
A Hand Grenade on Kalwaryjska Street
Two Lithuanians Dead
More about the Bombardment of Vilna
They Shoot and Break Windows

April 11 [1942]
The Ninth Lit. Artist. Meeting
Hunger in the Ghetto
100,000 in Warsaw

April 12 [1942]
Saviors or Gravediggers

April 15 [1942]
How a Sadistic German Whips Women

[*Page 354 begins in the middle of an entry about an execution of girls who had been whipped. An eyewitness account by Bebe Epstein (YIVO Archive, Eyewitness Accounts of the Holocaust Period Collection, 1939–1945 [RG 104]) tells of a case of the whipping of the girls in the Gestapo, where Epstein worked. This might be the same case mentioned in the entry.*]

[. . .] getting advice from me about what to do.

The mother tells: after the execution of the girls in the cellar, he led a group of older women there . . . and ordered an older Jew to whip them, just as he had done with the young ones. After whipping them, the German whipped the whipper so he should know "once again how to whip." . . .

APRIL 15 [1942]

AUCTIONS OF JEWISH PROPERTY

The local Polish newspaper of April 14, 1942, reports that on the 15th of this month, i.e., today, there will be an auction of 14 lots that once belonged to Jews. That inheritance of Jewish property will be done in the building of the Housing Office, Zygmuntowska 16, second floor.

Thus they are already dividing Jewish real estate.

WITH A KNIFE IN THE LUNGS

On the 13th of this month, on Szpitalna Street, a woman stabbed her fictive husband in the lungs with a knife. The reason for the murder is jealousy.

How a woman could be jealous of her fictive husband would be hard to tell on these pages. But it is an interesting example of the circumstances and customs of ghetto life.

Thus we see that a plain fictive husband became, it seems, a real husband, and the case became one of "getting even."

The woman is in the ghetto prison.

A SECOND BATH IN THE GHETTO

Yesterday the formal opening of the second bath in the ghetto took place. The first bath has room for 20 people, the second for 26 people. After that formal opening, Murer himself came for a visit.

WHY WITHOUT A PATCH? OR A FEW WORDS ABOUT THE FISHMAN-GENS INCIDENT

A typical incident between the police chief and a member of the Judenrat, Mr. Fishman.

As we know, the chief is formally subordinate to the Judenrat. But as we have frequently mentioned, the chief often allowed himself things that went far beyond his jurisdiction. The Judenrat's fear of the chief and the chief's arrogance toward everyone consist of the fact that the chief has good contacts with the German military authorities (Murer et al.), and the Germans, seeing the brutal way the police treat the population, placed great confidence in the chief.

As a result of this (and later of something else . . .), the chief, former commissar Oberhardt, Dessler (commissar of the second precinct), and Mrs. Lili Reszańska, an employee of the police command, have become very haughty because they have special permission to walk on the sidewalk, to go without the patch, and more . . .

The ghetto would have swallowed all this. Horses wash in dirty water. But the trouble is that it is not only the ghetto that suffers; so do the ghetto inhabitants and the wretched little ghetto social life.

For example, take the Fishman-Chief incident:

[Yoyel] Fishman, member of the Judenrat, is coming home from work with his fellow workers—a group of shoemakers. Among them is a 64-year-old shoemaker carrying two bundles of wood. Levas, the famous beater at the gate, jumps on the old man for the crime of smuggling wood and beats him horribly. Fishman, intervening for his fellow worker, tells Levas that even Murer wouldn't have allowed himself to do that. For that moral reproof, the chief threatened the chairman of the Judenrat that he would go to Murer and demand the removal of Fishman because, as he says, he is not fit to be a member of the council. Naturally, the Judenrat stopped him from doing that, and the incident seems to have been settled.

APRIL 20 [1942]

WE STAND ON OUR OWN

Concerning sociocultural activity.

The inhabitants of our ghetto are beginning to stand on our own. This interesting process is occurring exactly as it does with a child: in stages, slowly and cautiously. After the establishment of the Literary-Artistic Association [Association of Writers and Artists], several other corporations, as we know, were established, and each in its own area set itself more or less the same task. After the literary-artistic assemblies, the doctors began to organize similar assemblies. Every Friday these assemblies take place, featuring lectures on medical subjects. These assemblies are called medical-scientific meetings.

Every Friday, as we probably noted earlier, there is an assembly of teachers, where lectures are delivered on subjects of popular science.

In one of the local prayer houses (Jogiches Prayer House),[79] there are lectures on the history of the Jews, organized by the local Mizrahi.[80]

In the afternoon, the so-called gymnasium courses directed by Turbowicz take place (the so-called afternoon group).

The local religious circles are establishing a heder [traditional Jewish grammar school].

Two choirs have been created in the ghetto, a Hebrew one and a Yiddish one. The Hebrew one is directed by the musician [Volf] Durmashkin,[81] the Yiddish choir by the former director of the VILBIG choir,[82] Slep.

79. At 1 Szawelska Street. It was built in the first half of the nineteenth century by one of the most famous of the public leaders and wealthy men of Vilna, Yankev ben Yosef Jogiches.

80. A moderate religious Zionist party.

81. Son of a Vilna cantor. He was a director and singing teacher in the Akiva schools. In September 1944, he was killed in the Estonian camp Lagedi on Rosh Hashanah, one day before the Liberation. For his biography, see *Teachers' Memorial Book* 1954:125–126.

82. VILBIG is Vilner bildungs-gezelshaft, or the Vilna Educational Society.

Chess groups are created in the ghetto. We read announcements such as this one:

> The newly established chess circle wishes to buy chess sets and chess boards, even incomplete ones. Apply to Rudnicka 17 in the kitchen, from 6 P.M. until evening.

There are no chess sets in the ghetto; they even buy incomplete sets to save the situation.

In short, the ghetto is standing on its own. A sociocultural life is beginning to beat.

THREE MONTHS OF GHETTO STATISTICS

The Office of Statistics has already finished the first three months of statistics for this ghetto. The figures are so interesting we shall present some of them here: [*The statistics are missing.*]

MURER COMES TO ME . . . AS A GUEST

The Vilna Ghetto experienced two sensational events. The first was at about 6:30 this evening. Suddenly, the Jewish police started driving people off the streets, beating people murderously—sparing neither big nor small.

At about 7 in the evening, as I was walking in the street, a panting, frightened policeman caught me and said I should go with him immediately because Murer himself had asked for me. On the way to Rudnicka and Murer, there were whole groups of policemen running around looking for me. The street was glowing with excitement. . . .

"If Murer's looking for Kruk, who knows what has happened. . . ."

At the gate of Rudnicka 6, Murer and his staff, including Colonel Kin, were waiting for me. With them was Commander Gens, his adjutant Smuilikowski, and Police Commissar Dessler.

He asks me my name; I answer. He glares at me in an interrogative way, asks me several questions, and then orders me into a room.

We all go into the chief's private apartment. Everyone's eyes are on me. People are sorry for me, and . . . I feel how the people in the courtyard, before whom we parade, are already mourning for me.

Behind me and around me, I feel eyes. I turn around, and behind me is Judenrat member Mr. Gukhman. He gives me a warm glance of pity, poor soul, for falling into "his" hands.

But the commander winks at me, as if to say: Don't be scared, it's nothing. . . .

In Mr. Gens's room, there is an investigation in which both Murer and Kin participate. It turns out that my brigadier, who was visiting a house to take books for the "Rosenberg Task Force," took along two Jews—on the advice of Glazman, the member of the police command—intending to take a Yiddish typewriter from one of their apartments. As it turned out later, they not only looked for the typewriter but also . . . for something else.

Questions fly: Why did they go there? How did I allow it? Why did my brigadier allow it? Then an order: bring the brigadier. I wait and he appears. Another investigation ensues, and again it is clear that the two were sent by the member of the police command Glazman, and when Murer sends for the two, it turns out that neither is in the ghetto. The case is even more suspect, and Murer orders them to be brought to him tomorrow morning.

Thus Murer came to me, and the ghetto citizens were beaten and tortured because of it for more than an hour. . . . How this will end is not yet clear. But it is certain that I personally came out fine. Meanwhile, the most awful legends arose around me:

—The Judenrat was disbanded and Kalman[owicz] and I were appointed to a new Judenrat. . . .

—I was arrested as the vice-president of the literary association [Association of Writers and Artists].

When I came home, the door kept opening all evening. Everyone asked questions and was worried.

The second sensational event took place about an hour ago. At about 10:30 in the evening, I suddenly heard heavy airplanes. I went out and saw an airplane emitting smoke, two giant rockets fell, and I heard the roar of motors. The rockets lit up the whole city with enormous force. An alarm was heard somewhere. The airplane left, and now we all stand expectantly—it will surely come. . . .

WHO MAY AND WHO MAY NOT

We have often written about the dreadful scenes that are played out at the gate when groups of workers return.

Yesterday I observed it carefully. The scenes cannot be conveyed. One person carrying three kilos of potatoes was beaten and they were taken away from him, while others bringing in 20 sacks of salt were . . . kosher.

Jews curse bitterly, and the police beat sadistically and relentlessly.

I AM THE SUPPLIER OF THE GHETTO

The guards at the gate are amazed. I bring desks, tables, benches, cabinets, card catalogues, sleeping boards, etc., etc., into the ghetto. The Jews in the ghetto are amazed at how I obtain them, and only a few know that I've got a special permission in my pocket. But no one knows that under the furniture, I'm smuggling a mass of books for the ghetto schools into the ghetto. An enormous number of old prints, rare books, very valuable paintings—for example, that famous oil painting by Yankl Adler, "two soldiers" in tefillin—etc.

This [is] for the library, the schools, the future ghetto museum. I am also the contractor for the Aid Society. . . . For them, I bring in sleeping boards, straw mattresses, and pillows. For the Judenrat, I fill the role of a supplier of desks, and for myself, I am the smuggler of all above-mentioned valuables. . . .

A sense of accomplishment that pleases me as much as climbing the high Carpathian Mountains once did. . . .

THE GHETTO SEWS BANNERS

For Hitler's fifty-third birthday, the Germans have brought a lot of red cloth into the ghetto, a lot of old Communist banners, and in the tailor workshops here, they have turned the banners from Communist to Hitlerian.

People say that yesterday, in a lot of places, a sickle and hammer were visible behind the swastika. . . .

THE BATH BURNS

The bath just completed has already had a fire. Something broke, and everything around was enveloped in fire. Meanwhile, the bath hadn't yet been used, and now there are repairs to be made. The fire happened on the nineteenth of this month.

GERMAN PRECISION

In front of me is an interesting document—a receipt from a Wehrmacht bordello on Wielka Pohulanka Street. The receipt of the company is written out precisely, with the names of the woman partner, the number of the room, the date, etc. Aside from German precision, we see that our former descriptions are correct. On Subocz there is an official whorehouse, which uses women who once had been snatched off the street. . . .

APRIL 18, REVIEW AT THE THIRD POLICE PRECINCT, "TOMORROW WILL BE GOOD"

I attended this review. The performance is at a high level. But its character is low. The police praise the commander, the commander responds and praises the police. The actors praise the commander and finally Weiskopf, king of the ghetto. Weiskopf is satisfied that the ghetto knows about him, and the commander . . . [is satisfied] that the police appreciate him.

In terms of performance, the program isn't bad.

I learn that the same program will be performed six or seven times. I attach the program.

[*The program is missing.*]

HUNGER

A phase of hunger comes. Bread grows more expensive in the ghetto every day. In the city, bread is very hard to get.

Lietukis[83] transmits telephone cables saying not to sell even a kilo of grain. Everything is for military purposes. Everyone is warned against hoarding flour or other things.

Hunger knocks at the door. Misery increases from minute to minute.

Murer orders: he will tear someone to pieces for allowing even the smallest thing brought in. Murer orders, and the Jewish police do everything to please him.

LEATHER

This week, another big melina of leather, cloth, et al., was found on Szpitalna Street. It is estimated to be of great value.

THE GHETTO WILL BE ENLARGED

Rumors circulate that our ghetto will be enlarged. Our Housing Department also confirms this. According to information so far, the enlargement will mean that we will be allowed to use many of the buildings on the edge of the ghetto.

THE PERMITS ARE BEING EXCHANGED

The Labor Office of the Judenrat began to exchange permits for workbooks. Meanwhile, the permits are exchanged according to units.

A workbook costs 20 rubles. Of that, 3.50 goes for the Aid Society (?). Thus a social institution is allowed to take a tax from the population; the reason for which can be explained only by the Judenrat . . . and the chairman of the current Aid Society, Milkanowicki.

APRIL 23 [1942]

WHAT IS MISSING IN YIVO

According to the stock taking I did with friend Kalman[owicz], YIVO is missing the entire press archive of 10,000 newspapers, and a large number of books from the general library, especially the old editions. Twelve hundred volumes of Y. L. Cahan's[84] [folklore] collection are missing, as is part of Alfred Landau's[85] library. Several manuscripts are missing, along with rare items, like the IKA archive, Perl's[86]

83. The official Lithuanian trading agency for agricultural products.

84. Yehude-Leyb Cahan (1881–1937), a major collector and scholar of Yiddish folklore.

85. Alfred Landau (1850–1935), a Yiddish linguist and folklorist. He lived in Vienna and wrote in German. His life's work, materials for a Yiddish etymological dictionary, was given to YIVO, where it was destroyed in the Holocaust.

86. Joseph Perl (1773–1835), a prominent Yiddish and Hebrew writer of the Haskalah, whose unpublished manuscripts were in the YIVO Archive. Some of them were saved, wound up in the Hebrew University Library in Jerusalem, and were partially published.

Antigone manuscript, Mendele's manuscripts, many of Peretz's and Sholem Aleichem's manuscripts, and many, many other things.

Now, as for what more will be missing.

The question of what will happen to the remaining YIVO treasures is still hanging in the air of the "Rosenberg Task Force."

The "Hebraist" we mentioned before has already come. He is a military man in a party uniform. A tall man who looks like a Jew and seems to be of Jewish origin.

His name is Dr. Pohl. He studied at the Hebrew University in Jerusalem for two years. Published several works on the Talmud, etc. His behavior is courteous, even gregarious. But you can't get anything out of him. What will happen with his work at YIVO we can't even guess. The issue is hanging in the air.

No one knows what the "Hebraist" wants or what his plans are. . . .

APRIL 24 [1942]

THE ACTOR SIMKHE LIPOWSKI DIED

Simkhe Lipowski, the adopted son of the old Lipowski family of actors, died today at the age of 31 after a brief illness (typhus), leaving a wife and three children.

Lipowski's funeral took place today. Before the coffin was taken out, H. Kr[uk] spoke on behalf of the Literary-Artistic Association [Association of Writers and Artists], and Blacher spoke on behalf of the stage actors. The funeral procession looked unique: in front of the coffin marched the members of the association, two by two, led by H. Kr[uk] and Kalman[owicz]. Behind the coffin were many relatives and friends. In front of the ghetto gate, the row of artists divided into a gauntlet, and in the middle, the coffin and Lipowski's colleagues went through.

TWO YESHIVAS

To the previous entry "We Stand on Our Own," we want to add that the Orthodox Jews in the ghetto are not sleeping either. There are already two yeshivas in the ghetto: a Great Yeshiva and another one—a Little Yeshiva.

THERE ARE NO LUNATICS

This is typical for our time and our life. In a normal community of about 20,000 people, there would certainly be frequent cases of madness. Here in the ghetto, where everything is so strange and abnormal, there are hardly any cases of madness.

Everyone here is nervous, memory is weakened, there are specific ghetto illnesses, but it doesn't go as far as madness—the ghetto has no lunatics. . . .

BOILS

One of the illnesses that are particular to the ghetto and frequent here is boils. The illness comes—as the doctors explain—from abnormal eating, bad blood circulation, etc. To cure these ulcers requires Ichthyol ointment. Unfortunately, that cannot be attained.

Masses of people walk around the ghetto with bandaged necks, ulcers under their arms, etc.[87]

SOMETHING IS ROTTEN AMONG THE GERMANS

Rumors reach us from everywhere that something is rotten among the Germans. Demoralization is rising over their heads. Through the intervention of Jews, Germans buy gold and furs, they take money left and right, deal in Jewish property and estates, etc.

Most of the soldiers, from the lowest to the highest rank, are drinking horribly. They themselves recognize that going to the front is certain death. . . . The certainty of victory has long vanished from their mouths; on the contrary, sayings mocking the Führer abound, showing clearly that the stem is rotting away.

A CHARACTERISTIC JOKE FROM THE ECONOMIC BOSS

At Strashun 6, they are tearing down several destroyed buildings to make a sports field. A few days ago, a Jewish laborer was killed at work, crushed by bricks from a falling wall. He broke his spine and died.

In a noisy meeting of the Judenrat, people talked in Fried's presence. The boss listened and answered coldly and unemotionally:

"Died. The payroll will be reduced by one position. . . ."

APRIL 25 [1942]

Kalman[owicz] in Minus

We have often written about the rescue of culture done in the ghetto by Comrades H. Kr[uk] and Kalman[owicz] together.

The former received permission to bring all the furniture of the YIVO building into the ghetto. Kalman[owicz] was happy about that. With this permission, it was also possible to bring all the YIVO card catalogues into the ghetto. This included the library catalogue, the card catalogue of the Bibliographical Center, the press card catalogue, subscriptions to the YIVO-bleter;[88] in short, all kinds of cards, which are actually the soul of YIVO.

But in his fear, Kalman[owicz] cannot calm down, and suddenly he runs eagerly to the "Hebraist," Dr. Pohl, and tells him about the permission of the task force. Dr. Pohl is amazed and changes his treatment of his subordinate, Dr. Müller—permission to take out the card catalogues is withdrawn.

87. Concerning boils in the Vilna Ghetto, see Dworzecki 1946:193.

88. The scholarly journal of YIVO.

Another case: Noah Pryłucki once wrote a lot about a little book he discovered and which apparently was the one and only copy in the world. During the sorting of the secular books and holy books from YIVO, another copy was discovered among the YIVO books.

The little book is by the author Markuze and is titled *Seyfer refues*.[89] Unable to bear the joy, Kalman[owicz] takes the little book to Dr. Pohl, who is very happy about it and satisfied with what Kalman[owicz] has done.

The deed is hard to retract. Close friends who told me about this, the poet Abraham Sutzkever and the painter Olkienicka, trembled with anger.

It is hard to give the act a name. Put it down to Kalman[owicz's] nervous confusion, absentmindedness, and helplessness vis-à-vis the powers that be.

DOCTOR SPECULATORS

Speculation has not missed the Jewish doctors of Vilna. Yesterday several searches were made among the local doctors Goldman, [Lazar] Buzanski, and Lederman. A lot of medications that are almost impossible to obtain in the ghetto, or even outside the ghetto, were found in the possession of each of the three. The doctors prescribed the medicines generously and . . . asked for high payments.

Thus as we see, ghetto demoralization has not missed the local doctors.

ARRESTS AND EXECUTIONS

Yesterday, in a unit working somewhere in the fifth regiment in Loszówka, two Jewish workers who allegedly read a May Day appeal were arrested. The workers had obtained the appeal from a Christian woman, and they quickly denounced her. All of them are in Łukiszki Prison.

16 Executed

Today the local press reports the execution of 16 Christian workers in Vilna, as punishment for carrying out Communist acts of terror.

Thus we learn again of the terrorist acts of the Communists. . . .

IN HONOR OF MAY DAY

With the approach of May Day, which will be celebrated here as a holiday from work, the newspapers are already carrying big headlines about the preparations for Hitler's May Day.

Red banners with swastikas (renovated from Bolshevik cloth and with Bolshevik threads) are ready for sale. There are communiqués about the program of the celebrations, etc.

89. This refers to the rare Yiddish book *Seyfer refues ha-nikra ezer Yisroel,* by Dr. Moyshe Markuze. This edition, of great linguistic and cultural value, was printed in Poryck in 1790. A study of that edition with reproductions was published by Noah Pryłucki (1917:5–56).

May Day will be celebrated with the slogan: "Liberate labor from the Bolshevik yoke." . . .

■ ■ ■ ■ ■ ■

APRIL 27 [1942]

PALACE "REVOLUTION"

Another palace revolution. After those famous events—the incompetence of the Judenrat, Fried, the Cultural Department, etc.—the police started a new fight today: schools!

Gens came to the Judenrat today and demanded that because the Cultural Department had decided on two persons to direct it, there was also a need for two persons to head the Child Education Department. He demanded that two persons be appointed, specifically, that Glazman should be added to Yashunski.

Another policeman!! . . .

But the Judenrat decided this with a majority. Yashunski then resigned his mandate.

Incidentally, during the discussion, the "chief" managed to say that according to his information, the Bund is preparing a May Day demonstration in the ghetto.

His adjutant Smuilikowski repeated the same thing somewhere else and advised caution. . . .

OPENING OF THE GHETTO THEATER

Last night, in the renovated auditorium of the former so-called Little City Hall, the premier performance of the Ghetto Theater at the Cultural Department took place.

The auditorium is renovated; everything is smooth and makes a good impression. The furniture and benches are of various sorts. After the opening words by the director, Engineer Gukhman, there was a concert of the Little Symphony Orchestra, conducted by Durmashkin—a piano concerto and several dramatic performances. The performance was pure, the selection was chaotic, at best without a plan.

The auditorium is arranged so that the first rows are occupied by the elite: the Judenrat, the police commissioners, Avrom Siedschnur, the engineers, leaders of the Technical Department, and also . . . writers, artists, and others.

The Association of Writers and Artists, as such, was not invited to the performance. . . . In revenge, it seems, for the Peretz memorial and perhaps even an expression of relations between the police State Theater and the not-much-loved Literary-Artistic Association [Association of Writers and Artists]? . . .

We attach a program.

[*The program is missing.*]

BREAD — INSTEAD OF 65 — 130 DECAGRAMS

By order of the district commissar, the Jewish working elements are aligned with the non-Jewish workers in the area of food. Until now, a non-Jew had received 130 decagrams of bread a week and a Jew 65. Now every working Jew is to receive 130 decagrams.

We see this as a need for Jewish workers and, of course, as a guarantee that the situation in the ghetto is stabilizing.

SADISM

Meanwhile, the chairman of the district commissariat, the hero Murer, sent the Jewish Labor Office sealed letters to be delivered urgently to the German and Lithuanian unit leaders.

I learn that the letter said that Jews are an inimical element. One may not concern oneself with Jews, converse with them at work, or help them purchase food, etc.

Murer could not send this letter directly to the units but arranged it so that it was done by Jews.

The wanton sadism in all this! . . .

APRIL 29 [1942]

THE DOWNFALL COMES

Hitler's last speech in the Reichstag asking for special powers to fight the rebellious (as if he doesn't already have that), the news coming from individual Germans, the frequent executions of German soldiers for desertion, etc.—everything indicates that in Germany, the downfall is under way, the decline is coming.

Similar news is also coming from the front. And that is seen everywhere in the German communiqués from the front.

For example, a German just returning from vacation relates that he won't go back to Germany any more for the duration of the war; Germany, he says, is now a hell. The Eastern Front is the grave of the German men; Germany is the grave for German women. The bombings, he tells us, are dreadful there. In Hamburg, for example, where he spent two weeks, he was in the air raid shelters for eight days; whole parts of the city were completely destroyed. Berlin, where he lived for three days, is nervous and depressed. There are frequent revolts of women. They are shot en masse. Hitler's speech depressed both the German people and the soldiers.

In the fifth Vilna regiment, the chief, upon receiving the letter (see the entry "Sadism" above) tore it up in front of the Jews. . . .

Others openly laugh at the letter.

MORE ABOUT THE SCHOOL DEPARTMENT

Two days ago, we noted that the police wanted to put one of their men in the Child Education Department, although everyone in the Judenrat recognizes that all the work so far has been done well and irreproachably by Yashunski. Yashunski announced that he would not have anyone placed over him against his will. If, he says, the Judenrat decides to add another person, he asks them to release him. Nevertheless, the Judenrat decided three to two that Yashunski stays alone, as before, but . . . in all questions, he must consult with Policeman Glazman. Yashunski replied by resigning from the department.

A delegation of Bundists talked with Fried and Gukhman, warning that the police would introduce politics into the school, that they were opposed to that, and that if it happened, they would drag the politics out before the people.

The issue meanwhile is hanging in the air.

A MARIONETTE THEATER IN THE GHETTO

The ghetto has a new marionette theater. And like all other "theatrical pieces" in the ghetto, that also came from the . . . police.

This time the evening was arranged by the gate guard with Levas, the major beater and repulsive executioner in the ghetto.

The tickets were distributed at very high prices. The "better earners" in the ghetto paid big money, and Levas didn't spare the theater guests a good supper. The supper itself was estimated at 100 [per person] at least. . . .

The marionettes, they say, were very well done. The texts were a compliment from one police commander to another; often good and successful jokes.

The performance was attended by Gens and . . . the executioner Hering. Levas was the major speaker! . . .

JEWISH POLICE AND MAY DAY

After all that has been noted here about May Day, the finale came today. In the evening, the [police] command came—in the persons of Gens, Glazman, and Smuilikowski—and invited Mr. Kr[uk], and Gens asked him if the Bund is really organizing a demonstration in the ghetto on May Day. K[ruk] laughed in his face and answered that his informers are exactly as informed as when he came with the story of a Communist leaflet published by the Bundists with five signatures. . . .

Gens accepted this explanation and asked Mr. K[ruk], as a member of the presidium of the Literary-Artistic Association [Association of Writers and Artists], to tell him the contents of the literary and artistic evening titled "Spring." He said he was suspicious of it; it smelled like a May Day festivity.

Kr[uk] sent him for information to his police colleague Mr. Glazman, who is a member of the board of the association.

A SOPHISTIC DEBATE ABOUT 1,500 JEWS . . .

Murer learned that there were 1,500 more Jews in the ghetto than he allowed and ordered that the 1,500 Jews should not exist. He advised that they register for work in the peat bogs and forest work (lately Ponar is not mentioned). The German Labor Office didn't agree to send Jews from Vilna to the peat bogs because the Jews are needed for militarily important work. Murer lost the struggle and surrendered.

Today the chief of the Jewish police ordered all unemployed men between the ages of 16 and 60 to register in the Labor Office every day at 6 in the morning to be sent to work. Once more: the German Labor Office demands a lot of workers.

"RABBINICAL SANCTION" FOR GENS

Today the chief of the Jewish police obtained an official license for everything he has done so far without an official document.

Murer writes:

1. The chief of the Jewish police in the person of Gens and his policemen are responsible for the ghetto.
2. The police must maintain order in the ghetto; they must carry out the orders of the district commissar, see that the workers go to work in columns.
3. The gate guard must ensure that no food is brought into the ghetto.
4. For not executing these orders, the police chief is threatened with the death penalty.

The letter also includes a long tirade with points and subpoints. In short, a complete "Constitution"; for Gens it is status quo. In fact, it is nothing more than a written justification for all he has done so far without a piece of paper. . . .

APRIL 30 [1942]

THE EVE OF MAY DAY

Now, late at night, I can write how the eve of May Day, the evening of April 30, has passed.

This evening, in several places in the ghetto, groups of 10–12 people gathered and celebrated "*Erev* [Eve of] May Day." Because the Jewish police would predictably go out of their way [to suppress] May Day, it was decided that the May celebrations should take place on April 30, May Day eve. In every group there were two speeches, and the crowd spent the rest of the evening in conversation.

At about eight in the evening, the police started pushing into the houses and later arrested everyone in the street, asking where they were coming from and where they were going. Even the passes issued by the police were revoked this evening. . . .

Like every other police, the Jewish police also contributed to popularizing our May Day.

HUNGER BECKONS TO US

After yesterday's order from Murer to Gens forbidding the bringing of food into the ghetto under the threat of death, the ghetto experienced a hard day today.

Hunger beckoned in the homes. People everywhere are scared of what will happen. Everyone in his own way imagined the starvation threatening the ghetto inhabitants.

Today, indeed, at the gate, they searched those entering as never before. Food, even in the smallest amounts, was taken away from many people.

The price of a kilo of bread rose from 36 rubles to a full 50. Nevertheless, there were cases of merchandise brought in. Yesterday at about 11 at night, a German truck drove up to the door of Weiskopf's "tailor shop" and delivered sacks of flour, salt, etc.

While bringing furniture into the ghetto from YIVO, my unit also brought a few score pounds of potatoes, wood, etc.

Unofficially, people continue to risk their lives and bring things in.

SHOPS IN THE GHETTO

Recently many shops have opened in the ghetto, reminiscent of the former wretched little suburban shops:

In an open window of a private apartment, they put out a shop [with] cheese, butter, onions, bread, and even fresh plums.

Elsewhere, in a former shop, is a little table with candy, cakes, cookies, a paper bag with about two or three kilos of sugar, a bit of honey, and such things.

On Jatkowa between Szawelska and Szpitalna Streets, a secondhand consignment store has opened, and for the first time in the ghetto, I saw a trimmed display window with shoes, clothes, a mirror, a . . . doll, two plates, a table cloth, etc.

Thus we see that trade is flourishing, especially when we observe the courtyard gates: a little bowl with hot potatoes, candy on a plate, tobacco and cigarettes in a military bread sack. All in all, trade is flourishing. . . .

PLANK BEDS

As we wrote before, I succeeded in bringing furniture and other things from YIVO into the ghetto. Now I cannot walk through the street—everyone asks me for plank beds. People come to my home, my office, I really can't hide. For several dozen plank beds, there are already twice as many candidates.

They run after me in the streets.

MAY 1, 1942

MAY DAY, THE WORKERS' HOLIDAY

This May Day has reminded me of the May Days of the past three years. In 1939 we celebrated May Day in Warsaw for the last time. That evening I entertained a large group of comrades at my home, including the chairman of TSISHO, Comrade Kh. Sh. Kazdan; Bernard [Goldshteyn]; the writer [Mordkhe] Tsanin; [Moyshe] Perenson; and many many others.[90]

By 1940, I was in Vilna as a refugee. There the Lithuanian police of Vilna took strict measures against May Day celebrations.[91] Police, soldiers, and more: a May Day—not to mention it in the same breath—as just before the Revolution of 1905. . . .

Another May Day—1941. The Bolsheviks celebrate their Red military parade, and my friends and I are in hiding. Secretly, in my room (Makowa 5, apt. 24), we hold the last liquidation meeting of the Central Committee of the Youth Bund, Tsukunft, in Poland.[92]

Today is the fourth May Day, this time in the Vilna Ghetto, under the rule of Hitler's Germans and terrorized by the Jewish Revisionist police.

Do we need to add anything more? . . .

This May Day is celebrated here in Vilna as a national holiday of work and . . . liberation. A mass meeting is being prepared, and Communists are shot for . . . banditry.

In most units, Jews are released from work today from noon on (holiday! . . .)

The ghetto proletariat has not forgotten May Day. Here, in the ghetto, May Day started yesterday, the thirtieth, with meetings we have already described.

The celebration was arranged here together with the "Reds," our first successful enterprise with the Red partners. . . .

Today began with most of the Judenrat employees coming to work half an hour to an hour late, following the initiative of the B[und]. In some departments,

90. Kh. Sh. Kazdan immigrated to New York. Bernard Goldshteyn ("Comrade Bernard"), a veteran Bundist activist and author of *Five Years in the Warsaw Ghetto and Twenty Years in the Polish Bund,* died in New York on December 7, 1959. Mordkhe Tsanin is the former editor of the Yiddish newspaper *Letste Nayes* in Tel Aviv. Moyshe Perenson was the leader of the dramatic studio of Tsukunft in Warsaw; he immigrated to New York.

91. Vilna, renamed Vilnius, was in the hands of quasi-Fascist Lithuania. In May 1940, the Red Army occupied Lithuania.

92. The Central Committee of Tsukunft was only ostensibly "liquidated" under the Soviets. Even in the underground, opposition parties had to be dissolved so as not to endanger their members. As a Socialist party, the Bund was especially persecuted by the Soviets, with its leaders arrested and either exiled or killed.

that demonstration was 100 percent, for example, in the Departments of Health, Provisions, Library, etc. In the schools, classes were interrupted an hour before the fixed time.

At eight in the evening, a regular teachers' meeting took place, where May Day was secretly celebrated.

Later in the evening, the committee of the B[und] and B[undist] members of the Judenrat met and enjoyed themselves until late at night. At parting, Fish[man], Pati [Kremer], and Miriam [Gutgestalt] kissed me.

This is how May Day 1942 was spent, celebrated in the Vilna Ghetto of tragic fame.

MAY 2 [1942]

ANOTHER MAY CELEBRATION

This time it concerns a big, well-planned May Day celebration, which the chief of police was very interested in.

It has already been established in the ghetto that every Saturday a literary-artistic gathering takes place, and every time, as we know, those meetings are devoted to specific topics. This time the meeting was devoted to "Spring." And although no one said anything about it, the entire Jewish labor force and working intelligentsia understood that that meant a May Day event. The request for invitations was extraordinary. The result: in an auditorium that can hold 120 people, more than 300 gathered. The mood was May Day–like. The evening was opened by Mr. Kr[uk] (speech attached).

[*The speech is missing.*]

An introduction was given by Hersh [Gutgestalt], and then there was a literary and vocal part. The evening was carried out in a holiday spirit.

This was the close of the May Day celebration in the ghetto.

THE SCHOOL CRISIS IS OVER

The crisis about the police chief's demand that in the School Department, as in the Cultural Department, two persons should govern (the Cultural Department: Gens and Gukhman? . . .) is now over.

A delegation of the B[und] visited Messrs. Fried and Gukhman and explained to them that the innovations concerning the School Department threaten to disturb the peace in the ghetto, that this would not be tolerated, and that the two unaffiliated members in the Judenrat (Gukhman and Fried) must not stand for that. The next day, Gukhman invited Mr. Kr[uk] as a mediator. Mr. Fried also called on him for the same thing that day. From the other side, Mrs. Khyene [Borowska] had a conversation with the "chief" about it.[93] The result: Gens withdrew his suggestion.

Thus the school crisis concluded peacefully.

PLANK BEDS

Germans were once stationed at YIVO and left their plank beds there. Now, as I have written, I received permission to bring those plank beds into the ghetto. For the past 24 hours, the issue has been so popular it is hard for me to walk through the street. Hence I have stopped distributing the plank beds and have turned them over to the Aid Society.

MAY 3 [1942]

HUNGER KNOCKS AT THE DOOR

We have written that hunger has come. Now we feel it. Hunger is knocking at the door. Now a kilo of bread in the ghetto has increased in price to 80 rubles, a kilo of potatoes 35 rubles. People are walking around hungry and often tell of cases of fainting at work.

In my office, someone asked me today to give him work where he could sit, because he can hardly stand on his feet.

In the Rosenberg Task Force, at YIVO, Dr. Feinstein complained: for three days now he hasn't eaten any bread. If he could only get carrots! . . .

In contrast, the dread of hunger here in the ghetto is so great that despite all orders, people risk their lives and bring in food and more food.

Not even the order about the death penalty helps very much!

YOU CAN'T GO OUT ON SUNDAY

According to the last strict order, you can't leave the ghetto on days when you don't work. Thus on Sunday the ghetto is closed for all those who do not go to work.

THE LAST CHORD OF MAY DAY

This evening we experienced the last chord of the mutually celebrated May Day in the ghetto. In a small building, the leaders of the B[und] and the Reds celebrated our first joint action, which was also a celebration of triumph in the al-

93. Khyene Borowska was a nurse, at first a member of Ha-Shomer ha-Tzair and later an active Communist leader. She was the representative of the Communists in several ghetto agencies and assumed a position of leadership in the FPO, the United Partisan Organization. She was a partisan in the forest with her husband Shmulke Kapliński, a Bundist. Both survived the war and lived in Vilnius. Her intervention in this case demonstrates the underground's increasing influence on Gens.

ready mentioned School Department and the retreat of the arrogant Jewish policemen.

Her[man Kruk] spoke on behalf of the B[und]. Someone also spoke for the Reds. After the speeches, the assembly quietly sang the "Internationale."

THE FATE OF THOUSANDS OF JEWISH CHILDREN

Thousands of parents were taken to Ponar. But thousands and thousands of parents have settled their children so that regardless of whether they themselves survive, the children will.

Often Christian neighbors did this themselves, on their own initiative. People took Jewish children, often converted them, kept them in their homes, and brought them up.

I know an intelligent woman who lives in my neighborhood in the ghetto, whose only child lives with a Christian in a village. The mother will risk her own life, but she will not play with the fate of her child.

Here's another tale:

A Lithuanian soldier brought to the Jewish police an old Christian, a certain Marian Bylinski, who lives at Wileńska Street 22 with a two-and-a-half-year-old Jewish child who comes from a known Vilna family, Kulbis.

During the purge, her father was taken, the mother was taken to Ponar, and the Christian Bylinski took the child.

The Christian, former vice-president of the District Office of Insurance Companies in Vilna, seems to be a very conscientious and decent man. He did what he did, it seems, from a purely human point of view.

The Christian has already been arrested twice. He was taken to the Gestapo and did not want to confess that the child was a Jew. Finally he was forced to surrender, and the child was turned over to the ghetto police.

There sits the Christian in the Jewish police station, playing with the child, and on the table are the toys he brought for the child. He weeps bitterly, and the child, sensing that they want to part them, cries out to the Christian:

"Papa, I want to go with you, I don't want to stay here!"

All those who stand around see the tragedy of "Papa," the tragic child, and all the sadness of the affair.

The child remained with a woman in the ghetto who was once divorced by the child's father, Kulbis. Now the divorced woman has adopted the orphan of her divorced husband's second wife. . . .

This is how tragedies are rolling. . . .

MAY 6 [1942]

SUTZKEVER'S POETRY EVENING

A great deal has occurred since May Day, and yet I have not written. But today I cannot be released from immediately writing what I have just experienced.

The Literary-Artistic Association [Association of Writers and Artists], with the goal it posed for its work, has so far forgotten one thing: it has become famous in the ghetto. People come to it, people group themselves around it. Its evenings are talked about, its Peretz evening roused great satisfaction, etc. But internally, among the members, little has been done until today.

At one of the last meetings of the board of directors, I raised the question, and this evening was the first result of it.

In the company of fifteen of the most distinguished writers and artists, Mr. Sutz[kever] read his new poem, "The Grave-Child," as he calls it—a dramatic chronicle. The work was greeted with great applause by the audience and, most important, with a great and long exchange of opinions.

The dramatic chronicle has a lot of visionary lyricism, as someone called it. After the author read the work, it was a long time before anyone said anything. The proximity of the dramatic events, the form of the work, and its sublimity had such an effect that everyone kept their mouths shut. Only after the first speaker, friend Dr. [Tsemakh] Feldstein,[94] did a broad discussion get under way, which lasted for three hours. This is, I think, the first sublime evening of great creative excitement.

Those who participated in the evening were: Dr. Feldstein, Kalman[owicz], Dr. Gordon, the musician Yankev Gerstein, the Soviet actor Yankev Bergolski,[95] the poetess Leye Rudnicka,[96] Hersh Gutgestalt, myself, and others.

JESZCZE POLSKA NIE ZGINĘŁA . . .[97]

From Vilna and the whole area, masses of young men are being taken for work in Germany. Yesterday one of those groups was led through Szawelska Street and a

94. A Ph.D. and writer, principal of the Hebrew Gymnasium in Kovno. In the Vilna Ghetto, he was a dynamic cultural activist, editor of the *Geto-yedies* [Ghetto news], who made speeches and wrote several essays. He was killed in Schömberg-Dautmergen, Württemberg. For his biography, see Dworzecki 1948:265–266.

95. Originally from the Ukraine, son of a cantor, and an actor in the Yiddish theater in Baku. In 1941 he came to Vilna at the invitation of the Yiddish state theater. He was very active in the Ghetto Theater. In early July 1944, a few days before Vilna was liberated, he was killed in the work camp HKP.

96. Born in 1916 in the Lithuanian town of Kalvarija. She belonged to the circles of young Yiddish writers in Lithuania. During the liquidation of the Vilna Ghetto, on September 23, 1943, she was sent to the "left." She was killed in Majdanek or Treblinka (according to Kaczerginski 1947: 212, Majdanek; according to Kaczerginski 1948:87, Treblinka).

97. The opening of the Polish national anthem: "Poland is not yet lost [As long as we live]."

lot of Jews saw them. In the street, guarded by Lithuanians, they stormily sang the national battle song, "Poland Is Not Yet Lost," and as they approached the Jewish ghetto, they shouted slogans:

"Long live the Jews! . . ."

A mood I only want to note here.

LAG B'OMER AMONG US

Lag b'Omer[98] this year is as thoroughly strange here as everything around us. Yesterday, May 5, during the children's Lag b'Omer holiday, when children go on outings in field and forest, it snowed heavily. One can hardly remember such a deep snow in May.

Like the Jews, so the Christians. The yeshiva in heaven is like the yeshiva on earth. . . .

OPENING OF THE READING ROOM

Yesterday we opened the reading room of the ghetto. The reading room really began back in autumn 1941. The winter months closed it down, and now, after repairs and renovations, it was reopened.

Among the local intelligentsia, the reading room has brought great satisfaction and even greater excitement because of the mood that reigns there.

MARKUS STOVES

Much as the ghetto lives its unusual life, it is interesting to note the following fact: the ghetto is creative in various areas. Here, for example, in the Technical Department of the Judenrat, works a certain refugee from Łódź, an engineer named [Shimen] Markus.[99] The man is very energetic, active as an engineer, and very often inventive. In the winter, when everyone was freezing because of the lack of ovens and heating material, Engineer Markus invented a sawdust-burning oven. The oven, made of sheet metal, was cheap and good. Now heating is very expensive, and Markus has also invented a fireplace that warms quickly and uses a minimum of wood. Such a fireplace is cheap: the price is 50 rubles, which is now equal to the price of one kilo of bread or five eggs.

Both the oven and the fireplace are called Markus Stoves, after their inventor.

SPRING TEMPTS WITH GOOD NEWS

From all around comes good springtime news. Good news everywhere from the front. They say that terrible things are going on in Italy. Around the world, great

98. Lag b'Omer, the thirty-third day of the counting of the Omer, is a semi-holiday commemorating the heroism of Bar Kokhba and Akiba ben Joseph.

99. An activist in the Łódź Socialist-Zionist party Hitahdut, and a member of the patrons of the Borokhov kibbutz. He came to Vilna as a refugee in 1939. In the ghetto, he directed the workshops and belonged to the ghetto court. He was killed in a camp in Estonia.

acts of sabotage are being carried out against Germany. The German offensive on the Eastern Front is collapsing. Stalin is aggressive. The last German speech emphasized that prominently.

Although it is still raining and snowing outside, in the souls of the ghetto residents it is springtime and aggressive.

Even pessimists have changed into optimists.

CRIME AND PUNISHMENT IN THE GHETTO

As part of ghetto life and concerning its crime, we attach interesting figures from the Jewish court in our ghetto.

The figures are from November 15 [1941] (i.e., when the court was created) to March 31, 1942.

[*The figures are missing.*]

MAY 7 [1942]

GHETTO STATISTICS

A few times we have told of the Office of Statistics in the ghetto. Now we have a final accounting of the first three months of ghetto statistics, for September, October, and November of 1941.

The introduction says:

> The area of the ghetto contains 34,500 square meters, of which only 23,000 can be used. If we assume that the aforementioned area was densely populated, granting only 7, not 9, meters per person, this means that 3,750 to 4,000 persons lived in the area before the period of the ghetto.

It goes on to state that in the first ghetto period, there were 29,000 people in the same area.

The first three months of ghetto statistics describe the harsh experiences in the ghetto. Thus, for example, we see the vacillation in the use of food supplies during the infamous Aktions. In November, the general count of the population falls almost in half, but the number of consumers of the soup kitchens rises.

We shall write separately about the protection of health and the hospital. But meanwhile, several pieces of information about instances of death:

The cause of death is hard to ascertain; the official institutions do not give any answers about that. Officially, in November the number of deaths was 6 percent higher than in September, although the population was sharply reduced in November. (In October, it was 35 percent higher than in September.)

There is a special section here on instances of death among children and [infants]. Officially, in September there were 6 cases (5 percent), in October, 29 cases (18 percent), in November, 54 cases (45 percent).

From the unofficial figures, I learn that in September, 6 children under the age of four months died; in October, 26; in November, 43; and in December, 37. Altogether, 112 children.

Typically, in the last third of October, when the Aktion of the Yellow Permits took place (October 24), there were 14 cases of children's deaths. . . . In the first ten days of December, during the Aktion of those transferred from the first ghetto to the second, we see again 24 cases of children's deaths. Incidentally, on a single day, 16 children were buried. But about them another time, because we want to devote a special chapter to graveyard tales, which is worthwhile.

BREAD CARDS FOR THE VILNA GHETTO

According to official information from the Provisions Department in the Vilna Ghetto, 25,300 bread cards were distributed in October; in November, 12,000; in December, 13,000; in January 1942, 13,600; in February, 14,746; in March, 15,850; in April, 18,500.

In sum, the so-called legal population in the ghetto numbered 12,000 in November [1941] and 18,500 in April [1942].

We attach a diagram about this.

[*The diagram is missing.*]

BOOKS AND READERS

A unique page of ghetto history is the Jewish reader.

Even in November, during the great Aktions, when the population systematically declined by about 30 or 40 percent, the number of books borrowed increased by almost a third.

How people read, and what they read, we have already written about in greater detail.

This, more or less, is the chapter on ghetto statistics.

DATA AND FIGURES ABOUT THE HORRIBLE EVENTS IN THE GHETTO

While preparing the history of the ghetto for Murer, based on my information, we have compiled the following calendar of the horrible events in the ghetto.

The dates are precise, the figures approximate. The final count of the events is therefore also approximate.

The collected data and figures are attached.

[*We present the following document here exactly according to the original. The calculations of totals are mistaken in some places.*]

STATISTICS AND MOURNING STATISTICS[100]

1. Until the German-Soviet War

According to the figures available to us and the accounting of the Polish statistician M. Balinski (see his book on the population of Vilna), in 1832 Vilna numbered 35,922 inhabitants, 20,646 of whom were Jews, i.e., 55.09 percent. In 1870 Vilna had a Jewish population of 30,882 (48 percent). In 1897, 63,900 (40.09 percent). The number of Jewish inhabitants in Vilna before the last world war, in 1931, was 56,500, or 28.09 percent. Right before the outbreak of the war, in 1939, it was estimated that Vilna numbered around 60,000 Jews. That number was later increased because at the beginning of the war, Vilna became a center for Polish refugees, where thousands and thousands from Warsaw and the surrounding area sought a temporary shelter. If we figure that a lot of refugees left Vilna for America, Palestine, etc., during the Soviet period, and if we also subtract the small number of Jews who succeeded (since most did not succeed) in fleeing with the retreating Bolsheviks, we can still ascertain that on June 22, 1941, there were at least 60,000 Jews in Vilna.

2. From June 22 until the Ghetto

About July, the sad period of snatching Jews began.

If we could rely on the report of the director of the Department of Forced Labor in the Jewish Committee (Strashun 6), it turns out that from July 11 to July 31, 1941, an average of 1,300 able-bodied persons were supplied daily for forced labor (10 percent of them were women). Aside from that, as we know, the so-called Snatchers were busy "mobilizing" Jews in their own unique way. If we assume modestly that the above-mentioned Department of Forced Labor daily supplied 1,200 men, the Snatchers did that much more intensively. Moreover, a lot of Jews found jobs for themselves in various German working places (units). Thus, as we see, these figures can reach several thousand every day.

How many of them did not come back we know from our own descriptions. But more precisely, in terms of figures, we can know only when they come to the ghetto.

3. Calendar of the Horrible Events in the Vilna Ghetto

To answer the question posed just now about the snatched Jews in Vilna until the time of going into the ghetto, we must ascertain:

29,000 Jews entered Vilna Ghetto 1, and 11,000 Jews went to Ghetto 2. Altogether, 40,000 Jews.[101] Relying on our estimate of a [round figure] of 60,000

100. Another copy of the typescript of these statistics was found in Israel. It contains corrections in Kruk's hand. We have accepted the corrected figures here.

101. The Yiddish edition has 11,000 for Ghetto 2, but from the typescript it is clear that the figure was typed as 9,000, then corrected in Kruk's hand to 11,000, but Kruk forgot to correct the total from 38,000 (as in the Yiddish edition) to 40,000 (as here).

Jews in Vilna, only 39,000 [?] entered the ghetto, which means that the Snatchers and all others dragged off or annihilated 21,000 Jews before the Jews went into the ghetto.

Now the period of the ghetto:

We have rounded off some of the following figures, but if we know some of them precisely, we consider it necessary to convey that precision. The total thus makes an impression of precise numbers but is really only an approximation.

The following will make it clear:

On the night of September 6–7, as we have already [. . .] said, on the way to the ghetto and from Lidzki Street, about [6,000] Jews disappeared. Soon after, on September 15, 3,350 people were taken out of [Ghetto] 1 to be sent to Ghetto 2. No more than 600 of that group arrived at Ghetto 2. On the way, 2,950 [?] people disappeared. Thus the following were lost:

On the night of September	6–76,000
On September	152,950
Total	8,950

Chronologically, the following account is:

On October 1, Yom Kippur, at 1:30 in the afternoon, dragged out of Ghetto 2: 800 Jews

The same day, at 6:30 in the evening: 900 Jews

The same night, October 1–2, people were taken from Ghetto 1 to the gate on the pretext of stamping their permits. From that walk, the number that disappeared: 2,200 Jews

On October 3 and 4, the number taken from Ghetto 2: 2,000 Jews

On October 16, the number taken from Ghetto 2: 3,000 Jews

On October 29, the number taken from Ghetto 2: 2,500 Jews

Then came the turn of the old and paralyzed:

From Ghetto 1: 80 Jews

From Ghetto 2: 60 Jews

On October 24, the first Aktion of the so-called Yellow Permits took place. The inhabitants with permits abandoned their ghetto homes and left [. . .] most of them with wives and children to their place of work in the units. The minority—the Judenrat employees—were gathered in the courtyard of Rudnicka 6. The remaining persons were dragged out of their melinas and taken out of the ghetto. Their number was more than: 5,000 Jews

On November 3, there was a roundup of Jews taken from Ghetto 1 to [Ghetto] 2, and meanwhile, the number destroyed was: 1,200 Jews

On December 3, people were taken out of the so-called ghetto underworld: 67 Jews

On December 4, more were taken out of the so-called underworld: 90 Jews

On the night of December 15, all the residents of the "Gestapo" block were taken. Not returned: 300 Jews

The last roundup so far was carried out by Lithuanians on December 20 and 21; there were additional victims: 400 Jews

Thus, from my verified entries, the sorrowful [. . .] in the ghetto for the time of September 6–7 to December 20–[21], 1941, the number of those taken out of the ghetto: 26,447 Jews [?]

Thus the sad balance is:

In both ghettos, there were about 40,000 Jews. On January 1, there was only one ghetto. According to the bread cards distributed, there were in this ghetto 12,600 Jews.

Thus, altogether:

Before the ghetto, as we have indicated, the number of those destroyed was: 21,000 Jews

During the ghetto period: 26,447 Jews

With a trembling hand, I calculate: 47,447 Jews

This tragic total is made public after it was checked several times and then given authorization in a council meeting of all those who knew anything about it.

With trembling hand and full responsibility to history, we have presented the figures as they must be estimated.

(Vilna Ghetto, May 1942)

MAY 8 [1942]

Mobilization of Three Cohorts

The order concerning a mobilization of a labor force made a strong impression in the city. The order was issued by the General Council for Labor and Social Affairs. The mobilization includes those born in the years 1919 to 1922 and relates only to men.

The Aryan population is truly scared and doesn't know [. . .]

400 Jews to Podbrodzie
Bread Again More Expensive
Lublin Judenrein
Lida
A German on Legionowa
Again Lida

[Page 376 of the journal is missing. From the continuation on page 377, we see that "work permits" were distributed. In connection with the aforementioned labor mobilization, it is not clear whether Kruk is talking about the Jewish or the non-Jewish population.]

[. . .] pages. The population was divided into people with "work permits" and the "permitless."

POLICE AND PROVISIONING

The police undertook steps to prevent a rise in the price of bread. Those who smuggle in more bread will be allowed to keep two kilos; for the rest, the smugglers will receive 65 rubles a kilo from the ghetto administration.

So the smuggler has the possibility of smuggling, and the ghetto has the possibility of getting bread.

The police negotiations with the bakers in the ghetto led to nothing.

Nevertheless, two people are now in prison for selling bread at high prices in spite of everything.

UNREST IN KOVNO

Various rumors are circulating about unrest in Kovno. We shall note the information as we know it.

Concerning the mobilization of those born in the years 1919–1922, the groups that came to Kovno for the induction were soon arrested on the spot. Not expecting that, the young people started running away. There were clashes, and many of them were wounded or killed.

The events provoked a demonstration. The demonstrators attacked Gen. Kaidolunas [Kubiliunas?] in his apartment and stabbed him.

Gen. Kaidolunas is one of those who signed the mobilization order. He is also the creator of the Lithuanian "autonomy."

NEWS FROM PODBRODZIE

The Jewish laborers recently sent to Podbrodzie send very good regards to the ghetto.

GUESTS IN THE READING ROOM

The renovation of the ghetto reading room has stirred great interest among the ghetto intelligentsia. Every day many people visit the reading room, and they wish success to the new branch of cultural work. The reading room is considered the nicest cultural corner in the ghetto.

MAY 14 [1942]

A "POLITICAL CLUB" IN THE GHETTO

The Jewish police create a full state machinery, with all the advantages and disadvantages of a normal state. This week, the "chief" arranged an audience in his home—a glass of tea, to enable listening to lectures and possibly having discussions in a homey setting.

The first meeting took place on May 13. Representatives of all existing trends in the ghetto and representatives of the intelligentsia were present.

After the host greeted the guests, there was a lecture by the former editor of the *Rzeczpospolita*[102] of Łódź, Nussbaum-Oltaszewski, on "Folk and Nation." Those who participated in the discussion, which lasted until three in the morning, included Kalman[owicz], Engineer Markus, Dr. Feldstein, and others. Our group[103]—four persons—was present but did not take part at all in the discussion.

[*The end of page 378 is damaged. The beginnings of 25 lines are missing. We present the existing parts here, with our additions in square brackets.*]

ACTIVITY OF THE CULTURAL DEPARTMENT

[Today] there was an announcement about a concert of two cantors—Litvak [and Edelso]n. The tickets [were distributed] in a day.

[SHOLEM] ALEICHEM COMMEMORATION

[The Association] of Writers and Artists in the Vilna Ghetto organ[ized for Sun]day, May 17, at 11 in the morning, a big Sholem Aleichem Re[cital. The tickets] are selling very slowly.

[The leader of the Cultural Departmen]t knows his ghetto [inhabitants better; cantorial concerts are] more valuable here than a Sholem Aleichem commemoration. . . .

[This is how . . .] the ghetto is.

PROFANED GRAVESTONES IN *ZARETSHE* CEMETERY

[Ever since the Jews entered] the ghetto, the Zarzecze Ceme[tery has been] without a caretaker, and the neighbors all around there do [whatever they want.] Trees are cut down for heating wood, they pasture [flocks . . . they have take]n the fence palings apart, etc.

[. . .] to that cemetery came a gro[up . . .] broke and damaged a large number of better [tombstones that had be]en decorated with photographs [. . .] thus altogether were disgraced [. . . includ]ing the tombstones of Binyomin Bunimowicz, Epstein [. . .].

THE NINETY-YEAR-OLD YOYEL LEVIN

[. . .] for some years, there lived and wo[rked a Jewish peasant, Yoyel Le]vin, with a property of twelve hectares [of land. He was a retir]ed Nikolai sol-

102. In Polish, "Republic."

103. I.e., the Bundists.

dier.[104] When the Jews were driven into the Vilna Ghetto, Yoyel Levin decided to leave his land and run away with his family among the neighboring peasants. Thus they live to this very day, and thus old Yoyel also lived.

With the mobilization of the labor force on the week of the ninth of this month, the surrounding villages were searched by Lithuanian and German soldiers. There the gendarmes noticed Reb Yoyel, arrested him, beat him up, robbed him, murdered him, and buried him at the side of the road so that his boots stuck up out of the grave. . . . As soon as the peasants found out about that, they went off to the village elder and asked for permission to dig him up and bury him in the Jewish cemetery in Vilna. The corpse was accompanied to the cemetery by a few Christians, who brought sheets to bury him in linen, according to Jewish law. They also proposed to pay for a nice plot for him. They will also pay for a Jew to pray for him a whole year.

The dead man was beaten horribly. The money the murderers found on the Jew was taken by the Germans, the fur coat went to the . . . Lithuanians.

The family of the murdered man continues to hide out with the Christian neighbors.

MAY 15 [1942]

UPSETTING NEWS

Lida. Here they affirm that in Lida, about 300 Jews were shot, which we have already written about.

Woronów. The shtetl on the border of Lithuania and Byelorussia was a labor camp until recently. The Jews lived there without a ghetto. There was only a Jewish police. On the eighth of this month, a rumor suddenly circulated that the town was surrounded by German gendarmes and the Jewish inhabitants were seriously threatened.

On Saturday night the Poles advised the Jews to save themselves. The woman who tells us the story, her husband and three children, and a group of more than 100 persons bribed the Polish policeman and set off for wherever their eyes took them. They walked at night and hid in the forest by day.

On the morning of the 14th, our narrator comes to the Vilna Ghetto and tells us that on the way, she lost her husband and children and ran to Vilna alone.

She says that peasants she talked to on the way say that there are no Jews in Woronów, and the same thing happened in Beniakony and Radun.

104. Nikolai soldiers were Jews who were taken as children into the Russian army of Tsar Nicholas I (1796–1855) to serve for 25 years. They thus became thoroughly Russified. Reb Yoyel, born too late to have been an actual Nikolai soldier, may have been a veteran of the army of the next tsar, Alexander II, who ruled Russia from 1855 to 1881.

The information, although not yet confirmed, created a great upset in the ghetto.

Concerning this, I copy here an authentic letter from Jews written to their friends here, in the Vilna Ghetto:

> Dear friends Karnowski, Kęski, Koryski, Puzeryski, write us about what's happening in your city. We are in great danger here. Can we come to the city. We send the letter to you with a special messenger; please send an answer with him immediately.

The letter has no date, and it was hard for me to find out where it originated. It seems to be from Woronów.

WEISKOPF — THE SENSATION OF THE DAY

All at once, the ghetto was captivated by a singular event: Weiskopf, the king of the ghetto, was suddenly dethroned. He and his staff, the son-in-law Glazman, Yofe, etc., were removed from their "tailor shop" and . . . and the game is up.

A few days ago, at 11 at night, Weiskopf was brought to Jewish police headquarters and detained there until 4 in the morning. Meanwhile, his private apartment was thoroughly searched, and as they later said, they found one sack of flour, a few bottles of brandy, wine, liqueur, and other goods.

Why did Weiskopf suddenly fall so sharply in the eyes of the police, who had exalted him so high until now?

This is the story they tell:

A few weeks ago, Weiskopf made a contract with the Wehrmacht to mend and patch 400 railroad cars full of clothes, and he had even started acquiring a new labor force for that work. The police chief then demanded that Weiskopf set up a special "tailor shop" for that work, and the workers were to be hired not by Weiskopf but by the ghetto Labor Office. Weiskopf refused. Hiring workers yourself means acquiring a new source of profit for giving work.

[*The right corner of page 380 of the original typescript is torn off. We present the surviving fragment, with the first editor's additions.*]

[To organize a] new "workshop" implies a lot of workers. Can he indeed [undertake] to organize the work himself in his own workshops. Instead of [employ]ing about 500–600 [new] people, to be satisfied with just [his previous ones]. The police opposed that categorically, [and so Weis]kopf thought it necessary to go to his Germans with it. [. . .] Got into a rage and worked it out [his way. In the end] the result is—a few searches in the "tailor shop" [showed that] Weiskopf's management is improper.

Weiskopf was thrown out as head of the "tailor shop," and his workbook was [taken away]. The police commissar of the third precinct [was appointed] head of the tailor workshop [. . .]

May 17 [1942]

A BEAUTIFUL SHOLEM ALEICHEM RECITAL

As we have written, in honor of the 25th anniversary of Sholem Aleichem [. . .] [*Page 381 of the journal is missing. Kalmanowicz's speech at the Sholem Aleichem Celebration mentioned above is in the* YIVO *Archive (Kaczerginski-Sutzkever Collection, no. 495).*]

Jewish Firefighters in the Ghetto

May 18 [1942]

Strange Rumors

Anigst, or a Story That Goes from Hand to Hand

News from Kovno

A Catastrophe with Three Jews

[*Page 382 begins with the end of an entry about a railroad catastrophe.*]

[. . .] Jewish women. One, Rive Feinstein, 22 years old, died immediately, another one had a hand amputated. The third was slightly wounded.

The women fell under the wheels of a train.

FOR DESERTION

Yesterday, in the fifth regiment, three Germans were shot. People say they refused to go to the front.

A SECOND CATASTROPHE

People tell of another railroad catastrophe. This time in Ponar. The railroad connection was interrupted for a few hours. A train with wounded Germans was one of those delayed there.

A GERMAN TO A JEWISH GIRL

I read a letter from a German to a Jewish girl: in the "unit," he cannot talk to her. He wants to help her as much as possible. He asks her not to treat him as a German. "Write to me. I am at your service."

At the end, a signature: "Vernichten Sie den Brief sofort, Herbert" [destroy the letter immediately, Herbert].

A LETTER FROM MY SISTER, A MESSAGE FROM MY BROTHER

Since June 1941, I have remained completely cut off from my sister, who is in Poland, and from my brother, who has recently arrived in America.

Today I received a letter from my sister, dated April 23, this year:

She was overjoyed to learn I was alive. Her friend, Comrade Koszerowski, who supported her there, and she, were both sick. He died (i.e., was arrested, therefore not alive?). She is with both children and in great need.[105]

From the same card, I learn that she is in touch with my brother Pinkhes [in the United States], who even sent her packages. He is very worried about my fate.

A NEW ROSENBERG TASK FORCE

The leaders of my Rosenberg Task Force have gone off to the front, and a new leadership has replaced them. Yesterday they visited YIVO, and today I introduced myself to them.

The main thing: they ask me to find a translator of a Yiddish book on the Jews in South Africa.[106] They tell me that 80 cases will soon be ready to pack.

Does this mean they are already starting to pack? . . .

MAY 19 [1942]

I GROW OLD . . .

I am 45 years old today and entering my 46th year. I shall get no flowers here—no one to give me anything. I will not celebrate—there's nothing to celebrate. I bear my 45 years all alone, and especially the brand-new experiences from the 44th year to the 45th.

As I said, I found my sister. And my brother. My wife—who knows if I will live to find her.

The news that comes every day from the surrounding provinces does not bode well for our getting out of this alive.

My birthday today is not accompanied by optimism. . . .

WITHOUT PATCHES

For walking in the street without a patch, you are taken to Łukiszki. Just today I went out into the street without a patch, and only on Zawalna did a Christian

105. Kruk's sister, Genya (Golde) Torner, was the wife of a high official of the Płock Socialist City Council. When the Nazis expelled the Jews from Płock, she went to Tomaszów Mazowiecki, where her mother-in-law lived, but did not find her there. The Tomaszów Bundist councilman Shimshn Koszerowski took her into his home. In the Tomaszów Ghetto, Koszerowski was very active until he was arrested by the Gestapo. Several others, including Kruk's sister, were arrested at the same time. (Kruk notes this with a euphemism, that she "fell ill.") After a long time, Mrs. Torner was released and went to the Warsaw Ghetto, where she was killed a year later. Koszerowski was shot by the Nazis, along with the Cracow Bundist activist Shmuel Yoyne Blum (who had also been taken in by Koszerowski). For Koszerowski's biography, see *Generations* 2:460–461.

106. I.e., the study of Leybl Feldman, *Yidn in Afrike*. The translation was later done by Z. Kalmanowicz.

stop me and point it out. I went back to the ghetto in great fear to correct my error. . . .

Good that it ended only with fear!

This is how we "save ourselves" from day to day. . . .

MAY 20 [1942]

HUNGER

Here in the ghetto, hunger encompasses more and more circles. There is already a feeling of shame at being full. . . .

Our friend receives a letter from Warsaw: his father, mother, and brother-in-law have died of hunger.

I know of cases of cooking potato skins, cases of poor people not wanting to take any money. They beg for a crust of bread.

People walk around half wild, mean, upset—doctors explain it as hunger. . . .

The same hunger increases many new diseases of hunger among us. But we shall write separately about that.

A MOBILIZATION OF NINE COHORTS

After the mobilization of three cohorts of work forces and all the incidents we recently wrote about, there is now a new mobilization—this time nine cohorts [of those born] from 1910 to 1918.

The mobilization is not even published. The house "administrators" have to present lists of the inhabitants. But the inhabitants do not appear and escape en masse into the surrounding forests. Both Poles and Lithuanians run.

The forests in the area of Landwarowo and Podbrodzie are full of such deserters.

HORSE MOBILIZATION

In response to the published mobilization of horses, horses have suddenly started dropping dead. Often the horses get various illnesses.

People tell about a German, a Lithuanian, and a few officials who recently went through the villages confiscating livestock and haven't come back to this day.

MAY 21 [1942]

MORE RUMORS

The additional rumors about the events in Woronów, Lida, etc., become clearer every day. Both in Woronów and in Lida, thousands of Jews have been shot.

The ghetto is truly electrified today.

Similar rumors are circulating about Radun and Iwje.

People anticipate escapees from all those places.

THE MURDER OF HUNDREDS OF POLES

They say that there were groups of partisans near Święciany who attacked several places. Recently, the (Polish) Vilna newspaper reports that the partisans murdered a lieutenant and two members of his escort. According to an investigation, this was done by Bolsheviks and radical Polish and Russian elements. Extensive measures were taken. And the next morning, about 400 Poles were executed there.

MAY 22 [1942]

THE RUMORS ARE TRUE!

Yesterday Vilna was shaken by two events. Twenty-three people came to the ghetto from Woronów. At the same time, there also arrived a few dozen letters and answers to questions about relatives of several Vilna inhabitants.

We shall write separately about what those from Woronów tell. Here, a few remarks about the arriving mail.

Dozens of letters, sent from Vilna with questions about relatives came back with the answer: "Killed on May 8."

On scraps of paper, I read in Polish: "Sick in his leg (shot)."

[*The rest of the page, about 15 lines, is damaged. We present here all the legible text.*]

[A] Polish letter comes back with the answer in Russian: "Killed on May 8."

[Another] answer: "All killed on May 8."

[I] read another answer:

> [My] Elye!
>
> [At] last we can send you a few words. My family and I [are] alive for the time being. But they are about to send us [off] to Lithuania [Lida?]. I beg you if we can move to [Vilna], we shall look for a chance to come, etc.

The letter is addressed to Elye of Eyshishok, who lived at Niemiecka St. 37, a for[mer] sewing-machine operator.

[Sim]ilar letters have come from Widze, Lida, and Oszmiana.

18,000 JEWS IN CRACOW

The *Baltic Newspaper in Estonia,* published in Riga on May 17, says that in 1933, Cracow numbered 500 Germans. Today, they triumph, Cracow already numbers 24,800 Germans. Moreover, "In the framework of the development of the German city of Cracow, the Jewish Question is also completely solved. A Jewish district, numbering 18,000 Jews, was set up on the other side of the Vistula [River]."

As we see, instead of 65,000 Jews in Cracow, indicated by the statistics of 1931, only 18,000 Jews remain. . . .

MAY 25 [1942][107]

POLES ARE TAKEN OUT

What the Vilna Ghetto experienced in November and December, the Vilna Poles are experiencing now. For a few days now, whole districts there have been closed, and the dead and the living are taken off. The arrested groups are taken to Łukiszki Prison. Larger groups are seen being taken to Ponar. . . .

On the 23rd of this month, a raid was carried out on Zarzecze, Zwie[rzyniec . . .]

A Dead Officer
More about the Murder of Poles

May 26 [1942]

With the Slaughtering Knife in Hand
Men Should Be Replaced by Women

. . . Recently to work outside the ghetto.

TWO SHOLEM ALEICHEM LETTERS[108]

A few days ago, an Attorney Uciechowski came to me and said he had three letters from Sholem Aleichem and . . . he proposed that I buy them from him.

The investigation proved that those letters were authentic. On the inquiry of the Judenrat, I suggested paying 3,000 rubles for the letters. My proposal was accepted, and today I obtained the three Sholem Aleichem letters from the Judenrat.

The letters were placed in the ghetto archive.

This is, I believe, the first sociocultural act of our local Judenrat.

The letters were written in Russian in 1914 and come from Petersburg, from the Hotel "Astoria" there, and are addressed to A. Leprovski [?] in Vilna.[109]

107. This is the heading given in Kruk's table of contents. In the Yiddish edition, "January 25" is given by mistake.

108. The Yiddish edition reads "Three Letters," but Kruk's table of contents clearly says "Two Letters." See the next footnote.

109. The letters were written during Sholem Aleichem's last trip to Russia (see Sholem Aleichem 1926:122). Very few of his letters from that trip are preserved: among the many letters in

FROM PONAR, CLOTHING IS SOLD AGAIN . . .

People say that from the recent mass raids of Polish inhabitants, a great many were taken to Ponar.

Now they say that clothing is being sold in Ponar.

The wheel turns. A few months ago, they said the same thing about Jewish martyrs; now it is the slaughter of non-Jews.

MAY 27 [1942]

YIVO CONQUERORS

Back in 1941, precisely on June 28, on the main entrance of YIVO, instead of a world map titled "YIVO and Its Connections in the World," which had hung there, the Germans painted a German eagle with an inscription:

"Deutschland wird leben und deshalb wird Deutschland siegen."[110]

Here, on the YIVO facade, it seems it will indeed triumph. . . .

Meanwhile, we learn new things every day. For example, we found out that instead of 12,000 volumes of newspapers and periodicals, about 200 remain. Of 110 paintings of various sizes, 20 remain. Of 402 portfolios of folklore, just a few. Of [. . .] portfolios of material of Y. L. Cahan's archive, 2 are left, etc.

So this is a genteel job. Essentially a purely cultural work under the aegis of the Jewish Scientific Institute. . . .

My offices in the ghetto have revived. Another carload of furniture was brought from YIVO; my offices are again filled with cabinets, bookcases, paintings, etc.

MAY 28 [1942]

AIRPLANES . . .

Yesterday evening Vilna was roused. Again a lot of airplanes flew by here, again they dropped rockets on the city, and again people say that four bombs were dropped on Antokol, near the barracks, and that there was even one victim there.

---

the *Sholem-Aleykhem-bukh* (almost 300), there are only 2 from that trip. During that trip, Sholem Aleichem also visited Vilna and did indeed stay with Attorney Uciechowski. Among the letters from Sholem Aleichem that were published for the first time in *Filologishe shriftn* 3, 1929:153–172, 2 letters (nos. 12 and 14, both from April 21, 1914) mention Attorney Uciechowski. The postscript to letter number 12 says: "Send through the same fellow all my works (the big ones), bound if possible, to me at my lodgings where I'm staying—Uciechowski, Yosef, 4th floor." Letter 14 is written on a sheet with the letterhead of the attorney's firm. The letters are written to the Warsaw publisher Yankev Lidski.

110. "Germany will live and therefore Germany will win."

It is also typical that Vilna didn't raise any obstacle to those pilots, who calmly flew over the city . . .

A CONTEMPORARY GHETTO CURSE

In the ghetto they curse:

"May you live to be buried in a Jewish grave. . . ."

CHILDREN IN THE GHETTO

Concerning the problem of trying to use the maximum forces in the ghetto, children have recently been drawn into the work force.

Children are employed as assistants to preserve order and cleanliness, to implement the blackout in the houses, etc. This element has really thrown itself into active work. But a demoralizing element has also crept in—some of them run to denounce people to the police. The children have thus learned to be denouncers. The Department of Child [Care] has intervened in the issue and will now take over the supervision of the children. Meanwhile, the police have won them over. The children are given ribbons with ranks from the police. They are assembled in the courtyard of Strashun 6, lined up like soldiers in a triangle—and before the commander comes to review, the children are drilled in how to greet him.

As soon as the commander appears, they shout in chorus: "Good morning, Mr. Commander."

The commander, the simple, primitive man with his military character, smiles, is satisfied.

Thus militarism intrudes into all corners of our filthy ghetto life. . . .

MAY 29 [1942]

JEWS AND JEWRY

The second evening in Gens's "political salon" was devoted to the subject of Jews and Jewry. The evening took place without my presence. This time I decided not to go. My presence there is superfluous for two reasons. First, the gathering of dubious elements, and second, you cannot speak what you think, and just speaking makes no sense. I considered it more suitable to stay home.

WEISS INSTEAD OF HERING

Recently, the famous German patron of the ghetto—Hering (we have written about him a few times)—has left for the front. In his place, a hero we know from October–December, the German [Martin] Weiss, has come back.[111] This is the

111. One of the most bloodthirsty sadists, responsible for the death of hundreds of thousands. He was the "chief" of Ponar. The YIVO Archive contains an eyewitness account of 31 pages by Bebe Epstein, "On the Accusation of Martin Weiss."

one who once calmly took a girl to the gate of Rudnicka 17 and shot her right there.

This is the one who is now in place of Hering.

WEISS'S FIRST APPEARANCE—A "SPEECH"

After the recent events in Lida and Woronów, a few dozen Jews from those two places escaped and came to our ghetto. The Jewish police thought it necessary to legalize them here, and Weiss demanded to see them. Yesterday there was a gathering of about 30 people. Weiss looked at their hands and decided they were laborers. He then gave them a short "speech":

"Twice you've saved yourselves from death and this time too, I give you life. . . . But you must work and work hard, because . . . " Here he broke off in the middle.

Work, that is, or. . . . And because of that "or" our blood freezes.

This is our reality!

ONE MORE APPEARANCE BY WEISS

Yesterday morning, an employee of the ghetto Labor Office, an M. Stupel, went out into the street. A drunken German stopped him and ordered him to show him where the Jews hid their weapons. As a result, Stupel was severely beaten in the middle of the street, and only the gate guard of the Jewish police, led by Weiss, rescued him and brought him back to the ghetto.

Stupel can thank God . . .

MAY 31 [1942]

HEAD TAX

We complain that we are "leprous" (as it says on the entrance gate to the ghetto). But it seems that, in many cases, we are not only not separated but are even considered equal.

For example, all Aryan inhabitants pay a head tax, and now, just like everybody else, the Judenrat also received an order—head tax from every Jew.

The tax must be paid: men from 18 to 20 years and from 50 to 60, 10 Marks; men from 20 to 50, 15 Marks. Women: from 18 to 20 years and from 40 to 60 years, 8 Marks; from 20 to 40 years, 10 Marks. So it is cheaper for women. This is even better "calculated" for persons who are unable to work. The tax for such people is reduced by 40 to 60 percent. Every child below the age of 16 gets a discount of 15 percent of the normal tax rate. So despite the boycott on bearing children in the ghetto, people nevertheless also have to pay taxes for children. Thus we are made equal to the Aryan population.

When you need a thief, you take him down from the gallows. It is a repeat of the history of the Middle Ages: for paying—yes; for the rights of citizens—no.

JUNE 2 [1942]

A LEAFLET IN HONOR OF THE FALLEN

Concerning the sad events in Lida, Woronów, and other places, the committee of the B[und] decided to post leaflets in the ghetto in honor of those thousands of victims. So yesterday a leaflet was posted all over the ghetto.

The leaflet said:

"HONOR THE FALLEN"

The leaflet had a black border, like a death announcement.

That leaflet stimulated a lot of comment in the ghetto.

FOUR POLICEMEN ARE "SITTING"[112]

Four Jewish policemen are now in jail for not protecting the streets properly and for allowing those leaflets to be posted.

Aside from that, the authors of the leaflet consider that they have settled an account with the commander who once threatened that if leaflets appeared in the ghetto, he would send them to Ponar. The authors and the masses in the ghetto are waiting for that!

JUNE 3 [1942]

MURDERED IN A ROBBERY

For the second time since we entered the ghetto, a murderous robbery has occurred. This time, the murderers were members of the underworld.

[Page 390 of the diary is badly damaged. We present here the remaining parts of lines, augmented from the typescript from Israel, and with bracketed additions from the editor of the Yiddish edition.]

The murdered man was the yeshiva student Yosef [Gerstein. . . .] The murderers promised him to sell gro[ceries for a very ch]eap price. Gerstein saw that one can [. . .] a sum of money, and for that he prepared [. . .] rubles. This morning he went out to [work as usual and did not] come back. At about 7 in the evening, when his relatives [went] to the Jewish police, it turned out [he was lying] murdered in a cellar. It was soon clear [that the murderers] were indeed the

112. The original Yiddish says *sheven,* a slang word derived from the Hebrew *yoshev* (sits), i.e, "serves time in jail."

underworld characters. The murder [of the yeshiva student natu]rally made an enormous impression. To the place, a cellar at Szawelska 1, soon came the [chairman of the Juden]rat, the police chief, the inves[tigating judge . . .] and others. They were led off in chains [. . .]

More details tomorrow.

■ ■ ■ ■ ■ ■ ■

JUNE 4 [1942]

THE MURDER IN THE GHETTO — A SHERLOCK HOLMES STORY

Early this morning the ghetto was ter[rified when people] found out about the further course of yes[terday's murder. . . .] Truly a Sherlock Holmes story:

The murderers of Yosef Gerstein [. . .] as many as five murderers (Yankl Polikański, [Yitskhok and Elye, the brothers] Gejwusz, Hirsh Wituchowski, and Leyb Grodzenski). [It turned out that the] murderers not only killed G[erstein but they are the heroes] of another murder they [carried out to rob] Hertsl Lides, and they [killed him and buried him in a ce]llar at Strashun 9.

The ghetto court sen[tenced the murderers to death] by hanging. The sentence [was carried out . . .] by Jewish policemen [in the presence of Comman]dant Gens.

The night before [the execution Gens told everyone in] Yiddish:

[*The rest of the page, with the first words of Gens's speech, is torn off. On another page, which does not belong to the diary but which seems to be a special description of the execution written by Kruk, we found the aforementioned speech, which we present here.*]

> Police, Judenrat,
>
> Of 75 thousand Vilna Jews, 16 [thousand] remain. These 16 must be good, honest, and hard-working people. Anyone who is not will end the same way as those who were sentenced today. We will punish every such case and will even kill with our own hands.
>
> Today we carry out an execution of six Jewish murderers who killed Jews. The sentence will be carried out by the Jewish police, who protect the ghetto and will go on protecting it. The police will carry out the sentence as its duty.
>
> We begin!

Soon after, the police did indeed begin the execution. A few policemen surrounded each of the guilty men. The condemned men were extraordinarily calm. All of them climbed onto the hanging benches with majestic calm.

Hanged along with the five murderers was Yankl Avidon, who was accused of stabbing a Jewish policeman in the line of duty.

The execution took place on Jatkowa Street in the courtyard of the former meat market. The gallows were six former meat hooks.

In the surrounding streets of the ghetto, thousands of Jews waited for the sentence to be carried out, and thousands more breathed a sigh of relief on hearing that the six condemned men were no longer alive and that everything went peacefully. The reason for this is the sad result of a similar case in Lida, when those sentenced to prison began "squealing" with no rhyme or reason, thinking they could save themselves that way.

For an entire day, the ghetto lived under the shadow of that case of murder, considering it a great social disgrace that in these ghetto conditions, such a sophisticated murder among ghetto Jews could take place.

A few Jewish inhabitants of the ghetto appealed this morning to the chief of police, asking him to let them be the hangmen. The first was the leader of the gate guard, Levas. Another Jew brought ropes and asked to use them for the hanging. So great is the bitterness against the murderers and so great is the instinct to cleanse ourselves of the social and historical disgrace.

JUNE 5 [1942]

THE GHETTO CALMED DOWN

As if nothing had happened. As if no great and tragic event had happened in our ghetto. All by itself and on its own initiative, the Jewish police hanged six Jews. The ghetto accepted the news very calmly and, to some extent, was grateful for the sentence.

There was the same feeling about the delayed sentence of Yankl Avidon, the murderer of a Jewish policeman.

Today at noon, posters were put up in the ghetto with the following announcement about carrying out the death sentence of the six murderers:

[*The announcement is not attached to the diary but is in the YIVO Archive (Kaczerginski-Sutzkever Collection, no. 57). We present it here.*]

SENTENCE

Vilna, June 4, 1942

The court of the Vilna Ghetto, in the case against Avidon Yankl, accused in the court of an attempt to murder the policeman Greenfeld Yankl in the Vilna Ghetto, has decided:

To pronounce Avidon Yankl guilty of the attempt to murder the policeman Greenfeld in the fulfillment of his official duty in the month of November 1941 and to punish him with death. The sentence is to be sent at once to the Judenrat for confirmation.

Srolowicz
Chwojnik
Markus

Deul

Notes

[On the other side of the sheet:]

At its meeting of June 4, 1942, the Judenrat decided to confirm the sentence.

Engineer A. Fried (signed in Polish)

G. Yashunski

G. Gukhman (signed in Russian)

S. Milkanowicki

Y. Fishman

ANNOUNCEMENT

On Wednesday, June 3 of this year, at 7:30 in the evening, the criminal division of the ghetto police was informed that at about five that morning, Mr. Yosef Gerstein left his apartment at 11 Rudnicka Street, Apt. 3, and did not return.

In this connection, at night the police arrested the following persons inside and outside the ghetto: Yankl Polikański, the brothers Yitskhok and Elye Gejwusz, Hersh Wituchowski, and Leyb Grodzenski.

After thorough investigation, it was determined that Yankl Polikański, Elye Gejwusz, and Hersh Wituchowski lured the Jew Yosef Gerstein into a cellar at Szawelska 1 to rob him and murdered him in a dreadful way and buried him.

During the thorough investigation, it was also determined that Yankl Polikański, the brothers Elye and Yitskhok Gejwusz, and Leyb Grodzenski had previously in the ghetto, also for robbery, murdered Hertsl Lides in an extremely brutal fashion and buried him in a cellar on Strashun 9.

The ghetto court has issued against the murderers a sentence of death by hanging, which was confirmed by the Judenrat and was carried out on Thursday, June 4 of this year, at 15:00 hours.

Chairman of the Judenrat

Chief of Police

Vilna, Ghetto, June 5, 1942.

[*We present here a few more details about the murder of Yosef Gerstein and about Yankl Avidon, which is also recounted in Chapter 9. The information comes from Yosef Fuchsman and Henryk Zagajski, who were both in the Vilna Ghetto. Fuchsman was a close friend of Yosef Gerstein and was the first to notice that Gerstein was missing. He discovered the murder and was rewarded by the leaders of the ghetto with 5,000 rubles and a formal commendation by the police. Zagajski was a commissar of the ghetto police. Both later became partisans and eventually lived in New York.*

In the Vilna Ghetto, Yosef Gerstein was known as Yosl Bialystoker. He belonged to the group of Musernikes, *who were refugees in the Vilna Ghetto. The Musernikes studied a "daily page" in the Jogiches Prayer House at Szawelska Street 1. For some reason, the chairman of the Judenrat ordered the prayer house closed. The Musernikes resisted; Yosef Gerstein was one of the most passionate opponents, and in the ensuing fight with the police he was wounded and his clothes were torn off. As a result of this serious conflict, the ghetto police revoked his yellow permit.*

When he did not come home, some people thought that the police had probably arrested him and turned him over to the Germans. As a person with a white permit, he was in constant danger. But Yosef Fuchsman knew about his dealings with underworld people, who had promised to supply him with cheap food for the yeshiva. Yosef Gerstein had collected money for the "trade" from various people. That led to certain suspicions and later to the discovery of the dreadful murder that had been carried out in the cellar of the same prayer house.

Perhaps the murderers knew about Gerstein's conflict with the police and thought that would make it easier to eradicate the traces of their crime. They might even have been the ones who started the rumor that Gerstein had been arrested. As for the police, they did everything to find the murderers, thus clearing themselves of the suspicion that they turned a yeshiva student over to the Germans.

Aside from the previously mentioned five murderers, Yankl Avidon was also sentenced to death for stabbing the Jewish policeman Yankl Greenfeld. The court file of that case (YIVO Archive, Kaczerginski-Sutzkever Collection, no. 339) shows that it *took place in November 1941. This Avidon was also involved in the robbery of the Russian Orthodox priest in Lida (see the entry of March 14, 1942). He also had a hand in the denunciation of the Lida Judenrat, which had helped Vilna Jews settle in the Lida Ghetto. Because of the denunciation, hundreds of Vilna Jews and some members of the Judenrat were killed in Lida. As a result, a decision was made to kill Avidon. His attack on the policeman was still remembered, and even though the policeman remained alive, the Vilna Ghetto Court sentenced him to death and thus eliminated a dangerous character.*]

The inhabitants of the Vilna Ghetto have gotten over the whole story and have gone back to the routine of their daily ghetto lives. . . .

37 JEWS RELEASED FROM PRISON

For the Vilna Ghetto, yesterday was one of the worst nightmarish days, yet it hasn't left the slightest trace; but the glorious event [today], the release of 37 Jews from Łukiszki Prison, was greeted with great applause.

After long negotiations, Commissar Dessler managed to save 37 prisoners, including 12 women, from the dreadful prison. All were jailed there for violating various permitted or forbidden things—for wanting to buy something, for walking without a patch, for being found in a Christian apartment, etc., and so forth.

The prisoners look as if they had been tortured. Sick and starving. The happiness is as great as if the people had come from the other world to freedom. They all return from prison to the ghetto, and here, under the supervision of their liberator, Commander Mr. Dessler, in the Judenrat courtyard, they are given an exceptionally warm welcome by the Judenrat and the chief of police. From there, they are invited to eat in the kitchen on Rudnicka 6. Here, amazing scenes take place:

Judenrat member Fishman brings them a gigantic bouquet of lilacs and distributes them to all those who came. When the ghetto women appear with bread, butter, and tea, they stretch out long, thin, hungry hands, which make the most painful impression. All the onlookers weep. But the prisoners cannot control themselves. They snatch up as much bread as they can; they eat and swallow as if they were doing it for the first time in their lives. . . .

Fried, Dessler, Fishman, and others distribute cigarettes. They [the released] sit surrounded by guests and relatives, and the tales they tell are beyond horror:

Their nourishment in prison consisted of 70 grams of bread and a liter of soup or coffee. Actually, they call it water.

Recently, a group of Jews buried 50 shot Poles in the courtyard of the prison. Why were they shot? They don't know. . . .

Treatment in prison is terrible. So as not to die of hunger, the prisoners took off their last article of clothing and traded it for bread, cigarettes, and other things. Now they are really naked—without shoes, shirts, jackets, or coats.

After they were taken to the bath and after a communal lunch, everybody dispersed in the ghetto, happy and contented. This experience was greeted here with great cheers, and the inhabitants are again reassured that things in the ghetto are stabilized.

THE STORY OF THE SIX HANGED MEN

I decide to expose the whole tangle of the events surrounding the murder of the six in a journalistic narrative. I project doing this as a criminal chronicle.

[*Pages 393–394 of the diary are missing.*]

June 6 [1942]

A Clash Between the Judge and the Chief of Police

June 7 [1942]

From a Report of a Meeting of the Aid Society

June 8 [1942]

An Engineers' Association in the Ghetto

Vilna Ghetto Without Books

Even the Blind Ask for Books

June 9 [1942]]

Social Welfare in the Ghetto

The French Jews, Too, Stand in Line

A Book Sale in the Ghetto

[Page 395 begins near the end of an entry about an institution created in the ghetto and directed by Kruk, apparently the book sale.]

[. . .] and its direction is in the hands of the ghetto librarian, H. Kruk.

AGAIN YIVO AND THE ROSENBERG TASK FORCE

Germans have now come to the YIVO building to carry out a final selection of the books they can use (to take them out! . . .). Seventy percent of the books from the YIVO treasures, along with the books gathered up from the city, were rejected and thrown into the trash as scrap paper. Andersen-Nexø in German and Shevchenko in Russian were thrown in the trash as Jewish creations. . . .

The Jewish workers employed on [the project] are literally weeping. Your heart can break as you watch. The ghetto administration takes pains to obtain discarded books for the ghetto.

THE CARICATURE OF A POLITICAL SALON

We once told about the creation by Mr. Gens of a kind of political salon. It turns out, based on participation in a few evenings, that that initiative was a mockery in the full sense of the word, and it is a waste of the hours spent there.

Such is the cultural level of the remaining cultured inhabitants of Jerusalem of Lithuania. . . .

JUNE 10 [1942]

FESTIVE OPENING OF THE GHETTO RESTAURANT

After much wrangling between the leaders of the Provisions Department and the police, the newly organized ghetto restaurant opened under the patronage of the police cooperative (again police! . . .). This evening, the festive opening of the restaurant took place. Aside from the representatives of various ghetto institutions, the Lithuanian adviser for Jewish affairs in Vilna, Mr. Burakas, was also present at the ceremony yesterday.

The restaurant looks very good. The general equipment, the furniture, utensils, and so forth—all of it, on the background of our ghetto, looks like an illusion.

Speaking of the furniture:

The furniture is decorated with patches, just like the customers who are to come there. The chairs and tables have patches on both sides. On [. . .]

[Pages 396–397 are missing.]

The Ghetto Obtains an Emblem
A Fine Celebration
A Permission That Is Simultaneously a Rescue

June 11 [1942]
Greenery in the Ghetto

June 12 [1942]
Children
Scrap Paper
Women Instead of Men

THE ANNIVERSARY OF THE WAR

The press writes about the great "gains" of Italy with her entrance into the world war. Around the second anniversary of that event, the entire press writes about Italy's great merit and that thanks to Germany's help, Italy has opened a window onto the world (?) and helped bring down the world plutocracy of England-America, along with their partners the Jewish Bolsheviks.

There is not a word about losing influence over the Italian colonies, no word about Abyssinia, most important is a window onto the world. . . .

The German press is also preparing celebrations for the first anniversary of the German-Soviet war. In all probability, there, too, they will seek victories. The only one they can surely celebrate is the victory over the Jews. . . .

JUNE 15 [1942]

CORRUPTION

The Jewish police increasingly take over the life of the ghetto. Recently, many private enterprises have emerged in the ghetto: bakeries, restaurants, teahouses, secondhand shops, all sorts of stands of newspapers, cigarettes. There are in the ghetto a saccharine factory, a seltzer-water factory, etc. Some of these enterprises do extremely well. In contrast, the intelligentsia of the ghetto have been the first to be embraced by hunger. The Jewish police, concerned about the hungry, consider it necessary, when granting licenses, to force the enterprisers to accept some of the hungry as partners. Naturally, in the first place, this leads to corruption, and in the second place, the police do it primarily for their own policemen.

400 PEOPLE FOR WORK IN THE FOREST

On the one hand, the slaughter of Jews; on the other hand, orders to supply Jewish labor forces.

Recently, the district commissar, Murer, ordered 400 Jews from the ghetto for work in the forest. That order is mandatory and urgent. The Judenrat ordered a few hundred male employees taken out and replaced with women. Thus the 400 workers can be provided.

MURER AT THE GATE

Today, at 5 P.M., Murer suddenly drove up to the gate and started examining the workers coming back from the city. Naturally, as always, Murer found a lot of food, delicacies, often in such quantities that really cannot be allowed. Murer got into such a rage he threatened to shoot and [. . .]

[*Pages 399–400 of the diary are missing. The end of the story of Murer's behavior at the gate is probably included in those pages. From the first sentence on page 401, it appears that an agreement was reached with him. From the entry of June 17, we see that Murer demanded 100 men for work as a punishment for smuggling food into the ghetto.*]

A Group of Painters—Young Artists

June 16 [1942]
The Devil of an Aktion
Burakas Visits the Library
43 Privileged Ones
Scholars in the Ghetto
The Quarrel with Murer Is Resolved

Only that the issue should be settled between them. . . .

THE GRAVE OF THE UNKNOWN . . . JEW

At the very end of Strashun Street, next to the fence dividing Strashun Street from Zawalna,[113] a few stones were torn out of the pavement, and flowers were sown, with a flower bed of a star of David in the middle. The ghetto inhabitants have their own humor. That star of David of flowers soon acquired a name in the ghetto: the grave of the unknown . . . Jew.[114]

JEWISH "BANDITS"

During the nervousness about Murer's demands for 100 Jews, there was a dread that he would come to the ghetto prison and take prisoners from there. Hence the head of the prison immediately released twenty of those who were arrested for minor offenses, and only when the danger was past did he summon them back again. . . .

A Jewish prison, Jewish police, and . . . Jewish "bandits."

THE NEWEST MELINA

In the next few days, I shall put into the melina all the artistic and valuable objects my friends and I dragged out of the demolished houses and synagogues during the winter.

The melina is in the center, and it looks like a typical underground alcazar.

113. Known in Lithuanian as Pylimo Street (see Appendix).

114. The joke is based on the slur that Jews did not fight in armies and had no graves of unknown soldiers to serve as national symbols.

JUNE 17 [1942]

THE FIRST 100 FOR FOREST WORK

Of the 400 persons who had to be supplied for forest work, the first group of 100 workers was sent off today.

ALL THE RESTAURANTS IN THE GHETTO ARE CLOSED

Recently there has been a flood of all kinds of restaurants and nightclubs in the ghetto, which are open until late at night. There people would run up bills of thousands and thousands. For those places, various smugglers have brought wine, cognac, and the most expensive foods into the ghetto.

Because of the recent failure at the gate, which made Murer demand 100 men, the Judenrat decided to withdraw the licenses from those places.

AGAIN A RISE IN FOOD PRICES

Recently nobody brings in anything. The gate guard watches and doesn't let anything in. It is no wonder that the cost of all basic food has risen greatly.

JUNE 20 [1942]

AN OPEN MEETING OF THE SCIENTIFIC CIRCLE OF THE LITERARY-ARTISTIC ASSOCIATION [ASSOCIATION OF WRITERS AND ARTISTS]

Today the ghetto experienced a great and beautiful holiday. A few dozen people took part in that celebration: the Judenrat, representatives of organizations, writers, scholars, et al.

The holiday consisted of the first open meeting of the scientific circle of the Literary-Artistic Association [Association of Writers and Artists] in the ghetto.

On the program was a formal introduction and two scholarly lectures, held in the building of the reading room.

The solemn speech in the name of the Literary-Artistic Association [Association of Writers and Artists] was delivered by Herm[an Kruk] (speech attached). Kalman[owicz] then took the floor, and finally two short scientific lectures were read.

[*Kruk's speech is missing.*]

The gathering made a strong impression on all those present.

JUNE 22 [1942]

A YEAR OF THE HITLER-SOVIET WAR

Today it has been a year since we heard the first German-Soviet shots. More precisely, German shots, since the Soviets really didn't manage to . . . shoot.

The bitterness against the Soviets following the "expulsions" of June 14 was dreadful.[115] But the disappointment that here is war and here the Germans are already crawling up our heels was nevertheless so unexpected and so sudden that people really lost their heads.

On June 22, 1941, at 7 in the morning, when we were informed by "female sources"[116] that there was a war between Germany and the Soviet Union, I let it pass through my ears:

"Female sources . . . "

But information soon began arriving that Oszmiana and Lida were bombed before dawn by the Germans. More information soon came that wives of Soviet [officers and functionaries] were loaded on trucks and were fleeing.

No one understood:

Barely a few hours into the war and they were already packing and running away? . . .

At 9 in the morning, the gates [of courtyards] were closed and no one was allowed out. Thousands of trucks were then taken to the railroad with [Russian] women and children.

Thus it was a fact—war between the Germans and the Soviets.

No matter how much we knew that it was supposed to break out at any moment, no matter how much orientation we had in the tense situation, the outbreak of the war struck like a thunderclap on a bright day. The fleeing, which soon became panicky, drove us out of our minds.

At 10:30 in the morning, Vilna was already feeling the first German bombs, and that was enough to change the city's appearance completely: shops were closed and Soviet patriotism was gone, as if wiped off, and the panicky fear of German Fascism crept out.

During the bombardment, at about 11:30 in the morning, Pati and I decided that a B[undist] organization had to be created now. If the Germans march in, God forbid . . .

The same day, I decided to flee.

Where?

115. I.e., the purge the Bolsheviks carried out in Vilna on June 14, 1941, involving the arrests of thousands of Jews, particularly former activists of earlier Jewish parties, notably Bundists and Zionists, along with members of the "Jewish bourgeoisie." A week later, on June 22, the Germans invaded the Soviet Union, and on June 24 they reached Vilna.

116. I.e., gossip.

I shall run toward my [. . .] eastward.

The day and the night passed under a hail of German bombs, and when I was dressed and ready to leave, came information: the Bolsheviks won't allow it. You have to have a special "pedigree." I threw up my hands and gave up.

. . . That is, it was barely two years ago that I ran away from Warsaw to be a refugee in Vilna, and now to be caught like a dog? . . .

Like a dog that jumps out of water, I shook off the whole horror and decided:

To make peace with fate. I'm staying and must risk it all, I shall be socially active. I decide: whatever I am destined to experience, I shall set it down on paper. Vilna will become Fascist. I shall have a picture of how the Germans make a city like Vilna Fascist. The Jews will go through a hard time—I will watch it, experience it, and leave a record of it!

During the whole time of the war, I had not set out to make a diary, now I decide:

I shall set out to write a literary chronicle of the city of Vilna.

Soon I take up the first pieces of paper, start numbering them, and there first emerges an introduction about the tasks of the chronicle, and that if someone finds it without me, they should please deliver it to the circles of Yiddish journalists and writers around the *Naye folkstsaytung* and the editorial staff of *Foroys*.[117]

Does this mean I start writing and cannot live through?

A new pulse began to beat, new thoughts started throbbing in my brain. And around my heart, it became hollow, something tore off:

My wife remains wretched and alone in [. . .] my sister, my brother, the child . . .[118]

It becomes more and more hollow, and I feel the whole personal and social tragedy—a new calvary!

It has now been a year of humiliation history has never seen. Personal and social insults have stopped playing a role in your feelings. Of 76,000 Jews, barely 20,000 remain. Today's Polish newspaper compliments itself on its achievement:

The first year without Jews!

> It is really unbelievable—goes the text—and yet it is true that all the Jews have been eliminated from the city. We don't have them in trade, the offices, institutions, or public places.
>
> And a year ago, there were 70,000 of them, active, moving around, and seen everywhere.

117. *Naye folkstsaytung* was the daily newspaper of the Bund in Poland; *Foroys* was the Bundist literary weekly newspaper. Both were published in Warsaw.

118. Henyo, the son of Kruk's brother Pinkhes Schwartz.

With such joy the Polish newspaper *Goniec codzienny* [Daily express] of June 21, 1942, comes out.

We know very well how all this happened, and we understand that joy dictated by German politicians.

Today a great holiday was declared here, an anniversary of the liberation. The streets are trimmed with banners; all Lithuanian institutions are closed. Several German units aren't working either. There are parades, and Burakas, the adviser on Jewish affairs of the city government, even thought it necessary to order the Judenrat that the ghetto institutions must celebrate.

So we are celebrating our day of liberation! . . .

At 12 o'clock tonight, the bells of all the Vilna churches will announce to the city that the hour of the new year is approaching—a year since Vilna was liberated!

Tens of thousands of Jews have been shot in Ponar. Thousands of Poles have experienced no better fate. Thousands were sent to work every day. Fermentation all around. Young people are running off to the forest; partisan groups are created. There are clashes, assassinations, and acts of vengeance. This is the atmosphere in which Vilna celebrates her dictated holiday of "liberation" and subjugation.

The Jewish population of Vilna and of all Lithuania is annihilated and lies crushed underfoot. But those who remain have hope and are certain of better times, times of a better and greater anniversary than this one today.

Meanwhile, we celebrate it under Burakas's dictate.

MY BOSS, DR. POHL

We have often written of our "Hebraist," Dr. Pohl. When he was here, we apparently did not know his genius. Now, accidentally, I learn from the German *B. Illustrierter Beobachter,* Munich, April 30, 1942, [that] Dr. Pohl is one of those doing *Judenforschung ohne Juden.*[119] Among other things, he is the director of the Hebrew Department of the library for research of the Jewish Question.

I attach the illustrated newspaper with the picture.

[*The newspaper is missing.*]

ONCE MORE ABOUT THE BLOODY ARTICLE ON JEWS ON THE ANNIVERSARY OF THE WAR

We cannot calmly ignore the revolting garbage article about Jews in Vilna. Suffice it to cut it out and attach it to my archive.

[*The clipping is missing.*]

119. "The study of Jews without Jews."

JUNE 22 [1942], AFTER MIDNIGHT

THE BELLS RING MYSTERIOUSLY

Following the order of the committee for celebrating the anniversary of the German-Soviet war, at midnight tonight the bells of all the churches in Vilna started ringing.

It was a horror symphony, a music that chilled the blood. Standing in the courtyard, listening to this night in the ghetto, I felt completely desolate.

It was a reminder of our past year. A movie show of everything we have experienced here. I really felt as if my blood had frozen.

CONSTANT ANNIVERSARIES

After that celebration of the sad anniversary, anniversaries will follow incessantly: a year since their march into the city, a year since we began wearing the patch, since we began walking in the middle of the street, a year of snatching or being snatched, and then a series of provocations: a year since the Judenrat was taken, a year since the provocations on Glezer Street, a year of taking people to the ghetto, and then. . . . Then a new series of anniversaries of Aktions and more Aktions. In short, a year of anniversaries!

But also a year of waiting even more than so far—a year of waiting for the end. . . .

JUNE 24 [1942], LATE AT NIGHT

IN FEAR OF A PROVOCATION

Our ghetto doesn't need much. Every rustle, every abnormal movement of life in the ghetto, is greeted here with trembling and pounding heart. Last night large groups of Lithuanians were transported to the front. As a result, in the evening in the city there were big fights between Lithuanians and Poles. A rumor went through the ghetto that they would get even with the Jews (?).

The Jewish police command first took security measures: reinforced guards were stationed at the fences; in the houses bordering the outside, the house commandants were alerted. In their fear, the house commandants alerted several inhabitants of the houses to be prepared for anything.

The word was enough to keep the inhabitants of some houses from sleeping and they "were prepared." In some of the houses, people even went into the melinas.

It has been a long time since the melinas were visited!

This is how the ghetto lives. Every rustle makes our hearts pound, every loud word [causes] fear, dread, and . . . a reminder of November and December. . . .

In the morning, the whole ghetto was saying that at night there had been attacks by Lithuanians, that. . . . And when people started getting interested in it, it turned out to be something of a false alarm—made up out of whole cloth.

SOMETHING SUSPICIOUS

Concerning what was just said, there is a suspicion in the ghetto that Weiss was in the ghetto at eight last night and that Murer himself was at the gate by six this morning. . . .

Could it be? Why those strange visits? . . .

WHAT DOES THIS MEAN?

At about 10 o'clock tonight, a ghetto gate at Rudnicka 7, leading to Niemiecka and Wielka Streets, was seen burning.

The people on the outside put out the fire. They say that a person was caught, suspected of setting it.

The ghetto police immediately informed the authorities outside the ghetto. In the ghetto, people were ordered to be alert. All these cases bear a suspicion of something that is so far unexplained.

JUNE 26 [1942]

THE GHETTO IS ENLARGED

We have already written that the ghetto might be enlarged. Now I learn that it is about to be realized—the ghetto will be greatly enlarged.

The ghetto inhabitants are happy about the new information—that is, someone is thinking about us, our living conditions are to be expanded; we are to be stabilized. . . .

Everything is measured here from one aspect—safe or not safe.

Go understand what safe means. . . .

ANOTHER 140 PEOPLE FOR FOREST WORK

Today, a second group was taken away—this time 140 people—for forest work.

JUNE 27 [1942]

CORRUPTION AND COARSENESS

We have already told how the Jewish ghetto police corrupt their people and how they wanted to do the same with several employees of the Judenrat. At a meeting, the Judenrat rejected as corruption the proposal to place employees in various enterprises, and decided instead to distinguish 43 employees by assigning them greater bonus rations. According to today's account, such a portion is worth at least 2,800 rubles a month. The salary of an employee comes to . . . 500 rubles.

The professional representation[120] which dealt with the question decided that this distinction in the ghetto is not permissible. The professional representation established that the distribution of food, which the Judenrat has, must be done equally so as not to create any special, privileged groups of officials.

WHENCE CAME THE FOOD DISTRIBUTED AS BONUS RATIONS

That food comes from what is taken from the population—from each person, several decagrams. The special distinction was thus made at the expense of the population.

GENS INVITES AND GENS THROWS OUT

Today all the members of the professional representation received an invitation from the chief asking them to come to him at 6 P.M. Everyone understood that this concerned the issue of the bonus rations, and everyone really expected the cursing out that the chief would give them.

After a delay of half an hour, the chief consented to receive the representation. He stood stiffly, like Napoleon, and announced, more or less: He is the ghetto and he, Gens, is responsible for everything. Anyone who resists will go to the forest (this is a new kind of Siberia . . .). No refusal, and no one has anything to say. In conclusion, he proclaimed: Now you can go. As soon as one of the "representatives" asked permission to ask a question, the chief shouted coarsely, and à la Napoleon:

"No questions, get the hell out!"

They all scattered.

In the ghetto, that statement was like a bombshell. Invited only to be thrown out. Who was invited and who was thrown out? . . . The representation included all the trends in the ghetto, the best and the finest of the ghetto inhabitants, people who came to the chief's home, are in good relations with him, etc.

Everyone considered this a horrible coarseness, a boorish act and soldier-like debauchery.

THE FIRST REACTION

A watchword spread in the ghetto—to boycott the chief: not to greet him, to avoid him, and not to come to him.

This was spread by the B[und] because that was their decision.

Moreover, because that act proved that without the chief's blessing there is

120. Consisting of representatives of all workplaces and institutions in the ghetto, such as schools, theaters, clinics, etc.

no social activity in the ghetto and that nothing can exist in the ghetto without the say-so of the chief, the B[und] decided to withdraw from all existing social institutions, leaving only those who want to go along with what the chief dictates.

JUNE 28 [1942]

THE FIRST SHOT

[*The end of the page is damaged. We present all the remaining parts of the lines, with additions from the editor of the Yiddish edition.*]

[Today] at the meeting of the Aid Society, the committee mem[bers] from the Bund stated that because of the previously mentioned motives concerning [the impossib]ility of carrying on social activity, they were leaving the management [of the] Aid Society and were prepared in the future to help in all their [activ]ity. Such declarations were made by Chwojnik, H[erman] Kr[uk], and [Gutgestalt?].

[The statemen]t impressed the committee members, and it [was . . .] decided to request the three members [to] re[view their de]cision.

[The Bundist representatives on] the Aid Society thus left the instit[ution that] they created.

[*Page 409 of the diary, containing entries from the end of June and the beginning of July 1942, is missing.*]

June 29 [1942]

The Man Refuses the Honor

A Guest in the Ghetto

A Sea of Concerts, a Mountain of Reviews, a Flood of Lectures

July 1, 1942

In Perspective

"We Arrive, We Arrive"

[*Part of Page 410 is badly damaged. We present the remaining parts of the lines, with additions from the editor of the Yiddish edition.*]

In these depressing times, I suddenly heard children [singing]. Are people really singing in the ghetto? Who dares to [sing] here?

[It turns] out that the children building the [sports] field in the ghetto sing. In moments of rest, they gather [. . . and] sing. What do they sing? I don't believe my ears—[the song from the] film of the Medem Sanitarium, "We arrive!" . . .

[In] the ghetto, it sounds like an echo of the past, a piece of [history from] a youth that lived and died for a better [and finer tomorrow].

[*The next entry is completely illegible.*]

July 2 [1942]
A Monument in the Ghetto

EVERYWHERE GEESE [GENS] (ABOUT LITERARY COMPETITIONS) [. . .] already here lately. Gens creates himself [a society] and surrounds himself with various classes and social groups; most important, [he] wants to obtain moral support from everyone active in the ghetto. If it [were not done] with special intentions, it might perhaps be welcomed. But this was calculated to acquire [influence] and thus have an effect.

Recently he has grown interested in the group of writers and artists in the Literary-Artistic Association [Association of Writers and Artists]. All of a sudden, he has become a frequent guest at the literary evenings. Moreover, he wants all the writers to give him their manuscripts so he can make an album of them. Then, he has invited a group of writers to read their works to him.

To the credit of the writer of these lines, it should be said that no matter how much the colleagues tried to talk me into going there to "read," I refused and was not there even once.

On one evening, Gens proposed to give 10 gold rubles (3,000 rubles) for a competition among the writers for the best ghetto work. When the issue reached the meeting of the board of the Association of Writers and Artists, my proposal was accepted not to hold any competitions, but for the board of the literary association to distribute two awards for literary and journalistic achievements in the ghetto. Gens noted the formulation.

WHO IS SINGLED OUT FOR A PRIZE?

At the meeting of the board of the literary association [Association of Writers and Artists] on Monday, July 2, the question of granting two persons an award for literary achievement in the ghetto was discussed. At Kalman[owicz]'s suggestion, the awards were granted to the poet A. Sutzkever for poetry and H. Kr[uk] for underground literary and journalistic achievement in the ghetto.

ANOTHER PROTEST AGAINST GENS'S "GET THE HELL OUT"

When the result of the literary award was announced, H. Kr[uk] took the floor. He gave thanks for the honor, saying that even if such a thing had happened in big Warsaw, it would not have been as festive and as much an honor as it is here for him, a foreigner, a refugee, here in the special and unique circumstances, in one of the most unfortunate ghettos in Poland, and for underground journalistic achievement—he is full of pride and joy that this has happened to him. However, he refuses the gold rubles of the award because they come from leprous hands, from the same hands that, a few days ago, scolded him with the famous "get the hell out."

He is grateful for the award but refuses the money that comes from Gens. At the same time, he announces that just as in the Aid Society and for the same reasons, he rejects future participation in the board of the literary association [Association of Writers and Artists], as vice-chairman. He will not be a fig leaf protecting Gens. He thanks his colleagues for their collaboration and resigns.

Comrade Gut[gestalt] joins Kr[uk], and so does the actor Szadowski. Friend Kalman[owicz] resigns as chairman; without Kr[uk] he does not want to work. The painter Y. Sher announces that he is also with Kr[uk], but he feels the association is collapsing and he does not resign from the board.

Friend Glazman and others try to persuade the colleagues to take back their resignations. The meeting ends with congratulations to colleagues who merited the award.

JULY 4 [1942]

PEOPLE CONGRATULATE ME

The next day is like a holiday for me. Everyone congratulates me for my literary award. Intellectual circles are full of the event. In literary and artistic circles, among the Judenrat and in the regular intelligentsia, my last step of refusing the gold is interpreted especially enthusiastically.

THE B[UND] AND THE GENS INCIDENT

The Gens incident with the professional representation was discussed at the last meeting of the "B[und]." It was decided by a majority of four to two, with one abstention, that:

1. Gens will be personally boycotted;
2. The Bund will resign from the boards of all social institutions, with participation only as simple members;
3. The Bund will issue a protest against the Reds for the ugly statement of teacher Mire Bernstein in the committee of the Aid Society that Fishman took Jews to . . . Ponar;
4. In light of the tense situation and the daring turn in ghetto politics, a conference of representatives of the fives will be called.[121]

All that created a tense mood in the organization among some of the members, who attempted to resist the accepted decisions.

The conference will finally solve the question.

121. Because of the conspiracy in the organization of the Bund in the ghetto, it was divided into "fives"; every five members formed an organizational unit and sent a representative to council meetings. The committee handed down its decisions to the membership through those representatives.

MORE ABOUT THE GENS INCIDENT

The incident is already [known] in the street. Our statement against Gens evokes various comments. The ghetto is on tenterhooks.

Dozens of people come and try to make us change our minds. Among others, the chairman of the Judenrat, Mr. Fried, came to me today and sat for two and a half hours. The Reds want to talk to me, but I avoid all conversation with them until they have purged themselves of the horrible statement of their comrade Bernstein about Fishman.

Today, as usual, I received an invitation from Mr. Gens (as if nothing had happened between us) to have a cup of tea in his apartment. I returned the invitation. Later I learned that all my comrades and some who are not comrades behaved the same way, without any coordination. Now I am told that the Judenrat has decided on several new "bonus" rations for its employees:

1. Members of the Judenrat and police receive full "bonuses";
2. The 43,[122] half "bonuses";
3. Now another 120 quarter "bonuses" are decided;
4. Finally, all the rest receive double bread cards (so-called green cards).

Because of all that, people try to make us change our minds about the refused "bonuses."

In short, because of our group's protest, the Gens incident has assumed a social expression. It is the first passive move against his arbitrariness.

A WOMAN'S EYE IS KNOCKED OUT

The beatings at the gate when people come back from the city do not stop. Not only do they take everything people bring home, often even two eggs in a bag, a half kilo of bread, and similar things, but it is all accompanied by ugly insults and bloody beatings.

Yesterday the following sad act happened here: the elderly Mrs. Trocka was returning from work with her group. At the gate they took a kilo of peas and a piece of bread away from her. Levas beat her severely and knocked out her eye. First Aid took her to the hospital, where Dr. Rucznik operated on her. But unfortunately, she is left without an eye. Levas, the murderer of the gate guard, justified himself by claiming that she must have fallen and struck her eye on the door latch. . . . In short, it cost a human eye. The ghetto is seething with this sad event.

ABOUT THE HORROR OF ŚWIĘCIANY

After May 25, we wrote about the horrible murder of Poles in Święciany. Now an illegal appeal in Polish is in front of me—an open letter to [von] Rentlen, the general commissar of Lithuania, saying that because the Soviet partisans shot three

122. See the entry of June 27.

Germans, as many as 1,500 Poles, peasants, intelligentsia, women, and children were brutally murdered. The murders were carried out by Lithuanian police.

The clandestine Vilna Polish publication, *Polska Ludowa,* no. 1, of June 1942, states that two villages were burned and a similar murder of 45 Poles took place in Olkieniki.

As with the Jews, so with the Christians.

A TYPICAL MESSAGE FROM BIAŁA WAKA

Many Jews work in Biała Waka. The attached letter tells a great deal about the present mood among those Jews in Biała Waka.

[*The letter from Biała Waka is missing.*]

A MESSAGE FROM THE OTHER WORLD

Today a message came from a certain Weines, a young man who was snatched off the streets of Vilna before the ghetto, around August 7, 1941. He was taken to the railroad station and from there to Mołodeczno. Now he is in a labor camp in Suwałki. The message from Weines was brought by a certain Mrs. Świrska, who recently came from there.

Thus we receive another message from the other world from one of those we mourned long ago. Thus the dead are resurrected.

A MESSAGE FROM ŁÓDŹ

Just received a message from Łódź. For us, Łódź is one of those cities from which you can obtain almost no information. Of course, the rumors from there are crazy and wild, and according to them, it is already certain that there are no Jews in Łódź.

Now I learn from two young people who were taken out of the Łódź Ghetto in March that Łódź has a ghetto. There is no shooting, and mass executions are unknown. The only thing is, people are taken off to work. They figure that about 10,000 Jews have recently been sent out of Łódź. Now the young people know what it means to be sent out to work. They are dragged around from place to place; they don't know where they are or what they are doing. From time to time, groups are pulled out and disappear, and they assume that they are shot. . . .

Both of the young men escaped from such a group, and after a week of wandering, they were arrested in Vilna [and taken to] Łukiszki and were released from there only two days ago. Here in the ghetto they were clothed, and soon they will be sent to forest work.

JULY 5 [1942]

WHAT HINGST NEEDS THE JEWS FOR . . .

After Murer took the furniture, a new order came from Hingst. An order for several rooms of furniture arrived: a man's room, furnishings for a veranda, he is building beyond Vilna in Wołokumpia, etc.

Yesterday Hingst visited the workshop to see his furniture. He was not pleased there, because it is taking so long, and he commented:

"If you don't make any furniture, why do I need you at all! . . . "

So once again, Hingst made us understand how much he really needs us and how superfluous we are to him. . . .

LASHES FOR NOT WANTING TO GO TO THE FOREST

The fact evoked great bitterness in the ghetto: Dr. Steinman received an order from the chief of the Jewish police to go to the forest for medical work. Dr. Steinman refused. The motives were really not essential, but he categorically and decisively refused.

Gens personally beat him horribly for that. The "operation" on the surgeon Steinman lasted fifteen minutes. One who witnessed it (Commissar Donin of the cooperative) was like a corpse; others could barely keep from passing out. Beaten bloody and flogged until he fainted—this is a step forward for our ghetto dictator.

Just so we're moving forward and not backward! . . .

WHAT DID THE BUND DECIDE ABOUT THE GENS INCIDENT?

As we already know, the B[und] decided to call a special council of delegates concerning the previously mentioned incident. The council was called for Saturday the 3rd, and it was stormy. The conference lasted from 7 at night until 6 the next morning, that is, 11 hours. The one who was most interested in the course of the council was 76-year-old Pati [Kremer]. She did not move from her place the whole time and watched the council.

It was decided to return to the institutions at the next possible opportunity. The reason being not to deny the ghetto our participation.

It was also decided to change the structure of the organization: The membership should be twofold. First, the closest activists; second, passive groups. The committee consists of only five members. Both members of the Judenrat come to the committee only in special cases.

Leyke [Yashunski] and Berl [Widman] were dropped from the new committee. In contrast, those who were against returning to the institutions were elected with the biggest majority. A strange situation emerged in the committee: three members who insisted on resigning from the social institutions and two who were for returning.

THE PAINTER Y. SHER COMPLAINS

There was no place for him to hide, what to do with himself, nothing to eat. So he decided, and like all the Jews of the ghetto, went to work in the street for the SS. That happened months ago.

[Yankev] Sher works in the SS as a painter. He paints fences, signs, boxes, benches. He paints pictures, landscapes, portraits. In short, "Ein Mädchen für Alles."[123]

He complains bitterly and sarcastically: at the time of the Bolsheviks, he had 50 pictures in the exhibition held at City Hall. A German he confessed to went to the exhibition to get the pictures. The answer: all Jewish pictures were destroyed long ago. As a sign of that, the Lithuanian director admitted that the pictures were signed in Yiddish—Y. Sher. The sign is correct, says friend Sher, the pictures really were destroyed. . . .

The German consoled him: when a house burns, you don't think about pictures. But Sher can't think like that.

Sher had many pictures at YIVO. Not one of them remains. All we dragged out of there was a drawing of Leivick's head. Sher was as pleased with that as with the best out of dozens.

Sher paints fences, boards, all sorts of grief and mishaps. Until recently, he brought his oils for landscapes to [work with] the Germans. But recently he "revolted" and announced that he has no paints. The Germans finally "understood" this and helped him obtain oil paints. Sher is content—once again he's gotten a little something to smear. . . .

AN ALBUM FROM THE GHETTO

We are not allowed to photograph. Therefore, on my initiative and under my protection, a council of young artists led by the painter Sher was convened. It was decided that every one of them should start drawing pictures of the ghetto. The result: one works on a series "Holes," the second draws the fences of the ghetto, a third makes pictures of internal life in the ghetto. The group is already working, and the work is progressing, creating interesting drawings, primarily historical documentation.

JULY 9 [1942]

THE DEATH THROES OF YIVO

The death throes of the Jewish Scientific Institute are not only long and slow, but like everything here it dies in a mass grave, along with scores and scores of others.

The library, the documents, the archives are all mixed up in one mess, and following the Germans' order, is segregated as they want, and most important, most

123. "A girl-of-all-trades."

of it is thrown away as scrap. A small part remains where it is, waiting to be transported.

Thus the death throes.

And the mass grave? Until recently we separately selected every collection of books, every library. Now it goes into two groups: Judaica literature and non-Judaica. One of the Germans selects from the one group, and another German from the other group. But from both of them, the mass grave, the "scrap paper," grows bigger every minute.

Seeing that destruction, several staff members picked out a lot of literature and brought it to Mr. Kapral.[124] Just in the past two weeks, he was given documents of the Ukrainian Peoples' Republic; of the Peoples' Ministry for Jewish Affairs; material from the archives of Noah Prylucki, Simon Dubnow, Ber Borokhov. S. Dubnow's work for the Ukrainian chronicle on the second destruction in the Ukraine (1768); a portfolio of materials about Isaac Meir Dick, consisting of a bibliography of his publications and material for his biography; a portfolio of proverbs from various countries and places. And there was an enormous amount of letters:

Letters from Sholem Aleichem and several of his manuscripts. Manuscripts of David Einhorn, David Pinsky, S. L. Citron, materials from Dr. Alfred Landau's linguistic treasure; photographs of the theaters and museums; and letters from Moyshe Kulbak, S. Niger, D. Charney, Chaim Zhitlowsky, Y. Opatoshu, A. Leyeles, Zalmen Reisen, Leon Kobrin, H. Aronson, Moyshe Nadir, Marc Chagall, H. Leivick, Jacob Gordin, Dr. N. Birnbaum, Jakob Fichman, F. [?] Elyashev, Zangwill's letters to B. Gorin, etc., etc.

This is just a fraction of the total that has been delivered here. I have indicated only those items to provide the barest glimpse of what people are trying to save and of how much they are doing.

The risk to their life by taking away any piece of paper is awesome; every scrap of paper endangers your head. Nevertheless, there are idealists who do it easily. At another opportunity, we shall mention these people to record their names for the future.

UNITED JEWISH COMMITTEE TO FIGHT THE OPPRESSION OF JEWS IN GERMANY

During a rummage around among documents, a large number of documents were found already separated and classified in portfolios—this was the Warsaw United Jewish Committee to Fight the Oppression of Jews in Germany (Warsaw, Orła Street 6, apt. 4). . . . The entire portfolio had disappeared out of our hands.

124. I.e., Kruk himself. Before the war, he had used the pseudonym Kapral (i.e., Corporal) in the Bundist press. That pseudonym came from the time he had carried out Bund missions as a soldier in the Polish army (1920).

If important documents might actually be lying in a heap of scrap, why shouldn't these portfolios not "stroll off" among scrap paper? . . . Why do they have to become research material against Jews?

Those documents did not reach their hands.

I attach one of the documents.

[*The document is missing.*]

PROFESSOR STUDNICKI, HIS ROLE ON THE ROSENBERG TASK FORCE, AND THE USE OF HIS ANTISEMITIC BROCHURE

We have written once about the role of Prof. Wacław Studnicki on the Rosenberg Task Force.[125] It turns out that this professor is employed by them in various work and serves them in every possible way. Just now he thinks it necessary to submit his old, unpublished brochure—"The Jews in Historical Lithuania." Among other things, the author mocks the Jews for considering themselves here as a Russian element, and he mimics how the Jews corrupt the Russian language. . . .[126]

I.e., the Rosenberg Task Force did better with Prof. Studnicki than with us, their organizers. . . .

IF THE WOMEN ARE TOO FAT . . .

The police chief of the ghetto wanted a sports field. For this purpose, he pulled down three ruins, put in a few months of work, and finally the ghetto has a sports field (in fact a little square), reminiscent of the good pre-ghetto days.

On the sixteenth of this month, the chief brought Herr Murer to show him the achievement. After looking at the field, Murer went to the bath in the same building. At precisely that time, women were in the bath. Naturally, Murer wasn't embarrassed by that, on the contrary, he was amazed at the naked women and "impressed" by them. In the process, he determined that the Jewish women are too fat. They eat up the men, and they must be sent to work. In the city they will grow thinner. The chief had to play along, smiling.

If you crawl in the mud, you smear your shoes.

A HOPE ESCAPES

(CONCERNING THE FIRST PART OF THE MANUSCRIPT)

Day by day, another hope escapes here. It leaves and goes away. Man grows poorer, more hopeless. Strength escapes. You eat, you drink, and from day to day, you grow weaker, sicker, more nervous—it is the ghetto, and everything is answered there with the same formula—ghetto!

125. The entry about Prof. Wacław Studnicki was probably on one of the missing pages.

126. He quotes a pseudo-Russian sentence, distorted in the Lithuanian Yiddish dialect.

We dreamed of spring. It has come, and with it, all hope has escaped. People had illusions: summer, the big offensive will come, and—that dream runs out between your fingers. It is already July, the . . . Germans push further and further, the Russians retreat. The fort of Sevastopol has fallen, the Crimea is in the hands of the Germans, Voronezh falls, an attack on Kursk advances—one hope after another, one dream after another . . . summer comes to an end and we remain here with a broken trough.

I carried a dream with me: my chronicle—the hashish of my life in the ghetto. I carry it as a mother carries a child, and I think: the harder the experiences, the more precious this chronicle, of more than a thousand pages of woe, pain, and dread. Today the manuscript has 1,012 pages. I have left the first 197 pages, along with some manuscripts, outside the ghetto, hid it in a melina and was sure: we shall survive and then I will come, liberated, and dig it up, bind it, and match it up with the hundreds of additional pages, and it will be the horror document of our hard and painful time. But finally I came to the conviction that it is better to have that first part of my manuscript with me. If it is not with me, at least it is close to me. Moreover, let three copies of it be made and it will be safer as a whole. If any one disappears, the others will remain. For going into an old flat [in the city], you are threatened with a bullet in your head. I take advantage of the permission to search for books and manuscripts. I go away to my melina and . . . my dream runs away: the whole house is hollow, empty. The attic, where the manuscript should have been, is open, as the doors of all the apartments here are open. The attic and nooks and hiding places are plowed up, turned up, and thrown about. My melina has disappeared. Searched, dug, scratched in dung, in dust—the bird has flown away. . . .

I come out trembling. My head is delirious, my feet don't carry me, and I see myself walk trembling . . . on the sidewalk. I quickly go into the middle of the street and am carried along with my pain, which is still not past—I have been orphaned. The manuscript is missing from June 23 to. . . . A piece of the chronicle that can't be reconstructed: the period of the "Snatchers" and the first period of Fascism.[127]

In my heart there remains a rip, a rip as after a lost closeness, a piece of a dreadful time—"Snatchers." . . .

THE GHETTO WILL BE ENLARGED AFTER ALL

The ghetto will be enlarged after all. The rumors about that have come true. In the next days it will be a fact. We are acquiring an area to settle 2,000 ghetto inhabitants.

127. Kruk later found the lost part of the manuscript. When and how this happened is not known.

THE GHETTO ACQUIRES A . . . BEACH

People talk about it and laugh—a beach. But that, too, is a reality. The ghetto is awarded a beach on the Wilija.[128] A few hundred Jews will be taken there to swim and lie in the sun.

The beach is a beach. The main thing is the trace of a little bit of hope that meanwhile perhaps we are safe.

128. The beach was near Zakret Forest, outside the ghetto. As told by Mowszowicz (1947), parents were afraid that the beach was a German trick to lure the children out of the ghetto. Trips to the beach lasted only for the summer of 1942. In the summer of 1943, people no longer went to the beach (Dworzecki 1948:211).

CHAPTER 5
PUTSCH IN THE GHETTO
JULY 11, 1942 - OCTOBER 28, 1942

JULY 11 [1942]

THE PUTSCH IN THE GHETTO

Yesterday afternoon Murer drove up to the ghetto and proclaimed that he is coming with Hingst at 11 this morning and they demand that the entire Judenrat, along with the chief, be on the spot.

This morning the ghetto was cleaned and scrubbed. At the designated time, the "guests" came. They entered the workshops where they are finishing furniture for Hingst and again ordered the members of the Judenrat to gather. The Judenrat assembled in Mr. Fried's room. Soon Hingst, Murer, Burakas, and one more person came in. The Judenrat and Gens stood in a row, and Murer asked that Gens's deputy be called in. The latter [Gens] called in . . . Dessler, who had been waiting in the corridor.

Hingst sat down, and Murer tore open a sealed letter and read out that whereas the Vilna Einsatzstelle Work Unit executes important work, and whereas the Judenrat does not always act fast but makes the work dependent on meetings and votes, the Judenrat is to be dissolved, and in its place Mr. Gens is to be appointed head of the ghetto. His deputy for administrative matters will be Mr. Fried; for police matters, Dessler. Read out and gone.

Meanwhile, the Judenrat building was occupied by police. No one was allowed in or out. Five policemen were lined up at the door of Mr. Fried's office. The guard was so strict that the first-floor staff were not allowed on the second floor. Finally, at about 12:30, what had happened became clear.

The news spread through the ghetto like lightning, making a depressing impact:

The emperor has no clothes! [?] . . .

Our retreat from communal activity has once again been proved justified today—there is now no place for communal activity in the ghetto.

Two hours later, Mr. Glazman told me he is leaving the police because you can't serve two gods. . . .

Clear, open words.

The meeting with Gens and the Judenrat took place at 4 in the afternoon. Gens has three deputies. The third is . . . Brojdo.

How is this? Gens replies: I will take care of it.

Gens asks all the members of the dissolved Judenrat if they want to work with him. Gukhman, Jasz[unski], and Fish[man] answer that they are ready to work with him, but only as employees. But Milk[anowicki] declares he is satisfied that events have happened as they have and is ready and willing to. . . .

Decided: at 10 in the morning, Gens will consult with his deputies. At 4 in the afternoon, the continuation of the meeting takes place.

The ghetto is in a turmoil. The putsch is not really a surprise. The only surprise is that Dessler will be the police chief. The police are altogether beside themselves. They bring flowers for his triumph and say openly: "Now we'll show who we are and what we can do. . . ."

In the corridors, they say that the whole thing was managed by Brojdo, Dessler, and especially . . . Dessler's wife. . . . In short, a kingdom with a palace overthrow, now a putsch, and the leadership is taken over by the best of the best. . . .

WHO IS DESSLER?

Dessler is the only child of a rich Jew, a philanthropist. The son is a rich son, spoiled and good-for-nothing, who never associated with anybody and never had any friends. Everyone avoided him like the plague.

In the city, they considered him a dolt—a big, tall, fat, broad-shouldered man, a highwayman type. The only thing in his life is his sudden career in the police. Here he becomes a *Nutzjude* [useful Jew], has the right to walk on the sidewalk, without a patch, to ride a bicycle, and most important, he becomes an associate of the Gestapo and a hero who saves Jews from Łukiszki, etc.

Now this former Vilna good-for-nothing and current Gestapo follower becomes, unselfishly, the chief of the ghetto police.

Jews shrug their shoulders and ask each other: Is it any wonder? . . .

AN EXPLOSION BEYOND PODBRODZIE

Today the German newspaper from Kovno did not arrive. Later we learned:

Beyond Podbrodzie, a few train cars went up in the air. They brought to Vilna the 30 wounded. There must be 70 dead.

They tell of a similar tale beyond Kovno. . . .

ANOTHER MESSAGE FROM THE OTHER WORLD

A brigadier friend of mine tells me that as he was leading his group toward Zwierzyniec today, someone came from the sidewalk and joined the group. It turned out this was a Vilna Jew living on Christian documents who came from Minsk for four or five days. He cannot come into the ghetto and wants to inquire here about several people. He says that a lot of Jews from Vilna and Kovno are working in Minsk. He will report more precisely on this on Monday.

So a new message comes from Vilna and Kovno Jews. We will write more about that later.

OPENING OF THE SPORTS FIELD

For a few weeks, work has been in progress on a sports field in the ghetto. The field is in a courtyard at Strashun 6, where the first Judenrat was located, along with the Burial Department and the Disseminators of the Enlightenment Library. Now the sports field of the ghetto is here.

The past days have been full of events, and only today do I write of the formal opening of the sports field.

The formal delivery of the field to the Sports Department was on Friday, the 10th of this month.

Speeches were made: as donor of the field, Engineer Gukhman spoke in the name of the Technical Department. Gens then spoke, and the one who accepted the field—Milkanowicki—and others.

The field is full of young people, those who helped to build it. There were an honor guard of athletes and a unit of police.

Among the speakers, a girl appeared who expressed gratitude for the sports field and gave flowers to Fried, Gens, . . . [Flora] Romm, and . . . Milkanowicki.

The celebration ended with songs sung by the young workers.[1]

LIBRARY, READING ROOM, BOOKSTORE

In the ghetto, the three institutions of Strashun 6 play the only possible cultural role for all inhabitants. I attach here a treasury report for a half year's activity of these institutions.

[*The report is missing.*]

JULY 12 [1942]

WE AWAIT THE DISTRIBUTION OF PORTFOLIOS

The putsch is completed. Now we wait to see how the "new" administration will establish its weekly activity. We await the distribution of positions and, most important—who will remain outside, who will remain in favor.

The B[und] decided not to oppose, and to accept any proposed administrative work. Yet to treat it only as work of an employee.

The result is already known:

1. The protocol of this celebration is in the YIVO Archive (Kaczerginski-Sutzkever Collection, no. 540).

Really only small changes. The Provisions Department is taken away from Yash[unski], and he gets the Cultural Department. But now the Cultural Department will comprise all branches of culture and art in the ghetto, that is, theater, schools, children's homes, library, archive, Office of Statistics, et al.

Glazman leaves the police and becomes the leader of the Housing Department. Apparently he is already superfluous in the police. . . .

The Labor Office is taken [from] Fish[man], but he does get the supervision of the small workshops. Brojdo takes over the Labor Office.

Gukhman stays only with the Technical [Department] and loses the Housing Department. The Sports Department is taken from Milkanowicki and given to the Cultural Department.

At the court, an appeals court is established.

The result: nobody cries over it, and nobody complains that someone has gone and someone else has come. Now the ghetto moves calmly to the day's order.

JULY 15 [1942]

THEY WILL PURGE . . .

I learn from reliable sources that the new authorities are not staying with the changes they have made so far. People say very seriously that a gradual purge is coming.

Whose turn it is, is not clear. It is obvious only who should be coming, according to how the "government" is going to govern.

[*Gens's announcement about the issue is in the* YIVO *Archive (Kaczerginski-Sutzkever Collection, no.* 11*). In the ghetto, the announcement was popularly known as Gens's Manifesto.*]

JULY 16 [1942]

A NEW VICTIM, SOMEONE SHOT, IN THE GHETTO

This evening, they brought into the ghetto someone who had been shot with three bullets—Yitskhok Portnoy, an employee in the Railroad Ministry.[2]

The man who was shot worked in Nowa Wilejka on the railroad. Today he was sent to the Wilejka Colony to pull up grass, but he used the time to sleep. Just then a railroad guard arrived and noticed Jews on the railroad line. The guard started beating them, and one of them ran away. The patrol shot at him and killed him with three bullets.

This evening the corpse was brought into the ghetto.

2. I.e., a worker in a railroad work unit.

JULY 17 [1942]

THE AKTION OF 84 OLD PEOPLE

Today the ghetto suffered a tremendous shock. At about 6 in the morning, the ghetto was closed off by the Jewish police. Policemen holding lists went around taking old people, the chronically ill, and the crippled. The pretext is that they are being taken to Wołokumpia, to the former TOZ villa. . . .[3]

What is this sudden concern for old people, cripples, and the chronically ill that they are taken out to a boarding house? . . .

There was a dreadful turmoil in the ghetto. Everyone understood that this was really an Aktion like all Aktions, but nevertheless all of those were directed by the Gestapo and carried out by Lithuanians with the participation of the Jewish police, while today—today the Jewish police took the place of all three.

Immediately all the melinas for old people were revived. The most awful scenes took place because they didn't want to give up old people. Some were thus saved, and 84 old people were taken away.

Really to the colony of the former TOZ? That is the only question the ghetto cannot get away from. . . .

JULY 18 [1942]

ECHOES OF YESTERDAY'S AKTION

More precisely, it seems that lonely and helpless old people were taken—74 altogether. [And] 12 from the Old People's Home in the ghetto. In all, then, 86.

The old and sick are "so far" in Pospieszki. A group of police accompanied them, as did Lejzerowicz from the police kitchen, who is to set up a kitchen there. They took along supplies, a kettle—in short, as if they were really to be *erholen* [recovered].

A question mark hangs over the whole ghetto: What kind of sophisticated game is this? . . .

Meanwhile, I discover that more old people will be taken. Perhaps some of them will come back to the ghetto, but some more will still leave the ghetto. . . .

What for?

It is a game for the devil. . . .

3. This is a mistake. The old people were taken not to Wołokumpia but to Pospieszki, a summer place beyond Vilna. There they lived in the TOZ children's colony named after Tsemakh Szabad, until they were taken away to be killed. Wołokumpia was also a summer place, a bit farther than Pospieszki. There might originally have been a rumor that the old people were being taken to Wołokumpia. In the following entries Kruk corrects it to Pospieszki.

THE FATE OF Y. TEPER[4]

I once said that the teacher and Communist activist Y. Teper went off to work and left a rumor that he was shot.

Now I learn from a reliable source that the rumor, unfortunately, was realized.

Once Teper went to the peat bogs in Szumsk (30 km from Vilna), and the rumor that he was not alive came from there. In Szumsk he worked for two months in a collective of five persons, including the member of Young Vilna Shmerke [Kaczerginski], Avrom Pupko (brother of the school activist Khayim Pupko), and others.

On the Sabbath, the eve of Rosh Hashanah of 1941, Teper worked in a tomato field. At 10 in the morning, it was announced from the estate that they had to return from work because Lithuanians were waiting for them. Only four of them, including Teper and Pupko, went; the rest ran away. Later the shepherd said they took their watches, knives, wallets, etc. They were ordered to take a few things, not much, God forbid, because . . . they were going away to work. Only later did it turn out that all the Jews from Szumsk, Kiena, Andrilishok (a Jewish village), and Miedniki were herded together in Wieluciany, where they were shot.

Among them, Y. Teper fell, and with him, the talented young man Avrom Pupko.

TRUTHS THAT SOUND LIKE FAIRY TALES

Fairy tale number 1:

Brigadier Marek has always liked cantorial singing, and, although not religious, he often dropped into synagogue to hear some cantorial singing. It's tasteful, he claims.

For three years now, ever since he has been a refugee, he hasn't thought about cantorial singing. It sings in his head. . . .

He walks with his group from work through one of the Vilna streets and stops with one part of the group to wait for the other part, which is supposed to join them there. He listens and thinks he is dreaming:

Cantorial singing!

Sirota! . . .[5]

He doesn't believe his ears. He asks and everyone confirms: cantorial singing.

Only then does Marek understand that it is really nothing. Whoever seized the apartment here also seized a gramophone with records, and now they are played and there is singing—including Sirota and his prayers. . . .

It sounds like a fairy tale. Vilna, July 1942, Mickiewicz Street, the main street of the city, and Sirota's cantorial singing. Marek can't get over it. An exciting experience. . . .

4. Teacher and director of a Yiddish gymnasium under the Soviets.

5. Gershon Sirota (1874–1943), a famous cantor.

Fairy tale number 2:

In Śnipiszki, somewhere in a garden, an old woman works along with a group of Jews. In the garden is a big villa, and a children's home was opened there. When the children were brought, the old woman suddenly recognized among them her . . . grandson. It did no good to persuade her, the old woman remained steadfast in her claim—it is her grandson.

During the Aktion in the ghetto, she says, her sister-in-law and two children were taken to Ponar and now—the grandson!

The Jewish police investigated, and it turned out it is correct: the child is her grandson. And that grandson is now back in . . . the ghetto. He doesn't understand Yiddish, and you have to talk to him in . . . Lithuanian.

JULY 20 [1942]

CONCERNING THE AKTION OF OLD PEOPLE

The old people are in Pospieszki, and the whole thing remains a riddle to everyone in the ghetto.

For the past two days, the ghetto has been afraid that another Aktion of old people is coming. Old people are sent off and hidden in melinas. Recently, five old women were detained and, as people confirm, were sent to Pospieszki.

Apropos Pospieszki, information from there is good. The old people are divided into several groups, are fed normally, and the ghetto administration takes care of them, as they don't do for the ghetto inhabitants.

A typical feature: various searches were undertaken among the old people. One of these, by the police, produced unexpected results: gold, a mass of gold dollars and gold rubles. . . .

About Pati:

On Friday I received a guarantee from the chief of police that nothing would happen to her. Today two women were sent there, and they brought back, in writing: "Don't touch her."

Others also run to ask for the same thing. They're trembling here about comrade [Froyim] Fein, Mrs. [Ete] Żel[eznikow], Weinstein, Eisin.[6] The last was de-

6. These are names of elderly people, Bundists. It was feared they might be taken during the Aktion of old people. Froyim Fein was one of the oldest school activists in Vilna. His biography, by Hirsz Abramowicz, is in *Teachers' Memorial Book* 1954:332–333. Ete Żeleznikow was the wife of Yankl Zeleznikow, the Bundist activist who was arrested by the NKVD in 1939 and taken to the Soviet Union, where he was killed. Weinstein was the wife of Leybl Weinstein, who was also arrested by the NKVD in 1939 and killed in the Soviet Union. Eisin, one of the older generation of Bundists in Vilna, was also active in the YAF, the Bundist women's organization. All of them were killed in various later Aktions.

tained yesterday and was released only after the intervention of friend Hersh [Gutgestalt].

According to what Gens said in one of his last speeches, the Aktion of old people must and will be carried out to the end. There can be no unproductive and sick elements in the ghetto. . . .

JULY 21 [1942]

RUMORS ABOUT WOMEN AND CHILDREN

There are various rumors here concerning the Aktion of old people. Recently a rumor has been circulating that they are considering taking . . . children, and maybe women too. Gens assures us that there is no basis for this. He has had two women whipped for gossiping.

THE POET BOREKH GELMAN SHOT

Today we learn that the young B[undist] poet Borekh Gelman[7] was shot along with his two brothers in the Byelorussian town of Widze. It happened a year ago, right after the Germans came in. Borekh Gelman was shot with 80 other Jews.

The poet Borekh Gelman was one of the pleiad of the youngest Yiddish poets—a poet who sang of the proletariat and its ideals. Just before the war, he wrote for *Naye Folkstsaytung, Yugnt-veker, Foroys,* and other publications.

Honored be his memory!

PATCHES

[*The following part of the page is badly damaged. We present here all the remaining parts and add conjectures on the missing parts.*]

Today a new order is posted: everyone must wear ye[llow patche]s of cloth and not of leather, tin, [and other materia]ls, as so far.[8] There is a standardized price for patches—three [rubles] apiece. [Anyone who] does not obey will be punished. But the police [. . .] Today a woman worker of my unit pointed out to me [that the police] cut an old patch off her with a piece [of her . . .] coat. . . . Naturally she still has to [pay the set fin]e!

Ghetto Folklore

[*The rest of the page is so badly damaged that it is impossible even to present part of the lines. The entry clearly concerns smuggling food into the ghetto; the food must be hidden in melinas.*]

7. For Borekh Gelman's biography, see *Lexicon* 2:306–307.
8. This order is in the YIVO Archive (Kaczerginski-Sutzkever Collection).

[. . .] *to melinate*—we already know the word. Either hide yourself or hide something.

NEW POSSIBILITIES, NEW PLANS

Mr. Sporket,[9] on the Rosenberg Task Force, has new possibilities. He assembled three trucks of documents and tried to figure them out. The first to exploit it was Kapral. He soon put an expert to work there, and within a few days, he has succeeded in finding several pictures of Hersh, his wife, and his son.[10] He fearfully tore off the inscription that it must be sent to Yoshke. . . .[11]

Everyone admired Kapral. All the things he takes on himself! . . .

Now it becomes apparent that there are new possibilities, not only for Sporket—but, as he promises, new plans for a corporal as well. . . .[12]

JULY 23 [1942]

SECOND AKTION OF OLD PEOPLE

All night the Jewish police carried out another Aktion of old people. Forty-some old people were rounded up, and thirty-some were released immediately. Seven or eight persons remained captured, and a few of them will be released.

Once again, the question hangs over our ghetto: What is this? What will happen to the old people in Pospieszki? How many of them have to go there, if there is a number at all? And most important, Who is the initiator of this? The Germans or the Jewish police itself? . . .

The ghetto has already swallowed it. We get used to everything. . . . But that question hangs like a sword of Damocles. . . .

The Aktion hasn't yet ended. All day today they keep searching for victims for . . . Pospieszki. The old people have melinated themselves and don't let themselves be snatched. It is a human game of cat-and-mouse.

A human game but a sad game! . . .

JULY 24 [1942]

STILL ABOUT OLD PEOPLE

In the ghetto, they're still seething about the Aktion against old people. Today it began with a new act. An old man, Minkov, is in the hospital. He is more than 80 years old.

9. One of the Germans on the Rosenberg Task Force.

10. I.e., Hersh Gutgestalt, his wife, Miriam, and their son Gavriel.

11. Dr. Yosef Lipshitz, chairman of Tsukunft in Poland (later in New York). The inscription probably meant that the picture should be sent to the Central Committee of Tsukunft.

12. "Kapral" and "a corporal" refer to Kruk.

[Parts of the lines are torn off. From what remains, it appears that the old man was to be sent to Pospieszki, to join the old people who had previously been taken, but Dr. Sedlis kept him, and as a result, three doctors and a nurse were arrested. Later, the entry indicates that at sundown, six old people who were ransomed were brought from Pospieszki.]

Meanwhile, I learn that there, in Pospieszki, five of the old people died [recently]. People shrug their shoulders, and each [interprets it] in his own way. . . .

In the Christian Old People's Home, it was suddenly discovered that one of the old people, one Teresa Kochanska, is a convert. Apparently, she was converted at the age of 15. The Christian woman was turned over to the ghetto authorities. And the ghetto . . . [turned her over] to the authorities of Pospieszki.

Thus that old woman is driven out of the Christian Old People's Home to end up in . . . Pospieszki.

JULY 25 [1942]

HINGST IS SATISFIED

Today Hingst visited the ghetto and, naturally, "his workshops," where furniture is made for him. The ghetto breathed with relief: Hingst is satisfied. . . .

BUT THE GHETTO IS NOT SATISFIED

Today a German came into the ghetto with a car and went straight to the hospital. It turned out that he was the commandant of the blackout in Vilna.

Gens went to the hospital, where the following conversation took place between the two of them:

"From the hospital, they're signaling to the Bolshevik pilots."

Gens stated categorically that that was not correct.

This [accusation was made] repeatedly, but Gens maintained his position. Then the German shouted:

"If you say 'not correct' one more time, I'll put you up against the wall and shoot you."

Gens remained steadfast. His behavior made him a hero in the ghetto. But people are generally dissatisfied with the matter. Who knows if this doesn't smell of provocation. Moreover, the enraged German said that if it happens again, he will shoot all the inhabitants of the ghetto with machine guns.

PONAR, AS HE SAW IT HIMSELF

This word doesn't go away. There are homes where people "nourish themselves" on it. Ponar means mentioning the father, in [other homes] it is mother, sisters, a bride, etc.

In some homes people keep on convincing themselves: are they alive, aren't they alive. According to the messages from some people, they figure that they might be alive. According to those who have gone through similar Aktions not only in Vilna, they obviously aren't alive. Nothing to hope for. . . .

Even in December–January (1941–1942), some young men undertook bold steps and went illegally toward Ponar, to see with their own eyes. They say the place is surrounded by a guard, and you are shot for approaching. Some of the men came back with full-blown stories from Christian neighbors who saw and heard everything up close.

It was clear to some of the neighbors that no one came out of there alive. To others, that people were segregated in Ponar and sent off in wagons, and that only some were shot in the woods.

These desperate steps stopped long ago. No one argues about it, and no one wants to convince himself of whether Ponar was death or . . . anything else.

Now I possess a 100-percent-authentic message from Ponar—the message of a Jew who was there, walked around among the mass graves and looked carefully, looked around carefully and brought me relics from there, which I attach here (2 two documents: a booklet from the Polish Health Insurance, number 5539, whose owner was Jakub Lewinson, and an extract from a rabbinical [record]book[13] [*Wyciąg z ksiąg metrycznych,* no. 12, of Rabbi Eliokim Landsman of Nowa Wilejka]). [*The documents are missing.*]

The first visit took place on July 11, 1942; the second, on July 13.

The purpose of the visit?

The purpose of the visit was really quite accidental. The German military unit, where the visitor works, needed lime, and there is lime in Ponar.

How does lime get to Ponar?

In Ponar, of all places, in the very center of events, the Bolsheviks built six underground tank shelters. The Bolsheviks didn't have time to finish that work [before the Germans occupied Vilna], but a lot of building materials remained there, including lime pits. Now a military truck had come for that lime, along with two Jewish workers, one of whom was my informer.

Where is Ponar, and how can it be described?

On the way from Vilna to Grodno, between the 11th and the 12th kilometers, on the side of the Warsaw-Vilna railroad, is a square more than a square kilometer wide.

That square is on the right side of the railroad, surrounded by a barbed-wire fence, about 1.80 to 2 meters high. The tank sites were planned for there, and now the death camp of thousands and perhaps tens of thousands remains there.

The square next to the Vilna-Warsaw railroad is divided by barbed-wire fences into three parts, connected with gates. The executions took place only in one part, which comes out on the Vilna-Grodno highway. In this part of the square there are a few gates. The square is covered by sparse woods and is completely dug with big

13. I.e., a birth certificate.

pits and ditches. The drums of gasoline were to be buried in the pits; one is even built in. The pits are 30–40 meters in diameter and 6 meters deep. There are also smaller ones. Every pit is surrounded by a rampart of dug-up sand. Some of the pits are half filled; others are completely covered with soil. According to the smell, you can orient yourself about what is there. The crows who hover around here in masses are also indications, as are the traces of wolves, the paw prints and the stories of the surrounding peasants. . . . In some places the "guests"—both crows and wolves—have dug up the ground, preying on human "carrion." . . .

When you approach, it becomes clear that it is here:

There are places where parts of human bodies are sticking out, often even whole uncovered corpses. All around are scattered documents, wallets, little mirrors, torn-up money, bullet cartridges, machine-gun bullets, and bullets from automatic pistols.

Now you come on a handkerchief, now some makeup, a shoe, other little things.

Climbing the sand of the pit, you feel under your feet that the ground is loose, that soft objects—human bodies—are underneath. The ground here is as soft as down. You can easily guess that this was the site of mass shootings of humans, and because of the mass nature of the murders, the people were covered with a little sand. The smell here is very sharp and distinct.

[*Page 431 is missing.*]

An Exhibition at YIVO
A Secret about 20 Trucks

[. . .]

[Today] the police chief came in a bad mood; they demand 300 heads from the ghetto . . .

The account?

Two hundred for one crime—for exchanging Jews from the prison—100 for bringing too much food into the ghetto. They started haggling. And they agreed on 80 old people. . . .

The story of this is a special case. But now the 80 old people are obviously being done away with.

An Evening Dedicated to Young Vilna
Why I Am Not Happy

THE YOUNG VILNA EVENING

The evening devoted to Young Vilna[14] was a great success, with more than 200 people in attendance. The evening included an exhibit of drawings, paintings,

14. A group of Yiddish poets, writers, and painters in Vilna. It was one of the most important Yiddish literary groups in the world during the 1930s; it included Abraham Sutzkever, Chaim Grade, and others.

and reproductions of the group of painters, including Bentsye Mikhtom[15] and Rachel Sutzkever;[16] documents of Young Vilna, publications of Young Vilna, etc.

I attach the introductory speech of H. Kr[uk].

[*The speech is missing. It can be found in the* YIVO *Archive (Kaczerginski-Sutzkever Collection, no. 493).*][17]

AN ALARM

Just now there was an alarm. After our return from the Young Vilna evening, airplanes suddenly flew by. Only later did the alarm come. Somewhere from the distance did [. . .]

[*The end of the page is torn off. It included the beginning of the account of the expulsion of the old people from Pospieszki.*]

July 26 [1942]
Soccer
Today—Handball Match "Ghetto"—"Kailis"
The Old People Taken to Ponar

[. . .] it finally happened. This morning a group of 25 Jewish police went to Pospieszki, rounded up all the old people there, 84 of them, and took them out; some were carried out of Pospieszki to the main road. There our notorious hero Weiss was waiting for them with some trucks. Thus the Jewish police turned them over to Weiss and his assistants, Lithuanian military men.

The trucks went off toward Ponar.

The abscess called "old people" has thus burst. The 84 old people were sacrificed.

More detailed information about it when we gather more precise material about this matter.

I learn that on the way to the execution place, two of them died.

ANOTHER LITERARY AWARD

Today the ghetto representative and the chief of police published an announcement about three awards for three literary creations on the subject of ghetto life:

1. Poetry
2. A Short Story
3. A Play

15. An artist who belonged to the painters' group in Young Vilna and illustrated several Hebrew and Yiddish books and textbooks. He was killed in Ponar.

16. A member of the painters' group in Young Vilna and a graduate of the Department of Fine Arts of Vilna University. She was killed during the liquidation of the Vilna Ghetto. For her biography, see Kaczerginski 1947:201–202.

17. The Yiddish edition did reprint Kruk's speech here. Because other missing documents are omitted from the English edition, we have decided not to include this one.

The work can be written in Yiddish or Hebrew and must be delivered by August 25, at 7 in the evening.[18]

JULY 29 [1942]

MORE ABOUT THE 84 OLD PEOPLE

The ghetto swallowed the matter without special pain, used to it. But a strange tension has been created. Everywhere people are convinced that they're preparing an Aktion of children.

All informed circles claim that the issue is just made up by irresponsible people.

Nevertheless, the ghetto lives under a question mark.

SEREBROVICH IN THE GHETTO

Today the ghetto acquired a new guest, our old friend Serebrovich. He came to Vilna from Kovno and apparently is staying here.

What will his role be?

Why does Serebrovich come to Vilna?

Naturally, he will live outside the ghetto and his children will study in public schools. The ghetto already knows all that, but the ghetto does not know his role in . . . Vilna.

JULY 30 [1942]

THE GHETTO IS IN TURMOIL

Two things had an effect here. The ghetto is in turmoil. There is such panic here that it cannot be controlled.

The Aktion of old people and Serebrovich's appearance in the ghetto, combined with the fact that the same hero has already appeared a second time during Aktions and now he is back again, which means that it smells like a purge.

The turmoil has gone so far that women had hysterical attacks; some have fallen ill. It has spread through the ghetto like wildfire. Even stronger was the panic when the ghetto learned that the Jewish police were gathering for something extra.

Later it turned out that the chief of police gathered all policemen and ordered them immediately to arrest all those who spread unfounded rumors. Then he guaranteed on his own head that there was nothing to worry about. Only now

18. The announcement about the competition is in the YIVO Archive (Kaczerginski-Sutzkever Collection, no. 464).

have the panic makers calmed down. The same night two dozen people spent the night in the ghetto prison for . . . spreading unfounded rumors.

AN EXHIBITION AT YIVO

The Rosenberg Task Force is busy. A big exhibition of Jewish books and objects and . . . Bolshevik literature is to be prepared. That is, in this way the idea of Jewish Bolshevism must be realized here. . . .

The sum total is that the Germans must use their Jewish specialists for that. The exhibition is designed so that everything Jewish really is Jewish and none of us need be ashamed of it. Everything Bolshevik is a fine Bolshevik angle with no tones of anti-Bolshevism. Yet the Germans insist that the Jewish workers help with everything here as much as possible.

The wolf is satisfied and the sheep is safe. . . .

[*The following lines on this page are thoroughly erased by Kruk in the original. Perhaps they are presented in another variant on the next page, which is missing, or perhaps Kruk later discovered that the information was incorrect and therefore crossed it out.*]

A MESSAGE FROM PINKHES?[19]

Sutzkever tells me that London broadcast that a conference of journalists took place in London. From America, among others, B. Singer and my brother P. Schwartz were there.[20]

Is this really a message from Pinkhes?

How glad I am, how much it hurts me. . . .

[*Page 435 of the diary is missing.*]

July 31 [1942]

What Is Happening in Warsaw?
The Actor Szadowski in Jail
The Actor Blacher in Jail

MORE ABOUT THE EXHIBITION AT YIVO

We have already talked about the exhibition the Rosenberg Task Force set up at YIVO. Now I want to mention some typical facts:

The whole exhibition was reminiscent of a provincial Jewish philanthropic institution just before the visit from the Joint or something similar.

The Germans only made an effort that, aside from the exhibition, every room

19. In Kruk's table of contents, this item is not mentioned in this place; perhaps it is the same item mentioned four headlines later: "Pinkhes in London."

20. This was a radio message from London, secretly heard. The information that Pinkhes Schwartz was in London was not correct.

should make an impression. To prove they are packing books to send away, they ordered the exhibiting of the empty boxes, with some of them filled with books. In the room where the boxes were, a note was posted: "Transport." Every room had such a sign. In short, everything possible was done to make an "impression." . . .

We shall collect paintings for the exhibition. A picture from a German official publication came into my hands: Prussia 1870. A Jewish [military] company stands in a field; in the middle is a field rabbi, and the German-Jewish soldiers are praying. On top of [the picture] a title:

> DO WE NOT ALL HAVE ONE FATHER?
> HAS NOT ONE GOD CREATED US ALL?[21]

[*The end of page 436 of the original is torn, and pages 437–438, from early August, are missing. In Dworzecki 1948:499 is a note reading "August 3—slaughter in Wołożyn."*]

We Do What We Can
Partisans, Partisans
Pinkhes in London

August 1, 1942
A Year
A Lecture in the Ghetto—Forbidden
Again YIVO
Bare and Naked
A Little Bit of Folklore
A Great Document for Psychological Research
Polish Books
Ghetto Museum

At an order from the ghetto representative and the police chief, a ghetto museum will be organized in the ghetto. Mr. Kruk was appointed chairman of the committee to create the museum. The committee includes: Dr. Feldstein, Z. Kalmanowicz, the artist Y. Sher, the architects Mrs. Romm and Borowski, and Engineer Markus.

21. This description surely refers to the picture portraying a military unit with a cantor during Yom Kippur prayers near Metz in 1870. There were several variations of the picture. One variation is in the office of the YIVO Archive. On top is a line in Hebrew: "Do we not all have one father, did not one God create us all?" and underneath is the German translation. And again in Hebrew: "Yom Kippur services, 1870, in a camp near Metz 1870," with translations into English and German. Under the picture is a poem in German in four stanzas. The picture was published in 1871 by H. Schiele Publishers, New York.

GHETTO COURT

Today the composition of the judges of the Ghetto Civil Court and the Court of Appeals was published. These include Milkanowicki, Chwojnik, Yashunski.[22]

AUGUST 10 [1942]

THIRD SYMPHONY CONCERT IN THE GHETTO

Yesterday the third symphony concert in the ghetto took place in the auditorium of the Ghetto Theater. Once more, the same thing. The ghetto is amazing in all areas. This last concert, conducted by V. Durmashkin (program attached), proves that even in music, the ghetto is not behind. Under ghetto conditions and with the ghetto possibilities, the concert is an achievement of the highest order.

One and a half hours of elevation and forgetting is a great achievement.

[*The program is missing.*]

ONLY GERMAN AND LITHUANIAN BOOKS

Today we were amazed: from now on, in the Vilna public libraries, only German and Lithuanian books will be issued.[23] Witness the excerpt from today's Polish newspaper.

[*In the original, an empty spot is left, but the excerpt is missing.*]

WHAT HAS BECOME OF ROMANIAN JEWS

The German press boasts that Romanian Jewry is shrinking. The former figure of 750,000 has been reduced by about 270,000.

I attach this item, too.

[*The item is missing.*]

A RACE IN THE GHETTO

Recently the ghetto has had a new enterprise. The sports un[it in the] Cultural Department organized [a race] over the streets of the ghetto of three groups with three prizes, for older runners, younger ones, and [. . . for the] first prize was assigned 1 kilo of sugar.

[*Pages 440–442 of the original are missing, from August 11 to August 18, 1942.*]

22. In the YIVO Archive (Kaczerginski-Sutzkever Collection, no. 325a) is Announcement Number 72 of August 6, concerning the composition of the Ghetto Civil Court: Chairman—Yisroel Kaplan; Associates—Solomon Deul, Avrom Notes, Shimen Markus, Nosn Gavenda, and Abrasha Chwojnik. The Court of Appeals: Chairman—Shabse Milkanowicki; Associates—Binyomin Srolowicz, Grisha Yashunski, Daniel Katzenelson; Secretary—Efroimczyk; Assistant Secretary—Ovsey Bobrovski.

23. This reflects the Lithuanian oppression of the Polish population, which constituted more than half the inhabitants of Vilna before the war.

August 12 [1942]
Saved Books
Half a Year of Public Feeding in the Ghetto

August 13 [1942]
Geto-yedies [Ghetto News]
I Prepare to Travel to Three Locations of Forest Workers

August 15 [1942]
They Make Walls around the Ghetto
Again Folklore

August 16 [1942]
Warsaw

August 18 [1942]
Dr. Biber Lives and Works
Warsaw

ALARM

Late at night we had an alarm. Long awaited, but there was nothing to wait for. Not until late at night was I awakened by noise. An enormous number of bombers passed over Vilna. . . .

A SAD CASE

In the forest where several hundred from our ghetto now work, partisans often come and . . . demand various things. At first, the Jewish workers took this as a big deal. There was even a case when the Germans announced that, for having relations with partisans, they would all be shot. The Jewish police gave an order to drive them away, clear them out. But unfortunately, somebody apparently wanted to be a hero, grabbed a Bolshevik soldier, and turned him over to the . . . authorities.

The case made a dreadful impression even on the police. . . .

MY BOSS IN THE GHETTO

I have been sick for a few days. Suddenly I learn that my boss is in the ghetto. I get dressed in a hurry and run. Traffic in the ghetto has already stopped. I learn that he is on Rudnicka, visiting the technical school. But when he catches sight of me, he leaves his retinue, greets me warmly, asks about my health, and tells me right away to go back to bed.

"Our business won't run away, you're sick, go to bed. When you're healthy, we'll talk. . . ."

The authorities in the ghetto were amazed by his relations with a Jew. In this case, to me personally.

Meanwhile, he orders the ghetto to make a big map of Vilna with the location of every prayer house and cultural and social institution in the former Vilna, as well as a map of the Vilna Ghetto. The maps must be provided with monographs.

The chief of the ghetto appealed to me to carry out that work. I agreed.

WHAT HAPPENED IN OSZMIANA?

About 40 km from Vilna is the small town of Oszmiana, which was annexed to Lithuania only this spring. Until recently it was quiet there. Yesterday a train passed through Vilna with Jews who tossed out about 20 letters to those working in the Vilna railroad station. From the letters, it became clear that the Jews come from Oszmiana and are being taken to work in Vievis, a small town 50 km from Vilna.

They write that they don't know where they are being taken. They were sure this was the end. Some ran away. Altogether, some 400 persons were taken. Some are in . . . the hospital; some were not taken because they are wounded. . . .

That means there was an Aktion, that Oszmiana has already been staked out.

AUGUST 19 [1942]

REMNANTS OF THE PERETZ GYMNASIUM (HIGH SCHOOL NO. 15, ZAWALNA 4)

For more than a year, nothing of the Peretz Gymnasium in Vilna has remained. But remnants of its library have survived. Now soldiers stay there, and the classrooms are full of bunks. Jewish workers who serve them couldn't bear this disgrace that Jewish cultural treasures were being destroyed, and on their own started bringing books into the ghetto and giving them to the library. To make sure the books get out of there as fast as possible, I have organized an expedition,[24] and as of today, we have taken out a few hundred books, which, in the current condition of books in the ghetto, is truly a salvation.

Thus has the ghetto inherited the remnants of the richest Jewish gymnasium in Vilna.

[*A "certificate" of the police chief for one policeman and two workers to carry books is in the* YIVO *Archive (Kaczerginski-Sutzkever Collection).*]

AUGUST 21 [1942]

PEOPLE AGAIN RUN FROM LIDA

Rumors come to me that a purge took place in Nowogródek and in Zdzięcioł. The population runs from there, and the Jews also run from Lida.

24. The Peretz Gymnasium was not far from the boundary of the ghetto.

AUGUST 22 [1942]

OPENING OF THE HOME FOR ABANDONED CHILDREN

Today was the opening of a home for abandoned children, which is part of "Yeladim."[25] In the "home" live 38 children who don't have anyone. The guardian of the "home," just like of Yeladim, is the police commandant, Mr. Muszkat.

The Yeladim transport office is on Rudnicka Street, the "home," at Strashun 4. The children from both institutions are called the "Muszkateers" in the ghetto.

HINGST RENEGES . . .

Today, the whole ghetto was on its toes. They said that Hingst would come into the ghetto and he himself would go visit apartments to determine whether people are living densely in the ghetto and if it should be enlarged or not. The whole ghetto "prepared for Passover."[26] People washed, aired, polished, and cleaned. It turned out that Hingst reneged and didn't come. The ghetto residents weren't offended. . . .

OUR "REVIEW" IN THE VILNA GERMAN NEWSPAPER

We have written before about the exhibit made by a group of Jewish workers for the Rosenberg Task Force. On the 20th of this month, an article about it appeared in the Vilna German newspaper. The article, which I attach, is really concerned with the exhibition, but first, the writer settles accounts with the Jews. The Jewish staff of the Task Force laughed heartily about that offense. . . .
[*The article is missing.*]

BULLETIN NO. 74

So far, we haven't said anything. Now it will be recorded. There is a joint daily bulletin of radio information here. No. 74 appeared today.[27]

More precise information at a better opportunity.

25. Dworzecki 1948 contains detailed information about the children's brigades Yeladim (Boys) and Yeladot (Girls). In addition, the YIVO Archive contains a five-page report on Yeladim (Kaczerginski-Sutzkever Collection, no. 393).

26. I.e., did spring cleaning.

27. Kruk doesn't tell anything more about that bulletin, but it might be mentioned on the missing pages. One such bulletin (no. 278, June 29, 1942) is in the YIVO Archive and was published in YIVO-bleter 30:138. As Kruk emphasizes, it was a cooperative bulletin, issued by GPK. (It is not known what those three letters mean. Perhaps General Press Communications or Ghetto Partisan Communications.) Abraham Sutzkever (1946:155) says: "So as not to be cut off from the world, the partisan organization in the ghetto, on Karmelicka 3, installed a secret radio. Every evening, a political bulletin was printed and distributed for the partisans." The bulletin included news from the front and events from around the world.

AUGUST 25 [1942]

ALL THREE DETAINED

A few days ago, Grisha Yashunski, his wife, Leyke, and Simon Palevsky[28] left for a rest. Returning to Vilna, they were accidentally detained by the representative of the district commissar (Vilna district) and were arrested by him. Meanwhile, they're in jail.[29]

A THEATER PERFORMANCE WITH PAINFUL AFTER-EFFECTS

Our ghetto leaders, incidentally not very successful politicians, wanted to make a theater concert not just for Jews but also for Germans and Lithuanians. They invited about 40 Aryans for that purpose. Fifteen minutes before the beginning of the concert, a Gestapo colonel came in and ordered the Jewish police to clear all the Germans out of the hall. The Germans took the hint and took off. The Jews felt whipped.

Now people say that the "ruling people" of the ghetto harmed themselves with that.

Of course, the concert did not take place.

[*The beginning of page 446 is missing.*]

August 27 [1942]

In Bezdany, Too, an Aktion

Warsaw

The Case of Grisha's Arrest

August 28 [1942]

THEY SNATCH FOR WORK

This morning, when the workers of the units were assembled to march out to their workplaces, they were suddenly surrounded by ghetto police, and a few

28. A Bundist activist in the ghetto who became a partisan in the forests. He currently lives in New York and is active in Nusakh Vilne, an organization of Vilna Jews in America.

29. According to Palevsky, the story was that Grisha Yashunski, his wife, Leyke, and Simon Palevsky had indeed gone off for a rest, but they had also been assigned a mission by the ghetto leadership. More precisely, they obtained papers stating they were carrying out a mission. In Zatrocze, not far from Troki, on an estate that had belonged to the Tyszkiewicz counts, was a work camp where agricultural work and peat digging were done. That camp had been created at the beginning of August 1941, and Jews from Vilna had been sent there a month before the ghetto was created. The camp was included in the German agricultural society Ostland. Those employed there included Dr. Abraham Ajzen; Lubocki, a mathematics teacher in the Jewish academic gymnasium; Moyshe Lerer, a YIVO employee; attorney Gutmol; the musician Lichtmacher; and others. The group of three decided to use the "rest" to collect information on the conditions

workers were taken out of every unit. The purpose: there is an order to send 138 workers to the Lithuanian-Klaipeda[30] border, for road work.

The matter was drawn out for a whole day. In the evening, there was an assembly of all brigadiers with the chief of the ghetto, and it was decided: whereas the 138 workers must be supplied and such a number is not yet there, every unit must select a few workers to go. The brigadiers presented lists, and police went through the houses and took people out of their beds.

SEPTEMBER 1, 1942

THREE YEARS OF WAR

Ever since June 23, we have regularly and incessantly "celebrated" anniversaries. The anniversary of having your loved ones "snatched," of all kinds of provocations, evil decrees, etc. Finally, we also celebrate the third anniversary of the outbreak of the war.

Three years ago, we felt the dread of war, but we hadn't yet understood what it could bring. Now we do. If only we didn't!

Why repeat all this? . . .

After three years of slandering the English as good-for-nothings who have lost the war, the local German newspaper writes today: "It cannot be imagined that England would be able to get back *all her lost* positions."

This means she will get them back, but not *all* her lost positions. If so, England is far from being lost.

Further:

A year ago, around August, the Germans regularly complimented themselves that Russia was already crushed, the Red Army collapsed. Nevertheless, the same newspaper now writes that the Soviet Union is the second [most powerful] military power on the European continent after the Germans. . . .

In his appeal today, Hitler called on the people to give their "voluntary sacrifice for the winter." He concludes that he "expects his homeland will do its duty in the fourth winter of the war." . . .

Doesn't it smell once more like a new "voluntary" winter collection of furs?

So we are entering the fourth war year. Stalingrad, Leningrad, Rzhev—all those cities are now involved in bitter battles. Europe is now waiting for a second

---

of the camp in Zatrocze. On the way, they were detained. Their mandates from the ghetto authorities were not recognized, and they were taken to prison in Troki and later to Vievis. Later entries tell of further stages of the arrest.

30. Memel (German) Klaipeda (Lithuanian) is a port and region on the Baltic; it belonged to Lithuania (as an autonomous region) between 1923 and 1939, and then it was annexed by Germany. Thus the work was to be performed on the German border.

front. Japan lost the Solomon Islands, and here, in our area, we are flooded with partisans, who perform miracles. In some places the Germans rule by day, and by night, the partisans.

For us, however, there is one point: if this lasts, it is our end. The only salvation is that the plague should be over as soon as possible. The fourth year will certainly decide this. We just do not know if we will live and if we will survive it.

With such tones, we enter the fourth year of this war.

ALL THREE IN VIEVIS

We begin the fourth year of the war with no good news. Comrades Grisha [Yashunski], Leyke [Yashunski], and Simon [Palevsky] have been transferred today from Troki prison to a work camp in Vievis.

[*Page 448 of the original is missing.*]

September 2 [1942]

An Outline of my Workplaces in the Ghetto
What a Jew Is Not Allowed to Do
A Story of a Little Table in the Ghetto

[. . .] (about the case of Mrs. Anna Pavlovna Vygodska).

Mrs. Anna Pavlovna published a book of memoirs in 19[38] [. . .][31]

The book has an introduction by S. Dubnow and received good reviews at the time. Now, coming into the ghetto, Mrs. Anna Pavlovna has decided to continue writing. But where can you write in the ghetto, since altogether she has here 1.80 meters of space, a corner where she can only sleep, and not even do that properly? She asks her neighbors to let her set up a little table in the anteroom—not really a table, just a shelf, which, if they want, can be hung down and not disturb anybody; and when you want, you can lift the flap to make a little table. But the neighbors won't allow it. The woman roams the streets all day with nothing to do. Finally, a reading room is opened in the ghetto, and Anna Pavlovna revives. But she cannot write because the reading room is always overcrowded. It is small. But she was told to appeal to H. Kr[uk], the manager of the reading room. For three months, the naive old woman looked for Mr. Kr[uk] and once, by accident, caught him in a private apartment, where she told him the history of her hunt for a little table and . . . asked him to let her sit at a separate table. Kr[uk] al-

31. Mrs. Vygodska was one of the most interesting figures in the Yiddish school movement. Although her native language was Russian, she decided to work in the Yiddish schools. During the ghetto period, she was already in her late seventies. She was killed during the liquidation of the Vilna Ghetto in September 1943. For her biography, by Regina Weinreich, see *Teachers' Memorial Book* 1954:144–145. The book Kruk mentions is *The Story of One Life* (in Russian, *Istoriya odnoy zhizni*), published in Riga in 1938.

lowed her, and the woman was suddenly happy. With tears in her eyes, she rejoiced.

Now she sits at her table and writes. The person revives and now feels as if she were born anew.

HOW LITHUANIA WAS FORCED INTO THE SOVIET UNION

On this subject, the entire Lithuanian-German press published a declaration, signed by the Soviet [Lithuanian] premier and Foreign Minister Prof. V. Krėvė-Mickevičius and others. I attach the declaration. What I know is that at the demand of the Gestapo, all the signers had to come to a designated place, where they were required to sign the declaration. When one of the signers (. . .)[32] did not come, he was telephoned and informed that it must be done. Of course, he understood and . . . signed.

[*The declaration is missing.*]

THE FIRST GRADUATION OF THE TECHNICAL SCHOOL IN THE GHETTO

Today an unusually nice celebration took place in the ghetto. Nineteen young people received diplomas for a course in locksmithing and electrical engineering.

Engineer Gukhman opened the graduation celebration of the first Ghetto Polytechnic. He promised that the second class would consist of 60 children. Other speakers were the director of the school, Engineer [Matthias] Schreiber;[33] Gens; and others.

Ghetto youths passed by the table, barefoot, skinny, and tormented. From tomorrow on, they will work in shops as "professionals." In the ghetto, this is called good luck. . . .

SEPTEMBER 4 [1942]

9,000 WORKING PEOPLE FROM THE GHETTO IN THE CITY

I now learn that 9,000 people leave the ghetto every day to work in the city, aside from the groups doing forest work in various places and aside from the few hundred employed in the ghetto.

Except for children, old people, and sick people, the ghetto works very intensively.

32. The parenthesis is in the original, but the name is not written in.

33. A distinguished activist and pedagogue in the technical instruction of Jewish youth and director of the Vilna Yiddish Polytechnic. After the liquidation of the ghetto, he was sent to Klooga, Estonia, where he perished. For a detailed biography, written by Hirsz Abramowicz, see *Teachers' Memorial Book* 1954:432–435.

VILNA IPATINGA

For the anniversary of the Vilna events,[34] I have gotten hold of a photograph of the Ipatinga (Snatchers). The attached picture is of a group that not only "snatched" but also liquidated Jews in Ponar. The leader of the group is the current Gestapo representative in the ghetto, the famous Weiss, who commanded the work at that time.

I attach the picture.

[*The picture is missing.*]

SEPTEMBER 5 [1942]

THREE YEARS

It is three years today since I decided to leave my home, my wife, and all my loved ones. It is three years today since my brother Pinkhes Schwartz left his wife and child and, along with the group of reporters of the Polish Sejm, left Warsaw.

We have gotten out of the habit of speaking about such things from our heart. Our hearts are dried out. Now we speak of such things dryly, dried out as our lives. Enough that we are capable of mentioning that date.

Tomorrow a new anniversary—one year of the ghetto! . . .

WARSAW, MY SISTER

Just got a message from Warsaw. People tell me again that in Warsaw, the Aktion goes on incessantly. Twenty thousand Jews a day are taken out. The Jews are taken toward Malkinia,[35] and there, there . . . they are poisoned with gas.

My party comrades write me in Polish: "Mrs. Torner is with us.[36] She lives where she once lived" (perhaps that means in my flat). "She was deathly ill. We managed to save her. She is with us.—Kwiatek."[37]

What more does the letter say? The printer Comrade [Moyshe] Szklar, the barber Comrade [Moyshe] Goldberg, and many of the rank and file have fallen.[38] Such are our messages—messages from comrades, friends, and loved ones.

[*Page 451, from September 5–6, is missing.*]

34. I.e., the anniversary of the provocation on Glezer Street, at the beginning of September 1941, before the creation of the ghetto.

35. I.e., the Treblinka death camp, not far from the Malkinia railroad station.

36. Kruk's sister had been in Tomaszów Mazowiecki but has now come to the Warsaw Ghetto. See the entry of May 18, 1942.

37. The pseudonym of Abrasha Blum (see the entry for February 16, 1942).

38. They fell in Warsaw on the bloody night of April 17/18, 1942, known in the history of the martyrdom of Warsaw Jews as the Black Night, when the Gestapo took a few dozen persons, mainly those suspected of underground activity, and shot them. Many of them were Bundists. Moyshe Szklar was an activist in the professional organization of typesetters; Moyshe Goldberg, originally from Kałuszyn, was active in Tsukunft. For his biography, see *Generations* 2:437–439.

The Rabbi Won't Allow

September 6
A Joke in the Ghetto
Ost [?] Monies

GRISHA ASKS TO BE RESCUED

About 10 days ago, we told of Grisha [Yashunski]'s case. When he was sent to Vievis, he paid 1,500 rubles for two letters so that the letters would immediately get to the Vilna Ghetto.

Grisha [Yashunski] was released and has been in the ghetto for a week now. Only yesterday did I get the first alarming letter of September 1, which I attach. [*The letter is missing.*]

WORKPLACES IN THE PROVINCES

Quite some time ago, the Vilna Ghetto began sending workers for forest work in the area around Vilna. The population dreaded that and saw it as an evil decree. Now good news comes from there. Groups are coming back and groups are leaving. Such workplaces are in Kernave, Gladtsishok [??], Sorok-Tatary, Wielkie Pole, and other places. In the ghetto now, a special department was set up to deal with those workplaces, directed by a certain Meyer Greenstein, a specialist in forestry. The object of forest work is chopping wood for the ghetto. The ghetto received the right to cut 20,000 meters of wood for its own use. As of today, the ghetto has cut about 2,000.

BATH AND BREAD CARDS[39]

At Rudnicka 7, there is a medical center for children who do not attend any school. These school-age children are examined here and advised about their intellectual and physical development.

The children's clinic on Rudnicka takes care of children up to the age of 7. There are now 1,050 children under their supervision.

The dairy kitchen at Strashun 12 distributes milk, farina, butter, biscuits, macaroni, marmalade, eggs, and sweets to children. The kitchen distributes 900 lunches daily.

There is also a children's home with 65 children, most of them orphans.

39. This heading does not coincide with the item's content. In Kruk's table of contents, the same heading appears here. The YIVO Archive (Kaczerginski-Sutzkever Collection, no. 124) contains an "activity report of the Health Department of the Ghetto Administration, to August 1, 1942." Point one says that without a bath card, no bread card will be given. The subsequent points concern medical help for children and the day care center discussed in Kruk's entry. The same collection (no. 27) also contains the later order of October 10, signed by Gens: "Without a confirmation of a visit to the bath house in September, bread cards for October will not be issued."

A day care center (nursery) has also been set up for 100 children from 1 month to 6 years old. The children will be there from 6 in the morning until 6 in the evening.

GERMAN AND LITHUANIAN PROVOCATIONS

We have already written about the horrible acts against the village population because of parachutists, partisans, etc. It is enough to mention the cases of Święciany, Olkieniki, Głębokie, etc. The partisans increase constantly. The Germans can't manage, and so the most awful provocations take place here. Gestapo agents come at night in civilian clothes and chat with the population; in the morning, they return as Gestapo agents and take anyone who said anything against the Germans. So, for example, a bum came to a village near Ponar and asked for something to eat. Meanwhile, he asked who they hated more, the Germans or the Lithuanians. The answer was: We don't see the Germans; the Lithuanians torture us and are hated. In the morning, a group of Lithuanians drove up, took the man who had complained of the Lithuanians the day before, beat him to death in front of his wife and children, and threw his body in the dung heap. The woman and children were taken to Ponar and shot at the execution place.

SEPTEMBER 8 [1942]

THE GHETTO IS ENLARGED

At last, the ghetto is enlarged by an area of about 4,000 square meters, where about 1,500 persons will be settled. It is at the back parts of the courtyards on Niemiecka Street 21, 23, 25, 27, 29, and 31, Oszmiańska Street, and part of Jatkowa. The gates of Jatkowa and Oszmiańska are moved closer to Niemiecka.

AGAIN THE HISTORY OF THE GHETTO

I was called to the chief of the ghetto to write a history of our ghetto. I refused. Dr. [Tsemakh] Feldstein accepted the job. His history now turns out to be useless. It is again offered to me and again refused. Finally, Fried comes up with a successful plan. I agree to serve on the editorial committee of that "history."

MY STORY "SIX GALLOWS"

[The tale] received more respect in the ghetto among individuals. I told it, and [it] evoked an understandable interest.

The story is written like a criminal literary chronicle of the events about the six men hung in the ghetto.

SEPTEMBER 9 [1942]

GRISHA [YASHUNSKI] IS REBELLIOUS

Yesterday, the chief of the ghetto assembled the Judenrat and a few close friends of Grisha.[40]

Grisha was appointed to the ghetto court. He refused. Unable to convince them to release him from the court, he came up with an argument that offended the chief of the ghetto.

He doesn't want to be a judge because, in a free Poland, he wants to be an attorney. The chief asks him why none of us think of what they will do after the ghetto. Meanwhile, we have one objective—to save ourselves. Moreover, why should only we do the dirty work while others wash their hands of it? . . .

"Their" opinion is that he must be expelled from the group of those who dominate the work in the ghetto. In the exchange of opinions, those who participated twice included Kruk, Dan Gukhman, Milkanowicki, Chwojnik, Fried, Glazman, Gutgestalt.

At 8 this morning, Kruk obtained the decision of the chief that Grisha is to receive a month's vacation without pay and they withdraw his . . . ration.

Thus his enemies used the opportunity to punish him with . . . a month without pay and a ration.

The sentence has annoyed people in the ghetto.

THE GHETTO IS WALLED IN

We have written before that the ghetto will be walled in. Now this is a fact. The passages from Strashun to Zawalna and from Niemiecka to Rudnicka are already walled in.

SEPTEMBER 10 [1942]

ONCE MORE ABOUT THE GRISHA INCIDENT

The ostensibly legal pretext of not paying him his salary and withdrawing his ration, the incident of his not wanting to be a judge in the ghetto court, stirred a lot of comment in the ghetto. Most are on the side of the victim.

Once again, the B[und] has slapped the face of the ghetto dictator. This is completely clear to everyone.

LITHUANIA UNDERGOES A RESHUFFLING

It consists of the following: Kovno will be brought into the Reich. For this purpose, thousands of Germans are coming to Kovno. The Lithuanians are driven out

40. I.e., the representatives of the Bund.

of . . . Kovno to Vilna. Kovno will thus be Germanified, Vilna will be Lithuanified. . . .

COURSES FOR PAINTERS, GLAZIERS, MASONS, BUILDERS, AND CABINETMAKERS

The Labor Office set itself a goal of training specialist workers in various professions. The first graduation will soon take place.

The glazier course is attended by more than 10 persons.

The courses in oven masonry began on the 2nd of the month. They are attended by 20 participants.

In the very near future, a course for builders is to begin. For that, it is first necessary to get the relevant materials. Producing the necessary building materials will be part of that course.

Aside from that, courses for electricians and cabinetmakers are also foreseen.

The director of the courses is Mr. Goldman.

WORK BOOKLETS FOR WOMEN

There is a plan to issue work booklets this September also to women working outside the ghetto.

5,285 WORK BOOKLETS

According to information from the Labor Office, up to the 2nd of this month, 5,285 work booklets have been distributed to the working people of the ghetto, instead of the previous so-called yellow permits, family permits, protection permits.

GALVANIZING UNIT

In the technical workshop, preparations are almost completed with all the necessary equipment for a new galvanizing unit, which is soon to begin work. They will mainly coat with nickel, which is very important for the operation of delicate machinery.

WOOD CARVING IS ENLARGED

Wood carving is expanded because the number of orders has greatly increased.

WOODEN SHOES FOR AUTUMN AND WINTER

In the wooden shoe shop, they have started preparing large numbers of wooden soles so that with the approach of autumn, they can meet the predicted demand for wooden shoes.

HARSH PUNISHMENT FOR DEMOLISHING HOUSES

In the lower court of the ghetto, Shimen Lichtenstein, Yankl Mantwilski, and Khayim Friedenstein were accused of systematically ruining the attic and roof of

Strashun 9. A house inspection uncovered entire beams and other torn-off parts of the building. Testimony revealed that the torn-off beams from the attic were sawed, chopped up, and . . . sold for heating wood.

The roof was so ruined it almost collapsed. Not only were the residents of the house endangered, but so was the community because, as is well known, the whole ghetto is responsible for the buildings remaining intact.

Sh. Lichtenstein and Y. Mantwilski were each sentenced to 6 weeks and Kh. Friedenstein to 1 month in prison. They have already served the sentence and have been sent to the forest.

A COLUMN LEADER IS PUNISHED

Recently, the column leader of a certain unit, Sh. B., was tried in the lower court. He was accused of using his position to obtain money and food from the Jews working outside the ghetto under his leadership. The court sentenced him to 1 month in jail. The punishment was appealed in the upper court.

STRONG INTEREST IN THE READING ROOM

The number of visitors to the reading room is very large. In August, aside from periodicals and newspapers, 4,364 books in various fields were provided to the visitors of the reading room; 27 percent of them were scientific books.

A special department was set up in the reading room for belles lettres of various foreign languages. The reading room is open every day.

MUSIC SCHOOL IN A NEW BUILDING

The music school is moving to Strashun 10 (in the courtyard) in a special hall. There are already 95 students; 82 of them are studying piano. Theoretical studies have been introduced.

THE CHILDREN'S CLUB AND THE YOUTH CLUB

[They] develop from day to day. In the Children's Club, 210 children have already been organized, and in the Youth Club, about 200 older students and working youths. The members are divided into various units, such as: a literary unit, a historical-geographical unit, a sanitation unit, a game unit, a unit for arts and crafts.

ACTIVITY OF THE SCIENTIFIC CIRCLE OF THE LITERARY ASSOCIATION [ASSOCIATION OF WRITERS AND ARTISTS] IN THE GHETTO

[*The bottom corner of page 456 of the original is torn off. We present here the legible parts of the lines with reconstructions by the editor of the Yiddish edition.*]

[A] very important and interesting activity in the framework [of o]ur ghetto life is developed in the five units of the so-called scientific circle. [The following are active]: a unit for mathematics and physics, a unit for che[mistry, a unit for descriptive natural science, a unit for linguistics, and] a unit for philosophy and social sciences. Z. Kalmanowicz is the delegate from the [Association of Writers and Artists. . . .]

[So far] eight general lectures have been held for all units together. Aside from that, systematic lectures for the individual units also take place, e.g., in mathematics and physics, linguistics and philosophy.

A technical laboratory has been created in the chemistry unit, affiliated with the Workshop Department of the ghetto administration.

In the philosophy unit, a course in ethnography, ethnology, and folklore was established. The lessons take place every Saturday at 8 in the evening, at Strashun 12.

SEPTEMBER 12 [1942]

ROSH HASHANAH IN THE GHETTO

Holidays in the ghetto are celebrated in a unique way: it was the same at Passover as it is now.

Today's Rosh Hashanah was quite festive. The whole population confirmed that. People looked for one another to give each other their best wishes. And there is only one wish—to get out of the ghetto.

The chief of the ghetto, Herr Gens, sent the following greeting [to] all institutions and [to] several individuals:

> HAPPY NEW YEAR
>
> I wish all ghetto residents a Happy New Year. I wish everyone health, peace, and a happy future!
>
> Ghetto Leader and Chief of Police
> (signature)
>
> Vilna Ghetto, September 12, 1942
> Rosh Hashanah 5703

The enormous inscription at the exit from the gate was impressive:

> WE WISH ALL JEWS A HAPPY NEW YEAR
> THE GATE GUARD[41]

At noon, the police were all assembled, and the chief, Mr. Gens, and the police chief, Mr. Dessler, spoke and wished them a happy new year.

My friends practically don't let me get through the ghetto. Everyone wishes a good year. Mr. Gens even sent me a personal New Year's greeting note.

41. A photograph of this poster, with the ghetto gate and a few policemen, is reproduced in Korczak 1946:112.

The prayer houses are full of people praying. It is reckoned that about 30 percent didn't go to work today. The ghetto institutions were supposed to work. At the last minute, at 9 this morning, an order came—celebrate! The technical workshops work only partially, as do the workshops of the district commissar.

SEPTEMBER 15 [1942]

THE FATE OF SHER'S PICTURES

We have already told the story of painter [Yankev] Sher's thirty-some paintings, which were once in the Vilna museum. The pictures now suddenly turn up at YIVO, in the building of the Rosenberg Task Force. The pictures were described precisely and may be transferred to . . . Germany. Altogether there are 28 oil paintings, watercolors, and pastels here.

WARSAW AGAIN

Hardly anybody here doubts that dreadful things are taking place in Warsaw. But we look at that somewhat differently: when you stand face to face with danger for a long time, the danger stops being frightening. Fear doesn't increase, on the contrary, it shrinks.

We Vilna Jews have stopped fearing danger, and so, for us, every danger is smaller than small. We talk about the danger of Warsaw. We all feel that Warsaw is dying in blood, and yet we talk about the place as if there were no danger.

Today I have again learned: a Jew from Piotrków tells that 50,000 Jews are left in Warsaw. And he says that at the railroad station in Malkinia, he came upon a train with people from Warsaw. Women, children, and a few men. At the railroad station, he was told that "they" were being taken to be destroyed not far from Malkinia.[42]

Here we think the number is much exaggerated. We are already going [?] on information from letters from eight days ago that 250,000 Jews were taken out of Warsaw. But today a Christian comes who has just returned from Warsaw and tells, short and sweet: only 50,000 are left!

We sit and wait. And have been waiting for six weeks for an answer as to whose fate is at stake.

So, we sit and wait. . . .

ALARM

Late last night, there was another alarm. Late at night, bombers flew by. Today the press says that East Prussia was bombed [by the Russians].

42. I.e., at Treblinka.

STRASHUN LIBRARY

The Strashun Library, which has been transferred from Żydowska Street to one of the buildings of the university, will finally be purged by the Rosenberg Task Force.

Our group also purges the library. Every single day, many many old books, manuscripts, etc., are stolen from there.

Who in fact purges whom, we or the Germans? The game depends on who takes whom first. If we do in the Germans, we are the winners; if they us, we are the losers here. . . .

COURSES IN VOCATIONAL IMPROVEMENT

On the 10th of this month, courses to raise vocational training qualifications began in the ghetto, along with the first graduation of 200 trained house painters.

A PAWNSHOP IN THE GHETTO

A pawnshop is being opened in the ghetto. The pawnshop gives two-week loans on a pawned object.

A DAY CARE CENTER IN THE GHETTO

A day care center will soon be opened in the ghetto. For the time being, the "home" will take only 30 children.

TEAROOM NO. 2

From the 15th of the month, at Szawelska 1, a second tearoom will be opened, where coffee will be sold from 5 to 9 in the morning. The building will be open all day as a resting place.

JAZZ CONCERTS, TOO, IN THE GHETTO

On the 9th of this month, the second jazz concert took place in the ghetto. To our great amazement, both times the hall was sold out.

SEPTEMBER 16 [1942]

WARSAW! . . .

We keep talking about it. People tremble at the thought of Warsaw. Some want to know, and tremble at the truth.

Either 250,000 remain, or 50,000, or the ghetto in Warsaw has already been completely liquidated. Such are the messages.

Your blood freezes in your veins—Warsaw! Your marrow dries up—Warsaw.

My sister, my sisters-in-law. Their children, my brothers-in-law, and hundreds and thousands of friends and comrades—Warsaw!

Now I am reading a card from Warsaw, which is reminiscent of that SOS from Vilna Ghetto 2:

The letter left Warsaw on August 27. Evidently, Ela and Hela left the ghetto to go to the Christian woman who is writing. That means nothing has happened to them. And she hopes nothing will happen to them in the future. Juzia, however, has left Warsaw.[43]

Vilna a year ago: people were running from the ghetto; they were escaping from Vilna; there was liquidation taking place.

How long will it go on? . . .

BLACK CLOUDS

Since the last announcement of the ghetto chief to the brigadiers, a black cloud has once again drenched our ghetto. People walk around with bent heads.

The fourth Lithuanian police precinct, which includes the ghetto, acquired a German commissar, who has taken the ghetto under his observation. The food confiscated yesterday was taken to the precinct. He himself stood at the gate yesterday and today, and watched those coming in. In the street, there were several arrests of Jews. Two dozen are once again in prison. Something is in the air. Black clouds arrive.

Can it be even blacker than it is? . . .

ŠIAULIAI

People here say that a big contribution was levied on the Šiauliai Ghetto. The reason given is that the ghetto Jews and the local Lithuanians have developed an illegal trade.

SEPTEMBER 17 [1942]

UNREST IN KOVNO

Because Kovno Lithuanians were moved to Vilna and Lithuanian peasants of the Kovno district to the Vilna area, since Germans from East Prussia were transferred to Kovno, there was major unrest in Kovno yesterday.

People tell of a demonstration and of deaths.

The Lithuanians distributed an appeal not to leave the land. The slogan: better to die in your home than to give up your own land. . . .

43. The editor of the Yiddish edition could not identify the three persons mentioned.

SEPTEMBER 21, YOM KIPPUR, 1942

It is a year today since the first "purge" and the famous Yom Kippur Aktion. Every nerve still trembles when we think about that Yom Kippur.

This Yom Kippur Eve passed very festively. People wishing one another a good year reached a new height.

Now, with the perspective of a year, I write about it much more easily. In fact, this is a memorial date after a whole series of Aktions that took place then:

At 1:30 in the afternoon, the first "purge" in Ghetto 2, which cost 800 victims. At night was the case of going to the gate of Ghetto 1, in which 2,200 fell victim. After 6:30, the second "purge" in Ghetto 2, with 900 victims. Superficially—according to estimates and accounts—3,900 victims.

This was only a prelude to a whole series of sadder Aktions (October 3 and 4, 16, 21, and 24).

This was how it was a year ago.

This year, preparations were made for Yom Kippur, but only under the impact of last year's events.

The ghetto prepared a great many prayer services. The [high point] was to be the prayers in the theater auditorium. Here, at their own risk, the staff of the Ghetto Theater organized an event—a prayer service in the Ghetto Theater, which soon turned into a Kol Nidre procession.

Here, the cantor of the Great Synagogue, [Yosef] Edelson,[44] prayed, accompanied by a special choir. Entrance was by ticket.

KOL NIDRE

The hall here was beautifully arranged. Full of light. [There was] an improvised Ark of the Covenant with a pulpit. The women's section was on the stage. In the front was an Eastern Wall.

[Who was] at the Eastern Wall? All the police captains, the Judenrat members, and several places bought by Weiskopf, the hero of the ghetto Oberhardt, etc. There you see Levas, Muszkat, etc. The hall is full, and everyone is waiting for the chief, Mr. Gens. He enters. There is a commotion in the hall.

Gens (incidentally, the husband of a Christian woman) puts on a tallis, and it begins.

The cantor sings, the choir, a bass, a young man. A holiday mood [prevails].

After Kol Nidre, [Tsemakh] Feldstein announces that Mr. Gens will speak.

Gens says: Let us begin with a kaddish [prayer of mourning] for those who are gone. We have gone through a hard year; let us pray to God that next year will be easier. We must be hard, disciplined, and industrious.

At the beginning of Gens's speech, a great lament broke out. It was the wind

44. The last Vilna city cantor. Originally from Warsaw, he came to Vilna in 1940. He survived the war and lived in New York. See Stolnitz 1957:58–60.

of Ponar, of death, of the children, women, and men who were torn away. Even Gens was strongly moved.

Yitgadal v'yitkadash sh'mey raba! . . . [45]

WEISS AND YOM KIPPUR

Even Weiss, last year's Yom Kippur murderer, had something to say at this year's Yom Kippur. An order came:

Everyone must go to work! . . .

That was enough to cancel all prayer services: in the ghetto, you can pray from 5 in the morning to 7 and from 4 in the afternoon. Everyone must go to work—this is announced in the name of the chief and the rabbis.

Today, the day of Yom Kippur, the mood in the ghetto is still solemn.

The employees sit in offices, but nobody is working. People wait: maybe one of the Germans will come check.

Not until 4 in the afternoon will the praying begin.

■ ■ ■ ■ ■ ■

SEPTEMBER 23 [1942]

COLLAPSE . . .

This is how it looks far from the front. And how is it close to the front?

In Vilna, German soldiers are executed a few times a week. Recently several deserters escaped through an underground tunnel from Stefańska Prison. Unknown Germans were supposed to have provided them with clothing, documents, etc.

Another case: In the barracks in Werki,[46] a non-commissioned officer, a pilot, was shot for having relations with the other side of the front. A soldier was also shot there for transporting a Jew to the Soviet Union.

It already smells of decaying corpses. It is a collapse.

LITHUANIA IS COLONIZED

In Kovno, a colonization commission—*Ansiedlungsstab*—is already functioning. First, Poles and Russians are sent out of Lithuania, and Germans are settled instead. Second, the businesses of those who have gone to the Soviet Union are taken over. Then Lithuanians are to be transferred to Vilna and the Vilna area.

Thus Lithuania will be Germanized, and Vilna will be Lithuanianized.

GRAIN IS BURNED

People say that the partisans burn the newly cut grain in many places.

45. "Exalted and sanctified be the name of God." This is the first line of the kaddish.
46. A summer place six kilometers from Vilna, famous for its historical buildings.

■ ■ ■ ■ ■ ■

SEPTEMBER 24 [1942]

FOR *RASSENSCHANDE*

Yesterday, Weiss demanded that the ghetto turn over a young woman. Apparently for *Rassenschande* [racial shame].[47]

THE ROSENBERG TASK FORCE "WORKS"

Recently the Rosenberg Task Force employees work with a new energy. Scores of books and documents are brought into the ghetto every day. The guard unit of porters has been much enlarged.

BANNERS IN THE GHETTO

It is the eve of Simhath Torah, and the ghetto is full of Simhath Torah banners.

The bookstore in the ghetto has children's banners, and the children in the ghetto are delighted with that novelty.

■ ■ ■ ■ ■ ■

SEPTEMBER 25 [1942]

SOMETHING HAPPENS AGAIN

Just as in the winter, something tremendous is happening again in the big world. For weeks Stalingrad has been besieged, and for weeks people have been fighting in the streets of Stalingrad. But Stalingrad is solidly in the hands of the Bolsheviks. People say that right now, the Germans have finally been thrown out of the last positions in Stalingrad.

The situation on several other fronts is similar.

And in Germany? The most awful news comes from there. The biggest German cities are blotted out. Whole quarters of cities lie under the ruins of the bombs. People are running away from the cities. Soldiers who go home on leave from our area come back dead and exhausted. They all bring back one refrain: we have lost the war, Germany will not hold out.

Be that as it may—something is surely happening. . . .

TO LIQUIDATE OR NOT TO LIQUIDATE THE KOVNO GHETTO

Vilna has been upset for the past few days by this question. What turned out?

Because of the Germanization of Lithuania, and first of all Kovno, a project originated among the Lithuanians: instead of driving Lithuanians out of Kovno, liquidate the Kovno Ghetto and distribute the ghetto apartments among the Lithuanians who have to leave their flats for the Germans. The Germans an-

47. Sexual relations between an Aryan and a Jew.

swered: this proposal can be accepted, but who will furnish 6,000 Jewish workers a day under the same conditions? The Lithuanian advisers didn't find an answer to that. They had only one piece of "advice": settle the Lithuanians on the site of the Kovno Ghetto and send the Jews away—some to the Vilna Ghetto and some to the Šiauliai Ghetto.[48]

The advisers remained outside. The ghetto in Kovno remains, and the Lithuanians, as German assistants, will have to leave their Lithuanian earth.

GETO-YEDIES AND THE KOVNO GESTAPO

The *Geto-yedies,*[49] which has been appearing for a few weeks, has mysteriously reached Kovno and from there . . . the Vilna Gestapo. Those Gestapo agents are amazed at the "broad autonomy of the Vilna Ghetto."

The matter is true and without exaggeration.

VIRBALIS

Here, in public forced labor, the situation has grown significantly worse. People work hard, don't eat . . . and are beaten unmercifully.

SEPTEMBER 27 [1942]

YANKEV GERSTEIN HAS DIED

The news of his death immediately spread through the ghetto. A delegation of literati, consisting of Kalman[owicz], Kr[uk], Blacher, L. Rudnicka, and Bergolski stood at his bed. The artist Rachel Sutzkever drew him.[50] An hour after his death, a memorial service was held, under the chairmanship of friend Kr[uk], of writers, teachers, a representative of the Cultural Department in the ghetto, and a delegation of graduates and students.

In the street, obituary posters of the literary association [Association of Writers and Artists] and the Teachers' Union were put up.

The selected funeral committee held its meeting at 8 this evening.

The funeral will take place tomorrow, at 4:30 P.M. Gerstein receives a place in the cemetery near the teachers Bastomski and Pludermacher.

48. Vilna, Kovno, and Šiauliai were the only three ghettos that remained in Lithuania at that time.

49. A weekly publication of the ghetto administration, edited by Dr. Tsemakh Feldstein, sometimes with the help of Herman Kruk. The first issue appeared on August 24, 1942. The YIVO Archive contains almost a score of issues of *Geto-yedies*. The last issue in the YIVO Archive is from August 15, 1943 (no. 52), i.e., a month before the liquidation of the ghetto.

50. That drawing is reproduced in Kaczerginski 1947:80–81.

SEPTEMBER 29 [1942]

A DAY OF MOURNING IN THE GHETTO

Yesterday our ghetto experienced a strange day of mourning for the dead teacher, writer, and musician Yankev Gerstein.

Gerstein was part of Jewish Vilna. Hundreds and thousands of students, graduates, former pupils, and current teachers all loved, esteemed, and respected the teacher Gerstein. His death in the impoverished Vilna social scene, which tore one more out of the remaining small group, made an obvious impression among the Jewish intelligentsia, writers, artists, and common people.

According to the decision of the funeral committee, the body of the deceased was to be put out today before dawn in one of the rooms of the hospital.

At 6 in the morning, a few hundred workers filed by there. They came there in closed ranks with their brigadiers, before they marched out to forced labor in the units.

The unit Beutenlager filed by, under the leadership of Mr. [Dovid] Kapłan-Kapłański.[51]

The units of nutrition and others filed by here. Masses streamed all day long [. . .] youth.

[*The end of Page 465 is torn off.*]

[. . .] honor—may the earth lie light upon him.

I attach the poems by A. Sutzkever and Opeskin.[52]

[*The poems are missing.*]

THREE SUKKAHS IN THE GHETTO

The religious Jews of the Vilna Ghetto do not let themselves be deceived. In the ghetto there are three sukkahs, made as God requires, even covered with greens, brought with great efforts from the woods. . . .

GREEN FIELDS FOR THE SEVENTH TIME

The Ghetto Theater has recently produced Hirschbein's *Green Fields.*[53] The show has been performed here seven times.

51. A distinguished social activist, born in Białystok in 1899. He was chairman of the Society of Friends of YIVO in Vilna. In the ghetto, he was the chairman of the Brigadier Council. He was killed in Schömberg Camp on December 6, 1944 (indicated as no. 552 in the list of those killed in the camp). For his biography, see Abramowicz 1958:143–146.

52. A. Sutzkever's poem is published in Sutzkever 1946a:22–23, under the title "On the Death of Yankev Gerstein." Leyb Opeskin's biography was published in *Teachers' Memorial Book* 1954: 21–22. He was killed in July 1944 in the HKP Camp.

53. Peretz Hirschbein (1880–1948) was a major Yiddish playwright.

ANOTHER ASSEMBLY OF BRIGADIERS

As soon as trouble comes, there comes an assembly of brigadiers, as they joke here—an assembly of the workers' and delegates' council. Such an assembly took place recently, on September 28.

The ghetto chief, Mr. Gens, demands: don't walk in the streets in fancy clothes—it attracts our enemies' attention. [He] calls their attention to the fact that women should not use makeup, should not be friendly with Germans, and should not spend time with them.[54] So far, the ghetto has turned in a few women for Rassenschande. It would be a disgrace if this were repeated; it could also have worse consequences. . . .

[We are] not to stroll in the streets and not to simply roam around through the main streets. Murer shouts that the Jews are infecting the main streets for him. . . . The brigadiers are responsible for bringing [food] through the gate.

At 2 this afternoon, after that assembly, it was already felt in the ghetto. Bread is already significantly more expensive. Several other foods are also more expensive.

AN ECHO OF THE CONTRIBUTION IN 1941

We have often noted several variants of the Vilna contribution from just before the establishment of the ghetto. Recently, friend Srol[owicz] took me to an abandoned house and pointed to a wall. On the wall an accounting is written with a pencil.

This is what the historical accounting on that wall looks like:

	669,200	
	100,	
	64,	
	6,100	
	1,	
	6,500	
	104,500	
	100,500	1,051,800
5/8	107,400	
	130,	1,289,200
9/8	34,500	
11/	55,800	
12/	40,500	
13/	31,500	

54. The YIVO Archive (Kaczerginski-Sutzkever Collection, no. 29) contains Announcement Number 83 of the ghetto administration, saying that women, not heeding the frequent warnings, go to work too richly and elegantly attired, with modern hairdos, hats, and lipstick. In the future, says the announcement, such women will be detained by the gate guard and punished.

14/	16,200	
16/	14,600	
18/	14,	1,496,300

Aside from gold.

The accounting consists of entries according to the dates as they were paid as contributions. No one received any receipt for this. To know for himself, someone had semi-officially written on the wall. The writer has gone long ago, to Ponar. The wall has remained. Today the boiler for the bath is there (Strashun 6).

The entries are written in rubles. This talks only about currency because gold was delivered specially, about 16 1/2 kilos.

HOW THE NEW DISTRICT WILL BE OCCUPIED

So as not to allow the arriving residents in the new ghetto district to damage the arrangements of other still-vacant buildings, the Housing Department decided to distribute all orders for suitable buildings and not to leave any vacant apartments. The orders, to be received a few days earlier, will be valid for one day (from morning to evening), so all apartments in one house block are to be occupied at the same time.

THE RESIDENCE AREA IN THE NEW DISTRICT

From a more precise survey of the newly acquired district, it was determined that more than 75 percent of the apartments have water.

It is a positive phenomenon that there are a lot of apartments of 1, 2, and 3 rooms in that district.

The apartments are in good condition.

More precise details about the occupation of the new district will be published a few days earlier on the public boards by the Housing Department. The composition of residents for the new district has already begun.

RASSENSCHANDE!

Three Jewish women have recently been arrested by the authorities for their intimate relations with members of the Wehrmacht. Jewish women who work in Rzesza units were warned to be careful in this respect.[55]

FROM RZESZA TO KIENA FOR WORK IN THE PEAT BOG

Some of the Jewish peat bog workers were transferred by the peat bog trust from Rzesza to Kiena, where they will also work in the peat bogs.

The uneasiness about that is apparently unjustified.

55. In a testimony by Bebe Epstein (in the YIVO Archive), there is more precise information about a trial and execution of four Jewish girls for Rassenschande. The names are given there: Zina Mirska, Tsviling, Puzerska, Klyoner.

BAD HALLS OF PUBLIC KITCHENS WILL BE CHANGED FOR BETTER ONES

Along with the annexation of a new ghetto district, a change of the buildings of the public kitchens is foreseen. First, the kitchen of Strashun 2 will be transferred to a new place, to the former Niemiecka 3, the hall of the Aquarium Restaurant.

The second projected "café," on Szawelska 1, is finally confirmed.

SUPPLYING HEATING WOOD FOR THE GHETTO HAS BEGUN

As of the 23rd of this month, they have begun to supply heating wood for the ghetto from the so-called ghetto forest. Meanwhile, heating wood is brought from Sorok-Tatary. Supplying the ghetto with heating wood for the coming winter is carried out according to a precise plan.

THE VILNA GHETTO APPOINTS A DOCTOR FOR THE OSZMIANA GHETTO

On the order of the district commissar of Vilna district, Mr. Schmalzman is assigned to Oszmiana as ghetto doctor there. He had already organized the medical and sanitary-preventive activity there.

CENTRAL HEATING FOR THE READING ROOM

The Technical Department will soon introduce central heating into the reading room and library at Strashun 6, using the steam left over from the bath underneath. This will be, apparently, the only building in the ghetto with central heating.

GHETTO SCIENCE[56]

In the scientific circles of the Literary-Artistic Association [Association of Writers and Artists], a cycle of lectures has been given on various subjects, in the building of the technical school, and there is a considerable attendance.

The last public lecture was by Dr. [Daniel] Feinstein, on the subject "The Near and the Far." On Sunday, in the same building, two lectures will take place on scientific subjects: (1) by Dr. Feinstein—"The Origin of Jews in Light of Anthropology"; and (2) by Mrs. Dr. Biber—"Genetics."

THE FIRST SESSION OF THE COURT OF APPEALS IN THE GHETTO

On the 17th of this month, the first session of the Court of Appeals of the ghetto court was held. Eight criminal cases were dealt with. Mr. Milkanowicki chaired the first session. The associate judges were Srolowicz and Katzenelson. The secretary was Mr. Efroimczyk.

56. This term also encompasses the "human sciences," or *Geisteswissenschaften*.

A SWINDLER IS CONDEMNED

A certain Alter-Yosl Trinopolski promised Mrs. Twerdin to arrange it so that her husband would not be sent to work in Virbalis.

But the "enterprise" didn't succeed, and Mr. Twerdin was sent off with the others to Virbalis. The whole issue surfaced. There was a trial in the ghetto court and Trinopolski was sentenced to jail.

PUNISHMENT FOR THEFT IN A FOREST CAMP

M. Lubocki stole from his neighbor in a forest camp of the Vilna Ghetto. During the investigation, the stolen watch and some of the money was found on him. The ghetto court sentenced him to jail and court costs.

IN THE BEUTENLAGER WORK UNIT

In the Beutenlager, there are now 141 workers, 3 of them women. People work in Burbiszki and in Pioneers Park. During the past year, 3 comrades lost their lives and 8 were wounded at work. But everyone is precise and conscientious about their jobs because they are all aware that the major reason for the ghetto is work.

In the same block on Rudnicka 7, about 400 people live in the greatest density. With the annexation of the new ghetto district, living conditions may become easier.

The workers have a larger hall here, where they can drink a cup of coffee and relax after work.

GHETTO THEATER

Because of the Days of Awe, our Ghetto Theater has renewed its intense cultural work.

If September was a month of repeating old beloved repertoire plays, October must be a month of premieres of new things that might quickly please the theater audience.

First of all, a new review is being prepared, titled "You Can't Know a Thing"[57] —something, as we see, in harmony with our uneasy, indefinite wartime.

People ask if you know anything, and you have no idea. You can only put on a secretive face and say, in a serious tone: "You can't know a thing," and you are exempt from all other talk, and among young and old, you are a patented sage.

Yes, you can't know a thing! For example, both our choirs, the Yiddish one and the Hebrew one, are secretly preparing programs with very important items: oratorios, chorales, operas, not-yet-performed folk songs—in a word, innovations. But don't ask what or when; it can't be divulged.

"You can't know a thing."

57. A suggestive Yiddish idiom, literally: "You can't know at all"; or: "You can't know anything," implying among other things: "Who knows? You never know. Don't be so sure, it may still turn out well."

ON THE SPORTS FIELD

Exercises of various units that are preparing for championship contests take place [on the sports field]. The following have registered for the contests:

For Basketball	16 teams
For Volleyball	18 "
For Football-Tennis	10 "

The best teams were presented by Kailis, the ghetto administration, the gasoline camp, and military clothing.

The contests are held every day from 17:30 on both fields simultaneously.

On Sunday, the 28th of this month, the first performance of the men's gymnastics group on bars takes place. Aside from that, championship contests take place in distance jumping and high jumping.

CLOSED SPORTS HALLS

All sports events will soon be transferred from open fields to closed buildings. The groups of active games will train in the sports hall at Rudnicka 7. The gymnastic groups get a new hall at Oszmiańska 4, in the building of the former large fabric shop of Mr. Wołożynski (entrance from the street), which will be taken over by the sports unit within a few days.

More Than 1,200 Persons

More than 1,200 persons have recently exercised on the sports field. There were 33 groups, aside from the school groups, dormitories, and police groups.

SEPTEMBER 30 [1942]

THE MIGRATION OF THE JEWISH ACTORS' UNION ARCHIVE

To my great amazement, the artist Blacher brings into the ghetto archive several documents from the Jewish Actors' Union of Poland, i.e., from Warsaw.

"How did you get that Warsaw archive?"

And I learn: a Jewish actor is now working as a bookbinder. One-sided papers were brought there for use, including an archive of materials from the Jewish Actors' Union.

How did the archive of the Actors' Union come here?

Apparently, the general office of the ghetto bought the paper. It was brought by a Jewish worker employed in the Rosenberg Task Force, and the paper comes from YIVO.

This is the course of wandering: the Rosenberg Task Force purges the theater archive. Most of the documents go into the trash, and the Jewish workers take it out of the trash to sell it in the ghetto, which lacks paper. The Jewish actor, the ghetto bookbinder, cannot accept it, and the "trash" wanders again into the archive of the ghetto. . . .

A thousand and one nights of all the hundreds of days we have gone through since August 1, 1939.[58]

LAMENTATIONS FOR WARSAW

Again I must weep for Warsaw. My tears dried up long ago. From time to time, I drag out a tear and wipe my tormented face:

My comrades, my friends, my sister and her children, my brothers-in-law on my wife's side, my sister's husband, and hundreds of acquaintances, the Jewish workers and masses of Warsaw.

Again comes a message, and again my mind congeals:

Warsaw almost does not exist. Once I told here with disbelief that 100,000 were taken from Warsaw, later 120,000, another 250,000. Recently I told that 50,000 remained in Warsaw. Now, people say, Warsaw, Jewish Warsaw, almost doesn't exist. Only 20,000 remain there!

The poisoned blood congeals, but you just cannot believe it.

Twenty thousand Jews in Warsaw?

And what does the messenger bring:

Six weeks ago, [they] demanded 40,000 Jews from the Judenrat in Warsaw. The Judenrat refused. The Jewish police undertook it—7,000 a day. . . .

It is hard to say what happened to the Judenrat. People know only that the Jewish representative, Mr. Czerniaków, took his own life and the Judenrat was dissolved.

The Jewish police snatched in the streets, later started taking by houses, finally the Germans themselves started . . . taking by neighborhoods.

Two months like that. People were taken to Pawiak and from there delivered in trains in an impossible manner.

EXECUTIONS

[Executions] are supposed to have taken place somewhere near Malkinia. People are forced to leave their clothes in the trains. From there, they are driven to underground trenches, and they don't come back.

How it is done is still a secret.

She [?] tells:

Kielce and Lublin are *Judenrein* [free of Jews]. Białystok expects an Aktion. In Biała Podlaska and in Międzyrzec—no Jews.

She tells:

58. This date is a mistake. He certainly means August 31 or September 1, 1939, when Hitler's Germany attacked Poland.

The director of the Joint, [Yitskhok] Gitterman, is not alive. [Dovid] Guzik "is still alive."[59]

"And my sister? . . ."

Go shout into the open world. Honor to your memory, thousands, tens of thousands, and hundreds of thousands of my brothers.

Honor to your memory! . . .

SEPTEMBER 30 [1942], 1:30 IN THE AFTERNOON

I WEEP

I weep, and I am amazed. I have seen death so many times and have controlled myself. Have experienced so much torment, disgrace, and humiliation, and called myself the eternal optimist. And now?

What is my life worth even if I remain alive?

Whom to return to in my old home town of Warsaw?

For what and for whom do I carry on this whole pursuit of life, enduring, holding out—for what?!

Where are the workers and masses for whom I used to struggle, suffer, and rejoice?

Where are my near and dear ones?

Whom to return to?

Orphaned Warsaw streets, mournful Warsaw!

Talk to me, you slaughtered, at least in sleep. Talk to me, because death and melancholy do not frighten me. My heart has no more strength for sorrow—it is all ache. Blood has lost its color, it doesn't scare me.

My sister, where have you gone, abandoned and alone?

My comrades, where are you in your bitter struggle?

Talk to me at least in sleep!

The Vilna Ghetto is in an uproar and doesn't sense what is taking place all around.

And perhaps somewhere there is a verdict on our little remnant, too—to wipe it out to the last one? . . .

The experienced Vilna Ghetto doesn't think about that at all.

Is this possible?

My bones, rotting somewhere in the forests of Malkinia, come to me in a dream!

All right, then, let me weep—death doesn't scare me anymore. Let me weep! . . .

59. Dovid Guzik was another director of the Joint, who was killed in an airplane crash in 1946. Gitterman and Guzik did a great deal during the German occupation, both for the Warsaw Ghetto and for other towns in Poland with which they were able to make contact.

OCTOBER 5, 1942, SIMHATH TORAH

45 YEARS OF THE BUND

Today, to honor the 45th anniversary of the Bund, a group of worker activists got together and modestly and quietly celebrated the holiday date. The old comrade Pati [Kremer] was also among the participants.

After the opening, in which the sad situation of the Jews, the situation of Warsaw, etc., were mentioned, Hersh [Gutgestalt] gave a lecture titled "45 Years of the Bund." Herman [Kruk] then read an extract from V. Medem's article "The Bund." Finally, [Comrade] Abrasha [Chwojnik] read an extract from an article by Martov about Arkady and Pati.[60] The chairman greeted Pati, who was present, and then read a letter from the sick comrade Miriam [Gutgestalt] (attached). [*The letter is missing.*]

The quiet celebration ended with mention of recent events in Warsaw, Kielce, Lublin, Międzyrzec, and other places.

A lecture titled "45 Years of the Bund" was to be delivered to the groups.

OCTOBER 6 [1942]

ANOTHER ACT OF RASSENSCHANDE

The ghetto was shocked today when a young beautiful girl was taken out, ostensibly because of Rassenschande.

The girl was taken away by the infamous Weiss.

WARSAW

The most varied information comes again from Warsaw. One [piece of news] contradicts the other. The last information: the Aktion took only 125,000 Jews. I write "only" because, according to the news I have already noted, it would be a new miracle in the series of miracles we have recently prayed for. Unfortunately, we live only on miracles. . . .

FROM A SYNAGOGUE—A CIRCUS

In Vilna there is an interesting Lithuanian, a certain Narusis. He is a drunkard, a playboy, a close friend of Hingst and Murer. He goes hunting with them, visits women with them, etc. But at the same time, he also has many friends among the local Jews and does everything possible for them.

Narusis is the head of the [city] Housing Department. Recently Hingst wanted

60. Julius Martov (1873–1923) was one of the leaders of the Russian Social Democratic Workers Party, later a leader of the Mensheviks. Arkady Kremer, a founder of the Bund, was influential in the first years of the Russian party.

to change one of the most beautiful Jewish synagogues in Vilna, the so-called Choral Synagogue (Zawalna 35) into a . . . circus. They got the building, the organizer agreed, but Narusis diverted it onto a very different path: it is a shame to make the building into a circus. Better make a circus in the bigger building, in the empty Halles marketplace, which is bigger and more comfortable. The reason was apparently accepted, and now he is glad—it is 99 percent sure that the building of the Choral Synagogue will be avoided. . . .

Narusis talks about it as a victory over the destroyers. . . .

OCTOBER 9 [1942]

ANOTHER LAUNDRY IN THE GHETTO

A second laundry to serve the ghetto residents is now planned. The laundry will be on the corner of Dziśnieński and Jatkowa.

NUMBER OF EMPLOYED GHETTO RESIDENTS

According to the information of the Labor Office, up to September 25 of this year, the number of those working among the Vilna Ghetto residents reached 5,759 men and 3,049 women, together 8,808 persons.

A SEVENTH TEAROOM

[A seventh tearoom] will soon be opened by the Health Department.

SUBSTITUTE VITAMINS FOR FALL AND WINTER

The vitamin laboratory is now about to expand and develop its production.

First of all, what is noteworthy is the imminent production of vitamin D, which will substitute for cod-liver oil. Other interesting experiments are also done to find means to substitute for several vitamins—rich nourishment through a proper substitute, for example, black bread with yeast (a substitute for meat), etc.

AN ORDER FOR TOYS

The universal store or, as it is now called, *Deutsches Kaufhaus* (German department store), has ordered from the [ghetto] Workshop Department samples of wooden toys, which it plans to take in great quantities.

IN THE TAILOR WORKSHOP

A great deal of work was done on orders from outside the ghetto, especially for the so-called Pramprekiba.[61] From the latter came orders for large lots of men's

61. A Lithuanian distribution network.

suits, which have already been completed. Now they are about to fill an order for women's suits.

WHO WILL BE SETTLED IN THE NEW DISTRICT

The composition of the population for the new ghetto district is already completed. For that purpose, more than 300 places were visited in the entire ghetto district, which must be thinned out. The complement is being put together according to a special plan, considering that the additional area must be used so that living conditions in the ghetto are to be not only more comfortable but also fairer and more rational in the hygienic-sanitary sense.

An overview of that settlement plan shows that it envisages the transfer to new apartments in the new districts of about 500 people living in kitchens, about 200 from corridors, about 100 from buildings uninhabitable in winter, and about 150 from buildings needed for the expansion of social institutions and offices and workshops. That makes almost 1,000 people.

There is also a plan to create a place for 600 persons who have appealed directly to the Housing Department. That is, the settlement of the newly annexed ghetto district will include up to 1,600 persons.

TAILOR SHOP OF THE FIELD COMMAND

One of the oldest work units is the tailor shop of the field command, where 243 laborers now work. More correct, it is a universal workshop. Here you find departments of tailoring, shoemaking, hat making, gloves, furriers, underwear sewing, knitting, and other departments.

THE COURT DISTRIBUTES THE CLOTHING OF "DISAPPEARED PERSONS"

[. . .]

[*Pages 476–477 of the diary are missing.*]

Awarded Projects for Furniture of the Ghetto Court

October 10 [1942]

Warsaw

A Raid on the Ghetto Club

An Outpouring of Enterprises

Winter Aid Action in the Ghetto

October 13 [1942]

From Ghetto Life

We present several entries here from the internal life of the ghetto.

NEW VOCATIONAL COURSES

New vocational courses will soon be offered. First, courses for chimney sweeps, who are in great demand for work in the city. The course will last a month. In the evening they will learn theory, and during the day they will practice work. Moreover, courses for tailors of men's clothing and military uniforms will be offered, as well as for cabinetmakers, locksmiths, and electricians.

WOMEN, DRESS MODESTLY!

According to an order of the ghetto representative, all women must go to work in clean work clothes and without feminine hats. Wearing lipstick is strictly forbidden.

ONE YEAR OF THE KAILIS BLOCK

On the 10th of this month, it was one year since the workers of Kailis were set up in their own special house block.

THE LABOR POLICE

During September, [the labor police] punished 141 persons for walking without a permit, not going to work on time, etc.

THE PRODUCTION OF WINTER AID CLOGS

[This] is now the most current issue in the workshops. A special band saw has been installed for the purpose, and with it, they prepare for a production of, more or less, 100 pairs of clogs a day. The previous manual labor on clogs has ceased.

The whole production of winter clogs now goes for the Department of Social Welfare, and is designated first of all for the forest and other provincial workers. A special stitching workshop is engaged in the production of winter clogs. They also hope to get enough material soon for the production of bootlegs for the clogs.

All the machines for woodworking (cross saws, band saws, etc.) are now installed in one room, to rationalize the work process.

[*Page 479 of the diary is missing.*]

In the Furniture Factory
Medical Personnel to Provincial Camps
Second "People's Health" Recital in the Ghetto Theater
Sanitary Police at the Disposal of the Health Department
Monthly Medical Checkups of Working Jews
Institutions of Nutrition, Education, and Hygiene
Bath Cards Must Not Be Misplaced

[. . .] not for one time, but permanently. You have to keep the card and have it stamped at least once a month; without that you won't get a bread card.

THE OCCUPATION OF THE NEW GHETTO DISTRICT IS POSTPONED

According to an official announcement from the Housing Department, the occupation of the new ghetto district has been postponed until the 18th of this month, that is, a week from Sunday.

The issued instructions and orders to move and such are in effect.

They say that a week from Sunday, the houses will be occupied at Oszmiańska Street 4, 6, and 8, and Niemiecka 25. The courtyard of Niemiecka 21 will also be partially occupied. The remaining houses of the new ghetto district will be occupied a week later.

PUBLIC INSTITUTIONS IN THE NEW DISTRICT

In the new ghetto district, the following receive lodgings: (1) the sports unit (two big halls); (2) the school unit (a building for a new educational institution); (3) Health Department (a building for a tea house); (4) the scientific circles (two big rooms for a laboratory); (5) Food Supply Department (a building for a public kitchen); and (6) a large building for a children's clinic.

ONE YEAR OF PUBLIC KITCHENS IN THE GHETTO

In early October, it was the first anniversary of the public kitchens in the ghetto. The oldest kitchen, on Rudnicka 6, was a year old last Tuesday, the 6th of the month.

During the year of the existence of the public kitchens, more than 1 million lunches have been distributed. Now, about 3,500 lunches and dinners are distributed daily in the kitchens.

IMMEDIATE HELP FOR GHETTO WORKERS

Not waiting for the results from the winter help campaign, the Department of Social Welfare of the ghetto administration has taken concrete action: they have procured a certain number of sacks, which have been made into pants, shirts, and overalls, and distributed in the forests for the workers who most need them there.

This week, 70 pairs of clogs will be finished. The first installment will be distributed among the workers in the forest and the workers of Panemune and Virbalis.

APPEAL OF THE WINTER HELP CAMPAIGN

A mixed commission of representatives of the Aid Society and the Department of Social Welfare has been created, with the goal of carrying out the winter help campaign. The commission has already held a few meetings and issued an appeal to the ghetto residents to contribute to the maximum.[62]

A lottery has also been arranged for the same purpose.

62. The appeal of the Aid Society is in the YIVO Archive (Kaczerginski-Sutzkever Collection, no. 13). It is also reproduced in Dworzecki 1948:455.

PAYERS OF THE HEAD TAX

Because of the obligation to pay a head tax, persons who do not receive an announcement about the head tax must come themselves to room 17, where they will be registered and given the announcement in hand.[63] So far, only a few people have responded.

Therefore, such persons were again warned not to neglect the issue: whoever cannot present proof by the 20th of this month that he has settled his head-tax matter will not receive a bread card for October.

OFFICIAL ANNOUNCEMENTS OF THE COURT

Announcement No. 1: The ghetto court announces that on November 2 of this year, the request of Słonimczyk Boris concerning the confirmation of the right of inheritance from his late brother Słonimczyk Meyer will be considered.

Persons who have inheritance or property claims from the late Slonimczyk Meyer can present written announcements in the ghetto court, Rudnicka 6, Room 11 (File No. 4F).

Announcement No. 2: Persons who have claims to the property of the late Slonimczyk Meyer or have some information about the property of the deceased must announce it to the court-appointed trustees: A. Dimitrovski and G. Refes at the address: A. Dimitrovski, Police Office.

MILITARY UNIFORMS OF THE LW[64]

This is the biggest unit of Jews working outside the ghetto, numbering about 350 persons. Of these, 147 work in the workshop of the unit and the rest in the warehouses and transport department. The unit works exclusively for the military, making new clothes and repairing old clothes.

Not only do men do this work, but so do a great many women.

The brigadier of the Jewish workers is Hugo Gronner.

THEATER LIFE

Theater life in the ghetto plays a big role here. We take that into consideration and present a sample review of the theater in the ghetto.

The two reviews were published in the ghetto bulletin, *Geto-yedies,* no. 8, October 11, 1942.

"YOU CAN'T KNOW A THING"[65]

This secret and playful, intriguing saying is the leitmotif of the new review in the Ghetto Theater. It has been performed four times now and every time to

63. On August 27, 1942, the Vilna mayor issued an order stating that the ghetto residents had to pay a head tax of 10 Marks. A reproduction of the announcement Kruk mentions is in Korczak 1946:259.

64. I.e., the unit that worked for the Luftwaffe, the German air force.

65. Several songs from "You Can't Know a Thing" are in Kaczerginski 1948.

a packed hall. The review is delightful and amusing. Most of the numbers come from our ghetto reality, present pictures of our life pleasantly and humorously, often a bit satirically exaggerated. A new one is the number "Melokhe-melukhe" [A trade is a realm], which popularizes the idea of productive work. As a first attempt, it is quite successful. But we shall have to think seriously how to find the proper manner to combine good artistic acting with the propaganda of useful ideas. If such performances are to attain their objective, they must not be boring. One must not see the white threads of agitation. Of the other numbers, no doubt the most interesting is "The Goblet"—a new adaptation of S. Frug's "The Cup," well done by Kasriel Brojdo.[66] Also interesting is the finale, "The Cue," where you can see how ghetto gossip is fabricated.

The cast becomes more accustomed to the roles and performs better each time. We should mention Kasriel Brojdo, the productive author of six successful numbers; Leyb Rosental,[67] the author of three interesting numbers; and Iser Wexler,[68] who created most of the music and conducted the orchestra very beautifully. Tasteful decorations were made by Uma Olkienicka, Rachel Sutzkever, and Yudl Mut. Technical production was by Shmuel Efron.

The general artistic direction is in the hands of Yisroel Segal. Our workers' crowd, which needs peace for the soul after a hard day, enjoys itself and laughs with gusto. The review has already made itself a good name.

"A CHAMBER CONCERT"

On Saturday, September 23, the long-awaited chamber music concert took place. The playing of the ensemble was consistent, beautiful, and noble, and you felt you were in a beautiful and fine musical atmosphere. Shimshn Khaykin (violin), Max Seiderman (cello), and Roza Nodelman (piano)—each one played with heart and gave his best.

Adolf Rumszyński sang lieder by Marsini [. . .], Chaninov, and others.

[. . .]

25,000 PERMITS FOR WARSAW

After all the foggy information [that has so far come from Warsaw, we] know that the great Jewish Warsaw has acquired the right to 25,000 permits. What this

66. Born in Vilna in 1907. He graduated from the Hebrew Gymnasium and devoted himself to acting. Brojdo perished in January 1945.

67. Born in Vilna in 1916. He belonged to the famous Rosental family of Jewish printers. Author of countless songs and refrains, he also wrote creative texts for theater reviews. His sister, Khayele Rosental, popularized his songs, and the whole ghetto sang them. He perished in January 1945.

68. Born in 1907. Here Wexler, the conductor of the ghetto orchestra, is called Iser, but in Kaczerginski 1948, he is called Misha. He perished during the liquidation of the Vilna Ghetto in September 1943.

means, we can appreciate properly. But we can also estimate that 25,000 permits probably means 100,000 people. Assuming that about 30,000, about 20,000 are outside the ghetto, it comes out to the wretched figure of 150,000 Jews remaining in Warsaw.

THREE YEARS IN VILNA

On the 10th of this month, it will be three years that I have been in Vilna as a refugee. I came here with a group of 60 writers, authors, and journalists. I spent many months here in the literary dormitory of TOZ (Sadowa 9). Later, with Pinkhes Schwartz and Ber Rosen, I moved to a private flat at Piwna 7, and later to Makowa 5. There I did a great deal of work for TSISHO, which was then in Vilna.[69] Wrote a book—*Three Years with the Yiddish Children's Reader*—which was scheduled for publication by TSISHO. Worked as a press representative of the Vilna OZE. Later, after the departure of my brother (Pinkhes Schwartz), moved to Kovno, from there back to Vilna, and settled at Kijowska 4 along with my brother-in-law. From there to the ghetto, where I have lived until now.

SIX JEWISH WOMEN KILLED

Going to trade along the railroad to Biała Waka, six women were shot.

UNREST IN THE SCANDINAVIAN COUNTRIES

From time to time, we have said that there is not complete calm in Lithuania. Not long ago, we told about the result of elections in Sweden.[70] I learn from the radio that there was unrest in Norway as a result of the fact that 700 people were arrested and 7 were shot.

Similar events take place in Denmark.

The case of Finland in general is in question. The radio talks about that often. In short, the Scandinavian countries are not at all in order.

OCTOBER 15 [1942]

GHETTO PROPERTY GROWS

An interesting fact of economic life in the ghetto. Despite all difficulties, despite the dozens and hundreds of obstacles, nevertheless it turns out that the property in the ghetto is growing constantly. Today ghetto property is worth 7,900,000 rubles, a figure which, in our conditions, is truly amazing.

69. The leaders of TSISHO, who were in Vilna as refugees in 1939–1940, carried on extensive activity, especially in publishing, until Lithuania came under Soviet control.

70. Probably noted on the missing pages.

JEWS IN FRANCE

The newspaper bureau [DN]B[71] reports from Vichy that the Jews' Secretariat made a survey of Jews in occupied and non-occupied France. They have established that about 300,000 Jews are supposed to have been living in France. From the report, it turns out that many Jews have refrained from registering as Jews.

The German press is amazed! . . .

■ ■ ■ ■ ■ ■

OCTOBER 17 [1942]

MRS. SPIRO IS BURIED AS A RUSSIAN ORTHODOX CHRISTIAN

Mrs. Spiro, one of the finest bourgeois ladies in Vilna, was registered as the wife of a Warsaw refugee, Trockenheim (the former deputy of the Polish Sejm). After a long drudgery in the ghetto, she decided to go out to her Christian friend. She spent a long time in Vilna in an attic room. But the Christian saw that Mrs. Spiro wouldn't go on for long like this, and she had a Russian Orthodox document made for her. Mrs. Spiro went to the sister of her Christian friend as a Russian Orthodox woman, Mrs. Ewalina Nowicka. Thus, Spiro-Nowicka lived for several months in the village of Podpliszcze, near Głębokie. On November 6, Mrs. "Nowicka" died and was buried in a Russian Orthodox cemetery with all the ceremony of a Russian Orthodox woman.

Mrs. Spiro was 58 years old and left a daughter, Oppenheim, here in the Vilna Ghetto.

This is another one of the dozens of stories of current life-styles.

GUESTS IN THE GHETTO

Yesterday, the 16th, the whole ghetto died. Apparently Hingst, Murer, and four more Germans suddenly showed up in the ghetto.

Who are the Germans?

Someone said that it was Lause from Kovno, the governor of Lithuania, who presumably came to visit the Vilna Ghetto. Someone else said that a group from the press was with Hingst. Only later did it turn out that the last tale was correct—a press commission. The result of the visit: in one office, an employee, Mr. Gut[gestalt], did not stand at attention for them. This annoyed Murer terribly, and he asked Fried to reprimand him. In another place, Hingst asked the police chief, Glazman, where he got such fine boots and when he had bought them. Altogether: he left satisfied, and the ghetto breathed a sigh of relief.

A "PURGE"—FORTY-FIVE HUNDRED PEOPLE

Before noon, people were nervous because of Hingst's visit. After noon, because of information that came into the ghetto through the workers of HKP, a rumor cir-

71. The official German news agency, Deutsche Nachrichtenbüro.

culated through the streets that there would be a purge in the ghetto. Forty-five hundred people are demanded. Some of the workers of HKP have even taken their families out of the ghetto. The news spread quickly in the ghetto, and there was intense anxiety. Gens went out into the street especially and returned completely calm.

The ghetto breathed a new sigh of relief . . .

IT SMELLS OF POWDER!

I learn that in several little towns, which have been transferred to Lithuania this spring, Jews are assembled and transferred to some centers, where district ghettos are set up. I think this smells like a "purge."

First, it is easier to make a "purge" in 3 or 4 places, instead of in 12 or 15.

Second, those little towns haven't yet had a "purge." So is my guess correct? I wish it weren't.

OCTOBER 18 [1942]

A PAINFUL "CELEBRATION"

The ghetto Jews celebrated. The Jewish police are getting a uniform. If so, it is a sign that the Jews in the Vilna Ghetto are assured of their lives, and what more does a Jew in the ghetto want? . . .

This is how it was yesterday. Today it is already different. Today the Vilna Jews have learned that the policemen (about 20) who got the uniforms with a star of David are going to Oszmiana this morning, where they will "distribute" permits. So far, the Jews there haven't known the taste of a permit. Now this will be carried out with the help of the Vilna Jewish police. This means, thinks every Vilna Jew, that if they give out permits, it means . . . a "purge"? This is more than enough to dim yesterday's glow of the newly uniformed policemen and for people to see them as a kind of Ipatinga, a group of assistants in Aktions.[72]

In sum, it is like this: 20 policemen received military caps with a crown—a star of David—yesterday. The same 20 also received good leather coats, and this morning the group went to Oszmiana with several commissars.

Early in the morning, Weiss came to the ghetto with his big truck (incidentally, the same truck with which he took people out of here) and took the policemen. Leading the expedition were Dessler, Levas, even Bronschweig, as the recorder of permits, and others. Weiss himself also went along. . . .

72. The YIVO Archive (Kaczerginski-Sutzkever Collection, no. 31) contains Announcement Number 85, from the ghetto chief, dated October 20, 1942, stating that because some of the Vilna Ghetto police have left for Oszmiana and only a few policemen remain in the ghetto, he requests the people to behave properly and keep the peace themselves. That announcement says that the police have gone to Oszmiana because of "the enlargement of that ghetto."

The police even wore Russian military caps from tsarist days. The color, brown; for the commissar, garnet.

People tell from reliable sources that the police carried with them 2,250 notes as auxiliary documents to the permits. Similar cards were distributed here during the famous Vilna night before distribution of the yellow permits. . . .

Thus, after the purge of the old people, the Jewish ghetto police put themselves at Weiss's disposal to carry out another purge—in the "Vilna realm."

Today the ghetto is not happy anymore, today the ghetto is upset again.

The town of Oszmiana is 90 km from Vilna. I learn that the issue of Oszmiana does not come from the district commissar of Vilna but is an order from Wulf, district commissioner [of] Vilna district.

I learn at the last minute that an extra messenger went to Oszmiana to warn the Jews of what is being prepared for them.[73]

PEOPLE "MOVE" AND . . . CURSE

Many residents moved into the new part of the ghetto today. For a few hours, the new part was very lively. Of course, many of the new residents viciously cursed the Housing Department. The complaints, perhaps justified: a door latch is missing, a pane is out, etc. The director of the Housing Department jokes:

"I 'move' them and they curse me. . . ."[74]

MELINA NO. 3

On Saturday, with a group of friends, I finally went to Melina No. 3. The first one contains the 3,790 holy books of the Mefitsei Haskalah, about which I have often written. There are more than 200 Torah Scrolls there, copper, etc. In the second one are copper ware, candlesticks, cantors' pulpits, curtains of the Ark of the Covenant, and *kapoyres* [ark coverings]. In the third one are old holy books from the fifteenth, sixteenth, seventeenth, eighteenth, and nineteenth centuries, silver, old pictures, etc.

A NEW SOURCE FOR MY COLLECTIONS. . . .

Once the Bolsheviks took the Vilna Archive to Minsk. Now the German authorities have brought the archive back to Vilna. The local Polish newspaper announces that archive materials have already arrived in 30 cars. I know only one

73. The agent, Liza Magun, was sent by the underground movement, the FPO. She came to Oszmiana as an Aryan, contacted the local Jews, and warned them of what was awaiting them. The Jews, however, trusted the Vilna Jewish police and did not heed her call to go to the forest. Liza Magun, born in Vilna in 1920, was a member of Ha-Shomer Ha-Tzair. In the FPO, she was a contact with the Aryan side. She was captured by the Gestapo. The mobilization password of the FPO contained her name: "Liza calls!"

74. In Yiddish, a pun: "Ikh 'zidl' zey ariber un zey zidlen mikh."

thing: of the material that was brought, they bring me a great many very important and interesting documents.

A new source for documents.

THE THIRD STATISTICAL BULLETIN APPEARS IN THE GHETTO

We once were told that the Office of Statistics in the ghetto is about to issue a series of bulletins, each of which is devoted to a special problem in the ghetto. So far, three such bulletins have appeared. The first was devoted to the question of supply, the second to health protection, the third to the problem of social aid. All the bulletins cover the period from January to June 1942, i.e., the first half of 1942. Each bulletin contains an introduction explaining the problem to which it is devoted, a series of statistical tables, and some well-drawn diagrams.

In the ghetto conditions, such a publication is indeed a pleasant phenomenon. This is a document of historical significance, a reflection of the appearance of the ghetto.

OCTOBER 23 [1942]

WINTER AID

Overtly, the campaign for winter aid is well organized. But at every step, you sense that circles close to the ghetto kingdom are concerned with it. The members of the action committee are: Mrs. Fried, Mrs. Dessler, Mrs. Gronner, etc.—mostly women who have never had anything to do with Jewish public life. That is also felt in the question of the campaign. For example, Rudnicka Street was decorated with a big propaganda banner over the whole width of the street: "Warm Hearts Fight Cold." The slogan is translated from Polish: "Gorące serca zwalczają mróz." The Yiddish translation, done in the heart of what remains of Vilna, sounds grotesque, reflecting the uniqueness of this ghetto.

The action in and of itself is successful. The people participate as much as they can.

A KNIT SHOP IN THE KAILIS BLOCKS

The Workshop Department organizes a knit shop in the Kailis blocks, where Kailis women will be employed.

LADIES' TAILOR SHOP

A ladies' tailor shop will now be organized. Four qualified artisans and several apprentices and assistants will be employed there.

VITAMIN DISTRIBUTION IN THE SCHOOL MEDICAL CENTER

The Aid Society has provided means to distribute vitamin B, drunk by 50 poor and weak children.

A PAWNSHOP IN THE GHETTO

On the 15th of this month, an institution was opened at Szpitalna Street 11 for small loans. The brief existence of the pawnshop shows that the pawnshop is justified. People who need short-term credit show a distinct interest.

They give loans of up to 50 percent of the estimated value of the pawned items.

GHETTO COURTS

BECAUSE OF AN OVERTURNED TSHOLNT.[75] Recently, at Szawelska 8, apartment 27, there was a fight between Mrs. R. L. and Mrs. S. Sh. The latter knocked over a tsholnt of the former, and the case came to court. The injured party demanded a big compensation, but the court merely sentenced the defendant to 3 kilograms of potatoes.

FOR STEALING A GLASS in the café at Rudnicka 13, Mrs. Khaye Kwas was sentenced by the court to one week in jail, a five-mark fine, and two marks to cover court costs.

FOR DEMOLISHING THE ATTIC of Strashun 2, the court punished Mrs. Reisman, Khaye, with seven days in jail.

FOR STEALING A PIECE OF WOOD from the storeroom of the police kitchen, the court sentenced the minor R. Wiesenberg and turned him over to the protection of A. Dimitrovski (official supervisor of minors).

IN THE WORK UNITS — ONE YEAR OF KAILIS

Kailis is outside the ghetto. The workers live in special blocks near their work.

The new colony of Jewish workers had to start life without any experience or proper assistance. Now it is more or less normalized. In charge of each block is a committee, each member of which is responsible for a special area, such as food, work, culture, etc.

In the blocks themselves, social aid is very well developed.

The discipline of the Kailis residents is good. Now, when the area of the ghetto is enlarged, a few dozen Kailis residents, no longer working in Kailis, will move to the ghetto. That will also ease living conditions in the Kailis blocks, which are very crowded.

THEATER LIFE — RECITAL OF THE MUSIC SCHOOL, SUNDAY, THE 11TH OF THE MONTH

In the ghetto, there is also a music school for children. The lessons take place in schools. It is an itinerant school.

The morning recital, organized last Sunday by the directors of the school, proved that the devotion of Jewish teachers and the talent of the children can

75. A Sabbath stew. The book says *ibergeshtanenem* ("overdone"), but the context and Kruk's table of contents make it clear that the correct word is *ibergekertn* ("overturned").

overcome the most difficult conditions. One after another, 16 students performed piano, violin, and vocal pieces.

Some of the children are apparently very talented. The teachers—Hirszowicz, Feygus, Rechtig, Zublewicki, Boy, Bunimowicz and Khaykin—can be satisfied with their results.

The piano playing of Hindele Felman and Rivele Bernstein deserves special mention.

MORNING CONCERTS FOR WORKERS

On Sunday, the 25th of this month, at 11 in the morning, is the first concert of light stage music in the Ghetto Theater. The orchestra consists of 12 experienced musicians. Such concerts will take place now every Sunday morning.

OCTOBER 25 [1942]

IT SMELLS OF POWDER . . .

In the last issue of the *Geto-yedies,* this entry was published:

> FROM VILNA DISTRICT
>
> JEWISH LIFE
>
> We learned that the Jews of the Vilna district, living in small towns, were transferred to big centers in Oszmiana, Święciany, Michaliszki, and Soly, where suitable conditions will be created to supply everyone with work.
>
> A few Jewish specialists, employed in important local work, remain in every little town.
>
> The transferred Jews may take almost all their property to their new residence.

Unfortunately, this is a matter to calm [the readers]. Now it is clear as day—it smells of an Aktion in all the towns listed.

Moreover, this time, the Aktion will be done by the hand of our Jewish ghetto police. For the commander, Mr. Gens, this means saving Jewish souls. For us, this is an Aktion made by Jewish hands.

The Vilna Ghetto lives in great tension. The group of police, now in Oszmiana, write to their loved ones that everything is fine.

What does "fine" mean to a policeman? . . .

OCTOBER 27 [1942]

OSZMIANA

All ghetto residents are now talking about it. It is now clear. Jews were taken to Oszmiana from everywhere, especially old people, women, and children. The Jewish militia makes order there. "Order" consists of beating, prohibiting bringing in [food], etc.

The 30 Jewish police there are splendidly set up; they eat and drink the finest and spend their time with the local girls. None of the local residents believe in an Aktion—this is the major achievement of sending Jewish police there!

Not regarding the brutal treatment of the ghetto Jews there, the Jews of Oszmiana and the surrounding area consider the Jewish police as their salvation. . . .

If only it were true.

WHAT DOES G[ENS] SAY TO US

Abrasha [Chwojnik] and I went to try to get Comrade Bat'ke[76] out of Staroświęciany, which, we think, is threatened. In a chat, he [Gens] affirmed that nothing would happen to him [Bat'ke] because . . . he would segregate! . . . The same old song. He does this because he thinks he thus saves Jewish heads. He also says that Murer recently argued with him that there are only 15,000 Jews in the ghetto. We infer from this that this is left for us as a soap bubble, that . . . something can come out of it, and here, too, he will be the one who selects. . . .

MORE INFORMATION ABOUT WARSAW

From someone who just came from Warsaw, I learn that the Aktion lasted two whole months. The Polish police were removed from around the ghetto, and their place was taken by police from Latvia and a regiment of Bolshevik deserters. The Jews from there were taken, as has been mentioned, to Bełz[ec] (near Lwów) and to a forest around Malkinia. There the Jews are put into special underground entrances, poisoned, and burned.

Aktions in Otwock and Falenica. The Jews of Otwock and Falenica were shot on the spot.

The borders of the ghetto in Warsaw are Zamenhof-Nowolipki to Smocza-Gęsia and Gęsia to Zamenhof. Dzielna is included from Zamenhof to Smocza, Pawia the same. Between them is a section of Karmelicka and Nowolipki to Dzielna. The tiny Więzienna at Pawiak and the little street Nowa Karmelicka.

The Germans are now occupied with the Jewish property and take it out.

76. The teacher Motl Gilinski, known as Bat'ke. He graduated from the Yiddish Teachers' College in Vilna and then worked in the Medem Sanitarium. During the liquidation of the Święciany Ghetto, he moved to Vilna, and when the Vilna Ghetto was liquidated, he was sent to Estonia, where he perished. For his biography, see *Teachers' Memorial Book* 1954:93–96.

KIELCE, RADOM, CZĘSTOCHOWA, LUBLIN

Aktions were carried out in all these cities and their surrounding areas. There are Jews in Lwów.

RADIO KOŚCIUSZKO ABOUT THE POLISH MILITIA IN WARSAW

The illegal Polish radio reports that the Polish militia in Warsaw has betrayed and is in the service of the power.

What would the same radio say about the Vilna Jewish police? . . .

OCTOBER 28 [1942]

HOW JEWS DESTROY JEWS (ABOUT THE SLAUGHTER IN OSZMIANA)

After the Aktion of old people, the Vilna Ghetto is once more in an indescribable depression. Now there is the question of Oszmiana.

Whatever we may have foreseen and written about many times, it is all hardly a fraction of the actual situation.

Writing when your hair stands on end, when none of us can believe it, would mean to tell only a minimum of the factual [situation]. Let the facts speak.

Facts

As I learn from unofficial sources:

When the Jewish police from Vilna came to Oszmiana, Jews had already been gathered there from Szafrany, Solum, Smorgonie, etc. All of them brought many things, often even furniture. Learning that the Vilna Jewish police ruled in Oszmiana, the Jews were beside themselves with joy. Most of those who came were old, sick, women, and children. Up to 2,300 Jews were gathered there. All were given permits, and the Jews grew calm.

The police commissioner, Mr. D[essler], came to that Judenrat there and demanded 1,500 Jews. During the discussion he played with a revolver, not, God forbid, thinking of anybody in particular, he is just playing, as if nothing had happened. . . .

How did Mr. D. get a revolver?

How is it that the same Mr. demands that they should turn [Jews] over to him? . . .

And what are the Ipatinga from Kovno and Vilna doing here?

Why did they, too, come here?

Is Mr. D. their spokesman?

The chair[man] did not agree to turn over Jews. Mr. D. went to Vilna and returned with an answer—ostensibly bargained down to 600 . . . sick people, old people, and cripples.

How Does It Happen?

On Monday, the 23rd of this month, an order was issued that all Jews must appear in a city square. The Jewish police were divided into three groups. One drove the Jews from houses, the second from prayer houses (where the transferees were gathered), the third was occupied in the square.

Segregation and the End

No one suspected any threat. Nevertheless, not everyone went to the square. There the Jewish police officers themselves segregated and decided who would go right and who would go left. . . . Jews saw themselves caught in a net and started thrusting money. For example, a woman voluntarily gave away 800 gold rubles. This is how 200 sick people and 392 old people, 592 altogether, were selected, and 410 of them were sent out of town.

On the square, among the "condemned," a Jew suddenly began singing aloud "El Male Rahamim."[77] The whole square wept, and tears flowed from the eyes of some of the Jewish policemen.

The 410 selected people were sent out of town, where 150 peasant wagons were waiting. From there, they were sent 8 kilometers beyond Oszmiana. The execution took place in the presence of 8 Lithuanian and 7 Jewish policemen.

The leaders of the whole "enterprise" were Mr. D[essler], [Nosn] Ring, [Moyshe] Levas. All of them had revolvers.

Postscript

A postscript after the dry report is superfluous. Nevertheless, let it be said:

1. In the few days the Jewish police spent there, the 30 policemen drank 100 bottles of brandy. There was a special "libation" among Jewish and Lithuanian police. The Judenrat furnished a roast sheep to one of the "gluttons."
2. The policemen brought whole sacks of jewelry and money to Vilna. This applies mainly to Messrs. D[essler] and Levas. They came from there with full sacks!
3. Aside from that, the Jewish police who worked in Oszmiana got special rubber truncheons. . . .
4. People tell more: when the Jewish police were already in the wagons, leaving Oszmiana after accomplishing this job, one of the heroes, our long-famous hero Drezin,[78] sang to the assembled Jews:

We made ourselves happy and bright,
You, too, have yourselves a fine, good night.[79]

77. A prayer for the dead.
78. The identity of Drezin is unknown.
79. A couplet closing a traveling amateur show.

During the Aktion, the Jewish policeman [Ayzik] Averbukh became hysterical and had to be revived.

Finale

When the Jewish police came back to the ghetto, in "full splendor" (uniforms and sticks), they marched into the ghetto as in a victory parade. Two days after their return, there was a police assembly in the ghetto, where Gens justified the treatment with the motive of saving Jews. Dessler spoke about everything openly and with no restraint. Most of the police ascribed to the theory of the commandant and reacted even by cheering. Policeman Friedman openly pointed out that even if you are unanimous, about such a matter, you should not clap your hands.

The mood in the ghetto is still terrified. The tragedy is that the policemen don't breathe a word about it. Nevertheless, something reaches the public, and the tragedy is that the . . . public mostly approves of Gens's attitude.

The public figures that perhaps this may really help. The Jewish police made money, and that certainly was allowed in order to corrupt them. It is quite probable that a similar Aktion must soon be performed again, and then the Jewish policemen will themselves volunteer. . . .

This is the sad summary of the sad end of the Oszmiana Jews.

PEOPLE MOVE AND . . . PEOPLE CURSE

We have already written about the Germanization process taking place here for some time. Concerning [that], there have already been many tragic incidents, which we have unfortunately not recorded. Now, in the local press, an article appeared about it, which must be mentioned because of its cynicism.

The DNB reports that because of the transfer of Lithuanian peasants who belong to the German nation, which has been going on for some time in the Vilna area, and because certain elements have started inciting in this connection, it is officially announced:

The following districts are included in the transfer: Pobierze—327 landowners; Rudomino—6 landowners; Mejszagoła—5; Rzesza—7.

Thus, only 345 Lithuanian families are transferred. The communiqué announces that everything possible will be done so that those who must leave their homes are treated properly and given suitable work. Of course, for annihilating livestock and "dead" inventories, for destroying food, etc., people will be punished even with death.

SOMETHING IS HAPPENING AGAIN

Lately there have been many suspicions that in the big world, something is happening again. Persistent rumors come from German units, telling that peace is imminent between Germany and the Soviet Union, that negotiations are already being conducted, that Litvinov is in Germany, etc., etc.[80] Nevertheless: Russia is celebrating the 100th day of the siege of Stalingrad. A great offensive is advancing in Africa, as we have already interpreted—a second front to clear Africa and the Mediterranean Sea and to head for the weakest and least threatened boiling pot—through Italy to the Balkans. Now, it turns out to be probable. The offensive in Africa has already started and (as the communiqués report) in a scope never seen before. From Rome, they say that an air battle took place over El Alamein on the 20th, in which 400 planes participated—the biggest air battle in Africa.

They also tell from Rome that a "mighty" attack of English bombers took place again on the 23rd. At the same time, there were bombardments of Genoa, Turin, etc. There were bombings of Milan, Navarre, Genoa again, etc.

Is this really the beginning of a second front?

DESSLER CALLS — GENS INVITES

I got out of bed today. I have had a cold for a few days. During that time, Mr. Dessler had me called; Gens, invited. Yesterday, because of my illness, I couldn't come, and Gens postponed the meeting. Apparently, he did it because of me and Dr. Feldstein, who is also ill.

What can Mr. Dessler want from us? And why must Mr. Gens have me in his home late in the evening? . . .[81]

80. Litvinov was the Soviet commissar for foreign affairs in the 1930s (a Jew).

81. Dworzecki 1948:415–416 contains material on the meeting at Gens's home, at which Gens justified the Oszmiana Aktion. Dworzecki says that a protocol of that meeting exists.

Herman (Hersh) Kruk.

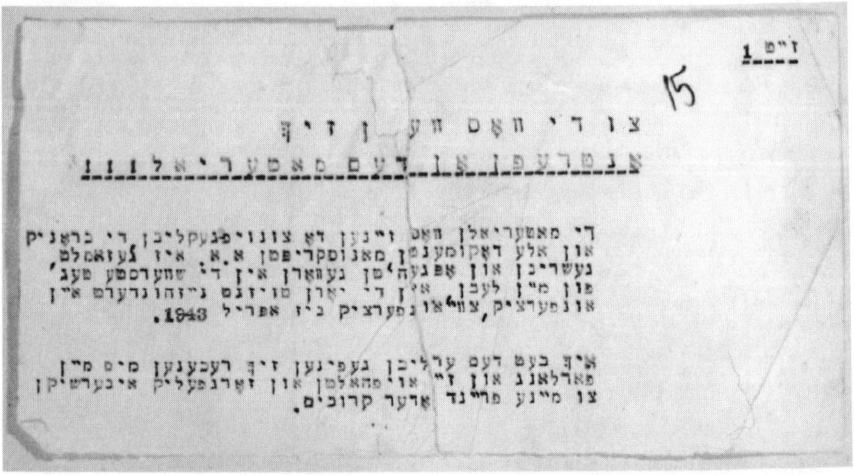

ז"ט 1

15

צו די וואס וועלן זיך
אנטרעפן אין דעם מאטעריאל!!!

די מאטעריאלן וואס זיינען דא צונויפגעקליבן, די כראניק
און אלע דאקומענטן, מאנוסקריפטן א.א. איז געזאמלט,
געשריבן און אפגעהיט'ן געווארן אין די שווערסטע טעג
פון מיין לעבן, אין די יארן טויזנט ניינהונדערט איין
אונפערציק, צוויי אונפערציק ביז אפריל 1943.

איך בעט דעם ערליכן געפינער זיך רעכענען מיט מיין
פארלאנג און זיי אויפהאלטן און זארגפעליק איבערשיקן
צו מיינע פריינד אדער קרובים.

A note found with Herman Kruk's papers, hidden in the ruins of the Vilna Ghetto: "To those who may find this material! The materials gathered here—the chronicle along with all the documents, manuscripts, and other texts—were collected, written, and preserved in the most difficult days of my life, from 1941 to April 1943. I beg the honest discoverer to respect my wish, preserve the materials, and carefully ship them to my friends or relatives."

A view of Vilna from across the Wilija River, ca. 1930s.

An entrance to the Jewish quarter at Jatkowa Street 15, later part of Vilna Ghetto 2, ca. 1936. Photograph by Alter Kacyzne.

A glimpse into the Synagogue Yard, summer 1939.

The reading room of the Strashun Library, 1920s.

The YIVO building at Wiwulski Street 18, in the 1930s. The Yiddish Scientific Institute (YIVO) was founded in Vilna in 1925 as a modern research center for the study of Jewish history, culture, and society.

Students from a Yiddish high school visiting an exhibition at YIVO, 1930s.

Young refugees at the Ramayles Yeshiva, Vilna, 1939.

Zelig Kalmanowicz (right)*, well-known scholar and editor, with F. Halpern at YIVO, 1930s.*

Shmerke Kaczerginski (left) *and Abraham Sutzkever in the Vilna Ghetto, July 20, 1943. Poets of the* Yungvilne *(Young Vilna) literary group, they were also instrumental in rescuing and hiding books and other documents from the Nazis.*

Dr. Jacob Wygodzki (front row center)*, a physician and an esteemed leader of Vilna's Jewish community, with other members of the* kehile *(Jewish community council), Vilna, 1920s.*

Hans Hingst (left)*, Gebietskomissar of the city of Vilna, with Franz Murer, his aide-de-camp in charge of Jewish affairs.*

A search by the Gestapo at the Rudnicka Street gate to the Vilna Ghetto, ca. 1942. Courtesy Beit Lohamei Haghetaot—Ghetto Fighters' House, Israel.

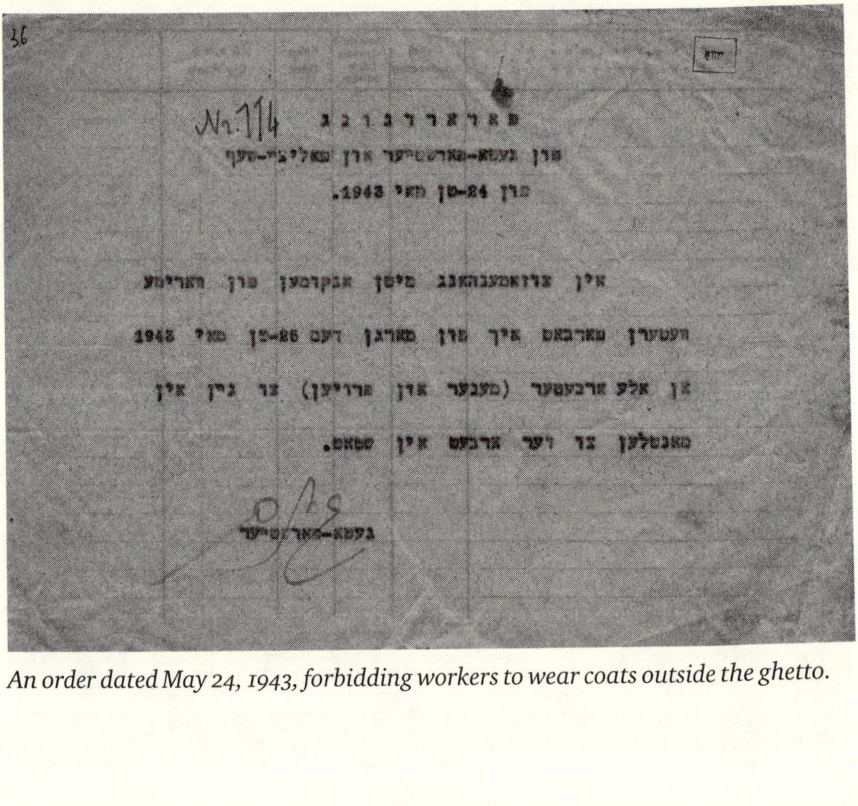

36

Nr. 774 פארארדנונג

פון געטא-פארשטייער און פאליציי-שעף

פון 24-טן מאי 1943.

אין צוזאמענהאנג מיטן אנקומען פון ווארימע

וועטער פארבאט איך פון מארגן דעם 25-טן מאי 1943

אן אלע ארבעטער (מענער און פרויען) צו גיין אין

מאנטלען צו דער ארבעט אין שטאט.

געטא-פארשטייער

An order dated May 24, 1943, forbidding workers to wear coats outside the ghetto.

Portraits of Jewish police who served as guards at the entrances to the Vilna Ghetto, ca. 1942. The larger portraits at upper right are of Jacob Gens (left), *head of the Judenrat, and Police Commissar Salek Dessler. Courtesy Beit Lohamei Haghetaot—Ghetto Fighters' House, Israel.*

An aerial view of Łukiszki Prison, Vilna, 1929.

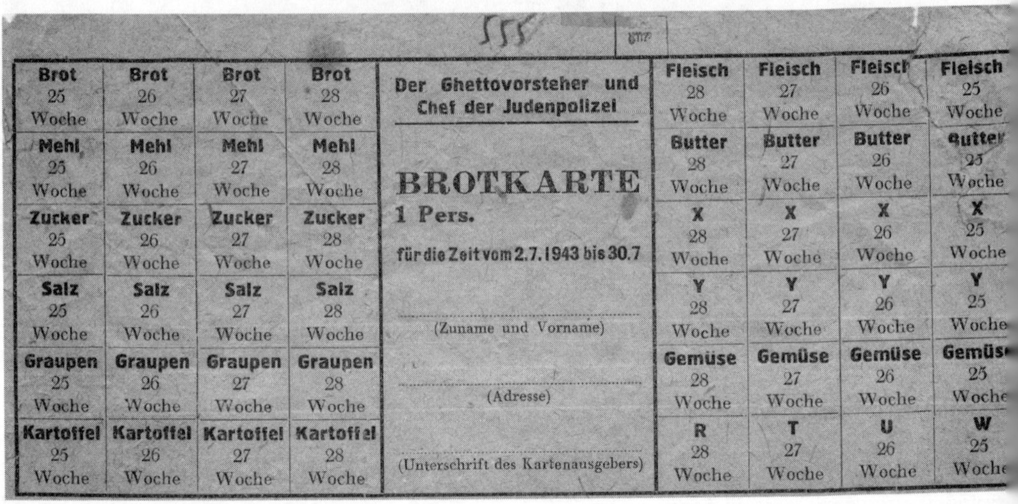

555

Brot 25 Woche	Brot 26 Woche	Brot 27 Woche	Brot 28 Woche
Mehl 25 Woche	Mehl 26 Woche	Mehl 27 Woche	Mehl 28 Woche
Zucker 25 Woche	Zucker 26 Woche	Zucker 27 Woche	Zucker 28 Woche
Salz 25 Woche	Salz 26 Woche	Salz 27 Woche	Salz 28 Woche
Graupen 25 Woche	Graupen 26 Woche	Graupen 27 Woche	Graupen 28 Woche
Kartoffel 25 Woche	Kartoffel 26 Woche	Kartoffel 27 Woche	Kartoffel 28 Woche

Der Ghettovorsteher und Chef der Judenpolizei

BROTKARTE
1 Pers.
für die Zeit vom 2.7.1943 bis 30.7

(Zuname und Vorname)

(Adresse)

(Unterschrift des Kartenausgebers)

Fleisch 28 Woche	Fleisch 27 Woche	Fleisch 26 Woche	Fleisch 25 Woche
Butter 28 Woche	Butter 27 Woche	Butter 26 Woche	Butter 25 Woche
X 28 Woche	X 27 Woche	X 26 Woche	X 25 Woche
Y 28 Woche	Y 27 Woche	Y 26 Woche	Y 25 Woche
Gemüse 28 Woche	Gemüse 27 Woche	Gemüse 26 Woche	Gemüse 25 Woche
R 28 Woche	T 27 Woche	U 26 Woche	W 25 Woche

A ration card for July 1943.

A set decoration from a play entitled One Less Hannukah Candle, *performed by children at the orphanage at 4 Strashun Street, Vilna Ghetto, December 6, 1942.*

A theatrical performance in the Vilna Ghetto. Courtesy Yad Vashem, Israel.

The Hebrew choir in the Vilna Ghetto. Courtesy Beit Lohamei Haghetaot—Ghetto Fighters' House, Israel.

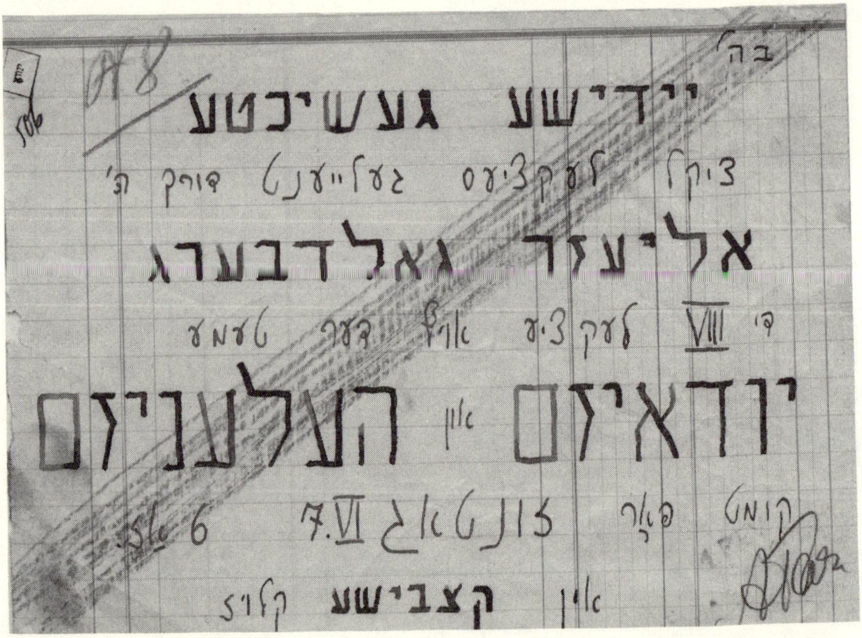

A poster advertising a lecture titled "Judaism and Hellenism," part of a series of lectures by Eliezer Goldberg.

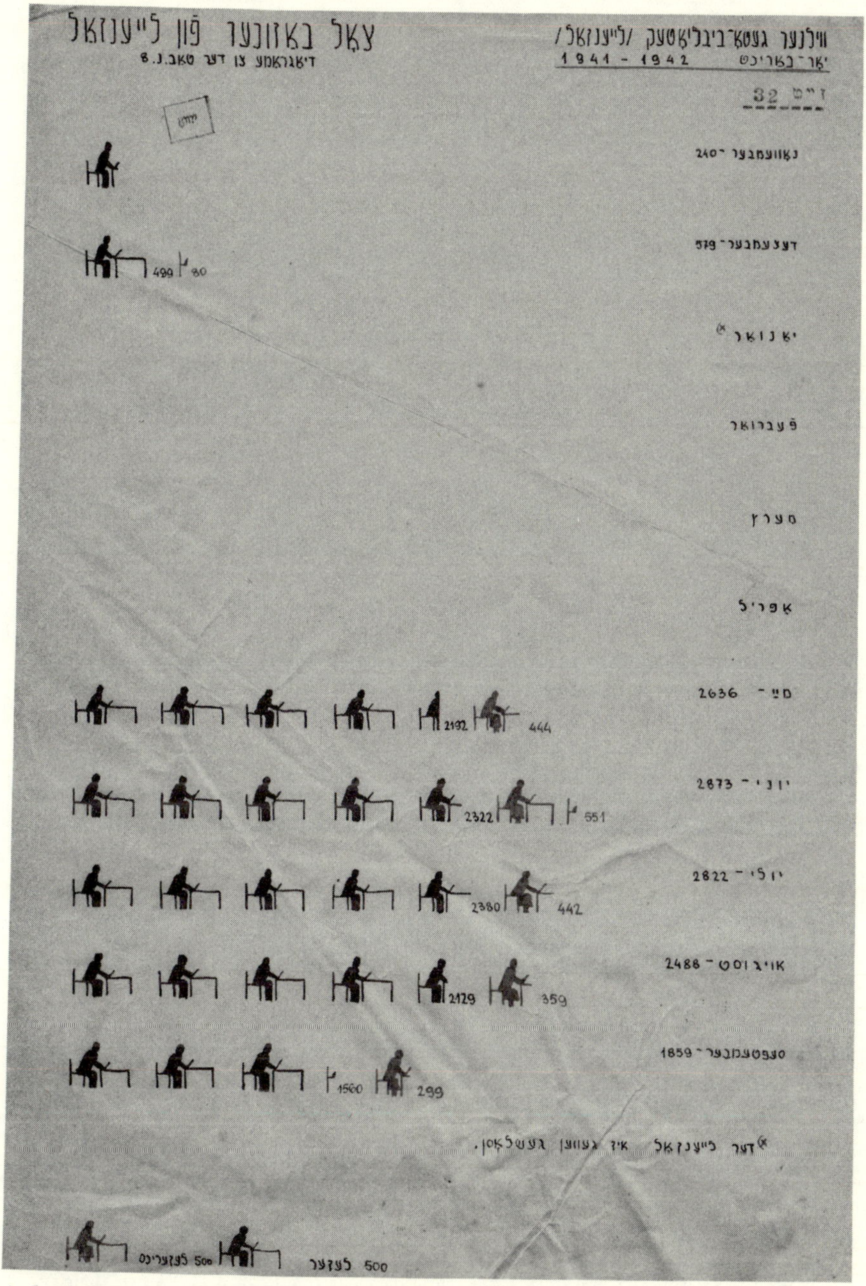

A chart from a report, "A Year of Work in the Vilna Ghetto Library, September 15, 1941–September 15, 1942," showing number of readers per month from November 1941 to September 1942. The library was closed from January to April 1942. From May onward the number of readers is broken down by gender, with the figures in skirts representing female readers.

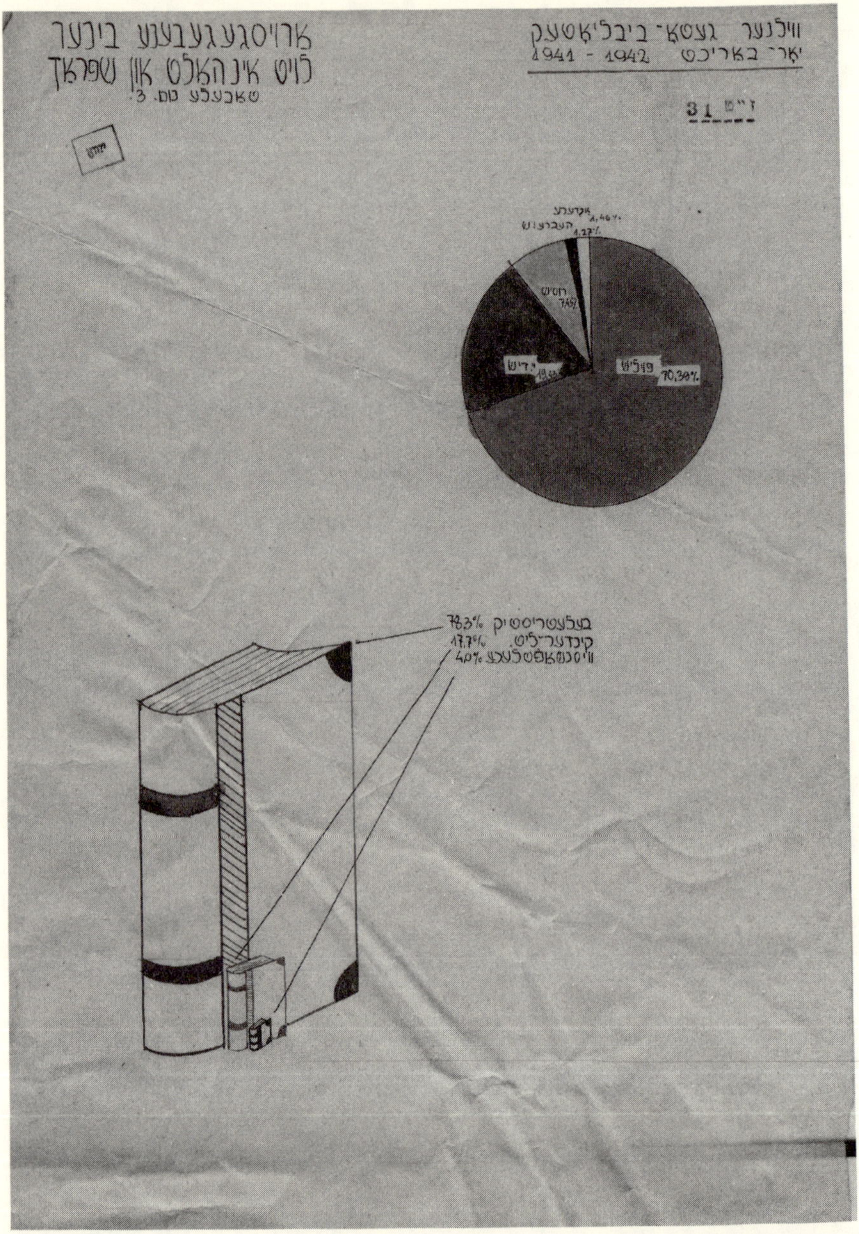

A page from a report, "A Year of Work in the Vilna Ghetto Library, September 15, 1941–September 15, 1942," analyzing borrowed books by language and subject matter. The pie chart shows that books in Polish accounted for most of the materials borrowed, followed by books in Yiddish, books in Russian, and books in other languages. The diagram indicates that fiction was the most popular genre, followed by children's books and scholarly works.

Workers sorting books for the Rosenberg Squad in the YIVO building, 1942–1943.

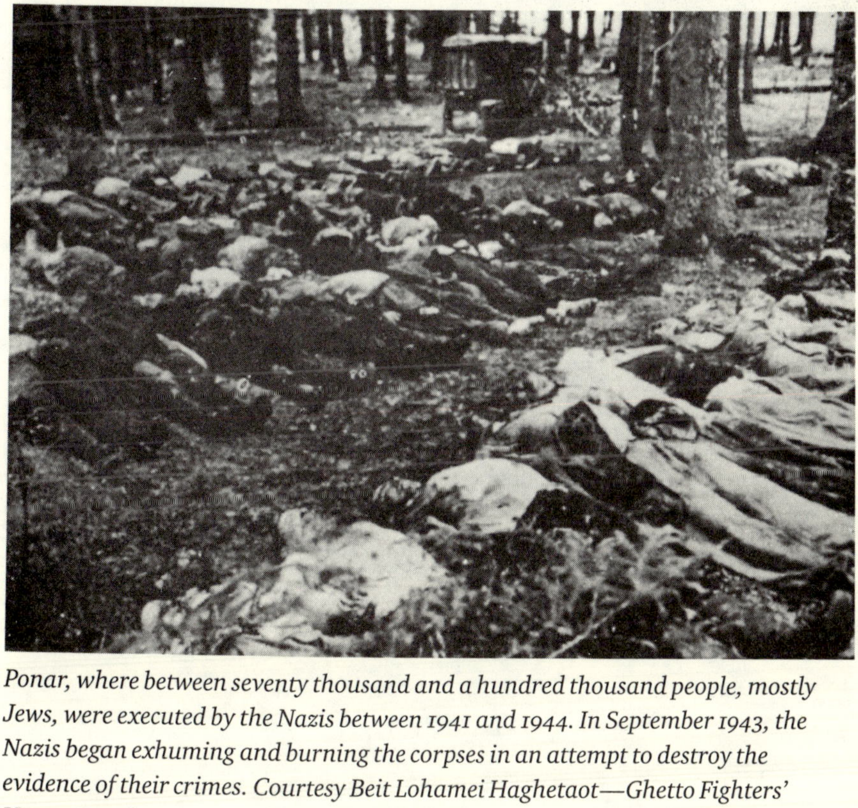

Ponar, where between seventy thousand and a hundred thousand people, mostly Jews, were executed by the Nazis between 1941 and 1944. In September 1943, the Nazis began exhuming and burning the corpses in an attempt to destroy the evidence of their crimes. Courtesy Beit Lohamei Haghetaot—Ghetto Fighters' House, Israel.

A ramp used to move corpses at Ponar. Courtesy Beit Lohamei Haghetaot—Ghetto Fighters' House, Israel.

A melina *(hiding place) for children in the ghetto. Courtesy Beit Lohamei Haghetaot—Ghetto Fighters' House, Israel.*

*The secret headquarters of the FPO (*Fareynikte partizanerorganizatsye, *or United Partisans Organization), the underground resistance organization in the Vilna Ghetto. Courtesy Beit Lohamei Hagetaot—Ghetto Fighters' House, Israel.*

Jewish partisans who assisted in the Red Army liberation of Vilna in July 1944. Among them is Abba Kovner (back center), *a leader of the FPO.*

Ruins of the Vilna Ghetto, ca. 1945. Courtesy Beit Lohamei Hagetaot—Ghetto Fighters' House, Israel.

Soviet soldiers in the Klooga concentration camp in Estonia, soon after its liberation in 1944. About three thousand people, half of them Jews from Vilna, were murdered there.

CHAPTER 6

THE SECOND WINTER

OCTOBER 29, 1942 – MARCH 18, 1943

OCTOBER 29 [1942]

THE SECOND WINTER

Here in the ghetto, people are preparing for the second winter. Some say the last, really the last, because soon they will finish us off. . . . But in the meantime, we live and prepare: the ghetto is excited about winter aid. Everyone is preparing for winter. Once again people put up the iron stoves, little ones with small panes instead of big and light windows.

Everywhere, people pull out old rags. The better clothes have already been sold. From the old things, they intend to alter clothing. They patch, darn, re-knit. They make soles out of an old belt; from two pairs of torn underwear, they patch together one. Poverty now creeps into the street. The clothes, the rags—everything shows clearly the distance from a year ago to now. All statistics show this: the lines for social aid, the distribution of free lunches—everything says that the ghetto is growing poorer. But Jews do not lose their courage. And everyone is satisfied: we are getting a winter, "they", a disaster. And a comrade helps me:

"A nastoyashtsher brokh! . . ."[1]

WINTER AID CAMPAIGN

As reported in the last issue of *Geto-yedies,* a new commission was appointed to run the entire winter aid campaign. It says there that to coordinate the winter aid better, the ghetto representative appointed a special commission: Chairman—Engineer A. Fried, and members—chairman of the former Aid Society, Mr. Milkanowicki; director of the Department for Social Welfare, Mr. Srolowicz; senior police inspector, Mr. Muszkat, Mrs. Dessler, and Mrs. Raf.

More news about the successful and active progress of the campaign.

The center of the winter aid campaign is seething with work. Diligent women, girls, young men are numbering, assembling, and arranging the collected clothing.

The campaign is well under way. You have to figure that they will finish visiting all ghetto residents in the next four or five days. We must say that the campaign

1. Half-Russian, half-Yiddish: "An honest-to-goodness disaster!"

was well understood by everyone and the collectors encountered great friendliness everywhere. Aside from the ghetto districts, they will work on the Kailis blocks, where everything is not yet prepared in advance.

Now everything will be set in order and checked. Because most of the clothing must be repaired, it is given to the tailor shop and the shoe shop.

GREAT DEMAND FOR SKILLED WORKERS

Because the demand for skilled workers is so great and there are almost no unemployed male skilled workers, the demand for skilled workers is now answered by women.

In this regard, it is noted that unemployed people will not be tolerated at all in the ghetto, not only able-bodied males but also able-bodied women capable of working.

THE *GETO-YEDIES* WARNS OF PASS PERMITS

Those who walk alone in the city with pass permits must join a bigger column that comes along at the first opportunity. It is even advisable to wait until a bigger column arrives.

Contrary behavior can easily lead to very great unpleasantness. At the least, it can end by confiscation of the pass permit.

WORK ON THE ISOLATING WALLS OUTSIDE THE GHETTO

In the new ghetto, [they] are already completed. In the next days, they start building the walled ghetto gate. These works take up a lot of material, especially lime, clay, and sand. Not only that, but most of the bricks from the ruined buildings that were demolished (almost 59,000 pieces) were used up.

To make it less complicated to take refuse out of the new district, a passage will soon be opened from the courtyard of Rudnicka 7 to Niemiecka 31 and from Jatkowa Street to Niemiecka 27.

WORKSHOPS

A New Stitching Workshop. A stitching workshop is being set up at Niemiecka 27 (entrance on Jatkowa into the new ghetto district). The workshop will be opened any day.

Ink is already produced in the technical-chemical laboratory. The ghetto's own ink will soon be on the market.

Chalk for the Ghetto Schools. The school unit appealed to the technical-chemical laboratory for chalk, which is necessary for normal teaching. The technical-chemical laboratory accepted the task.

In the Ghetto Barber Shops, 7,112 customers were served during September. Women will be employed in the new barber shop.

The Production of Washing Liquid in the technical-chemical laboratory looks good. Permission to import ashes from the municipal and government factories has already been obtained, and they will certainly be able to satisfy all orders. They predict a production of 1,100 liters a month.

OBLIGATORY VISITS TO THE BATH EVEN FOR RESIDENTS OF APARTMENTS WITH BATHTUBS

Until now, residents of apartments with bathtubs have been exempt from visits to the bath and were given bread cards even without bath notes.

Now, according to a specially published announcement, the ghetto representative also orders all residents of apartments with bathtubs to bring bath notes in order to get bread cards.

Not only must a person go to the bath, but it is important that his clothes also be disinfected.

WALK TO THE RIGHT IN THE STREET

The police calls to the attention of the general ghetto population that, regardless of all previous warnings, people in the ghetto are not very careful about keeping to the right when walking in the street. Because ghetto sidewalks are very narrow, the order to stay strictly on the right is more than justified—it is a necessity of ghetto life.

In the future, they will be stricter and will punish people for not walking on the right side.

ALFRED ROSENBERG SPEAKS

All around us is blood and bloodthirstiness. Warsaw, Kielce, Radom, recently Oszmiana, and in the midst of it all, a speech by the head of the Alfred Rosenberg Institute.

A day of art was held in Düsseldorf, and the main speech of the celebration was by none other than . . . my boss Alfred Rosenberg. What he said there is not important. But what interests us here are his remarks on the Jewish Question:

> The Jewish Question is now being brought to its last stage. We must remove Jews from all European countries so they will no longer interfere in their affairs.

Jews blink, ask, terrified, what that means—does it mean they will finish with the Jews forever? . . .

After Warsaw, Kielce, Radom, Częstochowa, Oszmiana, etc., it is no wonder Jews are scared. . . .

ŚWIĘCIANY'S TURN HAS COME

After Oszmiana, it is now Staroświęciany's turn. Most likely, this will also be carried out by Jewish hands—the hands of the Vilna Jewish police.

This evening, the older policemen, Bernstein, Levas, and Averbukh, left for this purpose.

MORE ABOUT OSZMIANA

This evening, eight [automobiles] with things from Oszmiana came to the district commissar of the Vilna district. According to the account of the Jewish police, 410 persons were shot in Oszmiana—old people, sick people, and cripples. But children's objects and clothing, which certainly did not come from any old people, were brought to the commissar of the Vilna district. Altogether, the clothing is estimated to be much more than they told us.

The German drivers say 800 Jews were murdered there.

A typical case: the automobiles with clothing were unloaded by Jewish workers. A barefoot girl spotted a pretty pair of women's shoes and asked a German if she could take them. He told her that if she knew where the shoes came from, she would surely not want to use them, even if they were made of gold.

So the German explained. "Now," the German added, "if you want, take them."

Of course, the woman took the shoes.

SETTLING THE NEW DISTRICTS

The settling of some of the new districts a week ago Sunday is 80 percent completed, according to the calculation of the Housing Department. The occupation of the apartments was done in orderly fashion. All arriving residents found their names marked on the rooms assigned to them.

A week ago Sunday, about 500 residents moved into the new district. This Sunday, the second 500. Meanwhile, the courtyard of Niemiecka 21 remains completely unoccupied because the repairs have not yet been completed.

THE PRESIDENT OF THE LOWER COURT OF THE GHETTO COURT HAS DIED

Last Monday, the president of the lower court of the ghetto court, Attorney Yisroel Kaplan, died in the hospital at the age of 62.

Born in Leningrad, the deceased had been a well known and distinguished attorney in Vilna for many years. He had long been legal adviser of the Vilna City Council and a member of the Vilna Attorneys' Council.[2]

DAY CARE CENTER IS EXPANDED

The day care center has filled almost all 100 places, but there are many applications by those entitled to use it. Therefore, the day care center is to be expanded to 150 places, and the place will be enlarged.

2. The funeral notice issued by the ghetto leadership concerning his death is in the YIVO Archives (Kaczerginski-Sutzkever Collection).

300 FAMILIES FROM KOVNO

According to reliable sources, 300 families were taken out of the Kovno Ghetto and sent to Riga this week . . . for work, they say. The families include as many as 1,100 persons.

AFTER ALL, SOMETHING IS HAPPENING . . .

Amid all the dreadful and painful events, a sunbeam sometimes comes, too: In Africa, a big campaign is developing against the Germans. Almost all big Italian cities are bombed every single day.

Ciano[3] has flown to Berlin. Berlin again justifies itself to the world [by saying] that England is telling lies, boasting that Germany allegedly proposed a truce.

Something is happening after all. . . .

OCTOBER 30 [1942]

IT IS LIKE AUTUMN

From outside, people bring into the ghetto what looks like "good" news—information that "something is nevertheless happening." Eyes shine with joy and grief at the same time. The good news brings joy; Oszmiana, Michaliszki, Staroświęciany don't let us rest. . . .

Over my head Messerschmitts roar and search. In the ghetto, nobody knows what—rejoice? So, what is this hunting? Something isn't calm, they say. I know that, unfortunately, this has nothing to do with us, nevertheless the roar is upsetting.

Outside, it is late autumn. I am not allowed to buy a flower in the street, although I am among the happy ones, who have the right to "pass." So I gather beautiful golden oak leaves. Instead of a flower, a leaf, a dried, yellow autumn leaf.

It is autumn and sad in my soul. . . .

A NEW MEANS OF TERROR

Near Podbrodzie, a new kind of forced-labor camp has recently been created. Those who have not registered "voluntarily" for work in Germany are sent there.

NO ONE WANTS TO BE MINISTER

Reliable sources tell that it was again suggested to the Lithuanians to create a Lithuanian government. But there is one obstacle: no one wants to accept a ministerial portfolio. . . .

People say that such persons might be found, but they are afraid of a bullet in the head. . . .

3. Count Galeazzo Ciano, Mussolini's foreign minister.

A MASS MURDER OF WARSAW JEWS

The underground [Polish newspaper] *Niepodległość*, which appears in Vilna, tells in issue 6 of a mass murder in Warsaw.

It says that in August, 300,000 Jews were murdered in Warsaw. The murderers were Lithuanians, Latvians, and Ukrainians, who did this on the spot, in the ghetto. Some [Jews] were taken on trains to Treblinka near Malkinia, many were conveyed as far as Bełz (in the Lwów district),[4] where they were poisoned en masse with gas or killed with electrical currents in the former soap factory there.

FROM THE "THIRD" FRONT

The same newspaper tells of Soviet paratroop landings: around Mir a battle occurred which lasted a few days. The "contest" was between a Soviet landing force, Germans, Byelorussians, and police . . . in which the Germans are said to have suffered heavy losses. The groups moved into the forest. The Germans didn't enter the forest.

In Głębokie, Szumsk, Szczuczyn, and Lida, there is unrest caused by groups of [Soviet] paratroopers. Near Varmunt [?], a train was blown up by a mine. Five train cars exploded.

OCTOBER 31 [1942]

HE WILL NOT SAY A BLESSING

According to the radio, the Pope has sharply condemned the slaughter of the Jews in a radio broadcast. He also said that until it stopped, he would refuse any blessing. It was supposedly a fact that a unit of Italian soldiers asked for a blessing and "His Highness" refused. Jews relate this and are satisfied. They think the conscience of the papal world is rising. Naive people—the terror of the last bombings in Italy is rising. When you're whipped from behind, it creeps into your head! . . . For Jews, this is also a consolation.

JUST A RUMOR

We reported that an Aktion presumably took place in Staroświęciany and that our Jewish police had already been sent there for that purpose. Now I learn that it is only an empty rumor.

GUESTS IN OUR PANOPTICON

The ghetto is like a panopticon. If District Commissioner Hingst wants to show off with his Jews, he brings [visitors] into the ghetto. If guests from Berlin come to

4. I.e., to the Bełzèc death camp.

Vilna, they are taken to the ghetto. Ever since yesterday, the ghetto has been seething with a commission from Berlin.

Whose commission? What commission? Nobody even asks. Everybody repeats "commission," and that is enough to drive people off the streets and to scrub and clean them.

Thus things were seething here yesterday from 12 to 3, and today from 9 in the morning to 1. Finally, a group of guests came. It turns out they are journalists. They strolled around here, observed, photographed the dead streets, and left.

Typically, the Jewish police paraded for the past few days, as we know, in their new uniform hats and without patches. Now, because of the Berlin guests, there was an order to doff the hats and don the patches. . . .

Apropos hats: one of the four who rule the Ghetto, Mr. Fried, apparently could not bear not getting a uniform hat, and he ordered himself a navy blue hat, similar to the uniform of the Jewish police commissars, of course without the gold insignia of rank. The ghetto laughs at him. . . .

As the group of journalists left the ghetto, the police went home immediately to change clothes. Now they parade once again as the sole rulers in full uniform.

HOW DOES IT LOOK FOR THE WINTER AID IN THE GHETTO?

Nothing is yet to be seen. They write, classify, and calculate. The distribution of things doesn't begin until the beginning of November. Meanwhile, I have learned that there are already 10,000 collected items, mostly underwear, shoes, most of them in bad condition. There is some warm underwear. The items are now being cleaned, patched, and straightened up.

The women on the committee say that aside from that, there are already 8,000 RM [Reichmarks] in the treasury, which means 80,000 rubles.

A REFLECTION OF WHAT IS GOING ON IN GERMANY

The Rosenberg Task Force, which has taken over the YIVO building, has recently shifted its "activity" from cultural to practical affairs. The cellar of the library storehouse and the safe have been emptied, and they bring potatoes, wood, and such. The shelves from the library have been taken apart, carefully packed, and 700 meters of shelves have recently been sent to Germany. Similarly, 30 balls of paper left over from the YIVO publishing house have gone, along with 12 cases of periodicals, 2 cases of Bolshevik literature, and other items. Shelves from Vilna to Germany! It is truly a reflection of what need Germany is in.

MORE ABOUT TODAY'S VISIT OF THE GERMAN JOURNALISTS

Those who know about it are satisfied and consider it a good sign: during the visit of the journalists to the workshops of the Technical Department, Murer explained that the workshops are being greatly enlarged and that he already has big orders for them.

Jews think: if the workshops are enlarged, if big orders come, this means that we are safe here. More than this, a Vilna Ghetto inhabitant doesn't demand.

TEN WOMEN OUT OF THE GHETTO

A week ago Saturday, when a group of Jewish and Polish workers returned from Nowa Wilejka, 10 Jewish women were detained at the railroad station. The Christians, on whom smuggled food had been found, had been detained on the spot. From the Jews, the food had been taken and they had been released. On Thursday, the Gestapo came with a list of the 10 released women. For two days, negotiations went on between the ghetto leadership and the Gestapo about whether the ghetto itself should punish the 10 women. Nothing helped, and the ghetto had to turn over all 10 [women].

THE LITERARY-ARTISTIC MEETINGS ARE CONTINUED

The meetings the Association of Writers and Artists began a year ago this winter are now being continued. An evening devoted to Judah Halevi[5] will take place tonight.

NOVEMBER 1 [1942]

GLAZMAN ARREST

This day is marked by a great sensation. The chief of the ghetto, Mr. Gens, decided to arrest his friend Glazman, the current head of the ghetto Housing Department. Gens thus rebelled against his ideological colleague, the Revisionist leader Glazman.

What is going on here?

All active society has recently been against Gens. Mainly for his actions during the Aktion of old people, and recently for the Aktion of Oszmiana. For this reason, Gens called a meeting of his officers this week and then a meeting of social activists and even later a meeting of brigadiers. Everywhere he publicly raised the issue of his calculations, because in this way he saves Jewish lives.

At the assembly of brigadiers, he tried to talk about the "stinking ghetto intelligentsia" who were against him. He even said he didn't give a damn about them. Now apparently he is setting out on a new path—to force the "stinking intelligentsia" to participate in those activities so that they too will be responsible along with him.

Yesterday Mr. Gens ordered his comrade Glazman to go with him to Staroświęciany and organize the Housing Department there. Glazman argued that that

5. Judah Halevi (ca. 1075-1141) was a Hebrew poet and philosopher, an exemplar of the so-called Golden Age of Spanish Jewry.

was national treason, and refused. At night, the police searched and arrested him. He was taken to the prison on Lidzki, the prison he himself had set up.

The sensation preoccupied the whole ghetto and, naturally, was commented on in various ways.

STAROŚWIĘCIANY

Early this morning Gens left the ghetto, along with Brojdo and a few others, for Staroświęciany. So Gens is riding around to take over several places, which are to be placed under his control. So we are becoming an . . . empire.

ARCHIVE OF COURT PROTOCOLS IN THE GHETTO

Attorney Milkanowicki, chairman of the high court of justice; Attorney Povirsker, the chairman of the lower court of justice; Attorney Rubinow, leader of the civil court; Attorney Nussbaum, prosecutor; and Mr. Kruk have been appointed to examine the archive of court protocols and set aside for the ghetto archive only those that are socially useful.

For me, the issue is especially interesting, because here, too, is a chance to save many historically significant court protocols. I personally can observe here a new aspect of ghetto life.

GITTERMAN — SOLOVEICHIK

With the sad news from Warsaw, I now learn that [Yitskhok] Gitterman took his own life.[6] The Soloveichik family is alive.

They say the Warsaw Ghetto is open; it has been turned into an open neighborhood.

20 PEOPLE TO VIRBALIS

Yesterday 20 workers came from Virbalis. Today people are snatched up in the street to replace the 20 who came—[they are being taken] to Virbalis.

NOVEMBER 2 [1942]

THE GLAZMAN CASE

The ghetto cannot calm down. Everything is full of the latest ghetto sensation: Glazman. Glazman is in jail, and everyone who talks about it is dissatisfied. Everyone thinks Gens is now pulling the strings and that everything is done under the pressure of his servants.

But few know the truth of these events. We who know understand that what is

6. False information was probably circulating in the ghetto. According to other information, Yitskhok Gitterman was shot by the Nazis.

at stake is not the freedom of one man. Gens wants to start a campaign against the "stinking intelligentsia" who are not with him. He wants to show them what power is.

May Gens not miscalculate. May he come to his senses and shake off his advisers. . . .

WHO ARE THE FELLOW EXECUTIONERS OF THE OSZMIANA PURGE

Only now received a list of names of Vilna policemen who were the closest assistants in the Aktion.

Those who led those condemned to the square of the execution included Brauze, Lak, Gurvich, Shapiro, and—the most horrible—Zubak, who even beat those condemned on the way to the execution.

As for who took part in the execution itself, I shall know more precisely later.

NOVEMBER 4 [1942]

GLAZMAN GOES INTO . . . EXILE

Yesterday morning Glazman was released and, at the same time, was dismissed as director of the Housing Department. He was also ordered to be sent for work to Sorok Tatary.[7] Thus [. . .]
[*Pages 505–506 of the diary are missing.*]

Glazman's Substitute
Shots at a Jewish Policeman
Daily Obituaries
About Jewish Properties
Ghetto Life in Staroświęciany Is Getting Organized
In Oszmiana, Too, a Ghetto Life Is Organized
The Chief of Police in Oszmiana
About the Shot Aimed at Schlossberg
What Belongs for the Time Being to Our Empire
A Council of Brigadiers
Also a Statute for Brigadiers
Brigadiers Are Punished, Too
A Plastic Map of the City of Vilna

By order of the district commissar, the Technical Department began working out a plastic map of the city of Vilna. For this purpose, the hall at Rudnicka 6 was divided so that the order could be filled without disturbance in the fenced-off part.

7. A labor camp, 15 kilometers from Vilna, where a group of 100 Jews worked in the forest, preparing heating material for the Vilna Ghetto.

The map will be made to a scale of 1:2,500 cm and will be about 4 by 5 meters in scope.

VOCATIONAL IMPROVEMENT COURSES FOR LOCKSMITHING AND CARPENTRY

[The courses] are already organized and will begin soon. There are many candidates for the courses.

SECOND GRADUATION OF GLAZIERS

The vocational improvement courses of glaziers held their second graduation last Tuesday. Forty-three persons graduated. Those who remain are held over for the new course that has been organized.

A NEW WORKSHOP FOR LEATHER PRODUCTS

A workshop for making gloves, briefcases, handbags, purses, wallets, etc., is organized.

POLICE WILL COLLECT LIBRARY BOOKS

There are subscribers to the library in the ghetto who do not return their borrowed books. Now such "frozen" readers are put on a special list to be given to the police. The books of such subscribers are recalled by force.

In especially malevolent cases, people will be punished for keeping library books.

GHETTO ADMINISTRATION RESETS THE TIME

By order of the chief of the ghetto administration, the clock will be set back one hour, as of Tuesday, November 3, just as in the whole city, by order of the proper authorities.

So far, all work and office hours will remain unchanged.

A NEW PLAY

Man Under the Bridge is now being prepared by the theater. The rehearsals are already in progress. This is a play of the European genre.

NOVEMBER 5 [1942]

SAD ANNIVERSARIES

Since the beginning of September, we have entered a series of anniversaries, one sadder than the other: September 6, going into the ghetto; the 7th, the already famous story of Lidzki Street, which cost 3,000 victims. Then a series of Aktions. October 1, Yom Kippur, in Ghetto 2, two Aktions, 800 and 900 people at night, people being driven to the gate with a loss of 2,200 people. Then a year ago today, October 3 and 4, Aktions in Ghetto 2 with 200 victims; after a small sigh of relief, more Aktions on the 16th, 21st, and 24th, which cost more than 10,000 heads.

A year ago today, we were at the high tide of the river of blood. But today, a year later, it doesn't feel as if we shall ever get out of the bloody sea. We splash and splash. We drown and drown. The wave has receded from Vilna for the time being, but it will inundate Byelorussia and now floods Crown Poland.[8]

Warsaw, Kielce, Lublin, Częstochowa, and others. We drown incessantly in a sea of blood and bury one another.

May this be mentioned on one of those bloody anniversaries.

IN THE WORK UNITS — "BOOTY-COLLECTION-CAMP OF THE LUFTW[AFFE] 7" (BENZYNÓWKA)

This is one of the most popular labor workshops in the ghetto, but also one of the units where the work is tense and hard. Two hundred and ten Jews work there, 100 of them as transport workers and 110 as specialists, such as: locksmiths, auto mechanics, carpenters, etc. The special work departments are also run by Jewish specialists.

Up to now, they have worked 10 hours a day. But as of the 1st of the month, they work 8 hours a day.

FREE BATH TICKETS

[These] must now be distributed in larger quantities because, since there is obligatory attendance of the bath, there have been several requests to receive free bath tickets.

During the past month, a thousand free bath tickets were distributed.

GLAZMAN GOES INTO EXILE . . .

Glazman is released from jail, released from . . . his office as director of the Housing Department, and is now again released from "ghetto freedom." The chief of the ghetto is sending him off in a provincial unit for forest work.

For not subordinating himself to an order, Glazman, his closest friend and ideological colleague, receives—exile.

In conversation with a representative of a social group in the ghetto that advised the chief not to exile social activists for refusing to carry out social missions against their conscience, Gens again elaborated his "theory" that he calculates mathematically. That he wants to save Jewish heads. That [in] Oszmiana, only 18 people under 40 were killed, etc., etc.

8. Ethnic Polish territories that until 1918 were part of tsarist Russia and were ostensibly autonomous under the Polish crown.

"AKTION" IN GRODNO AND ENVIRONS

Rumors reach us that in Grodno and environs, Aktions are taking place. Ghetto 2 in Grodno is presumably already liquidated.

All around blood, blood, and more blood. Mostly Jewish blood.

NOVEMBER 6 [1942]

CANNON FODDER

At 12:30 today, in the local Bernardine Garden[9] there was a swearing-in of Lithuanian soldiers. The German speaker asserted that the soldiers are of the best Lithuanian sons, ready to shed their blood for a new Europe. After the playing of "Deutschland, Deutschland über Alles," the Horst Wessel Song, and the Lithuanian anthem, the "ceremonies" ended.

IN KOVNO — CONSCRIPTION

They say that a conscription of 18- to 35-year-olds is taking place in Kovno. If this is correct, it should be understood that Lithuania has finally acquired a new government, which no one has so far wanted to enter.

NOVEMBER 7 [1942]

SCHLOSSBERG DEAD

At 4 o'clock this morning, in the ghetto hospital, the Jewish policeman Nosn Schlossberg died at the age of 34. The deceased was a lawyer. Here, in the Vilna Ghetto, he had a very bad name. In the village, where he was wounded, he behaved very badly. Apparently, Jewish workers complained about him to the . . . partisans, and apparently the latter decided to teach a Jewish servant of Hitler's Germany a lesson.

The police treat this as a matter of Schlossberg having fallen at his post. The police wear mourning for a whole day. An honor guard of policemen stands at his coffin. The funeral is planned with great pomp. Suffice it to say that for the first time in the ghetto, by special order of the district commissar, a score of police will accompany the coffin to the Jewish cemetery.[10]

The funeral takes place tomorrow, the 8th, at 9 in the morning.[11]

9. In front of the Vilna Catholic Cathedral.

10. The Jewish cemetery was situated far outside the ghetto, on the other side of the Wilija River.

11. The YIVO Archives (Kaczerginski-Sutzkever Collection, no. 300) contain the announcement, distributed by the ghetto chief and the police, for the funeral of policeman Schlossberg.

NOVEMBER 8 [1942]

TWO FUNERALS

Today it was crystal clear that the ghetto is divided into two distinct worlds. Each of them is a world apart from the other.

When the teacher Gerstein recently died, all those who strove for and lived with modern categories came to his funeral. But none of the ghetto authorities were there. Nevertheless, Gerstein was a name and one of the most popular Jews in cultural Vilna. But the authorities don't know anything about that and aren't interested in it.

Today, more than ever before, this division has become more prominent than ever.

THE FUNERAL OF NOSN SCHLOSSBERG

As we said before, the wounded policeman Nosn Schlossberg died yesterday at 4 in the afternoon in the hospital. The ghetto police declared mourning. At 6 in the evening, a memorial assembly was held in the hospital, where Gens, Dessler, Muszkat, and others spoke.

The funeral took place at 9 in the morning. The procession moved from the hospital to the sports field, where the coffin was placed on a special catafalque. Cantor Edelson and his choir sang psalms. Then the ghetto representative, Mr. Gens; Rabbi Jochelson; Mr. Fried; Mr. [Dovid] Kapłan-Kapłański; and Mr. Kammermacher spoke. Then the cantor and the choir sang "El Male Rahamim," and the funeral procession went back through the streets of the ghetto to the gate. The coffin was carried the entire way—from the hospital to the athletic field and from the athletic field to the ghetto gate.

The Jewish police in [their new] hats, and a small group of the ghetto population, took part in the funeral. A special kind of group. During the funeral, the ghetto population was driven from the streets to the . . . gates. Thus the funeral had another "attraction." The police received permission for a few dozen people to go to the cemetery.[12] The police column in their festive hats marched to the gate. There they had to take off their uniforms and became "civilians." Thus they marched with the funeral. The operetta made a bad impression. The policeman's funeral didn't leave any trace of sympathy at all. . . .

DR. MOYSHE HELLER

The referee on statistics from Strashun 6 had been sick for a long time. From time to time, however, he would come to work. Recently he went back to the hospital, and after an illness of three days, at 4 P.M. on the Sabbath, November 7, he died.

12. I.e., to march through the city of Vilna.

Soon, a meeting of the funeral committee took place under the chairmanship of H. K[ruk], including the Teachers' Union, the Association of Writers and Artists, representatives of the Office of Statistics, representatives of Kailis, and Grisha Yashunski of the Cultural Department.

Obituary posters soon appeared in the street in the name of the committee, the Office of Statistics and his co-workers, and the Youth Club.

The funeral took place on Sunday at 3 in the afternoon. A large group of cultural activists, intelligentsia, etc., took part. At the open coffin, the director of the Cultural Department, Mr. [Grisha] Yashunski, and the teacher Yankl Kaplan[13] made short speeches.

WHO IS DR. MOYSHE HELLER?

The deceased, born in a village near Zbaraż (eastern Galicia) in 1894, received a Doctor of Law from Vienna University and studied humanities in Lwów and Vilna Universities. For 20 years he was a teacher, since 1924 in Vilna. He taught history in Vilna Jewish educational institutions and was beloved by his students.

Dr. Heller also did research in history and Jewish statistics. In the ghetto, he directed the Office of Statistics in the ghetto library. His death was mourned deeply by all ghetto circles.

Both funerals on one day, but each with a distinct appearance. People regarded the funeral of Nosn Schlossberg as [that of] a stranger. Dr. Heller's funeral roused in the ghetto the old Vilna, which had been washed away in blood.

The ghetto is divided!

THE MEMORIAL SERVICE IN HONOR OF DR. MOYSHE HELLER

Aside from the participation of the workers in the funeral committee and the special funeral announcement, a memorial gathering took place on Sunday at 12 noon in the office. H. Kruk and Olicki, on behalf of the teachers, spoke. The leadership of Strashun 6[14] did everything to ensure that the son[15] of the deceased, who has been working here for a year as a volunteer, should now inherit his father's position. There are promises about that.

13. Born in 1907 in Vilna, and a graduate of the Yiddish Teachers' College. He was a Communist activist and a member of the Communist Party in Vilna. From 1943 on, he belonged to the staff of the FPO. During the liquidation of the Vilna Ghetto on September 23, 1943, he was hanged by the Germans (along with Abrasha Chwojnik and Asye Bik). For his biography, see *Teachers' Memorial Book* 1954:366–367.

14. I.e., Kruk.

15. Gabik Heller, born in 1928, was 14 years old. Other family details about Dr. Heller can be found in Rudashevski 1953:18–56. The original Yiddish manuscript of Rudashevski's diary is in the YIVO Archives (Kaczerginski-Sutzkever Collection).

NOVEMBER 9 [1942]

A CHAT WITH THE CHIEF

While settling several official matters—like getting 20,000 rubles to acquire Polish books for the library, taking pains that the ration of the deceased Dr. Moyshe Heller should be inherited by his son along with the father's position, etc.—the chief chatted at length with me about recent events in the ghetto.

The issues of Oszmiana, Glazman, and finally the attack on Nosn Schlossberg. The chief exhibits a certain nervousness. He feels that it is not all right. True, he behaves courageously. He tries to justify himself. Through me, he wants to get to the so-called Vilna society. Considers that, in Oszmiana, he saved Jews and, at the same time, tells me about the—

KIEMIELISZKI DESTRUCTION

Weiss ordered him to carry out a purge also in Kiemieliszki. He says that the history of Oszmiana and its painful effects made him hold out on the Kiemieliszki proposal. Now, he says, the whole Jewish town was indeed shot. He is sure, he says, that if he had taken it in hand, he would have saved many Jews.[16]

GLAZMAN

"I don't consider him such a saint," he [Gens] says. A year ago, he [Glazman] himself segregated Vilna Ghetto residents during the distribution of protection permits. How come he now wants the role of a saint? Should I now be defiled by him?

He is also very annoyed by outside intervention. He means Sorok Tatary, with its sad finale—the shooting of the Jewish policeman.

Obviously the chief is nervous; he feels that things really aren't all right. He is looking for people with social understanding to settle accounts with. You feel the influence of strangers moving him and persuading him to all those actions.

Our chief is torn apart and is seeking support.

EMBEZZLEMENTS

Meanwhile, the ghetto rots from day to day and from hour to hour. One person grabs another's hand; one person points to another. Now, as they say, there is a big embezzlement of wood in the ghetto. The embezzlement includes up to a million rubles.

If this is true, it raises the specter of a series of filthy tricks of the former Obmann and current economic manager. People say his position is shaky.

16. An eyewitness account of the destruction of Kiemieliszki was published in Kaczerginski 1947:164–166.

WINTER AID CAMPAIGN. THE DISTRIBUTION OF CLOTHES HAS ALREADY BEGUN

In the warehouse of the winter aid campaign, the distribution of clothes has already begun.

A special committee was chosen for the distribution of items, consisting of Mesdames Fried, Kuller, Solodukha, Gronner, and Kammermacher, and Messrs. Pińczuk and Muszkat.

A BRIGADIER COUNCIL IS APPOINTED

After the last assembly of brigadiers, the ghetto representative and the candidates nominated for the Brigadier Council appointed the following to constitute the Brigadier Council: Chairman, Mr. Kapłan-Kapłański (Booty Collection Warehouse); Vice-Chairman, Mr. Kammermacher (Gestapo Unit); Secretary, Lidowski ("City Command"); and members, Pinsker ("Benzynówka"), Kaufmans (Gr. H. Bauleitung), Steinhauer (Heinrich Tabatsh), Golomb (Spanish War Hospital). Candidates are Messrs. Ozerlanski (Field Command) and Woron (Sanitation Gathering).

A special statute for the Brigadier Council is now drafted.[17] As always, Kapłan-Kapłański pushes himself in everywhere. . . .

DOCTORS' COMMITTEE GOES TO THE PROVINCIAL CAMPS

With permission received from the district commissar, a special doctors' committee has recently gone to the camps of Jewish workers in Vilna district to set up proper medical-sanitary checks against possible epidemics. The commission consists of Doctors Brodski, Epstein, Weinryb, and Seidler. It will visit the camps in Biała Waka, Rzesza, Kiena, etc.

WHAT BECAME OF THE CHILD CRIMINALS AND WHAT THEY HAVE BEEN TURNED INTO

We once talked about the establishment of a workshop for delinquent children. With time, from that initiative came a new initiative like the transport brigade Yeladim, the home for homeless youth (Strashun 4) with its workshops, etc.

Now it is a half year since the transport brigade Yeladim was founded. We extract a few figures from the item published in the last issue of *Geto-yedies*.

Since it began, the brigade, which consists of the neglected half-orphans and children who are compelled to undergo self-improvement training, has achieved great popularity among the entire ghetto population. Every single day in the streets of the ghetto, you see the youngsters harnessed to the loaded carts they pull, involved in a healthy atmosphere of productive work.

17. The statute (regulations) of the Brigadier Council, confirmed on November 20, 1942, is in the YIVO Archives (Kaczerginski-Sutzkever Collection, no. 223).

At first, the brigade numbered 28 youngsters, but by now there are 71. The office of the transport brigade (Rudnicka 14) has a monopoly on transport labor in the ghetto. There are 10 carts, and the children work in two shifts, for six hours a day.

During this half year, the children have transported about 100,000 bricks and 4,000 cubic meters of wood in the carts. This is in addition to food for the bases and shops and private orders.

Clothes and shoes from the winter aid campaign are expected for the children.

The children also receive a school education. Moreover, a choir of the children's brigade is also active. Now, to commemorate a half year of the brigade's activity, a public performance of the choir is being prepared.

In terms of budget, the brigade is connected with the Department of Social Welfare, but the management of the work and practical activity is in the hands of a special committee.

NOVEMBER 10 [1942]

ANOTHER MASS OF BOOKS

In the Rosenberg Task Force in the YIVO building, books rain down again. This time Yiddish ones. In the cellars, where the YIVO library once was, on one side they load . . . potatoes, on the other, the books of the Kletzkin and Tomor publishers. The whole cellar and several side rooms of the ground floor are crammed with packs of those book treasures. Whole sacks of Peretz and Sholem Aleichem are there, bags of Zinberg's *History of Jewish Literature,* sets of Kropotkin's *Great French Revolution,* B[erl] Mark's *History of Social Movements of Jews in Poland,* etc., etc. Your heart bursts with pain at the sight. No matter how much we have become used to it, we still don't have enough nerves to look at the destruction calmly.

By the way, at my request, they have nevertheless promised to let us take some books for the ghetto library. Meanwhile, we take them on our own. We will, naturally, use the promise. . . .

AGAINST PREGNANCY

In the ghetto, you are forbidden to give birth. We recall again the dreadful order the Germans once issued about it. Now a social campaign is conducted here against pregnancy.

A BENEFIT EVENING OF THE SYMPHONY ORCHESTRA

On Sunday, the 8th of this month, a rich concert program took place in the Ghetto Theater. The best pieces of all the concerts so far were played. The soloists were the singer Lyuba Lewicka, the pianist Miss Sladkin [Zlatkin?], and violinist Shimshn Khaykin.

STATISTICAL BULLETIN ABOUT THE WORKING GHETTO

The latest statistical bulletin devoted to the question of the working ghetto has just appeared.

NOVEMBER 12 [1942]

PEOPLE ARE HAPPY AND TREMBLE

Great events around us. In Africa, there is a great destructive offensive on the German and Italian army. Germans run away and Italians surrender. There are already 60,000 prisoners. An enormous quantity of ammunition has been captured. More than 400 kilometers have been taken from the enemy. The English are now 150 kilometers from Tobruk.

Algiers and Morocco are occupied by English and American soldiers. Hitler occupies the second part of France, unoccupied France. Pétain protests and Hitler writes an appeal to the . . . French people.

The radio news pours out, and you can't keep up with it. Sidi Barrâni taken. In Tunisia, American landings take place at the same time as German landings. . . .

The Germans report that the battles at Stalingrad have been concluded. England reports that the Germans lost more than 400,000 men there.

Concluded with what, if Stalingrad is still in the hands of the Red Army? . . .

Churchill says that the time for being only on the defensive is past. Now comes the second phase—to break the enemy. Stalin again affirms that there will be a second front, certainly in Europe.

Even the ghetto now feels that the German bluff to conquer all the Mediterranean Sea is no more than a bluff. There, the English are the bosses. The second front does come to Europe—to clean out Africa, to drive the enemy from the Mediterranean Sea, to set out for Italy, to go to the Balkans—the second front in Europe.

. . . Nevertheless, people tremble. They build melinas at a new pace. People prepare.

In his last speech, on November 9 in honor of the Munich [Beer Hall] Putsch of 1923, Hitler stated, among other things: "The Jews wanted the war to exterminate the European races; the war has been turned into an extermination of Jewry in Europe."

This is how his speech sounds in the original. The local Polish newspaper did not print this passage. . . .

NOVEMBER 14 [1942]

SOMETHING CHEERFUL. — PALESTINE AND THE JEWISH COLONIZATION IN THE ENTIRE WORLD.[18] — 100 RUBLES[19] FOR THE DESTRUCTION OF THE JEWS IN KIEMIELISZKI

The events in Africa, Tunisia, and Morocco, the occupation of unoccupied France, and everything taking place around it, have cheered the ghetto. The ghetto suddenly saw another force, aside from the Bolsheviks, starting to work—the English and the Americans. It is cheerful in the ghetto, and there is no lack of jokes.

"Where will the Germans get so many people for . . . prisoners?"

But in the ghetto, everything goes on as if nothing has happened:

Yesterday, in the court[room], there was a lecture by the Chief Dr. Pohl, titled "Palestine and the Jewish Colonization in the Whole World." . . .

My fellow worker, Comrade [Shloyme] Bin[der],[20] who collects material for me in the university library, says he was in the reading room of the library. The librarian came to him and showed him a letter. In the letter was 100 rubles. . . . Why now?—She said a student gave it to her with a request to give it to the Jew. Binder is looking for the student, but meanwhile he has disappeared.

KIEMIELISZKI

Commandant G[ens] tells me:

I refused and now they did it themselves. In Kiemieliszki, between Landwarowo and Troki, 30 kilometers from Vilna, 800 Jews were murdered. People assume that only 80 were saved, escaping into the nearby forests.

IWIŃSKI HAS GONE TO THE PARTISANS

Today I heard that Ester Iwińska's[21] only son [Wiktor], who fought in Spain with his wife [Bronye] and who, in the last war years, came here as a refugee, has re-

18. The Yiddish edition had "German Colonization," but the typescript found in Israel, and Kruk's table of contents, make it clear that it is "Jewish Colonization."

19. The Yiddish edition had "100 Thousand Rubles," an obvious error, as indicated in Kruk's table of contents and the following entry.

20. A journalist who worked on the Kovno *Folksblat* and *Yidishe shtime*. He was also the correspondent from Lithuania for the Warsaw *Folkstsaytung*. In the ghetto, he was one of Kruk's informers about Lithuanian society. In 1943, he was sent to Camp Uligurme, in Estonia, near Tartu. He died of starvation and scabies in 1944. For his biography, see *Lexicon* 1:295–296.

21. A distinguished Bundist in Poland, one of the first Jewish women lawyers in Warsaw and a member of the Warsaw City Council. She was a sister of Wiktor Alter. She survived the war and lived in Brussels, Belgium.

cently gone to the partisans, where his wife has been for a long time. More precise news about it in the future.[22]

THE "BLACK" WEISS[23]

A policeman who often goes to the Gestapo tells, among other things, that the Gestapo call Weiss "the Black Weiss." You would think [of this as] a Gestapo camaraderie, but nevertheless there is a sense of uneasiness in those words. . . .

I don't need to say another word about who this "Black" Weiss is. . . .

A small thing, Weiss in the Vilna Ghetto? . . .

THE OSZMIANA VASSAL

We know now that the Oszmiana "chief" from Vilna is the famous Jewish policeman Drezin. Incidentally, the one who betrayed melinas freely, who sang the famous song "We Made Ourselves Happy" after the last Oszmiana Aktion, etc. As we said, he is now the governor of Oszmiana. Today, in a private conversation about the court in Oszmiana between him; myself; the president of the ghetto court, Mr. Povirsker; and the commissar for criminal police, Mr. Zagaj[ski], the "boss" answered thus:

"I am the only law in Oszmiana. My right hand is the criminal police; my left, the law. Both together are justice." And he smiled with his friendly, vagabond, good-natured smile. . . .

Thus he splendidly and succinctly characterized the "justice" of ghetto rulers around here.

WHAT IS NEW IN LITHUANIAN SOCIETY?

Actually, we must ask if there is a Lithuanian society at all now. That question is answered by a former Lithuanian activist, who replies that in fact, it almost does not exist. There are no movements; there are only individuals with this or that point of view. There are even circles that issue appeals, a newspaper; in general, however, those are not movements.

The mood in the Lithuanian society is such now that no one has any more illusions about the Germans. In this respect, Lithuanian society is completely sober. General Kubiliunas[24] went to Berlin a few weeks ago and has not come back, and

22. Either Kruk does not keep his promise to tell about the Iwińskis or this information was written on the pages we don't have. Biographies of Wiktor Iwiński and his wife, written by Chaim Nussbaum, who was with them in their partisan group, are in *Generations* 2:454–457.

23. *Weiss* means "white."

24. An extreme Lithuanian nationalist and antisemite. Just before World War II, he tried to make an uprising against the Smetona regime, which was too "liberal" for him, and wanted to transfer the power to Valdemaras, the leader of the Lithuanian Fascists. When the Germans took Lithuania in 1941, he created a Lithuanian regime of "general advisers," which did everything the Nazi rulers demanded. Now it seems that this Quisling felt deceived in the German "pro-Lithuanian" attitudes.

people think he was arrested for not agreeing to carry out a mobilization. A few weeks ago, 13 persons also went to Berlin on a would-be trip; in fact, it was supposed to be a Lithuanian government. They haven't come back, either. People think they have also been detained.

The Tautinikas (Death's Heads), Lithuanian nationalists on the far Right, in fact Lithuanian Fascists, issue an illegal newspaper; nine issues have already appeared.

Clearly, sobriety is even coming here.

LITHUANIANS TO POLES

Recently an appeal has been distributed in the city, from Lithuanians to Poles. It talks about the brotherhood of both peoples, the common enemy, and a common aspiration to fight the enemy, the occupier and exterminator.

NOVEMBER 16 [1942]

WE ARE INVITED BACK TO THE LITERATURE ASSOCIATION

Recently I was visited by a delegation from the management of the Association of Writers and Artists in the ghetto and presented with a unanimous decision to ask friend Hersh [Gutgestalt] and me to return to the management since they believe we can help them a great deal because, ever since we have been gone, the work has died out.

The actors Blacher and Szadowski were in the delegation.

At a meeting of the B[und], it was decided to reply with the same "no" that we gave to a similar invitation of the Aid Society.

PEOPLE SIT IN MELINAS

Recently the building of melinas has once again become topical in the ghetto. Warsaw and all similar events have once again put the ghetto residents on guard. Lately, Christians had regularly been spreading a rumor that a purge was to take place in the ghetto on November 15. In recent days, there has been alarming information that in Białystok and Grodno, "purges" are going on. All that together, apparently, terrified some of the ghetto residents so much that many people spent the night of the 15th–16th in melinas.

Now people here say that it is calm in Białystok and Grodno. But "purges" are said to have taken place in the small towns around Białystok.

Meanwhile, people are not staying behind. Jews are building melinas. . . .

THE GHETTO ADMINISTRATION RULES. — ARRESTS OF REVISIONISTS

In connection with recent events concerning Glazman, Gens is uneasy about the interparty cooperation. He is annoyed mostly by the Revisionists.[25] Again, appar-

25. I.e., his own party.

ently, new rumors are circulating in the administration about cooperation,[26] and this time, he is furious. He attacked other Revisionists, reviled some of them, arrested some, and put Police Commissar [Ayzik] Averbukh (a close friend of Glazman) under house arrest.

Yesterday, Milkanowicki was also called in. Gens scolded him for "cooperation with the parties" (?). Today Milkan[owicki] received a letter saying that the Aid Society (which he chairs) is dissolved and that he is authorized to compose a new leadership of the society. According to that letter, that leadership must include three brigadiers, one representative each from the Department of Social Welfare, Winter Aid (?), . . . the Labor Office, and others. A second letter said that Milkan[owicki] can also include people from the ghetto society. . . .

So why dissolve what was merely a shadow of a society and its social activity? In our circumstances this is not a question. In any case, a question that cannot be answered.

RUMORS

To the series of rumors about Aktions and melinas comes a series of inside rumors, which have recently had a great success in the ghetto.

A few days ago, a rumor circulated that the former member of the Judenrat and leader of the Technical Department, Engineer Gukhman, was dismissed. The rumor turned out to be wrong. Today, another rumor: Fried is resigning, and the commissar of criminal police, Zagajski, replaces him. This, too, is nothing more than a rumor.

Who is spreading the rumors? People say here that it is interested parties. But about that in the very near future.

A few ghetto residents were arrested yesterday for spreading rumors.

THE ACCOUNT OF 1942.—VILNA IS POLISH AND FREE OF JEWS

In the latest issue (7) of the illegal Vilna [Polish newspaper] *Niepodległość* of October 1942, the editor conducts a statistical battle with the Lithuanians over whether Vilna is Polish. It says there:

In 1916, Vilna had:

70,620	Poles
3,699	Lithuanians
61,233	Jews

26. Apparently implying the unified front of the underground partisan movement, which embraced all parties in the ghetto and included Glazman in its leadership.

In 1931:

127,479	Poles
1,413	Lithuanians
54,607	Jews

In 1942:

97,000	Poles
33,000	Lithuanians
12,000	Jews

The last numbers are based on the survey made this year. The number of Poles stands out. It has fallen to 97,000 from 127,479. The Lithuanians have increased, Jews . . . 12,000.

The *Niepodległość* emphasizes that of 55,000 Jews, 12,000 have remained; they claim that some committed Communists left with the Bolsheviks and that about 40,000 died in Ponar, murdered by the Germans with the hands of the Lithuanian "Ponar shooters."

The newspaper is satisfied: in spite of all machinations, Vilna is Polish. The lack of 40,000 Jews is a joy, for one thing; for another . . . something to regret, and perhaps really a joy that Vilna has been freed of Jews by foreign hands.

November 17 [1942]

The Goal to Kill Glazman While He Is Still Alive

Gens has learned that before Glazman was chief of police, the Revisionists used gold from Ghetto 2 for party purposes. As administrator of the Housing Department, he [Glazman] supposedly distributed apartments first to Revisionists. He thought about the party first, etc.

Because of that, police officer Averbukh was arrested yesterday in his flat; another one, Borke Schneider, was beaten by Gens so badly that he is in bed today.

I learn today that an investigation about the gold is going on, and Averbukh has admitted to some tens of thousands of rubles.

This evening, the police called an assembly of all policemen. Gens reviled the Revisionists for using money for Revisionist purposes, and from the lectern, he ordered Averbukh sent immediately to Lidzki [Prison]. His comrades, the policemen Salzstein and Salzwasser, are thrown out of the police and are to leave the hall at once.

Then Police Chief Mr. Dessler also cursed and told the guilty ones to go to hell.

Thus, apparently, they want to justify the ugly treatment of such a close person, as Glazman was. They try to turn him into a criminal, and there are those who help do that. . . .

NOVEMBER 18 [1942]

THE PIKE STINKS FROM THE HEAD . . .

Changes are taking place in Lithuanian society about which we mustn't waste any words. What I recently told about them is enough to make the matter absolutely clear. But once again, to show that Lithuanian society is trying to break out of its mold, it is enough to read the Lithuanian article in *Naujoji Lietuva,* no. 267, November 11, and the denial the next day. We attach the excerpts from that newspaper with their full translation in Yiddish:

[*The original excerpts are missing; the Yiddish versions have been translated here.*]

> LET US CONTRIBUTE GLOVES AND SOCKS
>
> Many Lithuanian youths now work in the transport service. Even beyond the Lithuanian borders, there are self-defense battalions.
>
> Lithuanian society must take care that the men of the transport service and the soldiers don't freeze their hands and feet in the winter. For this purpose, our own people are asked to contribute gloves and socks.
>
> Anyone with a spare pair of gloves or socks is eager to take it to the "Mutual Help," Wielka St. 12. Donations are accepted from 8 to 14 o'clock.
>
> If only Granny had a mustache . . .

It all seems fine, except for the addition: "If only Granny had a mustache . . ." But the next day comes an apology and a correction:

> In the news chronicle in the previous issue, the first item, "Let Us Contribute Gloves and Socks," a sentence was included by error of the proofreader which had absolutely nothing to do with the information itself.
>
> For that unpleasant matter, we beg the readers' pardon.

Thus, a lapse on the part of the proofreader. But I learn that this lapse will cost the typesetter dearly.

DR. WYGODZKI'S WATCH

Who Dr. Wygodzki was for Vilna needs no elaboration. Why Dr. Wygodzki was taken out of Vilna we have often mentioned. But no one—more precisely, few—remember that a very old wife remains and she is lonely and helpless. After long and hard efforts, the Judenrat remembered her and endowed her with a quarter ration. This is how much people think about her!

Of all the Vilna Jews, she has not had anyone to turn to but . . . me: the woman is isolated and abandoned, and now a doctor shows me she wants to send Dr. Wygodzki's watch into the street and sell it.

"We want to ask you," he appeals to me; "we think you can achieve something here. It is," he says, "a disgrace for Vilna to let the watch go into the street. It would not hurt anything for the Judenrat to buy the watch so the old woman won't be upset about it. . . ."

I decided to get involved, asked for a letter from the wife stating that the watch really belongs to her, and I went to Fried. Fried agreed that I was right, and now I am waiting for their decision about what the watch is worth to them.[27]

FIGHTING THE MOODS IN THE GHETTO

In the ghetto, they fight . . . moods. As we said recently, not only do people spend the night in the melinas, but a great many stay all night fully dressed.

How does the ghetto leadership fight this issue?

First, he ordered the arrest of a few people who spread rumors. Second, he ordered that theater productions are to be performed regularly and entertain the people. Thus the ghetto population might get out of the lethargy of moods and rumors.

In the auditorium on the 18th of the month there will be a light concert, presenting the second part of the review "You Can't Know a Thing." On the 18th is the program "Jazz 6" and part of "Rye Years and Woe to the Days" . . . [28]

In short, people are entertained . . . woe to the days.

WHAT HURTS THEM

In the Vilna (German) newspaper, there is a splendid writer. He does it in a few lines, each time short and sweet.

In today's issue, there is a little article:

[*The article is missing.*]

The "writer's" concern here is in what he cannot swallow, that the first thing the Americans did when they penetrated North Africa was to cancel the orders of Pétain's regime concerning the Jews in Algier and Morocco. That is: the Jews can again take an active part in public life. . . .

A JEW SHOOTS A GERMAN?

From Kovno, they tell the following dreadful event:

A Jewish resident of the Kovno Ghetto, one Mek, tried to get out through the ghetto fence. A German saw this and started shooting at him. The Jew shot back with a revolver. Mek was captured with 350,000 RM [Reichsmarks] on him, as well as gold and jewels and a Swedish passport (?). The whole case is being investigated. Meanwhile, 20 Jews are said to have been shot.

They say the ghetto meanwhile is guarded, almost surrounded. . . .[29]

27. Mrs. Wygodzka's thank-you note to the Judenrat for the 2,000 rubles she got for her husband's watch is in the YIVO Archives (Kaczerginski-Sutzkever Collection, no. 591).

28. A pun: "Korene yorn un vey tsu di teg" (rye years and woe to the days) sounds like "Korene yorn un veytsene teg" (rye years and wheat days).

29. Mek was hanged on November 18, 1942. The information that 20 Jews were shot in connection with the Mek case was apparently false. More precise facts about the issue are told in Gar 1948:130–133; Oshri 1951:102; and Garfunkel 1959:index.

WHAT IS GOING ON IN THE LITTLE TOWNS AROUND GRODNO?

I learn that in the little towns around Grodno, an Aktion has been going on since November 1. Only skilled workers have been left in the little towns. All the rest have been destroyed.

AND WHAT IS GOING ON IN GRODNO?

The remaining Jews from the surrounding little towns like Druskieniki, Marcinkańce, Szarkowszczyzna, etc., have been gathered in Grodno. Now all those who are not specialists are taken out of there to Dębówka. What will be done with them there, one can only imagine. . . .

WHY ARE THEY DOING THIS?

On the pretext of money embezzlement, as we wrote yesterday, Glazman was brought back from the forest by the police, and the prosecutor interrogated him. After the interrogation, Glazman was once again taken to prison at Lidzki.

After the interrogation, in the police station, I met with Glazman. Policemen asked us not to talk to one another. Nevertheless, we exchanged a few sentences. He said he felt cold and untouched by the entire matter. . . .

The whole ghetto is on Glazman's side today. Everyone asserts that if he's a thief, how come they remembered it only now?

Really, why are they doing this?

16 JEWS SHOT

People here say that the 10 women who were taken out of the ghetto for smuggling from Nowa Wilejka have been shot today. Another 3 women and 3 men were shot along with them. Altogether, then, 16 persons.

A few Christians were also in the group.

WE ARE REINFORCED CONCRETE

Yesterday the first theater performance took place . . . to intoxicate the population. The ghetto representative took the floor and said, among other things, that there is nothing to be scared of. The ghetto is now safer than ever. The population must be calm, disciplined, and must work.

SPAIN MOBILIZES

People here say that the radio said a mobilization is taking place in Spain.

Why on earth is Spain mobilizing?

Clearly, you have to be prepared for everything. What if the Americans and the English might want to capture it? . . .

The press doesn't yet write a single word about it!

NOVEMBER 20 [1942]

[Pages 525–530 of the original are missing, for the period of November 20–25, 1942. Kalmanowicz 1951:48 contains an entry dated November 20, 1942: "A day of commotion in the tents of Jacob. An order was issued to register those who eat and don't work. The commandant [Gens] declared that the one who was carrying out the order, his permanent assistant [Dessler], changed the order himself and took the permits from all Judenrat employees and assembled them all in the theater. A rumor circulated all over about evil decrees. People started hiding. Doors were shut. The order was soon withdrawn."]

November 20 [1942]
Glazman in Jail

November 21 [1942]
"Battle in the East" for the Destiny of Europe

November 24 [1942]
Melinas
Kovno and Michaliszki
Again Warsaw
[Only] in Fives in the Street
What the* Geto-yedies *Are Telling: Order in the Michaliszki Ghetto
Economic Council of Five Persons
First Graduating Class of New Chimney Sweeps
The Smithy Is Enlarged
Also the Tin Shop and Carpentry Shop
Before the Enlargement of the Turner Workshop
Gevald! Where Is Sholem Aleichem? (Tragicomical Events in the Ghetto and Outside It): The Street Aktion?!
Commandant Muszkat in Jail! . . . The Ghetto Looks for the Culprit
The Hero Shapiro

November 25 [1942]
Muszkat
Two Times Two Is . . . Lidzki

[Page 531 begins at the end of an entry from which it can be inferred that Police Commissar Muszkat was demoted. From an entry in Rudashevski 1973, dated November 25, it seems that Muszkat was too energetic about the registration order, creating a panic in the ghetto, and this behavior led to his arrest.]

[. . .] times two is . . . Lidzki.

The above-mentioned lecture was repealed, and the Jewish police were happy: "He is finished. . . ."

"The night devil," as they call him here, "is a goner. . . . "

The ghetto administration also punishes him. Today the Ghetto Theater took away his regular . . . easy chair in the theater auditorium.

It is not clear how Muszkat will end.

. . . AND GLAZMAN STILL SITS!

He sits. He is interrogated. Papers grow. His friend Averbukh is already half free, only under house arrest. A few more searches took place this week, but the main hero, Glazman, is sitting.

What will come out of this?

LITTLE LIBRARIES FOR FOREST WORKERS

The ghetto library provides several forest-labor camps with little mobile libraries. Such little libraries have already been set up in a few places, including, in recent weeks, Kernavė.

GREEN LIGHT IN DANGEROUS DARK PLACES

The Housing Department has decided to install green lights in all dark passageways and such, which can be dangerous for the ghetto residents in the long winter nights, when the street is slippery.

UNTO THE THIRD GENERATION

So it happens. Not only do Jews suffer from the yellow patch; often half and full Aryans do, too. We have often talked of cases of baptized Jews being driven into the ghetto. There was such a case a year ago, when baptized peasants were brought into the ghetto and later taken to Ponar. There was a similar case during the Aktion of "old people" in the ghetto, when old Tereza Kochonowska was killed. In Warsaw, the converts even had their own Catholic church (on the corner of Leszno and Karmelicka). In Lida, a group of baptized Baptists were in the ghetto. Extraordinarily, during the march past the gate (to check the Vilna Jews), the Lithuanians spared them and did not kill them. Nevertheless, on May 8, 1942, the Baptists of the ghetto were sent off with hundreds of Jews to the "other world." In the same way, my baptized friend, the PPS member Dr. Antoni Pański, died in Łukiszki Prison.

Hundreds, perhaps thousands, were taken out of the world like this. Staying far from the Jews, but yet as Jews unto the third generation.

NOVEMBER 26 [1942]

YOU NEED MELINAS . . .

Yesterday the most dreadful news has been brought into the ghetto. First a rumor circulated that Himmler issued an order to destroy all the Jews of Europe by

January 1st. Later that order became a speech, supposedly reported on English radio.

People ask one another; everyone seeks the truth. Women tell men they know something but . . . don't want to say anything.

Once more: you need melinas! . . .

This evening Messrs. Gens and Brojdo went into the restaurant at Rudnicka 13 and announced publicly that all rumors are false; people must calm down. But nobody believes anything. . . . They don't calm down. . . . You need a melina. . . .

Things go very well on the front. The Germans are beaten in Stalingrad, and the English and Americans are advancing in Africa. So Jews tremble again. If they are being beaten, will they get to us. . . . The conclusion—melinas. . . .

Jews are at sixes and sevens. Everything is good, but everyone trembles and fears tomorrow.

A REWARD FOR PARTISAN WORK

In Jaszuny, the Gestapo shot a few dozen local Jews, Poles, and Gypsies . . . because the Bolshevik partisans attacked three German railroad workers.

FROM 450,000 TO 35,000

Number 8 of the illegal *Niepodległość* says that in Warsaw and several other cities, gallows have been set up in squares and sentences are carried out publicly.

The Warsaw Ghetto has been reduced from 450,000 to 35,000 Jews. The newspaper swallows this without a word from the editors. . . .

November 28 [1942]

About Himmler

The world "is dealing with" us. It sounds like mockery. We're expiring in blood, and there, there in the big world, they're constantly "dealing with" us. . . .

[*Pages 533–535 of the original are missing.*]

"Shots on Mickiewicz"

"Series of Obituary Notices"

Sleep Calmly! Premiere of the Ghetto Theater

"The Man under the Bridge"

December 2, 1942

Bent Over

Workers from Virbalis and Panemunė [?] Return to the Ghetto

The Brigadier Council

The First Board of the Plastic Map Is Ready

G[ens] Will Judge . . . Glazman

An Award . . . a [Loaf of] Bread

December 3 [1942]
A Guest Brings Regards

[. . .] Today, a guest from Starošwięciany stayed here—Bat'ke. Now he is a real big shot there, and today he came here on official business.

Bat'ke is far from what he was in the Medem Sanitarium. He is generations away from the one who took part in the M[edem] film.[30] He swallows every word from us here, wants to know, wants to understand, wants to learn—maybe to use our "practice" in his little town. Twice we met. Parted warmly and got a promise: he will make an effort to come more often.

THE TEACHER H[ERSH] GREENBAUM

I learned that the teacher Greenbaum[31] and his wife and child were living in Brasław. He was saved; the wife and child were murdered.

Where is Greenbaum?

The speaker looks around, blinks his eye as if he hesitates, and says, quietly:

"He has gone to the forest. . . ."

"In our area, there are about 60 young people in the forests. . . ."

"Young people in our place want . . . to die like heroes. . . ."

He looks around to see if the walls are listening and breaks off. The rest—another time. . . .

NEW REGULATIONS FOR JEWISH WORK AND JEWISH WORKERS

According to a proposal from the German Labor Office, the district commissar of Vilna City confirmed new statutes introducing a new regimen for Jewish work outside the ghetto. According to the new regulations, more precision and clarity will be introduced into the arrangements of the so-called Jewish work unit, reward for Jewish work, pass permits, release from work, etc.

The precise text of the decision is being translated into Yiddish and will be publicized.

100,000 BOOKS IN THE GHETTO

In November, the ghetto library went beyond the figure of a hundred thousand books distributed to readers. Because of this, the library is organizing a big cultural morning recital, which will take place in the Ghetto Theater on Sunday, the 13th of this month, at noon. On the program: Opening by G. Yashunski, welcome from the ghetto chief, writers, scientific circles, teachers, and the Youth Club. Dr.

30. The Yiddish film on the Medem Sanitarium, *We Are Coming*.

31. Born in Warsaw about 1908. He graduated from the Yiddish Teachers' College in Vilna and was active in Bundist organizations wherever he was a teacher. In 1939 he left Warsaw as a refugee and settled in Brasław, his wife's home town. He did not survive the war. For his biography, see *Teachers' Memorial Book* 1954:117–118.

Ts. Feldstein will speak on "The Book and Martyrdom," then a lecture by H. Kruk, "100,000 Books in the Ghetto." The second part will be a concert of words and music.

The finale: distribution of gift books to the first reader in the ghetto and the youngest reader of the library.

[*Page 537 of the diary is missing. Kalmanowicz's entries for the same days (1951:50) tell of arrests at the ghetto gate for smuggling books. Some people were beaten. He also reports that the workers in the Rosenberg Task Force were working on the periodicals. The paper was being delivered to warehouses to be recycled for industrial purposes.*]

Warsaw
Vilna
They Dig in Ponar

December 5 [1942]
They Don't Dig, They Burn!
Glazman and Averbukh Released

[. . .] after long writing, making protocols, etc., Glazman and Averbukh are free. The files show there is no one to accuse. But the chief cannot give up holding a trial. After several negotiations, a conversation took place between Glazman and Gens. Glazman is released and Averbukh is again a policeman.

The quarrel in the Revisionist family is thus resolved.

HANUKKAH IN THE GHETTO

We have often written that the ghetto maintains traditions. Every holiday, no matter what, is enthusiastically celebrated here. Thursday, the 3rd, a big Hanukkah evening took place in the theater auditorium, arranged by the police. After speeches by the "leaders," medals were distributed to all policemen who have been in the police since its first day. In the second part of the evening, there were satirical review numbers, where policemen mocked each other.

One of the speakers was Levas: he thinks that, like Judah the Maccabee, the Jewish police will also lead the Jews out . . . of the ghetto.

People ask: Then where will the Jewish police be?

Another Hanukkah celebration was organized here by the religious circles. According to the playbill, this is called a Hanukkah Commemoration.

In the ghetto, lighting Hanukkah candles was allowed only with one candle for all eight days. The reason given was that candles are expensive and we can't afford them.

The Judenrat employees received an extra Hanukkah "ration"—two kilos of bread, two packages of matches, and one egg.

8,958 WORKING

According to the information from the file section of the Labor Office, the number working outside the ghetto on November 25 amounted to 5,695 men and 3,263 women—together, 8,958 persons.

10,000 LITERS OF WASHING LIQUID

Pramprekiba ordered 10,000 liters of washing liquid, which is produced in the technical-chemical laboratory in the ghetto.

Washing Cream—there are plans to produce it. Materials necessary for this are being prepared.

Tests of shoemaker's wax for making shoemaker's threads have been made in the technical-chemical laboratory. The tests are successful.

They are also about to produce tailor's chalk.

A GHETTO HOSTEL

In the building of the former Old People's Home on Jatkowa 4, a hostel will be opened in the ghetto, intended for those coming temporarily from outside, for example, [those from] forest camps.

IN QUARANTINE

At Rudnicka 23, for the first month of its existence, 33 persons have gone [through the quarantine]. From Zezmer, 9; from Vievis, 20; and from other places, 4.

THE SANITARY POLICE

During November [the sanitary police] wrote 759 tickets and made 246 arrests.

In that period, the number of children in the day care center was enlarged to 105; in the children's home, to 69. Milk, semolina, and macaroni, obtained from the municipal distribution center especially for children, were distributed to the children.

In the hospital, on the 1st of this month, there were 171 patients. During the previous month 244 new patients came in, and there was an average of 166 patients a day.

In the outpatient clinic during the previous month, there were 6,445 visits and 732 house calls to patients.

NEW CONDITIONS FOR WORK IN THE FOREST

From the 1st of this month, new working conditions have been introduced in all forest camps by the ghetto administration. According to these conditions, forest workers have to do one and a half cubic meters a day. Within that daily norm, they are paid 50 rubles for a cubic meter of heating wood. Over the norm, they are paid 100 rubles a cubic meter.

The previous payment for the work with food and meals has been canceled.

HANUKKAH IN THE GHETTO

In addition to our information about Hanukkah celebrations, we also note: the Yeladim made a Hanukkah play in the Ghetto Theater on the 13th of this month.

At 6 in the evening on the same day, a special Hanukkah enterprise was organized in the theater with a rich artistic content.

On Friday the 11th, the children's club organized a Hanukkah evening with "latkes." The evening turned from a Hanukkah evening into a splendid evening of the Vilna children from the former Yiddish secular schools. The evening ended with the anthem of the TSISHO schools. . . .

In the ghetto, as we see, there were a lot of Hanukkah celebrations. But the last enterprise turned from a miracle of Hanukkah into a miracle of youth, eager for a new free life. . . .

CURRICULUM IN THE SCHOOLS

In the five ghetto schools, five committees of pedagogues have been formed to work out the following curricula:

1. Yiddish and Hebrew; 2. Religion; 3. Jewish and general history; 4. Arithmetic; 5. Natural science and geography.

DECEMBER 13 [1942]

100,000 BOOKS

The ghetto library, supervised by the Cultural Department, held a ceremony today in the Ghetto Theater in honor of the fact that 100,000 books have been read in the ghetto library. That celebration was made with great pomp, and among the Yiddishist and cultural circles in general, made quite an impression.

Aside from the festivity, the bookstore in the ghetto set up a demonstration booth of books that can be obtained in the ghetto. The booth, artistically arranged, showed that despite all pain and suffering and despite the hard and bitter situation of the Vilna Ghetto, a cultural heart is beating here. One indication is that you can get the best books in the ghetto. Externally, too, the ceremony was tastefully prepared. The stage was adorned with nice big diagrams of readers and reading in the ghetto. The ceremony was opened by [Grisha] Yashunski on behalf of the Cultural Department. H. Kruk, the director of the library, read a lecture titled "100,000 Books in the Ghetto," analyzing the ghetto readers. The lecture is attached.

[*The lecture is missing.*]

Friend Leo Bernstein[32] spoke about the book and martyrdom. Greetings were

32. Born in Skuodas, Lithuania. In the ghetto, he was primarily active in Hebrew cultural work, was the director of the Youth Club, and was connected for a time with the ghetto police. A member of the Revisionists, he finally fell into disfavor with Gens. He was in a partisan unit. Af-

then delivered on behalf of the Association of Writers and Artists by [Yosef] Glazman, on behalf of the scientific circles by Dr. [Daniel] Feinstein, and on behalf of the Brigadier Council by [Dovid] Kapłan-Kapłański. After the second part, which consisted of a concert, there was another word from the director of the library, who mourned all the perished librarians and readers and finally distributed two gift books to the oldest and to the first readers of the ghetto library.[33]

RIVKE EPSTEIN IS HONORED

In the closing words, a member of the library staff who was honored was Comrade Rivke Epstein, the veteran and popular B[undist] activist in Vilna.

HOURS OF THE GHETTO LIBRARY

For the convenience of the readers, as of Sunday, the 6th of this month, the hours in the ghetto library have been shifted. Readers are served from 11 in the morning until 5:30 in the evening.

FOR SPREADING FALSE RUMORS,

the ghetto court sentenced ghetto resident D. to seven days in jail.

PARTISANS

In Bezdany, on Thursday the 10th, at night, a train carrying soldiers, military ammunition, and instruments was blown up.

IN WIELUCIANY, TOO . . .

In Wieluciany, a little town about 12 km from Vilna, there are also partisans. There they are in complete control. They come in the middle of the day, and the Germans are terrified to show their faces. All the partisans there are Russians.

ORDERS ARE ISSUED

Through the radio, we pick up orders for the partisans. Among other things, they are told: Group 82 filled its order. Group 32 is ready. Attention, Group 76, you are warned. Such and similar codes are heard often.

From one day to the next, the matter is apparently more organized and centralized.

CLOSED LITTLE SHOPS

In recent weeks, many little shops have been opened in the ghetto. This week, all of them have been liquidated and the merchandise confiscated. The reason is that

---

ter the war, he lived in Israel and the United States, where he was a professor of mathematics; he died in 1984.

33. The poster of the ceremony, "100,000 Books in the Ghetto," is reproduced in Kaczerginski 1947:64–65.

in German units, the word spread—it was popular among the Germans, that in the ghetto you could get food that can't be obtained in the city. The Poles and Lithuanians already know this. . . .

The matter could do very serious damage to the ghetto. So the police liquidated the trade.

Whether this will help is hard to say.

DECEMBER 14 [1942]

IT IS TOO GOOD

People have recently been joking in the ghetto that it is too good; nevertheless, it doesn't hurt to have a . . . melina.

Recently in the ghetto things really have been good. Considering all that surrounds us, the residents of the Vilna Ghetto are really not living badly. Great amounts of food are brought in, flour, potatoes, etc. There is no lack of bread; vegetables can be acquired. There is wood. However, the need for clothing is great. Here, no one can help. The committee for winter aid has done little to alleviate the great need for clothing.

But in general, it is still bearable in the ghetto. Indeed, from time to time, entering at the gate is interrupted, but afterward, another chapter goes on—they smuggle!

People are secretly envious. After all, it is the fourth year of the war, 15 months in the ghetto, and seldom does anyone die of hunger. But the fear is incessant, and people seek and build melinas en masse. . . .

Nevertheless??, you have to have a melina! . . .

POLES ARE TAKEN OUT OF LUBLIN

These days, the radio says that Poles are being taken out of Lublin.

NORWEGIAN JEWS ARE TAKEN TO WARSAW

English radio also talks about that.

AN ANNOUNCEMENT IS POSTED AGAINST BUYERS OF STOLEN GOODS

An announcement signed by the ghetto representative was posted, warning against buying stolen goods and threatening severe punishment. According to the announcement, the buyer is responsible for the theft. This has to do with the disasters that might come from goods stolen from German units.

AGAINST WEARING JEWELRY

For the second time now, there is a warning against wearing jewelry. Even fake jewelry is advised against.

By order of the ghetto representative, those married to Aryans must register with the police by the 14th of this month.[34]

OPENING OF NEW VOCATIONAL IMPROVEMENT COURSES

The Labor Office continues spreading more vocational knowledge among ghetto residents, to help older workers improve their skills in their vocation and to prepare the young as soon as possible for their future working life.

In the past four months, courses have been completed for glaziers, house painters, furnace masons, and chimney sweeps. Now four new courses are available for workers who are especially in demand for construction: locksmiths, cabinetmakers, carpenters, and welders. It was very hard to set up the courses because of a lack of tools, but these difficulties were somehow overcome, and on December 3, the formal opening of the new courses for 250 students jubilantly took place.

The ghetto hostel is open. Bedding and linens are scarce.

The special bath for the unclean on Szpitalna 13 is already finished and will be presented to the Health Department.

A project against bath deserters and people with lice has started across the entire ghetto. The sanitary police seek them out and turn them over to the sanitary-epidemiological unit of the Health Department.

GHETTO INDUSTRY

As we have often noted, we are making constant advances on the road to creating a big industrial center in the ghetto. More precisely, this is the road taken by the Germans. They'd push the ghetto to make Jewish production for military purposes. The following entries will demonstrate this more clearly.

RATIONAL COORDINATION OF ALL GHETTO WORKSHOPS

By order of the ghetto representative, as of the 1st of this month, the management and activity of all existing workshops in the ghetto are reorganized. The Technical and Workshop Departments, which have existed so far, are combined into one Department for Ghetto Industry. Engineer [Grigory] Gukhman was appointed head of the department.

The new Department of Ghetto Industry consists of: 1. Technical workshops, managed by Engineer [Shimen] Markus; 2. Light workshops, managed by Mr. [Yoyel] Fishman. Brush making, braiding, bookbinding, cardboard sections, etc., were added to the latter.

An order office, to take orders from outside the ghetto, is already active in the department, under the management of [Bore] Beniakoński.[35] But a build-

34. The official announcement is in the YIVO Archives (Kaczerginski-Sutzkever Collection, no. 33).

35. From Kovno. After the Gestapo shot Chief Gens, Beniakoński was chief of the ghetto for a very short time.

ing outside the ghetto, on Zawalna near the ghetto, has been planned for the office.

A project office is active in the department under the management of Mrs. Engineer [Flora] Romm. The project office is flooded with work. All kinds of orders for furniture, toys, writing materials, etc., are drawn. Almost all the orders are from outside the ghetto.

Both tailors' workshops are combined in one big tailor factory, which will soon be moved to a new, very spacious and appropriate building.

They are planning to set up the technical laboratory in one of the present tailors' workshops. The laboratory will be expanded and rationalized. The production of several new, useful items will be introduced.

FRESH POLICEMEN

Because of the expansion of the Vilna Ghetto empire to the surrounding smaller ghettos, the police will also be expanded. *Geto-yedies* announces that everyone who thinks he is well built, healthy, and fit for the work of a policeman can register in the police headquarters as a candidate for a police job.

Free wood is now being distributed by the Winter Aid Committee to ghetto residents in need. Applications for that are being accepted.

AN EVENING FOR THE 25TH ANNIVERSARY OF THE DEATH OF MENDELE MOYKHER-SFORIM

[It] is being prepared for the 20th of this month in the Ghetto Theater. A lecture and an artistic program are planned. On the 8th of this month, it was 25 years since his death.

IN THE SO-CALLED WORK UNITS.— *DEUTSCHE SICHERHEITSPOLIZEI*[36] (GESTAPO)

This is one of the oldest units of Jewish workers, dating back before the ghetto. This unit has existed since July 1, 1941. Now the unit numbers 130 workers, including 20 women. Of the 130 workers, 100 persons work in headquarters itself. About half are employed as skilled laborers: shoemakers, tailors, cabinetmakers, masons, locksmiths, auto mechanics, tanners, etc.

It must be noted that the productive and good work of the Jewish workers has had a very good effect on the relations with employers. When invited by the Jewish labor police, the employers responded very positively about the work of their laborers.

The brigadier of the unit is Mr. Nosn Kamenmakher [Kammermacher?].

36. German Security Police.

Thirty Days since the Death of Dr. Moyshe Heller

Last Tuesday evening, a memorial service was held in a closed circle in the teachers' club, devoted to the end of the thirty days of mourning the death of Dr. Moyshe Heller. The teacher [Yankl] Kaplan presented a broad portrait of the deceased. Kaplan had been his student and recently had daily working contact with him. Teacher Yisroel Lubocki shared memories about the deceased.

Anniversary of the Death of Engineer M. Idelson

Last Thursday evening, a memorial service devoted to the first anniversary of the death of Engineer [Mark] Idelson was held in the teachers' club in a teachers' social group. The deceased was described by the principal of the technical school in the ghetto, Engineer [Matthias] Schreiber. He emphasized Engineer M. Idelson's great virtues and, most of all, his moral purity. Two pupils of the technical school spoke very briefly about the deceased.

DECEMBER 15 [1942]

BLOODTHIRSTY INNOCENCE

History repeats itself. The crucifixion in the name of the crucified God repeats itself after a delay of 700 years in the name of the German Huns and the "New Europe." The history of the Crusaders[37] of the thirteenth century has been renewed and modernized by the Fascists of the twentieth century. In the past, they burned books and a few individuals as well, heretics and rebels; today they destroy presses, and they burn Jews en masse by the hundreds and thousands.

Philip the Fair (early fourteenth century) followed the path of Philip Augustus, of the most dreadful exploitation and robbery of the Jewish masses. If they could not extract enormous sums from the Jews for their own empty royal coffers, they did not refrain from dealing in Jews as if they were animals. Philip IV bought from his brother Count Charles de Valois all his Jews, paying 20,000 livres for all of them.

History repeats itself: The Vilna Ghetto is a work station because the current German authorities are interested in it. The Vilna Ghetto produces for the war effort, and as long as that goes on, it is good—the Jews retain the right to live. But this is not done with the sophistication of the times of the Crucifixion and Inquisition but with the hypocritical sophistication of German Fascism.

In the Polish press today, we read an innocent item: "The wage rate for Jewish workers will be raised."

37. The Yiddish edition has "Inquisition," which is surely a mistake or meant as a metaphor.

How bloodthirsty that innocence is, is indicated by this fact: Jewish workers were indeed told yesterday that they were getting a salary increase as of December 1. But therefore, working time will be increased from 8 to 10 hours.

How does the raise look?

1st category of unqualified	receive 30 pfennigs an hour
2nd category of semiqualified	receive 34 pfennigs an hour
3rd category of skilled workers	receive 38 pfennigs an hour
4th category of skilled workers	receive 44 pfennigs an hour
5th category of brigadiers	receive 50 pfennigs an hour

But as of today, all categories together receive no more than 15 pfennigs an hour. The rest is taken by the district commissar, the real boss of the ghetto. In sum, it is like this: it is announced to the world that the Jewish workers are getting a salary raise. The employers, who have to pay more, will get a longer work day, increased from 8 hours to 10 hours. The Jewish worker, the slave, gets a . . . quiet order, increase in all categories (thus to increase the income of the district commissar). The Jew is filth, his blood is good to drink, and not only do they drink it but they also bathe in it.

The case of the ghetto production is similar. The ghetto sets up workshops, comes up with all kinds of inventions, and produces for outside the ghetto. What does the ghetto get out of it?

The Germans thus earn an average of 25 pfennigs an hour for every Jewish worker, which makes 2 RM a day.[38] Close to 8,000 workers go out of the ghetto every day as slaves. Their earnings come to 16,000 RM a day, a half million RM a month.

DECEMBER 16 [1942]

PEOPLE PRAY FOR US, PEOPLE SPEAK ABOUT US, PEOPLE WEEP FOR US

This is our situation. Ourselves helpless, we have stood for almost two years like oxen to the slaughter, with outstretched necks, waiting for the knife. Death no longer frightens. Yet as long as we are alive, the heart nevertheless throbs and reacts to every rumor, every piece of gossip.

An Aktion in Warsaw is a rip in the heart; an Aktion in Lithuania, a message that we are again in line. . . .

And the world—what does the world know about it? Only now has it understood and begun to shout in alarm. They broadcast pro-Jewish radio programs,

38. Kruk calculates thus: the payments for the different categories, minus the 15 Pfennig the Jewish worker gets, equal an average of 25 Pfennig.

they speak, they threaten, they cry about us, and . . . they pray. Jews fast, and Jewish newspapers come out with black frames in honor of our loved ones, in honor of our friends, in honor of all those torn away from us.

Rumors reach us that in Sweden, they have started a campaign against the bloodbaths of Jews. Sweden calls upon all neutral countries to protest, and people say that countries, neutral and half-neutral, are joining that project. Churches ring, clergymen preach, and the masses cry over the fate of the people of Israel.

MINSK PARTISANS

The Minsk partisans have made themselves known in that area and really control several places. At the beginning of this December, the Germans sent a special pacification expedition against them. After a few days, they returned with about . . . 400 dead. The objective nevertheless wasn't achieved, and the partisans go on doing what they can.

AT SIXES AND SEVENS — PEOPLE ARE PREPARING FOR NEW YEAR'S EVE

Here in the ghetto, people are making big preparations for St. Sylvester's.[39] By order of the ghetto chief, the ghetto must celebrate. So the café at Rudnicka 13 is preparing a New Year's Eve celebration. An evening party is being arranged in the office of the booty unit (Rudnicka 7), and in the theater, at 7:30 in the evening, there will be a performance of the review "You Can't Know a Thing"; at 10 in the evening, a solo concert; and at 12:30 at night there will be a review and jazz until late at night.

The chief wants us to forget, hence his order.

That's how it is—the Rebbe ordered us to be happy. . . .[40]

LITHUANIANS ON THE SLAUGHTER OF THE JEWS. — IN LITHUANIA, 46,000 JEWS REMAIN

Every child knows that among the Lithuanians, there is a lot of caterwauling. Moreover, we have often talked about it. Now an illegal Lithuanian newspaper is lying in front of me, *Niepriklausoma Lietuva* (Independent Lithuania) no. 9, of December 1, 1942. The newspaper is put out by the populist, Smetona nationalist, and Catholic circles. This issue states, among other things, that in the territory that is now Lithuania, 46,000 Jews remain.

According to estimates, there were once 250,000 Jews here. Thus, 80 percent of the Jews were annihilated.

39. I.e., New Year's Eve, but called by its Christian name and without its contemporary (American) secular connotation.

40. An allusion to a Hasidic song. "Rebbe" is the title of a Hasidic leader.

JEW MURDERER . . . TO THE FRONT!

In the same issue of the illegal paper, I learn that all Lithuanian soldiers from the execution battalions of Jews, etc., have been sent to the front. So, apparently, this is how the Germans get rid of the eyewitnesses to the slaughter in our area.

MORE ABOUT JEWISH PROPERTY

Today's press announces, as several times before, that whoever will not supply information about Jewish property will be treated as if he were stealing from the . . . Third Reich.

Of course, you draw the appropriate conclusions from that.

"A NEW COOPERATION WITH WORLD JEWRY"

Under this headline, the local press wrote yesterday and today that next Sunday, in all English synagogues and other places, demonstrations will be organized in "honor of the poor persecuted Jews" (their quotation marks). The press writes against Hitler and his partners, and so the Jews, along with Churchill, Roosevelt, etc., want to start a new anti-Hitler campaign. The newspaper is angry that even before Christmas, Churchill will devote a special session [of his government] to the Jewish question. They predict the issuance of a joint declaration in favor of the Jews. The local press quotes the English newspapers that the campaign should have a large scope and will be one of the biggest enterprises in the history of the Jews for the past thousand years. The newspaper says that during the campaign, what has happened to Jews in the East must be told.

The local press concludes that this is another proof of Jewish Bolshevik-plutocratic cooperation. . . .

DECEMBER 18 [1942]

THREE MINUTES OF SILENCE

Only now has the world grasped that the Germans are murdering Jews by the hundreds of thousands. Only now!

We have already noted that campaign undertaken on the other side of the front. Today, I learn from the radio:

The governments of London, the Soviet Union, and the United States issued a joint declaration today about the persecution of the Jews in all countries occupied by the Germans. The signers of the declaration include the governments of Belgium, Poland, Holland, South American countries, and others.

THE DECLARATION

The declaration says: "In view of the persecution of Jews, taking place all through the German-occupied countries in a way unprecedented in history, aiming at the annihilation of the Jews of Europe." The declaration was supposedly broadcast simultaneously on Moscow, London, and Washington radio.

[British Foreign Secretary Anthony] Eden told, among others, of materials he has outlining a total extermination plan in Eastern Europe which was carried out in an unfathomable manner. Among other things, he says that not long ago, a half million Jews were taken from Western Europe to the East, and all of them, with few exceptions, were killed. He says that the nations will take steps to punish the guilty with all severity and . . . save the future of the Jewish people.

Hearing that, a local Jew smiles behind his mustache, and seeks his murdered wife, his child, his near and dear ones between the lines. . . .

"If they had remembered [us] a year ago," more than one says mockingly.

"How can this help?" say a lot of people here, in great despair.

The local Jews, tested and soaked in blood, don't believe in help from anybody. Nevertheless, people lend an ear. It warms [your heart]. . . .

In all countries, three minutes of silence were proclaimed yesterday. And Chile even proclaimed a ten-minute general strike. In the entire civilized world, mass protests are taking place. An "El Male Rahamim" was broadcast on London radio.

And so they honor us, so . . . they are silent about our fate, and so they say "El Male Rahamim" for us.

Harshly tested and turned to stone, without sisters and brothers, without fa[milies]. . . .

[*Page 550 of the diary is missing. This page probably included the end of the entry about the declaration and the first entry about the 23 garden workers Kruk refers to on page 551. Rudashevski's diary (1973) for December 19, 1942, says that these workers came from the Sołtaniszki(??) estate. They were detained at the gate as they came from work. Flour was found on them. At Murer's command, they were taken directly from the gate to Łukiszki Prison.*]

The Ghetto Is Enlarged Again
Arrested and Released
When the Ghetto "High Life" Celebrates
Not the Culture Department but . . . G[ens] Himself

[*The end of the first entry on p. 551 concerns the literature competition that Gens proclaimed, on condition that it be in his own name.*]

[. . .] so everything is good. It must only be in his name.

MY CANDIDACY

A few days ago, [at the announcement] of the project, Grisha Yashunski asked me if I would agree to be on the jury for literature. I told him I had nothing against it here and under the conditions. But now, after the answer from Gens, I withdraw: I will not be on a jury for a prize that must be in Gens's name![41]

DECEMBER 19 [1942]

BETWEEN FIRE AND WATER

So they look helpless, people emptied of the most minimal human demands, people who have not only been turned into serfs, owned bodies, but condemned people waiting their turn.

Yesterday, because of the pro-Jewish campaign on the other side of the corridor and [the news] here, that the ghetto would be enlarged, the mood in the ghetto seemed to be more cheerful: the world remembered us, even though too late, yet . . . nevertheless. The ghetto will be enlarged, what could be better? . . .

Today it turned out badly and everything has gone . . . bad.

The 23 garden workers (as we said yesterday) have been released from Łukiszki and, in the evening, were brought to the ghetto jail until the release. But at 10 this morning, the ghetto trembled. Two Gestapo agents came back to take the 23 workers. One of them said that he was very sorry for the men, but he had to do it because that was the order.

Four of the 23 were released, and the other 19 were taken to Łukiszki by the two Germans and Jewish police. The chief, Mr. Gens, tried unsuccessfully to intervene. In the evening, there was a rumor that the 19 were no longer in Łukiszki. . . .

The Dante-like scenes in the courtyard of the ghetto jail and the impression the whole tale made here soon turned the ghetto into a ball of nerves—everything stands under the sign of the 19.

We have sobered up from the sympathy announcement of recent days, and the ghetto population asks if this can be good for the Jews? If this will help?

[Some] joked and thought it couldn't be worse than it is, but some [thought] that this will only provoke and . . . Who knows [what may happen].

In short, there are pessimists and optimists. Fear and—satisfaction.

A third issue has joined the fray: the ghetto is enlarged. For what? Because they are liquidating many camps and bringing the Jews into the Vilna Ghetto? Or perhaps they are being concentrated to carry out an Aktion here?

The thought ripped through us like an explosion, and everything together combined to make the ghetto gloomy and dreary again in the evening. Optimism was rare.

41. The YIVO Archives (Kaczerginski-Sutzkever Collection, no. 472) contain the statement of the director of the Cultural Department about setting a competition for literary, musical, and artistic creation in the ghetto (dated December 15, 1942). On that statement is a note from Gens that he agrees, but that it must be in his name.

This is how people look with no support, no perspective, not the slightest gleam of hope. All bridges are torn up behind us; for us there is no spark of anything better. Smashed, dishonored, and humiliated—can it be otherwise?

80 JEWS ARE DYING!

A friend, who was in the area of Kiena with a German automobile this week, says that about 80 Jews work there. The people are half dead—with overgrown hair, infested with lice, and dirty. The only thing they asked of him was "*lekhem*" [bread]. They work loading big, heavy wooden posts onto wagons. The work is done under the drill of the whip, with which the "Todt" people lash them.[42]

The Jews are from Baranovitsh. Coming from work with permits, just as here, they were stopped, taken off the street of Baranovitsh, and brought here. It happened in July. Since then, they have been enslaved.

THE LITHUANIANS TURN THEMSELVES INSIDE OUT

After all the recent changes in the mood of the Lithuanians, it is interesting that all that is also expressed in relations to Jews wherever they meet them. The 23 Jews told of extremely friendly relations from the staff in Łukiszki Prison. The same with relations to Jews in all other Lithuanian offices. The Lithuanians are really turning themselves inside out to demonstrate their friendship to the Jews. . . .

Times are changing: a suffering man sympathizes with a suffering man. How long has that been unthinkable?

BRIGADIERS HAVE EXPENSES

The Christian holidays are approaching, and [the brigadiers have] rolled up their sleeves. They are collecting money and [gathering gifts to have something] "to please" the Germans or other mis[fortunes. . . .] How can it be without a holiday gift from the slave to the lord?

Just as it goes with Jews, so it goes with Christians:[43] even in the ghetto, they give holiday gifts.

At 11 tomorrow morning, a group of invited guests will have the chance to admire the so-called plastic map of Vilna. So far, only four plates have been finished, the center of the city. That gift will be sent on Monday to Murer, and by Murer to Hingst. We will probably write more about the other gifts.

42. Todt is the name of an official German economic and industrial company, which used slave labor in the occupied areas. Established by Dr. Fritz Todt in 1938 to construct military installations and special highways to accommodate armored vehicles, the Todt Organization was administered by Albert Speer after Todt's death in 1942.

43. A reversal of the Yiddish idiom reflecting the influence of general culture on Jewish behavior.

THE 20TH AND 21ST — AN ANNIVERSARY

Tomorrow and the day after tomorrow are the anniversary of the last Aktion in the ghetto, a year ago—a year since the last 400 people, whom the Lithuanians then had to supply, were torn away from us. As we said then, the Aktion lasted two days.

It was the last big Aktion of the series a year ago of "Aktions in Vilna."

Is this really the last and final Aktion? The little cluster of the Vilna Ghetto is feverish to this day about it.

POLICEMEN RUN AWAY

Interesting for the mood among the Lithuanians: a lot of policemen, who not long ago enthusiastically threw themselves into the arms of the police service, have recently been asking for "discharge." But because that is not given, they really run away and disappear. . . .

FOREIGN JEWS IN THE VILNA GHETTO

Until today, Jews from the surrounding provinces have come to the Vilna Ghetto. Here are workers from places like Virbalis, Smorgonie, Soły and Nowa Wilejka, Panemunė, and Kiena.

A NEW BIG "UNIT"

The Vilna Ghetto is like a railroad station. On the one hand, people have been brought together here recently from various places, and the ghetto and the population are enlarged; on the other hand, new workplaces are created for the newcomers. They don't let their flesh and blood rest. Now a new railroad station is being built and new cadres are to be put together for it, a new big unit of about 1,500 workers. On Monday, the first group—200 workers—will march from here.

■ ■ ■ ■ ■ ■

DECEMBER 20 [1942]

IMPOTENCE AND PERFECTION

At 11 this morning, in the theater auditorium, the first six plates of the Vilna map were shown for the first time. Altogether, the map is to include 40 tablets. These plates contain the most inhabited quarters of the city, like Zwierzyniec, Śnipiszki, Mickiewicz Street, Antokol, Zarzecze, Wielka Street, the ghetto area, Rosa, the New World, etc.

At the opening of the showing of the six plates, the director of the Technical Department said, among other things, that a week ago, Friend Kruk, at the ceremony "100,000 Books," expressed the idea that the ghetto is impotent, that nothing the ghetto achieves can be perfect—it is diseased. Pointing to the six plates,

Engineer Gukhman says that he does not agree with the idea; a proof of that is the achievement in the production of the map. . . .

So, the map proved that the ghetto is perfect! . . .

ONLY BRIGADIERS HAVE THE RIGHT TO WEAR WATCHES

This is because they must keep track of the working hours of their work groups.

ACCOUNTS OUTSIDE THE GHETTO

Accounts outside the ghetto were drawn up for November at a sum of 3,871 RM.

CAMPAIGN AGAINST PREGNANCY

We know that Jews are forbidden to give birth. But now the ghetto administration has begun an open campaign against pregnancy. So tomorrow, the 21st of this month, there will be a women's assembly for that purpose, attended by hygienists from the sanitary police, women block commandants and apartment commandants. A lecture will be read, titled "Means to Prevent Pregnancy," and all necessary instructions will be given.

Evil tongues say that the owner of the factory of means [of birth control], a local ghetto resident, encouraged that action because there is big business latent in it. . . . If so, it is now clear why the ghetto administration only now mentioned that dreary order that Jews are forbidden to give birth!

TWO FOOD CARDS FOR WORKING JEWS

The food card "Set 2" will be given for hardworking Jews, and it is identical to a double card. The card "Set 1" is for [. . .]

[*Pages 555–557 of the diary are missing.*]

A Dormitory for Abandoned Girls

A Ghetto Saying

120 *Families, for More Than 2 Million Articles of Clothing*

December 22 [1942]

With a Smile on Their Face . . .

Jews Are "Honored" in the English Parliament

What Happened in Łyntupy

Tragically Perished

It Gets as Far as

Holiday Gifts

December 23 [1942]

Blood, Blood, Blood

Third Aktion in Baranovitsh

Mołodeczno

Smorgonie

Grodno

BURNED DOWN WITH GASOLINE

This is told as 100 percent reliable: yesterday, a German and four Lithuanian soldiers entered the headquarters of the local Lithuanian criminal police and took the chief to Mickiewicz St. to the Gestapo. Half an hour later, he was separated from the Lithuanian guard and taken to Ponar in an automobile. There they poured gasoline on him and burned him. The entire story happened in one hour. What happened and why is not clear for the time being.

DECEMBER 26 [1942]

A HALF MILLION

We think of how the ghetto trembled when, a day after their release, the 19 workers of the Burbiszki gardens were returned to prison. Altogether, 75 kg of flour were found on 23 persons. Now they have been in prison for two weeks, and every day, the most varied rumors circulate about them.

Now it is clear what kind of a "principled" issue is involved to save the 19 people: if a half million rubles are paid—maybe; if not? . . .

They are already collecting in the units. Yesterday, up to a fourth of a million was attained. Let us hope it will be. [Is there] a choice—it must be! . . .

LEVAS IN DANGER

Eight days ago, Murer suddenly stopped a wagon filled with boards at the gate. It turned out that the wagon with boards was bought illegally. Murer made a great issue of "principle" about it, threatened and cursed.

Three days ago, a Gestapo agent stopped a "Jewish wagon of flour." The case was blown out of proportion, and now the issue is that Levas, who is responsible for the gate, was summoned to the Lithuanian police commissar of the fourth precinct. He was released over the holiday on condition that he must be on Lidzki.[44] On Monday, after the holiday, he has to appear, and there is a suspicion that he may indeed be arrested.

Our authorities are very nervous about it.

GLAZMAN JUST A [MANUAL] WORKER

[*Pages 559–560 of the diary are missing.*]

A Camp of Warsaw Jews

December 27 [1942]
Monotonous

44. The ghetto jail was on Lidzki Street.

December 28 [1942]
Levas Affair
They Close the Cooperative
Apropos Levas
A Joke about Levas
25 Years after the Death of Mendele
As on a Stormy Sea

SOS — GRODNO

Alarming rumors come from Grodno. Everything you read says that there is a real slaughter in Grodno. The alarms are accompanied by sentences familiar to us: hurry, it might be too late; it is the last minute; send an automobile; do what you can, etc.

From other sources, I learn that several thousand have already been shipped out from Grodno. All are supposed to have been sent toward Malkinia, where Warsaw Jews have been annihilated. On the way, orders were supposed to have come to send them all back to Grodno, and thus thousands were presumably saved.

People talk about all that here. Grodno is just two hours by train from Vilna, but now that seems like hundreds of kilometers. Everything is veiled, everything is unclear, and most important, everything is uncertain.

THE PRISON ON STEFAŃSKA IS EMPTIED

Don't look for Grodno. Now they tell a story that happened much closer than Grodno: here, in the prison on Stefańska Street, a 10-minute walk from the ghetto, all arrested German prisoners were smuggled out. Gestapo agents came with orders and took the arrested Germans out. At 4 in the morning, on the 25th of this month, searches were made by German military police in the whole area of Wielka Stefańska Street, Kwaszelna Street, Ponarska Street, Kijowska Street, Nowogródzka, Sadowa, Chopin, etc.

If this turns out to be true, it will be the second case in recent months. We have written above about the first case.

[*No previous reference has been found.*]

DECEMBER 29 [1942]

"GOD, LOOK DOWN FROM HEAVEN!"

The vocabulary has become impoverished. Concepts lose their clarity. Everything that was dreadful and terrible is pale and put to shame. Words stop affecting and influencing. It reminds me of another expression of helplessness in a similar period, at the time of the persecutions in Spain:

At the time of the attacks of the Almohades on the Spanish Jewish communities [in the twelfth century], Rabbi Abraham ibn Ezra wrote about his experiences:

The nation weeps, persecuted and oppressed by the slaves,
and trembles and prays "God look down from heaven!"

I remembered that poem after the events of yesterday at the gate guard. God, look down from heaven and behold our helplessness, dejection, and humiliation.

WHAT OCCURRED YESTERDAY AT THE GATE GUARD

As I wrote before, the major issue yesterday was whether the commissar of the gate guard, Levas, would have to go to Łukiszki or not. His arrest was not only an individual matter but concerned the entire ghetto. Levas had to appear for arrest at 6 yesterday evening.

At about 3:30, Murer showed up at the gate, entered, and gave an order to search a few Jews who were within reach. In fact, what he always does in such cases. But by chance, during the search, one of the Jews lost 290 Marks. Murer noticed that and ordered all of them searched for money. Everything down to the last bit was taken.

"Jews may not and must not have any money on them. . . ."

Three search rooms were set up (gate guard, workshop at Rudnicka 16, and office of sanitation at Rudnicka 16). Everywhere, 20–30 people were allowed in, men along with women, and told to take out all their money. Later, individuals were taken out and searched thoroughly. The ones they found money on were . . . whipped.

This was done in those three places. Those who were searched were forced to strip as naked as the day they were born. Men and women were forced to undress in the very same room.

All that took place under Murer's supervision. When an ashamed woman turned her face to the wall, he ordered her to turn around because, in sadistic language, you must not be ashamed in front of Jewish police.

All those on whom they found money, who had dared not to give it away, were whipped: one girl was whipped because she had dared to bring in not money but . . . 30 decagrams of bread. On another woman, they found . . . 15 pfennig. One woman who was whipped left all her clothes and ran away in her overcoat. . . . They found 50 Marks in the shoe of an old Jew. Murer, already tired, ordered . . . one lash. When the police sergeant, Mr. Witkowski, had done his job, he suggested to the whipped man that he thank the representative of the district commissar. Of course the whipped man thanked him. These and similar scenes occurred in those places.

Meanwhile, on the street stood a line that stretched from the gate to the Jewish hospital on Zawalna. Jewish police meanwhile enlightened the people to give the money to them.

[*Pages 563–569 of the diary are missing.*]

The Levas Affair Is Liquidated
Children Play in "Gate Guard"

December 31
Today Is Sylvester [New Year's Eve]

[*We have one page, torn up and without a number, which is certainly from the missing pages. We present that page, with additions by the editor of the Yiddish edition.*]

[And what] the world will make of this is hard to say. We and the [world] are two separate conceptions. What is [Worldly] in the world is Hitlerian in our circumstances. [But] Worldly and Hitlerian are two poles.

So we here, under the bloody Hitlerian atmosphere in the Vilna Ghetto, in the central cemetery of Lithuanian Jewry, will take leave of the past year and greet the new.

Why write about the past year? If I get out of here, I will leaf through the press, and with time, will become familiar with it. But if I do [not] survive, others will leaf through my notes and will be able to empathize with what we have gone through and experienced here.

Today my loved ones will remember, and I, how can I forget them.

In New York, my brother, my sister-in-law, and Henyo—a lump of terrible longing.

In Warsaw—if she and her two children are still alive—but I am sure my only sister and her two children are not alive, victims of the bloodbath of Warsaw. And my wife, where will she remember me today, if in Siberia? Who knows how she is? If in central Russia, where will she remember!

Where is Felicja,[45] where is our old friend Ber Y. Rosen, where are my dozens, hundreds, thousands of comrades and friends, with whom I spent years of friendship?

Today I will look at Sylvester in the ghetto. Here in the ghetto, New Year's Eve is noisier than outside the ghetto. Today at 10:15, a special "New Year's Review" will be performed in three places in the ghetto. In the ghetto restaurant, at Rudnicka 13, and in the club of a unit, Rudnicka 7. At 11 in the evening, the same review will be repeated formally in the Ghetto Theater.

We members of the B[und] meet today in a small group and will make an accounting of the past year.

45. Wife of the Yiddish writer Dovid Kasel of Warsaw. She came to Vilna as a refugee, then left Vilna with a "Japanese Visa." She survived the war and lived in Washington, D.C.

GHETTO ROBBERY BY THE "GATE GUARD"

[To] all that we have already written about the events in the ["Ga]te Guard," for the sake of truth, we must add:

The [gen]eral opinion in the ghetto is that the whole story with Murer [. . .] was staged. People met Murer's [. . .] instincts, the Levas incident was played out, and . . . the ghetto [administra]tion did not lose anything, and nor did the ghe[tto pol]ice.

[The sheep is whole] and the wolf is full.

[In connection w]ith that sad entry, I learn that Murer [. . .]

They drink to Levas's "bachelorhood"
Today Levas's Wedding
Drugi 1918 rok *[A second 1918]*[46]
Partisans
Murer Exercises

January 1, 1943
New Year 1943
Drunkards Invite Jews
Theater in the Ghetto
Illegal Polish Schools
Levas's Wedding
A German Asks a Favor from a Jew . . .

January 2, 1943
They Fraternize . . .
A German from the Rosenberg Task Force Describes the Ghetto
The Ghetto Starts Collecting Folklore
They Collect Exhibits for a Planned Ghetto Museum

January 3, 1943
Smiling Faces
Second Students' Concert of the Children's Music School in the Ghetto
Attempts to Gather Potato Peels[47]

It has been calm for a few days, even pleasantly calm. Nothing special has happened. Better and better news comes from the front. It grows clearer by the day that a big breakthrough is coming. The Germans are running away from the

46. This heading signals the independence of Poland after almost a century and a half of foreign occupation.

47. The following paragraph is not listed in Kruk's table of contents; it may belong in another place. The section that appears next in the Yiddish edition, "They Whip and . . . They Threaten to Whip," has been transferred to January 27, according to Kruk's table of contents.

Caucasus. The Stalingrad-Rostov and Rzhev-Rostov fronts have bigger successes from one day to the next. Today, as I write these lines, the Reds are 120 kilometers from Kharkov and a few dozen from Rostov. Leningrad is liberated [from the siege], and the Germans are driven out of Kronstadt. Today Leningrad celebrates the liberation of the city. In short, it is calm in the ghetto, even pleasantly calm.

100 FROM ŚWIĘCIANY

On Monday, 100 Jewish workers were expected from Święciany, to join the new unit of Smorgonie and Soly Jewish workers in depot work on the Vilna railroad station of the so-called Giessler Building Group.

IN THE JURY COMMITTEE FOR THE NEWLY ANNOUNCED ARTISTIC COMPETITION

The following composition is decided:

1. FOR THE LITERARY COMPETITION: Dr. Ts. Feldstein (Chairman), B. Lubocki, and H. Kruk.
2. FOR THE MUSIC COMPETITION: A. Slep (Chairman), T. Hirszowicz, and Sh. Khaykin.
3. FOR THE PAINTING COMPETITION: Engineer Smorgonski (Chairman), Mrs. Romm, and Engineer Rabinowicz.

THE GHETTO LIBRARY

[It] takes pains to enlarge its number of books in all languages.

As we have written, the library has now been reorganized in two sections: (1) for children and (2) for adults. This was done to remove the great pressure at the circulation desk.

Both sections work in the same place, Strashun 6, every day (except Saturday and holidays) from 11 to 17:30.

ALL WHO HAVE BOOKS TO SELL

[All] can sell books to the ghetto library. You have to present a list of the books and their prices in the library office to director H. Kruk.

IN THE READING ROOM

Because of the great demand, no children under the age of 10 will be admitted. Children over 10 can enter the reading room without books, with only a notebook and pencil.

[*Page 570 of the diary is missing.*]

January 4 [1943]

Collective Living Quarters
Tragically Perished
A Second Joke about Levas
Another Joke—NKVD
How Far Does Our Empire Reach

[. . .]

To govern all the places and to have complete control of them, the Vilna administration has delegated its police staff.

WORKERS FROM THE VILNA DISTRICT[48]

[They] will work here, as we have said, in "OTE,"[49] on the railroad station. For that work, people have been brought together from the entire surrounding area. Now they are housed in collective quarters. Such residences have been prepared on Oszmiańska 4, Niemiecka 29, and Strashun 3, 8, and 15. The Technical Department is preparing 500 wooden bunks for them.

A COUNSELING CENTER AGAINST PREGNANCY

As we said earlier, a counseling center against pregnancy was set up in the ghetto. In short, they are carrying out the order that "you must not give birth in the ghetto. . . ."

YOU MAY NOT CARRY MONEY

Out of the ghetto, it is forbidden to carry money. Every sum that is found is taken away.

A HOME FOR GIRLS

Following the model of child welfare (Strashun 4), a home for wayward girls is now organized. The Department of Social Welfare is busy with the selection. In the home, they will study tailoring, sewing, knitting, etc.

OUTSIDE THE GHETTO — A JEWISH OFFICE TO ACCEPT ORDERS

With the increase of the number of workshops in the ghetto and the number of orders from the city, the district commissar ordered a Jewish office set up outside the ghetto to take orders to be filled in the ghetto. The reason for this: customers should not "stroll around" in the ghetto. The office will soon be opened right in front of the entrance to the ghetto, at Rudnicka 29.

48. From here until January 6, the entries are not listed in Kruk's table of contents.

49. The same as Todt (see n. 42).

JANUARY 6 [1943]

MAY IT INCREASE

Today's radio news brings a new breath of hope along with a shudder of terror. The Bolsheviks are advancing. Victories on the Caucasian front. On the middle front, the "Reds" are advancing. The Russians are 150 km from the Latvian border. In Latvia, there are already arrests as the Bolshevik front approaches. All this is indeed good news, and Jews wish each other: May it increase.

But a shudder quietly passes: Will they leave us?

WE ARE NUMBERED

Today I learn of an order that every ghetto resident will have to wear a number around his neck. I already know of such cases from the provinces. I am trying to wait for more precise information about the justification for that order.

HOW BIG IS THE ADMINISTRATION OF THE GHETTO

From statistics prepared for the authorities, I learn that the ghetto administration employs:

Men	950
Women	821
Children below the age of 14	20
Total	1,791
Police	244
Total	2,035

As we see, a staff has been put together in the ghetto which could serve all Vilna, including its Poles, Lithuanians, and others.

OPENING OF A YOUTH CLUB IN THE GHETTO

For several months, a Youth Club has existed in the Vilna Ghetto, but only today did its opening take place. For months, the building was repaired, changed from a ruin into splendid quarters, which, even if it weren't in the ghetto, would certainly remain a splendid club. Like all such institutions in the good old days, the club was built in bits and pieces with great difficulty and drudgery.

The opening consists of several performances, including "Puppets" by [M.] Gilinski and [Yankev] Trupiański, Sholem Aleichem's "Enchanted Tailor," and others. The hall is beautifully decorated with pictures of Jewish writers, a beautiful stage with wings, and—as it later turned out—splendid sets.

[*The upper part of the original page is badly torn. According to what remains, this is evidently the end of the report of the opening of the Youth Club. We present the rest of the legible parts of the page, with additions by the editor of the Yiddish edition.*]

JANUARY 8 [1943]

LIKE NEW WINDS

Recently there have been [several signs indicating] that new winds are blowing in the ghetto. [You see it in the situation at the] gate and the gate guard. The incident with the 19, which the Gestapo [. . .] taken them; the issue of Levas; the gym[nastics in the] workshops; the entrance into the ghetto and the search for money; [the whipping of men] and women together; recently, the order about [wearing numbers; and] finally the events of today:

Today Murer came into the ghetto, stopped a group [of workers, and] ordered them to do exercises on the ground in the snow. The reason: [they] didn't greet him properly. Then he came into the workshop at [Rudnicka] 16 and ordered the women to go under the tables [. . .] he slept.

As we know, outside the ghetto, not far from the ghetto gate, a so-called order place is to be opened, an office to take orders to be filled in the ghetto. Now Murer has ordered the wage lists of all the units also to go through the order place, so they can control them. Now, fresh news: the office will have control of importing into the ghetto. A German woman official already sits in that office, one of those loyal to Murer.

All this portends a change in the relationship to the ghetto. A new era seems to be coming.

THEY WANT TO TAKE OUR MONEY

I learn from a reliable source that there is a plan to take from the residents of the ghetto the right to use mon[ey]. Instead of money, workers in the units will get scrip for food, the ghetto administration will pay . . . in food, etc. Meanwhile, this is a plan presented to the ghetto chief.

This information is part of that series we fear.

ARRESTED 6

The 19 have recently been increased by 6. Six workers of the so-called "Nachschu [. . ."] were arrested and sent to Łukiszki [. . .]. Expensive drinks were found on the 6: wine, liquor, etc. In the [ghetto], their fate is considered serious.

PASSPORTS

There is a plan for the ghetto reside[nts] to get passports, possibly soon. Simple, normal passports with "Jude" on them. The [plan] exists; it is still in the early stage.

JANUARY 10 [1943]

[NAFTOLE] WEINIG IS ALIVE

Yesterday, lying in bed, I learn the good [news that] friend Naftole Weinig, the Vilna Yiddish writer, is alive [. . .]

[*The remaining part of the page is badly damaged. From what remains, we can infer that information came from an employee of the Ghetto Theater that Naftole Weinig was living near the Constantine Estate, not far from Vilna. The employee went to get wood and met him there. Weinig asked him to give a message to Kalmanowicz and Kruk. From other damaged entries on the page, we find the following information.*

On January 9, Kruk was supposed to deliver a lecture in the workers' auditorium of Kaplan-Kaplanski's units. The subject was to have been "From the Library Center in Poland to the Ghetto Library." Unfortunately, he could not do this because of illness.

For the same reason, he could not participate in the meeting "For People's Health." There, he was to have read the article "Hygiene of Reading." His article was read by the co-editor of People's Health, *Dr. Kalmen Shapiro.*

A mobile library for the Zatrocze labor camp was set up.

[*Pages 575–579, for January 10–15, are missing. On those days, the ghetto population was upset by events at the gate. A few times, Jews were detained with smuggled luxury items. Murer, who led that activity, also arrested two persons, including the famous singer Lyuba Lewicka,*[50] *with some peas.*]

January 10 [1943]
Because of My Illness
A Mobile Library for the Zatrocze Work Camp
Weiskopf Restored; His Grandson Does Not Appear
A Second Café Is Opened
An Assault In Kailis

January 12 [1943]
Depression
Five of the Six Released
1 of the 19

January 13 [1943]
106 Furs Valued at More Than 4 Million Rubles
82 Persons Arrested
I Order Two Scale Models
The Ghetto Industry

50. Also known as Zublewicka. She performed in operas and was popularly known as the songbird of the ghetto.

Quarantine in the Ghetto
The School Program
A "Reserve" Communist Party
In the Work Units—HKP

January 14 [1943]
The Situation Becomes More Acute
The Ghetto Police Are Also Nervous
The Ghetto Archive Intervenes
Zalmen Reisen Is Alive, Too

January 15 [1943]
One Year of Ghetto Theater
Visitors in the Ghetto
Gens Complains

[*Page 580 begins at the end of Gens's complaining to Kruk.*]

[. . .] "Kailis has become a base for butter for Vilna. If you wanted it, you went to Kailis and got whatever you liked. Who suffered from it? Me. My prestige declined. My prestige means the respect of the ghetto, of the ghetto Jews. For example, take the fact with the six people five of whom are already free. Do they sit in prison for wanting to save themselves and bring in a kilo of bread for wife and child? No. They must be treated as disturbers and saboteurs. On the six Jews, they found no more and no less than 23 bottles of liquor and . . . 20,000 cigarettes. What does this mean? This means that the ghetto drinks liquor and smokes the most expensive cigarettes.

Isn't it undermining the ghetto? Isn't this a slap in the face for me, the representative of the ghetto, who constantly and incessantly complains about the bad situation of the residents of the ghetto?

Who suffers from this? First of all the masses, the 19 Jews [who] had 75 kg of flour altogether, the two poor souls [arrested] yesterday, [Lyuba] Lewicka and [Monye] Stupel."[51]

Thus the ghetto chief laments to me.

Isn't there some truth in it?

[*The rest of the page is destroyed.*]

THE 25TH GATHERING OF WORKERS

We have written of the gathering at Kapłan-Kapłański's [to] talk and lecture to the workers of his unit. [Now, I learn] that back in December, that institution cele[brated an important] anniversary—25 meetings.

51. Brother of Khaye-Sore Stupel, the wife of the popular Vilna Bundist leader Borekh Wirgili-Kahan. Monye Stupel, born in 1904, studied at the Sophia Gurevich Gymnasium in Vilna and the university in Liège, Belgium. He was active in VILBIG, the Vilna Educational Society. Before the war, he was an employee in Bunimowicz's Bank in Vilna.

Now, since the Brigadier Council has become a whole "[. . . "] in the ghetto and Kapłan-Kapłański its nominated chair[man,] the institution has turned into an everyday [. . .] the workers from all units. Of course, with [. . .] Kapłan-Kapłański [is occupied].

JANUARY 16

A YEAR OF GHETTO THEATER

Last night's celebration of the "year of the ghetto theater" looked as we had foreseen. It [was] first of all a happy occasion not for the artists, but an evening in honor of the "operators" of [the ghetto]. All those who *gave* demanded orations, and the orations contented [them].

Two of the speeches were interesting. The first by the actor Blacher (I attach the speech), the second by the speaker of the Association of Writers and Artists. The rest of the speeches, by Yashunski, Gens, Fried, Kapłan-Kapłański, and Dr. Feldstein, were pale and said nothing.[52]

[*The speech by Blacher is missing.*]

The artistic part was an abridgment of the first performance of a year ago and part of the last, current program. The same with the symphony orchestra—parts of the first and the last programs.

In general, the artistic part of the celebration was done without exaggerated solemnity and with a measure of intelligence. After the evening, the actors and theater activists went to a café on Rudnicka for a cup of coffee.

WHY EXACTLY THE TWO SCALE MODELS

Because of the impending construction of the two scale models mentioned above, at 7 this evening in the building of the PPV,[53] an assembly was held of all engineers of the Technical Department, the whole staff of the PPV, in the presence of Commandants Gens and Muszkat, the painters Olkienicka and Sutzkever. The lecturer, H. Kruk, spoke about "why scale models and why exactly these scale models."

I attach the lecture from the minutes of the meeting.

[*The lecture is missing.*]

After an exchange of opinions, everyone assures us that both scale models will come out much nicer than the first—the map of Vilna.

52. The speeches by Gens and Grisha Yashunski were published in Korczak 1946:264–265.

53. The collective where the plan of Vilna was produced was called the Plastic Plan of Vilna (PPV).

JANUARY 17 [1943]

PEOPLE SNATCHED FOR WORK

Today, Sunday, they were again snatching for work outside the city. More than 100 workers were sent out of the ghetto like this.

Even on Sunday, they don't let you rest!

GLOVES ARE CONFISCATED

Because many women were snatched for work cleaning snow today, by order of the ghetto chief, a few hundred gloves were confiscated.

The confiscation took place by house searches. Often gloves were taken off people in the street.

A TRAGIC EVENT

A tragic event occurred yesterday to a Jewish worker of the HKP unit, Mr. Salomon. On Saturday, he went with a German and a few Christians in a truck for wood. Four km from Širvintos, the automobile went down a steep incline. A few died in the catastrophe, including Mr. Salomon, who was brought to the ghetto.

It made a depressing impression here.

SENTENCED TO DEATH AND . . . RELEASED

Such things also happen. In the unit *Feldbekleid an der Luftwaffe* [Field clothing of the air force], two Jewish workers left work half an hour early. Somebody informed on them. The SD[54] arrested them and sentenced them to death.

This happened on December 9. On the 14th, a death sentence was issued.

Police Chief Dessler intervened several times, and both shoemakers were saved from death and . . . released.

A WOMAN CONVERT MAKES A PILGRIMAGE TO THE GHETTO

For many years, the Lithuanian shoemaker Frieškaila lived in Vilna with his Jewish convert wife. The couple had seven children—five sons and two daughters. About half a year ago, the shoemaker died, and the family began to quarrel. A sister of a daughter-in-law of the shoemaker denounced the old woman as a converted Jew. She was arrested and sentenced to death for not being in the ghetto.

After several interventions, she was spared the death sentence and was sent to the Vilna Ghetto in December.

On the day before the holiday, December 23, the convert ran away from the ghetto and once again was "denounced." On January 14, they brought her back to

54. I.e., Sicherheitsdienst, the Nazi Security Police.

the ghetto and asked that she be treated well. Social Aid in the ghetto is now taking care of her.

FIRST CASE OF A SENTENCE TO A JAIL [TERM]

[*The end of the page is badly damaged and impossible to decipher. It concerns important material gathered about the smuggling of goods through the ghetto gate.*]

January 19 [1943]

"CONTRABAND" IN THE GHETTO

[. . .] through the gate. The material presents a picture of an enormous underground ghetto enterprise. Naturally, Levas, as commissar of the gate guard, played a considerable role in it. We must say that in spite of everything we have written about him, he is a bold and daring fellow. If not for him, that contraband would never have gotten into the ghetto.

In fact, we must admit that Levas is personally responsible to the authorities for it. I attach a document proving this.

[*The document is missing.*]

CONSTITUTION OF THE GATE GUARD

The gate, as the major artery of ghetto life, has its own "constitution." To have a picture of the competence and possibility of activities of the gate and the gate guard, I attach an extract of that statute. Here is also the paragraph of our previous entry, concerning Levas's responsibility for the gate.

[*The extract is missing.*]

WHY ARE THE JEWS ISOLATED IN THE GENERAL GOUVERNEMENT?[55]

A document that just arrived gives an answer to that rhetorical question: *Sonderdruck Nr. 1,* published by: Ostland, Halbmonatsschrift für Ostpolitik, Berlin. The publication is titled: *Die Jüdische Wohnbezirke in General Gouvernement.*

What is the publication?

It says that the Jews have been gathered in specific districts: the most important are in Warsaw, Cracow, Radom, Kielce, etc. This was done for the following reasons: (a) sanitary reasons: Jews are dirty and very resistant to dirty diseases; (b) political reasons: Jews and Poles are united [in their opposition to the Germans]. And the Jews still have a big influence.

[*The rest of the page is destroyed, and pages 584–590 of the original are missing. Number 23 of the Geto-yedies* appeared on January 24. The issue is in the YIVO Archive (Kaczerginski-Sutzkever Collection, no. 264A).]

55. *Generalgouvernement,* an administrative unit including the territories of occupied central provinces of Poland, governed by Dr. Hans Frank.

[WHO IS] ALFRED ROSENBERG?[56]

[I attach] an interesting document by the journalist Franz Schell [showing that] Alfred Rosenberg, the Hitlerian leader, the [editor-in-]chief of the *Völkischer Beobachter,* etc., is a Jew, a Jew of very [high] origin.

[Aside from] the fact that the document appeared in 1936 and [was printed] in Tilsit, East Prussia, I nevertheless attach it as a [. . .] for further interest, for which I now have neither desire nor possibility.

[*The document is not attached.*]

January 21 [1943]

They Will Whip

A Strange Trial and a Strange Verdict

Possibilities of Traveling to . . . Palestine

Letter from Shanghai

Today a Commemoration Evening on the Eighth Anniversary of Dr. Tsemakh Szabad's Death

They Catch Fish

Levas Wants to Enter . . . History

"If There Is No Bread, There Is No Learning"

A Year of the Ghetto Theater

Sensation about a Woman Convert

The Ghetto Is Freezing!

40 Police Batons

January 23 [1943]

In the Ghetto, Everything Is Possible

What Is Happening to the Arrested [People]

January 25 [1943]

Warsaw Is Bleeding

For Trouble You're Beaten

Instead of a Letter . . . a Package

Renewal of the Lit.- Artist. Evenings

5 of the 19 Released

There Are No Maps of Vilna

Hundreds Arrive and More Will Come

January 27 [1943]

Cannibals

56. In the Yiddish edition, this entry was incorrectly placed at the end of December; here, we have placed it according to its position in Kruk's table of contents. The conjectures in square brackets are those of the editor of the Yiddish edition.

THEY WHIP AND . . . THEY THREATEN TO WHIP

Yesterday morning, an assembly of ghetto employees took place to help the police catch ghetto deserters. In the ghetto, there are indeed some who are avoiding work. At the assembly, the chief of the ghetto announced that every labor deserter will be whipped. The first time, 25 and Lidzki; and the second time, Łukiszki.[57]

So Murer's teaching is not lost. They whip and they will whip.

This morning, the day began with a hunt for people in the streets. This happens very often. Germans come and no one is allowed in the street. Soon the Germans arrived with a new boss from the Gestapo. All three visited several institutions and left satisfied. The ghetto sighed in relief: they came and went away satisfied. . . .

But the day is not yet over. Soon Murer came, and by his order, a box appeared at the ghetto gate, and the workers coming in were required by the Jewish police to put their money in the . . . box. Not many were eager to do it. Some people, on whom they did find money, were whipped until they were bloody, depending on how much Murer ordered. For one and the same "crime," one got 25 lashes, another only [. . .]

YEAR OF FPORG[ANIZATION]

On the 25th, one year of the FPOrg[anization] in Vilna was celebrated.[58] The commanders and representatives of all groups connected with it attended this celebration. Speeches were made by the chairman, two members of the B[und], a representative of the Revis[ionists], and one of Ha-Shomer Ha-Tzair. The command issued a daily order to the groups. The celebration was conducted in a very serious mood. The seriousness of the day and the concern about the fate of the ghetto and its almost 20,000 Jews hovered over all heads.

COMPLETION OF THE TRACTATE *KIDDUSHIN*

In the religious kitchen in the ghetto, Szawelska 5, the completion of [study of the] tractate *Kiddushin* was celebrated on Sunday, January 24, in the evening. Several religious men gave speeches. Among the many guests were representatives of the official ghetto leadership.

57. I.e., first offenders will be sent to prison inside the ghetto; second offenders will be sent outside, into the hands of the Lithuanians and Germans.

58. Most of the social and political groups in the ghetto belonged to the FPO. It is not clear if the FPO was founded on January 21, 23, or 24, 1942. The command of the FPO consisted of Commander Itzik Wittenberg (Communist) and command staff members Yosef Glazman (Revisionist), Abrasha Chwojnik (Bundist), Abba Kovner (Ha-Shomer ha-Tzair), and Nisn Reznik (General Zionist).

SOVIETS OVER VILNA

We have often gotten messages from the "other world" recently. For example, the Soviets flew over Vilna on Monday, the 25th, at about 1 in the morning. The next day, Tuesday, the 26th, the alarm sounded in Vilna. Later, in the afternoon, once more.

JOKES

A joke is going around about the liberation of Leningrad and Stalingrad:

Hitler's temperature is 2 degrees colder. Now his temperature is 34 (Celsius). How come? The answer: He lacks 2 degrees [Yiddish "*grad*"]—Stalingrad and Leningrad. . . .

A BON MOT

Each of the four governors of the Vilna Ghetto is ordered to sign documents in a separate color.

Now the four governors are called: the four pencils. . . .
[*The end of the page is damaged.*]

A Tormenting Day

[. . .] when they kill thousands, we say it is painful, inhuman, beastly; and when seven are killed we say almost the same thing. Where is the proportion? [. . .]

Not only have we lost everything else, now we have also lost our sense of proportion. We cry for 1,000 just as for 10,000. Did we then mourn less for the 30,000 annihilated Vilna Jews than for the hundreds of thousands of Warsaw Jews?

As the poet says: "Niechaj umarli grzebią umarłych."[59]

As Heine says:

Jewry is not a people—it is a misfortune. We are drowning in that misfortune and forgetting what is white and what is black. Is it any wonder?

Warsaw lost hundreds of thousands, Vilna only tens of thousands, Kovno even less. And Baranovitsh and Michaliszki and hundreds and hundreds of other cities!?

Nevertheless, not everything in us has yet atrophied. A trivial thing strikes and everything shudders as seldom before.

Such a thing happened today. The whole ghetto trembled. After all, it isn't thousands who go to the stake here but "simply," in our language, really simply, only seven persons altogether.

Monye Stupel

Yesterday, 47 persons, including 7 Jews, were shot at Ponar. Who were the Jews who were shot?

59. In Polish, "Let the dead bury the dead." The quotation is from the New Testament. Kruk probably quoted a Polish poet who repeated the phrase in his work.

Those who lived on Aryan passports: a mother and two children from Kovno and a woman from Grodno. The brigadier of Camp Nachschub, Vitin, was executed for stealing, in fact, for trading in brandy. The last of them were the employees of the ghetto Labor Office, Monye Stupel, and the popular Jewish singer Lyuba Lewicka, both of them because they were alleged to have stolen beans. . . .

We have already written the story of their arrest. From then until the past few days, people said that Lewicka sang and became the songbird in the prison. The guards used to stand at the door and ask her to sing. From the Christian cells they applauded and admired her.

Now it is clear that aside from the others, Stupel and Lewicka were executed in Ponar. For stealing one kilo of beans apiece.

The news struck the ghetto like a thunderclap. Few wanted to accept it, few wanted to believe it.

A shudder passed through the ghetto!

We will write in more detail about the two victims. Today we will only mention:

Lewicka is one of the best Jewish singers.

Monye Stupel was one of the beautiful pleiad of Vilna Bundists, one of the small group of Bundists in the ghetto, a brother-in-law of the Bundist Wirgili-Kahan.

The Bundist group in the ghetto bows its head for its last victim, the dear, good comrade, the unusually likable Monye Stupel.

Honor to his memory!

SOON PASSPORTS AND NUMBERS

As we have written, the citizens of the Vilna Ghetto are getting passports with a number on every passport. Aside from the work permit, the citizens will get those two more "toys." Those who have protection permits will exchange them for passports, and the protection permits will be taken away.

ABOUT THE REGISTRATION OF CHRISTIAN CHILDREN

The turmoil about the registration of Christian children in Vilna has now been cleared up. Apparently the registration was carried out because of an affair of falsified so-called additional cards for children. This way, the authorities will know how many children there are in the city between the ages of 2 and 14, when one receives the additional cards.

WARSAW UNTIL NOON AND WARSAW IN THE EVENING

We are hurled from cold to hot and back again. As for the bloody events, I learn from a "reliable source" that Warsaw is very depressed. Christians are snatched by the thousands and sent to work. The little ghetto risks its life, etc. At about 9 that same evening, I get some more "reliable information" from a Christian who arrived from Warsaw only yesterday. He says that in Warsaw, Christians are snatched off the streets and sent away. Christians fight with the snatchers and it gets bloody, right in the middle of the day. Moreover . . . the Jewish ghetto is completely liquidated.

After a pause for breath, I learn, as it were, more precisely:

Two thousand Jews were demanded from the ghetto for work. The ghetto refused, and as a result, the ghetto was "liquidated."

It is hard to say what really happened. Meanwhile, our nerves pitch us from cold to hot and . . . back again. What we were told today before noon turned into nothing by supper.

FROM 14 TO 18

In December, 18,026 people went through the bath in the ghetto. The number of daily shifts grew from 14 to 18. So obviously, every citizen in the ghetto visits the bath at least once a month.

THE BIGGEST UNIT FOR JEWISH WORKERS. MORE THAN 300 FROM THE PROVINCES

The newly formed unit, the so-called Giessler Building Group, which is working on the railroad, now employs 810 men and women.

The unit includes almost all those who came from the provinces. The unit is being systematically increased, and they still expect a lot of Jewish workers from the provinces. So far, more than 300 persons are lodged in ghetto dormitories. The Technical Department is preparing up to 1,000 bunks for those arriving, two and three on each level. Thus, four to six persons sleep on a bunk. The Department of Social Welfare is providing food for 230 persons.

EVERYONE MUST SPEND THE NIGHT IN HIS OWN HOME

Such an order has now been posted by the ghetto leaders. For not being able to find a person, his family is held responsible.

THE GHETTO PRODUCES

A. IN THE WEAVING SHOP. The weaving shop, which has so far produced various footwear out of hemp, has recently shifted to other kinds of weaving, for lack of raw materials. Now, straw mats for car radiators are being produced here, as well as straw mats, straw house slippers, straw boots, and light shoes.

B. IN THE EMBROIDERY SHOP various handbags of all colors are being produced.

C. THE CARDBOARD WORKSHOP is filling orders for the "German Department Store"—they are producing cardboard boxes for it.

D. CENTRALIZATION OF CLOTHING. The workshops of the tailors and the furriers are now centralized into one big workshop, which will take up two floors at Rudnicka 15.

E. AMOUNT OF BUSINESS TRANSACTED FOR DECEMBER. The amount of business in all workshops for last December amounted to 29,327 RM. One thousand orders were filled.

COFFEE AT HOME

Something new has been introduced for the winter months: in the early morning, coffee will be given to take home.

JANUARY 30 [1943]

10 YEARS OF THE HITLERIAN REGIME

Today, it is "with congratulations" 10 years since Hitler seized power in Germany in a bloody way. It is a holiday for the bloodiest events the world has ever seen.

Ten years after that, Hitlerism and its Führer face unprecedented successes and at the same time, even today, they face the abyss of defeat.

The great free-world press probably writes a great deal about that. I, in the ghetto, mention that fact as a reminder that we here do not forget it either. A sign that we are still alive and feeling. . . . What we were brought to is also a result of Hitlerian cannibalism and sophisticated, incomprehensible sadism.

Today, in honor of his great holiday, Hitler was to speak on the radio from Berlin, but instead of Hitler, his closest deputy, Göring, spoke. His speech, which was to begin precisely at 11 in the morning, started an hour late. Why? Precisely at 11, English bombers appeared over Berlin and congratulated Berlin on her holiday. . . .

It started at 12.

What was said in honor of that holiday? Everything was staked on victory. We are victorious, we will be victorious, because we must be victorious!

This is how the Hitlerian 10-year holiday was celebrated today, and with that old refrain came the Führer of German Fascism.

LITHUANIANS AND SS UNIFORMS

Yesterday, the uniforms of all Lithuanian soldiers were changed. They [. . .] [*Part of page 596 is damaged. We present all the lines and fill in the torn-out places, wherever possible, with conjectures.*]

Their own Lithuanian clothing was taken [and they were changed for] SS uniforms, leaving them [with only the Lithuanian emblem.] Thus from the supposedly [independent Lithuania,] only the horse [remains].

Lithuanians in the city tell that [many Lithuanian] servicemen deserted and fled.

NEW LEADER OF VILNA GESTAPO SAYS THE JEWS WILL BE ANNIHILATED[60]

We have already said that the Vilna Ges[tapo got] a new boss, named Neugebauer. At [first glance] he makes a good impression and looks like an interesting [type]. In a conversation with Mr. G[ens] he said, among other things: If we win the war, we will give the Jews a corner of the world somewhere and they shall live there. But if we lose, the Jews will be annihilated.

Well, so a Gestapo boss said. Nevertheless, for the group that knows about the "saying," it is a fine insinuation, indeed.

I SEEK MELINAS

"Nevertheless, it's better to have a melina." This is what everybody says now, even the most "frivolous" optimist. I have also recently been delegated to take care of the issue of melinas. Wandered around, looked around, visited buildings and cellars, and it seems we can get to work. . . .

LICENTIOUSNESS

We know our life in the ghetto is very licentious; ou[r feel]ings are dulled and clumsy. But everything has a limit. Today I was stunned: the day after the story of Lyuba Lewicka, a fine, decent, and intelligent man came. . . . Demanded Lyuba Lewicka's room.

Licentiousness!

LEVAS'S REPRESENTATION FUND

Accidentally, because of a trial in the ghetto court, the commissar of the gate guard, Levas, was brought in as a witness. During his testimony, it was discovered that Levas has a representation fund of hundreds of thousands a month.

IS IT INDEED THE LIQUIDATION OF THE "RESERVE" PARTY

From my pre[vious en]tries, we know about the [supposed] Commun[ist] party, "tolerated" and even protected by Police Commander D[essler].[61] The same source says that not long ago, the members of that party collected money ostensibly for the activity of the Com[munist] party "outside the ghetto" or for POWs.[62]

Now the issue has burst. Apparently the local authorities have finally realized that the matter can become serious.

60. This heading is given according to Kruk's table of contents.

61. This matter is not sufficiently clear. It probably concerns a group that was kept in reserve, in case the "Reds" won the war. The group would then be able to show off their work for pro-Soviet elements in the ghetto.

62. Russian prisoners of war who were probably supported by the above-mentioned "reserve party."

Yesterday the chief of the ghetto called in one of them, Mr. Zaydshnur, gave him a good scolding, as they say here, "cursed him through his mother" and fined him 10,000 rubles for the Aid Society. He scolded the leader of the "party," Shapiro, and kicked him out. Now the "circles of power" are thinking about what to do to make him harmless.

The story of the liquidation of the reserve party circulates and is commented on in various ways. We shall see how the matter will end.

FEBRUARY 4, 1943

A YEAR OF THE AID SOCIETY

Yesterday evening in the Ghetto Theater, an annual reporting meeting of the Aid Society was held.

As we know, the Aid Society was once taken out of the hands of its initiators[63] and has remained with the "stock company" partnership of the Reds, Zionists, Orthodox, police commissars, and . . . gate guard. The figures of the annual report showed it most clearly. The [Aid] Society is not based on society. It is supported mainly by the police and has in fact become their organ. The chairman, Mr. Milkanowicki, who delivered the report, regularly bowed to his police chiefs, thanked them for their help, and called on the ghetto residents to take an example from them.

The second speaker, Gens, talked about givers and takers and laughed at the "shitty" 190,000 RM that last year's budget reached. He said it is a "shitty" sum, and people should give more.

Mr. Fried spoke very "modestly." He said there are no rich and poor today. Today, he says, it is a disgrace to have more than someone else. Everyone looked at his elegant clothes, his fur, his shoes with spats, the rings on his fingers, and was ashamed of him for having more than others without being ashamed.

By the way, Milkanowicki, as always, did not say a word about the founders and initiators of the society. It looked as if it were his initiative and that he took credit for creating the society.

[*Pages 598–604 of the diary, for the period February 5–12, 1943, are missing. At that time, number 25 of the* Geto-yedies *appeared (its prospectus is in the* YIVO *Archive, Kaczerginski-Sutzkever Collection, no. 275). On February 7, the painting competition took place (a communiqué concerning that is also in the Kaczerginski-Sutzkever Collection, no. 468). On the 12th, the ghetto library requested the ghetto court to sue 15 persons who had taken books from the library and not returned them (Kaczerginski-Sutzkever Collection, no. 374).*]

63. I.e., the Bundist organization.

About 10 *Years of the Hitler Regime*

February 5 [1943]
A Black Day in the Ghetto: Fried's Last Chord
It's Dark in the City
Horrible Terror
Lida, Grodno, Białystok, Warsaw
Passes in the Ghetto

February 6 [1943]
Fried Gets a Job
Ginzburg, Too
Melinas

February 7 [1943]
Hunting for Work Forces
A Dead German
Fried Becomes Chief Accountant
Weinig Back in the Ghetto
Congratulations, the Ghetto Has a Clock

February 9 [1943]
The Ghetto under the Sign of the Crisis
Searches at Night
50 Jews
A Guest Performance by Murer
A Celebration
A Year of the Gate Guard
25th Issue of Geto-yedies
New Workers

A SPECIAL ROOM FOR WOMEN'S CONSULTATION

In the clinic, a special room has been set aside for a women's consultation, with its own special waiting room.

THE BATH IN JANUARY

During January, 19,007 persons attended the bath. In brief, almost the entire ghetto.

YEHOASH CELEBRATION[64]

On Friday, the 19th of this month, the Literary Association [Association of Writers and Artists] is making a big Yehoash celebration in the ghetto theater in honor of

64. Solomon Bloomgarden Yehoash (1872–1927), a major American Yiddish lyrical poet, author of a masterful translation of the Bible into Yiddish.

the 16th anniversary of the death of the great poet and translator of the Bible into Yiddish. There will be lectures on Yehoash as a poet and as a Bible translator, and an artistic program.

A NEW PROGRAM OF THE HEBREW CHOIR will be presented in the Ghetto Theater next Saturday, the 13th.

FIRST ANNIVERSARY OF THE DEATH OF MALKE CHAIMSON-BASTOMSKI

The 8th of this month is the first anniversary of the death of Malke Chaimson-Bastomski, wife of the teacher, cultural activist, and children's writer Shloyme Bastomski.

FEBRUARY 13 [1943]

IN THE SHADOW OF CRISIS

For a whole week, the ghetto has lived in the shadow of a "ministerial crisis." Fried is thrown out. Fried stays in the government or is kicked out. Fried himself is not loved in the ghetto. And no wonder that those who became interested in the issue, made it all grotesque. Meanwhile, everyone has forgotten that in spite of his dreadful defects, Fried has given the ghetto something. First of all, he is one of the chosen few, almost the only one left, of all the earlier Judenrats. When everyone tried to desert, only Fried stayed in his place. Good or bad, he carried on. But he stayed with the ghetto and—formally—bore responsibility for it.

This is how it is. This is essentially how it is in the ghetto. Either they shout hurrah or they destroy. The ghetto knows no middle ground; justice seeks [. . .]
[*The beginning of page 606 of the original is ripped off and begins with the end of the entry about a crisis in the ghetto leadership.*]

[The "cri]sis" is over. Fried has gone the way of Tshi[. . .] [Both] remain without influence, but both have been provided with [new] jobs.

One more thing is typical about it: instead of the ghetto chief taking pains to surround himself with better, more decent people, he surrounds himself ever more with a gang of nobodies in the full sense of the word. All members of the previous Judenrat are pushed aside, and their place in the responsible offices is taken more and more by people of little worth.

ROSENBERG TASK FORCE AT YIVO

Again recently, 35 cases of books were sent toward Frankfurt am Main. There are 9,403 books in the cases. That is, as we know, the second transport.

I attach a copy of the inventory.
[*The inventory is missing.*]

A DISTRICT COMMISSAR DISAPPEARS

The Lida district commissar, Bell, has recently disappeared. Bell is the commissar of Lida district. Incidentally, [he is] the executioner of Lida and Woronów Jews. The circumstances of his capture are not known. But obviously, this is a job of the partisans.

In Vilna German circles this has made an understandable impression. Here, too, the whole Gestapo is on alert. So far, the result is absolutely zero.

FEBRUARY 16 [1943]

COMMOTION

In Lithuanian society there was a great commotion. There is not a single Lithuanian today who doesn't understand the game. The Germans are sending them to the front and to the most dangerous sections of the front. They are driven off the land, and Germans come to their land. The Lithuanian soldiers, who are to be sent to the front, often run away. I have already written about such events. A similar event occurred a few days ago. A German officer shot a Lithuanian student in the street. The student allegedly demonstrated against the Germans. Yesterday rumors spread that demonstrations would take place during the funeral today. Incidentally, today is Independence Day for the Lithuanians. The holiday was forbidden by the Germans, and there was a public announcement that the 16th is a normal working day. People assume that the Lithuanians will turn the student's funeral into an Independence demonstration.

There wouldn't be much to interest us in that if the ghetto wasn't involved in it, which consists of the fact that no one, even with a permit, can leave the ghetto today. The reason: just in case, it is better not to be in the streets.

A YEHOASH EXHIBIT

For the anniversary of Yehoash's death, a beautiful Yehoash exhibition has been put together by the Youth Club. The exhibits are presented with great taste and show a clear picture of the major writings of the great poet and Bible translator. Several letters in the poet's own hand to his contemporaries and letters to the poets, including a few letters to the poet Y. L. Peretz, are in glass cases. There is a rich collection of Yehoash editions and an informative selection of works about Yehoash in various languages. Special placards give the necessary biographical and bibliographical information. The exhibition is a consolation in our present situation.

MESSAGE FROM DAUGAVPILS

Precise information about events in Daugavpils has recently arrived. More precisely about it—elsewhere. In the meantime, we note that the reporters from

Daugavpils give an old message from the Warsaw journalist B. Singer, who once stayed in their home.

IT DISAPPEARS LIKE CAMPHOR

My Rosenberg Task Force unfortunately has bitter luck. Our chief, Dr. Pohl, was assigned to go to Egypt. The result of this is an empty egg. Instead of Egypt, the Germans are already leaving the . . . African shores. Another chief, Sporket, was supposed to leave these days for the Caucasus. Now it is clear that the Caucasus have disappeared from their hands. He will not see the Caucasus. Now he is preparing for a trip to France. Who knows if France won't also disappear like camphor. . . .

THE RESULTS OF THE COMPETITION FOR LITERATURE, MUSIC, AND PAINTING

[. . .]

[*Pages 690–611 of the original are missing, for the period February 17–24, 1943. Some events of that time must be noted. Liza Magun was shot on February 17; on February 19, a recital took place in honor of the 16th anniversary of Yehoash's death; on February 21, the 33rd workers' assembly was held in honor of Moyshe-Leyb Halpern (Kaczerginski-Sutzkever Collection, no. 523).*]

They Bring Radios

February 18 [1943]

The 25th Anniversary of Lith[uanian] Independence

Children Who Break In

Iksnazhbod Arrested

A Message from Białystok; Mourning Messages from Grodno

Recital to Honor Yehoash; a Year of "Unity"[65]

A Serious Moment

February 25 [1943]

Shooting in the Ghetto

Today the Camp Workers Leave the Ghetto

Ghetto Seals

Today the Holiday of the Red Army

A New Institution of Yeladim

Opening the Hall for Ghetto Athletes

Again, 68 Persons Shot

[*The first half of page 612 is missing. We present the entire remaining part.*]

65. "*Fareynikung*"—referring to the United Partisan Organization, FPO.

WHO BELIEVES THEM?

It is barely the end of February. The rivers are already melting. The Vilna Ghetto is drowning in mud, and so is the front. The battles are weaker because the fields of snow are melting.

The rivers are melting, and along with them, hands drop. The mood is falling, and even the stubborn and obstinate optimists bend. Nothing to hold onto.

A bloody purge is taking place in Białystok. One says 10 thousand, one 20 [thousand]. Nobody knows exactly. Grodno is *Judenrein*. One talks about 500 remaining; another, a few dozen. Suddenly a rumor spreads in the ghetto: Hitler is supposed to have issued an order to exterminate the Jews of Poland. Right after that, new information: Hitler made a speech in which he is supposed to have ordered the extermination of every single Jew. Women have spasms. Some of them stand in front of the gate and wait for the men to come. People secretly ask each other what they heard outside the ghetto . . . etc., etc.

Because of that panic, the ghetto chief called an assembly in the Ghetto Theater of all staff and office heads last night. In his speech, he said that he and Dessler had gone to the district commissar, later to the Gestapo and the SS. They told [in those places] about the panicky mood [in the ghetto] and asked for candor about what is going on. The chief of the ghe[tto, Mr.] Gens, said: "Everyone laughed at the rumors. They [don't know] what is going on in Białystok and Grodno. But they empha[size that] in those cities, Jews live in ghettos; here in Vilna [. . .] there are labor camps. Jews must be calm and work." And the socially naive Gens calms them all. He demands that we work and not be concerned with foolishness! . . .

Naive Mr. Gens. Does he really believe the soothing words of the bestial murderers of the district commissar, the Gestapo, or the SS? If he does, let him know—the masses in the ghetto don't. He spoke, perhaps he calmed some of them, but no one believes, for how can you believe?

Who believes them at all?! . . .

ABOUT DRINKING

In his speech yesterday, Gens said: in the past, the "big shots" used to drink here; today, the lower echelons drink. He demands that alcohol be abandoned. . . .

ABOUT WHIPPING

He also talks about the trend of whippings, which he has recently introduced. He announces that he personally will whip everyone who commits something filthy against the ghetto, and he will whip them so that he will be remembered. He also says that he considers it better for him to whip them than the Gestapo.

ABOUT CRIMES

He says that everything can be done and everything must not be done—a Jew must not be caught in a crime. It brings damage to the criminal and can bring the greatest damage to all ghetto residents.

Everyone listened to the "presentation," most even applauded, and some were even calmed by it.

Today the ghetto is somewhat calmer. Nevertheless, the mood is still quite depressed.

CONCERNING HIMMLER

The last issue of *Niepodległość* includes an item [reporting] that Himmler allegedly ordered that, by January 1, not a single Jew is to remain in Congress Poland. It is now the end of February 1943, and only now, apparently, has the information come into the ghetto as an order allegedly issued only now. The order, as the Polish government from London announces, is old, and that is how it is to be regarded. Moreover, the same order was commented on widely here back in December 1942.

Thus, one of the rumors that have stirred up a panic in the ghetto is no longer current.

HOW MANY JEWS DOES THE GOUVERNEMENT NUMBER NOW?

[. . .]

[*Page 614 of the original, with the statistics of Jews in the General Gouvernement, is missing.*]

Kazanye [?] a Center of Partisans
Białystok Was Indeed Bleeding
Grodno Is Also Bleeding
"Surprise" Again: Murer

[*Page 615 begins in the middle of an entry about a "stroll" by Murer through several workshops of the ghetto.*]

[. . .] answered that he gets that from "good people" who love him. Levas got a brotherly clap on the shoulder, and Murer left. Soon he came to a second house, right to the bibliograph [Yudl] Anilowicz,[66] and found him reading a book in bed. Asked why he was lying down, Anilowicz answered that he was sick. Murer looked at the book and gave it back to him. Later it turned out that the sick man was reading the geography of the USSR. Murer apparently didn't get it. . . .

THEY ALREADY ISSUE PASSES AND NUMBERS

For a few days now, they have been issuing passes and numbers. The process of distribution will last about three months.

Jews joke: until then, who cares?

66. A graduate of the Yiddish academic gymnasium in Vilna. He worked in the bibliographical center at YIVO and belonged to the Reds. He died in the ghetto. For his biography, see *Lexicon* 1:126.

FEBRUARY 27 [1943]

MURER AGAIN, ANOTHER SCANDAL

Once again Murer dropped in on the ghetto, and once again, as he had done recently, he dropped in on a few apartments. This time, he visited Rudnicka 6. Among other things, he strolled through a window into the bath and found women there. When they became embarrassed, he ordered them strictly not to cover their breasts and pointed out that most of them were fat. The same song as a while back, on his visit to Strashun 6.

He also dropped in on the flat of Commissioner Gronner, director of one of the "tailor shops" outside the ghetto. Here he opened the closet and found sausages and flour. In another place, a mass of linen, onions, etc. He muttered to himself that his men don't see what he finds here in the ghetto (probably a hint at his visit to Levas).

At 3 in the afternoon, Gens had to be at Murer's. Among other things, he [Murer] advised him [Gens] to watch out for his policemen.

After a "private" conversation between the chief and Commissioner Gronner, it became clear: Gronner will be dismissed as police commissioner, released as director of the "Tailor Shop," and will be sent to work on the railroad.

Thus ended another ghetto career of another star in the police, Engineer Gronner. Although a calm, assimilated Jew, Engineer Gronner sometimes treated ghetto citizens as the chief treated him. Sometimes Gronner hit and beat not like an engineer, but like the lowest of the low. Now this star also declines. Certainly no one will sigh over his fate or be interested in it.

THE FINALE OF THE COMPETITION

Last night, in the Ghetto Theater, the finale of the literature-musical-painting competition was held. This has recently taken place, and we have already given the result. The program consisted of a lecture on "Literary-Artistic Competitions Outside and Inside the Ghetto." After the reading of the minutes of all three juries, came the second part of the evening—the productions of several creations of the ghetto laureates. The poets [L.] Opeskin, A. Sutzkever, and L. Rudnicka read. Then there were excellent musical pieces.

SOME GHETTO FOLKLORE

1. A German asks a Jew to lend him 20 rubles. The Jew immediately takes the sum out of his pocket and gives it to him. The German wonders:

"How can this be? You don't know me at all and you trust me with such a sum?"

"I have the fullest trust in the Germans," answers the Jew. "You took Stalingrad and gave it back; you took Kharkov and gave it back. I am sure that you will give me back my 20 rubles."

2. What is the difference between General Rommel and a watch?

"A watch goes tick-tock and goes forward; Rommel goes tock-tick [that is, tactics] and goes back [retreats]. . . ."

3. What is the difference between the Germans and the sun?

"The sun goes up in the east and down in the west; the Germans went up in the west and down in the east. . . ."

4. Why can't there be an understanding between the fighting sides?

"Because Hitler says that the war will be won by the . . . race [Yiddish *rase*]; Stalin, that it will be won by the . . . masses [*mase*]; and Roosevelt, that it will be won by the . . . Treasury [*kase*]."

5. What city is the longest in the world?

"Stalingrad, because it took the Germans months to get from the outskirts to the center."

ONLY ONE KILO OF FLOUR

Because of recent events in the ghetto, the ghetto chief ordered no more than one kilo of flour allowed in private dwellings. Larger supplies will be confiscated.

Yesterday the ghetto police searched for larger supplies.

HARD TO GET BREAD

By order of the ghetto, all melinas through which people smuggled in flour, etc., are to be closed. As a result, the price of bread rose terribly. It is almost impossible to get it.

REGARDS FROM ZALMEN REISEN AND BERNARD SINGER

We once talked about an alleged letter from Bernard Singer, who is supposed to have been in London as a delegate from America to a journalistic congress. Now a letter from him has arrived in Vilna. The letter has to do with the Reisen family. Zalmen Reisen is alive but not yet free. Bernard Singer, the writer of the letter, is in Turkey, in Istanbul.

The wife [of] Zalmen Reisen received the letter.

MARCH 3 [1943]

LETTERS TO THE WORLD

For the past week, I have tried to get in touch with the world. The world probably buried me long ago. Why should I be better off than the millions of European Jews? They have already said kaddish and tried gradually to forget. But I'm still alive and want to live—a lot—and hope to get out of here and perhaps enjoy my near and dear ones—those, of course, who are alive.

So I have started running through the world, and as I said, for the past week, I have regularly sent letters like Noah from the Ark. Maybe, maybe, one of my friends will carry the news about me, and maybe, maybe, one of my loved ones will get through to me with their messages.

So I am waiting for answers from Geneva, Japan, Manchuria, Turkey, and elsewhere.

Maybe, maybe . . .

THEY WHIP AGAIN

Murer is back again, yesterday and today. Yesterday everything went peacefully. Today, because he came, they are already whipping; money, bread, and a few potatoes are taken.

Clearly, Murer lets them know he's here.

STIPENDS FOR POOR TALENTED CHILDREN

The ghetto administration has set up stipends for 15 pupils, including 2 from the technical school and 1 from the music school. The stipend students are between the ages of 11 and 16.

For the ghetto, this is a welcome act. After the ghetto, we will be admired for our nerve—what we all achieved! . . . The answer: life is stronger than steel.

A SANITARY CHECKUP IN KAILIS

In both blocks of Kailis, the sanitary ghetto police has recently made a thorough checkup to establish the same sanitary-hygienic situation there as in the ghetto apartments.

IN THE LABOR UNITS — "FIELD UNIFORMS" — A DEGENER GROUP[67]

Now in the unit are 246 Jewish workers, 135 of them women. They work in four places. The central workplace is Burbiszki. Most Jewish workers are skilled laborers, such as shoemakers, tailors, blacksmiths, locksmiths, joiners, masons, etc.

The main difficulties of working in the unit are the great distances to and from work and in the workplaces themselves, especially [when you are] working in an open field with little food and clothing.

Recently, working conditions here have improved considerably, because the former manager, the sadist Degener, whom we have frequently had the sad opportunity to write about [?], has gone to the front and has been replaced by a decent person.

WATCHING OUT FOR BLACKMAILERS OUTSIDE THE GHETTO

Recently uniformed Lithuanian officials have taken the workbook from Jewish workers to extort money for it later. The Jewish police have recently turned over two such characters to the Lithuanian police.

67. There is a pun here: *degener,* in Yiddish, means "imbecile" or "degenerate."

HOW THE MANAGEMENT IN THE GHETTO LOOKS

The ghetto management changes quite often, too often. To keep up with the picture of the ghetto management, I attach here the full list of ghetto departments, sections, institutions, and enterprises, as of today, March 3, 1943.

[*The list is missing.*]

A FULL SCHOOL SYSTEM

At the opening of the girls' boarding school, a teacher commented that the ghetto now has a full school system. I think that is correct. Let me now examine it.

As of now, we have in the ghetto: 3 grammar schools (Strashun 12, Szawelska 1, and Niemiecka 21) with a daily attendance in February 1943 of 1,245 children; high school groups of 129 children, 2 groups in Kailis—1 and 2, with 113 children. Now there is a day care center for children of working parents, where 114 children up to the age of 6 are registered. An orphanage with 72 children and a children's psychological clinic, a children's kitchen and a dairy kitchen. If we add the technical courses, which have already had two graduations and now include 60 students, the music school for children, the boys' and girls' boarding schools, the Yeladim transport brigade, the Youth Club with its extensive activity, etc., etc., the picture is heartwarming.

Is all this possible in the ghetto?

Has this really been achieved in the Vilna Ghetto?

The future historian, the future cultural scholar will often ponder this cultural wonder of the Vilna Ghetto.

GHETTO LIBRARY AND GHETTO READERS

In honor of the first anniversary of the ghetto library, which occurred on September 15, 1942, a big and interesting publication titled "Ghetto Library and Ghetto Readers" has just now appeared. The collection contains an historical article on the emergence of the ghetto library, 10 tables of the activity of the ghetto library and the reading room for the year; and an interesting treatise on the ghetto readers, with diagrams illustrating the whole activity.

The publication is typed; the tablet and diagrams, made by hand. In general, the publication makes a good impression. For the future historian, this will certainly be a good contribution to research on the cultural activity and the psychology of the readers in the Vilna Ghetto.[68]

68. The publication, titled "A Year of Work in the Vilna Ghetto Library," is in the YIVO Archives (Kaczerginski-Sutzkever Collection, no. 370.) It has 32 pages, with the following contents: "Introduction"; "A Year of Work in the Vilna Ghetto Library"; "Ghetto and Ghetto Readers"; "Tables and Diagrams."

MARCH 5 [1943]

ON YOUR HEAD! . . .

[. . .]

[*The end of page 619 of the original is badly torn. From the remaining pieces, it appears that Kruk discusses the mood in Germany and other countries, and in the Vilna Ghetto, in view of the German defeat at Stalingrad. The beginning of page 620 is also torn, where Kruk discusses the impression Stalingrad made on the Lithuanians.*]

HOW THE MOBILIZATION LOOKS

Yesterday, in Vilna, men between the ages of 19 and 24 whose names begin with *A* or *B* had to report. By 1 in the afternoon, apparently not one of the men had showed up. . . . Today 68 Poles and 2 Lithuanians reported.

But, on the other hand, there was an enormous . . . flight to the villages and . . . the forests.[69] We hear that in Kovno, because of that mobilization, serious events took place. What those events are is not yet known.

Aside from the fact that none of those who were conscripted will strengthen the German striking capacity, that they don't want to go and are hostile to Germany, it is also clear that Germany is doing that out of exigency. Clearly, if the mobilization succeeds, this is a gangrenous element that will not only not strengthen Germany, but will infect and weaken her.

That the Reich does this anyway is only because it probably sees this as its last straw.

A REGISTRATION OF FURNITURE IN THE GHETTO

The German landlords apparently still have too little. Now a registration has been made of the remaining furniture in the territory of the ghetto. Never did that area have any special furniture. After all the events this district has experienced, everything was destroyed, and the furniture along with it. But even that is not enough, and if there is still a piece of a broken bed, a rickety cabinet, or a broken chair, it will probably soon be taken. The registration surely has only a single purpose. The statistics for the registration will show that almost 18,000 Jews who live in the ghetto own altogether 1,691 beds, 1,058 of them without mattresses. So, 16,000 people have no bed. Of these, 584 lie on trestles and 261 on bare mattresses. Thus altogether 2,536 people sleep somehow. The rest lie either on the bare ground or, at best, on boards.

The entire population uses 595 cupboards, 922 tables and little tables, 2,788 chairs, 187 mirrors, and 142 electric hanging lamps.

Now they are registering this poverty, and as we have said, apparently they won't let the ghetto have this either.

69. I.e., to the partisans.

SMOKING FORBIDDEN

[Parts of the following lines were torn. We present the remaining part, with conjectures about the missing pieces.]

[In the ghetto] smoking is forbidden. No smoking materials, not even matches, may be [found] in the ghetto offices. This [is the] latest order of the ghetto chief, issued under [pressure of M]urer.

THE LATEST GHETTO JOKE

[What] is our ghetto?

"A kingdom standing on goose feet. . . ."[70]

WHAT IS AN ARYAN?

The answer: the bottom part of a prolet-ARIAN. . . .

MARCH 7 [1943]

WHAT IS THE STATE OF MOBILIZATION?

I have written about the mobilization a few times. From reliable Lithuanian sources, I learn that for every 100 Poles, 3–4 Lithuanians show up. The interpretation is:

In Lithuanian society, there is a big campaign against the mobilization. The Lithuanian police and all others do what they can to help. So, for example, the Lithuanian police make documents for families and those who remained under different names so they won't suffer as families of deserters (to be shot, according to the order). The Lithuanians have other calculations as well: first, everyone here thinks there is a better chance of staying alive in the forest than on the front; second, if you aren't mobilized against the Soviets, you remain a hero in the future, thus covering up all the filth committed up to now. Poles, by contrast, do not have the same police machinery to help them as the Lithuanians have. So they have to appear.

From Jewish sources, I learn that several barracks have prepared a lot of places for the supposed mobilization. The Germans are waiting, and so are the barracks. Meanwhile, no mobilization is seen.

Obviously, the mobilization is increasing the ranks of the partisans.

A POLISH APPEAL

In connection with the recent incident between Stalin and Sikorski about the Polish borders, an illegal Polish appeal appeared, calling for struggle against Germany and the Soviet Union. The password: "Prepare and wait for a password."

70. A pun. The usual expression is "on chicken feet," indicating weakness. "On goose feet" here refers to the ghetto chief Gens (the Yiddish *gendz,* pronounced like *Gens,* means "geese").

NEWS FROM THOSE EXILED TO RUSSIA

I learn from a reliable source that the famous Vilna attorneys Zacks and Feldstein, exiled by the Bolsheviks to the Soviet Union, are now in Persia.

After the news from B. Singer, this is further proof that even from Russia, a lot fled abroad.

KAILIS IN THE GHETTO THEATER

Yesterday a few hundred residents of Kailis came to the ghetto for a special performance for them. For the performance, Ghetto Chief Mr. Gens gave his subjects the gift of a meaningless speech.

MARCH 8 [1943]

MURER SEARCHES

For the past two weeks, Murer has not only been a frequent guest in the ghetto but has started a new course here. He wanders around the ghetto, drops in on various apartments, searches and rummages around, and very often finds and takes things not allowed in the ghetto.

Today he was in the ghetto again, sniffing in all holes. Now he drops in on some Jew, a hat maker, catches him at work, and orders a case brought against him. The same thing happened with a tin smith. He also dropped in on a pawn shop on Jatkowa. He wondered how Jews in the ghetto obtained such valuable things and ordered them confiscated. Nothing good will come to the ghetto from all this.

RATIONS ARE "REGULATED"

For some days, the ghetto officials have been discussing that among themselves. At first, the new distribution of rations evoked a serious attitude. It looked like a fair allocation, where they took into consideration both your salary and the size of your family. Now the issue has exploded, and people joke in the ghetto: rations are distributed: (1) according to whom you know . . . ; (2) according to . . . salaries; (3) according to the size of the family. The first point is dominant. This is how the just food distribution among ghetto employees looks.

AGAIN THE ROSENBERG [TASK FORCE]

The work the Rosenberg Task Force began a year ago should have lasted no more than four to six weeks. By now, it has lasted more than a year, and it looks as if the Rosenberg deserters themselves want to keep the shop as long as possible.

1. REDUCTION. Now they are carrying out a reduction among the Jewish workers, as they themselves say, so there will be fewer work[ers] and more work for the remaining Jewish workers. Clearly, the pretense mainly has something to do with the party deserters from the Rosenberg Task Force. . . .

2. ADDRESSES. We once attached the first specification of the cartons sent out. Now I attach the second. This specification is connected with the address of our first specification.

I also attach an instruction with a Yiddish translation. In the letter there is, first, the address of the Riga center for the occupied areas (Latvia, Estonia, Lithuania, Byelorussia), and for the special center, Smolensk. The letter contains the address where the transports are to be sent.

[*The documents are missing.*]

3. FURTHER WORK. Another order comes from them: historical and architectural descriptions of all Vilna churches, all palaces, theaters, archives, libraries, colleges, etc.

[We] undertook the work with great diligence. The answer to the query is extremely topical. To describe churches—to get a special permit to confer with priests, to get into the churches, etc. The conclusion: contacting all of them means obtaining [information about] potential melinas, literature, etc. It is worth the effort. . . .

I TAKE MY SWEET TIME WITH THE BOOKSTORE

A year ago May, a book sale was set up in the ghetto. The purpose: morale—a bookstore in the ghetto! Second, the very fact that books are distributed in the ghetto; third, the books collected were made good use of; and above all, the ghetto administration didn't lose anything in it.

Now, because of recent events—especially the strict supervision Murer exercises over ghetto enterprises—the ghetto chief and police chief asked whether to liquidate the bookstore, or at least to hide it. We hide it, and it will be set up through a "back door" into a courtyard.

It is indeed interesting now to know what the book enterprise in the ghetto has performed so far:

From June 1942 to March 1, 1943—a period of nine months—the bookstore sold 3,396 books, 2,349 in Yiddish, 471 in Hebrew, 449 religious.

TEXTBOOKS AND PRAYER BOOKS, ONLY IN SINGLE COPIES

Recently, the ghetto police chief ordered all ghetto inhabitants to turn all books in to the library. In private homes, there can be only a single copy of textbooks and prayer books. The books must be turned in by the 12th of this month; afterward, searches will be made of houses.

Thus is the order. The announcement made an understandable impression on the ghetto inhabitants. Who wants to part with the few books acquired in the ghetto? . . .

JEWS MAY NOT BUY NEWSPAPERS OUTSIDE THE GHETTO

By order of the ghetto chief, ghetto inhabitants are prohibited from buying newspapers, journals, and such outside the ghetto.

AFTER THE PROVINCIAL CAMPS HAVE BEEN REMOVED

The rooms on Oszmiańska 10 have been disinfected, and the so-called collective home is to be set up there. First of all, families are to be located there who have to be isolated from their current apartments for cleanliness. Then the so-called single people. The homes are set up under special supervision to maintain cleanliness and internal order.

The buildings are repaired and well ordered. They have running water, plumbing, and toilets. Wooden beds are provided for all residents.

WHAT THE WHOLE GHETTO PRODUCES

[. . .]

[*Pages 625–627 of the original are missing.*]

What Do They Have in Their Heads? . . .
What Else Do They Have in Their Heads
But What Do "They" Have in Mind

March 11 [1943]

The Sword of Damocles Hangs over Us
500 Books for the Ghetto
Gens Calls a Conference

March 12 [1943]

Old and New Accusers [?]

[*Page 628 begins in the middle of a debate about Jewish education in the ghetto.*]

[. . . art]ists and Jewish education, about teaching respect for your own people, love of labor, etc.

As usual, friend Kalmanowicz finds it necessary to shout that the spirit of the Jewish schools is not Jewish. Here of all places, in the ghetto, he wants to settle accounts with the former Vilna Academic Gymnasium for not teaching Hebrew. Brojdo, as always, takes the floor and fights for national Jewish . . . dances. His speech, as usual, is taken as a review number. Glazman doesn't see any danger in Yiddish. For him, it is important that it be a national spirit.

All such moods are defended by the former principal of the Vilna Yiddish Academic Gymnasium, Comrade [Leyb] Turbowicz, and the teachers: Rokhl Brojdo, Khantshe Mann, Miriam Gutgestalt, and G. Yashunski, as the director of the Cultural Department.

In the whole mess of speeches and thanks, Rabbi Jakubson also spoke. . . . He thinks not only that they should teach religion, but also that they should not teach anything that might be against religion. Typically, almost all the speakers nevertheless spoke against religion.

Finally, of course, the chief spoke. He thinks that two speakers here had integrity, that is, Wittenberg and Glazman. The first wants Bolsheviks, but in the ghetto that is impossible. The second, with whom "he" [Gens] agrees, supports the nationalist attitude.

March 15, [1943]

NO COMPARISONS!

Years ago, I happened to read S. Anski's book *The Destruction of Poland, Galicia, and Bukovina.* I remember, as if it were now, how much pain and grief I experienced as I leafed through those volumes. That was how it happened then, years ago. Now I have leafed through those memoirs again.

The book is full of horrible events—race hatred, antisemitism, pogroms, victims, and such. But when I compare what is now going on around us with what I have just read, I can't figure it out: if that was destruction, what is this now? . . . I share my thoughts with friend Weinig from Vilna, who says: "If these events here are called destruction, those events in Poland, Galicia, and Bukovina were an idyll. . . ."

The pogrom in Lwów produced . . . 18 dead. So it was called the bloody pogrom of Lwów.

In one place in those books, Dr. Oder[71] laments: "A few Jews have suffered from the pogroms. There is no livelihood, people are being grabbed for work." In short, he says, "Jewish life is unbearable here." If it was unbearable there, what is our life?

I look for comparisons:

There are certain parallels, which can be traced through the whole chain of Jewish history: robbery, thievery and . . . annihilation. We have a lot of such parallels.

The Russian soldier, the officer, the general, sees Jewish spies everywhere to blame for their defeat. He shouts: "You, Yids, must all be slaughtered, driven out!" Today's exterminator sees us as enemy number 1—a race that undermines the existence of the world, a people that must be destroyed. They don't see Jews as spies but as partners of Roosevelt and Churchill. Who is making the war? The English-American plutocrats, for the sake of Jewish Bolshevism.

Returning to the destruction of Poland, Galicia, and Bukovina, I want to find a definition—if that was destruction, what is this?

There is really no comparison! . . .

RUMORS, RUMORS, AND MORE RUMORS

After all the daily rumors, a new rumor: all Jews in the surrounding camps and the entire area are rounded up and sent to Vilna. Jews begin blinking, their blood runs cold. Is last year's spring starting again? . . .

71. I.e., Dr. Oder of Tarnów. The quotation is from vol. 4 of Anski 1920–1925, in the second part of "The Destruction of Jewish Poland, Galicia and Bukovina," 176–177.

FOURTH GHETTO CONFERENCE OF THE BUND

On the evening of the 13th of this month, in the lib[rary] building, the fourth conference of the Bund organization took place. Twenty-two delegates and [invited] guests participated in the conference. Three lectures were given at the conference: an overview of the war situation, conditions in the ghetto, and a report of activities. After a discussion of three and a half hours, a new committee was elected. All members of the previous committee are back on the "new committee." Of the 15 delegates, Simon [Palevsky] got 14 votes; Herman [Kruk] and Abrasha [Chwojnik], 13 for each; Hersh [Gutgestalt] and Shmulke [Kapliński], 9 each. The conference lasted more than six hours.

The result was the acceptance of a resolution confirming the tactics up to now. But the new committee is ordered to be more watchful as to the current events of ghetto life.

We must mention here that in the result of the "screeching," which took place in last year's conference, is at the beginning [. . .]

[*Pages 630–631 of the diary, from March 15–18, 1943, are missing. The end of the Bund conference in the ghetto is missing. Rudashevski (1973) has the following entry for March 16: "People came from the city today with news. The editor of the Polish newspaper* Goniec, *the hooligan, was shot in church. . . . In all Lithuania today, there were mass arrests in the highest circles. They say the Lithuanians have issued a manifesto not to show up for the mobilization, until the Germans sign Lithuanian independence." Kruk discusses the shooting of the editor of* Goniec *in several subsequent entries.*]

Connections

Among Priests

A Purge of the Lithuanian-Byelorussian Border Strip Is Begun

Liquidation of the Warsaw Ghetto Is Continued

It Is Not Yet Clarified

The Latest Slogan

Something about Partisans

[. . .] in the Miadzioł area the partisans ordered the liquidation of the community administration of Wiśniewice, to transfer it to Bakda [?] [. . .]

The order was carried out, and I know that no step has been taken there so far, even to save their so-called prestige.

From all that, we can see once more that in some places, the partisans do not feel like a second power that terrorizes, but like a power that issues orders which must be carried out. . . .

A SUSPICIOUS CONVERT IN THE GHETTO

Recently the local Gestapo has brought a convert to the ghetto, Tadis Blumberg. Apparently the convert was a janitor in the Vilna City Council. He lives here in

Vilna with a wife and children. Recently he was arrested and, after an investigation, turned over to the ghetto.

Here in the ghetto, however, there is suspicion that Blumberg has been sent to the ghetto as a "sniffer."

The ghetto authorities are keeping their eye on him.

TO EASE GHETTO TRAFFIC

The ghetto is crowded. The streets are narrow. Every additional person blocks traffic. Therefore, steps have been taken to create several passages in the ghetto, which should ease communications and not make traffic harder. For this purpose, a passage from Szpitalna 18 to Rudnicka 17 is now being cut. The new passage will be very broad so wagons can also go through it.

A second passage is made from Szpitalna 4 to Strashun 7. This will be not only a passage but also a drive through, which will surely be a great relief for the ghetto population. Until now, coming from Szpitalna to Strashun has been difficult.

AN ORDER CONCERNING THE ORGANIZATION OF THE PROTECTION OF CHILDREN IS POSTED

By order of the ghetto chief, a special "patronage" office will be created to supervise all children up to the age of 16. The office will supervise the brigades of working children, the children's homes, boarding schools, regular schools, day care centers, etc.

Children with no parents are admitted to the children's homes and the boarding schools, and so are children whose parents are in great need, and also children who live in a morally harmful environment and have to be isolated from it because of their special inclinations. Children up to the age of 10 will be accepted in the children's home, and in the boarding schools, [. . .]

[*Page 633 of the original is missing. The end of the item about the order for the protection of children is certainly there.*]

Smoking Forbidden in Ghetto Institutions

March 17 [1943]

Events in the City

[*Page 634 begins at the end of an entry about events in Lithuania, in connection with the mobilization order and Lithuanian resistance.*]

[. . . ev]ents in Kovno. There, too, the university is occupied. The professors and students have been arrested.

I learn that the expert on Jewish affairs of the mayor, the "hero" Burakas, is hiding in the ghetto, along with the chief of the housing department in Vilna, Mr. Narusis.

Times change—now they seek shelter in . . . the ghetto.

People say that machine guns have been set up in some streets.

Who shot editor Ancewicz? Why do they occupy the university? Why the arrest of the mayor? And what is going on in Kovno? It is hard to talk about all that right now.

IS IT REALLY POSSIBLE?

After the information from Polish radio *Świt* about 20 Bundists [killed in the Soviet Union], after the other information from *Goniec Codzienny* about two Socialists who were shot, I now learn that the same radio reported that Bundists were shot, including [Wiktor] Alter.[72]

We shrug and don't understand: Is it really possible? . . .[73]

MORE INFORMATION ABOUT THE EVENTS IN THE CITY

11 *at night*. I now learn that the mayor of the city was not arrested, only his deputy, Grigas. People also say that the rector of the university, Mikołaj Birzyszko, and several professors, teachers, students, etc., were also detained. They talk about hundreds of arrests.

Yesterday, people saw how Weiss and his group took students of the technical school from the Holendernia.

Burakas, who spent a few hours in the ghetto yesterday, later went out, and now, in the evening, they say he is arrested.

Today an appeal was distributed in the city, calling on the Lithuanians not to report for army duty. Among other things, it says there that every Lithuanian policeman, soldier, etc., who helps snatch Lithuanians will be sentenced to death.

MARCH 18 [1943]

WHAT IS GOING ON?

Only now is it beginning to be clear what is going on in Vilna. Yesterday's events and the shooting of Ancewicz have nothing to do with one another. The shooting of Ancewicz apparently was an "honorarium" for his pro-Nazi and anti-Polish attitude. Yesterday's events must be connected with the proclaimed [Lithuanian] mobilization.

[We] have often talked about the many who deserted from the Lithuanian legion, about those who ran away from the barracks before being sent to the front.

72. The leaders of the Bund in Poland, Henryk Erlich and Wiktor Alter, were arrested by the Soviets in 1939 and taken to Russia. In 1941, as Polish citizens, they were released, but in December 1941, on Stalin's orders, they were again arrested and killed. The news reached the ghetto belatedly.

73. I.e., that the Soviets also liquidate Jewish Socialist leaders.

[We] have also noted that during the last mobilization, for every hundred Poles, three or four Lithuanians showed up.

We [also] noted that the mobilization was withdrawn. We must now deny that information. Not achieving the goal through mobilization, they began "snatching" again in the city.

Yesterday's Aktion in Vilna (about Kovno, and other places, we don't yet know) is therefore a result of resistance.

Today's Vilna Lithuanian newspaper publishes an article followed by an announcement. The article: influenced by the intelligentsia, the mobilization in Lithuania went badly. This is a crime against the New Europe, a lack of consideration for their own people. In the future, the registration will be carried out *only for the labor army.* To avoid harsh punishment, the Lithuanian people must dissociate themselves from their politicking intelligentsia.

Then comes an announcement:

The university and all its departments are closed. A special representative will be appointed for education in Lithuania. Let us hope that, after isolating the politicking intelligentsia, the Lithuanians will follow the good example of the Estonians and Latvians. Thus obviously, the Aktion is a result of refusing to go into the army. They are trying to lull the Lithuanians by using the Estonians and Latvians, and most important, the mobilization is continued as a labor mobilization.

According to rumor, the governor of Lithuania, Dr. von Rentlen, has resigned.

PARADOXES

Our strange and extremely difficult situation here leads, among other things, to paradoxes no one would probably ever have been able to invent.

1. Jews are not allowed to stand near Aryans, and yet it is a Jew, on the RR Task Force,[74] who is given the job of describing the churches of Vilna. Not only describing and going around to their holy places, but having the honor of being conducted by priests, parsons, pastors, etc.
2. Jews are isolated from the Aryan world, and therefore [we have] the ghetto. But Aryans who want to save themselves from Aryan-German hands come for asylum to . . . the ghetto.
3. Germans have no trust in the Aryan Poles, Russians, and Lithuanians. But, on the contrary, their Jewish slaves are their best . . . co-workers.

Paradoxes, paradoxes, and paradoxes.

74. Reichsleiter Rosenberg Task Force.

CHAPTER 7

THE SKY IS OVERCAST AGAIN

MARCH 19, 1943 – MAY 10, 1943

MARCH 19 [1943]

THE SKY IS OVERCAST AGAIN

Our ghetto horizon is again overcast. The cleansing of the Byelorussian-Lithuanian border strip of 50 km has taken "real" shape. But reality becomes real in the context of our sad existence.

Experts say that it amounts to 10,000 Jews: Jews from Oszmiana, Święciany, Michaliszki. Several camps are involved, etc.

Every such resettlement can bring victims. In any case, it is a tryout for a blood tax.

Some say that moving the [Jews in the] provinces is the first signal. Others interpret: in the Gestapo, they think that things will be calm until July. Still others think we can be calm for another two months.

Meanwhile, rumors reach me: all side doors of the ghetto are to be walled up; a ghetto office of the Gestapo will be set up in front of the ghetto; the block of Zawalna 4, where all the Todt workers are now concentrated, is to return to the ghetto.

It is overcast.

The sky is growing cloudy! . . .

HENRYK, WIKTOR

The hand trembles. The pen stops writing. Is it really possible?

But there is absolutely no doubt about it—yes, it is possible, it is more than probable. It is almost certainly true. The last radio news from the illegal Polish radio station Świt announced that in Russia, a year ago, two Polish Socialists were shot, Henryk Erlich and Wiktor Alter. The same broadcast discussed big demonstrations about it in New York, where Jewish workers broke the windows of Soviet Ambassador Litvinov.

Is it really possible?

If it is really so, if the news is really correct, I bow my head to you, comrades and friends, Henryk and Wiktor. You, our teachers and leaders; Henryk of the handsome, aristocratic face; and Wiktor of the charming and shining head.

My heart pounds—is it not too soon to write about this?

MORE ABOUT THE RESETTLEMENT

I learn that the above-mentioned province, which is now undergoing resettlement, will be divided among three ghettos—Vilna, Kovno, and a new ghetto to be organized in Ponevezh. The families of the men who work in the Todt camps outside those boundaries will be shipped to them. Because that sounds too nice and "ideal," few people believe it.

THE BURIAL DEPARTMENT IN A STABLE

Everything is possible here. Because of the whim of a "dignitary" familiar to us—the ghetto controller, Mr. Ginzburg—the archive of the Vilna Burial Department finds no other resting place in the ghetto than in a . . . stable. That is what the director of the local Burial Department, the veteran Jewish social activist Mr. Flax, was forced to today.

So, the Burial Department, with its card file and cemetery records, now rests in a stable.

ABOUT RECENT EVENTS IN VILNA

I learn details about recent events in Vilna. Apparently the events were much more serious than we have written so far. In the streets, not only were machine guns seen but also small tanks. People say that by Tuesday evening at 8, the Gestapo netted 435 arrestees, most of whom were intelligentsia and military men. They even mention the archbishop of Vilna, Rainis, and other clergy. The searches in the schools were often linked to formal pogroms. Such pogroms, for example, took place in the technical school on Zarzecze and in the laboratory on Nowogródzka. From the former, they took seven . . . typewriters and smashed a lot of instruments, glassware, etc. Even now, they are still taking machines and other things from there. The supplies in the apartments of those arrested were plundered and even divided among Jewish workers (of the Gestapo, for example).

A TRAGIC SUICIDE

At 9 o'clock this morning, Police Sergeant Grisha Krawczyński hanged himself for the second time. This is the one who tried to hang himself a few weeks ago. This time he succeeded. In a letter he left, he wrote vaguely that his name was sullied. They have lost faith in him and he cannot

[. . .]

[Pages 638–641 of the diary are missing. Krawczyński's suicide is mentioned in Lazar 1950:88–89. Krawczyński was a member of the FPO*. When the Jewish police took pains to uncover and liquidate the fighting organization, Krawczyński was arrested. At his interrogation, he blurted out that he had once had a revolver but had given it to someone, he didn't remember who. When new searches began in the ghetto, Krawczyński knew they would come to him again, and he was under the delu-*

sion that it was his fault that Gens and Dessler knew that a fighting organization existed in the ghetto. Members of the FPO staff tried to calm him and convince him that the ghetto leadership had known about the partisan activity and did not need to find out about this from him. But he was unable to calm down and ultimately committed suicide. He left a letter for Yosef Glazman, in which he wrote that he had a strong sense of guilt and asked for forgiveness. It was this letter that proved the existence of the partisan organization to the ghetto police.]

An Assembly about Ghetto Deserters
An Overcast Meeting

March 20 [1943]
The Sky Is Clouding, a Storm Is Coming
Ponevezh
The Mood of Those Assigned for Resettlement

March 21 [1943]
Somewhat Milder
Under the Sign of Zawalna 4

March 22 [1943]
"The Last Purim"
Somewhat Calmer
About the Latest Events

[*Page 642 begins at the end of an entry about an appeal of the pro-German Lithuanians.]*

[. . .] the appeal, as we see, is signed not only by the remaining stubborn Lithuanian Tautinikas, but also by some who are considered the so-called folk elements and even leftists. Some of them were arrested during the recent events. Some of those who signed were apparently forced to.

THE VILNA UNIVERSITY LIBRARY IS REMOVED

The degree of vandalism the Germans have attained has been proved once again by their behavior during recent events, which we have already written about. Their murderousness has gone so far that they have slashed many precious tapestries in the university building with knives.

Now I learn from the Rosenberg Task Force that the university library will be removed from Vilna altogether.

SEVEN ILLEGAL LITHUANIAN NEWSPAPERS

Comrade B[inder], who has many contacts with Lithuanians, brings me the news that today alone he held in his hands seven illegal Lithuanian newspapers. He couldn't write down their names, but he did remember some: *Nepriklausoma Lietuva* [Independent Lithuania]; *Lietuva* [Lithuania]; *I Laisve* [Freedom]; *Laisves Kovotojas* [Freedom fighter]; *Nepriklausomybe* [Independence].

A NEW LITHUANIAN APPEAL

The same friend B[inder] tells of a stenciled appeal signed by the Lithuanian Committee for Passive Resistance. Aside from calling for passive resistance, the authors also [warn] all Lithuanian police stations, etc., that they are making the Lithuanians responsible for helping arrest or expose Lithuan[ian reb]els.
[*The rest of the page is torn. We present here the bracketed additions by the editor of the Yiddish edition.*]

VEIVIRZENAI — A CAMP OF JEWISH WOMEN

[I] learned that in Veiviržėnai, between Tauragė and Kretinga on the Prussian border, there is a camp of Jewish women who are employed in agricultural labor. It is not clear if the camp still [exists] today. In any case, someone visited it four months ago.

MARCH 23, [1943]

A STRANGE FATIGUE

[After a ha]rd Saturday, after the small relief of Sunday, a strange heaviness de[scended], a fatigue which can only be interpreted as that [people are] beginning to resign themselves, are tired of everything, and give themselves [up to] God's chance.

[. . .]

[*Page 643 of the original is missing.]*

For Three Sacks of Salt
For Matches

A Vilna lad was apprehended in Nowa Wilejka today with a box of matches. So how will we have to pay for this?

AGAIN PEOPLE REGISTER

We remember what it looked like at the end of 1941 when the Vilna Ghetto didn't stop listing, registering, adding relatives, re-registering, etc. Now this is being repeated, because of the accelerated passportization. In order not to remain "outside," people pay the price and add on relatives. They say that it takes 6,000 rubles to add relatives.

History repeats itself. . . .

THE EXHIBITION IS BEING PREPARED

The exhibition of plastic arts, organized by the ghetto Cultural Department, has been prepared in no time at all. So far, paintings by Rachel Sutzkever, sculptures by Yudl Mut, pictures by Yankev Sher, caricatures by G. Drezin, and drawings by the 9-year-old S. Bak and the 14-year-old S. Volmark have been accepted for the exhibit. Preparations are in full swing.

MARCH 24 [1943]

THE EVE, THE EVE

No amount of calming helps. Moreover, as soon as things look calm on the outside, something undermines and digs on the inside.

The question of resistance has become one of the most popular subjects in the ghetto. Apparently there isn't a single Jew who doesn't share the opinion that you mustn't let yourself be taken. . . .

Meanwhile, they are preparing to accept those from the provinces. Both schools and prayer houses have been emptied out. The sports hall, really the hall of the Brigadier Council, has also been taken for the purpose.

SOROK TATARY

The group of forest workers from Sorok Tatary came to the ghetto yesterday.

In the ghetto, a place was prepared for barracks—everything for those who come.

The chief of the ghetto is also preparing. Yesterday he went to Oszmiana. This morning he came back. Meanwhile, rumors circulate here that the 100 heads Murer requires will be paid with . . . Oszmiana.

If my visit to the chief finally takes place today, I shall perhaps be able to report more.

The police chief is also ready for the final reckoning: recently he gave the representatives of the Vilna society a revolver and undertook the task of getting 20 more. . . . Money for that purpose had already been allocated.

It is not only the eve of Passover, but the air here already smells of "The Eve . . . the Eve."

THE LITHUANIAN REVOLUTIONARIES CALM DOWN

Lithuanian hearts have calmed down. They think that recent events have rehabilitated them and they can now sleep peacefully.

The second group, those who signed the last appeal and called for obedience, are preparing the congress. They say that seven delegates from Vilna are going to the congress.

There are even rumors about the supposed demands of the Lithuanians to the Reich. They also talk of a point concerning Jews! . . .

IN MEMORY OF THE FALLEN LIZA MAGUN

Liza Magun, the active member of the FPO who was shot for living on Aryan documents, the one who was sent to Oszmiana during the Aktion there to warn the people of what was going on (see the entry of October 18, 1942, "A Painful 'Celebration'")—to commemorate her death, her friends, fellow members of the FPO, gave the organization a revolver and a machine gun.

MY PRIEST

My contact, a priest, who was to have put me in touch with other priests (see the matter of describing churches for the Rosenberg Task Force), has in the meantime gone into hiding because of events among the Lithuanian intelligentsia. I will be able to meet him soon.

FOUR HORSES FOR THE GHETTO

The ghetto administration has received permission to acquire four horses.

A DOCTORS' ASSOCIATION

A doctors' association was to have been created in the ghetto to reinforce professional ethics and seek means of bolstering the health of the ghetto citizens. Meanwhile the matter has dissolved into nothing.

IN THE LABOR UNITS. "GIESSLER BUILDING GROUP"

For some time now, the so-called Giessler Building Group of the Todt Organization has been active in Vilna; they are executing a big building project at the Vilna railroad station. Several hundred camp Jews from Žasliai, Nowa Wilejka, Święciany, etc., have been brought to Vilna for this. But the provincial camp Jews are not enough, and a labor force must regularly be drawn from the ghetto inhabitants, the units outside the ghetto, etc. Every day, about 1,000 Jews go to work at the railroad station, building a big new hall for locomotives, hauling and rebuilding railroad tracks, clearing the tracks of ice and snow, etc. There are almost no skilled workers there.

The camp Jews go to work from their block outside the ghetto (Zawalna 4). The Vilna columns leave the ghetto at 5:30 in the morning and are immediately, outside the ghetto gate, taken in hand by the Todt people. On Kwaszelna Street, the workers are counted, and from there the columns are sent to the proper workplaces. They work mainly with spades and pickaxes. The workers get supper at midday—soup and bread—and at about 5 o'clock in the evening, the work day is finished.

This workplace is now one of the biggest units in Vilna.

MARCH 25 [1943]

It seldom happens that I seek a talk with the chief and he evades it. This time it happened. The chief had postponed our talk from one day to the next, for five days now. Everything indicated that he had nothing to say, and admitting that he had nothing to say was not feasible for him.

How can you be powerful without power? . . .

But last night, our conversation did take place. Mr. G[ens] tries to apologize, excuses himself, and says:

The conversation six weeks ago about the 60 km strip of border area between Byelorussia and Lithuania has now become a reality. So far, there have been various combinations. All Jews from the liquidated ghettos had to be transported to Kovno, Vilna, and Ponevezh. Recently the matter took a new turn. Now it looks like this: camps remain in Zezmer, Vievis, Rzesza, Biała Waka, Kiena, Bezdany, Nowa Wilejka. The ghettos of Michaliszki, Święciany, Soly, and Oszmiana have been liquidated.

RESETTLEMENT PROGRAM

The inhabitants of the liquidated ghettos are being shipped out: skilled workers and their workshops from Oszmiana are being transported to Nowa Wilejka, along with their staff—32 men and their families.

The families of the men working in the camps that remained where they were are being sent to their men. For example, the families of the liquidated ghettos come to Zezmer and Vievis. The same with Biała Waka, Bezdany, Kiena, and others. Two hundred and forty persons from Soły will be sent to Biała Waka.

All who remain in the ghettos, who are not skilled laborers or have no family to go to, will be divided between Kovno and Vilna. About 3,000–4,000 will be sent to Kovno. To Vilna will come about 500 skilled workers, a few families of the workers of OTE, and the rest without any support. Altogether, they expect about 1,800 new people here.

The resettlement campaign started today. The resettlement of Oszmiana to Vilna, Kiena, and Nowa Wilejka is taking place with wagons, with the assistance of the Jewish police of the Vilna Ghetto. Those who are going to Kovno will be transported by train. The residents of Soly, Oszmiana, and Michaliszki have been gathered in Soly and will all be taken to Kovno in 40–50 wagons. The Jewish police will help them as far as Vilna. From Vilna, the Gestapo . . . and perhaps a few Jewish police. All Jews can take as many of their belongings as they can.

This is how the account of recent events looks, which keeps the ghetto very tense.

When I ask why the Jewish police will take the carts of Jews only as far as Vilna,

Mr. G[ens] answers that it doesn't matter. He is sure nothing will happen to anybody. For example, he admits that Murer demanded 100 men for salt this week. He, G[ens], was prepared to do it because . . . there was no way out. But here the Gestapo got involved and held things up because such an act might disturb the resettlement plans: Jews would run away and reinforce the ranks of the partisans.

The conclusion: from a qualitative point of view, in the sense that we are a labor force [*Einsatz*], the Vilna Ghetto will grow significantly worse, because many people are being added who will not be productive.

"Do you think we're on the eve of Aktions?"

The Chief was pensive, as if it were the first time such a question had occurred to him, and answered:

"For the time being, I don't think so, but . . . it is not out of the question."

MARCH 26 [1943]

A NEW ERA

Everything indicates that we are entering a time of new, hard experiences. Everything indicates that whatever must happen here is aimed at concentrating large masses, and then. . . .

All night long, the police were on alert in the ghetto and in part of the provisions detail. It was calculated that the first wagons would begin to come from Oszmiana at about 2 or 3 in the morning. Murer ordered that if they didn't arrive, he was to be woken up. They prepared to bring the food into the ghetto before anything else, and Murer would search the wagons only after they had first been searched by the ghetto police.

The plan unfortunately failed. At night, a few automobiles did indeed come into the ghetto, and with them, large amounts of supplies. The wagons didn't arrive until 7 in the morning. They all gathered outside the ghetto, and not until Murer came were they allowed in. Now—a surprise. Murer allowed potatoes (and even whole sacks of bread, etc.) to be brought in. He confiscated flour. In fact, the Oszmiana Jews brought enormous amounts of supplies with them: sacks of flour, meat, honey, and other things.

The wagons and their passengers made a dreadful impression in the ghetto. There were 105 wagons, packed full of sacks, bedding, sometimes a chair, a folding bed, quilts; and on top of them women, children, old people. It is estimated that up to 350 people entered the ghetto today.

There were many heartbreaking scenes, tableaux that told of the coexistence of these Jews and their Christian neighbors. Often, when the local peasants, owners of the wagons, said farewell to their Jews, they wept bitterly. They called out nicknames and sent regards; they promised to look out for this and that one.

And they whispered together about things the Byelorussian Christians have to watch out for.

The scenes were heartbreaking and made a strong impression.

THE PICTURE IS GROWING SHARPER AND CLEARER

Again comes precise and reliable information. They say that we can rest easy until the end of May. Why May? Reports come from the Gestapo that whereas up to 23,000–24,000 Jews will now gather in the ghetto, the number must be reduced to 15,000–16,000. So, apparently 6,000–8,000 Jews must be taken out of the ghetto.

Why the concentration, and why the end of May:

The monthly reports of the district commissar and the Gestapo are sent to Kovno, and from there to Berlin. It takes six to eight weeks for an answer to come back. So it goes with the replies to all reports so this is how we come up with the end of May.

The information is reliable and, I think, accurate and likely. The conclusion: the picture is growing clear and sharp. The Vilna Ghetto is on the eve of great events that we must expect and "prepare" for.

TOMORROW IS THE PREMIERE OF PINSKY'S "TREASURE"

Meanwhile everything goes on according to its pace. After long rehearsals, the premiere of [David] Pinsky's "The Treasure" will take place tomorrow in the Ghetto Theater. The tickets are already sold out for the performance tomorrow, i.e., Saturday, as well as for Sunday, Monday, and Tuesday. The last performance will be a festive one—a benefit in honor of Mrs. Lipowska's 40-year acting career.

ŁUKISZKI PRISON IS ONCE AGAIN FULL

Not long ago, we wrote with "joy" that there were altogether 3–4 inmates in Łukiszki Prison. Today the number has risen significantly. They say that once again it holds 30–40, and most of them are serious cases.

MARCH 29 [1943]

PEOPLE SETTLE IN

For the past three days, resettlement has taken over in the ghetto. On Thursday, the first groups from Oszmiana came; Friday morning, another 250 wagons. On Saturday morning, more groups came; Saturday evening, a train from Święciany; and Sunday, 400 wagons from Michaliszki. There is a satirical line in the ghetto about the resettlement: "It's no good because it is too good." Every family brings a wagon of things. People bring rags, furniture, enormous supplies, etc. Murer is "amiable," he confiscates, he allows. In short, he is amiable as never before. So, the line: "It's no good because it is too good."

The ghetto becomes more crowded by the hour; it grows by the hundreds, and the population of the ghetto increases like yeast (no evil intended)!

"Is this good, is this bad?" It's on everyone's lips:

"What's the nature of this element coming into the ghetto?"

The answer is: mostly women, masses of children, and a lot of old people. There are almost no young men, only middle-aged ones.

Will this qualitatively improve the working element of the ghetto? Obviously it will make it worse. Will the authorities tolerate it? Everything indicates that a question mark must be put here.

Meanwhile, people say that the fittest young people of those places ran away—most, of course, to the forests.

But we shall write about that later.

They say that the Lithuanians in those towns are very sorry that the ghettos have been liquidated there. For them, it was a "kosher pot with a kosher spoon," a perfect arrangement. They could rule the Jews, they took from them whatever they liked, and especially, they did . . . business and earned big money. They really should miss it!

The Jews, too, might miss it. They were not only driven out of their old homes, but they don't yet understand; they think they will go on living as they have. That they lived relatively well is indicated, for example, by the supplies and provisions the provincials bring.

A fact: a Jewish woman asks at the [Jewish police] station for help getting back . . . five buckets: one with butter, the second with fried fatback, one with honey, and the rest with similar delicacies. . . .

Another fact: a mother and a few children were lying on a wagon full of feather beds, furniture, and other things. From somewhere, she pulls out a loaf of white bread (the ghetto hasn't seen that for months now), takes a cooked chicken out of somewhere, tears it into pieces, and divides them among the children. The ghetto inhabitants, who don't even remember such food, look and admire. After they finish eating, the mother says to her children: now, children, we must go look for an . . . apartment. The ghetto inhabitants smile behind their mustaches. The woman is used to good things: white bread, chicken, and is now looking . . . for an apartment in the ghetto.

These people are still living by old concepts. Here in the ghetto, all that is strange by now, and it really has a screeching ring to it. If only the dreams of the provincials would come true. If only! . . .

PREMIERE OF DAVID PINSKY'S "THE TREASURE"

On Saturday the 27th, the premiere of "Treasure" took place in a full auditorium. Outside, the police guarded the arriving Święciany Jews, and here in the theater, as if nothing were happening—a premiere!

The performance is smooth, the acting pure, the sets really beautiful—as if it were not in the ghetto. The ditties introduced here were a bit shocking.

Y. Bergolski, Shabse Blacher, and Dora Rubina were the best. I attach a program of the performance.

[*The program is missing.*]

When we came out of the theater late in the evening, some of the resettled were still dragging themselves around in the street.

AN ART EXHIBIT

Yesterday, the 28th, at noon, in the lobby of the Ghetto Theater, the opening of the long-promised art exhibit took place. The entrance to the hall made a strange impression: Did we really need all this? But, entering the exhibit hall, you are embraced by warmth: pictures, paintings, sculptures, and projects, including a lot of original ghetto art. Y. Sher—a series of drawings of ghetto holes, Sedlis—paper posters for ghetto trades (glazier, cabinetmaker, mason, painter, tailor, woodworker). Then, a tapestry by the PPV. And an exhibit of their woodcutting; churches and a part of the unfinished Synagogue Yard, which is to form the scale model "Synagogue Yard" (work of young Notes). The splendid painter [Rachel] Sutzkever is represented beautifully with oils and watercolors. The works of G. Drezin (14 caricatures and 6 cuts of tin figures) are good and successful. Yudl Mut exhibits good works here: drawings, pictures, and two sculptures.

The drawings of the nine-year-old S. Bak attracted the most attention. The child is apparently an extraordinary talent, in every respect.[1]

The exhibit is heartwarming. But when you leave it, you are once again cooled off. There is another exhibit in the courtyard of Rudnicka 6. Lying here on their bundles are families with all their belongings, the newly arrived refugees from Michaliszki. The leader of the Cultural Department, Mr. Yashunski, talked about that in his opening speech, and the chief of the ghetto, Gens, at the closing.

MARCH 31 [1943]

I TREMBLE FOR TOMORROW

Events here in the ghetto have again begun to move so fast that you can't grasp and digest everything. Recently everything has pointed toward one thing—tremble for tomorrow. But dreadful as that may be, we become more inured every day.

No, we will not be taken like sheep![2] No, we will not let them.

In several conversations I have had recently, everyone answers: "If only the

1. Samuel Bak survived the Holocaust and became a prominent Israeli painter.

2. Here Kruk quotes from Abba Kovner's January 1942 call for resistance, which laid the foundation of the FPO.

initiative succeeds—it will be a happy moment. For me there is nothing to decide, I am decided!" I get such answers wherever I go.[3]

The air here smells of powder. Everything indicates that we are on the brink. We are doing all we can so as not to be taken like sheep.

OUTRAGEOUS BEHAVIOR

During the recent resettlement from Michaliszki, Święciany, and Oszmiana, the ghetto wondered why traffic was stopped in the streets when they entered the ghetto in wagons. People did wonder at the time. Now it is clear that apparently, many of those arriving were robbed here in the ghetto by vile characters. It turned out that those arriving, happy that they were finally in the Vilna Ghetto alive and among Jews, were robbed by those very Jews. . . .

A few dozen of the thieves, including three Jewish policemen, have now been arrested. This is why the ghetto Jews were driven from the streets! . . .

WHERE WERE THE ARRIVING JEWS PUT?

I learn that the arriving Jews have been put in the following collective homes: the Jews from Oszmiana took the hall of the sports club (Rudnicka 7), the houses at Szawelska 1 and 3, and Niemiecka 27, where there was a medical school center. The Michaliszki Jews were put in the building at Strashun 12 and in the building of the vocational courses on Oszmiańska Street. Those from Święciany are at Rudnicka 13, Niemiecka 19, and a small group of them at Szawelska 1. In the last building, there are 39 old people, who were placed in separate groups.

ABOUT THE STOLEN FOOD

We have already written about the big stocks of food brought by the provincials, and that much of the food was taken away at the gate. Some of that food has now been returned by the ghetto administration. To give a sense of the magnitude of the stocks that were brought, we extract a few items from the requests of those who were abused.

The Smorgonie rabbi Yitskhok Markus asks the chief of the ghetto to return 2 sacks of flour, 150 kilos of potatoes, 32 kg of salt, 16 kg of peas, millet, buckwheat, and barley, oat flour, etc.

Nekhame Glezer asks for 2 sacks of flour and 65 kg of peas; Świrski, Yitskhok, 2 sacks of flour. Incidentally, the Świrski family has four requests, all for 2 sacks of flour! Ziskind, Hersh, asks, for example, for no more than 4 cans of oil, 4 puds of flour, honey, etc. Masha Levin asks for her 2 1/2 sacks of flour and 5 kilos of fat. A great many ask for the return of large quantities of hard sugar and, especially, flour, flour, and flour.

3. Kruk alludes to people's inclinations to find contacts with the partisan organization.

MIRON ABELOWICZ

Yesterday was the funeral of the optician Miron Abelowicz, one of the last of several generations of famous Vilna opticians. He worked for the Germans in a Lithuanian optical collective. Today the director of his collective came to the funeral from outside, along with a representative of the workers and the famous Polish optician, Iwaszkiewicz. They say that the Lithuanian director wept bitter tears at a speech given by a Jew before the coffin was moved.

When the coffin passed the turnpike, and the Jews and the women remained in the ghetto, those three Christians went out with the Jewish coffin. A large group of Christian opticians and fellow workers from the Lithuanian opticians' collective was waiting at the gate.

The funeral, the visit from his colleagues to the ghetto, waiting for the coffin outside the ghetto—all made an understandable impression.

We should mention here that the wife of the deceased received a large sum of money from her husband's colleagues.

FEVER AGAIN

It is now 4 in the afternoon, and a new fever is raging through the ghetto: Murer and Hingst suddenly came into the ghetto at 11 this morning and left a few orders. What these orders are, we don't yet know. But people do know that there was soon a strong atmosphere of tension in the permit office and that at about 3 in the afternoon, all house commandants went to the apartments, ordering all those who don't yet have a pass to register at 5 this evening to get . . . passes.

Does this have anything to do with Hingst's recent order?

PEAT WORKERS ARE DRIVEN FROM THEIR WORKPLACES

The idea that all the tension about the resettlement had something to do only with the famous 50 kilometers of the Byelorussian-Lithuanian border was reinforced by the fact that workers still remained in work camps in Bezdany, Kiena, and Biała Waka. Now, a few hours ago, information came that 1,500 workers from these places are returning to Vilna. The tension increases by the minute. The thesis that we are being concentrated in order to be killed grows clearer.

APRIL 4 [1943]

FEVER

Our ghetto lives in a fever, and that's why I have been silent for several days. It is clear to everyone, with no exception: everything that has happened here recently is not only the brink, but it is really clear—we stand before a series of Aktions or, as is often thought, a brand-new permanent Aktion, whose beginning we already see.

From what we hear, the units are supposed to have received brand-new instructions about the Jewish workers. People say that a great deal was said about the front and its approach, about the fact that Jews are enemies, that they must be watched. Wherever possible, Aryans are to be used. Wherever this cannot be done, one must watch the hands of the Jews, not leave them in charge. Guards must be posted everywhere, and for the slightest thing—severe punishment.

So much for letters. Also, at the last Brigadier Council, the ghetto chief announced: the smallest trifle will be severely punished. He warns: for every trespass, not only will the guilty one be punished but the entire family as well—everyone will be held responsible.

He enumerates: it is dangerous not only to bring in anything, but also to go out without a patch. The patch must be good and sewed on as prescribed. Avoid walking in groups and, in general, anything that provides a pretext for picking on you.

The same night, a few hours after the warning, the first blow came: five families were dragged out of the ghetto at night for the crimes of their husbands and fathers. Five families, which consisted of 14 persons, and the tragic thing: [some were] not even families but strangers, "written-in." Now the 14 were taken from specific addresses, and on the same day, at about 1:30 in the afternoon, Jewish workers in the Gestapo received . . . their clothing for storage.

What their crimes consisted of we have already written a few times: six persons were arrested in January for smuggling liquor and cigarettes. The brigadier of the group was shot. The other five, released. Now, recently, they were taken again and shot along with the real and fictional family members.

During the past days, masses of people have been detained at work. The brigadiers of the units have been made responsible for the crimes of their fellow workers. The families of those detained scamper like poisoned mice. People hide in holes, and the ghetto is feverish—it is even worse than an Aktion. It is a permanent Aktion, donc under the cloak of legality, in which thousands and thousands will be taken away.

. . . And well-informed people say to all this: Do you think this will avoid an Aktion, too? . . .

TWO VICTIMS

People report from the peat workers in Biała Waka that on April 1, two Lithuanian Gestapo agents arrived there, went into a peasant's hut, called out two girls, and shot them on the spot before the gate.

Why? People say that several months ago, they were reported for trading. It was thought that the case had long been forgotten. Now, apparently, came the sentence. The last two victims are oil on the fire glowing in the ghetto.

APRIL FOOLS' DAY

On April 1, the ghetto did not shirk its observation of April Fools', even this year. Among several April Fools [pranks], even my staff didn't leave me alone on April 1. More about that at a better time.

MORE ABOUT THE HORROR OF 14

I learn that one of the local police, forced to look for the 14 family members, had to bring in his own sister.

Will the world someday understand the tragedy of our life?

PEOPLE RUN AWAY TO THE FOREST

The recent resettlement has once again reinvigorated the escape to the forest. This time, of course, it is young people who don't want to be resettled who run. As we have already reported, 80 young people left from Oszmiana. And 28 from Święciany. People tell of similar groups from Michaliszki, Soły, etc. More precise information about this when there is an opportunity.

MAREK IN THE GESTAPO

My friend Marek [Kozik] was arrested, as a brigadier, for the sins of his fellow workers, and he is in the [custody of the] Gestapo. The entire ghetto is reeling. The warning of the ghetto chief is taking on flesh and blood. The brigadiers are being held responsible for the "crimes" of their fellow workers.

29 PEOPLE WITH 29 FAMILIES

Twenty-nine people with 29 families are now at stake. The German of the *Feldbauleitung* [field building unit] at Porubanek told the Gestapo that 29 of his Jewish workers left their job on their own.

The ghetto is scared of what will result.

ADDRESSES OF THE VILNA PRAYER HOUSES

Two days ago, the ghetto chief summoned Mr. K[ruk], who once wrote for the Rosenberg Task Force about Vilna and Vilna synagogues.

Why addresses of the prayer houses outside the ghetto? Apparently they want to move people from the peat bogs into those prayer houses.

Is this not, God forbid, a way station to Ponar? No one here can say anything about it.

700 PEOPLE FROM BIAŁA WAKA AND RZESZA

People say that about 700 people from Biała Waka and Rzesza will soon arrive in Vilna, and that some of them will be quartered at Zawalna 4, where the workers of Todt were driven into the ghetto a few days ago.

ABOUT PARTISANS

Issue 9 of the illegal Vilna Polish paper *Niepodległość*, of Nov.–Dec. 1942, says: "In the area of Świr-Kobylniki and Wiśniewo, fights took place with heavy Soviet paratrooper landings. Recently attacks on German railway transports have also increased."

No. 11, of January 1943, says: "In December, near Lida, a German train with soldiers returning from leave was blown up. A few dozen of those killed were buried in Lida. A great many badly wounded soldiers were taken to Vilna."

Partisan activity is also indicated by the fact that all community offices from the entire area have been moved to Lida for fear of paratroopers who impose contributions and carry out sentences. The Germans here are so terrorized that they travel to the villages with a whole unit of soldiers with machine guns. On most estates, the paratroopers burned all supplies before the Germans tried to take them away.

No. 12, of February 1, writes about the partisans in the Nowogródzka region: "The community offices are terrorized here; they destroy the local dairies, burn mills and estates. They shoot the lords and their stewards en masse. The Germans avoid clashes with them."

IN THE LABOR UNITS. "SPANISH WAR HOSPITAL"

Right now, 70 Jews work in the unit, most as skilled labor: shoemakers, tailors, masons, joiners, glaziers, electricians, locksmiths, etc. But in this workplace, there is also non-professional work that is done by Jewish workers. This unit has existed since July 18, 1941.

The workplace of the unit is in the former railroad hospital in Wilcza Łapa, far from the ghetto. The workers are satisfied with the work. The attitude of the employers is satisfactory. They also get the proper workers' ration. The brigadier of the unit is Mr. B. Golomb.

JEWS ARE MURDERED IN BYELORUSSIA

Under such a headline, No. 12 of the Polish illegal organ [*Niepodległość*], of February 1, has published an article, which says:

In mid-November, a mass murder of Jews began here, carried out by Germans and Ukrainians brought specially for that.

In *Postawy* more than a thousand Jews were murdered.

In *Duniłowicze,* 800 Jews.

In *Łuczaj*, 60 Jews.

The Jews barricaded themselves in private houses and put up resistance. The houses were burned down.

In Duniłowicze, children, old people, and women were thrown into the burning houses.

About all this, the "neutral" Polish paper writes.

CONCERNING THE EXPOSITION OF OUR GHETTO CHIEF

We have already mentioned the words of the ghetto chief at the last Brigadier Council. Now we will add that at his exposition, the chief talked about the dilemmas involved in educating our generation. He reported on the discussion in his house, and referring to the words of Z. Kalmanowicz, he says: "I cannot say that all nations are equal. We must be nationalists, and as Z. Kalmanowicz says: 'I don't want to know, I only know that I am first of all a Jew.'" From what the chief said and from the pearls of wisdom in the quotation from the former co-director of the Jewish Scientific Institute, it may well be that a new order will further cripple the ghetto schools with nationalistic attitudes. No use, this is how it is in our "kingdom" of the ghetto dictator.

FOR THE STRUGGLE AGAINST THE HITLERIAN OCCUPIERS

An appeal has recently appeared in Polish from a union of those involved in active struggle against the Hitlerian occupiers. This appeal is the first published illegal document that speaks openly about Jews, the murder of the Jews, race hatred, etc.

The appeal is apparently "Red."

I BUSY MYSELF WITH POISON

Once, wandering around the ruins of the second ghetto, I came upon three vials of strychnine. I grabbed them the way a drunkard grabs a razor and kept them as a treasure. As the review in the Vilna Ghetto Theater says: "You Can't Know a Thing." They might, God forbid, be useful. . . . Now I have dug up the vials from my hiding place, and from the three little ones I made a full bottle, ready for any event. . . .

Is this not a product of the current atmosphere?

THE SECOND PART OF THE RESETTLEMENT

The first part is almost done. The groups that were supposed to have arrived in the Vilna Ghetto are in Vilna and have already been settled somehow. Now comes the second act of the drama—the rest of the small towns are to be taken to Kovno.

At 10 this morning, the resettlement began. The entire ghetto police and its supervisors have been mobilized. The police received the job of carrying out the resettlement alone, with its own forces. At 10 this morning, all those left from Oszmiana climbed into the wagons. Jews from other places are also arriving. At the railroad station, more than 80 train cars are waiting for those coming from the Vilna provinces. Two trains will go to Kovno. Commandants Gens and Dessler are personally supervising the resettlement and went to Oszmiana for that purpose. Accompanied by them, the resettlement reaches all the way to the Kovno Ghetto.

THE REMNANTS OF THE ABANDONED SMALL TOWNS

Yesterday I was given two transports of Torah scrolls, *kapoyres,*[4] etc., for my collection. Today another transport came with similar things. All of it was sent me as the last traces of the existence of Jews in those small towns.

WHAT SHOULD THE GHETTO THEATER PERFORM?

Now of all times, last Friday to be exact, the Cultural Department in the Vilna Ghetto found it necessary to organize a discussion on the subject "What Should the Ghetto Theater Perform?" Needless to say, this is not a topic of great importance in the ghetto, especially not right now when our ghetto stands on the brink of a great play and the tension is unimaginable.

In any case, even tactically, the discussion should have been postponed for a calmer time.

MY FRIEND MAREK IS FREE

Yesterday the ghetto was elated because, from among the recent arrests, the brigadier Marek, my friend, has been freed along with his two men. His arrival in the ghetto was a great celebration. He was "attacked" in the street and kissed by all and sundry.

The upshot: Marek behaved well as a brigadier. He was dreadfully beaten twice in order to [force him to] denounce co-workers who were engaged in so-called speculation. Naturally he was silent. Today he is sick and broken. Only now does he feel the blows.

A YOUNG JEWISH WORKER'S SELF-SACRIFICE

Recently, at one of the workplaces outside the ghetto, a Jewish worker, Ts., found himself in danger because the equipment wasn't in order. The guilty one had to be found or else worker Ts.'s first case could not be overlooked. It was a matter of a few minutes, and when the real culprit didn't step up, the young joiner Heshl Straż volunteered himself. Straż (Szawelska 2, Apt. 8) announced that he didn't have anything to do with it but was prepared to take the blame for it to help his unfortunate comrade. The courage of the young Jewish worker impressed even the non-Jews so profoundly that the whole issue was soon dropped.

IN HONOR OF HENRYK ERLICH AND WIKTOR ALTER

After the certain and half-certain information about the shooting of Comrades Henryk Erlich and Wiktor Alter, there was an item in the Lithuanian newspaper,

4. The short curtain above the *paroykhes,* which closes the Ark in a synagogue. Kruk, who was not very well versed in religious matters, may indeed have meant the *paroykhes*.

which I attach in a Yiddish translation, once again confirming the murder of the two leaders of the Bund. Once again, the ghetto committee of the Bund raised the question of how to commemorate the tragic event.

It was decided not to draw any political conclusions or to create a rift in the cooperation with the local Communists; at one of the meetings of the FPO, Abrasha [Chwojnik] was to announce the tragic event and not draw any conclusions about it. It was also decided to assemble all the groups and simply read the last announcement, hereby attached. After a minute of silence, the group dispersed. On the 3rd of the month, in the ghetto library, a memorial service of the entire organization took place. Comrades Hersh [Gutgestalt] and Herman [Kruk] spoke. The former evaluated the individuals, the latter presented their descriptions and characteristic traits. Comrade Pati [Kremer] chaired the meeting.
[*The newspaper item and the announcement are missing.*]

THE MEMORIAL SERVICE

Blinds down, cut off from the surrounding ghetto world, at 5 yesterday evening, about 80 comrades gathered in the ghetto library and sadly looked at the decorative inscriptions "Henryk Erlich—Wiktor Alter. Honor to their memory." After the commencement of the memorial service in the name of the committee of the Bund, Comrade Pati [Kremer] was invited to be chairman of the memorial service.

Comrade P[ati] delivered a brief but splendid speech about the meaning of today's memorial service in the ghetto. Her warm and fine words made a splendid impression on the audience. Comrade Hersh [Gutgestalt] spoke of the personalities of the deceased and described their role in the movement. Herman [Kruk] spoke last, describing his meetings with the two comrades, Henryk and Wiktor, and sketching their life and influence.

The memorial service made an understandable impression. For the party members, this was a great experience because, since the outbreak of the war and especially for the past several years, this was the first general meeting of the Bund in the ghetto.

THEY ARE SEALING WITH BARBED WIRE

Now I learn that the train cars at the Vilna railroad station were sealed with barbed wire. Why? So that those who are being resettled won't run away. Thirty Jewish workers were mobilized for this. This news evokes strange commentary.

WEISS OBSERVES

More unrest, provoked by the appearance of Weiss here. He walked around the train and supervised the wire fencing.

Can any place be good if Weiss is there? . . .

SNATCHING OF FAMILIES TO SEND TO KOVNO

There was unrest during the night. This time, not the German but indeed the Jewish police arrested a few families and sent them to the train station with women and children. The reason: [they were] underworld people, speculators and undesirables. Thus, the Vilna Ghetto will throw off onto Kovno what it wants to get rid of. A few of those detained argued themselves out of it. Altogether, nine persons left.

200 UKRAINIANS

A rumor circulated in the ghetto that the Gestapo are preparing 200 lunches for tomorrow, apparently for Ukrainians who are to stay there as "guests" of the Gestapo. Tension mounts.

Particularly today, 200 Ukrainians as guests of the Gestapo? . . .

THE MARCH OF 340

At about 4 in the afternoon, the streets were suddenly in turmoil. A unique picture soon emerged: 340 people, carrying bundles, most of them young, and a lot of old people, children, and women. All were driven to the train, which at 7 this evening is to bring the Jews from Święciany; from here, under the supervision of the Jewish police, they'll go to Kovno.

People were amazed at the strange march and shrugged their shoulders, nerves twitching—may they arrive safely. . . .

MORE THAN 17,000 PERMITS

So far, the permit office has distributed more than 17,000 permits. Efforts will be made to get more.

INSTEAD OF 15,295, MORE THAN 19,000

Last month, the Food Supply Department received 15,295 food cards for the ghetto. Now, because of those arriving from the provinces, the Food Supply Department demands more than 19,000 bread cards.

The Vilna Ghetto now numbers almost 20,000 Jews.

TWO BARRACKS FOR THE ARRIVING PEOPLE

On the site of the wall that was removed between Oszmiańska and Dziśnieński Streets, they are working feverishly to take away the rubbish. Soon the building of two barracks there will begin, one next to the other. The provincial Jews now coming into the ghetto will be situated there.

DEPARTMENT FOR GHETTO INDUSTRY

Recently 1,000 metal cans were ordered from Lietukis. Three thousand sets of cast-iron frames for cabinets were ordered from the big mechanical workshop by a German office outside the ghetto.

CONCERNING PERMITS

Concerning permits, employees of the ghetto administration must come under the same regulations as all workers of other units. They must avoid walking through the main streets, must walk fast, and must join approaching columns or individual Jews they meet in the streets.

GHETTO LIBRARY

Trials for not returning books from the ghetto library were recently held in the ghetto court for eight subscribers. Each was punished with one day of arrest on probation. To cover the loss of the ghetto treasure and the court costs.

BENEFIT PERFORMANCE FOR THE ANNIVERSARY OF ESTER LIPOWSKA

Recently, in the Ghetto Theater, for Ester Lipowska's 40th anniversary in the theater, there was a performance of "The Treasure." The hall was full.

After the second act, Ester Lipowska was congratulated by the director, Yisroel Segal, and the artists Blacher and Bergolski. The modest celebration, with its moving warmth and in the special circumstances of our Ghetto Theater, made a big impression.

APRIL 5 [1943]

RUMORS

Since early in the morning, the mood has been dreadfully unclear. The tale spreads from ear to ear that the trains from Oszmiana and Święciany were taken, along with the Jewish police, to . . . Ponar.

Nobody believes it, but they do listen. Soon come details: this morning, Gens supposedly came to the station to the Święciany train and ordered all Jewish police to get out of the railroad station immediately. He ordered the doctors and nurses summoned for that purpose to return. He himself was very upset.

MORE THAN 4,000 IN 83 CARS

It is afternoon. As I write these lines, the entire ghetto appears as if it were on the brink of an Aktion. As if we are about to play our last card. The last chord.

Everything we have written above is no rumor. Now it is clear: instead of going to Kovno, the trains from Oszmiana and Święciany went to Ponar . . . 83 cars with more than 4,000 Jewish victims were taken there.

THEY SHOOT!

As I write these lines, I know for sure that the executions are still taking place. The train cars are opened, and people are taken into the forest, one car after another.

Some run away. Shots are heard all over the area. Peasants say they are hiding Jews who tell about it all.

THE POLICE BACK IN THE GHETTO

At about noon, a group of police led by Gens marched into the ghetto. At the checkpoint, the column was dispersed and everyone ran home. Soon it was clear:

The group from the train with Gens experienced difficult moments. They were sure they were being taken to be shot. At night, when they saw they were in Ponar, Gens ordered the policemen to run away. He soon noticed that the train was surrounded by Lithuanians and ordered them to stand together since it was too late to run.

[*On the original page is a handwritten addition: "At the railroad station, Dessler shot a Jewish boy who tried to run away."*]

The leaders of the Lithuanians in Ponar asked the Jewish police to get out of the car. All were taken to the forest and from there were transported in a truck to the Gestapo. There, a good supper was waiting for them and a bed. At 6:30 in the morning, Gens was released on condition that he return soon. He ran to the train commanded by Police Chief Dessler. At 11 in the morning, an order came that Jewish police could return to the ghetto. And so at 12, the Jewish police arrived in the ghetto.

UNTIL WHEN?

There is no longer the slightest doubt. Everything we foresaw has been realized in a much uglier and more shameful way.

As I write these lines, the odor of more than 4,000 Jews bleeding to death is in the air. Four thousand, taken in a horrible way and deceived, lulled by promises, let themselves be taken to the sacrifice. Not only were 4,000 lives taken, but also all their goods and property, money, gold, and all they were allowed to take with them supposedly to Kovno.

The Ponar sea of blood and tears has not yet dried, and now we again bathe in laments and weeping.

Is there no end even to the curse?

Until when? How long?

MURER IN THE GHETTO

As if nothing had happened, at 3 this afternoon, Murer came into the ghetto; as if nothing had happened, he arrived at "his" workshops; and . . . as if nothing had happened, he asked the half-dead, beaten Gens a question: "What's new?" When Gens replied that he probably knew and asked him what he now thought about the ghetto, Murer once again, as if nothing had happened, answered coolly and calmly:

"The Vilna Ghetto is not under consideration. . . ."

The warm Jewish blood has not yet turned cold, and some already console themselves with Murer's words—the Vilna Ghetto is not under consideration.

THE COMMANDERS

People say that both commanders are lying in bed in their apartments. The doctor was brought twice to Dessler today. Except for Murer, Gens didn't appear for anyone.

Nothing to appear for! . . .

SIX ESCAPEES

Now, at 7 in the evening, there are six escapees from Ponar in the ghetto. One of the six is a wounded woman.

At about 8 in the evening, there were already nine escapees, including children between 8 and 11 years old.

LITTLE YOM KIPPUR IN SHOELKE'S PRAYER HOUSE

Just as the information about the new murder in Ponar was definitely confirmed, a Little Yom Kippur was declared by the Orthodox. Shoelke's Prayer House was full of Jews. They recited psalms. Jews wept horribly.

APRIL 6 [1943]

WHAT HAPPENED?

After all the events of yesterday, the first half of today gives the impression of being our last hours:

Weiss suddenly showed up in the ghetto and demanded 25 Jewish policemen to go to Ponar with him to bury the dead. Everyone shuddered. Why Jews, not to mention Jewish police?

Soon an automobile slipped into the ghetto and the chief of the Gestapo, Neugebauer, drove up in front of Rudnicka 6.

What is the head of the Gestapo doing in the ghetto today? . . .

The ghetto chief received him, and he invited himself to [Gens's] office. While the two of them were together, the ghetto was on pins and needles. It was clear to everyone that Weiss was taking the ghetto police and that the purpose of Neugebauer's visit was an Aktion, if not the complete liquidation of the ghetto. The turmoil increased by the second.

Meanwhile, another event: the chief of the fourth precinct[5] crept into the ghetto through a melina, thus discovering how people bring flour through there. . . .

5. It is not clear who this is, but certainly he was not a Jew.

By the time the street learned what was happening, the tension had risen to the highest degree. They say that people bid farewell to one another.

But soon it became clear: Weiss assured Police Chief Dessler that it was a "simple" matter—just to bury the Jews who tried to run away during the Aktion. They are scattered over the fields and have to be cleared away. He also said that he was taking [the police] and that he would bring them back.

Neugebauer's visit: his first question was about the mood in the ghetto. When Gens explained the situation to him and said that everyone is depressed about recent events, he said he had come especially because of that. He assured him that the Vilna Ghetto is useful, and nothing threatens it. Moreover, as he said, "As a German, he had to do it; as a man he regrets it very much."

The "visit" to express condolences to the ghetto, as it were, nevertheless did not soothe. Everyone is feverish.

And what about the discovered melina? The chief has taken a bribe, and the melina can go on serving "its purpose." . . .

THE 30

In the ghetto, meanwhile, people are busy guessing what might be happening to the 30 policemen Weiss took. Some say that Jewish policemen are used for this same purpose in many places, but that there are also cases where, after using them, the eyewitnesses are shot. The commissars [Nosn] Ring, [Moyshe] Levas, Bernstein, and others, went with the 30.

After the Gestapo chief left, Commander Dessler went to Ponar and came back calmer: they really are collecting corpses and will come back in the evening.

NINE WAGONS

The Labor Office in the ghetto soon received an order to send nine wagons with 15 men to Ponar. Purpose: to bring Jewish objects from the cars?! . . .

This sounds strange. But the order was immediately carried out.

EVERYTHING IS DEAD

In the ghetto, it is as if everything were dead. The offices aren't open. People aren't working in the workshops. No one understands the events that have occurred. Rarely is there clear and certain information. Everything is veiled in fog. Everything looks unlikely. Every rustle is blown out of proportion. Some say the executions were carried out by Latvians. Some know that they were carried out by the 200 Ukrainians brought especially for that. People say that Hingst and Murer didn't know about the events in Ponar. The street seethes and argues incessantly. No one works, not even in the German units. The ghetto and the ghetto Jews are truly depressed. Everything is dead.

PEOPLE BANG THE WALLS

Late at night on the 5th and 6th, I went through the ghetto and what I encountered sounded like horrible music. From all corners echoes of hammers were heard, which, in the quiet night, in the tormented ghetto, sounded like a song of blood and tears. People are banging holes for melinas. Recent events have led to this, and now people are speeding up the work in the middle of the night.

THINGS ARE BAD IN THE GHETTO LIBRARY

During the previous Aktions in the Vilna Ghetto, we often reported that after every Aktion, the library was full of readers who tried to soothe themselves with books. Now the library is silent. Only a few come to exchange books. The only intensive activity is among children. The ghetto reacts completely differently now from how it did back then.

THREE WOMEN AND SIX CHILDREN

Now, at 5 in the afternoon, three women who were rescued from the shooting have come into the ghetto with a group from a unit. All three are from Święçiany. One of them was wounded in the arm. I was present when her arm was bandaged.

Six children, aged 8 to 11, were also brought to the same courtyard (Rudnicka 13). One of them tells that he ransomed himself from a Lithuanian for three gold coins. The six children came with a group of Jewish workers from Porubanek.

The women say that their whole carload ran away. The Lithuanians who led them into the forest to the execution whispered to them to run because . . . they were going to be shot. Everyone ran away. The three women are sisters.

A TWO-YEAR-OLD CHILD

One of those who came from Ponar was a two-year-old child. A Christian woman who lives not far from the execution place heard crying all night. Before dawn, she left her hut and went toward the sound of the crying. There, among a heap of corpses, she found a crying child. She took it with her and brought it to Kailis, where it was sent to the ghetto.

THE POLICE BACK IN THE GHETTO

Now, at 9 in the evening, the 30 policemen have come back to the ghetto. Depressed and exhausted, they say they collected corpses scattered over railroad tracks, fields, etc. Altogether, they think they gathered about 300–400 persons.

We will tell more about this later.

LOOT

Soon after the police, nine wagons with the 15 workers were driven into the ghetto. Eight of the wagons were full of foodstuffs: potatoes, flour, bread, etc. One wagon was packed with clothing. Everything was turned over to the winter aid [campaign].

A WOUNDED PERSON AMID THE LOOT

On one of the nine wagons, a wounded young man was also brought. He was immediately turned over to the ghetto hospital. He was wounded nine times.

LIETUKIS ALSO TAKE AN INHERITANCE

Among the inheritance takers, the Lietukis also got 26 wagons of foodstuffs.

AND IN BEZDANY EVERYTHING IS FINE

Meanwhile, people say that the five wagons of Jews sent to Bezdany arrived there safely and everything is "perfectly fine."

People look at one another and don't believe it: everything is perfectly fine!

APRIL 7 [1943]

THE GHETTO CANNOT CALM DOWN

The ghetto cannot calm down. Why should it? Even the gullible don't believe the German conferences and the continuous reassurances. The irritation in the ghetto is incessant. Today the group of 30 policemen was again taken to continue their work in Ponar.

"LOOT"

All we have written so far about loot was only the beginning of a big "gift" the Gestapo is preparing for us.

All day today, they brought masses of things and bundles, just as they had been packed by their owners. They bring food, furniture, cutlery, and everything that was in the wagons. The inhabitants observing all this curse that the ghetto is taking it. . . . Jews stand and shake their heads, looking at the furniture:

"This is how they prepared for a life," says a Jew, watching them take a washtub off a truck. "Thinking," he says, "that they would arrange a life here." . . . Some women cry and cannot watch. Others think it is disgusting to look at it, that all this is a profanation. Nevertheless, scoundrels who immediately try to share in the inheritance aren't lacking either. People snatch, take advantage of opportunities, and steal—Sodom! . . .

WHAT THE BRIGADIER FROM PANEMUNE SAYS

A brigadier from the town of Panemunė, a railroad station beyond Kovno, spent today here. He goes to the Kovno Ghetto almost every day and is in contact with everybody there.

What does he say?

In Kovno, everyone is calm. There are 16,000 Jews in the ghetto. He says that a few days ago, Müller (the so-called Kovno Murer) received an announcement to prepare a place in the ghetto for 5,000 Jews from Vilna district. Müller did not want to take the Jews. The Jew Lipiec,[6] Gens's counterpart there, was of a similar opinion.

So Kovno received a letter to prepare a place for 5,000 Jews. Kovno refused.

THOSE WHO RETURNED FROM PONAR MUST REGISTER WITH THE GESTAPO

Today's announcement that those who came into the ghetto after the 5th of this month, in fact those from Ponar, must register with the Gestapo, once again struck like a thunderbolt.

What good are all these methods of calming anymore?

I attach the announcement about this.

[*The announcement is missing.*]

WHERE JEWS ARE NOT ALLOWED TO LIVE

According to a letter from the Gestapo today, Jews are not allowed to cross the threshold of the regions of Oszmiana, Święciany, Eyshishok, Jaszuny, Turgiele, Rudziszki, and others under penalty of death.

Hundreds of Jews have lived there and created a cultural life. Today, after the inveigling and killing of Jews, a "Pale of Settlement" is declared there. I attach a copy of the letter.

[*The copy is missing.*]

APRIL 8 [1943]

THE GHETTO HAS LOST ITS BEARINGS

All who still live and walk the streets of the Vilna Ghetto are truly lost and helpless; everyone is waiting for the end—for liquidation. Most workers don't go to work. Those who do, don't really work. Nothing is in your head—anyway, it is all coming to an end! . . . This is the mood, and this is how most Vilna Ghetto residents think. Naturally, this panic is the greatest reservoir of rumors and Jewish gossip.

CONCERNING ZAWALNA 4

As we said, the workers and their families from Rzesza and Biała Waka were settled outside the ghetto in the building on Zawalna 4. Some come into the ghetto—people are uncontrollable.

6. His name was Liptser, not Lipiec.

THE GESTAPO BECOMES THE BOSS OF THE GHETTO

In the course of events, a rumor circulated that the Gestapo is taking over the ghetto. So the ghetto is being taken out of the hands of the district commissar and turned over to the Gestapo.

Is this good? Is this bad? No one can say anything about it. It is hard to judge whether the rumor is true or only a rumor.

THINGS, THINGS, AND THINGS

Meanwhile, the things of those killed are brought here. The ghetto warehouses are crammed with things. "Tatters" for many millions flow in here.

GENS AND DESSLER VISIT THE GESTAPO

In the chaos, in the horrifying shudder of events, anything seems likely. All rumors come together, and no one can deny them. A brigadier, a certain Engineer Prużan, grabs his wife and mother-in-law and runs away from the ghetto—he won't spend another night in the ghetto. Supposedly, this very night, Zawalna and part of the ghetto will be liquidated.

Gens and Dessler, who have hardly left their homes up to now and haven't officiated or appeared for anyone, have nevertheless gone to the Gestapo, and once again reported on the rumors in a clear-cut way and requested the plain facts. The Gestapo was even offended, but once again they repeated that nothing threatens the Vilna Ghetto: if you want, you can take Zawalna 4 into the ghetto. They don't care. Once more, they gave assurances that the workers from Rzesza and Biała Waka would return to their workplaces as soon as barracks were built there. Incidentally, they said that Jewish workers were building the barracks. They also gave assurances that the camps in Bezdany and Kiena would remain as they were. The last two pieces of information are somewhat soothing. They were signs of the likelihood that this is not yet the final liquidation. Moreover, the two agents received a "reward." The announcement of the 6th, that all those who came into the ghetto after the 5th [must register], has been withdrawn. More than 10 Jews have been released from [the clutches of] the Gestapo. "Reward," "reward," and . . . "reward."

APRIL 9 [1943]

IN ANY CASE? . . .

Despite all reassurances, despite all the soothing, despite all objective signs that danger is not yet knocking on the door, a lot of people spent the night in melinas. In some homes, people don't get undressed. All night long, they work with spades, digging melinas and underground passages. The FPO is fully prepared. The membership has increased—just in case. . . .

THE CASE OF GARMIZE

In any case, meanwhile, a certain Garmize, Ber, who works in one of the local hospitals, negotiated with a German to buy a revolver and the German turned him over to the Gestapo.

MURER IN THE GHETTO. HE TALKS AND . . . BIDS FAREWELL

Early this morning Murer came here. He went off toward Oszmiańska, to the tailors' workshop. On Strashun, terrified people began running, falling, there was shrieking and shoving. Murer noticed all this and looked on, satisfied, as the little Jews trembled at his glance.

In the tailors' workshop, he assembled all the workers and delivered a speech calming them down, speaking as a "colleague," challenging them to work well and honestly, not to steal and, in case anyone, "God forbid," noticed such things, to denounce it. He is going on vacation. He is making efforts so that the workers will be better supplied on the Jewish holidays. The workers listened to him, went back to work, and said that this was the age of the Messiah, Murer talks with them as human beings. Nevertheless, it went in one ear and out the other.

GESTAPO IN THE GHETTO

At the same time, Mayer—the deputy of Neugebauer, the head of the Gestapo—came to the ghetto. He strolled calmly around the empty streets of the ghetto and calmly . . . left.

EIGHT IN THE EVENING, A MEETING AT THE HOME OF THE HEAD OF THE GHETTO

I have been summoned to a consultation at eight this evening at the home of the ghetto chief. Apparently all department directors were summoned to the meeting, along with the police commissars and some individuals, including me. People expect that the chief will talk at length about the events.

THE PROVINCIALS ARE TAUGHT THE ALPHABET

The "lucky ones" from the provinces who have been safely moved to the ghetto don't yet know the local customs and flout all accepted rules. Hence an announcement was published today, teaching them the Vilna alphabet.

We attach Announcement Number 105.

[*The announcement is missing.*]

APRIL 10 [1943]

THE MEETING AT MR. GENS'S

In the company of about 20 men, Mr. Gens began his speech. The mood among those present was tense: what will the chief, Mr. Gens, who was recently so horribly and so sadly exploited for the slaughter, say?

Somewhat nervously, he tells the story of the resettlement we have often written about. He knows, is fully aware, that the Germans devilishly exploited him. He also thinks that not all the German authorities who conferred with him knew about the plan.

What happened?

Murer didn't want to let new provincial Jews into the ghetto. Finally they convinced him to take in 1,010 Jews, families of OTE people who work in Vilna. Kovno got an order to take in 5,000 Jews. But neither Müller nor the Jewish leader Lipiec wanted to, and both refused at the last minute. It was at that moment that the idea of Ponar probably arose. If Vilna and Kovno had wanted to take all the Jews, the Aktion in this form would not have occurred and the resettlement would have been carried out peacefully. As proof, the chief cites the fact that the train permits for Gens and Dessler were already written out clearly: Michaliszki-Kovno and Święciany-Kovno (incidentally, their photos were attached). Even the Polish railroad workers had the route Vilna-Kovno on their train passes. Mr. Gens tells the rest of the story just as we have already written. A railroad worker reveals the secret that the train is going to Ponar. Gens tries to telephone Weiss, and they are now in Ponar, from where they are taken to the Gestapo. So, from 1 to 4 in the morning, he was with the police in the Gestapo. Weiss then comes to him and, at the chief's request, is allowed to go to the railroad station, where Mr. Dessler is to arrive with his train, to tell him of Ponar in time. Next, Gens's description of how he comes to the railroad station. And he tells that seven cars from the Święciany train were uncoupled, five went to Bezdany, and two, with the Judenrats of the towns, remain in Vilna. Dessler is immediately sent from Ponar to the ghetto, where he arrives at noon, and at about 1, Mr. Gens also arrives with his police.

ABOUT THE POLICE FOR PONAR

Civilians were demanded for burying the slain, says Mr. Gens. He was afraid of this, and he himself offered his policemen.

ABOUT THE PROPERTY OF THE SLAIN

Here, he considers morale and comes to the conclusion that the property must not be taken. Nevertheless, in the name of the ghetto, he argues that the ghetto inhabitants are naked and hungry, and here food and clothing are provided. How to justify the refusal? Why provoke?

Then Mr. Gens comes to another conclusion: rather than let strangers enjoy it, better that it should remain among Jews (? . . .). So he decided to take the things.

What will happen next? He cannot guarantee that there will be no more Aktions in the ghetto. There could be an Aktion of the non-productive element; qualitatively, the ghetto has deteriorated. The most important thing is to raise our productive capacity. Everyone who can work must work! Mr. Dessler and Mr. Brojdo also spoke along these lines.

Altogether, the council didn't produce anything new. Everyone present was silent. What you think, you can't say. No one wants to condone the deal. We listened and went home depressed, because what has happened is still far from the end.

So we are once again in line.

A "PALE OF SETTLEMENT" IN THE VILNA AREA

On the 8th of this month, the chief of the Vilna Ghetto, Mr. Gens, received a letter from the Vilna German Security Police and SD, dated the 7th of the month, saying:

Under penalty of death, Jews are forbidden from now on to enter these areas of Vilna district: the districts of Święciany, Oszmiana, Eyshishok, regions of Jaszuny and Turgiele (Vilna district), Rudziszki, Onuškis, Aukštadvaris, Semeliškės (Troki district).

I officially request that you notify the inhabitants of the ghetto. At the same time, the Jewish Labor Office must get the proper orders to obtain my permission before they establish a labor unit of Jews in Vilna district.

GRISHA'S NOMINATION

Even before the meeting at Gens's house, Grisha [Yashunski] told me that a committee had been formed today to deal with the property from Ponar. Those appointed to the committee include Mr. Fried as chairman and Yashunski as vice-chairman. Now he asks me if he should accept the job. I answer that I wouldn't do it. Yashunski is satisfied with my answer, since Abrasha [Chwojnik] had given the same answer. He even says that even if there were hints of repercussions, he wouldn't accept it. I advise him in further conversations not to make threats. He promises.

A REPORT ON THE WORK DONE

I learn that the Gestapo telegraphed a report on the work done. The wire reported that 5,000 (!) Jews were shot, and only 7 managed to escape.

As we now know, about 3,800 Jews have been killed. Why this increase of the number of those shot and . . . decrease in the number of escapees?

The ghetto leaders want to view this as one in a series of "gifts" to the local Jews. . . .

"LITHUANIA UNDER RED TERROR"

Under this headline, Prof. Krėvė-Mickevičius published a series of articles in early April in the German organ *Wilnaer Zeitung*. . . .

The newspaper congratulates itself on the fact that Prof. Mickevicius, the former deputy of the prime minister and foreign minister in the Lithuanian People's Government, has reached the conclusions he has come to. If we add that the two distinguished Lithuanian professors Mickevičius and Birzyszko have completely put themselves in the service of the German occupiers, it is once more clear how much the Lithuanian intelligentsia is protecting their own skin.

TWO ALARMS

On Saturday the 10th, Vilna was under alarm. For hours, bomber planes were heard. Yesterday the German press told of bombings in Eastern Prussia.

Last night there was another alarm, and Russian airplanes again appeared over the city.

APRIL 11 [1943]

WHAT DOES A POLICEMAN FROM PONAR TELL?

On Tuesday, April 6, along with 29 other policemen, following the order of the ghetto chief, he went to Ponar. Weiss and two Lithuanian military men from the Ipatinga went with the police. The police were obviously nervous. Two hundred meters before the gates of Ponar, the truck broke down and the police had to go on foot. Weiss declared that the graves had to be covered because, until now, they had been covered with a two-centimeter layer of sand. He also forbade the uncovering of the corpses. . . . Nevertheless, during the covering, some of [the police] uncovered [some] and saw a mountain of naked corpses—men, women, and children all together. The bodies were horribly shot.

Twenty-seven policemen were employed in covering the graves, and three went with Weiss to gather the corpses still scattered over the fields.

There are two big round graves there, each 5 meters deep and 8 meters in diameter. There is another grave, the biggest one, which is 6–10 meters wide and 7 meters deep. A special passage was made to this grave from the railroad station. The passage descends deeper and deeper to the grave. In the middle of the passage, people were forced to undress. Next to the round grave, near the railroad station of Ponar, there is a smaller grave, where there were 38 victims. That grave is still hardly covered at all. So much for the mass graves.

And about the gathering of the corpses? Most were lying toward the railroad, outside the barbed-wire fence. Those corpses were shot shamefully. In every one of the corpses there are a few bullets, often seven to nine shots. Most were really torn apart, with ripped-off pieces of arms and legs, ripped-up intestines, etc. Apparently they were shot with dumdum bullets. They all lie here in positions as if they want to run. A woman [. . .]

[*Page 674 of the original is missing. The account of the slaughter in Ponar no doubt continues there.*]

Today a Public Fast
What Does the Official Ghetto Publication Say about It?

PEOPLE GO TO THE FOREST

In despair, people run to the forest. Recently this has happened not only among Jews but also among Poles and especially Lithuanians. Running to the forest is not simply an ideal—partisans, the struggle against the Nazi occupation, etc. Here it is a simple matter of first saving yourself and your own life. In the forest recently there have been not only partisans but also just groups wandering around with weapons, whose only purpose is to stay alive. Often such groups as these commit robbery, etc.

Today a group of 12 young people left [the ghetto].

MEETING OF BRIGADIERS

Today a big meeting of brigadiers and column leaders took place. Just as on Friday in Mr. Gens's home, the course of recent events was recounted there. The main speaker, Mr. Brojdo, called on the brigadiers to restore the work to what it had been until now.

APRIL 12 [1943]

WHAT HAPPENED?

What happened? It is a shame to leave out a word of it. If we raise the question now, it is not to repeat the chronicle of events but to draw some conclusions:

First, it must be concluded that both Ghetto Chief Mr. Gens, with his popularity, and Police Chief Mr. Dessler, irrespective of their guilt in the case, let themselves be used as tools by the Gestapo.

Second, Jews, reduced to despair, will no longer let themselves be killed as before. This is seen in the preparation for struggle and the resolve of several cities and towns.

Third, a fact which must absolutely be emphasized is that the recent execution of the Oszmiana and Święciany Jews was carried out for the first time in the open and without concealment. The Gestapo removed every veil here. By letting in the Jewish police and Jewish workers, the Gestapo turned Ponar, which had previously been covered up, into an open matter.

Fourth, all efforts to calm the Jews of the Vilna Ghetto are simply a means to dull Jewish alertness. The Gestapo uses the soothing of the Jews as a means of carrying out its intentions. Therefore, its usual condolences and soothing words.

[The prepara]tion being made by the masses in order not to die a senseless death must be [brought out] eve[rywhere]. The duty of all those who are still alive in the ghetto is w[ar . . .] and not to let it weaken.

All the previous decisions of our organization[7] also proceed in this direction, and we preach it wherever we can.

WHAT DO THE ESCAPEES FROM THE EXECUTION TELL?

Events in our ghetto have recently taken such a tragic course that there has been no time or place to linger over details that, nevertheless, express a great deal. Today, more than a week after the events, we try to decipher the collected material.

What do the broken, tormented people tell, the ones who only yesterday had families and somehow led a family life, and from whom today everything is torn away? They are alone, wretched, broken, and embittered.

What do the escapees tell?

The refugee from Warsaw, a bakery worker, lived in Widze with his wife and two children. In autumn 1942, along with all the other inhabitants (except for 72 who stayed), he left the town and came to Święciany, where he worked as a baker.

On Sunday, April 4, Święciany Jews were loaded in cars. From there, the train, supervised by Jewish police, moved at 10 in the morning. The car windows were shut with barbed wire and the doors were sealed. There wasn't the slightest suspicion among the passengers that anything could happen to them. "Didn't we listen to the assurances of the Jewish police?" the narrator says ironically.

At about 11 on Sunday night, the train reached Vilna, where everyone spent the night in the cars.[8] Not until 10 on Monday morning did the train move, and in about an hour, they suddenly saw they were in Ponar and that the train was surrounded by German and Lithuanian soldiers. The commotion was dreadful. The weeping and shouting rent the heavens.

Soon several cars were opened and shooting was heard. The narrator says that his was the fourth car and wasn't opened until about 1 in the afternoon. Until then, they saw from the window how people were driven out of the car, how some ran away, how they were shot at. . . . They saw how people threw off everything and . . . In the narrator's car, there were 52 people. When the car was opened, they were all taken toward a fenced-in space. About 20 meters before the barbed-wire fence, our narrator decided to run, and almost everyone in the group imitated him. This was perhaps the greatest miracle, since they couldn't shoot all of them at once. Probably because of this, some of them were saved. He says that two of this group are in the ghetto. The rest, he hopes, will come.

7. I.e., the Bund.

8. The distance from Święciany to Vilna is about 50 miles, but the journey took 13 hours.

They shot at them. He went toward the forest, where he stayed until 3 in the afternoon. Until then, the shooting never stopped.

After 3 o'clock, things calmed down, and only then did he go to the village, where he spent a whole night. On Tuesday, the 6th, in the morning, he came with a peasant to Vilna, went to Kailis, and from there, in the evening, with a group of Jewish workers, he arrived in the ghetto.

Thus one man tells. The second? The second is wounded, a 16-year-old boy from Oszmiana. His name is Narob.[9] He came to Ponar at night on the Oszmiana train. On their arrival, the doors of the cars were opened but were later closed again. No one realized that the Jewish police weren't with them anymore. Through the window, they saw people carrying brandy. At 11 in the morning, however, they started opening the cars. From each opened car the people were taken out separately. As soon as our narrator was out of the car, he dashed toward the forest. A gendarme shot at him a few times and hit him in the leg. He threw himself on the ground. But he got a few more bullets. He could feel that he was wounded again, this time in the chin and arm, and he decided to play dead. The shooter pursued him, gave him a few more lashes with the whip, and left him alone. He lay in a swoon for a whole day and night. Not until morning did the Jewish police find him and bring him into the ghetto. The whole time, he was taken care of by a Christian woman who brought him water.

A third: the third, a 16-year-old youth, ran with a friend. Now he is in the ghetto hospital. He says: as soon as he was out of the tunnel before Ponar, he saw German and Lithuanian soldiers around the cars and noticed that the locomotive had been uncoupled from the standing train. He didn't yet understand it. He saw people let out of the first car and surrounded by several Lithuanians. Why are they being taken out? Only when there was a great commotion did he figure out in his childish naiveté that everyone was being taken to the forest, where they were being shot. His car was the seventh, and he saw how people were taken out of the previous cars. He saw how all of them were surrounded by soldiers, how a group ran and were shot at, and how they ran without stopping. Only then did the idea of running away take shape for both youngsters, to run before they came to take them. A Lithuanian guard was standing in front of the wagon, guarding it. They tried negotiating and agreed that the two would run and he [would] pretend not to see it. When he got the sum, he maintained that it was too [little]. [They all carried] quilt coats. With the elbows of the coats [they pushed away the] wire, released the window, and jumped out of the car, running toward the forest. The friend ran first and escaped; he was shot at and hit. But he dragged on a while longer. From the forest, he ran to Biała Waka and from there to Porubanek, from where he came into the ghetto with a group of workers. At the hospi-

9. Kruk uses the reverse-letter system. The name Narob probably should be read backward, as Boran. Such a name is mentioned in documents from Oszmiana.

tal, where he will spend a few days, I talked to one of his relatives, a hospital employee.

About 30 escapees all tell the same thing. Everyone just has his own version.

GUESTS IN PANOPTICON

Today the ghetto had guests, 18 persons led by Dr. Dietz. Since before dawn, as always, people were cleaning and scouring, [expecting] a cleaning commission, as it were. In fact, it was an outing of doctors who came to admire the Vilna Ghetto panopticon. They were very pleased with everything and left satisfied. They were most pleased with the hospital. Dr. Dietz is the director of the Health Department in Vilna.

MEANWHILE PEOPLE BRING IN

Murer is on vacation. The head of the Gestapo, Neugebauer, has gone away. This means that the gate guard has "relaxed," and meanwhile people bring things in like nobody's business. Everyone who can "smuggles," and so prices are reduced in the ghetto.

L'AFFAIRE GRISHA

The conversation between Yashunski and the ghetto chief went as I had foreseen. Grisha not only refused but also promised that he would not accept the nomination even if there were consequences. Mr. Gens, having in mind the previous incident with Yashunski back in the early autumn, did indeed make the decision that would lead to these consequences.

Now it is known that Yashunski has resigned and Leo Bernstein is taking his place.

All the cautionary measures taken in this matter by the B[und] and representatives of organizations active in the ghetto had no effect. The Reds have no desire to do even what they once did for Glazman.[10] The intervention undertaken in spite of it was unsuccessful.

30,000 FRESH VICTIMS

From the German press, I learn that the Jews must leave 8 of the 11 Dutch provinces. This means about 130,000 fresh victims. No one knows if the Jews will be sent to Eastern Europe to work or to be killed. Now it's the turn of the Dutch Jews.

10. They defended Glazman when Gens waged war against him.

APRIL 14 [1943]

YASHUNSKI OUT

G. Yashunski, the youngest member of all the Judenrats in Vilna up to now, one of the most energetic and perhaps the most capable, the current director of the Cultural Department, has finally been released from his office.

Yashunski is gone, and everyone who talks about it thinks it is wrong, although most people think he should have taken the job and . . . shut up.

As we know, this was not a personal matter [involving only] Yashunski but a move supported by a committee of the Bund. That the decision was right has been proved by an interesting statement made by police officer Smulikowski. Excited about the things being taken away, he says: Are they giving the things to us? They are loaning them to us. All the same, sooner or later they will be taken away from us! . . .

Giving us the things is another part of the permanent Aktion happening to us. The only purpose of the things is to lull us to sleep. We must fight against this with every limb of our body.

Yashunski the Bundist behaved like a Bundist and wouldn't be hitched to the wagon that would lull us to sleep. Yashunski the man, however, wasn't careful and must bear the consequences alone. From the 19th on, with thousands of others, Yashunski will leave his ghetto home and march out to work like a regular soldier.

Yashunski, who had achieved a great deal during this bitter time; Yashunski, one of the boldest members of the Judenrat; Yashunski, the first supply "minister" and the current cultural and educational minister, takes the same path as Glazman—both are regular soldiers, victims of Mr. Gens's ghetto dictatorship.

THEATER IS ACTIVE AGAIN

Because of recent events, all activity of the Ghetto Theater was interrupted. As of Saturday the 16th, all performances will take place again.

FOR THE GOOD OF THE PROVINCES

Hastily, increased crowding is being implemented in the ghetto apartments in order to gain maximum space for the new arrivals from the provinces. For this purpose, the officials of the Housing Department have begun surveying the apartments and checking where new inhabitants can be put.

VACANT SHOPS ARE TAKEN

The shops are rapidly being adapted for new ghetto residents and turned into apartments.

VILNA DISTRICT DEMANDS JEWS

A few days after the slaughter in Ponar, Vilna district ordered 100 Jews for work. The Vilna Jewish Labor Office replied that it didn't have any. . . . A few days later, the German Labor Office once again got in touch with the ghetto Labor Office and decided to give . . . 50.

THE CITY SAYS FAREWELL TO . . . THE CEMETERY

F., the emissary of the Vilna Ghetto, was in Oszmiana on March 30 and provides many details about the behavior of those Jews just before they left their old home.

Oszmiana has been a Jewish community for more than 500 years. Now the Jewish quarter there looks like the aftermath of a pogrom. Everything is in ruins. And what is not yet in ruins is now being turned into a final ruin. Jews are selling everything, and there is seldom anyone who wants to buy. The Jews will have to leave soon anyway—why pay "them"? Nevertheless, they are selling some things for practically nothing. There are some [Christians] who don't want to exploit the destruction. Belongings of those who have already left for Vilna are scattered over the town. The sales are illegal because Jews are forbidden any contact with non-Jews. But this is rarely obeyed. Jews go to Christians, and Christians contact their old friends, the Jews.

The town, especially the Jewish quarter, is strewn with half-destroyed furniture, sacks, dishes, etc. My narrator, the emissary from Vilna assigned to collect and bring the community property of the former Oszmiana to Vilna, gathers Torah scrolls, objects, parchments, and documents—everything will go to Vilna into the melinas crammed with things.

On Thursday, April 1, two days before the final departure from the city, a few dozen inhabitants, old and young, assembled and went to the cemetery to say farewell to their ancestors. They all threw themselves on the graves, and the lamentations pierced the heavens. Thus they wept at the graves of their great-grandfathers, grandfathers, parents, and children. The picture he conveyed made a terrifying impression.

In a dark mood, they returned to the town and again made preparations for the trip. The stables are full of wood, and no one wants to buy it. The cellars, full of potatoes. Everything will stay here. Even now, they see Christian children crawling through the doors and windows of those who left for Vilna a few days [ago]. This is how it will look two days later, when the Kovno group also moves out.

On the same day, at 4 in the afternoon, a guard is placed around the ghetto and no one is allowed to leave. The next morning at 10, the train departs.

The young people have not yet made up their mind whether to go to the forest or to Kovno. One group decides it is better to go to the forest.

On Sunday, the 14th, at 10 in the morning, the train leaves for Vilna.[11]

Our narrator witnessed a similar scene of saying farewell to the graves on the next day, Friday the 2nd, in Soły.

APRIL 16 [1943]

ALMOST A BLOOD LIBEL

Our ghetto has had everything except for one thing—a blood libel. Yesterday, that too might have occurred:

An automobile suddenly came into the ghetto yesterday with the representatives of the Gestapo chief, Mayer, Weiss, and a few others, because the wife of an Ipatinga member reported that Jews kidnapped her child and took him to the ghetto. A Jew was even supposed to have said: "You spill our blood, today we will draw . . . yours." No one in the ghetto knew what to say. When the Jewish police chief, Mr. Dessler, laughed at the claims of the Gestapo and made light of them, Weiss—incidentally, one of his acquaintances—said heatedly: "This is no joke, it might reach the point where we will have to 'take children's heads.'" Soon a horse-drawn cab of Gestapo agents came with the child's mother and announced that the child had been found in Maistas, outside the ghetto.

It is hard to say how it would have ended if the second part hadn't happened.

So now we have had an attempt at a blood libel, too.

CONCERNING THE DUTCH JEWS

I learn that for the past two weeks, two trains have been halted in Vilna, each with 25 cars of objects, apparently from the Dutch Jews. . . .

A NEW RAILROAD LINE IN PONAR

People here say a new railroad line has been laid in Ponar, which will go deep into the forest. . . .

MORE ABOUT THE DUTCH JEWS

Today a rumor is circulating that there are about 19,000 Dutch Jews in Vievis.

ARCHIVES FROM SMOLENSK AND VITEBSK

I learn that five wagons of archives from Smolensk and three from Vitebsk have reached Vilna so far. The Smolensk archive consists of old tsarist documents; the Vitebsk archive, of Bolshevik ones.

11. Probably an error in transcription. Kruk most likely meant April 4, not April 14.

ONCE MORE ABOUT THE DUTCH JEWS

Just now I succeeded in getting a Jewish sign from a Dutch Jew and a copy of the order of the Reichskommissar for the Occupied Netherlands about Jewish property (attached).

[*The order is missing.*]

APRIL 19 [1943]

Passover

Under the pressure of all the events and the realization of what awaits us, we are celebrating the second Passover in the ghetto. The best thing we can wish one another is that we may see each other a year from now.

By now, there seem to be no optimists among us. Everyone here is convinced that we are coming to the end. For, why should we be different from everybody else?

Europe will be purged of Jews. The Jews of Warsaw are being taken to be killed in Malkinia, near Lwów or near Zamość.[12] The Jews from Western Europe are being taken east; their wandering goes on. Transport has recently become very expensive to the Germans, maybe even more precious than money. But transporting for the purpose of ruining and deluding Jews is cheap—it's a war aim!

The Vilna Ghetto has lost all illusions. It is a war aim, and as such, it is the highest priority.

Murer is on furlough. The "Gestapo" has slacked off a bit, and in the ghetto, we spent this year's Passover eve getting drunk.

A lot of Seders were made in the ghetto, private and public. Everyone who can buys, eats, and drinks, and . . . forgets.

Religious Jews put all their passion into this year's Passover. The religious kitchen on Szawelska 5 is preparing a Seder for 100 Jews today, including the chief, the police chief, and rabbis.

A kilo of matzos in the ghetto costs 300 rubles, like 6 kilos of bread. Nevertheless, it seems there is not a single home without matzos.

The Youth Club is making a Seder. The Zionists use the religious kitchen for a Seder. Even Gens himself organized a big Seder at his home today.

Seders are also being made for schoolchildren. The first Seder night in the building of the Youth Club is for older students; the second, for younger students. The Hebrew studio also made a Seder with the Hebrew choir and the boys' and girls' boarding schools of Yeladim.

The remaining Święciany and Oszmiana Jews in the Vilna Ghetto will certainly swim through today's Seder in their own tears. . . .

12. I.e., at the death camps in Treblinka and Bełżèc.

APRIL 20 [1943]

THE NUMBERS ARE INSPECTED

Yesterday a group of workers from Lietukis was searched by the Gestapo. They were interested in whether the Jewish workers were wearing the famous tin tags.

WHAT THEY ARE BOASTING ABOUT

Recently the ghetto administration received two big orders to be filled in the ghetto workshop. One order from HKP, which is related to the Wehrmacht, is for repairing automobile parts, etc. Filling the order is to take five months. A second order is to mend up to 30,000 military uniforms. This, too, is to last from two to three months.

Naive people are satisfied with this. If this is the case, we have received a gift of a few more months.

What the ghetto consoles itself with!

APRIL 22 [1943]

LIKE A BLOW TO THE HEAD — WARSAW

For a few days it was calm, and then it came again, like a blow to the head: information spread like wildfire today that at 7 last night, radio Świt announced that there is unrest in Warsaw. The ghetto is being liquidated. Battles between Jews and Germans are taking place. The Jews are mounting a stubborn resistance. "First Aid" carts come from the ghetto, taking the fallen . . . Germans.

The radio pays tribute to the Jews and says that Poles are helping them. The speaker sounds the alarm to the whole world and calls on it to defend the innocent Jews.

The ghetto Jews are losing their heads. They say unrest has also reached Białystok. The ghetto, meanwhile, is feverish.

WEISS LAUGHS

Weiss spent today in the ghetto. Messrs. Gens and Dessler asked him about Warsaw, and he assured them he didn't know anything. Then they asked him about . . . Vilna. He laughed and . . . calmed them. In his words, nothing can happen to Vilna.

Mr. Sneg[13] told me about it, smiling, as if he didn't believe it all. This, apparently, is payback for recent events.

If you are whipped on . . . your behind, it gets into . . . your head.

13. To be read backward, as Gens.

APRIL 24 [1943]

ŚWIT DEMANDS THE BOMBING OF BERLIN!

Today, radio Świt is supposed to have announced that because of the events in the Warsaw Ghetto on the night of the 21st and 22nd, May Day will be celebrated in great mourning. Świt demands that, in reply to that bloodbath, as they call it—massacre—England should bomb Berlin. As far as we can deduce from this suggestion, two things are clear:

First, the ghetto has apparently not yet been liquidated; and second, the ghetto has again gone through hard, painful days.

APRIL 26 [1943]

WHERE ARE THE MILLIONS OF JEWS OF EUROPE?

In our chronicle, we have often written about the millions of shot and exterminated Jews of Eastern and Western Europe. For us, unfortunately, this is not new. It is new only for those outside our situation. Evidence of that is the brochure recently reported about on English radio, published by a league for the struggle against the extermination of Jews in Europe, reporting that 2 million (?!!!) Jews have been taken away and that the remaining 5 million are awaiting the same fate.

If everything on the other side of the cordon is as precise as the figure of the 2 million, then the question remains: What do they know about us?

We know, for example, that Poland alone contained more than 3 million Jews, and now—can you find even half a million in former Poland? However much we try, we cannot reach such a number. And the hundreds of thousands of Jews from Romania, Bulgaria, Yugoslavia, and the thousands of Jews from France, Belgium, Holland, and Czechoslovakia, who have gone through Lithuania in the thousands, who were shot near Minsk, at the Seventh Fort of Kovno, etc.? And the Jews from Lithuania and Latvia? Lithuania alone lost 85 percent of its Jews!

If everything on that side of the cordon starts being based on the same arithmetic as this last calculation, the world will soon learn that Eastern and Western Europe are already *Judenrein,* and those who are still here and hitched to the chariot of the Hitlerian robbery train will, in one way or another, sooner or later, be gone, onto the roads of Malkinia or Ponar.

HOW MANY ARE WE?

In the latest issue, of April 25, the official ghetto organ, *Geto-yediyes,* presents a few figures about the number of inhabitants in the ghetto. It says that after the distribution of passports in the ghetto, 20,192 inhabitants live there, 8,149 of whom are men and 11,343 are women.[14]

14. The numbers of men and women total only 19,492. Perhaps there was a different figure for children.

This much according to the official statistical information. And how many are there in the ghetto who are not included in the numbers? Of course, the official ghetto organ can't even hint at that.

In short, there are not over 20,000 of us here, but instead, more than 21,000.

REGISTRATION OF 14- TO 50-YEAR-OLDS

By order of the ghetto leaders, all men between the ages of 14 and 50 and women from 14 to 45 must register in the Labor Office. The registration concerns only those who do not yet have work.

HOW MANY PEOPLE WORK IN THE GHETTO?

According to the Labor Office, as of the 20th of this month, 10,115 [persons] were working in the ghetto, 6,139 men and 3,976 women.

INSTEAD OF BARRACKS, A GARDEN

Given the current situation, the planned barracks on the corner of Dziśnieński and Jatkowa are no longer necessary. On the site, instead of barracks, a vegetable garden or a warehouse for wood is planned. A final decision will soon be made.

LITTLE GARDENS IN THE COURTYARDS

As last year, so this year, many little gardens are planned for the courtyards, as, for example, at Szpitalna 5, Jatkowa 15, Szawelska 5, Lida 8, Strashun 3, Szawelska 1, and Strashun 15. Smaller gardens will be planted in almost all ghetto courtyards.

Instead of flowers over us, we will make our courtyards bloom for the time being.

A PERETZ MORNING

In the auditorium of the Brigadier Council, in honor of the 28th anniversary of the death of Y. L. Peretz, a lecture by Dr. Ts. Feldstein on Yitskhok Leybush Peretz took place yesterday.

[*Page 686 of the original, from April 27 and 28, 1943, is missing.*]

More about Grisha Yashunski
A Pottery Workshop

April 28 [1943]
For Which Good Deeds? . . .
A Gift for Weiss
They Are Haggling over the Carcass

MR. LEVAS, GIVE BACK THE MONEY!

Levas, the commissar of the gate guard, was required to give back 3,000 RM that he was supposed to have taken during the Aktion in Oszmiana. The issue might have been forgotten, but the case was discovered accidentally, and Levas didn't deny it. He will give it back, he claims; but meanwhile he doesn't have it.

They quarrel over the carrion—people such as Commissar Ring, who only a few days ago wept for the murdered Jews and recited kaddish for them; or commissar Levas, who went to rescue Oszmiana Jews a short time ago. All quarrel over the carrion, some rip their garments in mourning, and some pry loose purses with gold and such.

GHETTO DRUNKARDS

As never before, people in the ghetto are getting drunk en masse. This has gone beyond the four walls of [the homes of] the ghetto inhabitants and marches wantonly over the streets. The ghetto is drunk.

MAY 1, 1943

In local proletarian circles, people are preparing, as last year, to greet May Day. The celebration will be organized here among the R[eds] and the B[und]. The R[eds] meet with their comrades, the B[und] with theirs. A joint memorial is taking place, and a meeting between the leading comrades of both tendencies.

APRIL 29 [1943]

ANTISEMITISM AMONG POLES

So far, as we know from our entries, the Poles in the Vilna area and in Byelorussia have never shown any great concern over the persecutions of Jews or their extermination. On the contrary, there were often cases of the Christian population, Polish or otherwise, waiting for their Jews to meet their end. It was worth the wait. Jews left very valuable objects with them. If they remained alive, the Christians would have to give it all back. If they didn't, the Christians could keep it; often, this meant large fortunes. Until recently, it all appeared rather respectable. Now, since the Germans succeeded in the Aktion with the shooting of the supposed 10,000–12,000 officers in Katyń;[15] since the Soviet Union, because of that deed, ruptured its relations with the London Polish government—since then, the Poles have suddenly done an about-face: the hostile relations of Christians to Jews has increased. Antisemitic tricks have increased, and many an intelligent

15. In April 1943, German authorities discovered a mass grave filled with the bodies of 4,250 Polish officers in the Katyń Forest near Smolensk. They broadcast the news, accusing the Soviets of the massacre and producing documents suggesting that the killing had taken place three years earlier, in April or May 1940. The Soviets denied the accusation and blamed the Germans for the atrocity. In 1989, nearly fifty years after the massacre, Soviet scholars revealed that it had indeed been ordered by Stalin. A year later, President Gorbachev issued a formal apology to the Polish people.

worker who works with Jews in German units sees in his former fellow worker a kind of "Kaganovich"[16] [. . .] An irony of the partnership with the Soviet Union and not one of those comes out clearly, with no concealing that [. . .]
[*The beginning of page 689 is damaged. We present all the remaining lines.*]

For the Second Time, with Weapons
The Gold Treasure in the Ghetto Grows
Alarms
A . . . Zoo in the Ghetto

APRIL 30 [1943]

MORE ABOUT [MAY] 1

The German and local German and Polish-Germanized press is full of May Day. We too, as has been told, are preparing. Our mutual May Day commemoration takes place this evening in the café, on Szawelska 1.

WARSZAWSKIE GETTO KONA![17]

Yesterday Świt once again sounded the alarm to the world, and once again the radio announcer repeated, as if he wanted the world to remember, the Warsaw Ghetto is bleeding to death. The Warsaw Ghetto is dying! Warsaw Jews are defending themselves like heroes. For 13 days now, the Germans have had to fight with the ghetto for every threshold. Jews do not let themselves be taken and are fighting like lions—"Hello, hello, *Warszawskie Getto Kona!* The Warsaw Ghetto is dying!"

An SOS. The biggest Jewish community in Europe is drowning. The last nucleus, the last few dozen [thousand] Jews are bleeding to death.

Tears have stopped for us long ago. Speech has lost its magic force. The pen can't be held in the hand. I am ashamed to look my loved ones in the eyes. For me?—God forbid! I am ashamed for their pain. My brother-in-law has a wife and two children there—he is silent. My neighbor has a mother and a sister—she is silent. And my own sister and children? . . . I am ashamed of my silence.

HOW DID IT REACH US?

Through the radio communication of the FPO[18] the information came to us in the form in which we attach it. The daily report had a special addition, as already told, with a spray of blood.
[*No document is attached.*]

16. The Soviet leader Lazar Kaganovich.
17. Polish for "The Warsaw Ghetto Is Dying!"
18. I.e., a bulletin of GPK (Ghetto Partisan Communications).

ANOTHER COMPETITION

The literary competitions in the ghetto have assumed a special character. Competitions are ordered as if they were shoes and pants. After the last literary competition, the ghetto chief proclaimed a new competition. This time for a dramatic work (comedy, tragedy, grotesque, etc.) to be presented by May 30.

Thus, in four weeks, the order must be carried out.

I attach an announcement of the competition.

[*The announcement is missing.*]

DOCUMENTS CONCERNING THE DUTCH JEWS

We have already written about the packing up of 130,000 Jews from Holland and their transport to the East. We have also mentioned that carloads filled with goods from the Dutch Jews are in the Vilna railroad station. Now an issue that clears it all up—beautiful old furniture has been brought here, to our joiners' workshop, to be repaired. In the drawers people find Dutch documents, including documents from December 1942, which means that ostensibly, the Dutch were not taken to the East before January or February. Thus the Jews [there], as in Oszmiana, didn't know they were going to be exterminated. The rich Dutch Jews even brought bridge tables with them, in case, God forbid, such things wouldn't be found among the backward *Ostjuden* [Eastern European Jews]. Now it is clear that they were slaughtered, just like the Oszmiana and Święciany Jews. In our area, dozens of railroad cars are scattered, filled with Jewish junk, remnants of the former Dutch Jewry.

THE YOUTH MUST BE EDUCATED IN A NATIONALIST SPIRIT

Yesterday evening, the 29th, the new director of the Cultural Department, Mr. Leo Bernstein, called a meeting of all teachers. Their presence was obligatory. The gentle and always well mannered L. Bernstein said it was the desire of the ghetto chief that the schools should educate the children in a nationalist spirit. Mentioning the recent consultations concerning the incident with friend G. Yashunski, he continues that Hebrew will be introduced as a compulsory subject from the first grade on. A study of the geography of . . . Palestine will be established. Jewish history will be reinforced at the expense of general history. Mr. Bernstein also thought it necessary to promise that this will not keep him from evaluating every teacher on merit. The new program is similar to the Soviet one . . . because there, too, you learn the history of Russia first of all. He thinks finally that a little Hebrew won't hurt, and in fact, everything remains . . . as it was.

The new "minister," who doesn't understand much, finished and was painfully waiting for the participation of the remaining Vilna Jewish teachers. He asked if anyone wanted to say anything, and the hall responded with total silence. This hurt the feelings of the "minister." He apparently didn't understand anything.

Sat[isfied] that he had succeeded with his Hebraizing plan, he immediately adjourned the meeting.

MAY 1 [1943]

Last night, as I said, the hall of Szawelska 1 was crowded with an audience of workers and intellectuals. Even before the commemoration began, the entire hall knew it was a May Day demonstration in the ghetto. On the "Eastern Wall" of the auditorium hangs a big artistic poster (done by Uma and Sutz).[19] with a decoration of paper May flowers. The inscription: "Spring in the Ghetto." In dead silence and tense mood, friend K[ruk] opened the evening. I attach his opening speech. [Leyb] Opeskin spoke on the subject of "Spring Motifs in . . . Peretz." A young person sang the folk song about Hirshke (Hirsh Lekert). Then came poetry readings and a violin concert. The poet A. Sutzkever read a poem, and the chairman, H. K[ruk], concluded the evening with the following words:

> Time does not stand still. Now it is midnight, April 30. And as the clock moves, so does the . . . calendar. Tomorrow is May, and spring is with us!

We went through the celebration with tears in our eyes. Very emotionally, people shook hands and expressed their excitement and satisfaction. The evening went by under the sign of May and . . . an eye for an eye, a tooth for a tooth. . . .[20]

A few days later, people in the ghetto were still talking about the successful celebration as refreshing and stimulating.

THE BUNDISTS MEET THIS AFTERNOON

At 6 P.M. today, the Bundist organization meets with its closest sympathizers.

Tomorrow, May 2, a meeting takes place between the leading authorities, the partners in [the] May Day Celebration in the ghetto, 1943.

WHAT ABOUT ZALMEN TIKTIN?

Everything is done here to keep the issue of Zalmen Tiktin[21] from being blown out of proportion. Meanwhile, rumors circulate that Tiktin is no longer alive. The information is not yet certain.

19. The artists Uma Olkienicka and Rachel Sutzkever.

20. An allusion to the partisan movement.

21. Born in 1922 (or, according to another account, 1925). He worked in a unit, in a weapons camp in Burbiszki (a Vilna suburb). As a member of FPO, he used to smuggle weapons from the camp into the ghetto. One day, when cars came with ammunition, he sneaked into a car and wrapped himself with a bundle of grenades. He was caught, tortured horribly, and died. A precise description of the case is in Sutzkever 1946a:157–159.

MURER BACK IN VILNA. HE GIVES ASSURANCES

Murer, who was on vacation, is back in Vilna. Today he summoned the ghetto representative, Engineer Mr. Gukhman, leader of the ghetto workshops, and Mr. Beniakonski, administrator of the "*Eintragstelle*."

After hearing a report on the time of his absence, he once again assured them that the Vilna Ghetto is secure, that he, Murer, guarantees it personally, and that he has and will have work for years. . . . The ghetto must work, for this is its only support. People must work in three shifts, and more and more.

You can hardly find anybody today who believes all the assurances.

SZTANDAR WOLNOŚCI[22]

Today, for May Day, the first issue [of *Sztandar Wolności*] of 1943 appeared, with a sub-headline: "Organ Związku Walki Czynnej z Hitlerowską Okupacją."[23]

The May issue is naturally devoted to current problems. The recent murders of Jews in Ponar, and the shooting of the 4,000 from Oszmiana and Święciany are reported there.

An editors' note asks their organizers to collect money for the publication and to collect . . . funds for the struggle against the Hitlerian occupier.

It is a Red publication.

MAY 2 [1943]

ZALMEN TIKTIN HAS DIED

Yesterday, Saturday, in the hospital of Łukiszki Prison, 18-year-old Zalmen Tiktin, who was wounded on April 29 in Burbiszki for appropriating weapons, died of his wounds.

The information quickly reached the ghetto, where it spread like wildfire. But the ghetto doesn't know who Tiktin is and on whose behalf he was acting.

Tiktin carried out an important social mission and fell while carrying it out. He was one of the best in the ghetto cadre. His death evoked an understandable pain among his comrades-in-arms.

Honor to his memory!

Zalmen Tiktin was all alone. In the Aktion in the Vilna Ghetto, he lost his entire family. He was beloved by the Germans and Jews of his unit, who called him Gandhi (because he ran around at work half naked), or Gendzlke [Goosie], because he was as tanned [brown] as a gosling.

22. The Vilna Communist underground newspaper. The name is Polish for "Freedom Banner."

23. Polish for "Organ of the Association of Active Fighters against the Hitlerian Occupation."

MURER COMES TO THE GHETTO AT 3 IN THE MORNING

He has just arrived, and again he steps on our feet. Last night, between May 1 and 2, he suddenly popped in at 3 in the morning. He came to the gate guard. Everything was fine. All the guards were at their posts. He was satisfied and immediately announced: "Lucky for you you're guarding." That's what he said to those at their posts.

BUNDISTS MEET IN HONOR OF MAY DAY

Yesterday, for a second time, the entire Bundist organization came together [. . .]

[*Pages 693–694 of the original, from May 2–4, are missing. The pages almost certainly contain a description of the May Day meeting of the Bundists in the Vilna Ghetto. On May 2, number 37 of the* Geto-yediyes *appeared (in the YIVO Archive, Kaczerginski-Sutzkever Collection).*]

Heroic Warsaw

They Carry [?]

May 4 [1943]

Are All Nations Indeed Brothers? [24]

Awards for Conscientious Work in the Units

THE FINAL MAY CHORD

In conjunction with the joint proletarian celebrations in the ghetto, a meeting of the two leading authorities took place last evening. During the opening speech, an alarm occurred, which enhanced the speaker's May Day allusions. Over the heads of those celebrating here, waves of Bolshevik planes headed for East Prussia.

The meeting proceeded under the slogan of surviving until next year.

LANDINGS IN VILNA

Yesterday it was told as an old wives' tale, but today the local press reports it as fact. Apparently [Russian] paratroopers landed here. The Germans shot two parachutists and are searching for the third. They announce that anyone who points him out will receive a reward of 5,000 RM.

COMPULSORY SCHOOL ATTENDANCE

On April 28, the representative of the ghetto issued an order of compulsory school attendance for all children from 5 to 13 years old.

24. Allusion to a poem by Y. L. Peretz, beginning: "All nations are brothers,/Black, white, brown, yellow," which was often recited and sung by Socialist youths.

AGAIN JEWISH WORK UNITS IN VILNA DISTRICT

New work units may once again be set up in the provinces of Vilna. Such units are now set up by HKP—50 men—and Giessler Building Group—80 men in Mickuny and 80 in building work in . . . Ponar. Similar work is introduced: Collection Company—60 men for forest work in Ławaryszki, railroad work for a large group in Nowa Wilejka, and others. The ghetto Jews see this as a good sign. . . .

MAY 5 [1943]

WHAT ELSE IS HAPPENING TO US?

The sword hanging over our heads constantly oppresses and torments. All our predictions about the events in the Vilna provinces have unfortunately been correct. Now, more than before, we stand with ears pricked up and eyes alert to everything that takes place.

People are escaping from the ghetto en masse. Youths go to the "forest." Older people, with "better possibilities," find places outside the ghetto. Those who remain here provide themselves with what they can. People carry weapons, prepare incendiary materials with flammable liquids, dig melinas—prepare. . . .

By all our "accounts" and according to what I just heard, people are talking again about turning over some [. . .]

[*The beginning and the end of page 696 are missing. We present only the parts that are not damaged. The beginning of the entry almost certainly discussed ghetto residents who obtained weapons.*]

After recent events in the [ghetto of] appropriating weapons, two hours ago there [was] an accident. On Lidzki Street, two Jewish workers were arrested by Lithuanians in plainclothes. One of the Jews tried to run away and, while running, lost a revolver. One ran away, the other, with the revolver, was captured.

The matter is beginning to take on threatening dimensions. The Germans sense and speak openly about the fact that Jews are preparing themselves, and they will presumably do anything to the Jews to disrupt this phenomenon.

A YEAR OF THE READING ROOM

Today the director of the reading room received a vase of flowers from his staff in honor of the anniversary of the reading room in the ghetto. In honor of this, the director is trying to get his staff one-time food rations.

MAY 6 [1943]

AN OBJECT TO INVESTIGATE

Two people talk calmly and casually. Suddenly their discussion turns into a riot. They abuse each other and fight in an abnormal way. Today there was an Aktion.

People lay in melinas, and meanwhile, between one breath and another, someone robbed someone else. When one part of the population hides in the melinas, the other part goes into the abandoned apartments and takes what it wants.

Again* 10 *Victims

[*Page 697 of the original is missing. Page 698 begins with an entry about Zalmen Tiktin, which was crossed out by someone. We present it here with that caveat.*]

WHAT ABOUT ZALMEN TIKTIN?

No one can answer this question so far. One thing appears likely. It seems that the rumor that he is no longer alive is not correct. Only last night, before dawn, the Gestapo staff, Weiss and Mayer, came into the ghetto and went immediately to Tiktin's flat. With the help of the Jewish criminal police, they searched it and left. If he were not alive, the incident would be superfluous. That is, if they are still searching, he is alive, for now.

TREBLINKA

This is the name of that place near Malkinia where Jews from Warsaw, Białystok, and Grodno are killed. Here, as I said, the trains come and everyone has to undress to go into the woods, where there is supposedly a disinfection facility. Anyone who realizes what is going on, and doesn't want to undress, is handed over to a group of Jewish police, who throw the resisters into a fire; then you have to undress and be driven in, no matter where.

This work was given to 40 Jewish policemen. We heard it from two who escaped from Grodno—Yisroel Goldshteyn and Brojdo, one of the commanders of the Grodno Jewish police. Most of the group of 40 are from Warsaw.

HOW DOES THE EXECUTION TAKE PLACE?

The victims are driven into the disinfection facility. From the inside, the air is sucked out by a machine until the people die. The bodies then burst from the pressure of the air and are automatically thrown into a so-called crematorium, which burns the bodies to coal. The narrators say that ashes are scattered on the fields of the whole area. Clearly, the ashes from the burned people.

BIAŁYSTOK

A young fellow from Grodno, who just came here from Białystok, says that he was there from March 16 to 26 of this year. Not long ago, there were 50 thousand Jews in Białystok. Now 40 [thousand] remain there. The Aktion, which recently occurred there—the only Aktion in "fortunate" Białystok—cost 10 thousand lives. Eight thousand of them were taken and 2 thousand were shot.

The reason? A Jew shot at a German. The Germans then opened fire and murdered 2 thousand Jews. The 8 thousand were taken to Treblinka.

In the Białystok Ghetto, 25 thousand Jews work in the ghetto industry. All of them are employed in the textile factories, tailor shops, and furrier shops.

The ghetto is quite big there. It takes the whole length of the left side of Mickiewicz Street, as well as Nowy Świat, Kupiecka, Arowiecka, Fabryczna, Ciepla, and other streets.

ANOTHER CASE OF A REVOLVER

The story about the arrest on Lidzki Street is this: while the documents of one of the two arrested Jews were being checked, one of them ran away. All three Lithuanians chased the runaway. Meanwhile, the remaining one disappeared. During the interrogation, the arrested one in the Fourth Police Precinct argued that he didn't know anything, the revolver had been planted on him by one of those who arrested him, he considered this a frame-up, etc. As for the other one, who got away, all he knows about him is that his name is Srolik. . . .

At 9:30 this morning, Weiss, Mayer, and two other Gestapo agents came into the ghetto with the arrested man of Lidzki in chains. After he had been tortured for two and a half hours, he gave the name of his comrade. But he, apparently, is not here. His mother was arrested in his place, along with a fictively registered wife and a young brother. The fellow with the Gestapo agents left the ghetto at about 2 o'clock.

Now people tremble: already the third case of arresting Jews with weapons. So Jews are arming themselves. And how will the Germans react? Will they really let them arm themselves?

The fear is not in vain, and there is indeed something to be afraid of.

ABOUT THE 10 WHO WERE SHOT

Four of the 10 shot in Ponar were children. All 10 are from Podbrodzie.

MAY 7 [1943]

FRIGHTFUL ANTISEMITISM

So far this has not been lacking either. But in recent weeks, the open antisemitic instigations have truly been unbearable. The local Polish and German press spits fire. A special antisemitic jargon has been created: "Jew-war," "Jew-bombings," "Jew-twins" (England-America and the Soviet Union), etc. Here, they bungle it so badly that the headline is often antisemitic and the content of the article doesn't have a thing to do with Jews.

The case of Katyń and the recent press campaign about it are really unbearable.

BACK IN THE GHETTO

Today they brought back the one who was arrested for being caught with a revolver on Lidzki. Why he was brought back today is not known. But one thing is clear: the wife they arrested yesterday has been released.

DOCUMENTS, DOCUMENTS

Again [we] carried masses of documents out of the archive in the YIVO building. This time we managed to get out several documents concerning close friends: here I attach a study about the Bundist Aronowicz, a memo of the so-called historical committee in Vilna, presumably written to the director of the Joint for Lithuania, Mr. Bekelman, and in all probability, with an added note by Hersh G. (?)[25]

Below, we attach part of the document about the Binder case (entry about Hilgebrand no. 173),[26] more entries about Henryk Erlich's family, documents from the NKVD, part of a letter, no. 1243/2, a document—a letter from the files about Aronowicz, Anna Rozental, and Wapner.[27]

Finally, materials from YIVO: a copy of the list of materials about pogroms, which [Elias] Tcherikower[28] once sent, a document—a bill of a Jewish worker from [April] 4–8 to [April] 4–14, 1943. Finally, a document by the leaders of the Oszmiana Judenrat, in memory of the destruction of Oszmiana.

I attach an order from the Vilna Ghetto chief, framed in black, concerning the shooting of the Shulkin family.[29]

Finally, concerning the Binder issue, a light investigation was made, from which it is inferred that the entire story is a malicious slander by an irresponsible person.

All documents are attached.

[*The documents are missing; however, the declaration of the Oszmiana Judenrat is in the* YIVO Archive (Kaczerginski-Sutzkever Collection, no. 708A). We reproduce it here.]

> Vilna Ghetto, the . . . the former Judenrat of Oszmiana met with the delegate of the Vilna ghetto police, Commissar Nosn Ring, and wrote as a memory for

25. In October–November 1939, when the Soviets transferred Vilna to Lithuania, a historical bureau was created there, which gathered material about the destruction of the Jews and the German cruelties in Poland. The bureau was directed by Noah Pryłucki, the administrator was Hersh Gutgestalt, and the bureau was in his apartment (Vilna Street 20). As many as a dozen Yiddish writers, former staff members of Yiddish newspapers in Warsaw, were employed in recording and questioning the arriving refugees. The budget of that historical bureau was covered by the Joint, whose director in Vilna was then Mr. M. Bekelman.

26. It is not clear what case this was. Probably Binder was accused of being in close relations with the Germans, but it turned out that this was a slander.

27. Bundists who were arrested by the NKVD during the Soviet regime; this sentence probably concerns documents of their arrest and interrogation.

28. A Jewish historian who investigated the pogroms in Ukraine in 1919, after World War I.

29. That funeral notice is published in Korczak 1946:328.

future generations the following information concerning the liquidation of the Oszmiana Ghetto.

In Memoriam

The remainder of the Oszmiana Jewish community—1,850 people—were driven into a ghetto on September 5, 1941, 13 Elul, 5701.

With time, the Jewish community was enlarged by the remainders from the liquidated ghettos in the nearby towns of Smorgonie, Holszany, Krewo, Żuprany, and Gierwiaty.

On March 15, 1943, the day we received the order to resettle the Oszmiana Ghetto, our Jewish community consisted of 2,830 people. In addition, there were about 1,100 people in labor camps originating from those communities, or members of their families in Žasliai, Zezmer, Kiena, Smorgonie, and Vilna.

Meanwhile, the camp in Smorgonie was liquidated, and 74 people came to us; altogether we were 2,904 Jews.

After 18 months of the ghetto and in light of our situation, the information about our resettlement was accepted with trembling hearts. Broken and desperate, we started packing the little bit we could take with us to make new homes.

The families of those in the labor camps were allowed to go to the appropriate camps. For the rest, at first the cities of Kovno, Ponevezh, and other places were considered.

To regulate the resettlement and to liquidate the community property, the Judenrat and a few staff members remained in place until the last minute.

To help us during the evacuation, the Vilna Ghetto police sent 10 policemen whose task it was to maintain order and guard the fence of the gradually emptying ghetto.

The resettlement on peasant wagons to the railroad station in Soly began on March 19, 1943, 12 Adar II, 5703.

The O.T. Management Todt Organization (German Military Building Group) of the camps in Žasliai and Zezmer helped with the resettlement in their camps.

Thus the following went to:

Žasliai labor camp	695 people
Zezmer labor camp	604 people
Kiena labor camp	36 people
Vilna Ghetto	722 people
And part of the workshops in our ghetto (with more than 200 craftsmen) were transferred to Nowa Wilejka	124 people
Total	2,181 people

Those transferred to the places mentioned above arrived safely, not counting material losses and small vexations on the way.

The transport to the Vilna Ghetto went on wagons from Oszmiana to Vilna.

During the departure of the transport to Vilna, on Friday, March 26, 1943, Sholem Levin was brought into the ghetto and immediately shot in public for escaping from a labor camp (with the intention of joining his family). May God avenge his blood.

On March 31, we were informed that the 723 people still remaining in the ghetto would be sent to Kovno.

On the Sabbath *of Torah portion Shemini,* 27 Adar II, 5703, April 3, 1943, at 2 o'clock in the afternoon, the last wagons of the transport to Kovno left the ghetto gate, accompanied by the Vilna Jewish police. The city was Judenrein.

The ghetto representative from Vilna, Jacob Gens, went with the transport from the railroad station in Soly.

Among the transported was a dying man, Shetsik [?] peace unto him. A refugee from Baranovitsh. He was buried in a Jewish grave in the town of Soły.

Leaving the ghetto gate, we encountered the vulture eyes of the hordes of local inhabitants waiting for their inheritance, with mocking looks of the curious and, to tell the truth, with glances of pity from a few.

On Monday, April 5, 1943, 29 Adar II, 5703, we received the sad news that the transport to Kovno, along with the entire Jewish community of Soly (about 700 people) and parts of the ghettos in Święciany, Michaliszki, Gudogaje, and Ostrowiec, altogether about 4,000 people, were killed on the Vilna-Kovno road at the Ponar railroad station. May the saints and the pure be bound in life. And may God avenge their blood. A few were saved by a miracle.

And one more Old City and Mother of Israel, Osmina [Oszmiana], is destroyed.

Wednesday, 2 Nissan 5703.

MAY 10 [1943]

WITH THE WIND

The ghetto lives with the day. It lives with the wind. The wind drives away a cloud, and it seems [that it is] gone—redemption comes. But it is no more than a wind. And so we live now like a weakling, tossed by every breeze.

In the past four days, it has been extraordinarily calm in the ghetto. Truly as if nothing were happening here. As if we didn't need to be afraid of anything.

The reason? The wind through the radio waves has brought news of Bizerte and Tunis.[30] If so, it won't last long, and if not long . . .

30. I.e., the American advances in North Africa.

The Jews "help count the prisoners." They are happy; seldom is the question asked—What now?

Jews live with the hour, with the wind—long live life! . . .

HEBRAIZATION IN THE . . . GHETTO

You might think that because of the famous story of the Ponar case, Yashunski has gone. Formally, yes; but in fact, it is different. The ghetto leadership, wanting to pull the school system in the ghetto onto a certain road, took advantage of the opportunity to drive Yashunski out of the office of director of the Cultural Department. Obviously, Yashunski wouldn't have allowed the Hebraization to be carried out. Who agreed to do it? Leo Bernstein, a young man who, under the Bolsheviks, was a professor in the people's university; a policeman in the ghetto; and later, a teacher; and is now the cultural minister who is Hebraizing Vilna.

Leo Bernstein is a nationalist Jew from Klaipeda, an intellectual who writes German poetry on Jewish subjects. Now he is the one who dares to Hebraize the Yiddishist Vilna.

THE GOOSE AS A SYMBOL OF GENS[31]

The feuilleton of *Geto-yediyes* of May 2 provides an example of what now preoccupies the ghetto. The subject is the goose we have already written about, and the attached clipping from the feuilleton demonstrates what we mean.[32]

What preoccupies them here?! . . .

BOOKS FROM UKMERGĖ

The Jews of Ukmergė have been dead for a long time. All that is left are the books from the local Jewish library. Recently the books have also been taken out of there and brought to a "Jewish grave" to the RR [Rosenberg] Task Force in Vilna, which does *Judenforschung ohne Juden*[33] with Jewish brains. . . .

Seven cartons of books were brought here.

YOU MUST LEARN HEBREW

Just today we wrote about the Hebraization. Now a document comes to me: Friend Kozik will not allow his child's head to be confused by teaching him Hebrew. There was once a time when Hebrew was voluntary. Now he shows me the letter where it says that his son must study Hebrew, and he asks me what to do. I advise him to remain silent because this is how the matter has been received here—one is silent. . . .

31. *Gendz* (a homonym of the name *Gens*) is the plural of *gandz* ("goose" in Yiddish).

32. I.e., the plan for the Vilna Ghetto to have an emblem of a goose. Kruk probably wrote about it in the missing pages.

33. "The study of Jews without Jews."

CHAPTER 8
THE GHETTO WILL NOT CALM DOWN
MAY 12, 1943 – JULY 14, 1943

MAY 12 [1943]

THE GHETTO WILL NOT CALM DOWN

The ghetto will not calm down from recent events with the Oszmiana and Święçiany Jews. If the simple ghetto citizen has been somewhat calmer lately, it is only because he is alive, like a fly, for a day—if it is calm, he is also calm. Does he have any choice? But there is a group that doesn't want to and will not calm down. These are the ones who are grouped around the ghetto cadres.[1] An exceptionally life-risking work is going on here now. They are preparing for the final decisive act. During recent weeks, from April 1 to the beginning of May, they spent more than 500,000 rubles to increase the number of tools. Now a collection has been proclaimed in the ghetto to raise a quarter of a million rubles. As far as I know, there were already more than 400,000 three days ago. Tears come into our eyes when it is clear how people sell their own things and contribute; they give away all they've got.

The work for this has become the most important of the local social cadres. The last two victims—the deaths of Liza Magun and Zalmen Tiktin—heated up the mood around this matter even more.

Our Jewish "authorities" have also felt something. And although they would have liked to be silent, only last night they thought it necessary to search the Burbiszki group as they came through the gate. They didn't take food. So what were they looking for? Burbiszki is the unit where the recent event of Zalmen Tiktin took place. . . .

The ghetto doesn't sleep. Jews buy weapons on their own. People bring masses of chemical explosives, incendiary materials, etc.

It doesn't go any further—but if an Aktion comes that smells of liquidation, everything will go up in fire and sword.

THE LAST MESSAGE FROM WARSAW

The Sphinx Warsaw is silent. There are dozens of tales, but not one is 100 percent certain. Does a ghetto exist in Warsaw, doesn't it exist by now? No one can say anything about it.

1. Kruk's euphemism for the underground FPO.

Now we have received a few bits of information from Warsaw, which must be precise: on about April 20, the Germans demanded from the Judenrat of one of the Warsaw ghettos, from Śliska-Sienna, 5,000 Jews to work in the East. The Judenrat, wondering why Jews would be taken from Warsaw to the East, requested 24 hours' time.

The ghetto immediately contacted the Polish military organization (POW).[2] A hasty acquisition of weapons and a preparation for resistance began. The campaign was to be led by a captain and two officers.

On April 23, when the Gestapo came with their armed bands and tried to invade the blocks of Śliska-Żelazna, they were met with a hail of bullets. Seventeen Germans fell, and they quickly retreated. Not until the next day did they come back prepared, bringing Ukrainians and Latvians with them. The resistance was so hard that on April 27, the Germans pelted the blocks with fire bombs from airplanes. The impression made on the city is colossal.

We will possibly write more precisely about the further course of events in a few days.

ENGINEER [YOSEF] YASHUNSKI IS NOT ALIVE

Already written about it once. Now the information is confirmed: Friend [Yosef] Yashunski and his son Misha were taken out of Warsaw and killed in Zamość, where Jews were taken to be killed.[3]

PEOPLE SHOOT

Recently trains with Russian kolkhozniks[4] have come through the Vilna railroad station. The Jewish laborers on the railroad tell of the horrible poverty of the peasants who are presumably from the Smolensk region. The peasants said that they are being taken to work in . . . Germany. Now there is a persistent rumor that all of them have recently been shot in Ponar.

Is this why Weiss's vacation was interrupted?

WELCOME, NEUGEBAUER IS HERE

He has already come back. His vacation is over, and he visited the ghetto as a "guest."

PARTISANS

I learn that there was recently a partisan attack on a train of Lithuanian and German soldiers, which went through Święciany. The result—five cars exploded, 45

2. Polska Organizacja Wojskowa.

3. Misha Yashunski (brother of Grisha Yashunski), a medical doctor, was active in Bundist student circles in Warsaw. Zamość probably means Bełżec, the death camp near the city of Zamość.

4. Workers on collective farms.

dead, and several wounded. The train from Podbrodzie did not arrive in Vilna yesterday.

The Grodno train to Orany also ran into an obstacle. What happened to it is not yet clear.

MIDNIGHT

WHAT DOES THIS MEAN?

For several days, rumors have been circulating about an Aktion of old people. Two days ago, they were arrested and put into the ghetto prison. Last night, three more old men were arrested and sent to the ghetto prison. This morning, as I said, Neugebauer was in the ghetto, and when he left, he said that he hoped the ghetto would be calm.

A few hours later, at about 8 in the evening, I learned that old people are to be taken tonight. Now, at midnight, I discover that 10 people are being delivered, 9 old people and 1 young one, who has been in the ghetto prison for two weeks now, simply because, as a messenger in the first Jewish police precinct, he knew too much.

Why 10, and what meaning can this have for the larger appetites? Something doesn't make sense here. Well-informed police circles interpret this as a payback for those who escaped from Ponar. . . .

It doesn't make sense and requires a proper explanation.

1,500 – 2,000

I also learn that in the next few days a brand-new Aktion is to take place in the ghetto. It concerns 1,500 to 2,000 people, old, unemployed, etc. Four "house managers" are empowered to compile a list. Outside the ghetto they already know about the Aktion.

A NEW JEWISH IPATINGA IN THE GHETTO

A new group of Jewish policemen is now created in the ghetto to fill the role of Snatchers. Levas is to lead the group, which includes the policemen Seidel, a former Vilna butcher, Smulikowski, Zubak, Shapirke, and others.

The ghetto sleeps and doesn't know about anything. But we do know—something is again being prepared in our ghetto.

MAY 14 [1943]

TUNIS AND WHAT NOW?

The battle for Africa has been going on since October 1942. Now Africa is purged, and in view of the events, the world asks—what now?

It is clear to everyone that great deeds must come now. The war of the Allies must be shifted to the European continent, for the so-called second front.[5] Italy is in turmoil. Italy, which has carried on seven years of war now and has lost everything she conquered, understands very well that she is now playing the last card. No wonder Italian citizens, even the party members, are beginning to rebel.

Aside from the moralizing sermon Il Duce recently gave, there is a repetition by the [Fascist] party secretary. And Mussolini also talked about that to the Fascist council from the balcony [of] Piazza Venezia, where he said: "Nine years ago, the African campaign was completed and the Italian empire was created. Events are still not complete. Italy must and will come back to Africa," etc. Naturally, the audience applauded, and the press wrote. We would have been happy with all this, as you are happy with the defeat of your enemy. But for us, as for the entire world, there is the question—what now?

Ghetto Jewry is isolated from the world. For ghetto Jewry, under the horrible sadistic terror of Fascist cannibals, the question is much more concrete than for the world politicians. For us, the bloody question of "what now" is much sharper than for all others. We are running out of time. If it lasts, we will all be killed. If something significant does happen, then perhaps, just perhaps, we might "win" our existence.

The blood and the will to live cries out from us—SOS, what now? . . .

SHOT BEFORE THE ENTRANCE TO THE MELINA

Two days ago, a Jew was wounded with a pistol shot as he was going into a melina on Zawalna Street. The Jew was carrying a side of meat. The partners ran away. The smuggler nevertheless escaped from the shooter. The wounded man is now in the ghetto hospital.

SEVEN JEWS TURNED IN

For a few days now, the ghetto has been in an uproar because old people are taken and the case of Pospieszki may be repeated. Apparently the matter is not just an invention. For the past two days, a few old people, cripples, and lunatics have been arrested by the Jewish police. Yesterday seven of them were turned in.

What kind of reckoning is this? People say this is for those who ran away from Ponar during the execution of the Oszmiana and Święciany Jews.

How come? Haven't the Germans withdrawn their order about delivering the escapees from Ponar? But the answer to this says nothing. In fact, they demanded 10. They even say that Weiss, coming after the victims, had two complaints in the prison courtyard of Lidzki: first, they give him people he will not be able to show

5. The Russians, who bore the brunt of the land war with the German army, kept demanding the opening of a "second front" in Western Europe.

off with on the . . . field; second, he told the police command and Mr. Dessler that they owe him three more Jews. . . .

The ghetto swallowed the matter as if nothing had happened. Taken, led off, and finished off. . . .

YOSHKE MOTYKAŃSKI

One of the seven was a healthy, handsome fellow named Yoshke Motikanski.

Who is this Motykański?

He is 19 years old; he was an extraordinarily smart and talented boy, a handsome, charming young man. But he committed one big crime: the Jewish police chief, the assistant commissar, the commissar, and he himself as their servant in the precinct of the first district, had a lease on all the melinas in the area. In their name, he took care of the joint business, took money and objects. In short, he knew a lot, and sometimes even took to squealing. So a few days ago, he fell into the ghetto prison, where the police took advantage of the opportunity to get rid of him. . . . When they tied his hands, however, he promised he would drag half the ghetto with him.

Indeed, more than one policeman is shaking, waiting for the minute he will be finished. . . .

When Weiss saw the young Motykański, unlike the old people, standing in front of him, he stated contentedly: "This is the kind I need!" And his sadistic thirst was quenched.

BACK TO BIAŁA WAKA

As we now know, all those from Biała Waka have to go back to their old jobs. As they were once scared of being transferred to Vilna, now they don't want to go back to Biała Waka. By order of the commissar of Vilna district, the ghetto police arrested all those from Biała Waka on the night of the 12th–13th and transported them to their old workplaces.

THE GATES ARE WALLED UP

Everything in the ghetto trembles: what for? Recently the gates of the houses bordering the ghetto have been walled up, i.e., the gates where you could eventually escape from the ghetto.

Why were the gates walled up? I am told by official circles that this was done to avoid incidents of smuggling in the ghetto. Second, the naive ghetto leaders think that "in case of something," "they" won't be able to crawl in through dozens of places. But meanwhile, the gates are walled up, and the ghetto knows one thing—they are walling us in! . . .

WHEN WILL WE BE SAVED?

This archaic concept of being saved is on everyone's lips. Everything that happens is greeted with the question—is it good for us?

Stalingrad or Tunis, a diplomatic move or something else—is that good for us? And when we ask "for us," we mean first of all the ghetto. No wonder the ghetto grabs at straws, may it be for its own good. Often, people do everything to convince themselves that this will be for the good of the ghetto. . . .

Recently the ghetto invented a new tale, which we present here for posterity and because it is typical of the psychological condition of the ghetto dwellers:

A few weeks ago, it was three years since the death of the famous Vilna [chief] rabbi Haim-Ozer Grodzenski. People say that after his death, a sealed letter was found to be opened three years after his death. When the letter was opened, it said that a war would break out that would bring a great destruction. The Jews still alive when the letter was opened would remain alive. Ten weeks after the opening of the letter, that is, three years and ten weeks after his death, the destruction will stop and the Jews will be saved. . . .

So much for the tale. Naturally, the entire thing is an invention. But many in the ghetto don't want to know about that, and the story circulates from mouth to mouth.

MAY 16 [1943]

YUDL ANILOWICZ DEAD

Yesterday the veteran staff member of the Jewish Scientific Institute, the organizer and leader of the bibliographical center, Comrade Yudl Anilowicz, died at the age of 37. For years Anilowicz had suffered from severe diabetes. The ghetto period and the lack of insulin, which was his daily food, finally put an end to his difficult life. He spent the last weeks in the hospital, and yesterday, the 15th, quietly passed away there. His funeral, which took place at 11 this morning, was one of the most painful events, attended by about 30 people, most of them teachers. His colleagues from YIVO, his long-time chief Z. Kalmanowicz, were late to the funeral. Those writers and artists who came included the writer of these lines and the artist Blacher. Of his party members, only a few. No one cared about his funeral. The writers, absorbed in pursuing "literary honoraria" from the head of the ghetto, forgot that Anilowicz wrote several biographies, that he was a member of the Association of Writers and Artists in the ghetto. His comrades apparently have more important things to do, and Z. Kalmanowicz agreed to the suggestion of the secretary of the Association of Writers and Artists, Blacher, that someone should say a few words about the deceased. But no one said anything, and none of them were there.

Not far from the checkpoint, after the coffin had left the ghetto, Kaplan-Kaplanski, the teacher Olicki, and others showed up. His close friend, the poet Sutzkever, didn't show up on time to this funeral either.

The funeral was painful because of the neglect and weakness of the remaining local intelligentsia. Everything here has become diluted and gray.

Yudl Anilowicz lived quietly and passed away quietly. His funeral was a continuation of his quiet and modest life.

Honor to his memory.

THEY ARE HEBRAIZING THE GHETTO

Everyone here has had a hand in Hebraizing the ghetto. The new "cultural minister"[6] carries out his decision firmly.

The ghetto organ, *Geto-yedies,* describes it as a "reformed school program," where the study of Hebrew is reinforced and a special study of the geography of Palestine is to be introduced. Bible study will also be reinforced, and most important, Hebrew will be introduced in the lowest grades of primary school and the highest groups of kindergarten.

According to the leading article of the official organ, this means "internal school reform." The writer acknowledges the great achievements of the ghetto schools, but he thinks that something essential has nevertheless been omitted. Namely, the Jewish national moment, the ideal of Jewish "revival" and "ingathering" (?). In addition, the writer of the leading article, who is not from Vilna, says that Yiddish study is a Vilna specialty, that Vilna has not gone along with the Jewish nationalist stream, etc.

The Hebraization of the ghetto goes further. In the theater, they are preparing a gala Hebrew performance. Hebrew lectures with recitations are being organized. The Hebrew choir has become a frequent guest in the Ghetto Theater. Posters about a Bialik evening are decorated with white and blue, and some talk with satisfaction that Murer suddenly asked the head of the ghetto if he is a Zionist. . . . The teacher [Motl] Gilinski, who, through my pains, was employed as director of the Children's Club (replacing the current director of the Cultural Department), was not allowed to do this work—he isn't enough of a nationalist. The children of the Vilna Youth Club are fed on evenings of Hebrew.

ABOUT GHETTO INDUSTRY

The newly created pottery shop in the ghetto is active now: people work here in two ways—by turning and by pouring into plaster forms. So far, people produce pots, bowls, vases, etc. A glazing department will also be set up in the pottery shop. Ceramics of various colors will be produced here.

In the technical school, the number of students has reached 100.

The second tailor shop will soon move to Rudnicka 13. The workshop is enlarged by 50 more persons. Large military orders have arrived there.

WE WILL REMAIN AT 15,000

In recent conversations with the ghetto rulers, it is finally clear to me: we are on the eve of more events. Chattering, they say that Murer has recently said more

6. Leo Bernstein.

than once: "It is too bad we enlarged the ghetto, it should have stayed not more than those 15,600." The assistant chief of the Gestapo has also recently thrown out such a line: "Shouldn't have enlarged the ghetto."

Does this mean the ghetto will be reduced to 15,000? Doesn't this mean that not 5,000 but 7,000 Jews will be taken out of the ghetto? . . .

PEOPLE STEAL IN THE CEMETERY

People steal wooden boards from the graves in the Jewish cemetery. Instead of wooden boards, the ghetto administration will put in cement slabs.

MAY 17 [1943]

A VICIOUS CIRCLE

It is a vicious circle. Once they said that the area must be Judenrein in order to clean up the Byelorussian-Lithuanian border. Now the leader of the Gestapo says that if the Widze[7] youth had not had contacts with the partisans, what happened to the Jews of Oszmiana and Święciany would not have occurred.

Some weeks ago, just before those events, the same Neugebauer assured us, as we know, that all of those Jews would reach their places. Later came the excuse that it happened because Kovno didn't want to take them. . . .

When the order was issued that the escapees from those events (Ponar) must appear, a second order soon came, rescinding the first. The seven persons who were recently turned over had to be, incomprehensibly, a compensation for those escapees. . . .

After the events of Oszmiana and Święciany, all sorts of people started acquiring weapons. Today, as we shall soon tell precisely, we are at the fourth case of Jews captured buying weapons.

Although the ghetto is on the alert and you can feel in the air the impending Aktions; although the head of the Gestapo has recently assured us regularly and incessantly that the ghetto will be calm; although Murer and similar "good friends" keep reassuring—nevertheless, the ghetto does not calm down.

Suddenly, on Saturday, the 15th, the ghetto chief calls an assembly of brigadiers and directors and says that the head of the Gestapo is laughing about Jews buying weapons. If he wants, says the chief in Neugebauer's name, if he wants, he will manage anyway. But he advises Jews not to bring misfortune on themselves, because when he feels the ghetto is threatening, then . . .

And the ghetto chief, in his military manner, says to the ghetto residents:

7. The editor of the Yiddish edition assumed that a typographical error had been made here: the Yiddish read "Vitser" (joker), but it should be "Vilner" or "Vidzer." "Vidz" (Yiddish), or Widze (Polish), seems to be the best guess.

"Watch out. Everyone should watch everyone else, denounce every case." He himself will make them responsible. He will take their families, the residents of the apartments, the whole block, etc. In short, an internal means of [ensuring] collective responsibility. . . .[8]

The head of the ghetto has already forgotten everything. Again he takes to heart the words of the head of the Gestapo, and again he believes in his sincerity, not understanding that he is using the cases of weapons to have a free hand at any time—I must liquidate you because you are arming yourselves.

It is a vicious circle. Let yourself be taken—how long can we endure it? To try to resist means to assume the fate of the entire ghetto.

Be that as it may, the Gestapo is looking for an excuse for an Aktion.

ANOTHER CASE OF A REVOLVER

On Saturday the 15th, one [Sholem] Świrski from Kailis was arrested for buying a revolver. The case stirred great uneasiness in the ghetto. Apparently Swirski, a meat smuggler, a former butcher, had financial dealings with a Christian, from whom he was supposed to get a revolver that Saturday. The Christian apparently wanted to get rid of his creditor and told the Gestapo about the revolver. Whatever the case, the wife and her two children were transferred to the ghetto today, so three more persons aren't involved.[9]

THEY SEARCH FOR WEAPONS

Because of what happened on Saturday, the Jewish police searched the local ghetto residents all day Saturday, as they returned from work. In the ghetto itself, Leo Bernstein, Abba Kovner, Glazman, Averbukh, and others were searched. The ghetto police obviously stayed with Zionists, not touching anybody else who is also suspected of having such things.[10]

It looks as if the searches here are of an "educational character": if you buy a weapon, you must hide it well. . . . Apparently, those who buy them understood this before the gentlemen of the Jewish police began their education.

NO MORE MASS AKTIONS. THE GHETTO CALMS DOWN BUT DOESN'T BELIEVE

Early Saturday morning, Murer was in the ghetto, and they say he was in a splendid mood. He handed out cigarettes, asked about people's health, etc. People saw in this a new era. Is it a trivial thing that Murer is handing out cigarettes and behaving like a human being? . . .

8. Gens's speech is in Korczak 1946:366–367.

9. The case of Swirski is in Kaczerginski 1947:306. Bebe Epstein, in her eyewitness account in the YIVO Archives, tells of the execution of Swirski and his children.

10. The first three of that list were indeed partisans. Typically, the Jewish police were afraid to touch the Communists, because they were likely to be the next group in power.

Yesterday the brigadier from Ponimun, who has often come to Vilna recently, came to the ghetto. He says that the Kovno "Murer" there told the local ghetto representative that there would be no more mass murders of Jews. He also said that a meeting was held on that question in Munich, where that decision was made.

Jews connect Murer's behavior with the newly decided Munich tactic. They do indeed connect it and want to believe in it. Nevertheless, it is hard to believe—trust is lost! . . .

THE CONSPIRACY IS STRONGER

In view of the recent failures in acquiring weapons, and the searches in the ghetto, the situation in the ghetto cadres caused some work to be stopped for a while. The cadres themselves went even deeper underground than before: the conspiracy is doubled and tripled.

MAY 20 [1943]

CALM BEFORE A STORM. THEY SEARCH FOR WEAPONS

In the ghetto it really is the calm before a storm. No special signs for the time being. And maybe we think like this because we are not accustomed to "calm."

All cases of weapons, so far, have ended without special damage to the ghetto. The Gestapo was persuaded that Christians who are antisemitic and others want to provoke the ghetto. The last case is an example of that, and there is even hope that the Swirski case will go peacefully both for the ghetto and for him.

After the last speech of the ghetto representative and the "searches" for weapons, another series of searches came yesterday: police commissioners, the ghetto prosecutor, and a special trusted group of police. They tore up staircases, a concrete floor, etc. The result—zero.

I went to one of the organizers of the searches and asked: How come? What will they do if they do find something? Will they turn [the person] over to the German authorities? Wouldn't this be, God forbid, a misfortune for you police if you do find it?

The one who was questioned answered: we know very well they have it. We even guess who and how. The searches will not only go on, but we will regularly and incessantly keep the population tense. Those who have it must know how to hide. Today we are searching. Tomorrow, others might. . . .

So the searches have the purpose of educating those who have them. I would add—also to prepare for other searches.

If everything goes as they tell me, if it is all sincere—will this preserve our fate?

WE BURY OURSELVES DEEPER

The recent searches dictated transporting one arsenal all at once. Girls were recruited as carriers, young people as buriers, to bury deep underground. When everything succeeded, faces were shining—it's not a trivial thing, such an arsenal! . . .

THE BISHOP SPEAKS AND ŚWIT TELLS

Świt announces on the radio that the Kovno bishop spoke in the cathedral of the participation of the Lithuanians in the execution of the Oszmiana and Święciany Jews. They say he condemned their participation. At present, we do not know what is happening to the bishop.

AGAIN ŚWIT

The latest Świt broadcast linked its Jewish radio program to the latest anti-Jewish campaigns around the Katyń affair. They say that the Germans are trying to pin everything that happened on the Jews. They are doing this with Katyń and recently with the dam explosion in . . . Kassel.

The German press shouts that Jews had a hand in it, and Świt calls for vigilance. The Germans, the radio program claims, want to use the explosion of the dam as an excuse for a new slaughter of the last few remaining Jews. They warn and call for vigilance.

[MAY] 21 [1943]

SHLOYME[11] ZYGIELBOJM (S. ARTUR)

None of the news we get here is certain. The news that my friend and comrade Artur has died struck me like the death of a close relation. Artur suffered from stomach trouble for several years. Now I learn that Artur committed suicide and left a letter accusing the Allies of indifference to the murder of the Jews in Europe. Because he was helpless, because rumors had now reached him that his wife and children had been killed in Warsaw, with his suicide he drew the attention of the world powers.

The news had a double impact on me. A friend and comrade has fallen, the Bundist Artur. He committed suicide to draw attention to the murder of the Jews. At the same time, I have learned for sure that I have lost my sister and her children.

Just as I was leaving Warsaw, in September 1939, the refugee from Łódź, Artur, moved into my apartment with his wife and children. Recently my sister and her children also moved in there. The murder of Artur's wife is like the murder of my sister. And so the whole house has been wiped out.

11. This is an error; it should be Szmul.

This struck me twice.

But we are used to looking death in the face, whether of a friend, a relative, or a stranger. We sigh, stand still a second, and . . . go back to our slavish harness.

Have I [not] already wept for my sister? Now, however, I have touched it, and it has scalded again; but I am again forced to keep going.

Isn't it the hashish of our bitterness, the drunkenness of our time. How can we do otherwise? . . .

But Artur didn't die just because he couldn't take it anymore. His death is a shout to the world, a call for help for our spilled blood and for those who are next in line.

In recent years, Artur grew immensely. A tutor in Lublin, giving lessons for his lunch, he got the "ideal" of acquiring a skill and became a glove maker and came to know the labor movement; he became an active Bundist and advanced to the big city. Starving in Warsaw, he arrived—he obtained the position of secretary of the union of metal workers and rose as a worker-activist. In 1921, he was elected a member of the Central Committee of the Bund, became the secretary of the central council of the unions in Warsaw, was later the leader of the Jewish trade unions in Poland (national council), got involved in journalism, participated in several international conferences, and when the war broke out, he escaped from Łódź to Warsaw, where he was a member of the defense committee of Warsaw. Warsaw falls and Artur plays a major historical role in the Judenrat there. He escapes from Warsaw and shows up at the International Socialist Congress, where he tells of the heroic struggle for Warsaw. He then became a member of the council of the Polish Government[12] and appeared often on the radio.

Now—his last act.

Artur is a child of the Jewish labor movement. His life's path is that of a martyr. His death, a hero's death.

Honor to his memory.

500 FAMILIES SAVED

For several days, negotiations were held for the delivery of 500 families from Vilna ostensibly to Minsk for work. The transport was to contain some 1,500 persons. For the time being, [our representatives] have succeeded in canceling the evil; the 500 families are saved.

MAY 23 [1943]

WARSAW

As close as we are to Warsaw, all the messages we get from there contradict one another. One thing is clear: the Warsaw Ghetto is still fighting. Poland fought for

12. In exile in London.

her independence for 19 days—the Warsaw Ghetto has already been carrying on its heroic struggle for six weeks now.

Some say the Warsaw Ghetto is strewn with fire bombs from airplanes. Someone else says they are fighting with artillery. A third says no one is allowed near the ghetto. Shooting is heard. Others say that despite the events, groups of Jews are seen in the street going to work. How is all this possible?

Now there is another piece of information, supposedly from the radio: the leader of the fighters in Warsaw is a Bundist, Engineer Fishkop. Who is this Engineer Fishkop? People ask me and I can't answer. Is it the Fishgrund from Cracow? Or maybe the name is an invented pseudonym.[13]

Warsaw is indeed close. But we are as far from Warsaw as from China.

COMMUNICATIONS

All attempts thus far to create communications from the ghetto with the outside have, unfortunately, not succeeded. Some communications were cut off, some weren't even made. Thus our comrades of the PPS are ridiculous. Instead of helping us, they ask us how, etc.

ALSO A SMALL ART THEATER

Now we have everything; we lack only one small thing—a small art theater. Now we will have this, too. The small art theater will be in the café at Rudnicka 13. The first performance has recently taken place. The theater will give two performances a week.

A mandolin orchestra has also been organized.

RUDNICKA STREET — THE INDUSTRIAL CENTER OF THE GHETTO

The ghetto workshops are constantly enlarged and expanded. In the next few days, the number of workers is to reach 1,500. Now all inhabitants of ground-floor apartments on Rudnicka Street are removed from their apartments so that workshops can be set up there. Rudnicka Street will be the place where ghetto workshops are concentrated.

MAY 24 [1943]

CRACOW AND STANISŁAWÓW

Once again the radio alarms that the ghettos of Cracow and Stanisławów are liquidated. Just a year ago, more precisely, a year from May 17, the German newspaper *Baltische Zeitung in Ostland* joyously reported[14] that the Jewish Question in

13. This surely means the engineer Michal Klepfisz. The parts of his name have been inverted and disguised.

14. See the entry of May 22, 1942, "18,000 Jews in Cracow."

Cracow has basically been solved because . . . the other side of the Vistula River, in that Cracow suburb, was arranged as a "Jewish district," numbering 18,000 Jews. Then the "gain" was very large because, instead of 56,500 Jews in Cracow, a "Jewish district" remained with 18,000. So now the last phase comes—Cracow goes the way of Warsaw. . . .

We always end up with the same thing: When will our turn come?

LABOR PROBLEMS IN THE GHETTO

I learn from the circles of the Jewish Labor Office that, since the last letter of the district commissar stating that Jews must be employed only in heavy labor, a lot has changed. Most units are indeed appropriate. The work is getting harder. On the other hand, everybody is helpless. Jews don't want to work: it is the end anyway, why work? These are the complaints of most working people. The Jewish Labor Office is helpless here.

The Labor Office wants the maximum number of the more than 20,000 ghetto residents to be employed and registered as working. The Labor Office wants as many as 14,000 ghetto residents to be employed soon.

An interesting phenomenon: in many units, a serious neglect prevails both from the Germans and inevitably from the Jews, too. The Germans pull the wagon for the sake of appearance; the Jews have no interest in pulling anything. The Germans often speak openly with the Jews—there is nothing to risk your life for. The SS people say that the game is played out anyway. A girl, Frida Lubecka, gets a seven-day vacation from them—something one can hardly understand. The Germans often play brotherhood with the Jews here because, as they say, the only thing that stands between us is the murderer Hitler. . . .

TERROR

Two days ago, two Lithuanian secret agents were shot on Szeptycki St. The search in the house where the case occurred accidentally came upon an arsenal of weapons and an illegal press. The population of the entire block was taken to Łukiszki Prison.

The next day, at lunch hour, two more Christians were shot on Ludwisarska Street. No one knows who they are. People only know that they were running in the street, followed by a gang of about 15 persons shooting at the escapees. Both fell on the street.

MAY 25 [1943]

MURER MAKES AN "AMUSEMENT"

Murer once again desired to amuse himself and again selected victims for it—Jews of the ghetto. Once again he stood at the gate and this time, for a change, was interested in the Jewish patches. He searched for patches not only on coats, not only on jackets, but also on shirts. That's what Murer wants. Anyone who wasn't all right was . . . whipped, and this, of course, was done by the ghetto police. Anyone who got away clean from Murer yesterday felt newborn. . . .

Right after his "visit," a new order from the ghetto chief appeared: those who go into the city may not take coats with them. The order aims, simply, at making it harder to smuggle things in under coats. For the time being, it is quite cold outside. People must obey the order, and the ghetto hospital will acquire customers as a result. Naturally, Murer doesn't care about this. . . . [15]

THERE WILL BE MORE AKTIONS . . .

All our prophecies are coming true—there will be Aktions in the ghetto, there must be. It is only a question of when, how big they will be, and how they will take place.

All this became clear to me from a conversation with an influential person:

In the ghetto, he says, 14,000 Jews must work. The Aktions will include 3,000–5,000 Jews. Thus, about 16,000–18,000 will be left in the ghetto, including children and unemployed.

To what extent one can rely on these words is not certain. But one thing is clear: about 5,000 people will be taken out of the ghetto, and more than 15,000 will be left in the ghetto.

When will this happen? In fact, he says, it should already have been done. But as long as it is in his hands, he will drag it out.

As to the question of who will be the one who chooses, he answers—unfortunately, he. . . .

"How will they be chosen?"

I get a smile for that, a smile which is supposed to make it clear to me that such questions are pointless. . . .

As for the 500 families to Minsk, it is not as we presented it. The issue is not topical for the time being. But it is not altogether over. I think this is one of the first "tricks" they are trying to devise here! . . .

G. YASHUNSKI IS ALSO CARRYING NOW

The carrying in of books and documents [into the ghetto], which we established, recently received new followers. The recently "heretical" cultural minister, G. Yashunski, has gone to work in the city and is employed in the municipal archive. From there, he now brings not only books but also documents and printed matter of a special character. Thus, for example, I have already received from him a manuscript of Anna Rosenthal, a few books by P. An-man, including the Russian book

15. Order Number 114, about not going to work in the city in coats, was issued on May 24, 1943. This order is in the YIVO Archives (Kaczerginski-Sutzkever Collection, no. 36).

about Romanovka, written by himself as a participant of Romanovka.[16] The edition seems to be a rare one.

DYING GASPS OF WARSAW

A few rumors still come from Warsaw: Warsaw is still fighting, the Warsaw Ghetto has already given up the struggle, and the final chord—the Warsaw Ghetto has finally been silenced.

Now the radio says they are searching for Jews in Warsaw, outside the ghetto. For pointing out a Jew, you receive . . . 10 kilos of sugar.

A Jewish head is worth 10 kilos of sugar.

A LITHUANIAN GESTAPO AGENT — A CORPSE IN THE STREET

After the previous assassinations, another case: a dead Lithuanian Gestapo agent was found on Vilna Street. Who, when—no one knows. Once again it is clear—a terrorist organization is working in Vilna.

MAY 26 [1943]

THE "INFANT" FROM THE GHETTO

We have often written that aside from the two-legged horses, the Vilna Ghetto also has four four-legged ones. Now the fifth is born—a colt who is the "infant" of the ghetto. Even Murer was interested in that first legal birth in the ghetto. Yesterday traffic was stopped in the ghetto; people were beaten and driven into the gate. What happened?—Murer wants to see the newborn ghetto colt with his own eyes.

Jews are not allowed to give birth. Horses, even ghetto horses, may increase and multiply. Murer is indeed satisfied—one more horse in the ghetto.

A BORDER CORDON AROUND THE GHETTO

We have often written that an empty strip was to be created around the ghetto, to form a separation between the Aryan and the semitic populations. There was a rumor about a partition 60 meters wide. Now the matter is beginning to be real, and people are already talking about a partition of 100 meters. Some are afraid and think we are finally coming to an end. The proof: the partition—destroying the contact between Jews and non-Jews.

16. I.e., the famous Yakutsk Protest carried out by political exiles in 1904 in Yakutsk, Siberia. The exiles barricaded themselves in the house of one of the Romanovs, hence the name *Romanovka*. There is a considerable literature about this protest. P. An-Man's study, "Romanovka," was published in Russia after the Revolution.

AND THE GHETTO IS HAPPY

Why is the ghetto so happy? Finally a big dream has come true here. The Wehrmacht has begun shipping military clothing. The clothing must be washed, patched, and renewed here.

So far, eight train carloads of clothes have arrived. The ghetto can now complete at best up to 1,000 pieces of clothing a week. The order consists of washing and mending 30,000 pieces of clothing. Naive Jews are happy—for the time being, they see 30 weeks ahead of them.

For that, Murer recently comes here twice a day, and of course, twice a day, people are driven to the [courtyard] gates; Jews must not be too visible. Murer's task: oversee, make sure that the Jews are storing the clothing right. Meanwhile, you cannot recognize him here. He behaves like a gentleman: he doesn't beat, he doesn't bark. Jews now see all of this as a consolation.

THE CONSOLATION IS NO CONSOLATION

But in the ghetto, there are those who don't accept all the words of consolation. The FPO keeps burying themselves underground. To have "rest" in the ghetto, people must prepare for "restless times." All the consignments don't have much to do with whether you can be consoled. The only consolation—to arm yourself.

BUT IT DOESN'T GET TO THEM

The rulers know very well that the end of the ghetto is not dependent on a bigger or smaller consignment. Although they know that in spite of everything we stand before the abyss, they nevertheless cannot control the vulgar game in which they have often acquired fame.

Recently one of the most decent of the police officers reached his 50th birthday. This is the officer Attorney Dimitrovski, who is the liaison between the ghetto administration and the Gestapo. The police command decided to make a celebration for their colleague Dimitrovski.

In the café at Szawelska 1, the entire police elite gathered, speeches were made, and they enjoyed themselves. One of the main attractions was Police Chief Mr. Dessler's joke that if the third of the ghetto triplets, Brojdo, would dance in his underwear, he would put up two liters of liquor. Brojdo went to the next room with ghetto prosecutor Nussbaum-Oltaszewski as a witness. There he took off his pants and earned two liters of liquor.

The ghetto is contemptuous of all that. It is one more proof of how well the ghetto rulers know their role and don't connect their office with the time they live in.

ONCE AGAIN THE GHETTO GETS A FOREST AND A BEACH

Like last year, this year, too, the ghetto leaders got the right to use a part of Zakret Forest and a beach on the Wilija River.

50 WORKERS TO PONEVEZH

According to the order of the Ponevezh district commissar, 45 male workers and 5 women, including 20 skilled, are going from here to Ponevezh.

BACK FROM PANEMUNE

Recently 20 Vilna workers (16 men and 4 women) have returned from the construction work in Panemunė. Great pains were taken so that the rest of the workers would also return.

NEW ORDERS

The ghetto administration recently received several big orders to be carried out in the ghetto workshops: from the "local command" and the "field command" came new orders for furniture. An order was received from HKP for 400 gas generators. The embroidery shop also received several orders for slippers.

FROM THE GHETTO WORKSHOPS

In the sock-knitting shop, old socks are exchanged for new for a small additional payment.

The electrotechnical workshop now turns out electrical switches of specially turned wooden parts.

POLICE WILL BE IN UNIFORM

As we once mentioned, the ghetto police will soon be in uniform, consisting of a dark-blue military costume trimmed with blue bands. The police already wear a hat, as we have known for a long time. The costume is girded by a leather belt. In short: full uniform.

13 WATER PIPES IN THE GHETTO

The ghetto administration is about to build 13 water pipes, which can be useful in a catastrophe to supply the ghetto with water, etc.

MAY 30 [1943]

A SYMPHONY CONCERT WITH A PORTION OF . . . CRAP

Yesterday a symphony concert took place in the Ghetto Theater with a new, sixth program. The concert was one of the most successful in the ghetto. Especially outstanding was the solo of the young violinist Rabinowicz.

During the intermission, the director of the Labor Office, Mr. Brojdo, gave a speech stating that more than 5,000 women in the ghetto are not working. He appealed to the women to understand that the unemployed put themselves in a dangerous situation. The ghetto representative then took the floor, and in "harmony" with the splendid concert, he preached the unemployed a bit of morality, and as a dessert for the concert, he added a big portion of . . . crap. That expression was repeated more than once. The ghetto representative apparently wanted to influence the audience of the festive concert. . . .

Today, May 30, for the anniversary of the symphony orchestra in the ghetto, the same concert is repeated as a benefit concert for the conductor Mr. V. Durmashkin.

Will today's audience also get the portion? . . .

IN THE LABOR UNIT *HOCHBAUBAHNMEISTEREI* NO. 2

[This] is one of the oldest Vilna units. Now about 80 people work there. Workplaces are scattered over the city and occupy several places on the railroad to Ponar and even to Landwarowo. There they work at repairing the railroads, etc. The management is in the hands of the Lithuanian railroad directorate.

Most Jews are employed in auxiliary work. There are also qualified railroad jobs and special railroad repair work.

The attitude of the employers is relatively good. The unit is given soup on the job. The common life among the Jewish workers is good. The poor there receive lunch without [having to] pay. Some of them even receive support. The brigadier of the unit is Ber Zuckerman.

JUNE 2 [1943]

IT GROWS CLOUDY . . .

Not long ago, we wrote that the ghetto is calm as before a storm. Now it starts to be clear—a new storm is coming.

The 500 families to Minsk are hanging in the air. The quiet registration, done in the ghetto, is almost finished. Now comes news:

ZEZMER

The camp in which the Vilna Ghetto invested so much work, toil, and initiative, where 1,200–1,500 Jews were employed—a cloud has come over that camp. Nominally, they say that 300 persons are to be shipped from there to Vitebsk. But some of those to be shipped have to leave their wives and children behind. The accounting is thus: 220 men and 80 women. Children cannot be taken with them. By order of the SD, the Jewish police commissioner Levas is to leave for Zezmer tomorrow morning with a few dozen policemen for a "special mission."[17] Until 9

17. There is a three-page description of Zezmer in the writings of Herman Kruk in the YIVO Archives.

this evening, the uniforms of the policemen are being sewn, so they won't go as civilians, God forbid. Without them, apparently, this work cannot be done. . . .

Other camps were also at stake: in a few days, policemen are supposed to travel to perform a special registration of the workers in several camps subordinate to the Vilna Ghetto.

The Germans grow weaker. You can feel it everywhere. It is a month after the fall of Tunisia, and there isn't yet the slightest ray of redemption.

The sky grows cloudy, and the sensitive Jews of the Vilna Ghetto have smelled the fresh blood of a new catastrophe. . . .

40 PEOPLE TO PONEVEZH

By a special demand of the district commissar [of] Vilna district, 40 men are mobilized here for work in Ponevezh.

HOW DOES THE GHETTO SUPPORT ITSELF?

We know that the ghetto treasury once increased from day to day. We have also discussed precisely where that increase came from. Now, in the new economy, which the chief personally supervises, the ghetto property has been significantly decreased, in spite of much more progressive and increased production.

No surprise there. For example, I learn that in the April budget, representation expenses were 159,000 RM, or 1,500,900 rubles. In addition, there are "miscellaneous expenses" of 70,000 RM. So no surprise there. . . .

VILNA CELEBRATES

Today the city is decorated with Lithuanian national banners. What happened? A group of Lithuanian soldiers is leaving for the front.

THE CEMETERY IS DISMANTLED

We once wrote that the Zarzecze Cemetery in Vilna is being dismantled. Now I attach a copy of a letter from the district commissar about the fact that the marble tombstones of the cemetery are being taken off.

[*The letter is not enclosed.*]

JUNE 6 [1943]

AS TO A NEW LIFE

Everything that has happened recently in the ghetto might make it seem as if we want to start a new life. Ghetto workshops are built and developed. Units are enlarged. New units are created. The Vilna Ghetto is striving to attain a labor force of 14,000. Rudnicka Street is purged of private apartments, and all spaces are turned into ghetto workshops. Between 600 and 800 people work in the tailor shop. All other workshops are enlarged, and their staff is constantly growing. Masses of apprentices are taken into all workshops, etc. A registration of 14- to 55-year-olds takes place in the ghetto. Women are brought into ghetto production en masse, and the children's homes for their children are enlarged. There is a new reduction in the [number of] employees of the ghetto administration—everything for ghetto production!

Are we indeed on the eve of a new life?

When you look at all that and orient yourself to the situation, it becomes increasingly clear—we are far from the eve of a new life. But we are constantly on the brink. . . .

According to the registration that the police are conducting in the camps, and according to the sudden order to send 300 people from Zezmer, it must be clearly stated: If Vilna needs skilled laborers, why are they sent who knows where? And if that doesn't matter, it is once again clear that that migration of people, just like all the promises and guarantees, is worth an empty eggshell.

But the ghetto newspaper scribbles away about it. There is a series of licorice-sweet articles. They say there that work saves our lives and, in the interstices, a slogan: "Jewish woman, think! Work saves blood!" In other, more delicate words, they threaten an Aktion. That is the upshot of the "heroism" of the ghetto authorities. But the Germans do it differently:

Yesterday afternoon, a group of skilled workers left for Ponevezh—42 men and 8 women. Murer, who was at the gate of the ghetto, "blessed" them with a speech in which he said: "Preserve the prestige of the Vilna Ghetto. . . . If you work well, you will have food to eat and you will come back to the ghetto. If you don't, you will not only not have food to eat but you will also not come back to the ghetto anymore." When the director of the Labor Office, Mr. Brojdo, translated Murer's words in our mother tongue, he added that they not only would not come back, but also would not remain there. . . . If we add that we know they are preparing to liquidate the camps soon, it becomes clear whether we are indeed going to a new life. . . .

YISROEL FRIEDMAN

Suddenly this member of the ghetto cadre was arrested in the ghetto and sent immediately to the Gestapo office, where he has been for a few days now. Why? People say this is a provocation by a Christian for whom Friedman and two other Jews worked in agriculture a year ago. All three are meanwhile in Łukiszki Prison. The denunciation is that the ghetto "is preparing," that the "ghetto will not let them [go]," that two of the arrested bought weapons and the third brought them into the ghetto, etc.

Naturally, the Friedman case has stirred great unrest.

A CO-FOUNDER OF THE BUND IN VILNA HAS DIED IN THE GHETTO

Yesterday one of the oldest Bundists, the Vilna dentist Yakov Gerszowicz, died in the ghetto hospital. He gave the first May Day address in Vilna in [1892].[18] In recent years he has not been active. The Bund in Vilna called its sympathizers to the funeral, which takes place at 4 this afternoon from the hospital.

Dr. [Jan] Antokolski spoke of the deceased.

CONFLICTS WITH THE FPO

Ever since our group[19] joined the FPO, there have been various kinds of friction between the group and our representative.[20] First of all, there were problems about conspiracy, and now we have seen several mistakes in the operation.

The cadre recently decided that because relations between the cadre and Mr. G[ens] and D[essler] were growing worse from day to day, because those gentlemen have forgotten all their promises and are scared of the cadre as a great power in the ghetto, and because therefore there is a fear that the ghetto will try to assassinate the heads of the organization—for all those reasons, they decide that if the ghetto authorities try to crush the organization [the FPO], the latter will take up arms against them. This will be done even if there is an action against even one of the leaders. That senseless decision moved Herman [Kruk] to tell the party representative to call on the fighting organization to control itself. He and Hersh [Gutgestalt] introduce the following proposals:

1. To the representative of the B[und]: not to accept any fateful decision without previous agreement with us.
2. As for the FPO: (a) FPO is our organization as long as it defines its goal as the defense of the whole ghetto; (b) every armed struggle inside the ghetto is a provocation for the ghetto population and may not be tolerated by us; (c) [our aim is] to strengthen the conspiracy in the organization.[21]

WHAT INTERESTS ALL GHETTO PEOPLE

Yesterday, in the Bookkeepers' Association—a fiction invented by the famous ghetto comptroller Ginzburg—a lecture was delivered by himself on the subject "Political Structure and Legal Economic Foundations of the Vilna Ghetto."

18. Gerszowicz's real name was Ruvn Gerszowski, and his pseudonym was Yakov. In 1892, when he made the speech, he was a suspender maker, and later he became a dental technician. For information about that May Day celebration and the famous "Four Speeches" delivered there, see *Historishe shriftn* 3 (1939):610–625.

19. I.e., the Bund.

20. Abrasha Chwojnik.

21. Between the Bund in the Vilna Ghetto and its representative in the FPO, Abrasha Chwojnik, there were differences of opinion about several questions of principle and tactics. In these conflicts, Herman Kruk and Hersh Gutgestalt tried to interfere in the business of the FPO and were a minority in the committee of the Bund.

So we now have a political structure and, most important, legal economic foundations.

At least a laugh!

A second lecture, to take place today, is titled "What Is a Jew?" The lecturers: three from religious circles.

NOW THERE IS A PROJECT FOR A GHETTO GATE

The ghetto, as we once wrote, is supplied—it no longer lacks anything. Just one little thing is missing, and that little thing now occupies the minds of the ghetto leaders. The ghetto lacks a gate and, most important, a gate that would express something monumental. Now the *Geto-yedies* reports that, with luck, there is now such a project and that this project smells of pipe dreams. The gate will consist of five pillars and three entrances with a gate for driving in. Over the entire width of the entrance is a cornice with emblems representing the crafts of the Vilna Ghetto.

PEOPLE PREPARE FOR THE "COMING" THEATER SEASON IN THE . . . GHETTO

The ghetto is also intensively occupied with such things. The latest issue of [*Geto*]-*yedies* says that people are already preparing for the repertoire for the "new theater season." So obviously, our theater activists are preparing for the theater season for next year.

So why do they say it's bad in the ghetto. . . .

THEY "GRAB" JEWS

We have recently written about the uneasiness in Zezmer. We now know that the Jews of Zezmer have truly been "snapped up." Thirty people have been transferred to the area of Pskov. The rest, 800, were taken to the Kovno Ghetto. In Zezmer itself, 140 skilled laborers remained. The deputy director of the Vilna Gestapo was in Zezmer when Jewish Police Commissar Levas arrived. Levas was to transfer to Vilna the Jewish skilled laborers who were "grabbed" in Kovno a few hours before. The Gestapo chief admitted openly that they had to murder 4,000 Jews from Oszmiana and Święciany in order to compete now for every Jew! . . .

JUNE 12 [1943]

THE TRAGEDY GOES ON

Today the Vilna Ghetto was again shaken up. Why? The gate guard in the ghetto detained a fellow with weapons. The detained man opened fire. A Jewish policeman fell, and the ghetto chief, Mr. Gens, shot the shooter, who fell dead.

Independent of that event, and not indulging in an evaluation—the tragedy of the Jewish masses goes on and has already reached the point that not only are Jews attacked but Jews attack Jews.

The fallen Jewish policeman is certainly a victim, who fell at his post. But the one who shot—whatever kind of character he was—is a victim of the time and one of those who told himself, loud and clear, "they" won't take me alive! But the tragedy has gone so far that he fell like a hero, but in a battle with Jews.

No doubt both are victims of our tragic time. And both have fallen defending not themselves but their sad fate.

HOW DID THIS HAPPEN?

Since the events of the Święciany and Oszmiana Jews, Jewish youth in Vilna and its environs have been arming and going to the forest. Everything so far shows that Jews are doing everything to be armed. From the information I collect, I know that young people are intensively going to the forest.

Recently a group of about 30 men was supposed to go to the forest. Before dawn, part of that group left the ghetto. They were to have been led by two Święciany Jews, who had come especially for that. One of the two was one Khayim Levin. Two persons didn't appear at the designated place, and Levin went to the ghetto with a woman to find out what had happened to them.

Today, at about 5:30 in the morning, when Khayim and the woman got to the gate and the guard there started searching, Levin returned toward the city. Jewish police ran after him and brought him to the gate guard. The woman, meanwhile, disappeared.

The shooting. Levin begged them to release him because he was not kosher.[22] The Jewish police didn't want to get involved. When they took Levin by force, he turned a revolver on them. Locked up in a cell, they wanted to get him out of there. He started shooting, and the policeman Moyshe Gingold (a refugee from Warsaw) fell in a puddle of blood. The ghetto chief and the police chief were sent for. Levin refused to put down his weapon, and the ghetto chief opened fire and Levin soon fell dead.

How does it look from outside? For the German authorities, this would once again be proof that Jews are arming. But once again, the Jewish police took a position as protector of the ghetto against arming itself. Soon several representatives of the district commissar and the Gestapo came into the ghetto. Both saw this as the "bravery" of the Jewish police and decided that it was an internal matter. The revolver of the Jew Khayim Levin was turned over to the German authorities. The revolver of the police chief, Mr. Gens, became a "brave weapon" against the Jewish ghetto conspiracy.

The impression. The events have made a tremendous impression here in the

22. Kruk may mean that Levin did not have the proper documents.

ghetto. No one regretted anybody's death. There isn't even a question of that. . . . Everyone pondered one thing—how will the Germans react? But as soon as they learned that the Germans didn't take it to heart, the ghetto passed by the events as a side issue.

This is how the ghetto is!

Who are the victims? The policeman Moyshe Gingold came from Warsaw as a refugee. In the ghetto he became a policeman and served in the First Police Precinct. He was a quiet and serious fellow.

Khayim Levin was the former chief of the Święciany Jewish police. He was in his thirties and unfortunately could not boast of a fine past. People say that during the time of Lithuanian rule, he was a "stool pigeon." His role as chief of police is not clear at all. When the Jews were expelled from Święciany, he went wild with a group of his friends. He was constantly in motion, moving from Święciany to Vilna and on from Vilna. The group carried weapons, gathered groups in the forest. Such a person was the deceased Khayim Levin.

The funeral and the parade. At about 11 in the morning, in the second courtyard of Rudnicka 6, almost under the window of the apartment of the ghetto chief, a catafalque was set up on which the body of the shot policeman was laid. The coffin was surrounded by a police honor guard and several ghetto residents, for whom this is an event.

At 12:30, police units in closed ranks begin to gather. All kinds of ghetto police appeared: first precinct, second, gate guard, labor police, policewomen, and simple ghetto residents.

It is exactly 1 o'clock. The police form a gauntlet around the coffin. A command is heard: "Attention!" And Mr. Gens and Mr. Dessler appear, the ghetto chief and the police chief. The cantor takes the podium and sings a chapter of Psalms. The ghetto chief takes the lectern. He says:

> Today I used my police uniform, and today, for the first time, I shot a man—a man, but not a Jew. A Jew only by circumcision. In fact, a stranger. If he were a Jew, he would not have done that. This is the second victim among the ghetto police. The first fell by the hands of an Aryan,[23] this one by a so-called Jew.

The speaker says that there will be more police victims, not only from outside. The most awful enemy is internal here. The speaker promises that the police will not stop because of victims, for the ghetto is too dear to them. Then he appeals to everyone: "Today is Shavuoth [Festival of Weeks]. Help carry the yoke of the ghetto. May the life of the policeman fallen today serve as an example to us."

Police Chief Dessler spoke, and so did the police commissar of the first precinct, of the deceased, Mr. [Nosn] Ring. The cantor chanted "El Male Rahamim," and the coffin, carried by police officers, was borne to the gate with great pomp.

23. I.e., Nosn Schlossberg, who was shot by partisans.

There the casket was put on the [funeral] wagon and, accompanied by several police units, the funeral procession marched off to the Jewish cemetery.

About the dead Khayim Levin. An investigation took place about the dead Khayim Levin. First, the body was closed in the "cold room," and no one was allowed in. Soon the decision was changed, and all present were observed, and those who reacted as if they were relatives were arrested on the spot and sent for interrogation.

The Jewish police, apparently, had recently learned a great deal and brought all their knowledge into the Vilna Ghetto.

Khayim Levin's funeral took place on the 10th, the day after the funeral of his victim, Moyshe Gingold.

Painful results. Several painful results begin in the ghetto. First of all, arrests occur among so-called foreigners from Święciany and Grodno. Searches and bigger raids begin. Then come several speeches in which the ghetto representatives talk of exterminating the "conspirators" who bring weapons into the ghetto. They accuse the newcomers who enjoy the hospitality of the Vilna Ghetto and want to bring misfortune on the ghetto.

In speeches to the Brigadier Council and at the performance of Brit Ivrit,[24] they even speak of a planned assassination of the ghetto chief and of the consequences of such a thing.

Until late last night, searches and raids took place. Entire courtyards were locked, and there were searches for people, weapons, and other things.

THREE REVOLVERS AND ONE HAND GRENADE

I learn that in one place, two revolvers and a hand grenade were recently found.[25] Hidden in a dung heap in another place—one "machine." The cases were hushed up.

HISTORIC MEETINGS, HISTORIC DECISIONS

If not for the specific tragic situation in which the ghetto finds itself, none of our group would have agreed to cooperate with the Revisionists, Shomrim,[26] and Comm[unists]. Not wanting to remain isolated, we, too, were forced to join the FPO. Naturally, the Reds took over the institution. They harnessed the partners in the supposed organized self-defense while turning it into a fortress of their own. Having no alternative, our group swallowed all that.

Since the recent cases of weapons in the ghetto, apparently the Jewish police, feeling that any armed force can also be a threat against them, have begun to withdraw from the position they had taken so far and have undertaken an Aktion

24. The Hebrew League.

25. There is a discrepancy between the heading and the text. It is not clear whether there were two revolvers or three.

26. I.e., Ha-Shomer ha-Tzair, leftist Socialist Zionists, led by Abba Kovner.

against individual members of the organization. First came a decision that Abba [Kovner] and others have to leave Vilna and go to a camp. After long negotiations, the ghetto rulers calmed down, and apparently they didn't mean "them" (the Communists . . .), but they expel only the . . . Revisionists.

WHAT IS DECIDED?

Therefore, the org. decides that every such action is an attack on the entire ghetto cadre[27] and that such things must be opposed strongly. It goes so far that the org., as we have reported, decides to mount an active resistance.

Our opinion:[28]

1. The behavior of the police is a logical consequence of involving it in the activity of the ghetto cadre. The police now feel the org. as a hostile political force and want to paralyze its activity.
2. Every kind of armed resistance against the Jewish police is a provocation for the "outside" and can lead to complete liquidation of the ghetto.
3. Our participation in the org. means taking on the martyr's role of being able to die like men. An armed struggle with the ghetto authorities means bringing about the downfall of the ghetto.
4. We must try to influence the ghetto police. But by no means to allow a social and historical crime of exploding the ghetto.

These theses were decided 3 against 2. Our representative in the org. of the ghetto cadre stated that although he is for the accepted decision, he thinks that, unfortunate as it may be, we must submit to the adopted decision [of the FPO]. The minority thinks that in case of a stand on the decision [of a struggle against the ghetto police], we must go so far as to leave [the organization] and create our own armed group. But our representative thinks that he cannot depart from the accepted decision and cannot raise the question again. Hence he refuses to carry out the accepted decision. There is a scandal. The meeting, which lasted two evenings, is interrupted.

GHETTO POLICE ARE ARMED!

Once we wrote that a group of Jewish police received weapons. We knew positively that Dessler and Gens [had weapons]. Later the police were apparently given a loan of 45 rubber sticks. Against whom is this, if not the ghetto population? Some time later, brass knuckles were distributed among the police. Now, because of the recent shootings in the ghetto, certain policemen apparently received the right to bear arms in the ghetto.

Against whom is this?

27. Here and below, "org." means the FPO, and "ghetto cadre" means the staff of the FPO.
28. I.e., the opinion of the Bundist organization.

A HEBREW PERFORMANCE

Two days ago, the festive premiere of the Hebrew dramatic studio in the ghetto took place in the Ghetto Theater. David Pinsky's "The Eternal Jew" was performed. As we said, the students, most of them policemen, performed. The director was the Yiddish artist Bergolski (?); conductor, V. Durmashkin; choreographer, Mrs. Gina Gerstein; decorations, the artist Sher.

Given ghetto conditions, the performance makes a good impression, especially the mass scenes of the first act. The policeman Pesker and the policewoman Miss Bernstein act well. In general, the performance was a success.

GHETTO WORKSHOPS WORK IN THREE SHIFTS

As we have noted, work in the ghetto workshops goes on in three shifts. It was started by the weaving shop, where 540 women are now working. The workshops make straw slippers for the soldiers.

GHETTO INDUSTRY

The sock-knitting shop in the ghetto has now received a big order. As many as 100 women now work there.

The big tailor workshop is now filling German military orders.

THE GHETTO BEACH AND THE GHETTO SCHOOLS

The beach is open.[29] On Thursday, the 10th of this month, the first outing of the ghetto schools took place.

Ghetto schools are now open longer, first, because compulsory schooling has brought many new students into the school. Second, many children stay home all day to protect the house; only when parents come home from work can children go to school.

17 IN THE FOREST

Raids in ghetto buildings in a search for weapons have recently become a daily phenomenon. Yesterday, during such a raid, a fellow was arrested who was suspected of coming from the part[isans] and was badly beaten. He, however, demanded one thing: take him to Mr. Jacob [Gens]. There it became clear that he was a part[isan]. He had been sent to people here, and he demands that he be allowed to carry out his orders.

The result: "Go, if this is what you want. If we are in danger, come help us"—thus Jacob refused and didn't understand his own naiveté. Released, with a blessing for the road, the fellow left the gate this morning with 17 people. At the gate, there was a special guard to make sure everything was in order.

The group included a few in police uniforms, who even had work permits say-

29. The Vilna rivers and beaches were outside the boundaries of the ghetto.

ing that they travel as Jews to work. Two of them were Vilna Ghetto police and two were from Oszmiana. One of the four is from Grodno. More groups are leaving in the next few days.

JUNE 14 [1943]

THE FPO CONFLICT IS TURNED INTO A CONFLICT BETWEEN US

The meeting about the argument [in the] FPO was interrupted by the scandal that Comrade Hersh [Gutgestalt] made in reply to the chairman, who is also our representative in the FPO, [when the chairman said] that he will not submit to our decision. Afterward, it was decided that not the chairman but Herman [Kruk] will assume responsibility for calling the next meeting.

THE MEETING

Herman [Kruk] opened and proposed:

1. Because of yesterday's conflict about the party chairman's refusal to carry out the accepted decision, the chairman must submit his resignation. Because he doesn't do this by himself, he is asked to give up his mandate voluntarily.
2. Because of the difficult question and the composition of the committee of five, he feels compelled to propose that the committee should be enlarged again, from five to seven persons, and that the next candidates should be added to it—Leyke [Yashunski] and Berl [Widman].

The chairman does not accept the proposal to submit his resignation. The majority decided with two for, two abstaining, and one against that the chairman must give up his mandate.

The two new members are co-opted, and it is decided to call a meeting to deal with the present situation, make a decision on the issue of the FPO, and eventually constitute themselves.

After a long discussion, the enlarged committee decided with two votes (Shmulke [Kapliński], Berl [Widman]) that they are in complete agreement with the position of the FPO. Three (Abrasha [Chwojnik], Leyke [Yashunski], and Simon [Palevsky]) are in agreement with the position of Abrasha (chairman), except that he should do whatever he can so that the decision [of the FPO staff] is not implemented. Members Herman [Kruk] and Hersh [Gutgestalt] abstain from voting and do not propose anything new.

It was also decided, with a majority of five against the votes of Hersh and Herman, that the chairman must not resign and will be returned to his office.

JUNE 15 [1943]

MORE ABOUT THE FPO CONFLICT

After yesterday's decision, Hersh and Herman demanded an extra meeting of the committee,[30] where Herman made the following statement:

> Our profound conviction is that the last decision of the enlarged committee, accepted on the 13th of this month, is dangerous for the Vilna Ghetto. With the decision, the committee assumed responsibility for actions that were not carefully thought through.
>
> Hence we consider it necessary to state that regardless of the decision of the committee, we maintain our conviction that:
>
> 1. In the current war period, the armed force of the ghetto must engage in struggle only to protect the lives and honor of the ghetto inhabitants from an outside attack whose purpose is to destroy the ghetto.
> 2. The armed force of the ghetto must not be turned against the Jewish ghetto authorities and must not be used for actions outside the ghetto.
> 3. The armed force in the ghetto is too weak to fulfill its mission successfully without support from the ghetto population. The objective of the armed force is not to save it; it can save only its honor. In the present circumstances, an armed struggle with the ghetto police would isolate the fighting organization, create a common front of the ghetto population and the ghetto police, and instead of an heroic death of the Vilna Jewish population, would lead to a painful and horrible fratricide, which the Gestapo would finish.
> 4. An insignificant number of Jews remains in Eastern Europe. Every blood sacrifice must be weighed and measured. Warding off the danger of death is a gain which, in a favorable development of the war, can save those who are still left alive. It must also be taken into account that after the demise of Jewish Warsaw, Vilna has remained one of the largest Jewish communities in Eastern Europe and the only remaining capital of the Bund in Poland.
> 5. Unable to agree with the latest decision of the committee, which contradicts our above-mentioned conclusions, and not wanting to weaken our forces, we declare that while remaining loyal members of our party, we reserve the right to fight to abolish your decision—while observing all the rules of conspiracy and carrying out the previously mentioned principles of our fighting organization.

[With the committee] depressed and observing that, unfortunately, a faction has been created, the meeting was adjourned.

30. Here and below, this means the committee of the Bund.

The decision, written by the pen of Comrade Hersh [Gutgestalt] and with the mutual redaction of the two of us, was presented orally by Comrade Herman [Kruk] in an abridged form.

JUNE 16 [1943]

THE MOOD IS CHEERFUL

Here in the ghetto, the mood is cheerful. All rumors about liquidation have disappeared for the time being. A rapid building and expansion of the ghetto industry has been going on in the ghetto in recent weeks. Skilled laborers are pulled in from all branches for the enlargement of the ghetto workshops. Mobilization of the labor forces in the ghetto progresses at a fast pace. About 2,500 are working already in the ghetto industry. The work in several workshops is carried on in two or three shifts. Many apartments have been renovated and adapted to the new conditions of big centralized workshops.

Yesterday, District Commissar Hingst and Murer visited the ghetto. Both left very satisfied and "amused" themselves with the ghetto representatives. The ghetto breathed in relief. We ask—for how long? . . .

LUCIAN IN LONDON?

I hear that yesterday, the radio broadcast that at a London convention of the Labor Party, which just took place, Friend Lucjan [Blit] gave a greeting in the name of the Polish Bund.

Lucjan was with me in Vilna as a refugee from Warsaw. From here, he went to "work" [for the party] in Warsaw and was once arrested with two other comrades by the Lithuanian authorities. I then went and freed them on some pretext. Later he set off again, and on the Russian-German border, near Białystok, he was arrested as a Christian. For crossing the border illegally, the Christian Lucjan was sentenced to two [three] years of exile. Twice I succeeded in corresponding with him, even sending him packages. Now comes the happy news that he is in London and is carrying on Bundist social activity.[31]

It warms the heart and evokes the wish that if not us, at least our loved ones are out.

31. After the Sikorski Amnesty, in August 1941, Lucjan Blit was released from a Soviet labor camp and was for some time in the temporary Soviet capital, Kuybishev, where Henryk Erlich and Wiktor Alter also were. After the arrest of Erlich and Alter, Lujian enlisted in the Polish army that was formed in the Soviet Union. He served in the unit that was stationed in Kenimekh, Uzbekistan. In the summer of 1942, he was evacuated to Persia with the Polish army. After the war, he lived in London.

JUNE 18 [1943]

THEY ONLY TRUST JEWS . . .

Recently it is quiet again in the ghetto. As we have written, the ghetto industry is expanding. They're breaking down walls, supporting and non-supporting. No one considers such things. Big factory halls emerge. Big workshops are centralized and . . . it looks as if the calm will set in.

Jews rejoice today: yesterday the Gestapo asked the ghetto police to guard their big garden, on Rosy. Why should Jewish police guard their garden? Apparently they can't trust others now, so they trust only Jews, and especially the Jews of the Vilna Ghetto police. . . .

INTO THE FOREST

People again prepare to go to the forest; a group of comrades again make preparations for that.

A MESSAGE FROM THE AMERICAN YIVO

You have to be in the Vilna Ghetto, you have to have gone through what we have, to see what has become of the local YIVO, to understand what a miracle it is for us to get a message from the American YIVO and, especially, from all those who live there and are rebuilding the trunk of Jewish scholarship.

Dripping with sweat, breathless, Comrade Kalmanowicz dropped in on me today:

"This time good news, the American YIVO is alive!"

What happened?

Kalmanowicz tells me that today, a German from "our" Rosenberg Task Force came to him and gave him this message.

How did the German on the Rosenberg Task Force come to know what is going on with the American YIVO? Apparently our chief, the oft-mentioned Dr. Pohl, got a bundle of American *Forverts* (?) with a report of the YIVO convention there on January 10, 1943![32]

Kalmanowicz says that it was declared at the congress that because the trunk of YIVO has been uprooted, the American YIVO has become the trunk. Friend Kalman[owicz]'s heart is in pain, and tears appear on his aged and wrinkled face. Nevertheless he goes on, his eyes gleaming with joy and satisfaction; he gives me greetings from my childhood friend Moses Kligsberg. He tells me about my prewar chairman of the Cultural League in Poland, Kh. Sh. Kazdan. I learn that many—so many friends and comrades, now in America—carry on their cultural and social activity there.

Kalmanowicz calms down, and we wish each other that we may survive and

32. That was the 17th annual convention of YIVO, in New York on January 8–10, 1943.

tell the world about everything we have gone through, especially the chapter of YIVO. Although fate has been so cruel to us that we are among the burden-bearers of this particular tragic ghetto, we are fortunate and satisfied to know that Jewishness and Yiddishism live and carry on our common ideals. May our future fate lead us happily out of here.

JUNE 19 [1943]

ONE AGAINST THE OTHER

Every kind of totalism has the same nature. Every means justifies the end. No ethics, no restraint—anything goes. Anything to achieve the goal!

The Germans are assembling a Russian Orthodox legion against the Bolsheviks. Nevertheless there are Russian Orthodox who do not stop and who do the work.

If you need to fight the Jewish ghetto in Warsaw and exterminate it, you drive the Polish guards out the gates, and Ukrainians must take their place. In an Aktion in Kovno to catch the so-called deserters who don't want to go to the German army, they use Latvians, and to help them, Jews, Jewish police from the Kovno Ghetto. . . .

Jewish police from the Vilna Ghetto were used to persuade the Święciany and Oszmiana Jews that they were being taken to Kovno, and meanwhile, they were taken along with the Jewish "persuaders" to . . . Ponar to be exterminated (aside from the police, who were taken out of there, safe and sound).

One is used against the other, and all means are proper and holy.

JUNE 20 [1943]

ADDITIONAL AGE GROUPS ARE MOBILIZED

Yesterday an announcement was posted that after the mobilization of those born in the years 1919–1924, those from 1912–1918 and 1925, i.e., from 21 to 25 years old and from 18, are now called.

TWO YEARS OF NAZI OCCUPATION

On the 22nd of this month, it will be two years since the beginning of the German-Soviet war. Several celebrations in connection with that are organized in Vilna and Kovno.

THE ENGLENDER FAMILY

The Englender family lived for many years in Podbrodzie. Arn Englender was the correspondent of the Vilna *Tog* and the Warsaw *Naye folkstsaytung*. His wife and daughter were two good Bundists. For years, he was interested in folklore and published several studies in the YIVO-bleter. Recently, forced to leave Podbrodzie, he went to peasant friends in Niemenczyn, where they hid him. On Wednesday, the 16th of this month, he was brought to Łukiszki with his wife and daughter. The crime: hiding in the area forbidden for Jews. The entire family is now threatened with capital punishment. In the ghetto, they do whatever they can [to save them].[33]

DEATH SENTENCES FOR JEWS

People say that several death sentences for Jews have recently been issued, including against Weiskopf, the former popular ghetto king, who was arrested for selling furs. Świrski, who was accused of buying a revolver, and several others were also sentenced. Nine new death sentences against ghetto Jews have been counted. A few dozen Christians are in the last group [of arrestees].

PONEVEZH

The latest issue of *Geto-yedies* (June 20, 1943) tells with satisfaction that the district commissar "allowed" letters [from] the workers sent away to Ponevezh to be sent [to] their families in the Vilna Ghetto twice a month.

The first such letter has already been allowed to arrive. It is provided with 52 signatures.

But he allowed. . . .

JUNE 23 [1943]

A TRIP FROM VILNA TO MINSK

The Vilna Ghetto has learned to look suspiciously at everything that happens around it. In every German order, they try to seek meaning, to interpret, and to outwit.

33. Englender is not the correct name. Kruk certainly means the Eyngeltsin family. Arn Eyngeltsin was born in Podbrodzie in 1887, studied in the Slobodka Yeshiva, and lived with his uncle, the ritual slaughterer Szklarski (father of the publisher Moyshe-Shmuel Szklarski). During World War I, he was active in Poltava, where he was a refugee and became the secretary of the Bund and of the Cultural League. Later he returned to Podbrodzie and became a passionate collector of Yiddish folklore, one of the most devoted friends of the YIVO in Vilna. His wife, Khaye-Sore, née Fein, was also a devoted cultural activist and had a great interest in Yiddish folklore and Yiddish folk songs. The volume *Pinkes,* published in Vilna in 1913 by S. Niger, contains a few dozen folk songs sent by the Eyngeltsins. Both enriched the folklore collection of YIVO with hundreds of valuable items. Especially rich was the collection of folk songs they compiled, many of which were published in the YIVO publications. Their daughter, Leye, studied in the Podbrodzie Jewish grammar school and later in Vilna. Arn Eyngeltsin was killed during the slaughter of Jews in the town of Kobylniki. His wife and daughter were saved from the slaughter and hid with peasants. But in the end, they were caught and killed.

Suddenly an order comes from the Gestapo about sending 60 skilled workers from Vilna to Minsk. With the reinforced industrialization, Vilna lacks skilled workers. The Gestapo knows this. So how can we explain the latest order about Minsk? A suspicion—perhaps this is only a pretext? Perhaps they mean another Aktion? It doesn't make sense—an Aktion of 50 skilled workers? Or perhaps they will let the 50 go so that later, when the ghetto learns that everything is fine, they can entice more, much more?

This is how ghetto minds operate, and recently this has been the course of thoughts of Vilna Ghetto Jews.

To calm the spirits and their own consciences concerning the order about the 50, two representatives of the ghetto are sent to investigate the workplace and the conditions for the 50 on the spot.

How can they send them to investigate? Do they have the choice to refuse? And is such an "investigation" not to be interpreted badly? But in the Vilna Ghetto, lately, everything is possible. Connections here have become so extensive and . . . entangled that often there isn't a thing here that is understandable, and not [just] one impossibility is wholly possible here and capable of being carried out. In the labyrinth of incomprehensible things is also the case of Minsk.

Who are the two agents delegated from Vilna to Minsk? One is a representative of the Jewish Labor Office; the other, the police commissar of the labor police, Mr. Towbin.

The Gestapo issues a permit [stating] that Towbin travels as a Christian, without a patch, and he, the Christian, takes a Jew with him, the representative of the Labor Office, Mr. Mintz.

Why one as a Christian? Why does the Gestapo agree? Why the whole game?

Both leave and come back with . . . nothing. In Minsk, they were not allowed into the ghetto and first of all were informed that they were not permitted to talk to anyone. They were almost locked up in a room of the Gestapo and, in time, were told that the workers were needed in Minsk for various jobs.

This is the result of the investigation!

What did they see and what did they bring from that trip? As I learn on the side, they say that Minsk is destroyed. Bombed and burned buildings at every step. The road to Minsk is also typical in that, at every step, you come on many overturned, burned, and damaged train cars. Signs of sabotage or partisan work.

In the Minsk Ghetto, 3,000–4,000 Jews now live. Next to the ghetto is another ghetto. In the first ghetto are Russian Jews from Minsk, Slutsk, Baranovitsh, etc. In the second, there are altogether 1,500 German and Czech Jews. Each ghetto has its own Judenrat. The leader of the first ghetto is a Vilna Jew, a certain Zamsteinman. The ghettos give the impression of two separate worlds. Relations between the two ghettos are cold. The Germans relate more amiably to the German Jews; to the Russians they relate better as labor elements.

Russian Jews wear round patches and under them a white cloth with a number; the Germans, a star of David with the inscription "Jude" and also underneath a cloth with a number.

There are many women, children, and old people in the ghettos (?).

The German Jews are silent and do not talk. You really can't get a word out of them. It seems they received orders to that effect.

The appearance of the Jews is not bad. A kilo of bread costs 70 rubles there. In Vilna, 50–60 rubles. You see Jews going to work in columns, three in a row. A German soldier accompanies the columns.

The Vilna Jews who are still in Minsk are mostly from the former Elektrit.[34]

They obtained all the information from a Russian Jew who works in the Minsk Gestapo building, where the two agents spent all their time and achieved nothing.

JUNE 22 [?] [1943]

A KEG OF POWDER

The ghetto is like a powder keg. It can explode any minute. Such is the mind set. Any trifle can turn into a dreadful account [destruction?]. The FPO does everything so that things will not settle down. The amm[unition] dumps increase from day to day.

Herman[35] is back in his profession—he washes, makes stamps, changes, etc.

AN ACT OF SABOTAGE

Yesterday the railroad bridge that goes over Ostrobramska Street was destroyed. Two Lithuanians were killed.

JUNE 24 [1943]

THEY COME AND THEY GO

Lately it has become a regular thing: people are leaving the ghetto. Suddenly you find out that so-and-so is missing, and it is clear—he has left. Everyone admires the leaving and everyone envies them.

A few days ago, another group left the ghetto. Some simply went out into the world, some left for the forest.

This morning a group went out, among them more policemen, including the

34. A radio factory in Vilna that belonged to the Chwoles brothers. In 1939, when the Red Army occupied Vilna, they nationalized and evacuated the Elektrit factory and many of its staff to Minsk.

35. Kruk is speaking about himself.

police officer Fried and his wife and the policeman Friedman. Five men came from the forest and took out 15. They come and they go. This is what has already been set in place.

HEBRAIZATION

The process of Hebraization goes on in a sharper form. Among the little conflicts and quarrels inside the ghetto are also conflicts concerning Hebraization. The local children, for whom this new thing is a burden, are rebelling.

Here I attach a document: the children call on one another not to submit to it. *The document is missing.*

JUNE 25 [1943]

JEWISH VICTIMS IN PONAR

Yesterday a few Jews were shot in Ponar. Among them were the once very popular Weiskopf, whom we have already mentioned; Świrski from Kailis, for buying weapons; along with two children, one 7-year-old girl and one 8-year-old girl. Altogether, 17 persons were killed yesterday, Jews and Christians.

FRIEDMAN IS FREE

Friedman and two others, who were once arrested supposedly for trading in weapons, were released yesterday.

BATTLES WITH PARTISANS

Big battles between partisans and Germans took place today on the Michaliszki-Swir stretch. The result is not yet known.

AN ASSEMBLY OF POLICE

Yesterday, in connection with the exit of the already known Jewish policemen, an assembly of the ghetto police took place. The head of the ghetto and the police commandant explained how great is the danger that policemen are also leaving their positions and going to the forest. If the Germans found out about this, they would put an end to the ghetto. They consider every such action as a danger to the ghetto.

The police listened, were silent, and went on their way.

NEW GROUPS ARE FORMING

I discover that new groups are forming to go to the forests. Everything is ready, and they are only waiting for the "comers" and "leaders."

JUNE 26 [1943]

A NEW CHAPTER

Today our ghetto again experienced a new chapter. This time, the ghetto has entered a new era: if our ghetto has held out as it has so far, this new chapter can make us explode and destroy ourselves with our own hands.

What is happening?

For a long time, we have said that the authorities in the ghetto have been very anxious about the organized self-defense movement, about those who "are going to the forest" and those who are arming themselves. We have already written about the behavior of the latter groups, about the threat to exile the leaders of the FPO and the compromises concerning that.

Now the most recent: yesterday noon, the newly appointed commissar of the criminal police, Aster, comes to Glazman's home and orders him to take his things because, by order of the commandant, he is to be sent to Rzesza. Glazman declares he will not submit. Aster [says] that that puts him in a difficult position because he will be forced to take steps to carry out his decision. He left and soon came back with three tough guys from the criminal police, including the famous bully Seidel and Berke Mieszczański.

Glazman remains firm: he will not carry out the decision. Seidel declares that he must use force. G[lazman] answers that they can take him only by force. When Seidel orders his assistants to "take" him, nobody moves. Only when their commander threatens consequences do all three throw themselves on Glazman. A struggle ensues and they succeed in handcuffing him, and thus, beating him, they lead him through the street to the police station.

It isn't hard to imagine the impression this picture made in the ghetto. The cadre was soon mobilized. Special groups were created. In accord with the accepted principles (see our previous entries), it was quickly decided that if he were banished by force, they would resist.

At about 4 in the afternoon, a little wagon rushed out of the closed gate at Rudnicka 6, with Glazman handcuffed and chained to the car (!). The car drove quickly toward the gate. The street was cleared of people. The barrier was raised and everything was ready. Suddenly, on Rudnicka, between 14 and 17, people came running out of the gates, stopped the wagon, and, surrounding it in a flash, threw themselves on the police escort. A second group cut the chain binding Glazman to the car.

Most of the policemen, who had been standing in the street during the events, disappeared. Some were beaten and escaped. The street was empty of police and ruled by the so-called assassins. Glazman was soon free, and with a piece of chain, which was still hanging on him, [. . .] the group led him to Strashun [Street].

IN THE POLICE

Meanwhile, there is turmoil among the police. The first "test of strength" between the licentious police and the ghetto cadre has shown the nothingness of the ghetto authorities. They do have one force—the Gestapo and the district commissar. The policemen, who have not yet lost their heads, some of whom are in fact in contact with the ghetto cadre or are just decent people, moved off to the side. Some policemen even stood with the "attackers." The rest, "simple servants," wanted to save their skin and dispersed.

Rudnicka and other streets are ruled by the attackers. The police commanders, shaken by events, are lost. Their first order was to clear the streets, ostensibly because Murer had come. About 20 minutes after the event, police appeared in the streets and started clearing.

WHERE IS GLAZMAN?

Glazman was taken to the ghetto library, where the staff of the cadre was soon assembled. The entire street and the building is guarded by activists.

AN INCIDENT

Meanwhile, a few policemen came out of the ghetto prison, not knowing what was going on, and tried to throw themselves onto the assembled people. Policeman Fleshel threw himself on someone who looked suspicious, but in a wink a saw came down on his head and he was covered with blood.

NEGOTIATIONS

Apparently the ghetto leadership understood that, with their recent disgraceful action, they had set themselves against not only the organization but also the entire ghetto. But to save their prestige, they contacted the staff,[36] and the ghetto chief personally guaranteed that nothing would happen to Glazman. But, to maintain his prestige, he demanded that Glazman be sent to Rzesza today, and then the matter would not be aggravated. Wanting to avoid further collisions, the staff agreed to give up Glazman with guarantees. At the same time, the staff was invited to further negotiations (?).

MEANWHILE A CALM

At about 7 in the evening, the street cheered the departing Glazman. The ghetto did not understand exactly what was going on. According to the majority opinion, this was a quarrel between the Revisionists, according to others, a personal war between Gens and Glazman. Legends and old wives' tales are going around. But few know the real truth.

36. Of the FPO.

ACCOMPLISHMENTS

Today has an absolutely historical meaning for the ghetto. It was the first contest between the not-yet-dead ghetto society and the empty hollowness of the ghetto rulers. The street said that the police are undermined. The danger that the disagreements inside the ghetto will explode the ghetto hovers over everyone. For the time being, the incident is settled.

Returning to our p[arty]-conclusions and our resolutions about avoiding clashes with the ghetto authorities, we now see where that will lead the ghetto.

MEMORIAL SERVICE FOR DR. HERTS KOWARSKI

This evening, in the building of the Children's Club, a memorial service was held for the second anniversary of the death of Dr. Herts Kowarski.

The group of Jewish doctors, along with those remaining of the former school activists of TSBK, where Kowarski was active, have not forgotten their friend even in the ghetto.

Some of those who took part in the evening were the teacher Y. Senicki, chairman; the speakers were Dr. E. Sedlis—about Dr. Kowarski as a doctor—and the former director of the Jewish academic gymnasium, Turbowicz—about Dr. Kowarski as a cultural activist. The painter-worker Berl Widman and Dr. Jabrow told memories. N. Lubocki also talked about Kowarski as a friend to children.

The memorial service was a success and brought a breeze from Vilna in the old days.[37]

JUNE 28 [1943]

AFTER THE EVENTS

Today, two days after the events, we know that late at night, at the home of the ghetto chief, there was a meeting of the ghetto rulers and the staff. The discussion was very superficial. Every time the staff tried to raise the talk to a certain social level, the "rulers" dragged it back down into the mud. Even more than ever, it is clear that those people do not comprehend the situation or understand the surrounding world. Negotiations until 2 in the morning did not produce any thing.

Yesterday, Sunday the 27th, as every Sunday, there was a workers' evening in the Ghetto Theater, organized systematically by the Brigadier Council. Among

37. The YIVO Archives (Kaczerginski-Sutzkever Collection, no. 530) contain the appeal to the police commander of the ghetto to allow a closed evening (by invitation) on the second anniversary of the death of Dr. Kowarski. The appeal was made by Dr. Leyb Pomerantz and Alter Mechanik on behalf of the friends of the deceased.

other things, Moyshe Leyb Halpern's poem "We Are Not Adults, We Did Not Measure Up" was read, followed by Leye Rudnicka's poem "Red Snow." The chief, who has been very nervous lately, jumped up, cursed the chairman of the Brigadier Council, Mr. Kapłan-Kapłański, and dissolved the assembly.

Why did this happen? I interpret it with the "intelligence" of the chief. He was convinced that Moyshe Leyb Halpern wrote the poem "We Are Not Adults, We Did Not Measure Up" here in the ghetto.[38] He couldn't control himself and dissolved the assembly.

A GHETTO DEFENSIVE

For a long time, they have "kept an eye" on the local social activists. No money is spared for this purpose. Now we write a list of agents who do this work: the house managers Anigst (the former hero and gold thief on Lidzki Street), Emes, Katz Ite (Karmelicka 5), Mrs. Ratner (Niemiecka 25), Mrs. Shneling; the policemen Levin Dovid, Margolis, and Seidel; Schacher; the musician Oppenheim; Mrs. Dr. Kuceniacka; and Kolke Niemański.

Some agents and subagents are active in the big units, too.

OUTRAGED

"They" do not learn or want to learn. After the fall of their police prestige, Gens strolls on Rudnicka Street at sundown Saturday and, while walking, visits one of his recently fired commissars and confidantes, his party comrade [Moyshe] Brauze,[39] threatening to teach him something someday. . . .

Incidentally, all the bitterness comes from the fact that Brauze also took an active part in the Glazman affair. That's why he was fired from his police post.

The same evening, the chief spoke at the theater performance of "Peshe from Reshe" and, with a stream of small invectives, insulted those who had just beaten him, the very ones he invited to his home after the performance. . . .

All day Sunday, he ran around the streets and searched all those who had their hands in their pockets. People say that he hit three minors on Rudnicka Street just because they dared to keep their hands in their pockets. . . .

Thus, apparently, the chief wants to restore his lost prestige, and thus, apparently, he wants to fight against the assassination supposedly being prepared here for him.

Struck in the head. You can't come to any other conclusion!

38. This is impossible, as the Yiddish poet M. L. Halpern, of New York, died in 1932.

39. Born in Lithuania. He graduated from the Hebrew gymnasium in Ponevezh and was a student at Vilna University. He also graduated from an officer school in the Lithuanian army. One of the active Revisionists in the ghetto, he served in the police and, at the same time, was in the FPO. While in Glazman's unit, he was killed in Narocz Forest on Yom Kippur, 1943.

HEADS FLY . . .

Struck in the head. That really is it. People joke here: the great French Revolution on the backdrop of the Vilna Ghetto. "The gods are thirsty," etc.

After Saturday's events, after the impulsive behavior of Gens and his assistants and advisers, there was a purge in and out of the police ranks.

Suspected of participating in Saturday's "assassination," officers [Ayzik] Averbukh and Lutek Salzwasser were fired from the police, both being Glazman's sort of Revisionist. Averbukh is in fact a participant in Saturday's events. Others fired from the police were: Miriam Bernstein (criminal police), Peskin, Sturman, Lunski of the Gate Guard, Warszawczyk of the Labor Police, Anolik of the First Police Precinct, and Mire Goniądzka, secretary of the prosecutor.[40]

SANCTIONS

The police command is not satisfied with that. It has recently become fashionable to demote, punish, and exile from the ghetto to forced labor. This was how the foreman Commissar Brauzas was dealt with, as well as all those who were fired from the police. This morning, they were dragged out of their beds, and some were sent off to Porubanek to work in a stone quarry, the rest to other hard work.

THE DIRECTOR OF THE CULTURAL DEPARTMENT IS FIRED

Gens learned that his friend [Bern]stein was also connected with a group of ghetto activists; in addition, the policeman Friedman, of the same group, has gone to [the forest]. Hence the recently appointed director of the Cultural [Department, Leo Bernstein] was fired from his position. The teacher Dimentstein was [appointed] director.[41]

40. All those fired were Revisionists who had been brought into the police by Glazman. Later, when Gens took steps against the underground movement, they were removed one by one. Miriam Bernstein (who should be distinguished from her namesake, the prominent teacher and Communist) worked in the criminal police. Born in Lithuania, she studied at Vilna University; was a member of the FPO; played a leading role in Pinsky's "The Eternal Jew," performed by the Hebrew Dramatic Studio in the ghetto; and was killed in Narocz Forest. Gamke Shturman and Khayim Lunski were both in the partisan movement. Lunski (or Luski) did special services: as a policeman in the gate guard, he participated in smuggling weapons; while in Glazman's unit, he was killed in Narocz Forest. Mire Goniądzka, born in Lithuania, was a member of the FPO; she was killed in winter 1944 during a partisan action in Narocz Forest. (Biographical information is from Lazar 1950.)

41. This is a mistake in the name. The newly appointed director of the Cultural Department was named Yisroel Dimentman. Born in Węgrów, Poland, he came to Kovno in his youth, graduated from the Hebrew Gymnasium, and later studied at Kovno University. He belonged to the Socialist-Zionist movement. He was killed at Klooga, Estonia, in September 1944. For his biography, see Dworzecki 1948:270–271.

■ ■ ■ ■ ■ ■

JUNE 29 [1943]

MINSK

The issue of Minsk is again alive. Today another announcement was posted about 50 various skilled laborers for Minsk. It can be predicted that no one will be eager, and it is certain that the ghetto administration will be forced to appoint people to go. In this regard, the chief summoned a member of the leadership of the ghetto cadre today to reach an understanding that they won't make trouble in this Aktion. The answer was that they weren't interested in anything the police and ghetto administration did as long as it wasn't an Aktion that threatened the integrity of the ghetto. As can be seen from that conversation, the ghetto chief wants to start a course of mutual understanding.

GHETTO CENSOR

From a letter of June 21, 1943, from the Cultural Department, I learn that the responsible censor of the Cultural Department is Dr. Tsemakh Feldstein, incidentally the editor of the official ghetto organ.

BEARDS AND MUSTACHES

By order of the ghetto chief, all those with beards and mustaches must get rid of them.

Why?

INSTEAD OF MEAT

Instead of meat for its residents, the ghetto received cattle heads. The ghetto residents grabbed them like hot cakes. . . .

STAR OF DAVID AND SOVIET STAR

Today the head of the Rosenberg Task Force got a new problem. He is interested in knowing if there is a connection between the star of David and the Soviet five-pointed star. . . .

HOW MANY INHABITANTS DOES THE GHETTO NUMBER NOW

As of today, the ghetto numbers 19,989 persons.[42]

42. A secret report sent by the *Reichskomissar für das Ostland* to the central German authorities included information on the situation of Jewish ghettos in his district for April–May 1943. Point 5 says: "In the ghettos of Vilna and Kovno, during the period of the report, the workshops have shown a significantly expanded activity. This is favorable to the Wehrmacht, which carries out its orders there. First of all, this concerns the production of uniforms, cooking utensils, and shoes. . . . The demand for Jewish labor goes far beyond this number. It has become necessary to

HOW BIG IS THE LABOR FORCE OF THE GHETTO

I learn that the labor force of the ghetto in the past two weeks has risen by almost 2,000. As of the 20th of this month, 13,247 people worked here, which amounts to about [66] percent of the population. Soon the labor force will have to reach [?] percent.

■ ■ ■ ■ ■ ■

JUNE 30 [1943]

A DARK DAY

[The end of the original page is torn. From the lines that can be read, the "dark day" apparently concerns the labor camp in Biała Waka, where 6 Jews escaped into the forest. On the next page, we see that 67 Jews were shot as a result.]

[. . .] escapees torn away from the more than 300 Jews—67 and they were shot on the spot.

There is no more precise information yet.

MINSK

By last night, only one person had registered to work in Minsk. At night, the police, using a prepared list, arrested 40 skilled workers and their families. Now, as I write these lines, all those arrested are in the ghetto jail, and a final selection is taking place. Women and children cling to the barred windows of the jail; around Strashun Street 6 and on the sports field, friends and relatives gather, some with the idea of rescuing their loved ones from being sent to Minsk, and some with a bundle or something to eat.

Once again (for the nth time), a wind of death and destruction has blown over the ghetto. The ghetto has a dark day today.

■ ■ ■ ■ ■ ■

JULY 1 [1943]

THE MINSK PEOPLE ARE RELEASED

Yesterday, at 11 (A.M.), the information suddenly came that the Vilna Ghetto is released from the order to send 50 workers to Minsk. Those who were captured, and locked in the ghetto jail, gathered around the barred jail windows and begged for help to be rescued "from the misfortune." The order didn't reach the jail until about 11:30. The joy is indescribable.

---

create additional groups. In the future, 400 Jewish laborers are to be sent from the Vilna Ghetto because of the scarcity of laborers in Kovno. . . . The population of the ghettos is as follows: Kovno, 16,000; Vilna, 20,300; Šiauliai, 4,770" (YIVO Archives, Berliner Collection).

67 IN BIAŁA WAKA

Now we know precisely about the sad events in Biała Waka. Sixty-seven persons were murdered there, including 17 men, 43 women, and 7 children. This was done from a list compiled by the local Lithuanian police.

I learn that the Gestapo wanted the Aktion to be done with the participation of 40 Jewish policemen from Vilna. The police somehow got out of it, so the Aktion was carried out by the German SD.

MURER IS OFF TO THE FRONT

Everyone and everything comes to an end. We see no end to our bitter situation. Yesterday Murer also came to an end. He, too, is going away to the front and is replaced by his deputy, Lakner. For the ghetto, it is all the same. The ghetto is tired by now of thinking and worrying. Murer or Lakner—it's all the same.

A NEW JEWISH EXPERT OF THE GESTAPO

The Jewish expert of the Gestapo, Mayer, has [gone to the front] and was replaced by a new one from Riga. The new one [. . .] German, is a Gestapo man with a "great" pa[st and is an] actor. During the war, his specialty is [. . .] He held the office of Jewish expert in Paris [and . . .] also in Warsaw and recently in Riga. Now he [has come to Vilna].

[Everyone here is inter]ested in whether this is good or bad for the ghetto.

HIS FIRST APPEARANCE

For the past week, the new Jewish expert has taken pains [to] learn about everything in the ghetto. He has quickly made himself at home and comes privately to the apartments of the ghetto leaders. The director of [the] shoe workshop has already measured him for boots, and yesterday he apparently tried meeting with the ghetto Jews.

He and two assistants stood at the ghetto gate during the return from work. There was a series of searches, which generally went quietly. All units were immediately warned not to "carry" anything, and his first outing didn't yield any results. But therefore, this morning, he went through the ghetto and hit a few Jews for passing by him without greeting him. . . .

JULY 2 [1943]

TIRED AND INDIFFERENT

The ghetto grows more tired and, especially, more indifferent from day to day. Just recently, 67 Jews of Biała Waka have fallen on the altar of our time. The ghetto had many loved ones there but went through the case as if nothing had happened. People swallowed it, and life goes on.

Murer is gone, and maybe the ghetto should thank heaven. The one who humiliated, whipped, and insulted [is gone]—nevertheless, few are interested. Murer has gone and someone else has replaced him and no one is especially upset, either, as we once would have been. The same is true of the new Jewish expert of the Gestapo. Only a few are interested in this issue. The ghetto is cold and indifferent to everything.

"FOREST"—A MASS PHENOMENON

In our area, going to the forest is really a mass phenomenon, something we often consider superfluous to note. As soon as there is some "snatching," Christians run into the forest. Every so-called mobilization is first of all a mobilization for the forest. Jewish youth are going to the forest. Poles, Lithuanians, Byelorussians, Ukrainians—all are saving themselves in the forest. As soon as Lithuanian soldiers smell the front, they run away from the barracks, bag and baggage. Hundreds, perhaps thousands, pay with their lives; and thousands, perhaps tens of thousands, are preparing a bloodbath for the occupier, preparing themselves for a final accounting.

TERROR

Attacks and terrorist acts are now a daily phenomenon. In mid-May, about 300 police and Ukrainians left for the area of Święciany around Hoduciszki to [fight with par]tisans. The Germans came out of that with the greatest defea[t. In the fight,] which lasted a few days, participated [. . .] tanks. About 80 Ukrainians went over to the par[tisans].

AROUND PODBRODZIE

On the Vilna-Daugavpils railroad line, a great many attacks on trains have [recently] taken place. In the course of one [. . .] 15 railroad mechanics [were killed]. In the middle of May, a train with ammunition was [derailed]. There was [. . .].

LIDA

The Lida railroad junction, mainly [. . .] Wolkowysk have recently been attacked massively by partisans. Most police guards and police offices have been transferred to the cities. In Żoludek [?] for example, the Jewish Community Council building was burned. In Iwje, it came to a regular battle between police and partisans. Telephone and telegraph lines were systematically destroyed, along with bridges and other things.

AUTOMATIC WEAPONS

In early June, a train car with automatic weapons left Vilna, going toward Mołodeczno. On the way, the car was opened and the weapons escaped.

ASSASSINATIONS

On June 1, at 3 in the morning, in Mołodeczno, Major Belke was stabbed. He was found with seven deep wounds.

Near Swir, on June 4, an automobile with German railroad workers was attacked. After a brief struggle, three of them were killed, and the fourth, badly wounded, remained on the road. The automobile was driven off by the attackers.

Beyond Troki, at the end of April, an automobile with two Germans and [a] Lithuanian officer was stopped. The Lithuanian got out and tried to talk to the attackers in Russian. Meanwhile, the two Germans ran away. The Lithuanian officer was murdered on the spot.

PONAR

The illegal *Niepodległość*, no. 11, this year, says that 90 Poles and a few Lithuanians were shot in Ponar on May 13. Weiss supervised the execution.

On the model of the Polish *Sztandar Czerwony,*[43] on June 1, there appeared the first issue of a Communist organ: *Tevynes Frontas.*[44]

So Vilna now has three regular illegal publications.

MORE ABOUT THE WARSAW GHETTO

Various rumors are still coming to us about Warsaw. We don't even note them because one contradicts another. Now the illegal Vilna Communist *Sztandar Wolności,* no. 2, of June 1, this year, says that the liquidation of the Warsaw Ghetto began in mid-April, and Jewish resistance was so heavy that the Germans had to use tanks and airplanes. At the end of May, the struggle was still going on and [. . . shots] were heard from the ghetto.

The Vilna *Niepodległość*, no. 11, [writes, among other things,] that "the heroic struggle of the worker-move[ment in the ghe]tto is close to an end. Individ[uals] are still defending themselves. [There re]main about 3,500–5,00 peo[ple." They] also said that the Germans were for[ced to bring to the battle] artillery, airplanes. "The struggle has lasted for two [months. On the] German side, there have been 300 dead and about 1,000 wounded. [The losses among the Uk]rainians are said to be much larger."

A Christian who has just come from [Warsaw says] there is a sign at the Vilna railroad station in Warsaw [. . .]

43. "Red Banner." This should be *Sztandar Wolności,* "Freedom Banner."

44. "The Fatherland Front."

JULY 4 [1943]

A NEW METHOD

The new expert for Jewish affairs in the Gestapo has started on a new track. After the search at the gate, which we have already written about, and after the beatings for not greeting him, which we have already mentioned, he came to the gate on Friday, the 2nd of this month, at 6 in the morning. He stood there for an hour and a half and looked on contentedly as the columns marched out to work, greeting him as he demanded.

Today, Sunday, at his request, an unusual meeting of the brigadiers was called, at which the German expert for ghetto affairs is to make his first appearance.

The ways, as we see, are new and the method brand new.

MORE MILITARY ORDERS

The ghetto workshops are expanding, and so are their military orders. Now new orders arrive: 100,000 pairs of socks and 20,000 pairs of boots.

THE GHETTO IS TO BE ENLARGED SOME MORE

Rudnicka Street is being emptied of ghetto residents, and big ghetto workshops are set up in their place. Negotiations are now conducted for further expansion of the ghetto to the houses of Niemiecka [Street], which were once supposed to have been given to the ghetto. It seems that the ghetto will now be accommodated, and the area will be enlarged.

THE ROSENBERG TASK FORCE UNIT ALSO HAS A SNIFFER

Concerning our June 28 entry about the ghetto defensive, I have learned that there are already sniffers at several units. So, for instance, it is clear that one of the local transport workers, Isser Malkes, is a subsniffer in the unit of the Rosenberg Task Force.

ALMOST WENT OUT INTO THE AIR

[. . .] apparently, our head of the R[osenberg] Task Force was saved from certain death. Recently he was called to the center of the Task Force in Riga. His train was blown up by a partisan act, and his car came out safely. Thank God, we still remain with the chief. . . .

THE 50TH WORKERS' EVENING

The workers' evening, arranged by the Brigadier Council and about which we have often written, celebrated its 50th workers' evening today. Its founder and organizer, Mr. Kapłan-Kapłański, certainly deserves congratulations for that institution.

JULY 6 [1943]

ABOUT THE "NEW METHOD"

[*The rest of the page is badly torn. From the remaining text, it is clear that this entry is about the behavior of the new Jewish expert of the Gestapo.*]

THE FESTIVITY AT THE SPORTS FIELD

The festivity at the sports [field, which took place on the . . .] of July this year, was celebrated with a race. The runners were men, women, and youngsters. After the running, a handball competition took place at the sports field. Mayer's deputy, the new hero, Kittel, was present at all the competitions.

SPECIAL BRIGADIERS' ASSEMBLY

The special brigadiers' assembly, which, as we mentioned, was called to honor the new Jewish expert of the Gestapo, Kittel, did indeed take place on the 4th. Among others, Kittel also spoke, emphasizing that he knew all the ghettos in the east. No place has such great freedom as here, no theater, no sports field, etc. "You have to thank these two men that you live here as you do." He points to the police chief, Mr. Dessler, and to the ghetto chief, Mr. Gens. . . . He thinks we must obey the ghetto chief because, he says, "such a police [officer] is better than others. . . . " He understands that people bring in a piece of bread. But he will not tolerate butter. Jews may carry watches (!), they are even allowed "fountain pens," but may not possess any gold. He orders everyone to turn in their gold by Wednesday, the 7th of the month. And he announces that a Jew may have up to 300 rubles on him. He says he already has good information about who, what, and how—he advises that it is better to be in order.

PARADE OF CHIMNEY SWEEPS

At Niemiecka 22, outside the ghetto, there was a theft in an attic. Apparently the thieves left a chimney sweep's bucket at the scene of the crime. The Christians complained that Jewish chimney sweeps had robbed them. The new Gestapo chief came to the ghetto immediately and called an assembly of all chimney sweeps with their buckets. All chimney sweeps came with their buckets, proving first of all that none of them had left anything anywhere. Second, it turned out that the buckets of the Jewish chimney sweeps are quite different from those of the non-Jewish chimney sweeps.

The trick apparently didn't work. The Aryans, both the Christians and the German Kittel, are left with nothing.

So, as we see, the "new method" of the new German is unique. In any case, a method not yet familiar to us Vilna Ghetto Jews.

[*The end of page 748 of the original is destroyed. From the remaining lines, it is clear that two entries were there: (1) the second graduation of the ghetto schools took place, involving 172 students from the three grammar schools and an additional number (unclear how many) from the high school; (2) on Mickiewicz Street [Lithuanian: Gedimino Street there was a terrorist act against a woman provocateur. The continuation of the second entry is on the next page of the diary.*]

[. . .] where a female provocateur, Mrs. Wyleżańska, was wounded. She was healed and is back at work. The ghetto victim Weiskopf also fell because of her. The bulk of her activity was [in] Polish society.

This morning, walking on Ostrobramska, she was shot, and this time to death. Another Polish provocateur, whose name we don't know, also fell from a bullet on the same day. None of the attackers were arrested. Mass arrests of Poles are taking place.

JULY 9 [1943]

AVERBUKH — WITTENBERG

At about 11 this morning, two agents came into the ghetto and asked the ghetto representative for a certain Averbukh. When he was brought, he was taken to the Gestapo.

At about 12, when everyone was impatiently waiting for Mr. Dessler's return to learn what had happened to Averbukh, an automobile came in and the same two agents demanded a certain Wittenberg.[45]

Those who know the ghetto activists really became feverish. The wildest rumors soon began spreading. Wittenberg disappeared at once. The ghetto representative ordered all melinas in the ghetto surrounded, so that no one could escape. The ghetto jail was shut, and the key was given to the ghetto chief personally.

My office was immediately surrounded with a net of local sniffers. Abrashka and Abrasha,[46] who were waiting for the latest information, left the building immediately. The turmoil increased, and I myself went to get more information.

I learned that two Communists had been arrested a few days ago [in the city]. One became a provocateur on the spot. The other hanged himself in prison.[47] The provocateur dropped the name Averbukh, pretending that he had bought weapons from him for the . . . ghetto. In the confrontation with him, Averbukh denied it.

45. This entry proves that the Wittenberg case did in fact begin on July 9, 1943.

46. Abrashka is Avrom Żeleznikow; Abrasha is Avrom Chwojnik.

47. These were the Communist activists Kozłowski (who became a provocateur) and Vitas (who hanged himself in prison).

[The end of page 749 of the original is badly damaged. From the remaining lines, it is clear that this is the beginning of the Wittenberg affair, whose finale was played out in mid-July 1943 (see the introduction). On the same page, there was also probably an entry about the events in Bezdany, which Kruk mentions in additional entries below.]

ABOUT 1,600 RUBLES

On Wednesday night, the ghetto police made several searches and looked for money. People say that the police snatched 1,600 gold rubles during the night.

So Kittel's demand for gold was not in vain.

JULY 10 [1943]

KIENA, BEZDANY

Now it is clear. The Jews of the Kiena and Bezdany camps are killed. It is still hard to say how it happened. There are dreadful rumors here about that.

FOR 3,000 RUBLES — PONAR

Bentsien Okun, known in the ghetto as Bentske, has recently been shot in Ponar. His crime was being at a Christian's home with 3,000 rubles on him.

BEZDANY

Now, at 8 in the evening, I receive news from a fellow who just arrived from Bezdany. He is a refugee from Łódź, who worked in the HKP in Vilna. His unit sent 34 workers to work to the forest in Bezdany to chop wood.

He says that at about 10 in the morning, half a kilometer from Bezdany, an automobile with four Germans—two officers and two soldiers—got stuck. The Germans went to the Jewish camp to get their automobile repaired. When this was done, they passed out cigarettes, praised the Jewish workers, and asked for a barber. When they were shaved, they passed out cigarettes again and asked to assemble all the workers for a roll call. The Jews went to the workplaces to assemble the workers.

In the woods where our narrator worked, there were 12 workers from HKP. The narrator didn't want to report, and when they came for them, he slipped off to the side, among the wood. [. . .] only 11 went. Nevertheless, uneasy, he went toward the camp. Suddenly, [standing] on a mound, he heard shooting. Apparently, just as the [people were] assembled, two of the four Germans [started shooting] for no reason. Our narrator hid on the mound and [watched] the events. The attacked Jews started [hiding] in the barracks, where the Lithuanians threw hand grenades at them. The barracks began to burn, and anyone who jumped out of them was shot.

Thus our narrator was saved. He says that the entire Aktion lasted altogether from 10 to 11 in the morning. At about 2 in the afternoon, they gathered the local peasants to bury the dead.

IS THIS AN ANTI-JEWISH AKTION?

It is hard to answer the question. So far we must refrain from this description. On the surface, it looks like an anti-partisan campaign.

For some time, there have been various part[isan] attacks near the Bezdany camp. Unknowing and unwilling to hunt the part[isans] in the neighboring forest, the Germans wanted to strike the [partisans] through the Jews. One way or another, 240 people fell in Bezdany. As we said, [the camp] numbered 260 persons, including 7 children and [. . .] women. Some of them were not present. A few children were in the forest collecting berries, and so about 240 people from the camp and from the HKP group fell. It is not yet clear how many died in Kiena.

FOR RESISTING THE POLICE

In our kingdom, everything happens as in the biggest, nicest, most respectable one. Recently we also note public trials of resistance against the police. Today, here in the ghetto court, two such trials took place. One of young [Gavriel] Gutgestalt (son of H. Gutgestalt), the other of Dr. Trocki. The sentence: Gutgestalt is condemned to 14 nights in the ghetto jail; Dr. Trocki, 17 full days.

IN THE LABOR UNITS: *BAHNBETRIEBSWERK*[48]

This is a unit of hard workers. Twenty-two of them are mechanics and locksmiths. The workplace is in the big depot of the Vilna railroad station.

Jewish workers get supper at work, just like non-Jewish workers. They work 10 hours. Their relations with the employer are proper. The brigadier of the unit is Tevye Sheres.

THE AIR GROWS THICKER

It looks as if we are coming to the end. How many times has it seemed like this?

The air grows thicker. Like a mockery—everything around becomes narrower and narrower. The air grows thicker. . . .

Everything that happens around us: the sudden removal of Murer and Mayer, the sudden appearance of the character Kittel. The events of Biała Waka, Bezdany, and Kiena. Kittel's mockery of everything in the ghetto. The supposed conversations between Kittel and Weiss, that there is a mess here and he will clean up—all of it together: no one can touch it but everyone understands it—we are coming to the end!

48. "Railroad Operations Works."

ABOUT SEPARATING MEN FROM WOMEN

From ear to ear, it is going around here that they are about to separate men from women.

ABOUT A SEGREGATION

People are talking here about a supposed segregation to be done soon between men, women, and children. . . .

The air grows thicker.

YESTERDAY

If there weren't recently such an air of death in the ghetto, many of us would have drunk a toast yesterday. At 11 A.M. a rumor spread that the Americans landed in Sicily at 5 in the morning. At 3 in the morning, they were thought to have landed already on the Boot[49]—one piece of news better than the other. Only late in the evening did I learn that the entire story is empty fantasy. The only true thing is that American and English soldiers landed in five places, and bitter battles are taking place.

A YEAR OF THE TRANSPORT BRIGADE YELADIM

Today in the ghetto, a year of Yeladim in the ghetto was celebrated. The ghetto leaders didn't come. One of the commissars said that they didn't have a mind for that.

What happened? There are more important questions. . . . Can it be, what are the more important questions?

A question mark hangs over the ghetto. The air grows thicker.

JULY 13 [1943]

THE GHETTO IS UPSET

Nothing concrete. Nevertheless, the ghetto is upset today, too.

RZESZA

After the events of Kiena and Bezdany, all the workers of Rzesza are [. . .]

[*Pages 753–754 of the diary are missing. To the interrupted entry about Rzesza, we can add that after the workers of Kiena and Bezdany were killed, the workers of Rzesza ran away. They were brought into the Vilna Ghetto in an organized way.*]

Suddenly Gens appeared. He comes from the street. He smiles, and everyone is relieved. . . .

Is it possible not to catch the fever? No one knows anything. No guarantees at all, and yet I write. I have to write about it all!

49. I.e., Italy, which has the shape of a boot.

GLAZMAN IN THE GHETTO

Now I learn that Glazman has come back to the ghetto.

WHAT DOES HINGST SAY?

Mr. Gens says he was received by Vilna District Commissar Hingst. Gens told him about the panic in the ghetto, and Hingst assured him that nothing is threatening the ghetto: you are necessary with your unit, you can rest easy.

GENS SPEAKS TO THE DIRECTORS

At 7 in the evening, Gens called the directors of all the departments and told them of the conversation with Hingst.

THEY COME FROM RZESZA

They come to the ghetto from Rzesza in groups.

GENS SPEAKS IN THE THEATER

This evening, Mr. Gens once again spoke and told of his conversation with Hingst. The ghetto calms down.

JULY 14 [1943]

RELAXATION

Today there is relaxation here. But the relaxation only lets us think. If it was nothing, why the relaxation? So we must assume that something is going on, but the ghetto rulers—if they know and don't say anything, that is indeed a mistake that lulls us to sleep. This is bad, and we must not allow it.

WATCH OUT

Guard our fate!

Condemned men may know when their sentence is carried out. Don't we know positively that our fate is sealed?

It is a blank check that can be filled in at any time. . . . Most important is to watch out, so that in case of something, we can die like human beings. . . .

THEY COME FROM KIENA

Yesterday groups came from Rzesza. Today groups of survivors come from Kiena. Like the picture on the eve of Oszmiana and Święc[iany. Wa]gons drag over the narrow streets of the ghetto. Wagons with those re[maining b]its of poverty, and on them, with them, and around them, the rescued, toiling hands that left everything on the scale of buying [their li]ves for labor.

CONCERNING EVENTS IN BEZDANY

In a conversation between Mr. Gens and Hingst, the latter, among other things, was supposed to have given the reasons for the murder in Bezdany: many Jews went to the partisans. They were in constant contact with the camps. The Lithuanian guard knew about that, took money for it, and tolerated it. That is why Bezdany had such an end. . . .

HOW WERE KIENA JEWS KILLED?

Only now do we learn more precisely about the murder in Kiena: a Christian woman, a former maid of my ghetto neighbor, tells with tears in her eyes:

Kittel and three Germans drove into the camp. Two trucks of Germans were hidden at the side. Kittel gathered everyone in the barracks, told them they must work, because work is useful. They must not be in contact with "forest people," not smuggle, etc. As soon as he left the barracks, he whistled, and the hidden Germans attacked the Jews. The men were tied up and shooting began.

The Christian woman says that more than 240 Jews died.

Apropos, still during Kittel's speech to the Jews, Christians were digging the graves! . . .

74 PERCENT WEHRMACHT JEWS! . . .

Asked to provide a list of "Wehrmacht Units" of the ghetto and the number of their staff, the Jewish department sent a list, showing that 13,800 Jews work in the Wehrmacht units, which amounts to 74 percent of the ghetto population. A percentage that is really amazing.

. . . AND THE GHETTO INDUSTRY EXPANDS

What is happening here is not only amazing, it is truly a madhouse. We are waiting for the Angel of Death, and we stand in "foreign" workshops and help sharpen the sword against our own heads. Parallel with that, as we "expect" the slaughterer, we expand our ghetto industry—a cabalistic sign of salvation in our difficult situation.

The ghetto industry expands incessantly: recently a workshop for mirrors was opened, located at Rudnicka 19.

A workshop for peasant whetstones was also opened at Rudnicka 6.

Nearby, a workshop for combs was opened.

The technical-chemical laboratory is expanded.

The binding workshop is expanded. So is the pottery workshop.

The tailor workshops are expanded many times over.

In short, the slaughterer's knife hangs over our heads, and we are building "Pithom and Ramses . . ."[50]

50. Two treasury cities that the Israelites had to build for Pharaoh in biblical times.

CHEESE DUMPLINGS FROM SNOW . . .

The starch and syrup factory makes its products from potato peels. That enterprise goes through various stages. Now it produces potato starch: from starch is made syrup (molasses); the syrup is transformed into a weak alcoholic drink, an imitation wine that is very tasty. Lately attempts have been made to produce "ices." In short, they make cheese dumplings from snow.

GOITER AMONG CHILDREN

The children's clinic in the ghetto has determined that 35 percent of the ghetto children have goiter. Most of the cases are children between 4 and 7 years old—66.1 percent.

The disease comes from malnutrition.

HOW THE GHETTO OFFICIAL ORGAN WRITES ABOUT THAT

The latest issue of *Geto-yedies* tells of recent events in the Vilna area. We consider it necessary to quote it without any corrections.

Item number 1:

Unusual Punishment for Escaping from the Ghetto

Six Jews escaped from the Biała Waka peat camp. The German authorities sentenced 10 Jews from the same camp to be shot for every escapee, that is, 60 adults (not counting the children).

The punishment was recently carried out. Altogether, this punishment was used for 60 adult Jews and 7 children from the above-mentioned camp.

A similar punishment is also expected for the population of the Vilna Ghetto if such cases also happen here.

So much for item number 1. Now another item in the same paper.

Warning! The Peat Camps in Kiena and Bezdany Are Liquidated

The German authorities have determined that the peat camps in K*iena* and Bez*dany* have had contacts with partisans. Because of that, both camps have been liquidated.

And then comes an addition by the esteemed editor to "elucidate" the matter:

We determine that our repeated warnings have been and remain correct:

Jews are kept and Jewish labor is held in esteem only up to the moment when the German authorities obtain proof that Jews have contact with partisans or non-German elements, and in such a case, the whole local community is made responsible for the [. . .]

[Here the diary of Herman Kruk breaks off,[51] *on the eve of the dramatic day in the Vilna Ghetto known as Wittenberg Day, which is described in almost every published work on the destruction of Vilna. On July 15, 1943, FPO leader Itzik Wittenberg was arrested while attending a meeting with Jacob Gens. Members of the FPO attacked the Jewish police and managed to free Wittenberg, who went into hiding. The next day, the Germans issued an ultimatum that unless Wittenberg turned himself in, they would liquidate the entire ghetto. Under intense pressure from the ghetto's leadership and in the face of the panicked hostility of ghetto residents, the FPO reluctantly allowed Wittenberg to surrender himself to authorities. Realizing that he would be tortured to reveal secrets about the resistance, Wittenberg committed suicide by swallowing a cyanide capsule on the day he was taken into custody.*

Soon thereafter, the Germans began the final liquidation of the Vilna Ghetto. Thousands of Vilna's remaining Jews were deported to labor camps in Estonia. Others were murdered at Ponar or at the Sobibor death camp. About 2,500 Jews remained behind in labor camps in Vilna but were murdered shortly before Soviet liberation of the city. The FPO's call to the ghetto's Jews to resist the deportation and mount an uprising was largely ignored. After engaging the Germans in combat on September 1, most of the remaining FPO members fled the ghetto for nearby forests, where they fought on as partisans. By September 24, the liquidation of the Vilna Ghetto was complete.]

51. As noted in the introduction, Kruk continued to record entries in his diary after July 14, but these pages were hidden after the war for fear that his account of the FPO's surrender of Wittenberg, a Communist, might be viewed as treason by the Soviet authorities. The missing pages were either lost or destroyed.

CHAPTER 9
NARRATIVE CHRONICLES OF THE GHETTO 1941–1943

[*The narrative chronicles in this chapter were written in the same period as the diary of the Vilna Ghetto, which is presented in Chapters 2–8.*]

GENESIS IN THE GHETTO

In the beginning there was chaos, *tohu-vabohu,* all was desolate and empty. All around and around, darkness ruled, helplessness and fear. God lost his grip on the world, and everything all around was neglected, abandoned, and without God's mercy.

In the underground of this genesis, little flames already flickered—kernels of the future tree.

And it was thus:

In the pervasive desolation of chaos and neglect, here and there little eternal candles flickered, and from the eternal candles little fires flamed up, and among the little fires, sunbeams appeared.

Here and there, small groups of Bundists, Communists, and Zionists gathered in circles. In the ghetto you feel one of your own, as in thick blood. And they reached conclusions, and all of them came to the same one:

To live and survive.

Let us call for perseverance, let us sow hope, let us plow the field while weathering the difficulties, rising on your feet, believing in tomorrow.

Our yesterday was tragic, our today is anguish—let us bank on tomorrow.

To survive!

To endure!

In the gap between one Aktion and the next, in the breathing space between one destruction in Ponar and the next, the apostles of a new religion gathered, like Marranos: survive, endure! . . .

How daring it was, how much internal faith, external courage, willpower, and stubbornness was in it—to be able to bring forth the words: survive and endure.

In every home a destruction. Every person has a *shiva* [mourning]. Everywhere blood and tears. Out of 10, 9 are missing; out of 7, 3—mass murder, mass slaughter!

Everyone lives in anticipation. Yesterday my father. Today me. At night, my wife and child. Tomorrow me.

Survive!

Endure!

Today all this sounds mystical, yet it happened, it was.

On Strashun Street 2, through crooked, slippery steps to the second floor, through a long [external] balcony, from the balcony to further steps, a short corridor leads to an attic room. Here, in this attic room, in the apartment of Comrade Gut[gestalt], one by one the defenders of the Vilna Ghetto sneak in. Free [people]—to launch the first slogan of endurance.

Here, in this attic, the meeting occurs that proclaimed the foundation of the Aid Society in the ghetto.

To aid the most unfortunate among the unfortunate.

To help them escape from the ghetto, a piece of bread, a bit of soup, to fight against separating them as if they were lepers—mix them up with the still fortunate ones, the owners of "yellow permits." All present beat their breasts and repent:

Why only now?

Why so late?

And they pronounce: better late than never.

Thus the activity of the first social institution in the ghetto was proclaimed: the Aid Society.

UNDERGROUND GHETTO

Cats

When flocks of steel birds, roaring and shrieking, suddenly swooped over Vilmen,[1] covering the city with lead and fire, surely none of the pilots understood how much the city trembled with fear and terror and how closely the ghetto listened to the bang of explosions as to a mighty symphony, a greeting from the "other world":

Does it mean that everything is not yet lost? Does it mean that somewhere a pulse is still throbbing. . . . And the Vilmen Ghetto Jews inhaled this horror music like a good omen.

This bombardment left Vilna badly damaged: dead and wounded. Dozens of houses in ruins. Battered and destroyed buildings. The ghetto was saved as if by a magic hand, and only its border was left with a gaping window—a breach into the world. . . .

1. A code name for Vilna, used in Kruk's fictionalized writings.

In the hermetically sealed ghetto, a dividing wall was ripped out, and the wall pulled with it a huge space, which now stands as an open wound, after the noisy roar.

Ever since, the sealed ghetto has had a window into the world. The ghetto, with its inventiveness, began to improvise. People soon realized that the recent destruction might serve as a point of departure for a new ghetto. Smugglers[2] sniffed out new winds, and the torn-up wound was transformed into a cure.

"Why should we squeeze through chimneys, push through narrow doorways, cracks, and chinks?"

Even Dovidke, the 11-year-old smuggler, and his gang caught on to it. "Indeed, why not use it? . . . "

The torn-up wall at Oszmiańska 6 leads to a roof, where there's a passage to a neighboring attic, and beyond it, with a ladder, you can get to a higher attic, where a deliberately blown-up hole takes you to Niemiecka 21, outside the ghetto.

From the attic on Oszmiańska Street, a bare wall juts out. It lost its roof and is isolated from everything around it like a plucked chicken, bare and naked. Somewhere pieces of wallpaper still hang, here and there the string of a picture trails, along with the remnant of a curtain, a piece of a board, and such things. From this attic, they leap like cats up onto the bare wall, from there they slide down like cats to a lower floor, and then, through ruins and breaches, they get to the neighboring attic with a ladder; with a ladder they climb to the second attic and through the hole out of the ghetto. . . .

From the point of departure on the third floor of Oszmiańska 6, a wide panorama opens up: uprooted or scattered buildings, shaved-off walls, bare chimneys, mountains of bricks, and a large square around the Church of Saint Mikołaj standing like an orphan on the once noisy Mikołaj Alley. Below it, the ghetto—Jews, Jews, and Jews. In front of it, Mikołaj Alley, empty and abandoned. On the sides and all around, torn-up and exploded walls—destruction!

As in a desert, abandoned and solitary, God's house stands here, the Church of Saint Mikołaj, and around it, supported by all the saints, swarms a beehive:

Flour to satisfy the hunger in the ghetto. . . .
Potatoes. . . .
Salt for the ghetto. . . .

The ruin, a memorial of death and desolation, is transformed into a central artery through which sap and lifeblood for the ghetto is delivered at great risk. Day and night, almost 24 hours a day, there's traffic here. At night, contraband: large, heavy transports; in the day, anything that can be gotten—an open game, as if nothing had happened.

The Christians in the church square watch and keep silent—let them save

2. In the Yiddish, *vashovnikes,* literally "launderers," ghetto slang for smugglers.

themselves. Some out of pity, some for vengeance on the hated Krauts—it doesn't matter. The priest watches through the window of his parish house and pretends not to see. The Jewish ghetto police know, see, but cannot pursue them. . . .

Dozens of ghetto dwellers have gone to "the other world" for a kilo of flour, for two kilos of peas, for a pinch of sugar, for trying to lessen the misery, and for smuggling. Here: this way has not yet been discovered. Everyone who crosses here guards its "purity" like the apple of his eye.

During the day, long convoys stretching out, rows of black, sooty chimney sweeps, strolling like cats from attics to roofs, from roofs to ruins, and from there, leaping like cats, into the crowd of the Vilmen Ghetto.

The most active and agile, as everywhere, are the youngsters—children from 9 to 11 years old, gangs, whole hordes, like wild locusts they swoop down outside the ghetto. Over there, they move boldly and licentiously, with no Jew badge, and here in the ruins, they rule like witches in a demonic dance. . . . Mixed and linked in a camaraderie with Christian children, here is a chase of transports and deliveries. Christian children buy and bring to the ruins. Jewish kids, tired of running around, wait for their "buyers," "suppliers," and traders on "commission." Here among the ruins, they hide and help each other. From here, through catwalks, they pull the merchandise up the walls with ropes to sell it in the ghetto.

At night smugglers prepare iron plates, and the Christian neighbors, janitors and residents, deliver the common goods from their secret warehouses—meat, flour, salt—a mass transport of underground work.

Plates and ropes. Young cat legs, climbing like acrobats on straight walls—legions of smugglers performing miracles, putting their lives on the line.

Underground ghetto. . . .

Dovidke is devil-may-care. Three things influenced him: the Snatchers who savagely carried off his father, his mother and two sisters who were dragged out of their melina, and stories about Ponar. Three moments that influenced the 11-year-old child Dovidke, made him demoralized and depraved. Dovidke quickly turned into an orphan, and with him his 6-year-old sister, saved by chance just like him. At that time, Dovidke was 9 years old and his sister was 4. An uncle, a cobbler, took pity and registered them as his own. The aunt kept cursing him: they're guzzlers and parasites. We've got to throw them out and let them get lost.

Dovidke has a nervous tic, a kind of slurping as if he were eating hot noodles. His head is slightly over to one side; one eye seems to be sitting higher than the other. His first gaze—and you sense he doesn't trust you.

You cannot trust anyone! . . .

"There is no trust. All are thieves." Thus he is demoralized by the energetic 13-year-old girl Beylke, with her broad fermenting bosom and swift energetic action.

Beylke, the assistant in Dovidke's business, is also a fatherless child.

Dovidke, under the influence of events, under the pressure of remaining alone with a little sister, understanding that his evil witch of an aunt curses the blood in his veins—Dovidke suddenly stood up on his own feet. He scraped together several rubles, got out of the ghetto, went to former Christian neighbors, and they, the Christians, took pity on him, fed him rich food, gave him bread, a piece of lard, and on his way back, bought him merchandise to smuggle into the ghetto and make a living for himself and his orphaned little sister.

Dovidke lost all notion of fear. Getting caught, falling into a trap, death—those are alien concepts, and if he talks about them at all, they seem to be something he can't grasp.

"And if so?" he answers the "moral" preaching of the Jewish policeman.

"And if so, is there a way out? So who cares?"

"And how many did they knock off for no reason? . . . "

"And why did my father go?"

"And my mother and my grandmother and my little sisters?"

The Jewish policeman is embarrassed and begs him:

"So promise not to leave the ghetto."

Dovidke, the young "criminal," refuses:

"But I can't. I can't promise. I won't keep it. What can I do? . . . "

The policeman on duty is at a loss: what to do about him? Almost every dawn he's a "guest" in the police station. What can be done with him?

Dovidke, with all his licentiousness, understands very well: "They" always arrest him. And every time, they release him. To promise and not to keep it would make them furious, and his child's instinct makes him insist: better not to promise than to promise and not keep your word. . . . For would he be able to keep his word? . . . Everything around is against him, even those closest to him. He believes in nobody's help and has lost his trust in the world.

"Everything is whores . . . ," he says bitterly.

With this philosophy of life, Dovidke plunges into life and sees everything as being against him. Dovidke won't look anybody straight in the eye. His asymmetrical gaze creeps under your skin: he doesn't believe, he's suspicious, he's ashamed . . . of his own thoughts.

If a policeman threatens him, he answers, resigned and provocative:

"Okay, release me or don't, who cares?" (Sensing how he plays on the instincts.)

And the ghetto police are at a loss and can't make up their minds: if you don't catch him, what do you do? If you do arrest him, what do you do with him? If you release him, he immediately dashes, with his cat's walk, to "make up" for the paid fine, for the "damages." Nobody cares—let him do what he wants. . . .

He himself is a rare guest at home—he does indeed "what he wants." Sometimes he drops in, leaves a bundle of money, some flour, sometimes a roll, gives his sister candy and some change, and disappears—devil-may-care! . . .

Among the labyrinths of attics on the side there is an attic and next to it a "wasteland," an empty room, desolate and hollow. In this wasteland, debauchery teems.

A remnant of a bed, sacks, spread-out straw; here, a mixture of sweaty bodies, cigarette smoke, and liquor created a horrible brew, a stench of demoralization, dampness, and rot.

Boys and girls together: at night and at dawn there is the common game of smuggling and debauchery. During the day—card playing, a smoking contest; and half drunk, half weary, they lie strewn about here on a bed or on the floor, weak and helpless.

The room is covered with empty liquor bottles, the skin of gobbled sausages, eggshells, and cigarette holders. Here is the gathering place and the central point. From here, they embark on their way out of the ghetto; here they rest, they play and carouse.

Beylke is an expert: "What did you think?"

Dovidke's earnings swim first of all into Beylke's pocket, and she, the beauty with her yeast-fermenting womanhood, conducts the whole game. She's the apple of Dovidke's eye, hers is the ultimate decision. She herself pushes money first of all into her mother's hand to support the family, returns to the "gang" and brings delicacies to eat and guzzle for Dovidke and the group.

Now Dovidke is a big money maker. It's enough for everything, and his smiling aunt, in her falseness, takes an interest in him:

"Dovidke, will you come for dinner?" And Dovidke, as if she didn't mean him, tosses a few rubles on the table and gets away with no answer. In the "wasteland," Dovidke has a life, here he is joyful and has a good time. Here he sleeps hugging Beylke, and Beylke pulls her dress up to the knees, lies in his arms! Exhausted, worn out, snoring—you can go crazy!

There is a legend: on the graves of murdered innocents grow poisonous plants. And as long as the innocent blood that was shed is not avenged, those plants bloom, increase, and multiply, poisoning their surroundings, the air, and the atmosphere.

So what are morals for?

Morals are the business of priests: Dovidke, Beylke, their friends, and their surroundings have lost all meaning. Death and fear are worthless.

. . . When everyone, family and strangers, is raped and beaten, when all is hollow and naked, and everything is right before your eyes and cannot be hidden, why should we be amazed? . . .

Ghetto is amoral, and ghetto life in Vilmen is the lawlessness of the borderland between life and death.

4. Shooters and Launderers

The ghetto sleeps secretively. The moon, hanging on the right wing of the cross on the spire of the Church of All Saints, smiles roguishly into the crooked ghetto alleys. The brazen moon looks down and sees both—the ghetto and the outside.

She knows what the ghetto thinks and what the world outside does. The moon, watching the mysterious silence of the ghetto, knows it all and laughs devilishly for no reason:

"Ha ha, a world with little worlds. . . . "

The sky prophesies a splendid day. The ghetto alleys lost their hope long ago. Day—for whom is the day? . . .

The heavy jackboot steps of the Jewish ghetto policeman ring depressingly—night in the ghetto. The Jewish watchman, the guard of the ghetto, shuffles up to the mourning ghetto alleys, drowning out his sadness with melodies of the ghetto revue.

Shedding the leaden night, comes the day. Shaking off the night intoxication, the ghetto wakes up. Thousands and thousands bring the streets to life. The streets and alleys washed by the morning dew, wet and steamy, look languidly and sleepily upon the groups and knots of people gathering to march out to their "units."

What is the hurry?

What is the rush?

Day after day, in the early morning hours, the ghetto spits out its specialists, according to the accepted term *Facharbeiter* [skilled worker]. With saws and planes, with axes, picks, and spades, with crates of glass, locksmith's tools, and so on, they march in groups, in a row, each to his work, each in his place, punctually, with German discipline and German calculation.

"Specialists" of the remnant of Vilmen.

Exhausted, tired, and languishing, emptied of everything and anything, they carry with them into the world the mysterious Vilmen underground ghetto.

It is taboo, unclean, and forbidden, against the law and against regulations. Death for a kilo of peas. Death for a piece of wood—forbidden! Filth, insults. So what is not forbidden here?

Life, is it not forbidden? . . .

Life? What can you live on?

Jews don't live. Jews launder.

In the First World War, it was called smuggling. Bread to your fill was obtained by smuggling. Butter for a child was obtained by smuggling. Now one launders—a new term invented by the Vilmen launderers.

Outside the ghetto, they risk laundering clothes and other objects for sale. Returning to the ghetto, bread, butter, meat—a minimum to feed and survive.

Are there still things to be sold? People, bereft of everything, sold what they had long ago. There is nothing to trot out anymore, so how do they live here?

What is distributed on your bread card is not enough to live on, but also not enough to die on. For additional things, for laundering, there is nothing to draw upon.

But people nonetheless live?

Most of the ghetto lives from shooting, and shooting means simply to appropriate whatever possible. Here in the ghetto, this is the most normal element of the ghetto setup.

To shoot? It is the most obvious way to live. Is there another way?

Ghetto is confusion. . . . Ghetto is turmoil. Being hurled into the narrow ghetto walls means losing any ethics. Here everything has no status, no class, no principle. It is chaos, disorder, and derangement. Solidarity in the ghetto means covering for each other "in an organized way." Camaraderie—to be silent and keep quiet. The goal—to live and survive!

There is no integrity, everything is entangled and mixed up. The blacksmith with the engineer, the doctor with the tailor, the carpenter with the glazier are on "brotherly" terms with the former industrialist and landlord.

Faces whipped by winds and rain, frozen by winter frosts and snow. Every Jew has a face of a peasant in the fields: thick skin, weather-beaten, with coarse, callused hands, with hard and tempered fingers, heavy and massive. Externally, a slave for generations. Internally, as if he had years of exploitation behind him. . . .

Is it all really possible on eight grams of bread a day and five decagrams of sugar a week?

Among the columns marching out of the ghetto, in the uproar of ghetto castanets, ghetto clogs, and heavy jackboots covered with nails, you can sense the collective responsibility. One corrects another:

"Pull your belly in," you suddenly hear out of the blue.

The engineer understands, tightens his belt, squeezes his wife's suit, and his figure looks normal again.

"Straighten your right pant leg"—and the former haberdasher, today's glazier "specialist," pulls his pant leg inside his boot so his laundry won't stand out. . . .

Anyone who still has anything carries it. Anyone who has no more carries with him only tools, instruments for importing.

Why the empty bread sack carried to work?

Why carry an overcoat on a summer day?

In the bread sack he will launder potatoes. Under the coat a labyrinth of hiding places is sewn, a "corset" for flour, a "truss" to carry between your legs, a "brassiere" to launder . . . a "compress" to put around your body—terminology of the ghetto launderers in the struggle for a piece of bread, butter, meat—the minimum of a minimum.

But not everyone launders for himself. There are also tradesmen launderers. To trade three kilos of meat means to earn half a kilo for yourself. There are small launderers and big ones. Big, bigger, and very big.

It seems like a classless society, and yet there are nuances. It seems to be a ghetto, and yet there is no uniformity.

Poverty, languished and starving, looks at the sated, and the sated doesn't see the suffering and doesn't understand the starvation.

Those who will never go down, they will always get out and will always float on top like filth on muddy water.

Just like Berl, Leybl, and Hele, just like Arke, the shooters and launderers, too, crawled into the underground. Berl and his group are preparing to face a battle, Arke looks for a way for vengeance, and they—those who always float up, always ready for action, full of initiative and daring—they, too, live in the underground. The labyrinth grows bigger and bigger. The ghetto digs deeper into the underground. Above, a ghetto slaving and languishing; below, luxury, obstinacy, yearning for battle, and rebelliousness.

To live. They, too, want to live. Why should they be destroyed?

Thousands starve, nothing left to launder. Quietly and obediently, they lie with swollen bellies and watch how individuals and "the chosen ones" live in luxury and oblivion.

So why let your wife and child die?

So why stop at anything, consider any rules?

The shoemaker in his work unit is flooded with leather. So he cuts soles for German shoes and shoots for himself for laundering. . . .

Nails from the carpenters' shop are merchandise not obtainable in the ghetto. So they pound some into the boards and stuff the rest in large quantities into the bread sack and the boots.

The erstwhile butcher becomes again a meat dealer. He and his workmates, on collective principles, carry in bulk a hundred, two hundred kilos—all for the underground ghetto.

Cheese, disappeared from the canteen, creeps into the ghetto.

Liquor from the Nazi swindlerheads is sold in the ghetto.

The engineer working with electrotechnical instruments wraps around his body several meters of electrical cords, switches, burners, batteries—everything is merchandise. . . .

Peasant women come to the fence of the "units" and trade—buy and sell.

Stuffed corsets—it is flour for the underground bakeries. Boots, slippery and wet—it is fish bought to sell in the ghetto.

For some, laundering is to save themselves from starvation; for others, "to make a living."

Nuances of ghetto life: living to survive and living to "make a living." So groups and little clusters are growing, groups that starve, and groups that barely eat, and groups that live luxuriously. For them nothing is expensive, and they don't calculate the cost. A new class structure, a unique division.

When facing death, death is a trifle. When facing annihilation, everything is lawless and licentious. There are no limits, no boundaries. Need breaks iron, and licentiousness carries savagery.

Berl, Leybl, and Hele are waiting to face a battle. Arke is looking for a way to vengeance, and they—the shooters and launderers of all kinds—dig deeper in the underground to survive, to hold out, to live, and to "make a living."

Above, a ghetto, slaving and languid. Below, a network of luxury, obstinacy, yearning for battle, and rebelliousness. Like ants. Need swarms, the underground digs.

Two lives. The ghetto above, and its life in the underground.

Six Gallows in the Vilna Ghetto: A Criminal Literary Chronicle of the Vilna Ghetto

K. Herman

Vilna Ghetto

August 1942

INTERPRETATION

On June 4, 1942, the entire Vilna Ghetto was suddenly brought to attention. At 3 in the afternoon, six Jews condemned by the Jewish ghetto court were taken to the gallows. Dozens of Jewish policemen, under the leadership of the Jewish police chief in the ghetto, took part in the execution.

After hearing the prosecutor's demand for a death sentence on all six, one of the accused asked for a . . . cigarette, another one asked to be allowed to say goodbye to his wife, and a third declared that he was guilty.

Facing death at the site of the execution, they all quietly and very calmly accepted the carrying out of the sentence.

No one in the ghetto resented this act of justice. No one doubted the just verdict or the guilt of the accused. Everyone was relieved at the announcement that the accused would not be turned over to the "outside world," that their sentence would be carried out by the ghetto, and that. . . .

. . . When the Judenrat and the police chief posted announcements in the streets of the ghetto about the death sentence that was carried out, thousands read them calmly and very attentively. No one felt any "maybe," any doubt, any spark of sympathy.

The ghetto sentenced. The ghetto carried out the sentence, and the ghetto very calmly went on with its daily routine.

Why such truculence?

Why such calm?

Is it only because, of 75,000 Jews in Vilna, barely 16,000 remain?

Or perhaps because the inhabitants of the Vilna Ghetto have gotten so used to murder and are calm and indifferent? . . .

June 4 in the ghetto is, thus far, the day of the strongest emotions. Thousands fell here in Aktions. Thousands were caught by "Snatchers," and thousands remained orphaned, homeless, and without families; widows, broken and crushed people. For them, today has been one of the hardest days: the ghetto has to be purified. The Vilna Ghetto felt ashamed of that double bestial and wanton murder; debased and offended by the ten-time murderer Avidon.

Everything that happened here had one great purpose: in view of the great events, face to face with the horrible historical situation of the local Jews, the shame has to be wiped out.

The whole ghetto wanted to wash its hands! Therefore the "bloodthirstiness" of the Vilna Ghetto residents.

The author, with his journalistic sensibility, could not rest until he had registered this event for posterity. The story we chronicle here is reminiscent of a Sherlock Holmes story. Everything that occurs in this narrative is no more than a criminal literary chronicle based on the events of June 1942 in the Vilna Ghetto.

—Vilna Ghetto, August 1942

1. To Jerusalem of Lithuania

With deep hatred did Yosef flee from the enemy who exterminated Jewishness and the Jewish religion. The thirty-something yeshiva student, plodding from one yeshiva to another, relied on God and on his own Jewishness. When the Bolsheviks entered Białystok, he fled with his belief and carried it toward Vilna.

Vilna, the Jewish cultural center!

There he would again be able to study and hide himself along with all that was holy in his Judaism.

In the long, heavy winter of 1939–1940, a group of paupers is trudging in the deep heavy snow, and Yosef the yeshiva student is among them.

During the day, they lie in peasant huts. At night, no matter how strong the cold, they go deeper and deeper, closer and closer to the promised land—Lithuania, the Smetona regime, which tolerates Judaism.

Yosef can see that masses of Jewish yeshivas are fleeing from the Bolsheviks, and that most of them are running to Lithuania, mainly to Vilna.

It is clear to him: there he will get a place for himself, and there he can again study in peace and quiet. It thrills him.

Just to have a chance to study!

At 1 o'clock in the morning the wandering began again. Since 1 o'clock in the morning, the exhausted Yosef has been trudging. He thought Vilna was just around the corner. Yet this is the third night he's been wandering. With a dry crust of bread in his pocket. With continual fear and beating heart—how long can it last? Yosef begins to doubt, he gradually loses hope of reaching Vilna.

The dreadful frost, the constant fear, the continual vigilance as they approach the border, the getting up and lying down, the hiding by day in barns and walking at night—all that together begs for an end, and when the end doesn't come, he can't stand anything. The hope of the promised land dissipates, and the poison of pessimism drips into him more and more.

Today it must finally happen. Today or never.

Today the group must finally reach its goal—so states their peasant leader:

"We will soon cross the border, and after two or three hours of walking, Yosef, like Our Teacher Moses, will look upon his promised land. . . ."

A few steps further and another order: lie down. In the air is the flare of a rocket. Everything is beautifully illuminated and is as light as day—a rider, a soldier on skis, a bloodhound.

It is the border itself. You hold your breath. Yosef, in his great nervousness, feels that he is growing weaker and weaker. Nevertheless, he overcomes it—his dream comes true:

"With God's help, another hour, maybe in another hour he is on the Lithuanian side, he is in Vilna. . . ." he consoles himself and calms down.

It is already dawn. The fog dissolves and the horizon grows broader and broader, deeper and more visible. The tired Yosef barely makes it up to the top of a slippery mound and joyously recites a blessing—finally he has arrived. In two or three hours, he will be in Vilna. . . .

Thus the yeshiva student Yosef Gerstein got to Vilna and found his way to Reb Velvele, the Rabbi of Brisk, where he studied and had the opportunity to admire the new city. He studied very diligently and wandered from prayer house to prayer house, through the 105 prayer houses. . . .

As the Bolsheviks occupied Vilna a second time, Yosef returned to his little bundle of clothes and pawed it as if packing for a new trek. He looked at his "property" and calculated:

With the Germans it's impossible, and is it possible with the Bolsheviks? And again, as in Białystok, Yosef had the problem of how to retain an opportunity for study. Whole yeshivas are setting out for America, for Eretz Israel, and he, Yosef?

He is caught up by the Vilna fad. He makes fake visas and tries his luck—to emigrate, escape from there.

"Escape where?"

And Yosef Gerstein, swept by the stream, prepares to go to Eretz Israel.

Thousands of yeshiva students are going; so why can't he also rescue his Jewishness?

The pride of receiving a promise of support and preparing for Eretz Israel gave him new vitality, fresh courage, and fresh hope:

Eretz Israel! . . .

It's hard to get a visa. Where can you get it? And Gerstein let himself be persuaded—he had a forged visa made. The Bolsheviks tolerated that anyway. For them, it was an enterprise to get dollars. If not thousands, at least hundreds left that way, didn't they?

Why should he flinch from a forged visa?

Indeed, hundreds did go, but Yosef didn't succeed. He was denounced, fell into the Bolshevik prison, and after four months of starvation, avoiding nonkosher food and eating only dry bread and water, he was finally released at the outbreak of the German-Soviet war.

A person has to live. Eating is a necessity. Escaping from the Germans brought him back into the arms of the German armies.

Yosef's only way out is trading. Everybody trades, so he will try, too. And he establishes for himself a life of pursuing a small income and . . . hiding from "Snatchers," Lithuanian or German catchers. Until, until he is dragged into the Vilna Ghetto.

The worse life becomes in the ghetto, the stronger is his religious zeal. Precisely here, when everything around is oppressive and squeezed in the vise of pessimism, precisely here the feeling of hope and perseverance stirs in Yosef:

"Ghetto is not an eternity. The enemy must and will fall, and Yosef and everyone else will be liberated! . . ."

Perseverance? Life gets harder by the day. It's harder to make a living, and Yosef, chasing after survival, hurls himself like a fish into water. His trading sometimes succeeds, sometimes doesn't. And trading like this, he trades himself for eternity.

2. He Will Shoot!

The inhabitants of the Vilna Ghetto lived with a sensation: a group of Jewish police, goaded by the man in charge of Jewish affairs in the Regional Commissar's Office, the strict German officer Murer, have, at his orders, conducted a search.

The Jewish policeman Avrom Greenfeld, a short, broad fellow with head and throat bandaged, stood with Murer, who, enraged, still couldn't understand:

"A Jew, you say, an inhabitant of the ghetto?"

Greenfeld stood at attention and confirmed:

"*Jawohl,* a Jew, an inhabitant of the ghetto."

Murer was amazed. In the ghetto, one Jew stabs another one? But what infuriated him most was that a Jew dared attack a policeman.

A Jew? In the ghetto?

"How dare he?"

"You've got 15 minutes to deliver him to me!"

"Here on the spot I'll shoot him! . . ."

Murer doesn't need to give assurances. Here in the ghetto they know him. When Murer says he'll shoot him, it's clear as day—he'll shoot him.

Trembling, the residents of Rudnicka Street who watched this scene expected something horrible:

Soon they'll bring him, and Murer, as his deputy Weiss once did, will pull out his Browning and cut him down on the spot. . . .

The searching lasted not 15 minutes but two full hours. Murer left with nothing, and the police felt somewhat stronger—even Murer worried about them. . . .

"A policeman is a policeman."

"For touching even a Jewish policeman, he'll shoot. . . ."

But the murderer is long gone. In a peasant wagon and with a Christian document in his pocket, he shook himself and found no sign of remorse in himself. On the contrary, he seethed with anger for not having stabbed him to death.

"No matter what, he has to get out. No matter what, he is a murderer. So why then did he only wound him in his pig snout?" And swirling in his mind were oaths and curses against the wounded Jewish policeman from the Vilna Ghetto, whose honor was championed by Murer.

"Murderer! The devil take his father!" His anger at Murer the murderer seethed again. "Murderer," he went on, "one murders Jews, and the other one [in this case the Jewish policeman Avremele the Thief], the inhabitants of the ghetto!"

"Now he'll remember me, Avremele Ber, now he'll know you mustn't mess with Yankele Avidon. . . ."

"So what if I wanted to get in out of line?"

"Would it hurt him to let one of his own in without a line?"

"He wanted to boast, to show who he is, a policeman, a Jewish pig, and I taught him a lesson."

"Now will he remember that you don't mess with Yankele Avidon?"

Thus did Yankl Avidon, the actual stabber of Avrom Greenfeld, try to justify to himself the anger that burned in him toward his former "professional colleague," the thief Avrom Greenfeld, currently a policeman in the ghetto.

The small peasant wagon swayed, and so did the heavy and massive Avidon. He stretched out in the straw and slept like a log until they reached Lida.

3. Murder or Not?

The entire staff of the Vilna criminal police were pondering a case. The commissar pulled his goyish mustache, which seemed to have been stuck onto his pleasant face, and ruminated:

Murder or not?

The secretary reports that the hat maker Lides didn't get along with his wife. He didn't get a pass. He somehow made arrangements for his children and registered them with friends—clearly he took the money and ran.

Everything pointed to it: the hatmaker Hertsl Lides ran away with 27,000 rubles, for which he promised to buy 100 gold rubles. So it was obvious:

The promise to buy 100 rubles was a swindle. Lides swindled them and ran away.

But the wife doesn't want to give in: no, he hasn't run away. She thinks it's a murder and requests an investigation. But the criminal police comes to the following conclusion:

It is clear as day that Lides ran away. To divert attention, his wife shouts that he has been murdered.

Mrs. Lides has been arrested twice under the same suspicion. Both times she was in the ghetto jail on Lidzki, and both times she constantly and incessantly claimed: her husband has been murdered. She has a feeling and that's how she sees it. She is prepared to cover the losses of the victims. She will sell everything and she will pay up. But she asks that the case be investigated—murder or not?

The victims demanded their due, and Mrs. Lides gathered up everything she had and paid up to 70 percent of the debt.

She suffered doubly: shame that she is under suspicion because her husband ran away from her. Sorrow because she thinks he has been murdered somewhere. But not wanting to quarrel, she gives away all her property, just to avoid the shame of trudging again from prison to the interrogation and from the interrogation back to prison. Just in order not to remain under suspicion that she is a partner in the hijacking of the 27,000 rubles.

The police did try to deal with the case again. There were even witnesses who said they saw Lides being carried on a wagon out of the ghetto. They tried to look for him in Łukiszki jail. And again the leadership of the Jewish criminal police conferred and came to the same conclusion: the woman is indeed suffering, perhaps innocent and honest. Her husband left her, took the money and ran.

The matter was deprioritized. The criminal police gave up. Mrs. Lides grew weary of demanding, and the issue was hushed up.

According to the criminal police, Hertsl Lides remains a swindler and money hijacker. According to his wife, she is a desolate widow who cannot even find out where her husband's bones have gone to. Both children remain orphans, and the case has been dropped like a stone in water. On top of that, she was stripped of everything. Everything they had, they took off their bodies and sold. And still she remains an accessory to the swindle, or at least shamed and victimized.

Hardly anybody in the ghetto is interested in it. Big deal, a person. One person more or less, who cares? The Vilna Ghetto has lost more than one person; here the lost are counted in thousands and tens of thousands.

How many thousands were liquidated here?

The Vilna Ghetto continued its normal ghetto life. Every day a new chapter of fear. Every day new rumors. And a fresh commotion at the gate guard.

Big deal, the Vilna Ghetto! . . .

4. The School of the Gejwuszes!

The restaurant at Kwaszelna Street 11 is not only a restaurant, but something else—and that "something else" is more important than the restaurant itself.

The regular customers, the behavior here, the language, and everything around let every stranger know that that above-mentioned "something else" is more than the restaurant itself.

The Vilna family of porters Gejwusz boasted an uncle, and the uncle drew his spiritual nourishment from a far-and-wide past. Gejwusz's uncle is a regular visitor at Simke's, more precisely, Simke the Hundred, and Simke is the son of Urke the Hundred and also the owner of the restaurant at Kwaszelna Street 11.

Simke's father, more precisely Urke the Hundred, owns three courtyards. One of the three, at Kwaszelna Street 11, the restaurant with the something else, is run by Urke's son Simke. The word *restaurant* sounds here like Versailles. The place is referred to here much more simply as a pub; some find another term for it—*melina*. In this pub, a special kind of "nobility" would assemble, our kind of people, people with a "past," only such people as were trusted here, who would feel at home with the unique behavior, language, and manners here.

A "stranger" who dropped in there accidentally would be called an "idiot," and everybody would glare at him, for they hated outsiders. Such an "idiot" soon felt "unwanted" and understood that he should take off in time. . . .

Often, over beer and hard-boiled eggs, they told each other tall tales about some underworld character, some pig or other, about a new stool pigeon, about the prosperity of a new butcher shop, and so on. From here they would receive and send messages, here they would buy a rod, and here many a plan for gangster exploits was hatched.

The son, Simke, had someone to learn from. His father, Urke the Hundred, was a man with a rich, extensive past. He himself had been one of the "greatest" and "strongest" of Vilna and its environs. The first and strongest was Zelig the son of Khane-Bobke, or, as he was called, Zelig the Generous. But Urke was not far behind.

Zelig the Generous is a carter who, back during the revolution of 1905, helped Piłsudski in his bold takeover of a train in Bezdany. Since then, Zelig has gone "his own way," become a "wet" power broker (a thief who wields a knife). And . . . he made himself a name and became popular.

Old Urke once again established himself. His letters were delivered to this or that merchant informing them that they had to remit such and such a sum, and only a rare person would dare to refuse.

Vilna trembled before both of them. Before both Zelig the son of Khane-Bobke and Urke the Hundred. Once both of them were the most "popular" names in Vilna, and their wishes had more force than a government order.

Urke's son Simke was the boss of the slaughterhouse. People sang in the streets of him and his exploits. Zelig the son of Khane-Bobke, along with Sashka the dancer, were the leaders of a special organization, the "Golden Banner." Vilna trembled before it. From here, orders were issued, protection money was assigned, fees were taken from clerks and housemaids. Here sentences were passed: who was to be cleaned out, who was to pay for a privilege, etc.

In the past, both groups worked together. Later they quarreled over the spoils. And thus two enemy camps emerged.

Zelig the son of Khane-Bobke spent half his life in jail, and in the name of his great historical feat of 1905, Piłsudski would repeatedly get him out. Urke, in contrast, amassed a great fortune and settled down. From those ancestors, Gejwusz's uncle draws his inspiration, and through him, his relatives the Gejwuszes draw full buckets.

The uncle would often tell stories, and the Gejwuszes would listen to him with great interest and attention.

The son of Khane-Bobke knocked off a stool pigeon and got a life sentence for it. Yet he got out of it and didn't cease his professional activities. In 1937–1938, he kidnapped Lipkowicz's child and demanded ransom. He was denounced and got a five-year sentence. It was only the Bolsheviks who liberated him and [when they left Vilna] carried him off to Mołodeczno, and he came back from there and died.

That is how the uncle would educate his relatives, and all the Gejwuszes absorbed his teaching, so that in their sleep they dreamed of various heroic feats and of gangster exploits of robbery and murder.

The uncle, a tiny Jew with a thin pointed nose and cunning feline eyes, used to know everything, hear about everything, and keep a sharp eye on everything around him. He understood that he was growing old and the Gejwuszes could still be a source of pride. He sensed that every story was an infusion into their veins, and the quiet, cunning, and pointy little uncle wove a nest in which he enmeshed himself and his young relatives .

5. The Lida Tragedy

The population of Lida lived relatively quietly. They listened with pounding heart to the horrors of Vilna and went through every passing day, waiting with bated breath. Lida was the first sanctuary where Vilna people ran. Running to Warsaw, Białystok, or Grodno meant first of all running to Lida. With no money to run as far as Warsaw, Lida was meanwhile a temporary stop. Thus Lida was the first asylum from bloody Vilna. Here people would rest from the Vilna nightmare—from here, some would go on, and many stayed to wait it out.

Reassuring letters arrived in Vilna from Lida. The Lida Ghetto was not really a ghetto. The relations were, in general, bearable. In short, for a Vilna person it sounded like a fantasy paradise. For a Lida person it was a matter of survival.

In early November 1941, Avidon came to Lida, and the next morning he started working at his carpentry. For Avidon it was clear that the events of Vilna would be forgotten and here in Lida, no one would touch a hair of his head. From carpentry in a work unit, you don't get enough to eat. And he didn't just eat. Here Avidon and his whole gang carried on a generous and wasteful life, he ate, he drank, he played cards, and. . . . He soon realized that just working for the Germans made no sense.

. . . And everything went fine.

Cards sometimes succeed, sometimes don't. . . . What can you say. . . .

Lida suddenly trembled. The whole town was jolted. There was a turmoil in the Judenrat and a commotion among the Jewish population.

What happened?

What happened is this:

The town boasted a Russian-Orthodox priest. And the priest was perhaps one of the few who saw the Jewish tragedy with great sorrow and didn't just observe it, but also helped with words and deeds. Many were beholden to him for finding them a place among peasants and hiding [them] from unwanted eyes. A priest the local population could be proud of. But it so happened that this friend of the Jews became a victim of a robbery by Jews.

In town they reported that the priest had been badly wounded with brass knuckles to the head; that in the pursuit of the escaping bandits one of them lost a garment with a yellow patch, which made it clear that the murderer was a Jew.

The district commissar ordered, sharp and clear: in 10 hours, the Judenrat had to supply the murderer or else . . . 1,000 Jews.

At first the city thought the whole thing was a provocation, but soon enough, more precise information came from Kościuszko Street, the site of the attack. It turned out that everything was true.

The whole police force was mobilized. The local and the Jewish. The district commissar wouldn't listen:

"Either the murderer or 1,000 Jews. . . . "

The whole population went on the chase. Six suspicious underworld characters were arrested, including Yankl Avidon. Yankl understood that his head was in danger. He was prepared to "squeal" on condition that he would be freed. Thus Yankl accepted the role of a denouncer.

The Judenrat, he claimed, took money and dollars to make passports for all those who fled from Vilna, claiming that they were inhabitants of Lida.

An order was issued:

"Arrest the whole Judenrat!"

Again the city shuddered, and again reassurance came: the district commissar promised to free the seven members of the Judenrat, but meanwhile on a Sunday came an order that the entire Lida population must immediately appear in the marketplace. There a provisional gate was established, and on both sides stood two of the six suspects. One was the carter Olkienicki, the other was Yankl Avidon. The whole Jewish population of the city had to pass between them, and they were to indicate which ones were from Vilna and which weren't.

Of the 7,000 Jews in Lida, 75 were singled out as allegedly from Vilna. They went to jail, and after 10 days in prison, they were all shot in the jail yard with the members of the Judenrat.

Avidon attained his goal. He was free and vacillated—he couldn't make up his mind:

It was impossible to stay on in Lida. To go back to Vilna was risky. Yet it was attractive. He looked slyly in all directions, wandered from place to place, and finally decided. As soon as Avidon decided something, the decision itself calmed him:

Two cold eyes like two fiery coals gazed out of the deep fur collar, and in them gleamed a murderous calm not every murderer is capable of.

In early March, the Vilna Ghetto was suddenly seized by a sensation: in the ghetto jail was the murderer of the Jewish policeman Greenfeld, the robber of the Lida priest, and the one guilty of the death of 75 Lida Jews and their Judenrat. . . .

Everyone turned his head away in disgust.

Many quietly thought:

In jail, and what then? . . .

6. Murder for Robbery in the Ghetto

Every time the Gejwusz brothers passed by Strashun 9, they dropped their heads in shame and couldn't look each other in the eye. Of course no one knew about it and no one saw it.

The pious little uncle, the tiny, shriveled Jew with his pointed, beaked nose, and sharp eyes, regarded it somewhat differently. He had forgotten about it long ago and was now hatching a new little business, a little trade, which, if it succeeded, would again provide something to rely on.

He himself is not such a weakling as his "kids." They will either learn, get tough, and God will help, and it'll boil over. . . .

The widow of the hatmaker Hertsl Lides didn't know what was happening to her: Was she a widow or an abandoned woman? However, if she had known the Gejwuszes and their tough uncle, wouldn't the criminal police of the ghetto also know about them?

But then everything was still buried under the ground, and whatever is buried can rarely see the light of day.

The Vilna Ghetto lives with its own settled and "stabilized" life: at dawn, they rush to work; at night, they run home, to wife and children, to relatives and friends.

The Vilna Ghetto lives its own life: one unit or another unit. Whether you get dinner there or not. A long distance and you rip the soles of your shoes. Whether or not a work place is nearby—those are problems that absorb both poor and rich, former rich men and yesterday's proletarians. Everything here serves the Reich, and whatever remains alive has a right to life only insofar as it is needed for the Reich, and—mainly—if it can be subservient, obedient, and slavish.

The Gejwusz brothers, uncle Grodzenski, Yankl Polikański, and Wituchowski —not one of them is in a hurry to go home, although most have wives and children. They are all involved and intimate with the Germans—slaves from the land of slaves. They are always busy with business: here they whisper secrets, there they quarrel, and here again they have a drink together, eat fish, and bathe in goose fat. That quintet is in no hurry to go home.

Why hide it?

When the news ran through the ghetto like a thin thread that a murdered body had been found at Szawelska 1, the ghetto residents trembled:

A murder in the ghetto?!

A large crowd gathers on Szawelska. The police cannot manage. Now the crowd parts—the commander of the ghetto police is coming. Again they crowd together: the prosecutor is coming, the president of the Judenrat. They go, they come, and they go again. The criminal police are very busy. No one is allowed into the office of the criminal police. Still everyone knows:

A murder at Szawelska 1.

A murdered body has been dug up from a cellar on Szawelska Street.

"And who was murdered?" a passerby asks curiously.

A young man appears from somewhere; he knows that the murdered man was a Hasidic yeshiva student, a refugee. Soon it was known that the murdered young man was named Yosef Gerstein.

The same Yosef Gerstein who fled from Białystok to Vilna as a yeshiva student. . . .

All evening the ghetto seethed like a cauldron: a murder in the ghetto!?

A murder, moreover, a robbery murder!—some added.

People couldn't understand it. Others blushed with shame: after so much suffering and blood, after so much humiliation—a murder for the sake of robbery? . . .

The ghetto regarded the entire event with shame. Never had it been so interested in the smallest details as then. This time more than ever everyone wanted to find out exactly how low the ghetto outcasts could stoop.

No one noticed that it was already dark. This time, as always, the street took part in the events. The ghetto was aroused, and the ghetto residents were sent belatedly to their yards. Even the policemen with their whistles missed the curfew.

Eventually they all dispersed to their homes, thinking of the ugly event—a murder for robbery in the ghetto. . . .

The night was heavy and nightmarish. Only when the beaten and ashamed ghetto citizen went quietly home and rested his exhausted body, only then did the ghetto authorities raise the real alarm.

The whole police force was assigned to the criminal department. A series of searches began, complete with digging up melinas, interrogations, and confrontations; and every time a new discovery. Every time the mud became deeper. One murder led to another. The second one showed preparations for a third. One murder more horrible than the last. The third murder was still in process of being planned. . . . A Sherlock Holmes story, a labyrinth where you don't see the beginning and don't find the end.

So it seethed on June 3 until late at night and all night long.

7. The Avidon Problem

In the solitary cell of the ghetto jail on Lidzki, like a lion in his cage, Avidon paced back and forth and racked his brain to grasp his situation.

His pure, symmetrical face, his black, ardent eyes, his whole sturdy figure was taut as though facing the final, decisive contest:

Everything points to a need to save himself. To stay here means to wait for death. To escape from here to the ends of the earth. But how do you do it?

Just like Avidon in his cell, so did the ghetto authorities rack their brains and come up with the rationale for Avidon's arrest:

To let him live means providing an opportunity for evasion sooner or later. Any kind of freedom would again give him an opportunity to invent new libels. Yesterday against Lida Jews, today against Vilna Jews. *Avidon must be destroyed*; he certainly deserves death. No one doubts it. To let him live means to risk the lives of thousands. To destroy him—but how? . . .

It was a problem you couldn't get a handle on.

But Avidon is far from giving up. Within the jail walls, he is a model prisoner. He is quiet, obedient, disciplined. He lies in his cell all day long, looks at the ceiling, and is silent. He is silent and spits for no reason. In his gaze you can see him constantly weaving plans. Quietly, a thread with a thread, he weaves a web with a spider in it. . . .

Every day he asks, calmly and casually:

"How long will you keep me here?"

"Why?"

Even if you hack him to pieces—he's innocent and doesn't know a thing.

Even if you cut him up!

Everybody points to him as the one who stood at the Lida marketplace, at the gate, and identified Jews from Vilna, but he, even if you cut him up, knows nothing about it.

When he asks the prosecutor when he will get out, this was the calm, cold answer he received:

"It is healthier and better to stay in jail. . . ."

"Why?" he coolly wanted to know more precisely.

"Because they are pointing at you. . . ."

"Because they will stone you!"

Once he grew pensive and loyally suggested:

"If so, turn me over to the Lithuanians. . . ."

"And then?" the prosecutor asked suspiciously.

"Then, then I'll find a way."

The people from Lida used to say: he is strong, a giant. He is nimble. He is a brilliant stabber. He can run like a deer. And the Jewish police force was indeed afraid he might escape.

Others said of him: he had an 18-year-old wife. She was in her eighth month [of pregnancy]. They were both hiding in a melina when they were taken from there. On Rudnicka Street, he pushed her down, she fell, and in the commotion, he escaped. She went to Ponar and he got away. . . .

The police grew even more frightened. The watch around his cell was reinforced. They pulled him out of his carpentry work in jail, and he never grew weary of asking:

"How long will I sit here?" He cannot sit unless there is a reason.

Suddenly he learned that they knew everything about his past. They even knew that he was once in jail for three years and another time for eight months. He sensed that the investigation of his case was not yet over, and if they were still concerned with him, perhaps it would be better to confess? He broke down and began blabbing.

He did do things. He regrets. He didn't believe it would have such sad consequences. Had he known, he wouldn't have done it. So how long can he be in the dark about what will happen to him?! . . .

This "diplomat" was only 27 years old. . . .

Suddenly he insisted on knowing if he would live. . . . And when he heard that he would, he renewed his request:

"How long will I be in jail?"

After each such conversation, he calmly and casually went back to his routine. At first, to his carpentry work; later to his cell, where, as if nothing had happened, he read Sholem Aleichem or stared at some point for hours and spat incessantly. . . .

Everyone admired his calm; at the same time it frightened them:

Once at night, when Vilna was heavily bombed by Bolshevik planes, when all the prisoners screamed to be let out of their cells, Avidon quietly lay on his pallet as if they didn't mean him—a unique calm!

Suddenly he begged the prosecutor for a visit. A visit with a little girl.

"Who is that little girl?"

They suspected everything.

"A girl registered to me," he explained.

A few days later, the prosecutor made up his mind:

A visit on June 4.

Avidon was excited.

8. June 4 in the Vilna Ghetto

Tens of thousands of Jews were torn out of the Vilna Ghetto and taken to death and destruction. Every Aktion cut into the organism of the ghetto like a bad dream. Each such purge brought new victims, and every time, in suffering and pain, up to its neck in blood, the ghetto thought about the day of historical vengeance.

No wonder. In the great grief and helplessness, people grew closer together—all equal candidates for Ponar! . . .

Jews became intimate with each other—brothers of one destiny!

The plight is shared—every hesitation at the gate is a blow to everyone. Every scare is a tremble for everyone. Everything is equal and equalized. The ghetto knows no ambiguity, no dualism. The ghetto is shaped like lead—all is one and one is all! . . .

All for one and each for all.

Suddenly a blow to the collective, a gangster story—a robbery murder in the ghetto.

A robbery murder? This is not the right expression. It is too mild and delicate. It is a gangster story. A robber gang that has no equal. A thing that may be the first case in the history of the Jews.

Today, more than in the past, the ghetto was aroused:

On top of yesterday's murder at Szawelska 1, there has been another murder at Strashun 9.

The investigation went on all night. Since dawn a kangaroo court has been working. All five murderers confessed, and the sentence will soon be handed down.

The investigation learned that at Strashun 9, there is the long-ago-murdered Hertsl Lides, the hatmaker who was robbed of 27,000 rubles, for which he was supposed to get 100 in gold; instead, he was lured into the cellar at Strashun 9, where he was murdered in a bestial way and buried standing on his head. So only now did they find Hertsl Lides.

At Szawelska 1, they found Yosef Gerstein, who was murdered yesterday morning for the same reasons, and who was buried almost like Lides, in a cellar, his head pressed down with a heavy stone, so that if he were found, he wouldn't be recognizable. . . .

And Avidon? Just this morning, the investigators remembered Yankl Avidon:

Avidon must be destroyed! . . . This is the opportunity—now or never! Avidon has to be dragged into it! . . .

At 6 in the morning, the key screeched in Avidon's cell and the order was given: get dressed.

Today, June 4, Avidon arranged a visit with the child. Just a few days before, he had written a petition to be released. Now, at the order to dress, Avidon's heart lurched. Suddenly his arms and legs went limp. Pale and scared, he didn't even ask what it was all about. Calm as ever, his sharp eyes observed all that was happening around him and understood—his fate was sealed!

When he saw the large police guard waiting for him, when they suddenly pulled his hands behind him and bound them, he understood that all that had happened so far had been a game. He was duped, now lost.

Six persons now lie stretched out on the floor of the Jewish police headquarters. Most half naked, beaten, and bleeding. The large room is steeped in tension, sweat, and bloodstains. Around the murderers are the entire police leadership, the Judenrat, the ghetto court, and the criminal police. The prosecutor demands a sentence of death by hanging for the six accused.

In his last words, Elye Gejwusz begs to be given . . . a cigarette; Yankl Polikański begs to be allowed to say farewell to his wife. Hirsh Wituchowski admits that he stabbed Gerstein; he is guilty. Avidon also asks to say his last words. He has lost his calm. The gleam in his eyes goes out, and he says:

"I don't admit guilt. I ask to be released."

Everyone present looks around in amazement. The court announces a recess and goes out to confer.

After a brief break comes the order to stand up. In a dead silence, two sentences are read:

> In the case of Elye Gejwusz, Yitskhok Gejwusz, Yankl Polikański, Leyb Grodzenski, and Hirsh Wituchowski, accused of committing two murders in the Vilna Ghetto with intent to rob, the judges of the court of the Vilna Ghetto have decided:
>
> 1. To pronounce Yankl Polikański, Elye Gejwusz, and Hirsh Wituchowski guilty of carrying out, on June 3, 1942, the premeditated robbery murder of Yosef Gerstein.
> 2. To pronounce Yankl Polikański, Elye Gejwusz, and Leyb Grodzenski guilty of carrying out, in the month of February 1942, the premeditated robbery murder of Hertsl Lides.
> 3. For the above-mentioned crimes, to punish Yankl Polikański, Elye Gejwusz, Hirsh Wituchowski, Yitskhok Gejwusz, and Leyb Grodzenski with the death penalty.
> 4. To convey the sentence immediately to the Judenrat for ratification.

And then the second sentence:

> In the case of Yankl Avidon, accused of an attempt to murder the policeman Yankl Greenfeld, the judges of the court of the Vilna Ghetto have decided:
>
> 1. To pronounce Yankl Avidon guilty of the attempt to murder the policeman Greenfeld in the course of his duties in the month of November 1941, and to sentence him to death.
> 2. To convey the sentence immediately to the Judenrat for ratification.

A gust of death blew into the hall. Everyone fell silent as if he had lost his tongue. The reading was over and the accused were ordered to lie down again, and . . . only Avidon couldn't calm down. He seethed and shook. He was the only one who tried to beg for mercy, but. . . .

He doesn't understand the whole thing:

"How did it happen?"

"Hasn't his case been resolved? . . . "

They all lie on the floor face down, and only Avidon glares at everything that is going on around him. He seems to want to calm down and continue working on it—just maybe something will work out. . . .

The accused are guarded by a heavy guard, and apparently nothing in the world will help them except a miracle from heaven.

And perhaps they are waiting for that miracle?

After a brief consultation, the members of the Judenrat added the following to both sentences:

> At its meeting of June 4, 1942, the Judenrat of the Vilna Ghetto decided to ratify the sentence.

Thus everything is over. The sentence is ratified, and the ghetto authorities prepare the execution.

Meanwhile, the ghetto seethes like a cauldron. Everyone feels ashamed. The ghetto is ashamed. Among the clusters of people gathering and commenting, you often hear:

"It's the greatest disgrace of the ghetto!"

"It's a shame for our enemies. . . ."

The death sentence—six gallows in the ghetto—was a relief:

"The ghetto must wipe off the disgrace."

"It's a historic day."

"The ghetto must clean itself for history."

Six gallows in the Vilna Ghetto.

A Jewish investigation, a Jewish court and sentence, written in the Yiddish mother tongue—six gallows.

The ghetto is shaken by the events. No one is sorry. Everyone waits impatiently:

"The ghetto must wipe off the disgrace!"

"It is a historic day."

9. Preparations

The narrow little streets of the Vilna Ghetto now assume an unusual appearance. Everyone is in the street, and everyone is tensely awaiting the execution.

It is said that:

Many volunteers have reported to serve as hangmen.

A Jew brought a rope: he wants them to hang on his rope.

The youngest of the Jewish police commissars is red as a beet. His request to become hangman was rejected. . . .

There is one decision:

There are no hangmen in the ghetto. Policemen will carry out the hanging. Those whose duty it is to keep order in the ghetto . . .

No one person must have on his conscience that he is a hangman—everyone will share the role of hangman.

The tension increases by the minute. At first the execution was to be carried out only in the presence of the local ghetto authorities. But later the Germans expressed their desire to be present. The execution was postponed from 12 noon to 3 P.M.

An uneasy feeling burrowed its way into everyone's hearts:

"And perhaps 'they' will feel like investigating the case?"

"What will happen then to Avidon?" . . .

"Who knows what such a character may try?" . . .

The street seethes, and only the few who understand the entangled affair of Avidon fear the final consequences:

Who knows what such a character may try? . . .

On Jatkowa Street, in the butchers' yard, for years there was a meat market: butchers, butchers, and butchers. There, among the big, heavy pillars, flayed calves hung head down. There, the butcher would come with a knife and cut the piece the customer wanted.

Jatkowa Street, the butchers' yard.

Now they're preparing the site of the execution here. Six gallows for the accused. Instead of calves, ghetto Jews will hang here. Jews will hang them, and no one's hand will tremble. No one in the ghetto will moan!

Twenty thousand Jews against six, and twenty thousand are waiting for the moment of the end.

The sooner the better! . . .

Simple Jews—one lawyer, one student, one engineer, one clerk, and just a decent man—these are the ghetto judges.

For many years, a judge could work at his desk and live his whole life without pronouncing a death sentence.

These simple Jews, the Jewish ghetto judges, were cast by destiny in the role of pronouncing six death sentences.

They are all hunched over: the condemned certainly deserved it. The sentence must be carried out unhesitatingly, as soon as possible. But they signed it, and they are the ones who send six people to the other world.

Deep in their hearts, worms burrow, and somewhere deep, a pain gnaws.
The chief of police, the linchpin of the action, is in complete control:
It must happen and we must be courageous.
"It is our historical task!"
The ghetto waits tensely.

10. The Execution

The Vilna Ghetto looks like a film set, like a well-rehearsed event. Everything seems as though it were on a movie screen.

Thousands of heads stick out the front windows. Thousands are waiting for the procession to the site of the execution.

Three limousines slice into the ghetto: *Gebietskomissar* Hingst; his adviser for Jewish affairs, Murer; Hingst's chief-of-staff, Lakner, representatives of the *Schutzpolizei,* Gestapo, SS, *Sonderkomando,* and others.

Three limousines right to the site of the execution.

A procession is organized at Rudnicka 6: the six condemned, following one another, each surrounded by six policeman. All the condemned have their hands tied behind their backs.

People hold their breath:

"To the gallows . . ."

"Jews take Jews to the gallows, and Hingst and Murer are the witnesses. . . ."

Aren't they the ones responsible for the slaughtered thousands and thousands of Jews in Vilna? . . .

The procession goes to the site of the execution. The first one is Avidon; after him marches Yitskhok Gejwusz. Then comes Leyb Grodzenski, Yankl Polikański, Wituchowski, and Elye Gejwusz.

The streets are dead. The march of the procession beats on the stones like hammers hitting the heads of the spectators. It seems that the ghetto is holding its breath.

Regret—you won't see it in any one of the six. They "march" as though to a well-deserved punishment. They march and don't tarry.

The ghetto shudders!

The ghetto holds its breath. . . .

A small, square yard—the butchers' yard on Jatkowa Street. Six meat hooks and six stools. The ground is hard, covered with asphalt—a butchers' yard.

Each criminal is placed under a hook—here he will come to an end! The gallows ropes hang over their heads; before them stand the gallows stools.

Everything is waiting!

The Gebietskomissar allows the execution to begin. The chief of the ghetto police walks to the middle of the yard and is visible to everyone, his voice resounding in Yiddish:

Police, Judenrat

Of 75 thousand Vilna Jews, only 16 thousand remain. These 16 must be good, honest, and hard-working people. Anyone who isn't will end the same way as those who were sentenced today. We will punish every such case and will even kill with our own hands.

Today we carry out an execution of six Jewish murderers who killed Jews. The sentence will be carried out by the Jewish police, who protect the ghetto and will go on protecting it. The police will carry out the sentence as its duty.

We begin!

The words slice into the tragic ghetto history like a howl. The first one to put his head in the noose is Avidon. He hangs! Now it's the second one's turn—Yitskhok Gejwusz—but Avidon cannot rest. He tries to wrench himself out, and the whole square is filled with a clatter. Avidon has wrenched himself out and has fallen like a heavy stone on the hard asphalt.

The entire audience trembles. Dead silence. A horrible surprise, followed by the question: What now?

According to the universally accepted law, he must be released.

But can Avidon be released?

Would it be possible to let him out of the noose? . . .

Jews see it differently: his dozens of innocent victims begrudge him such a death. The German "guests" suggest that the Jewish chief decide. And he decides:

"We don't need him! . . ."

The beaten Avidon lies in a pool of blood on the ground, and the execution continues:

Yitskhok Gejwusz turned his head aside and grew stiff—his last tremor.

The little uncle watches and doesn't bat an eyelash. Soon his turn comes. He looks at his brother's son, observes his last convulsions, and doesn't take his eyes off him; now he himself puts his head in the noose:

"Shma Yisroel!"—he whispers into the noose.

And Polikański turns his head. His tongue hangs out. . . .

Those still waiting in the line watch and don't react.

Heroes!

Everyone admires their calm.

The Germans are amazed:

"Jews, such courageous Jews. . . ."

Wituchowski quivers, and here is the last one, Elye Gejwusz. He cannot wait any longer. Something pursues him. He climbs up on the stool by himself, and with his bound hands, he pushes his own head into the noose. The rope is pulled, the stool falls, and . . . the execution returns to the first one—Avidon!

Lying [on the ground] all the time, half-conscious and half-confused, he still understands he has to play dead. As soon as they pick him up, he opens his half-drunk eyes and looks at the big world for the last time.

Twice on the gallows, and the longest and most difficult death is Avidon's. He still twirls on the gallows and cannot finish. For a long time after everyone has left the site of the executions, Avidon's heavy body still bounces and apparently doesn't want to make peace with the death he deserved.

The street waited impatiently. Thousands of people blocked the roads, and thousands lined up to watch the six gallows. No one came to mourn. No one could believe it, and they wanted to see it with their own eyes.

They didn't believe their own eyes!

THE DREADFUL TRAGEDY OF THE BARANOVITSH JEWS

Written in the Vilna Ghetto, January 1943, by Herman Kruk

This time, my source is an intelligent man, an attorney from Warsaw, and since the war a refugee who reached Baranovitsh with his wife and child. Now he fills the role of an *Oberjude* in Eknaymsho [Oszmianka] OTE camp—near the town of Enaymsho [Oszmiana].

The narrator clearly understands the social situation we all find ourselves in. He is an active participant in several preparations we shall discuss. In the second Aktion in Baranovitsh, he lost his wife and child, and he decided to do anything to die like a man and not be shot like a pig.

Up until the "purge," Baranovitsh numbered about 12,000 Jews. The first "cleansing" took place on March 4, 1942, and lasted all day. Four thousand Jews perished. Eight thousand Jews remained in the city.

The second "cleansing" took place one day after Yom Kippur, on Tuesday, September 22, 1942. The "cleansing" lasted eight days. Of the 8,000 Jews, 5,000 perished. At that point about 3,000 Jews remained in Baranovitsh.

The third "cleansing" began on December 17, 1942, and lasted three days. The result was that, as of today, in January 1943, there are 200 Jews left in Baranovitsh.

About a month after the first slaughter, things grew absolutely calm. You might have thought that no more changes would be made there. But after April 13, it became clear that it was not yet over. Reliable information circulated that, in the surrounding towns, the Jewish population was being liquidated—the entire district would be *Judenrein*. Many people then came up with the idea of not letting themselves be slaughtered. The idea of preparing a resistance became popular.

The first to seize upon the idea were those whose families had been taken. They collected weapons and brought a lot of them into the ghetto. The idea of creating a self-defense organization crystallized. The first organizers were Khone Nivograsht [Czargowin], a former military man who now works, posing as a

Pole, in Eknaymsho; then came Yankl Kavon [Nowak]. Then came several intellectuals: Dr. Abrasha Iksvomarba [Abramowski], Lola Shtivonerb [Brenowicz], and others. The latter soon joined the leadership.

The whole organization was divided into groups. The groups by streets, the streets by sections, i.e., subgroups. A group numbered 25 people; a subgroup, 5 or 10. In its heyday, the organization included 500 members. In fact, a large number of Jewish nemecilop [policemen] joined, including the chief of police, Shtivekdar [Radkiewicz], and his deputies Repesh[3] and Iksvashrav [Warszawski].

Everything was done underground: under the meeting place of the Judenrat, a tunnel was built to serve as a workshop for composing and repairing snopaew [weapons]. There they were tested and cleaned, and also often distributed. A few more arsenals were scattered through the city. One of them wasn't far from the Jewish hospital. In that storehouse there were about 280 grenades, 100 rifles, 10–15 automatic submachine guns, CKMs, machine guns, and several thousand rounds of ammunition.

On Orła Street, there was a big, long bunker that also served as a shooting gallery. On the same street there was also a big arsenal. Another warehouse was in the rabbi's bunker.[4]

An underground architecture of melinas was created. A melina was dug under almost every house. The entrance was always from your own apartment or from the apartment of a neighbor who lived under the same roof. Thus they planned that during future Aktions, no one would have to go out to the courtyard or the street. Most of the entrances to the bunkers were made under the floors and were camouflaged, for example, under a bed, or covered with a pile of logs. Everywhere this was done so that no one would notice it and, as far as possible, no one would catch on.

The architecture of the bunkers is like this: you dig pits 5 meters deep. The bunker itself is 2 meters high. On top of it are 3 meters of dirt that have been dug out. To make sure that the pit won't cave in, boards are placed in the form of the Hebrew letter ח. Nevertheless, it was feared that because of the straight line, the dirt would cave in, and that gave rise to the idea of building zigzag canals. According to engineering calculations, that would make the walls more solid. Naturally the boards, as described above, were positioned accordingly. The canals were provided with running water, or water tanks, sewage, or an outflow, or at least with buckets and electricity. People usually drew electricity from the street so that no "meter" would move during an Aktion. The bunkers were usually ventilated by chimneys through tubes of boards that were connected to wells, disguised in sheds under woodpiles, extended out to a field and concealed with

3. This person, presumably someone named Sheper, is unknown.

4. The bunker of Słonim rabbi Shloymele Weinberg, who later perished in Camp Kołdyczewo.

plants, etc. In the bunkers there were benches and bunk beds made of dirt; often shelves for food were arranged. In some places, there were even special branches for children.

Only at night was it possible to work. The work was done from 11 at night until 4 in the morning. According to the calculation of the engineers, a space of 5 meters of channel could be dug in that time. Of course, a few such groups were working simultaneously. That is how thoroughly the work was calculated and systematized.

In case of an Aktion, the following plan was worked out:

The ghetto has three gates. One gate is completely closed, the second gate is to the workshops, the third is the main gate through which all traffic moves. To the right of the main gate is an alley. In the third house on the alley is the site of the Judenrat. Opposite the Judenrat is the Jewish police. In case of an Aktion, there are two possibilities:

1. An attack at night when everyone is inside the ghetto, or possibly on Sunday when almost the entire population is in the ghetto.
2. Penetration into the ghetto when the workers are outside the ghetto in their units.

The most active members of the organization were deployed so that they never moved far from the ghetto. Their places of work were always in the ghetto. Most of them were on duty frequently and regularly stood guard during the day or at night.

In the first case: during an attack at night or on a day of rest, they would open heavy machine-gun fire from the two buildings to the right of the gate (Judenrat and police). Surprised, the Germans would retreat. Two brigades would use this hiatus: one would set fire to the ghetto, the other would leave the ghetto and dash to the buildings of the district commissar and the post office: both would be set on fire. In the general confusion and tumult, everyone who could would flee.

In the second case—in the middle of the work day—the murderers would be met with the same firestorm as in the first case. The ghetto would be set on fire, and that would be a sign that all the workers in the city were to set fire to their units. Again, in the turmoil of the events, everyone would flee wherever he could.

The leadership was in touch with two outside forces—the partisans and the Poles. It is hard to judge how much of the contact was serious. The Poles promised that they were organized, that they would support the struggle whenever necessary. A Soviet Jew was in touch with the partisans; he was a lieutenant who stayed behind with his son and hid in the ghetto.

The groups not only learned to shoot and to accept discipline, and so forth. A system of alarms was also set up, for training purposes or when there was a suspicion that something was "in the offing." Often this was done not only in order to assemble the groups, but also to test their readiness, to dispatch them to various posts, duties, etc.

When the Germans suddenly entered the ghetto on the pretext of seeking men for work, the ghetto became like a ghost town, as described above. The only ones who remained aboveground were the chairman of the Judenrat, Jankielewicz,[5] and two policemen. Aside from that, the Germans posted three more men who later fell under suspicion. Among other things, those persons who remained during the Aktion received the task of burying all the dead who perished in the ghetto. About 200 murdered Jews were buried.

Because the entrance of the Germans clearly looked like an Aktion, no one wanted to leave the bunkers. The Germans, it turns out, knew all about them and understood it all very well. They wanted first of all to take out the men, and their caution in uncovering bunkers led to the suspicion that the Germans knew precisely and in detail about every step in the underground ghetto, and had been informed about the resistance they might encounter. Wanting to have an easy time of it, the Germans brought into the ghetto 20 Christian engineers, technicians, and 200 workers who, with axes, crowbars, and shovels, were to determine the locations of the bunkers.

In spite of the good preparation, it is a far cry from theoretical preparation to practical execution. The end of it was extremely tragic. Everyone was in a state of readiness, everyone was at his post, and from the side of the resisters, there was not one order of battle and not one shot.

After the Aktion described above, a great many of the best and most active were sent to the camps in the surrounding area. Naturally, among those "best and most active" were included many members of the self-defense groups. So, around July, the organization was badly weakened. Nevertheless, new people were attracted who somehow replaced those who were sent away. Yet the organization did indeed remain weak.

The second blow the self-defense groups received was that three days before the slaughter, one of the leaders, Dr. Baranovitsh [Abrasha Abramowski], left the ghetto, leaving no trace behind. People said he went to a lady friend who lived in that area.

Dr. Iksvomarba was appointed leader of the resistance. He had to direct the defense from a certain bunker. His fiancée, Mine Aksnayvrolov,[6] served as his personal adjutant. A courageous and energetic woman, she went to the gate as a nurse with a revolver under her cloak to see what was going on. Suddenly she was hit over the head from behind with a stick. She fell and was soon put in a car and driven away.

Did they find out anything about her? Perhaps someone had denounced her? . . .

5. Shmuel Jankielewicz survived the Holocaust and moved to Israel.

6. Mine Lachozwiańska (the inversion reads Volorvyanska), from Słonim, a registered nurse of the Czysta Hospital in Warsaw.

All posts were meanwhile manned. Aside from positions taken at the gate, there was a well-built bunker above the hospital where a machine gun was ready with 60 people armed from head to foot. The Germans already controlled the ghetto, and yet the order didn't come.

There was discipline, and no one would shoot without an order!

Dr. Iksvomarba, it turns out, knowing of the horrible end of the person closest to him, was dismayed and didn't give any orders. Not until 6 in the evening, when the Germans left the ghetto and it became easier to move, was it clear that the commander Dr. Iks[7] had moved to another bunker and it was impossible to find him.

As we mentioned above, the Aktion lasted eight days. The Germans introduced a normal eight-hour working day:

Every day at 8 in the morning, the White Russian and Lithuanian police entered the ghetto singing. Behind them, the SS men. Only after all of them came the groups of Christians mobilized from among the civilian population. The "work" lasted until 12 noon. Then came a lunch break. The work resumed between 2 and 6 P.M.

People from the discovered melinas were taken to the building of the Judenrat, where they were gathered and sent away in groups.

Jankielewicz was on guard. In the dark of night, he, along with others who remained, brought food to the pits. He did this from Wednesday to Saturday. On Friday the people who had been settled in the small ghetto were ordered to go back to the "old ghetto" on Saturday and Sunday in order to bring the things from their "old homes." On Saturday and Sunday, the Aktion was therefore interrupted. While carrying their things, a lot of people left the bunkers and joined the ones who moved to the "small ghetto," convinced that it was outside of any danger. The guard didn't prevent it.

On Monday morning, the "small ghetto" was surrounded. Only the able-bodied were allowed to leave for work. All those who were left were sent to be liquidated.

Facts that must be recorded:

Fact 1: Ismn, a local inhabitant, was loaded onto a truck; he said that if the Germans would let him live, he would show them bunkers. The Germans agreed. They seated him with great honor in a special armchair, gave him good food, and only after he denounced 15 bunkers was he sent to the execution square.

Fact 2: Once, in the place where people were gathered to be transported to the execution square, a German major appeared, removed more than 50 women, and loaded them onto a truck. When the Aktion was over, that officer brought them back, safe and sound.

After the first day of the Aktion, Tuesday night, when the murderers left the

7. Also Dr. Abramowski.

ghetto and the armed resistance groups started searching for their commander, it turned out that the latter had left his melina and had fled. So nothing more could be hoped for from him.

For two nights, his subordinates, with exceptional discipline and obedience, had waited for an order. At night, the hospital was guarded—from above, from the observation post with its full garrison; from below, by two men with automatic rifles. When the fighting groups finally saw their tragedy in all its nakedness, they gathered together and decided to leave the ghetto with their arms and go to the forests.

But to get out of the ghetto without a battle, they had to make contact with a White Russian policeman, to whom they paid 20,000 rubles. The policeman took the money and betrayed them. Suddenly, as they came to the agreed-upon place, a spotlight was cast on them, and under that light, they were shot at. Five of the fighting brothers fell dead; the rest ran away, 50 kilometers from Baranovitsh to the area of Telechany, and a week later were followed by a few more groups.

The work of discovering the bunkers in the ghetto was done with great caution and dread of the concealed army, which the Germans knew about. The Christians who were forced to do that work discovered that about 70 percent of those bunkers held axes, shovels, and other such tools.

During the dark nights, the chairman of the Judenrat, Shmuel Jankielewicz, and the deputy chief of the Jewish police, a local sawmill worker, A. Warszawski, were busy supplying food to the bunkers and transferring people from one part of the ghetto to another. They contacted the head of the guard, Titus, and for a bribe of 2,000 rubles a head, the business was concluded, only now with his help and knowledge.

A few times, the contraband succeeded. Suddenly, when they tried to move the people from the rabbi's bunker, including the wife and child of our narrator, all three were suddenly surrounded, and all of them, even those from the bunker, were detained and sent off in trucks.

Two days after that event, Warszawski was returned to the ghetto, half naked, barefoot, bloody, and so maimed that it was hard to recognize him. They demanded that he show them the arsenals, the bunkers with people, etc. He and another person were taken through the "old ghetto" under heavy guard. But Warszawski didn't lose his head. He led his executioners to those bunkers from which he himself had taken the people a few days before. . . . He was beaten dreadfully and finally . . . taken away. . . . The proud, idealistic Warszawski did not betray. He remained loyal to the Jewish masses to his last breath.

Jews watched the finale and painfully heard the cries of Warszawski and his companions. The helpless prisoners from the second, "small" ghetto clenched their fists and had to keep silent.

In the town, it was clear to everyone that those three were guilty of treason.

The third Aktion, for the remaining 3,000 Jews, began on December 17, 1942.

The Aktion lasted three days, to the 20th of the month. As an Oberjude of a provincial camp, our narrator came to the town by chance with his German boss. Seeing that the ghetto was surrounded and understanding what was happening, the German immediately drove away with him because he was afraid for his Oberjude. . . . Only later did our narrator learn that everyone was taken out of the ghetto to the outskirts of the city, and there, behind the tar pits near the village of Grabowiec, they were shot. Now he thinks there are about 200 Jews left in Baranovitsh.

Comments

The sad details, with a few comments, were confirmed by the Baranovitsh resident Motl Iksnalop [Polański], a veteran B [Bundist] activist, member of the local committee of the B and the Tsukunft. Some comments of a social nature were supplied by him.

The comments about some of the participants and their party affiliation or decency also come from the same source.

The Lublin refugee Namdlog [Goldman], a serious and responsible man, reports that the director of the arsenal on Sosnowa was Engineer Shtivobyel [Lejbowicz]. In this arsenal were two CKM heavy machine guns, 200 hand grenades, 7 pistols, 20 rifles, and 2,000 bullets.

Now I learn that on about March 28, 1943, the narrator went to the partisans with a group of 75 people.

August 15, 1944

WANDERING FROM NIEMENCZYN THROUGH SMORGONIE, OSZMIANA, RUDZISZKI, TO VILNA

The narrator is Rabbi Yankev Namdaynsh [Schneidman], who was born in Smorgonie and studied in Ramayle's Yeshiva in Vilna. He spent the years 1929–1939 in Radun in the Hafetz Hayyim Yeshiva. At the outbreak of the war, he went into the army. Participated in the defense of Lwów against the Germans, then went back to Smorgonie, left for Vilna, and continued studying. The yeshiva where he studied settled in Utena, and there he stayed until the outbreak of the German-Soviet war.

One week before the war, the Bolsheviks exiled 60 people from the yeshiva. Our narrator escaped and came to Niemenczyn.

His appearance: externally 100 percent Aryan. Also beautifully built, tall and broad. His arms heavy, a toiler's healthy hands. His face smiling and open. Everything he says he conveys good-humoredly and ironically.

Niemenczyn

The Sabbath before Rosh Hashanah 1942. Early in the morning came an order that all Jews must assemble in the synagogue, ostensibly to be taken to a ghetto.

Many inhabitants of the shtetl tried to run away, but they realized that the entire shtetl was surrounded by Lithuanians and that running away was risky. Hence they all went to the synagogue.

The Synagogue

The shtetl numbered 600–700 Jews, including 100 refugees, who in turn included 60 yeshiva students from Międzyrzec and three heads of the yeshiva. They all went to the synagogue with heavy bundles and sat there until 8 in the morning. Two Germans appeared and calmed the crowd, telling them they would be taken to a ghetto. One of them climbed onto the pulpit and ordered all gold, money, silver, and other valuables turned over to the Lithuanians at the exit of the synagogue. They also ordered the people to leave all bundles and take only small parcels. How frightened the people were can be seen from the following vignettes:

In the synagogue, someone demanded that everybody recite the Confession because the synagogue would be set on fire. Most of the Jews recited "Avinu malkenu." One local Jew, Avrom-Yitskhok Bezdański, says to his five-year-old son: "Up to now, I have reared you; now I turn you over to the hands of God."

At the exit of the synagogue, the Germans and Lithuanians conducted a strict and brutal search of men and women separately. In some cases they broke teeth made of . . . gold.

This lasted until 10 in the morning. All those who left the synagogue had to lie down on the ground, and thus the group lay there, surrounded by Lithuanian policeman.

The March to Slaughter

Everyone was then lined up, three persons in a row. Talking on the way was forbidden. Those who lagged behind were killed on the spot. Thus, the majority of victims were children and old people. Some two and a half kilometers from town, the column was turned to the right, into a grove, where it became absolutely clear that the road did not lead to a ghetto.

The Shooting

A lot of people decided to run. But no one dared share this thought with anyone else. Some 200 meters off the road, the front lines began screaming: "Here are our graves." This had the effect of an explosion. A mother took off the shoes of her 21-year-old son, Gershn Niemenczyński, so he could run faster. A sister wouldn't let her brother run, because if they must die, she wanted them to die together.

Running

The first one who dashed off was the 21-year-old Niemenczyński. He ran to the right, they shot at him, he fell, got up again, and ran on.

The narrator ran after him, and then a large mass of people dashed off. About two days later, he met some 10 escapees. The first one, Niemenczyński, was [later] in Vilna, worked on the railroad, and accidentally fell under a train and died in the Vilna Ghetto.

Summary

Of the more or less 700 inhabitants, about 100 were saved. The rest have to be counted as dead. As [the escapees] ran, they heard shooting all day long. Those who escaped hid in the forests, among the wheat in the fields, in peasant houses. But all ran toward Byelorussia, because the fear of Lithuania and the slaughters in the Lithuanian region became clear to everyone. Our narrator came to Bystrzyca; from there he went on until he reached Smorgonie.

Smorgonie and the Jewish Village Karke[8]

When the Germans entered Smorgonie, the shtetl numbered 1,636 Jews. The Germans marched in on June 26 [1941]. But as soon as they entered, certain elements set fire to many Jewish houses, with the intention of robbing them. Later, at the investigation, they accused the Jews themselves. For that, the Germans shot 40 Jews.

Two Ghettos

In September 1941, two ghettos were established here, one of them outside of town in the so-called Karke, a Jewish village one kilometer out of town. The second ghetto was in the town itself, in the quarter of the synagogue and cemetery. The Polish police ruled both ghettos and would beat the local Jews murderously. Later Byelorussian police arrived, who didn't beat people.

In the winter, toward Passover, Smorgonie was transferred to Lithuania. Until then, Smorgonie had to supply the Gebietskomissar of old Wilejka with anything he wanted. The "orders" included money, sometimes gold or silver, sometimes cloth, leather, toilet soap, etc. Fourteen such orders were given and filled. The city knew that this was a kind of extortion and paid silently.

Liquidation of the Ghetto in Karke

At harvest time 1942, the ghetto in Karke was liquidated. All the Jews of the village were transferred to Smorgonie. The Smorgonie Ghetto was enlarged. This lasted for a month, and then many of the ghetto inhabitants were sent to work camps. Thus, for example, 290 people were sent to camps, 170 of them to Zezmer, 120 to Rudziszki; others were sent to Olkieniki and Orany. The ghetto was fenced in, and 1,300 people thus remained in Smorgonie.

8. *Karka* is the Hebrew word for "soil," and its Yiddish cognate, *karke,* means "cemetery plot."

Liquidation of the Smorgonie Ghetto

In November, the Smorgonie Ghetto was liquidated. Some were transported to Oszmiana, some to Sol. In the city, only 150 Jews remained, as workers in a local camp.

From Oszmiana to Rudziszki

Oszmiana is a mixture of Jews pulled together from Holszany, Krewo, and some from Smorgonie. Oszmiana became a big ghetto. Some of the people from Krewo, Holszany, and the 170 from the Smorgonie Ghetto were transferred from here to the camps of Zezmer. The narrator was transported to a camp in Rudziszki.

Rudziszki

In Rudziszki there are no more Jews. When our narrator came there he found only 40 Jews. The old families, who had been there for generations, had been taken to Trok between Rosh Hashanah and Yom Kippur 1941.

Two Jewish Villages—Lejpuny and Żydownia

During the time our narrator spent here (ten weeks, until Sukkoth), he visited two Jewish villages, Lejpuny and Żydownia. He reports that during Sukkoth all Jews of Żydownia were gathered and sent to Olkieniki. After Sukkoth, they liquidated the Jews of Olkieniki, along with those of Żydownia and Eyshishok. Żydownia was settled by Lithuanians. At the same time, the village of Lejpuny was also destroyed.

End

Our narrator worked in Rudziszki for ten weeks. From there, he went to Kiena. In Kiena he worked at the Todt organization for six weeks. Then he escaped and came to Vilna in December 1942.
Recorded in January 1943

WITH HIS LIPS SEALED

I

Head high, his hair tossed back, his medium-sized figure stood provocatively, as if at any minute he were ready to contest everything that might stand in his way. This was Srolik.

His adult but still youthful countenance looked as though he had embraced independence early in his life.

Why be a burden to his father?

Why depend on the support of his parents?

Reyzele was one year younger than her brother. Her head, too, was held high, her gaze all-encompassing, and in her wide, plump face, there were two dimples hidden in the two corners of her mouth. Her face was always smiling, her look always full. Her eyes saw everything and took in everything around her.

By her feminine grace, their young mother betrayed her age.

"Is this a mother of two grownup children?" It was hard to believe. But you had to believe it. The children were a perfect copy of their mother.

The father, in contrast to the rest of them, was prematurely old, and all their youthfulness seemed to be at his expense. Every day he trudged along in the German unit, carrying his box of carpenter's tools. Under the double cover of his box, he "laundered in" either butter or sugar or tobacco—anything he could!

There are five mouths to feed. The parents, two children, and Reyzele's husband. The mother works in the ghetto workshop, a make-work job—12 rubles a day, yet she can be registered; working in the Wehrmacht workshops is a recipe for life. . . .

The son, Srolik, recently worked in the "heavy industry" of the ghetto workshops. Eight hours a day, he "keeps busy" in the mechanical workshop; he keeps busy but doesn't want to do anything: For whom, for what, why? . . .

Quietly he thinks about it. Is it sabotage? And he's happy.

His sister, Reyzele, doesn't understand politics—her work as a barber is perfect; she does it with energy and devotion. She knows that a woman coming to have her hair combed wants to leave happy, that a woman having a manicure in the ghetto is still thinking of her feminine graces. So she does her work with precision and calm. Until late at night, she works in the Ghetto Theater as a hairdresser. During the day, half legally, women come to her and she combs, manicures, and . . . talks.

Reyzele talks a lot, nonstop. Young, barely 18 years old, and talks with everyone about everything—an old soul. She knows everything, talks about everything, and hardly lets anybody get a word in.

For Reyzele, talking is a pleasure. A pleasure that costs little, often even nothing, entirely free.

Her husband? Barely 20. It started with "registration"; later they got married for real.

A marriage in the ghetto? Is that all they've got to think about. . . .

But Reyzele is happy with her Simke. Simke is tall, slender, healthy. He goes to his unit with his father. The father goes to his carpentry, and Simke goes to Pienocentras, where he distributes milk from churns. He "launders" cheese, butter. It's no small thing to feed five mouths.

<u>2</u>

The time for "registering" arrived, and with it a quarrel—who would register whom. Fathers registered as their daughters' husbands, sons became the husbands of their mothers, sisters became wives of their brothers, and brothers husbands of their sisters. A cacophony of registrations: adding to a registration, subtracting from a registration, changing a registration. Families became entangled and hardly ever got straightened out. Solitary people were surrounded by families as if by flies. An old bachelor suddenly acquired a father and a mother, a wife and children. That is how it went in the ghetto, and that is what happened to our mechanic, to Reyzele and her husband and her husband's sister—a cacophony that unfortunately resulted in tragedy.

During registration, the question of Reyzele's sister-in-law arose. Her husband, Reyzele's great and passionate love, remained alone with his sister. His whole family had gone to Ponar. Now that he was married and had gone to live with his wife's parents, his poor sister remained alone. Reyzele then suggested that she "divorce" her husband and register as her brother Srolik's wife. Furthermore, her husband Simke would register his own sister as his wife.

Everybody liked the plan, and the most grateful was her "real" husband. Simke, his sister's official husband, lived with his wife, Reyzele, and Reyzele's brother had a wedding contract with his own sister. . . .

That was no surprise to anyone. This is no secret in the ghetto for anybody, not even a special case. Everyone "registered" as he liked, and as was convenient. Even the ghetto authorities would "pair off": a Jew with a *Schein* [permit] needs a wife, and a wife with a Schein must obtain a husband. A Schein is the protection for a whole family, and to save as many people as possible, such families swell with wives, children, fathers, and mothers. Barely 4,000 Scheins gave the right to life to more than 15,000 Jews: matchmaking, families, registrations—that was life in the ghetto.

3

Reyzele's brother, Srolik, barely finished Sabbath School.[9] At 13 he went to work and underwent all the difficulties of an apprentice. When he finally became a genuine worker, he continued his association with the Komsomol.[10] Under the Bolsheviks, he was a representative of the Red youths in his factory, the most active of the activists. Srolik hated intellectuals. He couldn't stand intellectuals with soft hands. Srolik didn't get along with books, either. He hated to read: he had no patience. Reading was a game for intellectuals. He grew up in the Vilna suburb of Lipówka with Christian children; he absorbed a goyish mentality—a rigid, heavy logic, and the sort of wisdom that doesn't have any twists and turns.

"Only those who work are proletarians. And work is recognized. Intellectuals aren't recognized. They aren't workers. The intellectual Komsomol youths are only good for talk. For working they're worthless. . . . " He stuck to this rigidity

9. Elementary schools for Jews, which were conducted in the Polish language but observed the Jewish Sabbath.

10. The Communist youth movement.

until . . . the Bolsheviks left and the Germans marched in. Conditions changed, the ghetto came, and Srolik was forced to live with the Jews; his brain grew softer and his rigidity became more flexible. In the ghetto, Srolik was involved in an intellectual youth circle, and through it, was drawn into the fighting organization in the self-defense of the ghetto, actually, a partisan organization that undertook the defense of the ghetto population.

The FPO, the United Partisan Organization, guarded the ghetto against the final liquidation. If the FPO couldn't prevent it, at least they wouldn't let them fall like flies. People had to know how to die, and Jews in the ghetto would no longer let themselves be slaughtered like oxen! . . .

This was the teaching of the FPO. Srolik knew no twists and turns. He knew no tricks. Drawn into it body and soul, he exploited any possible opportunity. Suddenly Srolik brought a "rod"; tomorrow there would be another one. . . .

His comrades try to ask him, to find out, and Srolik answers, rigid and stubborn: "Nobody's business. You need it or not. If you need it, okay. If not, I'll stop bringing. . . ."

No tricks help. Srolik repeats the same thing:

"Conspiracy. Nobody needs to know where I get it from, maybe from the sky. What's important is I get it!"

There was no point explaining caution to him. He wouldn't let them talk to him:

"Give me a short answer—you want me to bring it or not?"

The answer was: yes, bring it. But the comrades wanted to know his methods, to take precautions. Srolik wouldn't hear of it; he himself understands the need for caution. You can count on him for that. He doesn't understand German, he used to say. He knows no tricks; if you need it, I'll bring it, if you don't, say no.

Yet they did learn something: *Beutenlager* [the booty camp]. There he has access to the arsenal, and that's where he gets it. Could you forbid him to do it?

4

The father goes to his unit, the mother goes to the ghetto weaving shop, Reyzele works at her profession. Her husband, Simke, works in Pienocentras.

"Where does Srolik work?"

They learned just one thing: Beutenlager.

"So why doesn't he 'launder?'"

Srolik makes excuses. He cannot, there's nothing there, it's hard. . . .

"So why do other workers at the Beutenlager 'launder?'"

Srolik is disgusted by the questions. He waves them away—"Stop pestering me"—and disappears. He doesn't explain, doesn't finish his sentences, and his parents don't understand:

"A strange kid that Srolik turned out to be."

"Nobody to talk to."

"Srolik changed altogether."

"Like talking to the wall. . . . "

As suddenly as he entered the ghetto workshops, so suddenly he left them and went to the unit in the Beutenlager. Why, what for, no one knows.

"Srolik," his mother often asked, "where do you work?"

"A mother isn't allowed to know either?"

And Srolik, a bit bashful, looks at his German military boots and answers, half seriously, half bashful:

"What do you mean, where? What's the difference? . . . "

"Srolik, is it a secret?" The sister cannot stand it any longer, and Simke helps out:

"What do you mean a secret? Of course it's a secret. . . . "

Srolik takes the joking in stride, pays no attention to all the questions, and answers sometimes evasively and sometimes: "What's the difference?"

That Srolik had a secret was understood not only by his sister and brother-in-law, not only by his mother, but also by his father. Always tired, never sleeping enough, the father would argue with no one in particular:

"Hiding it from your own family? . . . "

"Secrets among your own people?"

"A child shouldn't answer like a human being?"

The more secretive Srolik was, the more his family nagged him:

"Srolik, aren't you ashamed before others, where do you work, what is this Beutenlager." And talking to Srolik is like talking to the wall, not just that he doesn't answer, but it seems he doesn't even hear. He's not the same.

"Srolik, maybe you could 'launder' something in?" And Srolik, somber and arrogant, gets angry:

"We don't 'launder.' . . . "

Who is the "we," why don't they launder—like talking to a lamp.

Reyzele is insulted: She knew about everything, she talked about everything, but heard not a word about Srolik. So what kind of secret could Srolik have?

Srolik spends almost no time at home. At dawn to work. After work he washes, eats, goes out, and comes back late at night, tired and exhausted. Again to work, again late at night, exhausted, and . . . so on for weeks.

Srolik is almost a stranger at home. His family has stopped asking. Half mad at him, they don't talk to him, and he is silent, too.

Maybe he's in love? But Reyzele assures them he's not. She would have known it. . . .

And yet maybe? But Reyzele excludes the very thought: out of the question!

Reyzele knows everything. What anyone has hidden in his heart is evident to her. But what happens under her own roof is Reyzele's secret. . . .

She cannot forgive herself!

Nothing doing! . . .

The ghetto trembles with fear. The tragedy of the Święciany and Oszmiana Jews had just taken place. More than 4,000 were liquidated. Everybody around them thinks that the ghetto is coming to an end. Young and old live with tension and Srolik doesn't talk. At home he's an enigma, and in the organization he's a phenomenon.

He's a wild fanatic. Fear can't even be considered. And he won't hear of risk:

"If you do something, you have to take a risk. If you don't do it, no reason for taking risks."

In the beginning he would bring revolvers, later bullets, later hand grenades, eventually fuses for mines, explosives, and other things.

The organization discovered the secret—Beutenlager. He breaks in, takes from the wagons, and pulls out as much as possible.

The guard at the gate became stricter. Recent events with the 4,000 created a new hunt for weapons. Jews and simple ghetto dwellers—everyone buys weapons. The wish not to be taken empty handed excites everybody. They buy, carry, and hide. People carrying weapons are often arrested and shot. But all this doesn't mean a thing to Srolik. He argues:

"If you do it, you have to take a risk. If you don't, there's no reason to risk."

Short and sweet:

"If you do it, don't hold back. Certainly not in the ghetto."

5

On that day in May, the ghetto basked in the spring sun, and on that day the ghetto was jolted: scared and upset Jews kept asking one another:

"Is it true?"

"Another incident with weapons?"

Only a rare person inquired who and what. The word *weapons* was enough for the whole body to tremble. A fever swept through the ghetto:

"The fifth incident with weapons! . . . "

A rumor spread in the ghetto that it was not just a question of weapons but that there were dead and wounded people.

Only around 4 in the afternoon did it become clear that in the Beutenlager in the suburb of Burbiszki, there had been an accident. Jews had tried to steal weapons. There were dead and wounded.

The ghetto Jews run around like poisoned mice and keep asking:

"Burbiszki, caught stealing weapons? . . . "

Soon comes more information: the whole unit was in danger—collective responsibility!

The whole unit? Don't 120 people work there?

Not just simple Jews, but even the ghetto authorities, scared, try to find out. They send messengers, and soon relays came back:

In Burbiszki, in the Beutenlager, a young man was caught breaking into the arsenal. The youth, a certain Srolik, tried to run. The guard shot at him and wounded him badly. He was taken to the hospital in Łukiszki Prison:

"And what next?" curious people ask, trying not to miss one word, God forbid.

Next? . . . The fellow is okay. He claims he was looking for a weapon to commit suicide with. In great pain, lying on the stretcher, he told his comrades not to worry. He would be silent as a dog. He cursed the Germans who were busy around him, called them murderers, Jew-exterminators. The Germans were taken aback and almost apologized:

"What can you do, orders, duty. . . . "

"They ordered us to shoot, and we had to do it. . . . "

That means the whole thing is nothing. They have to shoot because what can they do, it's an order, it's their military duty, and duty is above all.

The local Germans, in their naiveté, were sorry; others self-righteously asked why Jews were taking up weapons. Meanwhile, the group from Burbiszki wasn't punished. Somber and scared, and maybe even angry, they returned to the ghetto as they did every day.

The ghetto was agitated:

"This is the fifth time they've caught people with weapons. . . . "

6

Three days passed. The whole thing was forgotten. Here we don't remember anything for long. Events pass by too fast. No one asked anymore, and hardly anyone was interested. The turmoil among the Beutenlager workers almost stopped. Srolik, though one of the most beloved, lay in the hospital in Łukiszki Prison, and nothing could be done. . . .

Haven't we had enough victims?

Nothing doing, Srolik will also be a victim! . . .

The ghetto authorities were worried. The frequent incidents endangered the ghetto. Yes, his relatives, but—aren't there many misfortunes in the ghetto? But mostly it hurt not Srolik himself but his comrades, brothers-in-arms, and especially the organization as such:

Will he talk or will he keep quiet?

His family reassured them: he'll be silent. He's 100 percent safe. He's got his lips sealed. But the organization couldn't calm down.

First of all, three of his fellow workers in the Beutenlager are in danger for helping him. By "carrying off" new people, they increase the danger of . . . denunciation, which again endangers the ghetto, calls attention to the whole organization, and then. . . .

Therefore, precautionary measures were taken immediately:

First of all, the three disappeared. For the time being they didn't go to work, and all three of them obtained doctors' certificates saying that they were sick. Second, for the time being, the carrying in was to be stopped. . . .

The gate must remain clean!

In Srolik's home, there was lamentation: the father, shattered, sighed; the mother and sister wept bitterly and mourned Srolik even though he was alive.

7

In the middle of a rainy night, three policemen were awakened and ordered to rouse Srolik's family from their beds and to take them to Lidzki.

The inspection officer on duty knew very well that the poor people were about to perish. . . .

Depressed and frightened, not suspecting anything, they got dressed and asked what had happened.

The inspection officer couldn't get it straight: according to the instructions of the registration bureau, Reyzele is Srolik's wife; but Reyzele is lying in the arms of a man she claims is her husband; Srolik only "registered" with her.

The family is made responsible for Srolik and his "crime." The women cry and beg for mercy. The policemen apologize and try to convince them that it is just an investigation. The inspection officer decides to save, for the time being, as many as he can:

Why carry away Reyzele's real husband, too?

It says that Srolik is her husband, so why sacrifice someone else? . . .

The family goes to Lidzki, and Reyzele is separated from her husband. The latter is held in the police station, ostensibly at the disposition of the police commissar.

The devil got his way. At around 11 in the morning, a car drove up to Lidzki Street. Kittel,[11] like a hungry wolf, took three persons with him: Reyzele, her father, and her mother.

A lock was put on the door, and hanging there it told everyone, short and sweet: Srolik and his family have gone to the next world, Srolik with his lips sealed and his family with their door sealed. . . .

Another tremor ran through the ghetto. Again everyone understood that the situation in the ghetto had become more serious, and again everything fell into oblivion, for nothing is remembered here for long. And this may be the most dangerous thing.

The rain poured incessantly and washed away everything that stood in its path. In the ghetto, [it washed away] the fifth incident with a revolver and the third death incident, actually six victims.

In the organization, everyone calms down. What can you do, as Srolik used to say: either you do or you don't.

"If you do, you must be prepared. If you don't, no cause for fear!"

Again a danger had passed. Srolik's fellow conspirators went back to work and the organization breathed a sigh of relief: nothing doing, that's fate! . . .

11. A Gestapo officer in Vilna.

It's good that he is no more, that the thing didn't spread. . . .

In the organization, Srolik is the second victim. The first was Leyke. The second, Srolik. Srolik went like a hero—with his lips sealed.

May his memory be honored!

8

The inspection officer, the director of services of the Second Police Precinct, was "happy": he had saved an innocent victim.

After the extradition of Srolik's family, Reyzele's real husband, Simke, the forced laborer at Pienocentras, was released from the police station. Only then did he learn of his tragedy.

Srolik had destroyed his wife. Poor Reyzele perished because of him. . . .

At first he was confused and didn't know what to do. He raised hell. His arms and legs shook with pain. He lamented and felt guilty. He tried to complain about the police who had separated him from his wife, and he understood that that was foolish.

What can I do. . . .

The door is sealed:

Should he open it and enter? His sister and the family begged him tearfully:

"Don't touch the seal. Stay away from the unfortunate house, stay with us and tomorrow we'll see." He seemed to return to his senses, accepted their arguments, and went with his family. The next morning, as if nothing had happened, he went to work.

Who could stop him? And why stop him? Perhaps he wanted to forget himself at work? . . .

In Pienocentras, at the churns, pouring milk, he didn't show the slightest sign of confusion—a stone, not a heart. The Jews who worked with him didn't understand: he clammed up. No sign of his tragedy of yesterday.

Why should we remind him?

Why rub salt on his wounds?

Like every other day, a truck drove in to get milk for the hospital. The German, like many who come here with transports, was easy, like one of us, friendly with Jews more than with non-Jews. Today, as always, he joked and gargled his fast German in his throat so that hardly anyone could understand. He approached the silent new widower and, as always, offered him a cigarette—he may smoke, for Jews in the ghetto were forbidden to smoke. . . .

Simke bent over some screw of the churn, stood still as a stone, and didn't move, as if he didn't mean him. The German stood with a cigarette in his outstretched hand, and Simke. . . .

. . . Suddenly he darted out, jumped up, and with foaming mouth, leaped on the German, with an outstretched hand:

"Murderer! Murderer! Jew-murderer! Ugly sonofabitch!"

Frightened by the sudden turn of events, the German recoiled as if he didn't understand, and retreated, pale, asking no one in particular:

"What happened?! . . ."

"Murderer! Jew-murderer!" Simke, drowned in blood, didn't let go of him.

The German retreated, and Simke stepped on his boots and wouldn't relent:

"Murderer!" A hollow echo resounded in the factory—"*Murderer!*" Then the Jews separated into two groups: some leaped on Simke, the others moved the German away and tried to explain it to him.

The German soldier sat a long time, flabbergasted. He couldn't understand it, couldn't grasp it, couldn't recover, and couldn't forgive himself:

Why him?

Why did he deserve it? Didn't he want to give him a cigarette? Pale as the wall, half confused and half furious, he again approached his "Jewish friend," again tried to communicate with him, to talk it over, perhaps to excuse himself. . . .

"Murderer!" Simke, enraged, lunged again for his eyes:

"You're murderers! Hitler is the greatest world murderer. You're robbers. Bloodhounds. Bastards!"

The German recoiled again. This time, decisive and determined, he quickly left the factory, got into his car, and without the milk cans, fled as far as he could. Before they turned around, he was gone. Only the sound of the wailing engine was heard.

Twenty minutes after the event, a car drove in with three Gestapo agents; the fourth one was our driver. Furious, enraged, almost unrecognizable, he dashed up to his former attacker, caught him by the hair, and the others pounced on him. Blows fell, thuds resounding in the factory as in an empty barrel. Beaten to a pulp, the unfortunate man was tossed into the car, and in the vapors of the car's engine, he went up in smoke.

In the ghetto, people said that an hour after this event, our victim was shot in Ponar.

This information came from the Jews who worked in the Gestapo.

His wife, Reyzele, perished because of her brother. He, because of his wife. And all of them together because of Srolik.

Vilna Ghetto
August 1943

OLD PEOPLE (SAD REPORT ABOUT 84 LIVES)

1. Dull

Weary and wretched, thousands of Jews from the Vilna Ghetto lie down and rest. Rest for the new working day that is in store for them.

From the distance, their dwellings look like garbage dumps, placed there without any order. Several people in every dump, twisted, crooked, and tangled up together under a blanket, a rag, or a heap of clothes.

The floors are full of sleeping people. On the shelves, on the tables, on chairs pushed together, on crates—everywhere—they are sleeping. One meter seventy per person and only sometimes can you straighten your leg, and now at the dawn of a midsummer day, everyone is sunk in lethargic fatigue.

The Vilna Ghetto is sleeping.

Thousands of Jews are preparing for a new day of toil!

Air.

Air in the Vilna Ghetto is like sense. Sense is hard to get, and it's even harder to get air. Beautiful, spacious Vilna condenses its Jewish population into the narrow alleys of Vilna Jewish poverty. In crooked, winding alleys, 20,000 Jews are twisted into an area that barely held 4,000 before.

Crooked and contorted with great crowding, the streets of the ghetto twist, along with its 20,000 inhabitant-prisoners.

Leaving the ghetto for slave labor means to breathe fresh air, to enjoy the beauty of Vilna, inhale the smell of a tree, of grass, of weeds.

Air.

The air in the ghetto is saturated. . . . Saturated with fear, insecurity, and helplessness—no mean feat, the Vilna Ghetto?! . . .

In the entire area of the Vilna Ghetto, there are only two acacia trees, but they are also dry and withered. Sick of their irregular lives, since everything around them is wretched and abnormal.

The air in the ghetto houses is the essence of the area around. The narrow alleys don't have enough air. The overcrowding in the apartments poisons the air, and the apartments full of sleeping people, crowded with sweating bodies, snoring and wretched, create the same density here from which every chemist is prepared to distill explosives, combustible material, or poison, which no doubt could be used as something valuable in the atmosphere of the present war.

Air.

The walls are heaped with clothes, rags, sacks, and pouches. Shelves on shelves. Walls—like blistered, sweaty, smoking bodies, forsaken by God and man, without a free inch—everything is pierced and porous with nails, roofed with boards and shelves.

Lines and lines of bags and sacks are hanging here, big ones, small ones, and tiny ones, like bunches of eggs in the guts of a slaughtered chicken.

Now the ghetto is sleeping, sunk in a predawn weariness. Soon heavy, stubborn steps will echo in its alleys, trudging in a procession of slavery.

The ghetto is still sleeping, but soon countless groups will be borne away, men and women, children and old people—all of them in the procession of slaves.

But for the time being, it's still night. The weariness of yesterday's labor is what inspires this heavy sleep, which now turns into a kind of dullness, not sleep but not yet waking. The night is over now, but the day hasn't yet come. . . .

The ghetto is dull in its predawn. Soon it will come. Day will come. . . .

2. Signaling

Strong men sleep, obstinate in their "athleticism" and stubbornness, saying to themselves:

"Endure, hold out!"

"Hang on!"

And even though they are sober and look reality straight in the eye, they poison themselves with rosy hopes and avoid all despair.

Optimists of the ghetto! . . .

And there are also others:

Stricken by the recent past, saddened and dejected by the blows and destruction—they no longer weep or rant. A profound pain gnaws and stings them:

"Why?"

"What for?"

Days of intoxication and long, drawn-out nights, sleepless nights full of nightmares and hallucinations.

The optimists try to fool themselves: it's entirely untrue. The pessimists, veiled in black, consider every new day superfluous, a heavy burden that sooner or later disappears, and along with it everything else also disappears—the shadow of life. . . .

Life? It's worthless.

Death? Something that no longer has any impact. Just a habit! . . .

In the great long night, she dreamed of her young, delicate sister-in-law, her brother. She saw them fondling each other and . . . suddenly their being dragged away half naked to be shot. . . .

Death.

And out of the hilly swarm that is lying unraveled and twisted there comes a heavy groan, and in her nightmare she sees demons, dead ones, walking with crutches, live ones, crawling on the ground and looking for a morsel. Among them are Eros and Psyche, then Peter and Lucia and then her brother and sister-in-law.

Heavy, tortuous nights and wearying, dull days.

And yet, sleep is somehow interrupted:

Like people are running. . . .

Like they're chasing each other. . . .

Like hearing fragments of conversations. . . .

But something's going on!

Something has happened?

Like shots from a heavy weapon, she's torn out of her bed, sure that something has happened: puts a coat around her shoulders and bursts into the street.

It's not yet 5 o'clock, and most of the tenants of the courtyard are already awake. Half-dressed people hurry up:

"Five in the morning—what's the turmoil?"

Groups gather. Everyone pricks up his ears:

"What's this whispering?"

She glances back at her room and sees how everyone is immersed in a heavy, half-awake sleep—a dullness. In the man's coat, like a bird out of her nest, she rushes to the neighbors, to the commotion, to the whispering group.

Like thunder playing, like lightning on a rainy day, sudden and unexpected—shots that didn't end, and only her voice echoes:

"Aktion, they want old people."

Now they recall:

At night they woke the neighbors. The police in the neighborhood.

Only now does she also recall:

"Police, right." She heard how they assembled the police.

Old people—and her father?

Old people—and her girlfriend's mother?

Like thunder playing, like lightning at midnight on a winter night. . . .

The secret signals of Vilna are borne on the air:

"Melinas. . . ."

People are borne on air, they don't walk, they rush:

"Melinas. . . ."

"A hiding place for my father. . . ."

"A corner for my mother-in-law. . . ."

"A mouse hole to hide in. . . ."

Death suddenly whinnied:

"*Ponar!*"

3. Separation

It's a struggle to survive. Simple common sense dictates—hold out.

But not everyone is capable of looking straight into the face of reality:

"And even if that's enough, how much more can you take?"

But logic and refusal is one thing, and the survival instinct is another.

Now, of all times, they want to live. The life instinct.

They plod on the stairs and through the corridors—melinas!

Old people trudge, shrouded in secrecy—melinas!

The gates are locked. Traffic is stopped.

And people are like ants. "Bedrooms," the heaps on the floor, uncover themselves, and as if in spite, the day takes them into their clothes early. In danger, half dressed, groping and searching. The keys to the attic now take on additional importance. You carry them carefully and lovingly in the safest pocket.

Suddenly the old folks seem to vanish from the houses to take their chances in the remote melinas.

It's already 6 o'clock, and the masses have to go to work. The gates are opened, and the nodding armies turn toward their workplaces. But not everyone is doing that today. Some stay behind to watch over their parents. Children guard their grandparents.

The Jewish police go to places that are a safe bet. They are searching, and this time they are satisfied: they don't find anything.

The neighbors gather in the yards and look on. The streets look like a terrified anthill. Old and young are alert. All of them are in the courtyards, all of them are in the streets, and mainly—the melinas have once again been repaired.

"This is no Aktion," wonders a Jewish youth, seeing that only the Jewish police are concerned with it.

"Whose Aktion is it, and whose business is it?"

"Can it be? Just the Jewish police all by themselves? . . ."

But only for now.

For now, the collection point for the captured is the new sports field. Here dozens of old people are assembled. Here the children come to separate from father and mother. Here heartbreaking scenes take place:

One elderly man comes to his old mother and weeps bitter tears. . . .

A girl clutches her old grandfather, who is condemned to stay here. The shaking hands of old people cling and tremble in their desire to tighten the embraces of their relatives. Clutch them to their heart, to express to them all that they are thinking now.

To divulge? And perhaps not to divulge? . . .

"Why should the son suffer?"

"What for?"

"Why make the separation sad? . . ."

And the elderly woman, the righteous grandmother, groans, mutters something, trembles, and mutters an explanation:

"Don't be sad. We're all in the hands of the Lord. He won't desert us. . . ."

"And if he does? . . ."

The old woman gropes with her skinny hand, shakes her daughter's shoulders, and mutters simply:

"My oldest daughter. The son in America. . . . Another son in the Soviet Union, one of the sons fell in . . . Spain, the youngest is in Palestine, and this one . . . this one. . . ."

And she hugs her remaining daughter with her trembling hands and kisses her. . . .

An old man is lying on a bench on the sports field and reciting his dying confession. To whom is he speaking if not to The Holy One Blessed Be He?

One son went off with the Reds, the second was stolen from him by the Snatchers. The third, his daughter, and his grandchildren were dragged off by the Lithuanians. . . . To whom does he turn in his hour of grief? . . .

An old grandmother entreats mutely, with gestures, and bursts out into wild shouts.

What is she saying?

Maybe she is pleading to be saved, maybe she means that she should be taken in by her children and grandchildren, who are scattered all over the globe? Or perhaps the grandchildren are already in Ponar, along with their mothers and fathers? . . .

And what is she saying now?!

Engelstern. All the time he worked as an unskilled laborer, worked preparing the sports field, and now they're dragging him off as superfluous—old. He walks around here like a caged animal:

"He built the sports field himself and now it turns into his grave?"

And she, the old woman in a carriage?

A bundle of bones. She can't walk on her legs anymore. A broken vessel. Put in a carriage and dozing off. Puts herself to sleep in time. . . .

Two young people. The two of them—blind men from Strashun 7. But both of them are full of life and lust for life. Just two weeks ago they appeared in the ghetto library and tried to find someone who would be kind enough to read to them from time to time—so that they too could enjoy a book. They are productive, busy weaving, on orders from the ghetto workshop. Now both of them are in the sports field, pleading to be saved.

A girl is chasing one of the police officers, Levas, known in the ghetto: "Mother!" and he releases her into her care.

Policemen lead old people, and mourners follow them, as if they're accompanying a corpse. . . .

Some of the old people are busy with their bundles. They barely move, like half-crushed worms. Another step and they're destroyed. . . . Some of the bundles are superfluous, and their owners all but ignore them:

"If life is abandoned, let the bundles be abandoned too! . . ."

The old people are ordered into the prison on the sports field. They are escorted and assisted so that they won't strain themselves, God forbid. Wailing comes from the cells. A group of old people dart to the window, and one of them attempts to jump out. These are the last moments, and the old people still try:

"Save us! This is the last minute!"

"Save while you still can!"

A strong hand takes the old man down from the window. The lamentations of a cemetery reach your ears. These are the last minutes, and they are mourning themselves. . . .

From here, we learn that they are loading them on wagons outside the ghetto. Loading them on wagons, onto plain, hard platforms.

Where to?

The street around Strashun 6 is teeming with people, relatives and family members. It's hard to bear it. A bitter smile on everyone's face—the devil's play!

"It can only be Pospieszki!"

"They opened a rest home for old people—the devil's play. . . . A bitter play. A play so as not to anger the ghetto residents.

A question mark hovers over the ghetto:

"Isn't it simply a deliberate act of sadism?"

"Isn't it just an operation of the Jewish police, who want to demonstrate their loyalty and prove that they can do something too? . . ."

A question mark hovers over the ghetto, a heavy question mark. Gloomy silhouettes with dull expressions.

"Play! Devil's play!"

For the fifth time, posters are put up in the ghetto for the musical "Rye Years and Woe to the Days."

They don't cancel the performance. It's forbidden to mourn in the ghetto! To hold out! To overcome!

Indeed, rye years and woe to the days! . . .

4. The Last Station—Pospieszki

The abandoned Pospieszki, the former TOZ rest home in Vilna, swallowed up a few dozen old and sick people. Not only old people. Also young people and incurables and even simply young people. Once the place hummed with the children of working and poor Vilna. They would come here in droves, children and parents, teachers. Sometimes guests would also come—grandfathers and grandmothers, to reap satisfaction from their offspring, while today. . . .

One old woman remembers those visits and weeps in isolation.

And the residents of Pospieszki still make a living. From the ghetto they are supplied with food. Here they are served. And from here—who knows and who can know? . . .

Of the memorial statue of Dr. Tsemakh Szabad, which stood in the yard, nothing remains except the bottom part. The top part, the portrait, has disappeared. On this remnant of the memorial, we read:

> On July 18, 84 old people were brought here from Vilna and are under the supervision of the Jewish police. On the 23rd, six more old people were brought. On the 21st, one died of natural causes. As for the rest, who knows?

And the walls say that all this is the devil's play. . . .

Loneliness pours grief onto the walls and the doors. It speaks from above the door:

Today only simple words . . .
Tomorrow historical documents
Signed: Kh. Sh.

And another inscription:

Yesterday, life, joy, hope
Today . . . grief, apathy.
Tomorrow life again,
For . . .
The people of Israel live!!!

Thus the current tenants of Pospieszki, the old and the condemned, speak their hearts. Thus they sing their hopeless grief.

One who left his heart in the Messiah's care, writing a report on the wall:

We here report to the wide world that 91 old people whom I have accepted in my care from my colleague are awaiting their fate. . . . At 10 o'clock at night an anonymous woman died here. At 12, Yitskhok Rudnik died. Later, another woman died, Rokhl-Leye, a well-known linen seamstress.

And then the inscription goes on:

A day in Pospieszki under the gaze of the dying brothers. . . .

And another adds:

Today 90 old people; tomorrow? . . .

Another wall and another report:

Yesterday, the 24th, at 1300 hours, a woman named Tereza Koranowska was brought here, a convert for the past 65 years. She converted to Christianity when she was 15 years old. So she is more than 80, and here she will end her life as . . . a Jewess.

And nearby, someone else tells a secret:

Yesterday the old people were led, one by one, into a special room, and everything they had was taken from them—money, gold, objects. . . .

And in the ghetto, they still rack their brains:

"A rest home for old people?"

"Better an honest play than such a sadistic farce."

"Can it be? What for? . . ."

The walls report that this is the devil's play. The ghetto talks and racks its brains, while the fate of dozens of old and sick people is already sealed.

5. Dance of Death

This is what they came back and reported:

Close to the hill, near the road that branches off to the right through the dirt road to Pospieszki, is a convoy of trucks with armed Lithuanian soldiers led by—Weiss! They gave in, and in exchange for the 300 they demanded, they made do with what there was: 84 people.

In the ghetto, it was business as usual. The revue, "Rye Years and Woe to Our Days," continued.

Trucks couldn't drive on the dirt road. Twenty-five Jewish policemen were sent there. They are approaching the denouement. The tragedy is reaching its end.

A dance of death on the dirt road coming toward Pospieszki.

A convoy of corpses is stretched out—old people, crushed, incurable. They lead them, carry them, drag them. The road from the boarding house to the trucks was the road from Pospieszki to the hands of Weiss.

A calvary of sighs, ravens' screams, an orchestral accompaniment to the dance of death.

The old people cling to the Jewish policemen, their "supporters," and groan softly about their dog fate. . . .

A last road of thorns in their lives! . . .

Four trucks are loaded. Eighty-four people. The trucks begin to rumble, set out, and at the crossroads 25 Jewish policemen remain standing, ashamed and as if they have been slapped in the face:

"With their own hands, they turned them over to the Lithuanian hangmen! . . ."

"By themselves, they delivered them to Weiss. . . ."

The trucks rush to Ponar, and the Jewish police, tearful and sweating, go on foot to report that the order has been carried out.

The ghetto will swallow that.

The ghetto will digest it.

. . . And afterward, in the ghetto, they repeated:

Two of the old people died on the way. Probably out of fear and perhaps even with curses on their lips. The ghetto swallowed that. The ghetto digested that. . . .

Vilna Ghetto, July 1942

THE VIA DOLOROSA OF MRS. MATZ

How the Family Split Up

Vilkaviškis is a district city in Lithuania, in the Suwalszczyzna sector, in the southwest corner of Lithuania, 25 kilometers from the Prussian border. After

Kovno, this place was considered one of the most cultured in all Lithuania. The city numbered about 12,000 people, 3,000 of whom were Jews. They were generally small traders, but the pride of the city was that it was the center of the brush manufacture, which was all in the hands of Jews, especially in the hands of the well-known pig merchant, Sobolewicz, one of the richest Jews in all Lithuania. And hundreds of Jewish brush makers did indeed make their living by processing pig bristles.

In this city, the 47-year-old Matz had lived peacefully for years now with his family: his wife and his two daughters. The family was one of the most important in the town. He, manager of the local popular bank; she, Khasye Matz, 38 years old, had a women's millinery shop. By the way, we should mention that one of the relatives was Yisroel Matz of New York, owner of an enormous pharmaceutical company, whose most famous product was the laxative Ex-Lax. Another relative is the famous activist of OZE in Vilna, Hirsh Matz.

Now Khasye Matz sits before me, alone and weeping: her husband was murdered in Vilkaviškis, her older daughter was taken out of the Vilna Ghetto, while she herself, and her daughter Dine Matz, take advantage of their Aryan looks to move among the peasants, as "Easterners" who remained behind. The two of them pretend to be Russian Orthodox, and thanks to that she is a servant in the homes of rich Lithuanians, one today and another tomorrow. When I ask the "Gentile" Khasye Matz for her name, she forgets her real name and bursts into tears: "It's been six months since I've met a Jew. I've forgotten the Yiddish language, soon I'll forget my real name. . . . "

When I learn everything and Mrs. Matz tells everything she has been through, I feel a chill throughout my body.

The First Wandering

On Sunday, June 22, a few hours after the outbreak of the German-Soviet war, at exactly 11 o'clock in the morning, the Nazi armies entered Vilkaviškis. The Matz family, like scores of other families, fled to the surrounding villages. The very next day, they were forced to return to their old house, but the house wasn't there anymore. The city was in flames, because the Germans, guided by Lithuanians, had gone to every Jewish house, smeared the wall with some sort of liquid, and set it on fire. She didn't know what the liquid was. Indeed, they burned down 80 percent of the Jewish houses in Vilkaviškis. The Matz family, which was homeless, went to live temporarily with relatives, the Goldin family, where they stayed for about six weeks.

The woman pauses and blurts out:

"I can't imagine that I'm really among Jews, just as I can't understand that everything I'm telling you now really happened to me."

The narrator is talkative and goes on:

My only goal in life is to tell and to be able to tell. Let the world know about it all!

On the first night that we found shelter with the Goldins, Germans and Lithuanians came in, beat us mercilessly, stole whatever they could put their hands on, and took all the men away with them. Such things happened in all the houses where there were Jews. They took the men to a local college for priests, and there yesterday's Communists and the newborn Saulists (Lithuanian Fascists) stood in two lines, 20 in each line, and forced the prisoners to pass between them, beating them as they passed by.

The fruits of that "reception" were three killed: Yosl Teicher of Vilkaviškis and two refugees from Wiżajny near Suwałki.

Even before the Saulists started executing, they carried out a precise search of all the prisoners and robbed them of gold, silver, foreign currency, and objects whose value the woman estimated at a million rubles.

(The Matz woman had means and had managed over the years to tour Europe with her husband several times, getting to know countries and people. She gave the impression of being a wise and insightful person.)

Of the 40 Saulists, the woman can name only 2. Recently, she has been having problems with her memory. She frequently forgets what happened to her only half an hour before. But she will remember those guys forever. One of them was Marutis. The other was the peasant Newricki. She can't remember the names of the others.

After that first night, they began escorting the men to work every day, and every day they would beat them severely. Once they sent them to work in the garbage dump, and as always they beat them brutally. They found the carcass of a cat there and ordered the Jews to say a eulogy for it. Then they forced them to dig a grave and bury it. This sadistic ceremony was directed by a German with help from a group of Lithuanian Fascists.

A second case:

Because Meyer Toboryszki, owner of a local oil press, didn't properly wash a bathroom, they broke his hands and smashed his eyes.

These torments lasted six weeks, with men constantly falling dead and wounded. One Saturday, they moved all the men from the college to the barracks. In the early days, they allowed women and children to visit there. But this "humane" act was set up so that the visiting time wasn't allowed before 7:45 in the evening, and by 8 all movement in the street was forbidden. There was a sense that something bad was about to happen.

The Last Time

On that critical Saturday, the German on guard said:

"Take a good look at your husbands for the last time!"

No one paid much attention to what he said, but Mrs. Matz was chilled to the bone.

Starting on Monday, they didn't let them go to their husbands. The women who came stood and waited unsuccessfully at the entrance. Nevertheless, they saw how they were leading away a small group of men. This lasted from 6 to 10 in the morning, and then a few cars with Gestapo agents entered the courtyard of the barracks, and right after that a volley of shots was heard.

The narrator slipped through a side street to get to a Lithuanian partisan that she knew and find out from him where they might be taking them to be executed. Her plan succeeded. Her Lithuanian acquaintance did indeed live in the place next to the execution site, the barracks courtyard. The Lithuanian removed a board from his fence and pointed to an area covered with tall weeds where she hid to see what was going on.

What Did Mrs. Matz See?

It really was too far to the place of execution for her to distinguish the faces. She saw a machine gun and a few military men around it. She saw a group of civilians they were shooting at, and they dropped and disappeared from the face of the earth. At that time, she didn't yet know that they fell straight into a gaping grave. Horrible sounds reached her, the helpless shouts of the victims. All that happened some distance from the barracks, in a place called the field of horrors, not far from the forge.

Because the Lithuanian didn't allow her to stay there for a long time, she went from there to Rosa and reported it to Mrs. Orinson. Some believed her; others didn't even want to hear.

The execution lasted from 10 in the morning until 2 in the afternoon. A policeman that she knew, Diksnis, stood guard at the gate. When he was asked how long the women would have to wait until they would be allowed to see their husbands, Diksnis answered calmly:

"At 3 you'll be able to see them and give them food. . . . "

But at 2, they opened the barracks and there was no one there anymore.

Mrs. Matz tells how she and Mr. Faktorowski entered the barracks yard and a German came from somewhere and threw them out.

900 Victims

For two days, they brought clothing, shoes, and linens from the yard. Then it was learned that during the execution, 900 men had fallen, including 65 Lithuanians, apparently Communists.

In spite of all that, in the city they didn't believe it. A rumor circulated in the town that they were taking men out. On Tuesday, a few women appealed to the German commander to find out what had happened to their husbands. The German replied that he would look into it. Meanwhile, he extorted money, convincing the mourning women that he would give their regards to their husbands and would even try to have them released.

Into the Ghetto

Three days after the execution, all Jews were ordered to take their things and move to the ghetto. Everyone was entitled to take 25 kilograms and 250 rubles in cash. The road to the ghetto was paved with blows and insults. They situated the ghetto in the same barracks where the 900 had been executed. A large part of the Jewish population fled. In the six weeks before the ghetto, about 200 men were shot because they had been pointed out as Communists.

Mass Graves

There, in the middle of the ghetto, in the barracks yard, were the mass graves of all those victims who had been shot there a few days before. There were two graves. The first measured 20 by 5 meters, and the second was 14 by 3 meters. The earth on the graves was leveled to the ground. A third grave was completely open (apparently they forgot to cover it) and hadn't yet been used. Only by chance did the people learn that their relatives were buried there. A pilgrimage to the graves began. They would weep over them, plead, and the place turned into an island of tears of the remnant of the Jews in Vilkaviškis. The Lithuanians, seeing what was going on, forbade them to go to the graves.

"We would stand at the windows," says Mrs. Matz, "and eulogize the innocent victims who fell at the hands of the Nazis and the Saulists."

We Get New Ones; Once Again the Sky Turns Dark

"Suddenly they started bringing new Jews from the immediate area to us."

> That was Monday of Rosh Hashanah. Unexpectedly the assistant commander of the local Saunuma (the political police), one Rainis, appeared in the ghetto. He was seen at 5 in the afternoon and again at 8. Those "visits" roused great suspicion. The first time Rainis was talking with Silber. The second time with Mrs. Yofe. Rainis pitied her very much for staying here. Silber's sudden disappearance made us nervous. But we were immediately relieved, and the ghetto inhabitants were happy: Silber returned! . . .

Expectation

In spite of the relief, no one fell asleep. Everyone was expecting something. At 11 at night, they knocked on the door. The tenants said that Silber had disappeared again and so had Toboryszki. Then they learned that at 11:30, Rainis had again visited the ghetto. . . .

Out into the World

There was noise until 1 A.M. Mrs. Matz and her 12-year-old daughter went out the gate, and from there she went not far from the barracks and hid. As dawn broke, they tried to flee from the spot, but they immediately saw a group of Lithuanian partisans approaching in the distance. They hid among the weeds. They heard isolated shots. Afterward they learned that they were shooting there at those who had tried belatedly to escape from the ghetto.

The two Matz women turned to the rye fields, and there they encountered other Jews who were escaping, including the Weber family. From there they turned to the home of a famous Christian family with whom the Matz family had deposited 10,000 rubles, a bit of gold, and a few diamonds. The family gave them a chilly greeting. During the day they didn't even let them into the house, and at night they put them up in the stable. From there, through the opening, Mrs. Matz could see how Jews were led along the road. After two days in the stable, the Christian family even threw them out of there. Once again the woman and her child confronted the question of where to go. And once again, she and her daughter turned at night out into the world. They went over fields and forests toward Gaudon [?]. In Pilviškiai, they stayed with Christians for four days, pretending to be Russian Orthodox.

Modern Marranos—Pilviškiai

One night, the lady of the house told her what had happened to the Jews and, in deep secrecy, pointed to the place where the shot Jews had been put. It was in a nearby grove. The lady of the house and everyone around her were pleased at everything that had happened. They had chanced upon a Jewish woman who had been shot with her child. At night, people came out of their graves, and the children shouted "mama." But when the Lithuanians found out about it, they killed everyone in the grave who was still alive. Such incidents occurred in Pilviškiai and in Niva.

Once again Mrs. Matz had to pick up her walking stick, once again came to the village, and once again was unable to stay there for more than four days. On the fifth day, they arrested her and took her to the political police. They turned her over to the German commander and he released her. Alone and weary, Mrs. Matz once again set out on her wanderings. The "Christian" Matz got herself hired as a maid and two weeks later was fired. Once again on the road, and once again a stop in some village where she got work cleaning house. There she worked for four months, changing her job to her present one, where she is working to this day.

This, more or less, is Mrs. Matz's story. She lost her husband, Zondl Matz, three sisters, a brother-in-law, and now, according to her story, her older daughter, too.

On Antisemitic Moods among the Lithuanians

Mrs. Matz sighs deeply, prepares to leave. As she puts it, the Lithuanians' hatred for the Jews is dreadful: they are happy that so many Jews have been shot and are waiting patiently for spring to murder the rest. Mrs. Matz says that this is what the Lithuanians are talking about in Kovno, Marijampole, and only around Vilna do you also hear of isolated instances of sympathy for us. Therefore she is preparing to escape to wherever she can.

Now Mrs. Matz is returning to her village. She thinks that because she has Soviet citizenship, they'll send her and her daughter to Germany. Mrs. Matz is convinced that the Lithuanians are guilty of 90 percent of all the horrors.

The Germans would frequently hide Jews, while the Lithuanians would betray them and shoot them. Mrs. Matz gives such an assessment of the murderousness of the Lithuanians she was born among, lived among, and who did her in while she was still alive.

As for Vilkaviškis: the Lithuanian partisans report that when the Jews were brought there to be shot, they were tortured horribly. They split their skulls, pulled out their tongues, poked out their eyes, etc. The Lithuanian partisans bragged of all that to Mrs. Matz, whom they thought was a Soviet citizen.

Recorded in April 1942

I WALK ON GRAVES (TOUR OF THE ABANDONED HOMES OF JEWISH WRITERS AND CULTURAL ACTIVISTS)

In the first months of the headquarters of the Reich, the Germans would demand that I provide information about the whereabouts of Jewish books, holy books, and museum exhibits. For this purpose, I obtained the addresses of synagogues, Jewish bookstores, etc. Afterward I discovered that on these visits, I could acquire things that might be useful.

There should be a lot of manuscripts in the apartment of Professor Noah Pryłucki. Why shouldn't I take them out of there under the aegis of my "iron permit"?

The Vilna Bundist Aronowicz—couldn't I visit his home and try to rescue whatever I can from there?

Because this is the way it was, I made up a list of addresses where I assumed something could be rescued. This list included the names of Sh. Bastomski, the principal of the Jewish academic gymnasium; Professor N. Pryłucki; M. Shalit; Rabbi Shub; Weinig; Pludermacher; the Tomor and Kletzkin publishing houses; Engineer Schreiber; Turbowicz; Attorney Shepsl Milkanowicki; the painter Olkienicka-Lerer; Krasny; the director of the Mefitsei Haskalah Library; and others.

Conversations with Janitors

Wherever I appeared, as an official agent of the authorities, I asked the janitors to escort me. The janitors would tremble: some of them out of dissatisfaction at being "pushed," because many of the Jews' objects were at his disposal and he was scared.

[The janitor thinks:] To take him inside would be bad. Not to take him inside? After all, he's an "official" agent!

There was also another kind of janitor, the kind every Jew once needed. He understood that the two of us together wanted to see them. . . . Moreover, through a Jewish agent it might be possible to find out about the fate of his tenants, who were taken out of there to the street, caught, and arrested, etc., night and day.

The janitor at Niemiecka 4, where I am looking for a synagogue, is confused. He replies politely, but I see that he wants to get rid of me. Better I shouldn't see. . . . And I do indeed see: the woman is ironing with a splendid electric iron. Nice furniture, beautiful tablecloths; in short, it's not good for him that I peep in. . . . The janitor at Niemiecka 6 shows me the two "prayer houses" and keeps assuring me that everything has already been taken. Of course, other people did it, not him. He gives me two shofars as a "souvenir," and wishes me good luck. . . .

At Niemiecka Street 21, the janitor does everything possible to get rid of me. He shows me the ruins of the Soviet bombing. . . . He laments the Jews who ran away from here, but I see that I am disturbing him, that he would like to see me outside and soon.

I go to the apartment of my friend Krasny at Pohulanka 24. The janitor is very glad. He lets me into his house, asks with great curiosity about several of the tenants of his previous apartments. His wife wipes away her tears. They want me to write down their names and give them their regards if I find them.

A second one tells me: my tenants aren't alive anymore. I'm sure of it. My wife ran after them. I know they shot them. All of them, women and children. . . .

"They stole the things, robbed them," another one tells me. "Anyone with hands and feet came in and pulled out. . . . "

Another janitor leads me, and the children call after him: "Thief of Jewish things." The Christian isn't flustered and says: "The neighbors dragged away all of the Jews' things, and now they make me out as a thief. . . . "

These are the kinds of conversations I have with the janitors.

On Graves

In every Jewish house I enter, I feel that I am treading on graves. Everywhere the pulse of life throbbed. Everything was full of life. Now I find only traces of looting and robbery. Or heirs who took our legacy while we were still alive.

At the home of the elderly director of the Mefitsei Haskalah Library, we meet two Germans who have been quartered here. They welcome me very politely. I'm in Krasny's office; I glance at his private library, and the German tells me that the Lithuanians burned all the books and left only . . . those Jewish ones.

Why the Jewish ones? In short, because the Germans stole the foreign ones.

Everything in the house looks untouched. The drawers the German opens for me are full of photos (of the owners) and of many friends. I pretend I am looking for museum exhibits, and he helps me. . . .

I record in the report: 90 Jewish books.

Another time, I go to the apartment of the writer N. Weinig. It is impossible to get into the apartment. Lithuanians live there, and they are at work now. The children in the courtyard take me to the trash cans and point to the garbage heap. Underneath the garbage heap, they tell me, books are buried. The neighbors explain to me: there was a lot of Russian literature here. The administrator didn't know what to do with it, and he buried it.

Are there a lot of books here? I ask. And the answer is: "Sir! Hundreds and hundreds. It is a pitiful sight."

I go to Piłsudski 26. My friend Aronowicz lived here. Lithuanian clerks live in his apartment. Everybody is at work now, but the guard is very interested in his Aronowiczes. He asks questions, and without any sense of unpleasantness, he shows me: this book is his and also the picture. "Why should strangers drag them off? If the owners come back, this is theirs; and if not, God forbid, why should the Lithuanian pigs gorge themselves with them?"

One day I went to my own former home at Kijowska Street 4. There was nothing to look for. Nevertheless, I went to feel once again the same feeling as when I left it, the night before we went to the ghetto.

The apartment was empty. The destruction here was so complete that the thieves had even removed the electrical wiring, the doors of the ovens, the doorknobs, etc. Here was my room where I used to hide during the time of the Bolsheviks, here was my melina where I fled when the "Snatchers" were searching in the time of the Germans. This is where my friends would come, and here, in this corner, I would pour out my tears, and here I wept a few moments before I left for the ghetto.

From there, exhausted, I went to a fresh grave: at Trocka Street 5 lived Felicja Kasel, the widow of the Jewish writer Dovid Kasel. Here she found shelter with her sister as a refugee from Warsaw, and I often used to spend time with her. Now I learn that Krever, her brother-in-law and sister-in-law, were sent to Ponar. Felicja Kasel is now in Japan, and I am here like a crow on graves. The apartment has been completely pillaged. Most of the furniture is gone; only broken pieces, trash, and books remain—and that's just what I'm looking for. In the neighborhood, in that very courtyard, is the apartment of my friend Professor Noah Pryłucki. Now it is occupied by an office, and there's no trace of Pryłucki.

Only from the guard, with the intervention of the sister-in-law of the painter Uma Olkienicka (wife of the folklorist Moyshe Lerer), do I learn something, and I am taken to Wileńska Street, and here, in one of the cellars, do I discover a full collection of Pryłucki's manuscripts, books, and some manuscripts of the Vilna poet Sutzkever. Pryłucki's manuscripts are taken to the melina, and Sutzkever's poems are returned to their creator, who is still alive.

And thus from house to house, from ruin to ruin, from nest to nest, I "stroll" over graves.

And if anyone of us gets out of this hell alive, and meets those mentioned above among the living, let him be consoled that within the destruction of Vilna, there is one who, to honor them, endangered himself and looked for their legacy to preserve it lest it be lost in the ruins of the destroyed Vilna.

HOLES

The Paper Walls of Jericho

Vilmen, enclosed in the ghetto, is surrounded by walls. The walls are desolate both outside and inside. From the outside, the walls are sealed like a border strip between the open city and the locked Jews' ghetto. Fenced off from the surrounding streets, the border strip stands barred and boarded up. Not just the ghetto strip; dozens of streets and hundreds, thousands of apartments, abandoned by their Jewish inhabitants, now stand deserted and closed. Walled in and boarded up, the doors and windows overlooking the border strip of the ghetto are witnesses that here, inside, the exiled are enclosed in a cage. The temporary border boards make a Chinese wall here, transforming what seem like puny boards into a horrible, unapproachable abyss.

The ghetto swarms like a beehive. An area for 3,000–4,000 people is occupied now by tens of thousands. Heads upon heads. One lies on top of another. Less than a meter per person, worse than in a cemetery.

For lack of space, a series of holes was breached: up front, several city blocks were closed off, so people broke into them. In back, from the middle of the ghetto on, bricks fall and holes grow: buildings on Lidzki gain holes through Strashun; yards on Zawalna are pierced from Szpitalna Street; from Rudnicka people break into Karmelicka Street. Homeless and roofless people, bent-over threefold, creep through holes in search of a roof over their head, a corner.

Ghetto filled up with holes. Addresses: Lidzki 5, entrance Strashun. Szpitalna Street 7 leads through a hole next to the garbage can to Zawalna 46. From Rudnicka 14, through two holes separating one yard from another, you get to Karmelicka 7. Addresses complicated, twisted and bent, like this life—twisted and bent.

Every yard is a street. Every street, a city. A swarming anthill: pushing, chasing, rushing—pain of pain. One on top of another, one above another. One person gets less than 1.20 square meters—worse than in a cemetery. Water doesn't flow—the pressure is too weak to serve such an overflow. Lines form for the toilet. Hell. "Crowded" is no longer a concept.

You cannot get through the streets—tens of thousands instead of 4,000. The beehive swarms—such swarming, probably, in hell. So they tear up the walls and shorten the way: from Strashun 7 there is a hole to Szpitalna—to walk and to drive through. From Shawelska 5 there is a road to Jatkowa—to walk and drive through. From Szpitalna 23 a passage leads to Rudnicka 17, and from Rudnicka 7 through Niemiecka 21. If you squeeze through at Jatkowa at the corner of Oszmiańska, you take a shortcut. If impossible through streets, you trudge through courtyards; in Vilmen they are called "through-yards." From Szawelska to Szpitalna, from Szpitalna to Rudnicka, from Rudnicka to Jatkowa. A labyrinth of holes—holes and holes and holes.

So you go here like a thief through back roads. You rush here like dogs driven through lairs past garbage bins, through holes leading downstairs and staircases leading up. They dig here like worms, like mice in the underground. A sieve full of holes—to delude yourself. An improvisation to make believe that the air gets thicker, purer, better.

The ghetto is hermetically sealed, and only the moon, the sky, and the stars witness the shifts and transformations of those still living—remnants in the ghetto. "Himl un erd vet undz hern / eydes di likhtike shtern" [heaven and earth will hear us, / (our) witnesses (are) the shining stars], the people sing in a popular song.[12]

So it was in the beginning, when there were still tens of thousands of Jews in the Vilmen Ghetto. Today it is 1943. A handful of Jews remain in Vilmen, very few of them from Vilmen itself. What is stuck away here is a mishmash of people driven out of the surrounding towns, or escapees from slaughters, from execution squares, from purges, from holes and hiding places. They have gone through horror and grief, have been purged in pain, have returned from hell. They are wild and wanton. Death is nothing to them, but they won't commit suicide. Trust is a ridiculous thing—trust no one, only rarely trust yourself! . . .

Vilmen—for some this is the last refuge. A place of challenge, of not letting go. For some, Vilmen is no more than a springboard. From the slaughter [in a small town] to Vilmen, from Vilmen a base to go to the forests, to bury yourself.

So Vilmen digs deeper and deeper: labyrinths, holes, underground passages. They dig under the cellars. Foundations strike their roots deeper, holes stretch down to human lairs, and with ingenious inventiveness, lairs for worms are often transformed here into architectonic wonders.

Above, the ghetto is like a sieve: holes leading from one yard to another, from one street to another. Below, a world with little worlds, an underground world burrowed by moles, prepared for a time of emergency, a trap with no way out.

Those who have money hide huge sums here, invest all their worldly goods. The melina should be as good and comfortable as possible, and as safely covered from above. Those who don't have money invest themselves and their skills in it, all their common sense and energy.

Everyone is digging deep, and the more they dig, the deeper they reach, the more inventive the diggers get, and more wonderful their achievements:

Melinas deep underground, unreachable . . . everything is taken care of: ta-

12. "The Oath"—the hymn of the Bund, written by S. Anski.

bles, benches, bunks, electricity, water, a radio, a listening device to find out what is happening outside, and a way to get out to observe what is happening all around.

The bitter experience of the horrible events, the maturity and suffering, give rise to a kind of shrewdness, an unparalleled refinement: electricity in the melina is drawn not from the nearest electrical outlet, but from the street, from the city network, because when events develop, the electricity of the ghetto will be shut off, and because every visible connection might give rise to a suspicion of a melina. The melina has its own water, independent of the general ghetto supply of water, because water might be cut off, and the people hiding in melinas would die of thirst. The deeply rooted melina digs even deeper—8, often 10 meters deeper than the melina. Wells, small water pumps, water closets are built. In what sort of fantasy could one have imagined it: distress breaks iron!

Underground tunnels lead from the cellars, through the underground tunnels you get to holes, from the holes they dig deeper and deeper—here is the melina. Only here is independent illumination, a deep water pipe, no eye should see it—your own electricity and, if you wish, your own stream, run by your own batteries, from your own generators. Contact with the world—a radio, not to be cut off from what is happening in the territory of the ghetto—a listening device that absorbs every sound from outside! When the ghetto burns, it will not reach the melina.

[*A page is missing here.*]

They will sit here underground, just to endure, perhaps survive, and not let them kill you like worms, not let them slaughter you like oxen.

The ghetto cadres, the fighting organization, whose goal is not to abandon the ghetto, does its duty. The arsenal gets bigger, the alcazar grows stronger, and the underground net wider and more complex.

CHAPTER 10

THE CAMPS IN ESTONIA

AUGUST 1943 – SEPTEMBER 1944

LETTERS FROM ESTONIA

[*The first exiles from the Vilna Ghetto to the camps in Estonia wrote letters home, which calmed the ghetto inhabitants and convinced them that being sent to Estonia did not automatically mean death. People from the ghetto were rounded up and gathered first in the Vilna suburb of Rosa before going to Estonia. Thus the Germans gradually emptied the ghetto until its final liquidation. The following excerpts from letters, probably copied by the Judenrat censors and typed on two pages, were in Kruk's archives.*]

1. Reyzl Kalmanowicz to Her Neighbors at Strashun St. 11, Apt. 12

. . . I have so many children I couldn't watch them.[1] The Jewish police have separated me from Meyerl. I was barely alive until I saw my child, M. . . . We are still in the same place. The G[entiles] who escorted us are better than the Jewish police. The Jewish police should be ashamed of the way they have treated us. I am writing this note, and God knows if I'll be able to write any more, if there will be someone to send it with. Other workers are 20 kilometers from here. I don't know where Shmuel is. I don't even ask about Shmuel, because I'm terrified that they will send me straight to him. I want to rest. I am so worn out from Rosa and the road.

2. Keyle and Yehoyshue Ziskind to Mane Kęska at Strashun St. 2, Apt. 14

. . . There is nothing to buy food with. There are no Christians here. God knows what will be with food. Bread is 300 rubles a kilo; potatoes, 60 rubles. . . . "It seems, we are going to live."

3. Unknown Correspondent to the Residents of Szpitalna St. 10, Apt. 11

. . . We arrived all right. How it will be later, God only knows. The previous [group of] workers are all working. Those who arranged their lives in the ghetto are smarter than we are.[2] Today it's too late. Go ahead, arrange yourselves in the ghetto. We should have followed our common sense when it was still possible. Hold out.

1. A hint that her children were taken away.
2. An allusion to those who hid in melinas in the ghetto.

4. Unknown Correspondent to Mrs. M. Lubocka at Strashun St. 5, Apt. 10

Vaivara near Narva, Estonia, August 27, 1943.

My dearest,

We are still alive and working. Our boss is Todt. Food is scarce. Forty decagrams of bread a day, work very hard, but the main thing for me is clothes. I am vice-commander of the camp and secretary. So, as far as food is concerned, it's better for me, but I don't have a coat or any underwear. It rains hard here and it's very cold. Conditions are hard enough. The impression of the current party[3] is harsh. Good that you stayed.

5. Leye [Surname Unknown] to Sore Kopanska at Rudnicka St. 7, Apt. 6

. . . He told me that Yitskhok Bruk and Sore Janiska are in another camp, 20 kilometers from here. I regret that my coat has not a single "button."[4] It is very hard without "buttons."

6. Shimen [Surname Unknown] to Markus [Surname Unknown] at Niemiecka St. 31, Apt. 30

. . . Here we met our brothers who have been here for some time (from the first party). The first word is . . . "Mire" with a capital M. . . . They give *lekhem* [bread]. More details I don't know . . . bread costs [?] rubles, if you get it, but you have no trouble getting tobacco.

[*A page is missing here.*]

Ida [Surname Unknown] to Efron Sasha at Niemiecka St. 27, Apt. 29

My dear ones! Today, Friday, we are about [. . .] The way was very good we are [. . . persons] in the wagon. This is the Judenrat, the police, [the hospital, the doctors], the nurses with the clinic. Berl was elected [. . .] the first impression is very good. The weather is [. . .] like in Vilna. The barracks are beautiful. The treatment of the [. . .] was very good. They gave us very good food. Cottage cheese, butter, sausages, and canned meat. It was so much that we brought bread and butter to our place. We saw several people from the earlier party. They say, here it is not bad. The work they are doing, as we saw, is not hard.

. . . So far, I don't regret that I went. They give enough food here. It cannot be worse than in the Vilna Ghetto. We won't starve from hunger here. As far as I overheard what people say, everyone is happy, and meantime the first impression is very positive. I greet and kiss you all. Don't worry. We are all here to live.

Alatka [?] to Reyzl Ansher at Karmelicka St. /1

They say more people will be taken [to Estonia]. If, God forbid, you will have to go, do not be afraid and take everything with you.

3. The current transport of Vilna Jews.

4. The letter writer probably means hidden pockets.

Moyshe Rabin to His Neighbors at Szawelska St. 6, Apt. 19

On the road, there was plenty of food, as in a pension. The work is not too hard, depends for whom. Women and children are separate from men. They meet after work. In general, it is better than they feared in the ghetto. Make an effort not to go [to Estonia], but if you can do nothing about it, don't worry. Clothes are welcome here. "Yellow sateen"[5] certainly. Take as much food as you can.

Perele Kles to Khane Tsvey at Rudnicka St. 19–21, Apt. 3

We traveled in closed wagons. From time to time, they would open. They gave us bread, sausage, butter to eat, and Vichy water, everything more than enough. The treatment quite mild. Gestapo and Lithuanians traveled with us. Here we met all the workers of the previous party. I have not yet seen my husband. He went to work but is healthy. The workers say that there is enough food. Don't worry. Everything is okay. We go without [yellow] patches. It is not very cold here. The camp leader is a good man. On the train, we had an opportunity to see the world: Riga, Tartu, and Daugavpils are large cities. No one knew that we were Jews.

THE LIQUIDATION OF THE VILNA GHETTO[6]

In Vilna

On Sept. 23,[7] 44,[8] a group of [Bund] Party comrades gathered at the home of Comrade Berl Widman (Szpitalna 11): Berl and his family, Zalmen Silkir [i.e., Riklis], Mila Aronowicz, and Bmolog [Golomb] with their families; at around 3 P.M. they left the ghetto for Rosa, where Berl Widman was put with 100 old people who could not run and. . . .

In Subocz[9]

Here we gathered at the church, where women and children were separated. In the street, the men were assembled. There were probably 2,000 people. They slept under the rain. At night, an orchestra played from a car, and various announcements were made, for example, that the men would soon see their wives, that they would be taken away at 6 P.M. for work in Vaivara, that there would be coffee in the evening, that all instruments, knives, forks, spoons, and tools had to be turned in. The area was enclosed in barbed wire. At night, the Ukrainian

5. Probably silk.

6. September 23, 1943, was the last day of the final liquidation of the Vilna Ghetto. The following text is written in Kruk's hand; it is not clear whether the author is Kruk or whether this is a testimony from another Bundist.

7. "August" was first written and crossed out, then "Sept." was written over it.

8. This should be "1943." On Sept. 23, 1944, Kruk was no longer alive. But he made this mistake several times, so clearly 1944 was often on his mind.

9. A suburb of Vilna.

guards walked among the half-sleeping people, robbed and beat them, fired a shot as a provocation, and ostensibly looked for the shooter, and so on.

Indeed, on the 24th in the morning, they took away the instruments; later we attended the execution of four comrades. Then followed the selection of 100 old people: Berl, Yitskhok Riklis, the owner of the house on the 3rd of May, Rashkes, and others. Finally, around 4 A.M., the trial of the four began.

The Execution

The SS men asked whether there was one Kovner here,[10] for he has to go over to HKP.[11] Later they were looking for Palevsky but didn't find him, either. Then they called Grisha Levin, who was pointed out to them as Palevsky's bodyguard. The German told him he would soon be shot with the others, and took him away. Later the verdict was read, charging them with attempting armed action against the Germans. The protocol was read by Weiss himself.

About the 100

Sitting in the field, the Ukrainians blubbered that the 100 were shot because 8 Germans were wounded. In exchange for this information, they wanted a watch. Comrade Mechanik gave him his watch. . . . They asked for another watch for information about what happened to the women. . . .

Travel

All the men were then marched before the four corpses!

On the way to the train, several women disguised as men were caught, beaten, and sent back to the women. On the road, the Ukrainians robbed incessantly.

On the 27th [the men] arrived in Vaivara, where they were led to the first camp.

Vaivara

Here three camps exist. Camp 1 at the railroad station; Camp 2 in Vivikoni, 10 kilometers from Vaivara; Camp 3, 5 km, at the gas factory. We 800 men were let into the Vivikoni camp.

Vivikoni

Here Finnish barracks stood, where we were lodged. A swampy area. Looks horrible. They took everything away from us and let us in, 40 people to a barrack, where we slept on the hard ground.

10. Abba Kovner, the commander of the FPO, left through the sewers, along with several hundred partisans, during the liquidation of the ghetto. The group went to the partisan forests.

11. HKP, the German industrial camp, was the only official Jewish enclave in Vilna after the liquidation of the ghetto.

Here we worked in the forest and on the highway. The others worked building barracks, the women worked on the railroad. Our group, along with the old ones, numbered about 11,000 persons,[12] including women and children. The women were lodged in separate barracks, and the children were also separated. But there was contact. Here, we spent two weeks.

Narva

On Oct. 7, we were transferred to Narva. Two groups of 800 men. Two hundred men to Vaivara. Several dozen remained in the workshops. Camp Leader Heiman left with his camera to build a new camp in Port Kulgai.

Separation of Women and Children in Vivikoni

A general roll call. Men on one side, women and children facing them. The children were taken away to a separate barrack; they cried and ran back to their parents. Mothers broke away to go with them. Children refused [to go] and screamed. The job was done by the G[erman] police.

In Narva

Here we found a camp with some 500 people. Together, about 1,250 persons. Women, but no children. Here we worked at anti-tank ditches and bunkers. Smaller groups at Wehrmacht, wood cutting, etc. We stayed four months, until February 1, 1944. During that time: radically unhygienic conditions. Covered with lice. Slept on the ground. Never bathed.

The camp was in the factory hall of the local flax factory at the knitting factory.

The Regime

Harsh. Everyone—young, old, sick—had to work. All the sick and weak had to stand at the wall (called "The Wailing Wall") of the factory and were then driven out to work. Later they were brought back in the yard and were beaten. As punishment they received as many as 25 lashes and were deprived of food. Screams of the beaten people. Motl a.g.v. also received 25 on his behind, but hurrah, hurrah, Motl is here again. All this during the roll call, which lasted about one and a half hours.

Stamped to Death

Around Dec.[ember], on a holiday, visitors came to the camp, friends of the camp leader. As an example, they took two old people, the Vilna man Fried, an usher at the Jewish theater, and another man, and started beating them on the ground, and just trampled them to death in the presence of everybody.

12. This figure should probably be 1,100, not 11,000.

The Leadership

A society of people, relying on two groups of *shtarke* [strong men]. One works in the kitchen and in transport. The second, at the best workplace in Port Kulgai. The camp elder is the Galician Jew Zieler; the camp registrar, Brojdo from Vilna.

The Transports from the Camp

Transports were sent from here: ostensibly Brojdo has 30 sick and weak persons in Vaivara. They arrived there and were sent on. Some say they were annihilated. The second transport of sick people was ostensibly sent to Vaivara. They say the group was liquidated.

Quarantine during an Epidemic

Around New Year we were quarantined because of cases of typhus. The first time for six weeks, and the other, six days. The typhus epidemics and cholera occurred here in Nov. And Dec. and Jan. About eight to twelve people died every day. Altogether, 400 persons died here.

Left Narva on February 1
Evacuation

First, the sick and weak were sent out, ostensibly to Vaivara, [and they did] arrive there. The rest, more than 800 men, left on foot on February 1 and arrived in Vaivara on the 2nd of this month.

They stayed in Vaivara for two days, then passed by [Kohtla-]Järve, Ereda, then Ereda-Holzman (two camps, 7 km from each other). Arrived in Kivioli only on the 7th.

Kivioli

Here there was already a good camp of between 350 and 400 men and women. The newcomers were arranged 2 km from the camp with the same administration, the so-called Eastern Camp. Nearby was a little camp of German and Riga Jews (about 120 persons, belonging to the first Kivioli little camp).

The camp elder was Cypelewicz, a Vilna Jew. In the Eastern Camp, the old administration of Narva, headed by Zieler, remains. The Eastern Camp [?] for O.T.[13] at the cold soap factory.

Of the 800, some remained in Ereda. The rest, along with a group from Camp Vaivara (the 100), arrived in Kivioli. Thus about 650 people remain here.

13. OTE—i.e., Todt.

TESTIMONIES FROM ESTONIAN CAMPS

Nosdniklaz [Zalkindson] Bernard[14]

On Sept. 3, 1944,[15] I left the hospital by myself—and went out the [ghetto] gate. From there I was taken by a truck to Rosa, where they let us sit in the square and ordered us to wait. People kept coming and coming. Among them were all doctors and staff members of the hospital, the group of chimney sweeps, and others.

Here, people caught in melinas had been waiting since the 2nd. The doctors were suddenly ordered to take off their white coats and follow. The chimney sweeps were ordered to go to work in the city, and they were all taken to Rosa.

There we were watched by Lithuanian soldiers, who assured us that nothing would happen, that we were all being sent for work in Estonia. Every few minutes, groups were sent to the train.

On the 3rd, the train moved. In our transport, there were about 50 wagons with 50 persons in each. Two or three people escaped from the neighboring wagon; the rest were prevented from running away [by the other inmates] for fear of collective punishment. In our wagon, two women were disguised as men. We arrived in Vaivara on the 5th of this month. From there, 500 went back to Kohtla, 30 km from Tafsee.[16]

From Kohtla we were taken to Ereda, 6 km.

Ereda: here we are taken by a group of Dutch marine commandos of O.T. and lodged in a Finnish barracks in a swampy area, where they slept on the bare ground.

There were already 500 people here, all from Vilna, from the earlier train. The next day we were divided into units for work: paving a highway in Kaike [?], barracks, and artisans worked on the railroad. The camp leader was a Todt man who stole a lot while the Jews were starving. He divided a loaf of bread among six persons, i.e., 20 decagrams. Later he raised it to 30 decagrams. A tiny bit of fat and marmalade. All of them were very hungry.

The men were allowed to receive packages of clothing from Vilna. Then a group of people was sent to Vaivara to fetch the packs, and there they were told: you won't get the packs, because we found revolvers in them. That was a great disaster, leaving people naked.

A week later, Sept. 10, a new camp leader arrived, an SS man with new Eston-

14. Bernard (Vova) Zalkindson, son of the famous Vilna surgeon Dr. Yehoyshue (Osip) Zalkindson, was a mathematical genius in the Vilna Ghetto. He was taken to Camp Ereda, then to Camp Klooga, where Kruk recorded his testimony. He perished with his father in Klooga. His mother, the ophthalmologist Dr. Paulina Zalkindson, was sent to Majdanek during the liquidation of the Vilna Ghetto.

15. This date clearly should be 1943, as it refers to events in the Vilna Ghetto.

16. Near the town of Kohtla-Järve, a central labor camp was established.

ian guards. The Estonians guard the camp, the Dutchmen at work. The "New One" forbids cooking potatoes; improves the nourishment, takes away all food for the camp inmates. He introduces a sharper regimen, and everybody must appear; even the sick have to appear at roll call. This continued until about the beginning of October. During this time, there was a group of Vilna Jews who went to Kivioli. They told of the liquidation of the ghetto. After informing everyone of the regimen and announcing that everybody must turn in their gold and their watches, except for doctors, he announced that assaulting the guard or trying to escape would be punished with death.

During that time, one person was shot to death for sleeping at work, one wounded for stealing potatoes.

On Oct. 3, the camp was dissolved and 750 were sent to Narva, taking with them all the sick and invalids. In Ereda 245 healthy people remained.

The only five women, who cut their hair like men, and 15–18 children also remained in Ereda.

Our narrator was one of those who remained.

Suddenly, about mid-October, the Dutch guard was recalled and was replaced by a Lithuanian guard. Two weeks later Ukrainians came, and two weeks after that, Estonians. All guards were good.

Everybody worked in units, the women in the kitchen of the children's camp. The dirt there was terrible. About November, changes were introduced. The people were transferred to different, dry barracks. They were deloused and began considering sanitary measures.

In early November, 140 women arrived from Kovno, were given easier work, and were not separated from the men.

In mid-December, a transport of Jews arrived, 250 men and 50 women sent from Kaiserwald. This group included several women from Vilna, discovered in their melinas.

Most men were from Riga or Daugavpils. There were many German Jews, and several from Kovno, but only a few from Vilna.

Meanwhile, a new camp leader, Trupin, an SS man from Klooga, the one who shot the Jewish policeman, arrived and began beating people. The regime remained mild. The food got worse, but they didn't starve, because people brought [food] from peasants.

After the new year, a transport of 100 women arrived from Tallinn Prison. Among them were three men, one Jew from Tallinn, one Soviet prisoner (an invalid), and one man from Berlin. The women were German and Czech Jews. All were still well dressed and in good health. In mid-January, several hundred (300) people were sent from here to Goldfilz, actually, mines of shale [?], brown burning stones, from which gas is extracted.

About 300 people remained in Ereda. The death rate was minimal. Altogether, 20 people died here, most of them German Jews. All were burned. One hanged himself in Welosing [?]. Twice, people escaped from the camp, four persons altogether. In both cases they were caught but not punished. At the inception of the camp, two people were brought who had escaped from Vaivara (still in September), but they were not punished, either.

In late January a new camp leader arrived, and the old one stayed on as his assistant. For the Aktion, sick people were often sent out (chronically ill, crazy, etc.). The first time six were killed in Vaivara; the second time, two, who lie in Vaivara.

In early January, a woman from Tallinn named Marocznik Wanda was shot, actually for "racial shame" [Rassenschande], though nominally for an attempt to escape.

In early February the front moved closer. On February 4, the camp of Vaivara, of about 1,600 men and women, including 500 people in the hospital, came here with the camp leader [Scherbel?]. From Vaivara, 1,200 more left for Goldfilz, and a similar group went from there to Kivioli.

Healthy people were put in barracks. The sick were housed in the bad barracks in the swamp. About 20 persons died every day. Nourishment grew worse. Some people were sent away from here: 180 to Zonge [?] and 40 to Port Kunda [?]. The sick were sent by train to Riga, and we even received news about them. Instead of the hospital, a group of 700 arrived from Vivikoni with their camp leader (Bock) and were lodged in the dirty barracks instead of the sick people. In some of the barracks, sick, old, and weak people were brought from all the camps and began dying en masse, an average of 10–12 a day. In mid-March, the sick were sent out again, ostensibly somewhere around Vilna (?).

In place of the Jewish elder comes Khayet, a Vilna Jew.

In early March, the camp of Järve arrived (a hundred and several dozens) and Kuremae (several hundred). They went from here to Goldfilz.

On April 17 we were selected, 100 people and 150 from Goldfilz, and sent by train to Klooga.

The Entrapment of the FPO Group at Szpitalna Street 6
[Eyewitness Account of] Nayv [i.e., Wein] Moyshe from Vilna

On Wednesday, August 1, [1943,] at 6 A.M., he was captured with the entire second battalion because they were denounced by Policeman Rok and Brigadier Heiman. Both of them indicated the forward position of the FPO at Szpitalna 6 and let the German police go through Heiman's apartment (at Szpitalna 6, from the street side). The purpose was to get rid of the youth who had barricaded themselves in the passage courtyard under the command of Grisha Shtivelepets [i.e., Cypelewicz].

They had no [weapons, because all the weapons] of the group were hidden. [Along with them] were five other groups and their commanders. [. . .] Among them were the group commander Policeman Kilona [Anolik], Moyshe Nayv

[Wein], Avreml Kinvotnog [Gontownik], Motl Epsoy [Yoshpe], Yitskhok [. . .]. The ranks included former students of the Real Gymnasium: Rebeyrsh [Schreiber] Zhozik, Rezelg [Glezer] Leyb, [Gebzor [Rosenberg] Yankl, Reneyv [Weiner] Zelig; and the Shomrim:[17] Iksnilod [Dolinski] and Letsid [Distel]. The group of 150 men was taken by the Estonian guard to the ghetto gate. About 25 people managed to scatter in all directions. The group had two gas-filled light bulbs per person, and the battalion and group commanders had four revolvers altogether. At the gate, they all dropped their bulbs, except for Comrade Nodrog [Gordon], who wanted to take them with him, and did. The rev[olvers] were transferred to a member of the [Partisan] Org[anization], a policeman who remained in the ghetto, so as not to remove them. The group was loaded onto two trucks and taken to Rosa. The group in the second truck [tried] to escape on the way. On Końska Street they [cut the can]vas of the hood, and at the corner of Bazyljańska [Street, next to the public] bath, the first three men jumped. One of them was Nayv; Gurman was arrested, beaten atrociously, and thrown back into the truck. The other two escaped. The guard of the truck was then reinforced, and at Rosa they were put into the second train car of the transport.

The group elected Kilona [Anolik] as car leader, and he became the temporary group com[mander] of the 50 men in the second car. The rest were in Car 1. Contact with the first car was immediately established, where the battalion com[mander] was Shtivelepets. Three hours later, there was a search, especially among the men of the first two cars. In Car 1, they found Comrade Yankl's rev[olver]. He was immediately taken away by the Gestapo. Fifteen minutes later, they took Comrade Lekheyr [Reichel] Velvl from the same car. In Car 2, Comrade Nodrog's bulbs broke. The smell was detected by the guard, who informed an officer about it, and the door of the car was shut for about three hours. Two Gestapo men arrived and conducted an investigation about the two bulbs, with no results. They didn't find the culprit. . . .

The train left the next day, August 2, at 1 P.M., in the direction of the [main Vilna railroad] station, and from there toward Nowa Wilejka. The train continued with tremendous speed to Bezdany, where they decided to escape from the car. Preparations were made immediately. The wood around the door lock was cut out. Suddenly the train picked up speed and rushed to Daugavpils [in Latvia]. The group could no longer jump out. From Daugavpils—via Riga, Tartu (Yuryev)—they reached Vaivara. The trip lasted three days and three nights.

The whole train contained 1,500 people, including about 10 women who volunteered to come. The transport was now sorted out, and 500 were returned to the cars, including about 40 members of the FPO with Shtivelepets. The same day, the train reached Kohtla. A Dutch guard took over and took them to the area of

17. Members of the leftist Socialist-Zionist youth movement, Ha-Shomer ha-Tzair.

Ereda, where a camp was erected; they were put in Finnish barracks (a drawing of a Finnish barrack is attached), 60 men per barrack.

[*The drawing is missing.*]

On the night of the 2nd, 500 more people from the ghetto arrived. With us were Mrs. Kalmanowicz, Mrs. Weinig, the teachers Berman, Kapliński, Anisfeld, and others.

For the first several days, the camp lived without water. People slept on the ground. They got 20 decagrams of bread [per person] and a thin soup and salt. The price of bread was 600 rubles a kilogram. Because of the influx of people, new barracks were built, and 40 men were placed in each barrack. The FPO group stuck together in barrack no. 12, which became the model barrack of the whole camp.

The FPO member Mordkhe Namdlog [Goldman] became the camp elder. The mat[erial] situation of the group improved.

A month later, on a[bout] September 1, the camp was dissolved. Two hundred fifty were transferred to O.T., and 750 went [by train] toward the city of Narva, among them the FPO group. There the train was transferred to the flax factory, where a segregation took place. Two hundred fifty went [by train] toward Soski. At Lake Peipus in Narva, the FPO group was divided, and 10 men were sent to Soski, among them Shtivelepets, Namdlog, Moyshe Nayv, Kinvotnog, Epsoy, and others. In Soski, they met 250 Jews from the ghetto, who had been there for three days. Comrade Mordkhe Namdlog took charge of the camp and became the camp elder.

After a week of building, the camp was established. Memb[ers] of the FPO were included in the leadership. The work consisted of improving the road from Soski to Vask-Narva, a town at [Lake] Peipus. The supplies [nourishment] in the camp were improved due to the building of a narrow railroad. In time, work became very hard there; the distances and the beatings made the situation unbearable. The camp elder then pulled all FPO mem[bers] into the staff of the camp.

Organizational Work Develops. After two weeks in Soski, a request arrived from O.T. for wor[kers] in Fort Gorodenko. Epsoy went with them to investigate the workplace. One result of his investigation: on the other side of the Narva River, eight kilometers from the shore, i.e., from Fort Gdov, there was a young part[isan] gr[oup]. Efforts were made at once to contact them. In exchange for gold, a peasant of that area arrived, and they tried to talk to him about the [possibility of] a contact. Three days later, the contact arrived. Both sides were extremely cautious. It was decided to create another contact to double-check the first one. Nayv Moyshe was sent to work at the SS guard, which consisted of inhabitants of the surrounding area who were exempted from being sent to a concentration camp at the price of joining the SS. The commander of the guard was a Balt from Rev[el = Tallinn], Lieutenant Balkhov. Comrade V. [Wein] began wo[rking] there. He decided to talk openly to one of them, Boris. The discussion took place at the camp fence, when that Boris was on guard duty. The result: he announced that on the other side was a [partisan] unit; that [propaganda] was being spread among the guards; and that the commander of the guard was one of them. If they went [to the partisans], they planned to take 10 strong men from the camp with them. The same evening, the first meeting of the group of 10 was held in the camp bath. It was decided to send two comrades to the other side to create contact and get orders for further work. Comrade Nayv was taken off the guard and appointed night stoker in the railroad depot, and was replaced by comrade Letsid. Nayv could get into the camp any time of the day or night, all the while observing the nocturnal movement on the highway.

The day after the meeting, the first orders arrived to carry out acts of sab[otage]. The first act consisted of destroying two big diesel motors used for pulling the narrow railroad train. Comrade Shtivovel [Lwowicz] was excellent at that. The anniversary of the Oct[ober] Rev[olution] was approaching. Ten more people were drawn into this work and attended the holiday meeting in the bath. The Order of the Day, read by Battalion Commander Shtivelepets, listed several regulations and assigned various tasks. It was decided to leave [the camp] if an opportunity should arise. There was a regular contact, conducted through the forest, where a Jewish forest column was at work; its members were selected by the FPO.

About the beginning of February 1944, it was finally decided to leave. But, swiftly and unexpectedly, the [Russian] front approached the camp, which was hastily evacuated. The plan was not realized. The camp then marched 20 kilometers to Kuremae, where it was integrated into another Jewish camp. Thus the FPO work was truncated. Of the group of 20, only the first 10 stuck together. But no more activity was carried out.

A month later, about March 1, the camp marched 60 kilometers toward Goldfilz, where the group commander was met by Kilona [Anolik] and a part of his group. There, too, the men stuck together. All lifelines were cut off. In April, 150 men were sent from there to Klooga, including, by order of Bat[talion] Com[mander] Cy[pelewicz], Comrades Nayv, Namdirf [Friedman], and Rebeyrsh [Schreiber], and others, to launch [organizational] work.

Nalpak [i.e., Kaplan], Yisroel, Originally from Holszany, Former Student [of Yiddish School], 15 Years Old: Rosa—Kaiserwald—Dünawerk—Kohtla—Goldfilz—Klooga

On Friday, August 23, 1942,[18] soon after the last Jews were taken out of the Vilna Ghetto, they fished us out of the melinas: 85 men and 300 women. At the ghetto gate, Kittel separated people older than 50 and children younger than 12 years old. The others were taken to the train. Thus, 85 + 300 = 385 remained. Another

18. This date is wrong. It should be September 23, 1943.

400 women from among those who remained in Rosa were brought to the train, altogether 700 women and 85 men.

Three days later, the train reached Kaiserwald near Riga, a concentration camp with 5,000 Jews, men and women, and a small group of Christians. Most people work here: women at cement, at the Riga railroad station, at gas, etc. Food not bad. Slept in barracks. Spent only three days here.

[I] was settled in Dünawerk, 2 km from Kaiserwald and 10 km from Riga, where 600 Jewish men and women, 170 men and 430 women, worked—at cement, transport, etc.

Spent two months here. In November arrived in Kohtla (Estonia). A group of 200 men. Two from Vilna, the rest German and Riga Jews, a few Czechs.

Kohtla was a camp for 170 men and women. Worked at transport, wood, etc. Now the camp has 370 persons. Lived in barracks, slept on bunks. Food not bad, but dirty. Here spent 10 weeks, i.e., until mid-January 1944. Then transported to Goldfilz.

Goldfilz. Found an empty field. Built eight barracks, where 170 men were quartered. Men and women. Later people arrived here from various Klooga camps, e.g., from Vivikoni, Narva, Kuremae, Fituni [?], Vaivara, etc. In mid-March the camp population reached 1,700 persons. The newcomers were from the camps liquidated during the Bol[shevik] onslaught. In Goldfilz, the death rate was high—3–4 persons a day. In Goldfilz worked at building barracks, railroads, transport, in mines of white stone used instead of coal, to extract gas from them, etc. Left Goldfilz in mid-April and after three days arrived in Klooga, where I work on the railroad, digging sewers, in the forest, carrying trees, etc.

P.S.

1. In Kaiserwald met, among others, the Vilna Ghetto actress Khayele Rosental.
2. In Kaiserwald they brought a Vilna Jew who had escaped from Vaivara. They took him in here as a prisoner of war and placed him in Dünawerk among the Russian POWs. There he stayed from morning to dusk; at dusk he crossed the Dvina on a boat and escaped again.

Bush [i.e., Shub] Sholem (Vivikoni—Ereda—Klooga)

Left Vilna during the Aktion, when the Estonians surrounded the ghetto. Was pulled out of the melina on Oszmiańska 10, a deep cellar with five persons. From there, arrived in Vaivara, where they were ordered to stand five in a row. The packages were left in the wagons. Thus they took 300 men to Vivikoni, 8 km by foot.

Vivikoni. In Vivikoni, two camps already existed—First Vivikoni and Second Vivikoni, Oil Baltic Company. He landed in no. 2, settled in wooden barracks, slept on bunks. Food: 25 deca bread per day, 3 deca [30 grams] butter, soup, and coffee. Work: among them were 900 highway workers, 30 in mines, and others. Later: in the oil factory in Silame, a port 12 km from Vivikoni, around the oil factory, mines about 100 persons, forest more than 100 persons, on the railroad Vivikoni-Vaivara, and others.

Life. The camp leader[ship] was in Estonian hands, later passed to the SS. Under the Estonians the regime was easy, harsher under the SS. Not allowed to cook, laws introduced, no food, no trade. Then, when the camp leader arrived, the regime got even harsher: everybody was harnessed to work. Forbidden to move from one work position to another, frequent searches and confiscation of possessions, harsh roll calls, confiscated all cooking utensils, etc.

Cases of Death. In six months five persons died, one girl was found dead in the forest.

Of the 900 persons there were 600 men and 300 women. All from Vilna.

In February, left Vivikoni for Ereda.

Lower Ereda. Six hundred and ninety-nine persons arrived in Ereda, including about 240 and some [sick?] among them sick on sleds. Here encountered two camps, Upper Ereda and Lower Ereda.

Upper Ereda stands on a hill. A camp and wooden barracks with bunks. The lower camp is 50 meters lower than the upper camp, divided as if they were different camps. Settled in small Finnish barracks, built 25 cm above ground in a swampy area. Here we, the newcomers, lived, later the sick, dragged here from all camps to be sent to Riga.

Here, in Lower Ereda, worked for Todt in jobs like: 25 km from Ereda, digging bunkers; women, 12 km [away] in Kohtla-Järve in an oil shale factory; a small group 1½ km [away] worked loading parts of the shale factory and oil shales that were shipped to Hamburg.

Mortality in Lower Ereda was high, about 1–2 persons a day.

From Ereda we went to Klooga, 100 men, including a great many sick and weak. Among the 100, there are 56 from Upper Ereda.

Camp Vaivara, Told by the Vilna Tailor Kupits [i.e., Tsipuk?]

1. *Torture in the Camps.* It is often impossible to record the names. He lost his memory.

In Vaivara, people were often thrown out of the hospital while they were still alive. They were thrown into the laundry room, where they would often expire. The camp leader (nicknamed "The Black One") would enter the hospital, and if he thought people were dying he would order them thrown out, and there they died. One of those he [Tsipuk] remembers is the dentist Katz from Vilna. The Black One often beat him unconscious. Katz then went to the hospital, where he was thrown out; The Black One even forced a young man to poison Katz by pouring some powder into his mouth. There must have been a dozen such cases.

Beatings. As soon as people began to fall down, growing weak or sick, and so on, they were beaten. The Black One would torture such people to death with blows to their head. He would order them to undress in the winter and would throw them naked into the swamp, then leave them for several days in the laundry room. For example, Ruvkin [. . .], a Vilna Jew from Rudnicka 13, a shopkeeper, was tortured to death in this way . . .

Typhus epidemics invaded the camp in the winter, November 1943. At first they were driven out to work with a fever of 38 degrees.[19] The death rate climbed. As soon as they recovered, [they] were expelled from the hospital. Only later did they keep the sick 10 days after recovery, and the death rate declined. Nourishment was also improved.

Later this camp became an assembly place for sick people. For example, a group from Tallinn was brought, about 40–50 sick people, and quartered in the hospital. From Higenburg [?], 40–50, and from Narva some 30 sick people. Thus more than 300 [sick people] were gathered here. Many of them recovered. There used to be 4, 5, or 6 deaths daily. All of them were burned.

With the evacuation of the camp, the whole hospital and its staff were transferred to Ereda (see protocol of Ereda).

[*The protocol is missing.*]

2. Camp Vaivara was a transit camp. People would come here, remain in groups for a month or two, and then the Jews would be transported to the surrounding area. In the camp, there was an average of 1,300. Of that figure, about 200–300 were permanently on the spot, including the administration of about 130 persons. The rest worked at various tasks.

3. There was a special children's camp here, where children aged three to seven were sent from various camps. There were 200 children, mostly from this camp. Meanwhile they would send out the mothers or fathers, but the children remained and were even treated relatively not badly. The director of the institution was Dr. Finkelstein from Kovno, assisted by a group of Jewish nurses. At the evacuation, this institution was transferred by train to Ereda, and from there to Riga, where the children arrived.

4. *Evacuation of Vaivara* occurred at the end of February 1944. Here they gathered the Jews from Narva, Vivikoni 2, Higenburg, and more. The trip took three days; [they] marched in the nights. Old and weak people were transported in wagons. Thus they made 60 km.

Other cases of Evacuation. Those walking behind were thrown into the sea. One case of three men is known; in subsequent groups there were more such cases.

The groups from Narva are now in Kivioli, or the so-called Little Kivioli. In March this year there were more than 600 Jews there. The rest were sick in Ereda. The children and sick were in Riga. The rest, from other camps, remained in Goldfilz, Ereda, and Kivioli 1.

19. Celsius (or 100.4 degrees Fahrenheit).

In Narva Died, Among Others: Z. Kalmanowicz, Moyshe Lerer, N. Weinig, Dr. Rivkind.

BOOK 6 — LIBERATION

[*Kruk planned a fictional account of the Holocaust, which was to be based on realistic descriptions of typical situations rather than daily journal entries, and presented through the narrator's emotional and often judgmental voice. Only parts of this work survived, and apparently Kruk himself made only incomplete drafts. It is remarkable that Kruk gave the final "book," several chapters of which are presented here, the title "Liberation." Indeed, the Germans clearly were losing the war, the Red Army was close, and the camps in Estonia were labor camps rather than death camps. Kruk was unaware, however, of the plans for a Final Solution and the Germans' devotion to their mission of ridding Europe of Jews.*]

Chapter 1: Klooga—The Metropolis of the Jewish Camps in Estonia[20]

. . . And Klooga did not fall behind the surrounding world. The surrounding world, whose economic and industrial life died out with the war. But on the contrary, a new industry rose, a war industry.

Klooga, the tiny dot in the tiny state of Estonia, rose from an empty place to an industrial point for the needs of the war. The Germans found several buildings here, and two or three old barracks. Apparently they decided to use this point for the economy, and thus an industry was built here, oriented 100 percent to the war effort.

When the many hundreds of Jews from Vilmen[21] arrived in Klooga, they found a large forest area, cluttered with boards and logs. Off in a corner, several women sat and twisted wires—ostensibly for the iron grids for the production of concrete.

Now 1,800 Jews work here. The forest area is filled with large and small barracks. The corner where reinforced concrete [is made] is one of the major branches, produced by Jewish prisoners. Around the "Concrete" buildings, adjacent to the walls, are stacks of tens of thousands of bricks for the construction of bunkers. "Concrete" now occupies a large area, and about [?] persons, men and women prisoners, work here. Concrete is no play; work in Concrete is the hardest work in Klooga, penal hard labor even for the Klooga inmates. If they need to punish somebody, they send him to work in Concrete. It is as hard to get out of working at Concrete as it is to split the Red Sea, for who would agree to work in Concrete? . . .

The boards and logs once strewn around here are nothing compared to the sea

20. An earlier title, "Klooga—Industrial Center," was crossed out.

21. A code word for Vilna, used in Kruk's fictionalized writings.

of boards and logs now flooding the camp area. Residential barracks, field barracks, carpenter workshops, [. . .] cross-saws, electric planes, [. . .]—an extensive wood production operation with hundreds upon hundreds of slaves, Jewish prisoners, trudging on the conveyor belt, driven by Estonian and German slave-drivers.

Locksmith shops, cobbler shops, tailor shops, a large wooden clog factory, a dye plant, painter's materials, many small workshops, huge warehouses, and storehouses, etc., etc.

Klooga already has its own electricity. Jewish prisoners produced an electrical network that covers Klooga. Jews built machines, erected barracks. They are productive and are harnessed to the labor wagon 14 hours a day.

Such is Klooga today!

. . . And Klooga does not stay behind. Everything here is enlarged and expanded. The enemy is knocking at the gates of Estonia, and here, 220 km from the enemy, everything is bubbling. If day work is not enough, night shifts work, too. If the Klooga people are not enough, a large part of the O.T. activity from Tallinn is transferred here, too. Tallinn, the capital of Estonia, is in danger, the Reds have invaded its sky, so O.T. transferred all its property to Klooga.

Until recently Klooga had just one SS man and three O.T. men. Today there are three German SS men and an Estonian SS guard of dozens and dozens.

Klooga was transformed from a desolate corner into an industrial town, just seven or eight months old.

Not to be sneezed at, what Klooga is for Estonia today!? . . .

Trains arrive, bringing dozens of wagons of raw material, wood, cement, iron. And they take hundreds of housing barracks and whole trains of barracks for the battlefields.

A broad and diversified transportation network of cars, trucks, and small buses connects us to Tallinn. People come and go, visit and . . . admire the Jewish "warmongers," the prisoners here, who have to produce for the "New Europe." . . . The Jewish camp, on whose shoulders rests the development of Klooga's heavy production, has long since emerged from its primitive beginnings. Here we have closed groups, work units, with their own interests, groups occupied with smuggling food, storekeepers with their portable stock in the blocks of the camp, and groups of people who made a pact to stay together, so they wouldn't drown in the vulgarity and demoralization of most camp inmates.

With the remnants of strength, an ideological group was also organized, a group of the so-called Marxist thinkers and radicals, aimed at protecting camp interests and helping to liberate the country. . . .

Not to be sneezed at, Klooga! . . .

Klooga is the largest of all Jewish camps in Estonia. The Klooga camp is considered the best-organized camp, with its own laundry, two baths (one for men and one for women), two disinfection stations, two clinics, two hospitals, a dentist's office, an internal tailor shop, a carpenter shop, a barber shop, and a Social Aid Committee to help the needy and hungry.

Things are bubbling in Klooga. By day at work, by night among ourselves. Germans get drunk and hold balls, using Jewish food, and Jews hunt for bread, organize into groups, and think seriously about the war that is already knocking at the gates of Estonia.

The depressed and exhausted Jews don't want to remain slaves in Hitler's wagon. The hour, some say, has rung, let us get liberated! . . .

Now groups of "runners" emerge. Some runners are "moneybags," as they are called here, and some runners don't want to run, even at the cost of their lives. The Reds are closing in, and the harnessed slaves think about breaking out of the vise, about liberation and salvation. . . .

Klooga, not to be sneezed at! . . .

[*Chapters 2–5 are missing.*]

Chapter 6: A Life—a Palliative

Such is the instinct of man: in every difficult time he seeks a way out, a support for his will to live. If he finds one, fine. If he does not, he invents it for himself—just to immerse himself in a game, evade danger, get rid of the uneasiness and fear of the uncertain tomorrow.

When the Vilmen Ghetto was suddenly liquidated, the Jews [Jewish men] were separated and cut off from their wives and children, whom they abandoned in Rosa, and alone, as prisoners, were transported to Estonia. In their great helplessness, they all, swiftly and seriously, circulated a rumor among themselves: any minute, the Baltic countries will be liberated. Just look how Vilmen will be free, and consequently the whole thing will be over, and we will remain here in Klooga for just a few days, at the maximum, weeks. Such a rumor was supposed to calm, perhaps even console, them. A drowning man will clutch even a razor blade. The rumor was believed, and the hope that we would remain here for only a short time calmed us; at least a palliative of calming took hold among most Vilmen men. It was no more than a lying delusion, an instinct that allowed them to endure.

Weeks passed. The Vilmen prisoners here were first liberated from the [yellow] patches, ostensibly no longer Jews. Later they acquired the honorary title of *Häftlinge* [detainees], with patches, numbers, and various insignia, designating their workplace.

The illusion dissipated, and disappointment came incredibly fast. The Klooga slaves, driven daily to work, succumbed to their lot. Klooga was the last road. From here, the final end would come.

"Either/or"—Shmulikl the Vilmen bakery worker sets the tone. "Either we get out of here liberated, or they will finish us off." Jews, divided into optimists and pessimists, swallow everything, overlook the prophecy of finishing off, and push the wagon.

Fearing that they may come to search any day, or just make searches and such, the Klooga prisoners carry all that has remained with them: every day they put on two or three pairs of underwear, one coat worn on top of another; thick, wide, and puffed up, they depart for work certain that every day gained is either closer to the goal. The goal . . . or . . . or . . .

Locksmiths became carpenters, cobblers became workers in reinforced concrete, specialists in sawing-works, transporters, and similar professions. Jews "specialized" in "new professions," established "new lives" for themselves and adapted to the new conditions incredibly fast. The workplaces were transformed into commercial centers, the commercial centers into exchange banks, where Jews would bring clothes and Estonians would carry bread, butter, and various foodstuffs, etc.

Jews who still had money would change fivers and turn gold into bread. Some of the Klooga inmates supplemented their food by exchanging clothes. Others by swallowing gold pieces. The newborn Estonian speculators demanded not "tatters" but gold. With gold they were safer. . . . Fivers, tenners, etc., streamed out of the camp, and gradually hunger settled in the camp. The gold ran out, the tatters were no more, and the problem of hunger intensified. . . .

A few dozen, who still have it, live and eat. Hundreds who don't, starve.

Poverty became a daily affair, hunger a phenomenon of most Klooga Jews. Jewish prisoners with swollen arms and puffed-up faces, Jews with bodies covered with boils—a plague from bad nourishment! . . .

In the forest, among the Klooga evergreens, among the new, well-arranged buildings, established by the Reds, back when Klooga was turned into a Bolsh[evik] military base.

The road that separates Klooga from Tallinn became the separation line between the so-called women's camp and the men's camp. To 700 men, 1,200 women!

Women are forbidden to visit the men, and men must not have any contact with women.

Women suffer poverty like men, and men do not want to be silent about it: Why separate us? . . .

Sooner than the men, women get entry into the men's block, and individual men push themselves to the women in the women's camp. Faster than men, women establish contacts with Estonians, with . . . Germans, with Christians inside the camp, and with Estonians outside it. Women who have the support of "acquaintances," local Germans or Estonians and others, often even risk contacts with former "Easterners"[22]—not only inside the camp but even outside the camp. Large-scale trade arises. The Jewish camp is supplied with the necessary

22. Russians, who immigrated from Russia to Estonia under the Soviets.

minimum. Contacts thrive between the men's and women's blocks, and the connections outside the wire fence develop fast and make life easier.

Jews do business and earn "tenners." Others exchange and support themselves; some cast their net and pull wherever it goes. But the rest remain helpless, watching how in the miserable Klooga [Yiddish: *in klogedikn kloge*] a life is established—a palliative so we don't go under.

Women must not have relations with men, and men certainly not with women. Nevertheless, threads are woven, friendships created—men are drawn to women and women driven to men. . . .

On Sundays, on the rare days of rest, often even in weekly evening hours, the blocks fill up: a mixture of guests, and of return calls—women visit men and men visit women.

Eyes shining with a starved smile, faces distorted and hiding life's drive. . . . Everything as it has been—women have relations with men and men have relations with women. . . .

On the bottom bunks, at each person's narrow corner, "guests" sit, talk about the situation, work conditions, perspectives, about freedom, and, mainly, they talk and talk about their recent past. Youths who do not like to philosophize stretch out, lie on the bunks, and sing aloud, songs filled with nostalgia, hope, and desire for life.

A life, a palliative to chase out the gloom!

A life only Klooga Jews can understand.

Shmulke the bakery worker lies on his bunk, embittered, thinks about his wife and child, who remained in Rosa, and cannot understand the men and women, from whose bodies a piece of living flesh was torn out, and yet . . . yet the will to live continues. . . .

Or, tired from work, sated, and often drunk, he lies on the bunk with his boots on, stinking like an ox in a stable. For him there is no life anymore. He lives because he works hard, because this is what the group wants, his friends with whom he carries the heavy loads and bears the days and weeks in Klooga.

And Abke?

He is perhaps one of the few who arranged a life here with no "why"s:

For here one must forget about everything;
Each of us has to begin from the beginning . . .
To overcome, just to survive! . . .
Isn't each of us today many times more precious than before? . . .
For how many of us are left altogether? . . .

A philosophy of a kind, deriving from a mixture of the worldview of the erstwhile Arke and the adaptability of his heir, Abke.

[Who is] Abke?

Abke is the first of the first; in the group of the Strong Ones [*di shtarke*] he sets the tone. Others are actually strong, most of all Berke, Samure, the Kukhele. But he is the guiding force. Abke worries and supplies. Berke became the favorite of the Six-Footer, and Abke exploits it. He becomes his prompter, initiator, and adviser.

Abke creates and acquires; his acquaintances reach not just the women's block or the Todt people in the men's camp. His extensive relations go far, far outside the camp. Every opportunity is exploited. If they travel to Tallinn for supplies, Abke whispers: "You have to use the Strong Ones for that. . . ."

"It is a good thing to be around supplies," says Abke to his buddies. And the buddies don't need much; Samura helps:

"The good years you can gain there. . . ."—and a whole business unfolds.

The Six-Footer agrees, and the Strong Ones establish a standard of living at the expense of the camp supplies. Again an opportunity arrives: special trucks are sent for potatoes, and as always, the first to go are the Strong Ones.

Every trip from Tallinn brings a profit, bread, meat, and what not? Every trip for potatoes—a surplus of hundreds of kilos of potatoes. The potatoes are eaten, and they are sold, and vodka is bought. Vodka becomes a daily thing for some and bread a holiday for others. And as the saying goes, "as with the Christians, so with the Jews": among the women too, a group of Strong Ones emerges. The initiator is again, as always, Abke.

Beylke, a friend of Abke's, who often lies on his bunk and already has the sardonic nickname Abke's Missus [*Di abikhe*], was the one who became the leader of a group of women who do various loading jobs. If men load logs, machines, barrels of gas, etc., the group of Strong Women do the same, unloading wagons of boards, loading cement, producing concrete-iron bricks, parts of barracks, and so on. Beylke, Abke's friend, is more man than woman. Wearing man's pants with wide jodhpurs shoved into her boots. On her body, a peasant fur coat, from which her full, red cheeks emerge, along with a pair of big, wide eyes, shining with lust for life and joy of life.

Beylke commands a whole "company." They come to her in time of trouble, asking for advice and help. And Beylke, the young, daring, strong, and well-built woman, the leader of the Strong Ones, finds her ways. She gets the Estonian guards to release confiscated items. Often she manages to twist the arm of Estonian swindlers, who catch things and don't want to fulfill their commitments. Beylke, perhaps more than Abke, is a rare bird among the Strong Ones and a famous name among the Klooga Jews. . . .

Beylke, Abke's Missus.

And around her? Not only Strong Ones gather around the golden Beylke. They are mostly bold women traders who dare to go outside the barbed wires, who are friendly with Germans and with Estonians, and who have a good time.

Both groups are steeped in business. On the one hand, they draw from the living and the dead, pulling from the camp whenever and whatever possible. On the other hand, a series of businesses: Abke acquires in the name of the men's group, Beylke for the women. People who need a favor pay for it, people who need to get to Beylke through Abke sleep with [him?]. . . .

A wagon of leather for the wooden clog factory, and some 15 ox leathers disappear as a payment that the whole group lives on for weeks! . . .

A trip to Tallinn brings big earnings. Another group unloads in Klooga the bread that was brought in. The "other group" takes again, pulls, and gets for it new loaves. Outsiders are not allowed—it all belongs to the "loading group." . . .

Tallinn is loading. . . .

Potatoes—loading, a series of loadings that bring in great profits.

[*A section of the manuscript here is unreadable.*]

And undertaking an extra job requires an extra food ration from the Jewish elder, remuneration for the "hard work." Everything gets to the Strong Ones, the Benjamins of the men's and women's blocks.

Berke, perhaps the most solid of the Strong Ones, swears "by his heart's beloved" that he doesn't take from the "Bride." "May he be as sick," he claims, "as much as he takes from her." So why does she crawl to him again? And Berke, with his sick, bass voice, answers modestly: "Well, she comes. . . . " "So what if she comes? . . . " "Why shouldn't she come?" Berke, the giant among the Klooga Strong Ones, sticks to his guns: "She comes, let her come, so what if she comes? Why not?"

The "Bride," along with Beylke, constitute the command staff among the women; Abke and Berke conduct both the affairs of the men and the "businesses" of the women. The conduct of the Strong Men is similar to the attitude of the Strong Women. Everywhere they are the first ones, everywhere they get the best deal, and everywhere people owe them change.

Vodka is a daily thing. Where do they get money for vodka?

Meat is a foodstuff used a lot here. So where do they get so much of it?

The Strong Women grow strong and healthy. The Strong Men eat, drink, and gulp vodka.

In the camps, people collapse. It is impossible to get rid of the swollen, hungry, starving. People here eat potato peels, use dried coffee instead of food. You see people picking scraps from the garbage. For hundreds, poverty, swollen bodies, boils, and potato peels; for the few, meat, vodka, and girls.

A life like a radish—bitter and harsh.

A life a palliative—an imitation of survival. . . .

Chapter 7: The Strong Ones of Concrete

The whole camp rings with noises that sound like the pounding of a blacksmith. Iron pounding on iron emits a gamut of echoes, and far and wide over the fields goes a music that, in normal times, we would call the music of work. But today this is certainly no music. It is the shouts of Klooga slavery.

In this place, people are making the iron grids for reinforced concrete. People are twisting iron to be enclosed in concrete bricks, which are produced in the nearby building. One group twists the wires. Another group stands absorbed over the concrete cases—"workbenches," as they are called here—and pounds concrete, shaping concrete bricks.

Concrete and iron grids are the main nerve of Klooga's production. Concrete, produced by Jewish prisoners, is used to build bunkers—war production molded by Jewish slaves, prisoners of Klooga.

In the long, half-dark barracks, with wide, long tables all around, stand trained "workbenches," and over each of them a pusher, a master of concrete. As long and as big as the building, from everywhere comes a mixing, a pounding; the iron-grid sounds deafen the concrete pounders, and the concrete pushers drown out the ringing of iron with their blunt thumps. Over them and around them is the growling of two mechanical mixers that blend cement with sand, transforming it into a mixture of concrete.

One hundred and twenty concrete workers. Ninety women serve the more than 50 iron workers—a mixture of 300 mouths who don't shut up, a tumult of people, a noise of wires, and the pushing of the concrete—an impressive symphony concert. A chase that looks like a drive to help build the New Europe.

That's how it looks when German supervisors turn up. An oversight committee.

In fact, the play here is different. Concrete is overcrowded. Instead of 50 people, 300 work there. People get under each other's feet. One disturbs another, and—as the concrete workers say—the greater the honor, the better the joy.

The big, long stable, the barracks there that was changed into the enterprise of concrete production, is full of people, a "competition" for pushing concrete, a race of women porters who carry the finished concrete bricks to be dried, a transport of finished concrete moved from the machine to the workbenches. Worlds are seething—a beehive. A full marketplace. It boils like a cauldron.

And in that tumult, Jews are trading furiously. Here come Estonians, the protectors and guards of Concrete, their friends and comrades. Here they conclude "transactions," and from here come supplies of bread, onions, flour, groats, etc., to the block.

Jews take off their last remaining clothes, and Christians with great greed bring food, cigarettes, brandy, and so forth, in exchange for them.

The Concrete barracks seethe like a cauldron. Women and men are absorbed in their calculations. People assess clothes. People feel, and people look at the merchandise, and people hide everything from prying eyes. All you need is the shout "Apple"[23] for everything to disappear; the concrete workbenches start pushing. The grid wires ring; the women, as if harnessed, rush with their carrying

23. A code word to sound the alarm that someone is coming.

boards, with concrete bricks. The biggest war enterprise in Klooga is the biggest center of trade and exchange!

The "better" Germans don't interfere. They smile and are satisfied with the Jewish activity. The worse Germans search, smell, and seldom succeed in finding anything. It happens that blows fall—they caught a group of Jews who weren't working. . . . Sometimes somebody shows up suddenly, catches one in the act and . . . intercepts a bundle, sometimes even clothes for exchange, sometimes food. The victims cry, calmer ones groan, and the trade continues—a market that never ceases. . . .

It often happens that Beylke is called right away to the scene of the "events." She looks for the "snatcher," dissuades him with her eye, and the snatched bundle soon swims back out:

"May she be our sacrifice, just so it is rescued!"

The sacrifice is a five-ruble ransom, two measures of brandy, or a gift of one kind or another. Moreover, Beylke's ways are manifold—who can know. Who wants to know? . . .

Everywhere there are Strong Ones. Not always does "Strong Ones" mean muscles. The Strong Ones set the tone, go by force, those who dictate and get their way. Concrete also has its Strong Ones, leaders, even though no one has given them the authority. Their head is Max. A tall, broad-shouldered, clumsy young man with a solid bass voice and solid big hands that push cement stones with the speed of an ace worker, thereby determining the size of the quota.

Once 15 stones a day was established here as the quota; later the quota was raised to 19. A Viennese engineer noted that Max and his gang managed more, and the quota rose again from 19 to 25. From there to 30, 32, 35. Max is already getting to 40, and everyone who is driven by Max's strong fists follows and drives out his last strength, the last bit of health.

That doesn't interest Max. His clumsy figure regularly shakes over the workbench. The women porters who take the mass of finished stones from him are worn out. The transporters, who have to deliver cement, curse bitterly, and Max, the German refugee, stands with all his cold-bloodedness and cracks jokes, as is his wont.

"*Faulenzer,* I hate lazy people. Don't let them get underfoot, let them dance. . . ."

And the weakling and the lazy guy do indeed dance, dragging heavy, overfilled barrows of concrete and transporting the finished stones that grow like mushrooms after a rain from under Max's strong gigantic hands.

His coarse face, lined with clumsiness, lights up with satisfaction, all his cronies standing around, the followers and fellow travelers, the quota setters and flatterers: they all "beam" at his wisdom and strength.

"Let them understand how we do things for Max," says one of his servants.

"Is it beneath them to work?" a small-town old-clothes dealer flatters him, seeking in "Comrade Max" support from a Strong One.

"They want to have a *resort* here. A *resort* in Klooga. A plague on their heads," fidgets a strong young man who is Max's factotum, an aristocrat among aristocrats!

All the Concrete workers chew and spit, driven by an unwieldy force—Max and his gang.

Nevertheless, not everyone takes it seriously. Some there don't care about anything: German-Shmerman, the world is lawless. You keep yourself busy with merchandise, as if nothing has happened. You trade and deal, close deals, and seek fresh merchandise.

"Maybe you know about a good leather satchel?" a graceful young girl asks a Concrete worker standing over a workbench, trying to catch up with the quota.

"And I'm looking for a pair of long scarlet pants," answers the other one.

"Wool socks! Who's got wool socks?!" a sportsman of Concrete shouts into the hall.

"An old dick for three loaves of bread," mocks a cement mixer.

No one listens to this. The coarse shouts have no effect on anyone. That is street talk, and no one is embarrassed. Women who still bear the signs of "good breeding" button up their dignity and pretend not to hear. Men who can't stand it don't react. Why act like a fool? . . .

Estonians walk around in the turmoil and feel like foreigners. Girls rummage around the Estonians, tease them flirtatiously, haggle, and do business. The "fair" is in full swing, like the sea.

There are hours when the work is in last place. First of all, trade:

"First priority to a piece of bread . . . ," a woman from the carriers apologizes. To whom? But the merciful one goes on:

"Bread-shmed, may they drop dead. Oh God, Master of the Universe," she goes on, in the tones of an old psalm chanter in the cemetery.

One who stands on "alert"[24] suddenly gives the watchword:

"Apple!"

"Apple" is repeated from one to another. "Apple," the "password," spreads like an announcement to watch your back.

And then a game is played: the wires start ringing and beating on the anvils, the pounders start pounding in the concrete cases. The transport jerks as if on the end of a chain. Bricks swim from the tables to the places where they are dried—a factory of Jewish prisoners, masters of competition! . . .

"May they have a sweet death . . . ," says a woman, walking through with her carrying board loaded with concrete bricks.

"May a cart with sugar run over you," responds a concrete maker with no purpose, not even knowing what provoked his words.

"May they be torn to pieces," a third doesn't refrain [from saying].

24. The word translated as "alert" is Yiddish slang: *zeks,* like the British *nix*.

"Every fingernail separately," another one adds pointedly.

"And the teeth? One tooth after another, may they be pulled like nails from a wall . . . ," a bitter concrete master plays it out sadistically.

The manufacturing goes full speed ahead. The enterprise bangs away, and the Germans passing by are satisfied, although many of them understand very well that everything there is a farce—a performance, as if directed by an invisible hand. . . .

Not only do men gather around Max. There are also women, carriers who take his finished stones and are not behind in driving the production.

Just like Max, healthy, sturdy maidens sit there; some of them sit like hens, protecting him, getting joy from his sturdy hands, looking him straight in the eye, laughing and taking pleasure in every saying of his. Max, such a sturdy fellow, a strong one, a joy to look at. . . .

"Hands like hooks," one says to another.

"When he embraces you, it melts in your bones . . . ," a neighbor holding a pick echoes. Max knows everything about them; he stands in the middle of his circle, shoots out proverbs, and is satisfied that his teachings have caught on and are carried around like a delicious dish.

Max, a trifle, Max in Concrete? . . .

. . . Max is the spokesman, the preacher and commander.

But otherwise, it's among the masses. Hostile glances are everywhere, cursing and reviling the "quota setters," Max and his whole gang.

"Max," the weak ones beg him, "you're driving us into misfortune. You regularly and systematically raise the quota"; and Max, with his clumsy coldness, with the calm of a sage among idiots, doesn't interrupt and answers stubbornly.

"So what?"

"What do you mean, so what?" the weaker ones ask. "And who has the strength to maintain the quota?"

"And why do I have strength?" answers Max bluntly, as if they didn't mean him.

"You're strong, healthy. But we, you can see for yourself, our legs are collapsing! . . ."

"Max, what is the limit? We're already maintaining a quota of 30! . . ."

For Max, this is like last year's snow. . . . He lifts his head, looks the "weaklings" straight in the eye, and says angrily:

"So who told you to work in Concrete?"

"Is there easier work!" the small-town tailor chips in.

"Work, what do you mean easier work? Who in Klooga is looking for work? . . ."

The complainers are tired, worn out, some feel ashamed of the mock answers, and some even rebel:

"Max, who is this one, a bag over his head and out of Concrete!"

"Let us talk with the Jewish elder. Let him react, let him intervene! . . . "

Cooled off, the anger dissolved, everyone goes back to the tables. One stands on lookout, others are involved in trade. From time to time, the shout "Apple" creates a disturbance, but everything together is mixed in the whole, in the wild brouhaha of the Concrete barracks. . . . The complaints of slavery carry on, and everything that is human and capable of life is crushed . . . oppressed and hushed among them. . . .

Most can hardly catch their breath, striving for the quota. People deal, people do business, people buy and sell. Most are hollow things; people who really earn money make it somewhere else, are organized into bands, have contacts, have their own people who stand on lookout and others who know when to shout "Apple."

Beylke, Abke's girlfriend; Max, who stands innocently shaping the concrete stones; Abke, the leader of the hall. And on and on. All those are leaders of "stockholder companies," whose businesses prosper and whose partners don't live, God forbid, on the ration. They eat, they drink, and they work, proving to the Germans and Estonians their efficiency, and in the meantime doing the greatest trickery of wheeling and dealing.

Max is the "leader." He already has his business people, the enterprise goes well, and Max walks around in the shop as a hen walks around her chicks.

[*A section is missing here.*]

Every workplace has its Strong Ones; in every unit a privileged group, aristocrats who carry on a life at the expense of the hungry. Handfuls of people carry on the good life; the majority is starving, working, and serving as meat on a butcher's block. So what is the wonder?

[*In his description of the slaughter of the Jews in Klooga just before the Soviets arrived, Dworzecki (1948) describes how the inmates were made to sit and observe the selected 300 Strong Ones carry logs to the forest. "Suddenly they saw one of the camp inmates, Max, throw down his log, run back to the camp, and scream: 'Jews, save yourselves, they are killing us!' And he was shot on the spot by an SS man" (p. 380). Could this be the same Max?*]

Chapter 8: Starvation

Satiation is no wonder. Everything is set up here so that the worm eats the radish, digs deep, makes holes in it, sucks it out, and the poor radish begins to rot until it expires. The radish is no longer a radish when the sated worm croaks together with his victim Mr. Radish. . . .

Thirty-three decagrams of bread is neither enough to live on nor enough to die on. The work is no work. The discipline lacks discipline, and the prisoners, apathetic toward themselves and neglecting everything, are afraid of no one and nothing:

"What is left to be afraid of?"

"So they will shoot you from the front . . . ," jokes Srolikl.

"So they will shoot you from behind . . . ," continues his neighbor.

"Shooting, who's afraid of being shot?"

"But still . . ."

The Germans beat, the prisoners writhe and move on to the point of order. They flog publicly, so you get up half-faint from the bench, pull up your pants, and with the beaten body of an invalid, who can neither sit nor lie, you keep thinking about one thing: bread. Where could you get a ration of bread? . . .

Bread is not only the major dream [?] that gnaws everyone. Bread in Klooga is a curse for some and a blessing for others. Can bread in Klooga be taken lightly? . . . Everyone lives here at the expense of the prisoners, the consumers who are slaves, obedient, and swallow anything that comes their way—a dog's nature, to catch a bone that is thrown back. . . . According to the monthly plan, a prisoner gets 35 decagrams of bread, and on Sundays, half a loaf per person! But they sit in the camp supply office and calculate: instead of 35 daily, 33. Instead of a precise measure, tens of kilos get lost—how can you weigh it and protest? . . . And on Sundays there is a change. Instead of one loaf for two, the prisoners receive one loaf for three. Again, they make a large chunk of holiday bread on the prisoners' backs.

A prisoner is supposed to get 2 decagrams of sugar daily. But we get sugar every third day, and instead of 6 decagrams, 5. And margarine, the only piece of fat, instead of 3 decagrams, 2½. The kitchens cook for 2,000 prisoners, and the kettles can tell you stories: the soup is water, the so-called piece of meat disappears by the kilo, the dinner is a thin brew, and the prisoners, always hungry, curse into the air, tired and crushed.

The Germans do it differently. They, the suppliers of foodstuffs for the Jews, do not dabble in trifles, do not take off a decagram of meat per person: three wagons of potatoes for the prisoners—and one disappears altogether. Cheese—where did the cheese brought into Klooga disappear to? . . . Prisoners starve and suffer. The Germans, the camp leadership, the supply department, the Jewish camp police—they all eat and drink. The Jewish bosses grow wider, glow as never before, give parties and celebrate holidays. Poverty grows in the camp, and the "leadership" amass "tenners." . . .

The rage of the many grows, and the luxury of the few ferments.

Hunger knows no restraints. A hungry person is ready for anything except for stifling the worm inside you, which gnaws and gnaws.

Jews stopped being cowards: Is hunger better than death? Jews stopped being choosy: What can be worse than permanent hunger? . . . Some do not succumb and find means to live. Others, bent over, fasted, succumbed, deteriorated—resigned and finished!

Orke was finished long ago, a man who will not be resurrected. Others, on the contrary, will not allow themselves to be pulled out by the root. They do anything possible, permitted or not, to overcome, to survive! The slogan is the same: to live. The marrow of your bones gnaws and gnaws—to hold out! . . . Men wander around here as if in limbo—strange and estranged. . . .

The Strong One is guarded as never before: the will to live grows into an animal instinct with no limit and no restraint.

Rubin left work and walked into a peasant's house to "eat." The German saw it, shot at him, and Rubin went to the world-to-come—his body burned out from hunger pangs

[. . .]

Could even this stop us? Hunger breaks iron!

"Okay, what can they find here."

Everything is crushed, bent, and writhing. As in fear of the flogging you can get here maybe just because you did not become a Strong One. Many an intellectual befriends a Strong One. And there are various kinds of Strong Ones: the group of Strong Ones who take by their fist, use force, and are the first ones everywhere; the local authorities—Jewish block elders, brigadiers—and just nimble guys with connections and supporters.

The simple prisoner, the average camp Jew, is driven by both the Germans and the Estonians but mostly by the camp elder in his block and the brigadier at work. Nevertheless, they fight for a piece of bread. Trade flourishes, the exchange system is widespread, and Estonians from near and far come to the fences with . . . bread, flour, grains. During the day the business is conducted in the workplaces, at night around the fences: a shot is heard, the Estonian watchman signals to the Jews to come over to the fence in the dark of night. Enclosed in barbed wire, hands push out, pointing and showing. They haggle, they quarrel, and the trade flourishes. Bread, herring, meat, cigarettes flow into the camp, prices rise and fall, and the majority in the camp observe closely, are indifferent to the speculations, and are hungry, terribly hungry.

Who is interested in speculations? The wealthy man doesn't care about the price, he buys because he has enough to buy. The one who has nothing, why should he care how much and how much.

The majority, who cannot help themselves, starve and expire. They are totally exhausted, crushed, walk around bloated. Bloated legs and bloated arms. Starving: now they run after a barrow of potatoes, taking the potatoes from the bunker to the kitchen. A dropped potato is the prize of the lucky one, just to fetch a potato is an indescribable prize. Germans beat [Jews] over the head, block elders drive without mercy, and the hungry chase like dogs after a potato, run after an opportunity and are not ashamed, either for themselves or before others. The more energetic ones give up standing for hours around the potato bunker and try to get potato peels. They sort them out and take the thicker ones. The potatoes are washed, ground, and cooked, making a black mass—a potato cake or potato balls, whose consumers often get stomach cramps from them. But the stomach ache passes and hunger returns. So they chase after a turnip again, moldy pieces of bread, and stuff their bellies with poison, with aches, just to drive out the hunger, the worm that gnaws and gnaws and won't stop. . . .

In a corner, in the dark of his lair, a prisoner hides, and with his thin, long fingers he soaks the moldy bread that the supply department distributes and some prisoners throw away.

Those who have bread may throw it out. But those who are hungry beg their neighbors, the "bread owners," to get the mold. The wealthy ones do it gladly. Often even magnanimously—let him know, let him feel that he does not begrudge him. . . .

In the kitchen they chase after peels, and this reaches only those who can smuggle in, have acquaintances, have pedigrees.

Reb Hertske works at the garbage can, an old, good artisan, honest and decent. He does not know the wild tricks of Klooga, or the trade business. But his stomach doesn't understand his decency; it drives Hertske, it torments him and wears him out. And Hertske, the artisan, changed beyond recognition, is employed in the camp block. Here, along with Segal, the intellectual refugee from Warsaw, they clean the toilet, watch the garbage can and the brooms, buckets, and scrubbers like the apple of their eye—the best and most devoted ones for the sake of the block! . . .

The intellectual Segal talks politics and explains, and the small Hertske listens and pokes a stick in the garbage can. Now he finds turnip peels, wipes them off on his dirty pants, and puts them in his mouth to soothe his hunger. . . .

Hertske the artisan, the consumer of the garbage can, and Segal, master of seven languages, his entertainer and explicator. . . .

Gloomy, they arrive in masses for coffee, fill themselves with dry fake coffee and the growling of their hungry stomach.

Coffee. . . . There are many ways not to let your health drown. . . . Segal the intellectual understands the value of brain marrow for the bones, and he gets the dregs of the German kitchen, the bones they throw out. He washes, grinds the bones, and cooks them. He gets a greasy mass he can trade: one part he keeps for himself, and another part he sells for half a soup of next day's dinner.

Inventions of swollen bodies, the means of rescue of drowning people. sos screams of the hungry.

Bloated, they report to the clinic, show their swollen arms and legs, and the helpless doctor can hardly help them. How can he tell them about the damage of the organism caused by lack of protein, fats, vitamins, etc.?

He cannot. He can do nothing. On the contrary, his only advice is not to drink. Not to eat, for there is nothing to eat; not to drink either, then what? . . .

The hungry complain of dizziness, and the doctor, helpless, answers: lie down. Perhaps you'll feel better. But it is forbidden to lie down. You are allowed to lie down only with a temperature of 38 Celsius, and often even then you must leave the block and go to work.

So the work is not work, the discipline is not discipline, and the Jewish prisoners are left to the mercy of God—so what is the difference? . . .

When the piece of bread comes, along with a twelfth of fat, the tiny bit of sugar, or other items, the brigade is enveloped in seriousness: the products, weighed and measured, are distributed by lottery—all divided in 12 parts. One of the 12 turns his face away from the products, and another fellow points at one of the 12 parts and asks: "For whom?" And the man turns around, lists them all, every crumb comes by a lot—hunger justice of the weightiest degree.

Thus the prisoners cut their 33 decagrams of bread, calculate so that it will stay until supper, and until the next day's breakfast . . . and the account doesn't work, it's not enough. . . .

Others swallow all of the 33 decagrams and are hungry until the next day: at least once a day to eat your fill and feel the taste of bread. . . .

The sated don't wait for this. They cook mashed potatoes, roast chops, and drink samogon [self-brewed vodka]. Children and hungry people watch and swallow the smell, bite their lips and . . . clench their fists.

The Strong Ones, it's all the Strong Ones! . . .

The worm eats the radish, digs in deep, makes holes in it, sucks it out, and the radish rots and dissolves. The radish is no longer a radish, and the overfilled worm croaks together with his victim, Mr. Radish. . . . Hungry people tell each other about good food, about things they used to eat, and . . . in the hard, wailing Klooga nights, they dream about food . . . about bread and about—liberty. . . .

Chapter 10

Everything here is built on sand. Such is the destiny of the area. Close to the Gulf of Finland, adjacent to the Baltic Sea, the entire Klooga area is in such a miserable condition[25] that all that is done here floats on the surface and cannot put down roots.

Klooga, the tongue of little Estonia, pushes like a peninsula to the Baltic Sea on the one side and to her relative, the Finnish Bay, on the other. If you dig your shovel deep, a stream of water spurts, as if the sea wanted to burst out here, with its insolence and murderous demeanor.

Everything is built on sand. Everything is undermined by the sea. Hard to strike roots.

It would have been tragic for the Estonians. But the Estonians live well here. The country has plenty, and the population is calm and happy with its tiny country and its tiny state, democratic in attitude and friendly to strangers.

And when the war intruded into the tiny land and Estonia was devoured first by the Soviet Union, then by Germany, the well-being of the country died out.

25. A pun in Yiddish, used by the camp residents: *kloge* ("Klooga") sounds like *klog* ("lament") and *klogedik* ("miserable").

The population grew restless. And the tiny country with its tiny state lost its independence, its democratic attitude, and its hospitality toward strangers: for who if not "strangers" has broken and shaken it?

For who if not strangers has devoured and swallowed it? Everything here is built on sand, and everything in Klooga is miserable and unsafe. . . .

Much more, and harder, it hurt the Jews, the prisoners who were exiled here and scattered and dispersed in Estonian SS camps.

When the Vilmen Jews weighed anchor in Klooga and saw that Klooga was not a temporary phenomenon, that they might have to spend a long time here, who knows how long and who knows how it may end, fermentation began, and groups and cells emerged among parts of Jewish Klooga. Groups of people close to each other. Groups of people with common goals. Groups of people who would run away and escape. Groups looking for contacts [with the outside world or with partisans] and groups—a flood of groups and cells.

Human beings here lost the appearance of being human. Humans stopped being human. Everyone followed his animal instinct, forgetting that he arrived here in the image of man—the crown of creation, the most beautiful of all creatures!

When all around became desolate and wild, when all around, built on sand and water, began to disintegrate, a few individuals arose, saw [?] their faces, and tried to save themselves:

An idea emerged from among the intelligentsia of Klooga's Jewish camp to create a collegium of intelligentsia-intellectuals. Gathered around a full table, covered with a white tablecloth and self-brewed coffee, the assembled people tearfully honored their fallen colleagues and praised the great event of being able to sit together, look at the white tablecloth, and talk to each other like human beings, forgetting about the surrounding world, the camp, the situation, and the perspective.

And the human beings suddenly felt like humans! . . . True, all of them were hungry. True, none of them settled down properly, had anything to sell, or could engage in commerce—but all those intellectuals devoured the fine table, the white tablecloth, the festive gathering, and the atmosphere, which was so far from Klooga and even farther from reality.

Everything here is built on sand. Things built on sand are weak and do not last.

The fear of meeting. The great risk and small return. . . . All of it was pointed out: the group of intellectuals would die before it was even born.

And a shudder went through the camp: there is an organization. An alliance of people, whose goal is: to arm themselves, to guard the lot of the Jews in camp, to create contacts, and in case of a catastrophe, to run into the forest. . . .

Henekh breathed easier: finally he found some meaning. The organization would create an alibi for him in case of [a Communist return], he'd cast his net and show himself in his full splendor, that even here in Klooga he was vigilant and toed the [Party] line. His line, broken and distorted. His past—perhaps he himself did not realize it—was ugly, horrible, and shameful.

So what, if under the Poles he had been an informer [against the Communists]?

So what, if under the Soviets he was an NKVD man?

And under the Germans? . . .

We remember well (see "Underground Ghetto," p. . . . Chapter . . .)[26] Henekh the agent and provocateur. We remember Henekh, who assaulted the FPO. So where does he come from—what is there to tell? . . .

Henekh understood that sitting in Klooga in the role of a royal official was just a delusion. And tomorrow, when liberation comes? . . . Henekh began seeking a purpose—he had to create an alibi for himself that would rid him of his past. But what? He is a Communist, he boasts of Communist ideas, his NKVD past will support him, he will rouse the camp, he will gather people around him and create a group—a [Communist] Party in Klooga!

But everything here is built on sand, and there is no solid ground. How could Henekh become a Party leader? And rumors spread in the camp: they will annihilate us. They won't let us out. No one knew where the information came from, but everybody repeated it, analyzed it, commented on it, and invented a rationale:

"We are broken anyway. We have nothing to lose, because we are lost anyway. . . . Let us unite. Let us come together and prepare, and when the time comes, let us be victorious or die."

These words, uttered by the greatest coward of the Vilna Ghetto, the founder and leader of the present Party, sounded like a joke; yet although all assembled knew who he was, knew him and understood his motivations, nevertheless they went along for a bit, for what could they lose here? . . .

Henekh became the Party leader. His comrades and collaborators were the moneybags packed with gold, adventurers, no worse than their leader, as well as naive people, believers, and just plain deluded people.

What would a Party be doing in Klooga?

Yet no one tries to analyze it. No one is interested in the substance. For the camp, it is a sensation, and a secret. Nobody wants to ponder how much of it is truth and how much is bluff, lies, and delusion.

Indeed, how come Henekh is a leader? He surrounded himself with secrets: he has connections outside, beyond the camp. A moment will come when they will break into the camp, remove the group, and with weapons in hand, take them to the forest.[27]

K.[28] lacks no w.[29]

26. A reference to a book Kruk was writing in the Vilna Ghetto, for which many notes survived. Two sections of "Underground Ghetto" are published in Chapter 9 of this book.

27. The words "group" and "weapons" [*gever*] were forcefully erased, apparently for fear of censorship.

28. Perhaps "Kh," the last letter of "Henekh."

29. Probably "weapons."

Under the buildings, covered with water, there is a [. . .][30] rifles and machine guns, small tanks, and . . . People watch his every word. Those who believe, believe. Those who don't believe are happy that he babbles and creates a diversion. The leaders around Henekh knew anyway that it was all empty words, phraseology. But they counted on the rich [. . .]
[*The manuscript ends here.*]

DIARY NOTES

[*Kruk wrote a diary in Klooga, but it was apparently lost. The diary reproduced here began in Klooga and continued in Lagedi, where Kruk was sent on August 22, 1944.*]

Addendum to Diary

JULY 7 [1944]

I have been silent for a long time. Unfortunately conditions for writing were nonexistent. During this time, many things happened. We shall only mention a few:

Chronicle: The artist Rotblum died. A victim of starvation and suffering in the camp. The [Jewish] Advisory Committee ["Bayrat"] has resigned from its activities. Because three bosses—Mintz, Ratner, and Meltzer—prevented it. Its achievement in lowering the price of bread has all but been forgotten. The price of a loaf of bread had been 62 marks. The dumping of bread on the market lowered it to 22 marks a loaf. Now, after their resignation, bread again has risen to 30 marks, and the trend is toward higher prices.

Recently the camp received potatoes for the winter. Eighty percent rotten. Nevertheless, the camp came to life. In the camp, mountains of potatoes are heaped up, and everyone can pick them. But the potatoes stink of rot, are reshuffled by hundreds of hands. The selected potatoes are hidden in bunkers and people cannot use them freely anymore. The resignation of the Advisory Committee and the prevention of the free use of potatoes again aggravate the situation of supplies in the camp. Nevertheless, recently there has been no starvation in the camp.

The situation on the fronts. The Germans are surrounded and we here are in the soup. Thus our camp is in danger (and even faces the problem of liberation? . . .). Pris[oner] groups are under a mobilization order. Night watch of the cadres, checkups, and so on. Yesterday an attempt to create one unit of all the forces in the camp.

30. A word is crossed out here: "melina" or "store(house)."

JULY 14 [1944][31]

Today, in mid-July, I cannot be silent any longer! I began my notes in the first hour of the Sov[iet]-German war. And if I am destined to survive, I shall finish them as I started.

Unfortunately, for a long time I could not write because of my last defeat, when I tried to do some proselytizing [?] in the camp. In connection with my activity for the Advisory Committee, I was punished and sent to Concrete, to the division of reinforced iron beams. The work is hard and dreadful. My arms swell, the veins of my arms and legs are puffed up. The skin is flayed on my arms, and cracks. My arms and legs are heavy, and I am totally exhausted, sleepy and tired.

In camp, there is a lot of work. The P.G. [Partisan Group] work takes all my time. The [work with] the cadres is like hard labor. The P.G. has already 56 mem[bers], the cadres about 20.

The Advisory Committee fell apart. Mrs. Meltzer, Ratner, and Mintz wanted to employ me for auxiliary work, check out the kitchen, and so on. But one thing succeeded: stabilizing the price of bread. Bread fell from 64 marks a kilogram to 22. Today, two weeks after the resignation, bread again costs 44 marks. . . .

Meanwhile, the Kovno artist Rotblum died at the age of 46, of starvation and overexhaustion. Another victim of the camp leadership.

Several days ago I had a failure with the camp quartermaster, who suddenly appeared during a consultation and confiscated my notes. I managed to save the notes, and the whole affair passed with only a scare.

The situation here rests on a razor's edge. Today, the [?]th, 19 days to the [Russian] offensive into the Baltic countries, the Soviets recaptured all of Byelorussia and Lithuania—Estonia, Latvia, and Kovno are in the soup. On the 13th, Vilna fell after a long battle with encircled Germans. The Germans are taking a stand 60 km before the Prussian border (Oarta) [?]. The Baltics are thus encircled and are about to be cut in two on the Daugavpils-Riga line.

What happens to us will be determined first of all by the camp. Evacuation is impossible. No place to go. Will they leave us [here]—who knows? . . . So we stand, perhaps more than ever before, on the boundary between life and death. The P.G. is preparing for such an eventuality. The camp is looking up to the groups. Three groups are consolidating. The Com. B. [battalion commander] is leader of P.G. and commander of the cadres.

31. This date may be incorrect. In the entry itself, Kruk indicates that the date may be the 8th or the 12th.

Vilna is liberated, and here we groan under the yoke, crying over our lot. The Vilna FPO is surely now marching victoriously through the alleys of the ghetto, searching and looking. I hope they also try to save my materials.

Here the situation is such that the army around us may evacuate at any minute. That means that over our fate hangs a serious question mark. The Germans themselves are terribly depressed and confess that they are jealous of the Jews. "Soon you will be liberated. And our lot is bad. They will slaughter us with no mercy."

Nevertheless, the regime here goes on as if nothing had happened. They build, they chase to work as before, and make plans for the future. Today the Wehrmacht left the railroad line (*Strecke*), and now the Todt stores are being evacuated. Wood for the motors comes right to the field. Masses of barracks are taken away, mostly to Tartu. *Signalka* is all but stopped. Other concrete-iron products still go to Daugavpils, although that city is surrounded and the Reds are 100 km from Riga? . . .

The "Sanitäter"[32] takes us to bathe in the sea and asks us to sing Sov[iet] songs. Behaves "collegially" and politely. Many Germans make peace with Jews. Even B. K., the camp leader, hints to his girl that we are in the soup and are stuck in the sh[it]. . . . But the J[ewish] authority still understands nothing and continues its ugly actions.

JULY 15 [1944]

After the attempt to establish a so-called Advisory Committee as a framework for surveillance, two weeks passed. The committee dumped bread on the market against the speculators at a low price, and the price collapsed from 64 to 22 marks. Meanwhile, 16 wagons of potatoes arrived in the camp, 80 percent rotten. The camp was flooded with potatoes. Whoever wanted could pick them up. Everybody cooked and ate their fill. Then [the price of] bread fell even more. Now, after the two sated weeks, hunger has returned. The price of bread is already 60 marks.

The grave situation in the Baltic and our fear for our destiny led us to concentrate all possible forces. Today the issue will finally be decided. In this situation, even the darkest pessimists suddenly become optimists, and I, the "perennial optimist," am calm and reserved. Now more than ever.

Angry at my initiative to create the Advisory Committee and to continue its work, the "leadership" of the camp takes revenge on me and bullies me as far as possible. They send me to Concrete, chase me to various jobs, and are hostile.

32. A German term meaning "first-aid attendant."

The artist Yisroel Rotblum was born in Kovno in 1902 and died in Klooga on July 5, 1944. On the 7th of this month, he was burned at the stake.

Various rumors are circulating, covering the distance from Tallinn to Riga. On Monday they will select the healthy men among us and take them away—incidentally, most people are calm and tensely waiting. People greet each other often with: "May we be liberated as soon as possible." Among our Germans, the fever is not yet felt. They just talk about how we are surrounded and that we will soon be liberated. . . .

JULY 17 [1944]

It turns out that they are indeed evacuating. The workshops are building crates to pack the saws of the Catons [?] and similar objects. In the meantime, they are gradually running toward Riga. What next? . . . Yesterday evening, the Baltic port of Tallinn was bombed. Today Dr. P.[33] went to the Jewish elder concerning H. [Herman Kruk], who is sick and must not work in Concrete. The answer was: "He had a taste for committees, surveillance; let him now know what a camp is. Let him not think he is in the ghetto. . . ." That is how the Jewish elder torments me for demanding public surveillance.

JULY 18 [1944]

The P.G. merged its cadres with two similar groups. A new committee was created, and there each group brings in its five-person cells. The united cadres had 15 cells of five on the first day. The P.G. itself continues to exist. Nothing happening around us seems like the "normal" life of the camp. Work is normal here, and the Sanitary normally takes us to the sea every day. Every day, between 100 and 200 people leave. Of course they are from those strata that are free from the yoke of labor. What should one think? . . . Again rumors are spread that we will be sent, along with the [. . .], to Danzig. . . .

It's symptomatic: evacuation to survive, surviving to die. This is the topic of the day. Germans from all sides calm us: *Das Kommt nicht in Frage*. That's out of the question. Still, two women, mother and daughter Salonowicz from Vilna, escaped. The camp leader did not take it to heart. Yesterday three more women escaped. Today they came back, supposedly went to do business. The consequences? Several smacks and nothing more. . . .

33. This could be Dr. Leyb Pomerantz, a well-known Vilna physician and public activist who perished in Klooga.

It's typical: the camp leader has himself well [?]. . . . As for the others, they are also making money through civilian pursuits. . . .

Like a sword of Damocles, the question hovers over us: we are again between death and liberation.

JULY 19 [1944]

Very little changes in the boat of our life. In spite of all that is happening around us, life in camp continues its normal ways. Every day, the "Arabs" bring delicacies from the railroad. In the camp, in the lower hall, trading begins that looks like a market fair in a shtetl. They sell butter, bread, lard, honey, challah, strawberries, berries, milk, canned food, cigarettes, tobacco, etc. Jews come here to buy, resell it, and . . . the Klooga trade is flourishing. The Klooga people, "English," and "Arabs" found a common life, and apart from some small antagonisms, the play is well rehearsed. The authorities, too, are continuing as if nothing has happened. Just yesterday, 33 wagons of concrete arrived. On the one hand, evacuation, and on the other hand, building. Signalka is not transported out; work here goes on at full speed.

JULY 20 [1944]

Today seems to be the decisive day for the lot of our camp. Everywhere crates, coffers, etc., are being constructed, and suddenly an order came for the camp leader and the commander of the Estonian guard to report immediately to Tallinn (?). They left right away. Clearly their trip has to do with us, and we are awaiting the result with great trepidation. . . . The *Haupttruppenführer* Otenik, a Pole Przesonek [?], left suddenly yesterday. No one knew. He told everyone something else: to one he said he was going on a two-week vacation, to another, just for five days, etc. He burned all his papers in the yard with his own hands. He asked his Jewish maid to keep his room in order and not to touch his papers. . . . Many Germans commission or buy civilian clothes from Jews. They all talk about the end of the war, and that here, all are condemned. The price of bread is rising. P.G. groups stand guard until the "Alliance" takes over.

JULY 21 [1944]

According to the Jewish calendar, today marks 10 months since we came to Klooga. Most Jews mention this date. Our situation and our expectations of an unclear tomorrow make an impact on everything. Yesterday's trip of the Estonian police chief and the camp leader turned out to be a simple matter. Both were called as witnesses in the case of Tshizhik [?], the former medic, who got drunk and shot an Estonian policeman. Typical: the Dutch were already packed to leave; suddenly an order came to unpack and stay. Has the situation improved? . . . On the contrary, it has gotten worse. The Baltic is blocked. What does that mean? Does it mean final resignation from rescuing, or just rescuing their own. . . .

2 P.M.

Since morning, rumors have been circulating about an assassination of Himmler. Later the rumor included Hitler. Now the daring event is already known: an assassination attempt on both Hitler and Himmler. The latter is dead, as announced on the radio by the wounded Hitler himself. The assassins are from the Wehrmacht.[34]

Here it has no effect. Every trifle may lead to a provocation. So we talk about it quietly and express our wishes to each other quietly. . . . Clearly the world is not asleep. The situation is coming to an end, and perhaps an end is coming to our camp. We live amid the tension of further news.

In the com[mittee] of the Alliance, I spoke in favor of Comrade Nayv [i.e., Wein]. I will not sit at the same table with Henekhl, the leader of that group I wrote about before [i.e., the Communists], and called him a polit[ical] charlatan.

JULY 23 [1944]

Yesterday was a day of some tension. The chief doctor for all the camps, Botman, came, called in three women, two of them melancholics and the third a lunatic, and gave them injections. Half an hour later they died. Then he gave an order to cut the hair of all women and to cut a stripe in the middle of the heads of all men. Yesterday a rumor spread here that 250 Estonians had fled from the nearby military barracks. In a forest farther off, 24 Estonians and 6 Jews were caught. Another rumor: in Kohtla (Estonia) there is a Sov[iet] parachute drop, which [the Germans] engaged in a fight. Yesterday, in the workplaces, they started digging shelters and trenches for us. Today, Sunday, all prisoners were mobilized for this work. The squares are being plowed up, and everyone here remembers the beginning of the war.[35] Today new rumors are spreading: the men will be castrated, the women sent to Königsberg. Several changes in my own condition: after I was

34. The attempt to assassinate Hitler and Himmler occurred on July 20, 1944. It is interesting how fast the rumors traveled. The camp inmates appear to be more interested in Himmler's supposed demise than in Hitler's being wounded. In fact, Himmler was not killed.

35. An allusion to the attack on Warsaw in September 1939.

removed from building barracks, I went to the concrete beams, hard work. Yesterday I worked again for 13 hours building barracks; tomorrow I have to go to the carpenters' workshop. Since the latest events on the Eastern Front, since the assassination attempt on H., since Estonia and the entire Baltic has been surrounded, our situation seems to be coming to a head. We are so upset, our nerves choke us, and every day is superfluous. Everything is more and more irritating. We count not just the days, but the hours and minutes: any minute we may get out of hell. When I write about it, I can hardly believe it. . . .

JULY 27 [1944]

The tension increases by the minute. Narva, Ostrov, and Pskov have already fallen. Daugavpils surrendered yesterday. Ponevezh went. The Baltic is hermetically sealed. Estonia is falling. And only here, it's as if nothing has happened. Work goes on as usual. The Germans clean and decorate the square. But they've become milder, and our relations [with one another] indicate the end of the war and our liberation. We wait, jittery about what may happen. But the Germans opened a new factory today to make Dutch slippers. Wagons no longer arrive; in the next few days everything will have to stop. [. . .] has nothing to do. The end is in the air. But the authorities do their duty. They count numbers, conduct checkups, and observe our every move. A stool pigeon strolls like a devil, observes, and doesn't say a word. They build [?], they build shelters and . . . trenches. Although there is no work, they drive us as before, 15 and 16 hours a day, as if we were doing something. . . .

The Estonian newspaper writes that there is danger of typhus in the Klooga Jewish camp, so the Jews must be kept inside. . . .

Dozens of rumors come daily, rumors about the lot of the Jews in the camps: barred wagons, Jews evacuated to Kivioli. In the end, it comes to nothing.

Women cover their heads—a fashion of colorful scarves.

JULY 30 [1944]

Today is the end of July and we are still in Klooga.

Everything is being liberated, even Warsaw (!!!), everything except us. Here we feel nothing yet. Our lot is as always; they turn things up, they search, they chase. The O.T. people go on doing their job, as if nothing has happened. However, we feel that they do it because they must. Every one [of them] continues moving to the beat, with no flair. He was ordered, so he does it. . . . Again we live in fear for our fate. Suddenly, two days ago, information arrived that in the railroad station in Klooga there are 15 wagons with Jews. Later it turned out that those were the same Jews who were yesterday in Tallinn, the camp inmates of Goldfilz and Ereda. Any minute, they'll arrive here. Soon the "Vaivarchik" came with the superintendent. A meeting, and he left. Soon after, the train left, too. How and why became clear. Two days ago they were sent out, perhaps to Königsberg. They had food for 10 days. Later it became clear that they could not go there, and it was decided to send them to Klooga. The building authority here doesn't want them; it doesn't have enough work. They don't need any more [workers]. Decision: to take them near Tallinn, where they will be divided into groups to work for . . . Tallinn. The enemy is only 100 km from the city—why are Jews here? Still, people calmed down. They don't send anybody, God forbid, by sea, something people are very scared of; but they stay in Tallinn, close to us. Now rumors spread, that for money a group can be transferred to us. . . .

The passersby left many letters. I guess that Friend Marek was among them; if possible, he will surely make an effort to come to his son.

The women cut their hair, and they all cover their heads with kerchiefs, make headdresses, and a series of colorful headbands is beginning to appear. Men cut rows in their hair.

People have calmed down. Explanation: they stayed in Tallinn. Why were they not sent by boat? Why try to send them to Klooga and back to Tallinn? It means they are seeking work, it means they are looking for a way out! . . .

People here stand on guard. We follow and observe everybody and everything. No signs of calm. Nevertheless? . . .

AUGUST 5 [1944]

Several weeks ago two women, a mother and daughter, left the camp. Later we heard a rumor that they were arrested by the building commissioner in Tallinn, who suddenly recognized them and turned them over to the Gestapo. Today they were brought back to us in camp. Their punishment: their hair was cut and they were covered with a sign: "*Hurra, ich bin schon wieder da.*" Hurray, I am back here. With this hanging on their body, they go to work in their old workplace, quiet, advertising themselves. . . . All night long and all day, we hear mighty explosions and bombardments. The situation grows tenser by the minute. Our royalty begin soiling their . . . pants, want to get something, are prepared for anything, and are . . . helpless. Their meeting ended with nothing. They try to make contacts with the camp cadres. Finally, with good luck, the supplies of the camp went out of Jewish hands and were turned over to the German superintendent. . . .

AUGUST 6 [1944]

I go to bathe in the sea bay.

AUGUST 7 [1944]

Again three prisoners of war escaped. Immense trains with junk pass by our camp: smashed cars, broken old wagons, etc.

AUGUST 8 [1944]

Direct-aim artillery is installed in the camp. Lately, many squadrons fly over our heads, especially friendly ones. Rumor has it that Warsaw is ruled by a Polish uprising (bravo Warsaw!).[36]

AUGUST 10 [1944]

I worked for three days 13 km from Klooga, in Laikola, 5 km from the Baltic. For the first time, I experienced a heavy bombing—there we were building a ramp from the south side. The beautiful area was developed under the Reds. Now everything is in ruins—late at night, when we returned to Klooga, the women were still standing at roll call. Apparently, the *Haupteinsatzführer* of the Estonian camps was selecting 250 old and sick women and children to send them to Tallinn to the Jewish camp, as it were. The men stood at the barbed-wire fence of the men's block with clenched hearts, waiting to see what would happen.

AUGUST 11 [1944]

At 3 A.M., there was a roll call of all the women. Those selected for transport were put aside. The shifts go out to work as usual. The rest go quietly to sleep.

At 11 A.M., the Einsatzmeister is called to the telephone, returns and cancels the deportation of the women. What is happening? No one knows what to say. The camp is happy, some are worried. Soon a rumor spreads that at 5 this morning the Tallinn Jews were loaded on ships, ostensibly for evacuation to Germany. The tension reaches its height. The rumor originated with the camp leader him-

36. The Polish uprising of the Armia Krajowa began in Warsaw in August 1944.

self. The women's transport is canceled, because the ship departed in the meantime. What next? What about us? . . .

People say that the Kivioli camp was liquidated and 400 Jews were shot to death. Why only 400? . . . Where is the truth? Who spreads the rumors? The cadres have a meeting. Want to decide: to go on the attack [?] or just hit the road. My advice: only an attack. [?] is an idea, "just" means desertion and betrayal of the camp.

AUGUST 12 [1944]

Again I work building barracks—they say we are the last camp in Estonia. The situation is tense. Mintz brings no news. Awesome excitement, we would smash the heads of the travelers. [. . .]

[. . .][37]

Rumors about the Jews of Tallinn: the Jews were loaded on the train and at 11 A.M. again unloaded—Jews were transported from the front in trucks? . . . Today in Laikola, a Jewish worker was shot to death for leaving his work.

AUGUST 15 [1944][38]

Today Comrade Moyshe Kantor, the veteran YIVO librarian, died. Various sources say that the Jews of Tallinn are in Tallinn in the same place as until recently. No one understands the new rumors. Yesterday there was a ball for the Germans. They drank, fought with each other, and seven were wounded. Some days ago we received a gift . . . overgrown onions. They felt like straw, and what a treat!

A new nasty disease has spread in the camp: our legs ache.

AUGUST 15 [1944]

The hoops around the Baltic become tighter. Estonia is attacked from Lake Pskov to Lake Peipus in the direction of Tartu toward Valk. Estonia is cut off. The evacuation is conducted with exemplary chaos. They carry rags and throw them into

37. Here the date 14 was written and then crossed out. Kruk's notations during these last days are shaky and barely readable.

38. Here the date 13 was crossed out and changed to 15.

the fields of Laikola, in our camp, etc. But it does not prevent our camp leader from carrying out searches, beatings, and insisting on the new Jew-sign—the stripe in the hair. . . .

The prominent cultural activist Engineer [Matthias] Schreiber is dying. His son is also very sick. And Comrade Hersh is still sick.

I work hard. I was in the hospital for two days. Tomorrow back to work.

Work in all local units comes to an end. Barrack building and [. . .] don't work, because no wood arrives, no boards. Therefore we are being pushed to transport work. Concrete stops—it is superfluous. Everyone is busy loading the evacuated wagons.

The past two days, the movement of trains was enormous. Mass trains with red crosses drive to the Baltic port. . . .

AUGUST 16 [1944]

From one day to the next, the evacuation emerges from hiding and becomes increasingly open. In addition to [coming from] Klooga and Laikola, Todt people arrive from Latvia—Latvians, Estonians, Ukrainians, Poles, and others. From Riga it takes four or five weeks to get here. There are strange cases: Today an *Obertruppenführer* came here with a big, beautiful dog. For three years now, he has taken his own two Jews along with him and doesn't let them out of his sight. No one but him has any right to them. . . . His private slaves. Many wander around here without food or a roof over their head. [. . .] from Vaikanis, and elsewhere. Yesterday letters arrived from the Tallinn Jews. Twice they were loaded on transports, together with Germans. They have been unloaded again, and are back in the camp, 13 km from Tallinn. This correspondence calmed our camp. Jack-of-Spades is the name of our third SS man, the front leader, an original character. [*Here the diary breaks off. During this period Kruk is transported to Camp Lagedi.*]

AUGUST 29 [1944] LAGEDI

Finally I arrived from Klooga at Lagedi. Once again naked and barefoot, once again a splinter hurled into the middle of a stormy sea. Lagedi is 7 km from Tallinn and 130 km from Tartu. Tartu has fallen, and the Reds are 25 km between Tallinn and us. We are almost at the train station, which is full of commotion. You can sense the front. Full trains to and from the front. All trains are guarded by anti-aircraft and machine guns. All around us is noise, pilots are being shot at and do not relent, day or night. A lot of shrapnel over our heads. We lie here in wooden field barracks, barracks I built when I worked in the Klooga barrack-building. Here we sleep badly on the [. . .], we work lightly on the railroad, to get something. The camp leadership is mild-mannered. Seems to be a camp for transporting us to Germany.

Here 2,000 from Estonian camps lived for three weeks. Among them, Marek from B[und]. They left by ship to Danzig. Today the guard returned and told us about it.

What is our destiny, it is hard to tell. However, the poverty, dirt, and lack of water say a lot about what will happen if we remain here.

I was chased out of Klooga in a dirty shirt with 2 marks in my pocket. My brother-in-law kept everything. The camp leadership did not make any effort, on the contrary, were happy. . . . My brother-in-law, Deul, Pomerantz, and Kalman[owicz] are surely even more orphaned.

Here I encountered the Warsaw tailor B. Hochman. He and the camp elder take care of me, get me a piece of soap, a towel, a plaid blanket, etc., and find a job for me as house elder. I live with Durmashkin, Rosental Lola, and Dimentman Dovid. Dr. Kholem is with us, and I met the famous ghetto hero Aster [?].

So far, I have slept on the bare ground. Today I built a lair for myself, boarded up the holes in the barrack—an achievement for Lagedi not for [?]. . . .

If possible, shall continue to record.

AUGUST 31 [1944]

Was sick for two days. Meanwhile got another report. The guards who took the Jews to Germany say that they left the Jews in Danzig. There are tens of thousands of Jews, who work in factories and fields. There are also other nationalities. The living conditions—clean, good living rooms, and not bad nourishment. News from Klooga: there are many SS men there. People work, [. . .], 130 Jews remained there. Eighty Jews went to the new camp in Laikola. Our departure from here seems unrealistic. Meanwhile, they say, we shall stay here for three weeks. In the barracks it is cold, the wind blows, and when it rains, it gets wet. Everything is damp. You can smell us rotting. [. . .]

SEPT. 5 [1944]

Sunday, we had some tension. The chief butcher came, the chief doctor. But everything remained as it was. Today again some anxiety. The commandant came here, the so-called Vaivarchik, the so-called Sortovshchik [Selectioneer]. . . .

We received news of the Jews transported to Germany. They landed in Danzig and are in a camp 30 km from there, where, they say, there are tens of thousands of people of various nationalities. There are about 20,000 Jews, including a large children's camp.

SEPT. 8 [1944]

Again experienced some anxiety: the Vaivarchik Dr. Botman was here, with Schwartzer, the whole "butcher shop," as it is called. Everybody was sure something horrible was imminent, in the best case, transport to Germany. The result is zero—we remain. He orders underwear, clothes, etc., sent; it seems we are staying. Thus we are playing for time.

On Sunday the 5th, the inmate Elye Peskin died. Yesterday, the 7th, his friends Dovid Dimentman and Volf Durmashkin held a memorial service for him.

On Wednesday the 6th, the inmate Yofe was shot on the railroad. He got a bullet for leaving his work post, and he fell on the spot. The same was met by another inmate of the camp, Finkelstein, who was shot a day later, Thursday, right in the morning. Yofe was buried in the forest, where the shooting took place; Finkelstein, next to the camp, where seven Jews are buried. Thus we already have 4 victims here: a man who died, a man who committed suicide, and two shot to death.

We're getting settled here. Today we acquired a floor and a small oven. Commissioned to make a pair of underwear from a blanket. For the first time in my life I received something I begged for. Yesterday, during the noon hour, went out of the camp to wash myself. At the well, there is a bench for Estonian forced laborers. When they saw *Häftlinge Juden* [Jewish prisoners], they showered us with bread, cigarettes, etc.

SEPT. 17, 1944[39]

What am I doing in the camp? Comrade Hochman protects me. He knows me from Warsaw from the Tailors' Union, and he "arranged" a job for me as a house elder. He watches me and takes care of me. Mrs. Gordon takes a German into the barrack. A quarrel erupts about racial shame [*Rassenschande*]—my worries. The end—I start trading and make money and eat. . . . I received a package—a pleasure. In the package, my Klooga manuscripts. Except for the "Klooga miniatures" and the Klooga "Notebook." Today, the eve of Rosh Hashanah, a year after we arrived in Estonia (by the Jewish calendar), I bury the manuscripts in Lagedi, in a barrack of Mrs. Shulma [?], right across from the guard's house. Six persons are present at the burial. My coexistence with my neighbors is difficult.[40]

39. This note, written in a trembling hand and with a thick pen, is Kruk's last entry, dated a day before his death.

40. A hint at the relations with the Germans, which were coming to a head.

[The next day, all Jews from Klooga and Lagedi, including Herman Kruk, were hastily exterminated. The inmates were ordered to carry logs and spread them in a layer, and then they were forced to undress and lie down naked on the logs, where they were shot in the neck. Layer was piled on top of layer, and the entire pyre was burned. The next morning, the first Red Army units reached the area. One of the six witnesses mentioned by Kruk in his final entry survived. He returned to Lagedi, dug up the diary, and brought it to Vilna.]

APPENDIX: PLACE NAMES

The place names in this book have posed a particular problem in the English-language edition because each had many variants—Polish, Lithuanian, Yiddish, German, Russian. For hundreds of years, as Benjamin Harshav points out, the Jews had their own names for places and people: a parallel Jewish geography. Although Kruk for the most part made use of Yiddish forms, he was not entirely consistent. Therefore, the general practice in this book is to spell place names in accordance with pre–World War II official usage, with occasional exceptions made for forms more familiar to the reader of English. In this table, place names in Vilna and the neighboring regions that have more than one form are listed as they appear in the text, followed by the post–World War II official name and the Yiddish name. The relevant language is abbreviated after each entry (P. = Polish, L. = Lithuanian, La. = Latvian, R. = Russian, Es. = Estonian, G. = German, U. = Ukrainian, E. = English, Y. = Yiddish).

Spelling used in this book	*Post–World War II official spelling (if different)*	*Yiddish name*
Alytus (L.)		Alite
Antokol (P.)	Antakalnis (L.)	Antokol
Antokolska (Street) (P.)	Antakalnio (L.)	Antokol
Aukštadvaris (L.)		Visokedvor
Bakszt (Street) (E.)[1]	Bokšto (L.)	Baksht
Baranovitsh (Y.)	Baranovichy (R.)	
Bazyljańska (Street) (P.)	Bazilijonų	Bazilyaner
Beniakony (P.)	Benyakony (R.)	Benyakon
Bezdany (P.)	Bezdonys (L.)	Bezdan
Biała Waka (P.)	Baltoji Vokė (L.)	Byalevake
Biržai (L.)		Birzh
Bosaczkowa = Karmelicka (Street) (P.)	Karmelitų (L.)	Bosakes = Karmelitn
Brasław (P.)	Braslav (R.)	Braslev
Brisk (Y.)	Brest (R.)	
Burbiszki (P.)	Burbiškis (L.)	Burbishok
Chełm (P.)		Khelem
Chopin (Street) (E.)[2]	Šopeno (L.)	Shopen
Daugavpils (La.)[3]		Deneborg
Dominikańska (Street) (P.)	Dominikonų (L.)	Dominikaner
Dorpat = Tartu (Es.)		

Spelling used in this book	*Post–World War II official spelling (if different)*	*Yiddish name*
Druskieniki (P.)	Druskininkai (L.)	Druzgenik
Duniłowicze (P.)	Dunilovichi (R.)	Dunilovitsh
Dziewieniszki (P.)	Dieveniškės (L.)	Devenishok
Dziśnieński (Street) (P.)	Dysnos (L.)	Disner
Eyshishok (Y.)	Eišiškės (L.)	
Gaon (Street) (E.)[4]	Gaono (L.)	Goen
Głębokie (P.)	Glubokoye (R.)	Glubok
Glezer (Street) ("Glazier") (Y.)[5]	Stiklių (L.)	
Hoduciszki (P.)	Adutiškis (L.)	Haydutsishok
Holszany (P.)	Gol'shany (R.)	Olshan
Jaszuny (P.)	Jašiūnai (L.)	Yashun
Jatkowa (Street) (P.)	Mesinių (L.)	Yatkever
Jonava (L.)		Yaneve
Kalwaryjska (Street) (P.)	Kalvarijos (L.)	Kalvaryer
Kernavė (L.)		Kernuvke
Kiemieliszki (P.)	Kemelishki (R.)	Kemelishok
Kiena (P.)	Kėna (L.)	Kene
Kijowska (Street) (P.)	Kijevo (L.)	Kiever
Kock (P.)		Kotsk
Końska (Street) (P.)	Arklių (L.)	Konske
Kovno (E.)[6]		Kovne
Kretinga (L.)		Kretingen
Krewo (P.)	Krevo (R.)	Kreve
Landwarowo (P.)	Lentvaris (L.)	Landvarove
Ławaryszki (P.)	Lavoriškės (L.)	Lavrishk
Legionowa (Street) (P.)	Savanorių (L.)	Legyon
Lejpuny (R.)	Leipunai (L.)	Leypun
Lidzki (Street) (P.)	Lidos (L.)	Lider
Lipówka (P.)	Liepkalnis	Lipuvke
Łuck (P.)	Lutsk (R.)	Loytsk
Ludwisarska (Street) (P.)	Liejyklos (L.)	Ludvisarer
Łukiszki (P.)	Lukiškės (L.)	Lukishkes
Łuków (P.)		Likeve
Lwów (P.)	L'vov (R.), L'viv (U.)	Lemberik
Makowa (Street) (P.)	Aguonų (L.)	Makove
Mała Stefańska = Kwaszelna (Street) (P.)	Raugyklos (L.)	Kleyn-Stefn ("Little Stephen's")
Małkinia (P.)		Malkin
Marcinkańce (P.)	Marcinkonys (L.)	Martsinkants
Mejszagoła (P.)	Maišiagala (L.)	Mayshegole
Memel (G.)	Klaipeda (L.)	

Spelling used in this book	*Post–World War II official spelling (if different)*	*Yiddish name*
Miadzioł(P.)	Myadel' (R.)	Myadl
Michaliszki (P.)	Mikhalishki (R.)	Mikhalishok
Mickiewicz (Street) (E.)[7]	Gedimino (L.)	Mitskevitsh
Mickuny (P.)	Mickūnai (L.)	Mitskun
Miedniki (P.)	Medininkai (L.)	Mednik
Międzyrzec (P.)		Mezritsh
Niemenczyn (P.)	Nemenčinė (L.)	Nementshin
Niemiecka (Street) (P.)	Vokiečių (L.)	Daytshe ("German")
Nowa Wilejka (P.)	Naujoji Vilnia (L.)	Nay-Vileyke
Nowogródek (P.)	Novogrudok (R.)	Navaredok
Nowogródzka (Street) (P.)	Naugarduko (L.)	Novigorod
Nowy Pohost (P.)	Novyy Pogost (R.)	Nay-Pohost
Olkieniki (P.)	Valkininkai (L.)	Olkenik
Onuškis (L.)		Hanushishok
Orany (P.)	Varėna (L.)	Oran
Ostra Brama (P.)	Aušros Vartai (L.)	Ostrobrom
Ostrobramska (Street) (P.)	Aušros Vartų (L.)	Ostrobrom
Oszmiana (P.)	Oshmyany (R.)	Oshmene
Oszmiańska (Street) (P.)	Ašmenos (L.)	Oshmener
Piłsudski (Street) (P.)	Algirdo (L.)	Pilsudski
Pilviškiai (L.)		Pilvishok
Piwna (Street) (P.)	Daukšos (L.)	Bir ("Beer")
Płock (P.)		Plotsk
Podbrodzie (P.)	Pabradė (L.)	Podbrodz
Ponar (Y.)[8]	Paneriai (L.)	
Ponarska (Street) (P.)	Panerių (L.)	Ponarer
Ponevezh (Y.)	Panevėžys (L.)	
Reval = Tallinn (Es.)		
Rokiškis (L.)		Rakishok
Rosa (P.)	Rasos (L.)	Rose
Różana (P.)	Ruzhany (R.)	Rozhenoy
Rudnicka (Street) (P.)	Rūdninkų (L.)	Rudnitsker
Rudnicki (Forest) (P.)	Rūdninkų (L.)	Rudnitsker
Rudomino (P.)	Rudamina (L.)	Rudomin
Rudziszki (P.)	Rūdiškės (L.)	Rudishok
Rukojnie (P.)	Rukainiai (L.)	Rukoyn
Rzesza (P.)	Riešė (L.)	Reshe
Sadowa (Street) (P.)	Sodų (L.)	Sadove
Safjaniki (Street) (P.)	Maironio (L.)	Sofyanikes
Semeliškės (L.)		Semelishok

Spelling used in this book	*Post–World War II official spelling (if different)*	*Yiddish name*
Šiauliai (L.)		Shavl
Širvintos (L.)		Shirvint
Skopówka (Street) (P.)	S. Skapo (L.)	Skopuvkes
Skuodas (L.)		Shkud
Slabada (L.)		Slobodke
Słowacki (Street) (E.)[9]	Mindaugo (L.)	Slovatski
Smorgonie (P.)	Smorgon' (R.)	Smargon
Śnipiszki (P.)	Šnipiskės (L.)	Shnipishok
Strashun (Street) (E.)[10]	Strašuno = Žemaitijos (L.)	Strashun
Subocz (Street) (P.)	Subočiaus (L.)	Subotsh
Święciany (P.)	Švenčionys (L.)	Sventsyan
Szarkowszczyzna (P.)	Sharkovshchina (R.)	Sharkeyshtshine
Szawelska (Street) (P.)	Šiaulių (L.)	Shavler
Szeptycki (Street) (E.)[11]	Ševčenkos (L.)	Sheptitski
Szpitalna (Street) (P.)	Ligoninės (L.)	Shpitol = Hegdesh ("Hospital")
Szumsk (P.)	Šumskas (L.)	Shumsk
Tauragė (L.)		Tavrik
Trocka (Street)	Trakų (L.)	Troker
Troki (P.)	Trakai (L.)	Trok
Turgiele (P.)	Turgeliai (L.)	Turgl
Ukmergė (L.)		Vilkemir
Uniwersytecka (P.)	Universiteto (L.)	Universitet
Utena (L.)		Utyan
Veiviržėnai (L.)		Varzhan
Vievis (L.)		Vevye
Vilkaviškis (L.)		Vilkovishk
Vilna (E.)[12]	Vilnius	Vilne
Virbalis (L.)		Verzhbolove
Węgrów (P.)		Vengreve
Werki (P.)	Verkiai	Verek
Wielka (Street) (P.)	Didzioji (L.)	Breyte ("Broad")
Wielka Pohulanka (Street) (P.)	Basanavičiaus (L.)	Groys-Pohulyanke
Wielka Stefańska (Street) (P.)	Šv. Stepono (L.)	Groys-Stefn ("Great Stephen's")
Wieluciany (P.)	Vēliučionys (L.)	Velitshan
Wilcza Łapa (P.)	Vilkpėdė (L.)	Viltshelape
Wileńska (Street) (P.)	Vilniaus (L.)	Vilner
Wiwulski (Street) (E.)[13]	Vivulskio (L.)	Vivulski
Włodawa (P.)		Bludeve

Spelling used in this book	Post–World War II official spelling (if different)	Yiddish name
Wołokumpia (P.)	Valakampiai (L.)	Volokumpye
Zakret (Forest) (P.)	Vingio (L.)	Zakreter Vald
Zarzecze (Quarter) (P.)	Užupis (L.)	Zaretshe
Žasliai (L.)		Zhosle
Zawalna (Street) (P.)	Pylimo (L.)	Zavalne
Zdzięcioł (P.)	Dyatlovo (R.)	Zhetl
Zezmer (Y.)	Žiežmariai (L.)	
Żydowska (Street) (P.)	Žydų (L.)	Yidishe ("Jewish")
Zygmuntowska (Street) (P.)	Žygimantų	Zigmunt

[1]Polish: Bakszta
[2]Polish: Szopena
[3]Russian: Dvinsk
[4]Polish: Gaona
[5]Polish: Szklana
[6]Lithuanian: Kaunas
[7]Polish: Mickiewicza
[8]Polish: Ponary
[9]Polish: Słowackiego
[10]Polish: Straszuna
[11]Polish: Szeptyckiego
[12]Polish: Wilno
[13]Polish: Wiwulskiego

REFERENCES

All titles appear here in the original language, followed by their translation into English. The language of the original work is provided in parentheses after the title: (Y) for Yiddish and (H) for Hebrew. If a work is referred to within the text by an abbreviation, the abbreviation has been placed in square brackets at the beginning of the citation.

Abramowicz, Hirsz. 1958. *Farshvundene geshtaltn* (Y) [Vanished figures]. Buenos Aires: Tsentral-farband fun poylishe yidn in Argentine.

Ajzen, Abraham. 1950. *Dos gaystike ponim fun geto* (Y) [The spiritual face of the ghetto]. Mexico City: Yidisher kultur-tsenter.

[Anski, S.]. *1920–1925*. *Gezamlte shriftn* (Y) [Anski's Collected Writings], 15 vols. Vilna: An-ski Publishers.

[*Arkady*]. 1942. *Arkady: Zamlbukh tsum ondenk fun Arkady Kremer* (Y) [Arkady: Essays dedicated to the memory of Arkady Kremer]. New York: Unzer tsayt.

Bernstein, Mordecai W. 1957. *Pinkes Zamoshtsh* (Y). Buenos Aires: Tsentral-komitet far Pinkes Zamoshtsh.

Dworzecki, Mark. 1946. *Kamf farn gezunt in vilner geto* (Y) [Struggle for health in the Vilna Ghetto]. Paris: OZE Farband.

———. 1948. *Yerusholayim de-Lite in kamf un umkum* (Y) [Jerusalem of Lithuania in struggle and demise]. Paris: Yidisher natsyonaler arbeter-farband in Amerike un Yidisher folksfarband in Frankraykh.

Fuks, Kh. L. (ed.). 1958. *Fun noentn over* (Y) [From the recent past]. New York: Congress for Jewish Culture.

Gar, Yosef. 1948. *Umkum fun der yidisher Kovne* (Y) [The destruction of Jewish Kovno]. Munich: Farband fun litvishe yidn in der amerikaner zone in Daytshland.

Garfunkel, L. 1959. *Kovna ha-yehudit be-khurbana* (H) [The destruction of Kovno Jewry]. Jerusalem: Yad vashem.

[*Generations*]. Hertz, Jacob Sholem (ed.). 1956–1958. *Doyres bundistn* (Y) [Generations of Bundists]. 3 vols. New York: Unzer tsayt.

Goldshmidt, A. Y. 1935. "Yidishe doktoyrim velkhe praktitsirn itst in Vilne" (Y) [Jewish doctors now practicing in Vilna]. In Jeshurin 1935, pp. 278–437.

Jeshurin, Ephim H. (ed.). 1935. *Vilne* (Y) [Vilna]. New York: Wilner Branch 367, Workmen's Circle.

Kaczerginski, Shmerke. 1947. *Khurbn Vilne* (Y) [The destruction of Vilna]. New York: Fareynikte vilner hilfs-komitet in Nyu-york durkh Tsiko-bikher-farlag.

———. 1948. *Lider fun di getos un lagern* (Y) [Songs of ghettos and camps]. H. Leivick, ed. New York: Tsiko-farlag.

Kalmanowicz, Zelig. 1951. "A togbukh in vilner geto" (Y) [A diary of the Vilna Ghetto]. YIVO-bleter 35:18–92.

Korczak, Reyzl (Ruzhka). 1946. *Lehavot ba-efer* (H) [Flames in ashes]. Merhavia, Israel: Ha-Shomer ha-Tzair.

Kowalski, Isaac. 1954. *Di geheyme drukeray* (Y) [The secret press]. New York: n.p.

Lazar, Khayim. 1950. *Khurban ve-mered* (H) [Destruction and revolt]. Tel Aviv: Masu'ot.

[*Lexicon*]. 1956–1981. *Leksikon fun der nayer yidisher literatur* (Y) [Lexicon: Biographical dictionary of modern Yiddish literature]. 8 vols. New York: Alveltlekher yidisher kultur-kongres.

Mowszowicz, Y. 1947. "Derinerungen fun shulvezn in vilner geto" (Y) [Memoirs on the school system in the Vilna Ghetto]. In *Pages About Vilna* 1947, pp. 19–23.

Musnik, Yosef. 1945. "Dos lebn un di likvidatsye fun vilner geto" (Y) [The life and liquidation of the Vilna Ghetto]. *Unzer tsayt,* no. 11 (November): 29–31.

Oshry, Rabbi Efroim. 1951. *Khurbn Lite* (Y) [The destruction of Lithuania]. New York: Horav Oshri bukh-komitet.

[*Pages About Vilna*]. 1947. *Bleter vegn Vilne* (Y). Łódź: Farband fun vilner yidn in Poyln.

Pomrenze, Seymour. 1947. "Operatsye Ofnbakh" (Y) [Operation Offenbach]. YIVO-bleter 29:282–285.

Pryłucki, Noah. 1917. *Zamlbikher far yidishn folklor, filologye un kulturgeshikhte* (Y) [Collection of Jewish folklore, philology, and cultural history]. Warsaw: Nayer farlag.

Pupko-Krinsky, Rachel. 1947. "Mayn arbet in YIVO unter di daytshn" (Y) [My work in YIVO under the Germans]. YIVO-bleter 30:214–222.

Rudashevski, Itsik. 1973. *The Diary of the Vilna Ghetto, June 1941–April 1943*. Translated from the Yiddish manuscript by Percy Matenko. Israel: Ghetto Fighters' House.

Sholem Aleichem. 1926. *Sholem-Aleykhem-bukh* (Y) [Sholem Aleichem Book]. I. D. Berkowitz, ed. New York:IKUF.

Silberman, Ephraim. 1948. "Geheyme post in kovner geto" (Y) [Secret mail in the Kovno Ghetto]. *Fun letstn khurbn* (Munich) 10 (December): 42–47.

Stolnitz, Nathan. 1957. *Negine in yidishn lebn* (Y) [Music in Jewish life]. Toronto: n.p.

Sutzkever, Abraham. 1946a. *Vilner geto, 1941–1944* (Y) [The Vilna Ghetto, 1941–1944]. Paris: Farband fun di vilner in Frankraykh.

———. 1946b. *Lider fun geto* (Y) [Poems from the ghetto]. New York: IKUF.

Szyk, Zalmen. 1939. *1000 yor Vilne* (Y) [One thousand years of Vilna]. Vilna: Gezelshaft far land-kentenish in Poyln, vilner opteylung.

[*Teachers' Memorial Book*]. Kazdan, Kh. Sh. (ed.). 1954. *Lerer-yizker-bukh* (Y). New York: Komitet tsu fareybikn dem ondenk fun di umgekumene lerer fun di Tsisho-shuln in Poyln.

[*These Will I Remember*]. 1956–1972. *Eyle ezkera* (H). 7 vols. New York: Research Institute of Religious Jewry.

Weinreich, Max. 1946. *Hitlers profesorn* (Y) [Hitler's professors]. New York: YIVO.

Zeldin, M. 1947. "'Tsukunft'-arbet in geto" (Y) [The work of Tsukunft in the ghetto]. *Yugnt-veker* 1, no. 2: 12.

Żeleznikow, Avreml. 1949. "Bundistn in vidershtand fun varshever geto" (Y) [Bundists in the Warsaw Ghetto uprising]. *Unzer tsayt,* nos. 4–5: 21–25.

INDEX TO PEOPLE AND PLACES

Italic type indicates towns and neighborhoods.